This Land of Ours

A New Geography of Canada

This Land of Ours
A New Geography of Canada

Ralph Krueger • Ray Corder • John Koegler

HBJ
HARCOURT BRACE JOVANOVICH, CANADA
Toronto • Orlando • San Diego • London • Sydney

Canadian Cataloguing in Publication Data
Krueger, Ralph R., 1927–
    This land of ours

ISBN 0–7747–1372–0

1. Canada – Geography. I. Corder, Raymond G.,
1939– . II. Koegler, John, 1926– .
III. Title.

FC75 K78 1990   917.1   C90–095140–0
F1017.K78 1990

The authors and publishers wish to thank Colleen Wassegejig and Valerie McGregor for their counsel concerning the information contained in this book about the people of Canada's First Nations.

Editorial Director: Murray Lamb

Senior Editor: Jo File

Editor: John Sabean

Editorial Assistant: Diana Semenuk

Production Editor: Karin Fediw

Photo Researcher: Liz Kirk

Permissions Editor: Sarah Byck

Director, Art and Design: Patricia Garbett

Text Design: Full Spectrum Art Inc.

Maps and Technical Art: David Hunter

Cover Design: Gary Beelik

Chapter One Map Illustrations: Malcolm Cullen

91 92 93 94 95   5 4 3 2 1

Printed in Canada by Friesen Printers

Contents

Chapter Three

Economic Development, Settlement, and Population

Chapter Four

Canada's Evolving Political Geography

Chapter Five

Urban Canada

Chapter Six

Water: Uses and Abuses

Chapter Seven

Fish and Fisheries

Chapter Eight

Forests and Forestry

Chapter Eleven

Canada And The World

Chapter One

From Sea to Sea

This land is your land, this land is my land
From Bonavista to Vancouver Island,
From the Arctic Circle to the Great Lakes' waters,
This land was made for you and me.

Canada in Perspective

This chapter will take you on an illustrated journey across Canada. It will show you the many different kinds of landscape and the results of human use of resources that are part of our country and affect our environment.

On your journey you will travel from west to east, generally following the route of the Trans-Canada Highway (Figure 1.1). This road is almost eight thousand kilometres long: the longest national highway in the world. Detours along the way will take you into parts of Canada off the highway route.

Some of the photographs you will see on this "journey" show Canada from the air. Aerial photographs help geographers to see patterns in our Canadian landscape that cannot usually be seen from the ground. They offer a different perspective and also make a point: on this "tour" you will be looking at Canada from more points of view than would a passenger in a car on the road.

FIGURE 1.1   The Trans-Canada Highway

. . . a kaleidoscope
of shapes and colours.

WEST
ORIES

BA

Pangnirtung

Iqaluit

ONTARIO

Fort George

Schefferville

NEWFOUNDLAND

Moosonee

QUÉBEC

Kenora

Thunder
Bay

Sault Ste.
Marie

Corner
Brook

Bonavista

Edmundston

Fredericton

Québec

N.B.

P.E.I.

St. John's

Montréal

Hull

Sherbrooke

Sydney

Sudbury

Ottawa

Saint John

Charlottetown

L. Superior

Halifax
Lunenburg

Kingston

N.S.

Toronto

Hamilton

L. Ontario

L. Michigan

L. Huron

Windsor

London

L. Erie

1

A Pacific Island

PHOTO 1.1   Long Beach is part of the Pacific Rim National Park, which lies on the west coast of Vancouver Island. Among the twisted driftwood and colourful shells on the sand, you may see, now and again, a glass fishing float carried by winds and currents from Japan.

PHOTO 1.2   The tallest trees in Canada grow along the west coast of British Columbia. Many of the larger trees are several centuries old, and some are more than one hundred metres tall and have trunks that measure more than 2 m in diameter. These trees are specially suitable for the manufacture of building lumber and plywood.

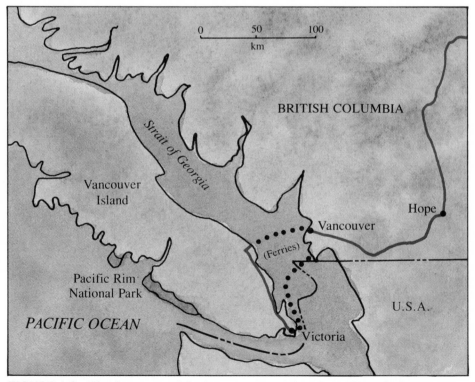

FIGURE 1.2   The first stage of the journey: from Victoria to Hope, B.C.

A Port City

PHOTO 1.3 Tall office buildings rise from the streets of downtown Vancouver, Canada's third-largest city. Stanley Park, in the background, offers a place for recreational activities. British Columbia's Coast Mountains form a scenic backdrop.

FIGURE 1.3 The image you see above is not a photograph; it is the product of *remote sensing* equipment.

A satellite orbiting in space receives radiation from the earth and converts that radiation into information that is stored as coloured images. It uses different colours to represent different features on the ground.

The colours in a Landsat image are not the natural colours that an astronaut would see from a spacecraft. In this image the forested mountains show up in dark red-brown, agricultural land in off-white, and city areas in light blue tones. You can see that Vancouver and the suburban communities that surround it have spread over most of the Fraser delta. The light blue colour of the water west of Vancouver shows silt that the Fraser River is carrying into the Strait of Georgia.

Flat Farmland and the Fraser's Fury

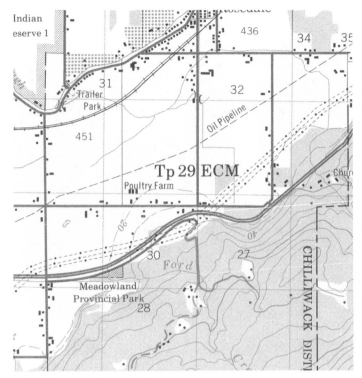

FIGURE 1.4   Topographic maps are large-scale maps that show much more detail than the usual maps in an atlas. This map has a scale of 1:50 000; in other words, the map is 1/50 000 the size of the actual area of the land it shows. The straight blue lines are grid lines, useful for locating items on the map.

Brown lines on the map join points that are at the same height above sea-level. They are called *contour lines*. A number of contour lines close together show that the land is steep or hilly. Flat land has very few contour lines.

Source: From National Topographic System map sheet #92 H/4 © 1980, Her Majesty the Queen in Right of Canada with permission of Energy, Mines and Resources Canada.

PHOTO 1.4   This air photo shows the same area covered by the topographic map (Figure 1.4). It is a vertical air photo, taken from directly above.

PHOTO 1.5
Newly hatched chicks are often shipped from hatcheries to chicken farms. Dairy, chicken, and egg farms are the most common kinds of farms on British Columbia's Lower Mainland. Farmers also raise pigs and fatten beef cattle. Important garden crops include berries and vegetables.

PHOTO 1.6   The Fraser River has cut a deep canyon through the Coast Mountains. Although the canyon provides the best land route through the mountains, it was a difficult area for railway and highway construction.

Ranches and Orchards

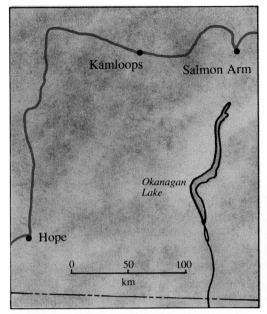

FIGURE 1.5 From Hope to Salmon Arm B.C.

PHOTO 1.7 The Interior Plateau of British Columbia west of Kamloops. A *plateau* is a high, fairly flat landform. Rivers often cut valleys through a plateau, giving it a hilly appearance.

PHOTO 1.8 Part of the Okanagan Valley at the Canada-U.S. border. The climate here is desert-like.

Mountain Passes and Railway Tunnels

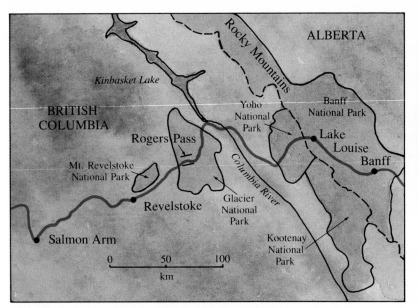

FIGURE 1.6   From Salmon Arm, B.C. to Banff, Alberta

PHOTO 1.10   The Rocky Mountains, particularly on the Alberta side, are world famous for their scenery. Lake Louise is just one of many picturesque areas visited by thousands of tourists every year.

PHOTO 1.9
Rogers Pass is the only usable route for rail and highway through the Selkirk Mountains. Up to 15 m of snow fall in the pass each winter. In early spring, *avalanches* of heavy snow thunder down the mountain slopes. The avalanche paths are the pale green sloped areas without trees. The Canadian Pacific Railway was forced to build more than 7 km of sturdy wooden structures called *snowsheds* over the track to protect its trains against the annual avalanches. Today two tunnels take the railway under the pass.

Skyscrapers and Black Gold

PHOTO 1.11   Calgary is located in the Interior Plains region along the eastern edge of the Rocky Mountains foothills. In the photograph these hills can be seen beyond the city. Calgary grew up as a regional centre for surrounding cattle ranches and farms. In the early part of the 20th century, the city was nicknamed ''Cowtown''. The development of Alberta's oil industry, which started in the late 1940s, triggered the rapid growth of the city into ''Oil Town''. The headquarters of many oil companies are in Calgary.

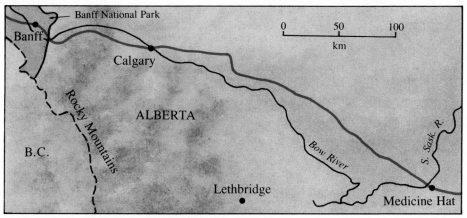

FIGURE 1.7   From Banff to Medicine Hat, Alberta

PHOTO 1.12   The east side of the Rocky Mountains marks the eastern edge of Canada's western mountain region.

Pioneers and Power

PHOTO 1.13   Sometimes large geographic regions can be subdivided into smaller areas called sub-regions. The Peace River area is a sub-region of the Interior Plains region. Farm settlement in the Peace River area dates mainly from the 1930s. People are still clearing land there today. The modern pioneers have replaced the traditional pioneers' axes and oxen with chain-saws and bulldozers. The logs and stumps are bulldozed into rows for later burning.

PHOTO 1.14   The Peace River region is also important for its energy resources. This refinery, near Fort St. John, handles both oil and natural gas. Pipelines carry oil and natural gas from Alberta to other parts of Canada.

PHOTO 1.15   During the 1960s, the gigantic Bennett Dam was built across the Peace River to produce hydro-electric power. The dam is located about 100 km upstream from Fort St. John.

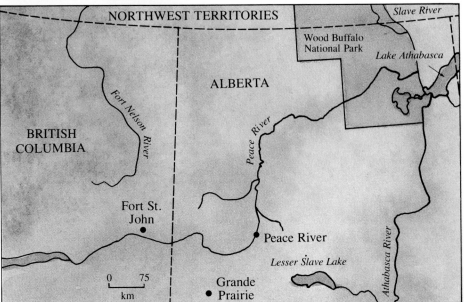

FIGURE 1.8   The Peace River District

Drylands and Oases

PHOTO 1.16 In southeastern Alberta the climate is too dry to favour crop growth. Some early explorers called the region part of the ''Great American Desert''.

PHOTO 1.17 In southern Alberta, people have altered the environment in some areas by bringing water to the parched land. They have dammed rivers flowing eastward from the mountains to provide water for irrigating crops. Canals carry the water from the reservoirs behind the dams to farming areas. The photograph shows an irrigation canal crossing a valley south of Lethbridge.

PHOTO 1.18
An irrigated
wheat field in
southern Alberta

Golden Fields and Prairie Towns

PHOTO 1.19 The surveyors of the prairies divided the land into one-mile squares called sections. Each section measures 1.6 km by 1.6 km. This air photo shows farmland a few kilometres west of Regina.

PHOTO 1.20 Prairie grain farms cover the land to the horizon. Between the golden fields of grain are fields that have been left unplanted. These *fallow* fields gather and store moisture for the next year's crop.

PHOTO 1.21 The harvested grain is brought to rail-side grain elevators for storage and shipment to Canada's ports. Inside the elevator, grain is lifted to the top of the building and then dropped into storage bins.

Mennonites and Hutterites

PHOTO 1.22   The Prairie Provinces were settled by people from many lands. For many people, the Canadian West represented freedom and opportunity. For example, it attracted people looking for freedom from religious persecution. Such people made up the group of about 7000 German-speaking Mennonites who moved from Russia to southern Manitoba during the 1870s. These Mennonites built 123 villages similar to the ones they left behind in Russia (now part of the U.S.S.R.).

   The Mennonite villages of Manitoba are street villages. The houses and barns are strung along both sides of a single village street. The farmers live in the village and go out each working day to their fields beyond it.

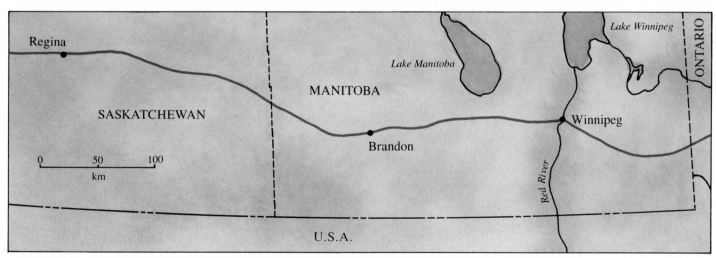

FIGURE 1.9   From Regina, Saskatchewan, to Winnipeg, Manitoba

PHOTO 1.23 Once the Mennonite villages were well established, many of the farmers built house barns. In these structures, the house and barn are attached to each other.

PHOTO 1.24 A Hutterite settlement in southern Manitoba. Scattered over the prairies are over 200 Hutterite settlements. Hutterites moved from Russia to North America mainly to escape religious persecution. Many who had settled in the United States later came to Canada to escape harassment over their refusal to do military service during the First World War.

Each settlement is made up of 50 to 150 persons. Hutterites share the work of operating their farms. Members of the community live in one-storey frame apartment buildings, where each family has its own private living quarters. All the members of the community eat their meals in a common dining room, which often doubles as church and meeting hall. Farm buildings and gardens surround the living quarters, and beyond the farms are the fields.

Where the West and East Begin

PHOTO 1.25   William Kurelek's "The Painter" shows the artist sketching prairie landscape in Manitoba. This Canadian painter grew up on the prairies.

PHOTO 1.26   The building of two transcontinental railroads made Winnipeg a railroad centre for Canada. On the tracks at Symington Yard stand dozens of freight cars. The city's tall business buildings mark the horizon.

Grain Port and Paper Maker

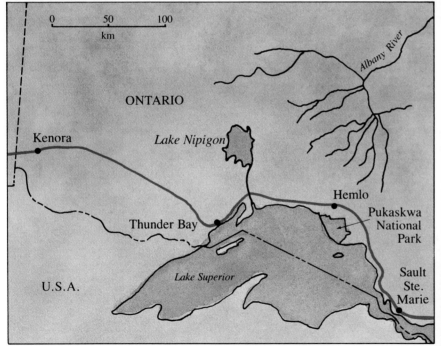

FIGURE 1.10   From Kenora to Sault Ste. Marie, Ontario. The Lake Superior section of the Trans-Canada Highway over the Canadian Shield was difficult to build. The rough terrain that made its construction difficult also provides spectacular scenery on the finished route.

PHOTO 1.27   Much of the grain grown on Canada's prairies is exported to other countries. Trains of boxcars bring grain from the prairies to Thunder Bay.

Thunder Bay has 15 terminal grain elevators, making it one of the largest grain-handling ports in the world. There grain is stored in elevators until it can be loaded onto lake freighters for transport to ports on the lower Great Lakes and the St. Lawrence River. Grain destined for Europe is then loaded on ocean freighters for the trip across the Atlantic. A few ocean freighters transport prairie grain directly from Thunder Bay to Europe.

PHOTO 1.28   One of the five large pulp and paper mills at Thunder Bay. These mills are the main employers in the city.

Old Rock and New Gold

PHOTO 1.29   In 1920, a group of seven Canadian artists joined together to discuss new ways of painting the Canadian landscape. The images that many Canadians have of Canada come partly from the paintings of this Group of Seven. Arthur Lismer's painting ''October on the North Shore of Lake Superior'' shows how this artist viewed the Canadian Shield.

PHOTO 1.30   A small part of the Pukaskwa National Park shoreline. This park protects part of the Canadian Shield landscape. Most of the park is difficult to reach by land.

PHOTO 1.31   The Trans-Canada Highway winding through a road cut. You can glimpse Lake Superior in the background.

Mines, Forests, and Clay Belts

PHOTOS 1.32 and 1.33 Elliot Lake is known for its uranium mines. The ore from several mines provides radio-active fuel for nuclear power plants.

PHOTO 1.34 Harvesting the spruce trees in Northern Ontario for the pulp and paper industry

PHOTO 1.35 A pulp and paper mill at Smooth Rock Falls, Ontario. Such mills are often located in a forested area beside a river that can be harnessed to make hydro-electricity to power the mill. The river also acts as a floatway for bringing logs to the mill. A nearby railway usually serves to ship the finished goods.

Canadian Shield: A Summer Playground

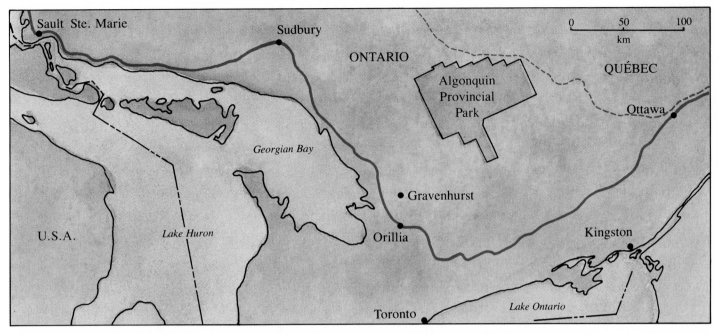

FIGURE 1.11   From Sault Ste. Marie to Ottawa, Ontario

PHOTO 1.36   A century-old steamship again sails the Muskoka Lakes north of Toronto. The steamship *Segwun* has been restored to its 1887 condition. Years ago, vacationers from southern Ontario used to come by rail to Muskoka Wharf in Gravenhurst, just north of Orillia. Here they would board one of the lake steamers to take them to their summer homes.

PHOTO 1.37   Today cottages are located on most Shield lakes within several hours drive of Toronto. To serve the heavy summer weekend traffic, a multi-lane highway was built.

Toronto and the Golden Horseshoe

PHOTO 1.38   Near the centre of the **Golden Horseshoe**, Toronto's distinctive outline glows against the night sky.

PHOTO 1.39   Large cities, like Toronto, offer many types of major sport, recreation, and entertainment. Ontario Place, in the foreground of this photograph, offers films, displays, and amusements.

FIGURE 1.12   The shores that edge the western tip of Lake Ontario are covered by almost continuous city. People call the area the Golden Horseshoe.

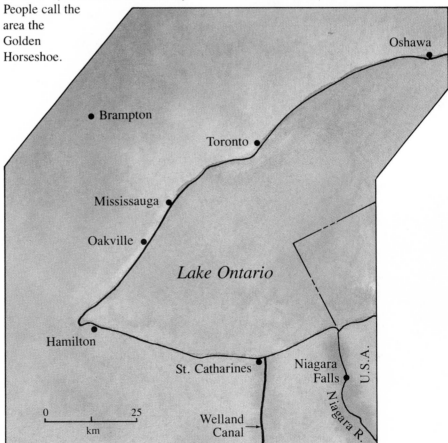

Oshawa

Brampton

Toronto

Mississauga

Oakville

Lake Ontario

Hamilton

St. Catharines

Niagara Falls

U.S.A.

Niagara R.

Welland Canal

0   25
km

Farms and Towns

PHOTO 1.41   West of the Golden Horseshoe lies rich farming country like this farmland south of Listowel.

PHOTO 1.40   A southern Ontario dairy farm

PHOTO 1.42   Scattered through the farmlands of southern Ontario are communities that serve farmers in the surrounding areas. The town of Milverton serves a farm area south of Listowel.

Energy, Steel, and Cars

PHOTO 1.43   People from all over the world visit southern Ontario to see Niagara Falls, which produces much of southern Ontario's hydro-electricity.

PHOTO 1.44   For almost a century, power plants in the Niagara Gorge below the Falls have run on energy provided by water redirected from above. The water behind the hydro-electric stations on the right came from above the Falls by tunnel and canal. This water will plunge through large, enclosed tubes of steel and concrete to the turbines that turn the electric generators.

The two power stations on the right are on the Canadian side of the Niagara River. The one on the left is in the United States.

PHOTO 1.45   Besides plentiful, inexpensive electricity, many Ontario industries also require steel. The province's largest iron and steel plants are in Hamilton. Find the piles of iron ore and coal in the photograph. These resources were brought to Hamilton by lake freighter.

PHOTOS 1.46 and 1.47   One of the biggest users of steel in Ontario is the automobile industry. At the huge General Motors plant in Oshawa, east of Toronto, this assembly-line worker is fitting the rubber seal to a car door.

An Inland Seaway

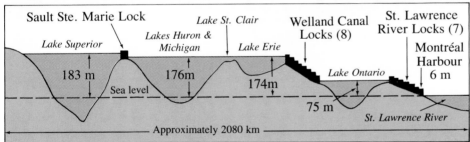

FIGURE 1.13   A profile (side view) of the Great Lakes-St. Lawrence Seaway. All but the largest ocean vessels can now sail almost half way across Canada, by way of the St. Lawrence River and the Great Lakes. Obstacles such as rapids and falls along the route have been overcome by building canals and locks.

PHOTO 1.48   Canal locks are needed to take ships around the rapids in the river. The photograph shows the Sault Ste. Marie Locks, which are on the U.S. side of the St. Mary's River.

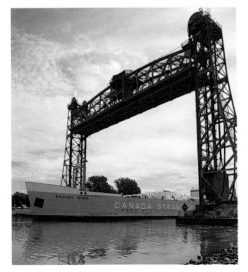

PHOTO 1.49   A lake freighter passing under a lift bridge on the Welland Canal

La grande ville

PHOTO 1.50 Montréal is the second-largest French-speaking city in the world. For 150 years it was Canada's largest city and main financial centre. Only recently has Toronto surpassed it.

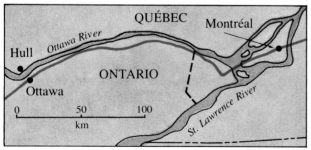

FIGURE 1.14 From Ottawa, Ontario, to Montréal, Québec

PHOTO 1.51 Montréal is older than Toronto. Near the harbour, in Old Montréal, many city blocks have been declared an historic area. Here the buildings are being restored to their 18th and 19th century appearance.

From Montréal to Arctic Settlements

PHOTO 1.52 Canada's eastern Arctic communities are supplied by ship from Montréal and St. John's, Newfoundland. This ship, loading in Montréal, may be taking on such items as food, building materials, and fuel. Ships supply each Arctic community only once a year.

PHOTO 1.53
A group of Inuit at Pangnirtung watch for the arrival of an airplane.

PHOTO 1.54 Inuit artist Jeetaloo Akulukjuk created this Pangnirtung print.

Long, Narrow Farms of Rural Québec

PHOTO 1.56   Some of the farms shown in Photo 1.55 appear in this photograph.

PHOTO 1.55   The air photo shows *rural* farm landscape in Québec. In Québec's early days, settlement took place along rivers because they were the chief means of transportation and communication. In order to give river frontage to each farm, the land was surveyed into long narrow lots. The same survey pattern was also used later along roads.

PHOTO 1.57   A Québec village along the St. Lawrence River

Canada's Oldest City

PHOTO 1.58   The citadel of Québec, built in the 1800s, overlooks the St. Lawrence River from the heights of Cap Diamant.

PHOTO 1.59   Ice sculpture is a special feature of the annual Québec City winter carnival. The old stone building in the lower part of the city is typical of the French-Canadian architecture.

PHOTO 1.60   The city's walls and gates are a reminder of Québec's past. The photograph shows one of the old gateways, the St. Louis Arch.

Three Québec Sub-Regions

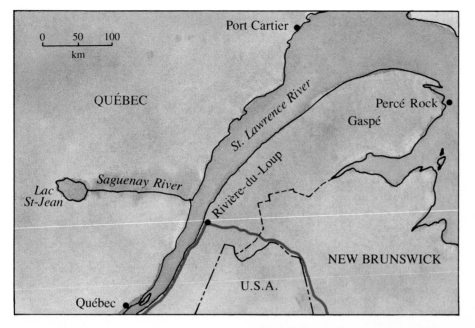

FIGURE 1.15   The Lac St-Jean–Saguenay sub-region lies on the Canadian Shield.

PHOTO 1.61   The rivers of the Lac St-Jean–Saguenay sub-region help generate hydro-electric power. Much of the electricity is used by the large aluminum smelter at Arvida, now part of the city of Jonquière. The smelter uses an electrical process to separate aluminum from its ore.

The Québec North Shore sub-region extends northeastward from the mouth of the Saguenay River.

The third sub-region shown on the road map is the Gaspé, a wide peninsula that juts out into the Gulf of St. Lawrence.

PHOTO 1.62   The Canadian Shield of the Québec North Shore sub-region contains iron mines. The iron ore travels to the Gulf of St. Lawrence by rail. Here, at Port Cartier, ships take on the iron ore and carry it inland to the steel plants around the Great Lakes. These same ships may be cleaned out and used to transport grain back through the St. Lawrence Seaway.

PHOTO 1.63   The dramatic silhouette of Percé Rock stands proud against sea and sky. Photographs of Percé Rock appear in many picture books and calendars about Canada. Try to find one that shows how the Rock got its name.

The Gaspé sub-region has a rugged interior, and most of its inhabitants live in small fishing villages along the shore.

Valley of the Loyalists

PHOTO 1.64   Many groups of people have sought refuge in Canada. After the American Revolution, many residents of the new United States of America wished to go on living under the British flag. They became known as United Empire Loyalists. About 14 000 Loyalist refugees landed on the north shore of the Bay of Fundy and began to carve out settlements in the Saint John River valley. This house is in St. Andrews, on Passamaquoddy Bay.

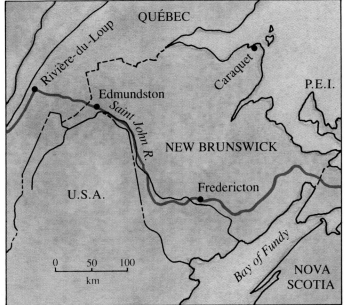

FIGURE 1.16   On through New Brunswick

PHOTO 1.65   This working, water-powered sawmill is at King's Landing on the Saint John River, near Fredericton. Here a living-history project reconstructs the life of a pioneer settlement in the 1800s.

In the early days, the forest industry was extremely important to New Brunswick and Nova Scotia.

PHOTO 1.66   When the Loyalists arrived, French-speaking Acadians were already living in some parts of New Brunswick. The photograph shows part of Caraquet. The first Acadians arrived here in the 1750s, after Britain had expelled them from other Maritimes' sites. Caraquet's main street is 13 km long!

A Garden in the Gulf

PHOTOS 1.67–1.69 The number of tourists visiting Prince Edward Island each year is more than 10 times the Island's population. No wonder, when the Island offers scenes like these!

PHOTO 1.70   To reach Prince Edward Island, road vehicles and railway cars must use a ferry. The photograph shows the ferry docks at Borden. The people of Prince Edward Island have a special love and pride for the Island.

PHOTO 1.71   Prince Edward Island is famous for its lobsters. A dockside inspector measures a lobster. If the size of the lobster from its eyes to the back end of its body shell is smaller than the measuring gauge, the lobster must be returned to the water.

From Fundy Tides to Halifax Harbour

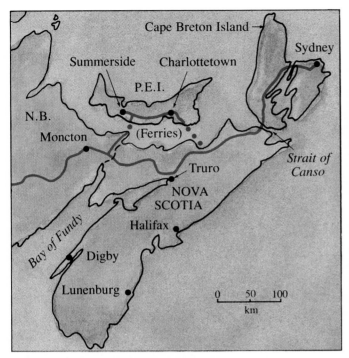

FIGURE 1.17   On through Nova Scotia

PHOTO 1.72   The harbour at Lunenburg.   The largest fish processing plant in Canada is located here.

PHOTO 1.73   The tides in the Bay of Fundy are the highest in the world. They may range more than 15 m from low to high tide. The observers in this photograph are watching the tidal bore at Truro, Nova Scotia.

PHOTO 1.74   Low tide in the Minas Basin of the Bay of Fundy

PHOTO 1.75   The Strait of Canso separates Cape Breton Island from the mainland. The Canso Causeway, completed in 1955, rises 66 m from the floor of the ocean in the strait. The causeway is 243 m wide at the base and 24 m wide at the top. Both road and rail traffic use the causeway.

Canada's Oldest and Newest

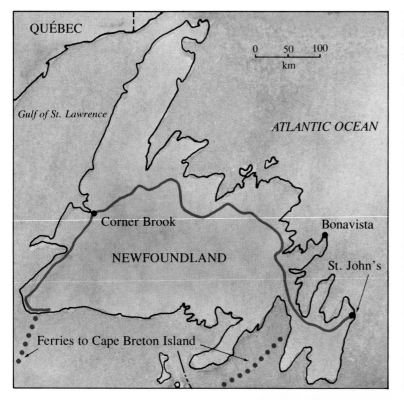

PHOTO 1.76 Western Newfoundland has enough forest to supply this large pulp and paper mill in Corner Brook. When the mill was constructed in 1925, it was the largest in the world.

FIGURE 1.18 Our journey ends in Newfoundland. Long before the first Europeans reached Canada's mainland, fishing ships were bringing crews from Europe to Newfoundland each year. Yet Newfoundland did not officially become part of Canada until 1949. The Province of Newfoundland consists of the island shown on the map and the large mainland area of Labrador.

PHOTO 1.77 Along Newfoundland's coast, small protected bays make good sites for fishing communities, or outports. The outport shown here is Tilting, on Fogo Island.

PHOTO 1.78 The old part of St. John's occupies land that slopes up steeply from the harbour. Fishing vessels from many countries come to St. John's for fuel, food, supplies, and repairs.

PHOTO 1.79   Cape Spear is the most easterly point in North America.

Questions and Activities

CANADA IN PERSPECTIVE

1. As you "cross Canada", you will see many traffic signs. Your own safety and the safety of others may depend on how quickly you recognize these signs, and how correctly you interpret them.

a) On a page in your notebook, copy the signs shown in Figure 1.19, and print beneath them what they mean.

b) Add and label sketches of any other traffic signs you know and that you think might be important on your journey.

c) Explain why you think it is important to know the information printed at the bottom of the chart. How might this information affect your driving habits?

d) Create a slogan to promote safe driving on a long trip. Design a logo for a sweatshirt or a bumper sticker to promote your slogan.

2. Using as a guide a map of Canada in this text or in an atlas, draw an outline map of Canada on a blank sheet of notebook paper. (Don't worry about minor details, but observe carefully the general shapes and their proportions. One way of checking proportions is to use a strip of folded paper. Make a paper strip the full length of your notebook page and twice the width you plan to use. Fold the strip in half lengthwise. Now fold your strip to half its length and crease the fold. Open the strip on the fold you have just made and fold its two ends so that they meet at the middle fold you have just creased. Crease the new folds.

Use the long edge of your strip to measure the proportion of the map(s) you are using as a guide. Relate these proportions to the map you are drawing.

You will use your map of Canada again later on.

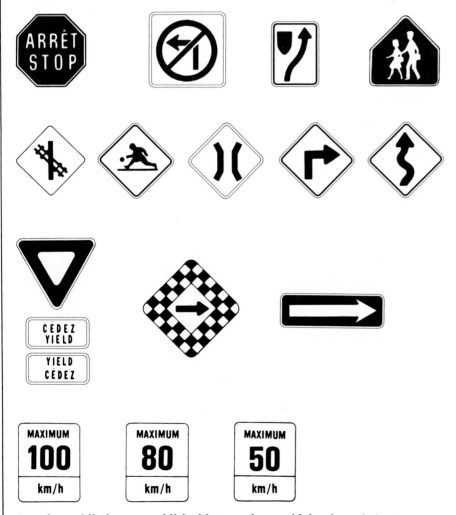

Actual speed limits are established in accordance with local regulations.

FIGURE 1.19   Some important traffic signs

BRITISH COLUMBIA

1. On your map of Canada, mark and label Victoria and Vancouver.
2. a) Look at the photograph of Vancouver (Photo 1.3). Why do you suppose many people wish to live in Vancouver? (Jot down your reasons.)
   b) Working in small groups and pooling the reasons you have jotted down, create an advertisement that Vancouver's Chamber of Commerce might use to attract people to the city.
3. Compare Figure 1.4 and Photo 1.4.
   a) What features show on the air photo that do not show on the map?
   b) What features show better on the map?
4. Look at Photo 1.8. How could people have changed part of the desert landscape into green orchards in the Okanagan Valley?

PRAIRIE PROVINCES

1. How do the foothills differ from the mountains in the background of Photo 1.12?
2. In an area of newly-cleared fields along the Peace River, strips of forest have been left standing (Photo 1.13). Explain why leaving trees is a good idea in a dry, windy area.
3. Draw a sketch map of the area near Regina shown in the air photo (Photo 1.19). On your map mark squares to represent the surveyed sections. Use symbols to show the roads and farm homesteads.
4. Photo 1.20 shows fallow fields on the prairies. About what proportion of the fields has been left fallow?
5. Photos 1.22–1.24 show Mennonite and Hutterite settlements on the prairies.
   a) Why are there no homesteads on the land between Mennonite villages?
   b) Suggest some advantages of living in a village rather than in homesteads on the land. Suggest some disadvantages.
6. As some people drive across the prairies, they are most impressed by the vast expanse of fields; others are most impressed by the ''Big Sky''.
   a) Which aspect of the prairies has Kurelek chosen to emphasize in his painting (Photo 1.25)?
   b) If Kurelek had chosen to emphasize the fields, how might he have changed his picture?
7. Locate and label Winnipeg on your map of Canada.

   Winnipeg has six large railway yards (Photo 1.26). Why do you think Winnipeg developed as such a large railway centre?

ONTARIO

1. Photo 1.27 shows grain elevators at Thunder Bay. Grain can be shipped from Thunder Bay to other parts of Canada and the world.

   On your map of Canada mark the route taken by ships from Thunder Bay to the Atlantic Ocean.
2. What might the presence of so many pulp and paper mills (Photo 1.28) tell you about the vegetation in the Thunder Bay area?
3. What feelings about the Canadian Shield does Arthur Lismer express in his painting ''October on the North Shore of Lake Superior'' (Photo 1.29)?
4. Part of the shore line of Pukaskwa National Park is shown in Photo 1.30.
   a) Use your atlas to locate Pukaskwa National Park on your map of Canada.
   b) You are a member of a Conservationist Group concerned with preserving the ecology of ''Wilderness National Park''. Or you are a member of a local Hiking Club and an eager all-season camper. Meeting with other members of your group/ club, suggest some arguments for or against opening up easy routes into Wilderness National Park.

   When you have collected your arguments, meet in committee with representatives of an opposing group. Give both groups' arguments a fair hearing, and then try to negotiate a compromise that will give access to the Park and protect its ecology.
5. Photo 1.31 shows a road cut in Northern Ontario. Why would

the construction crews blast cuts for the highway through the hard rock instead of building the road over the top?

6. Look at the photograph of a mine at Elliot Lake (Photo 1.33). Why might some people be disturbed by the changes in the landscape caused by mining?

7. Draw a rough sketch plan of the site of the pulp mill in Smooth Rock Falls (Photo 1.35). On your sketch, label the items that make the site suitable for a pulp mill. Using an atlas, locate and label Smooth Rock Falls and its river on your outline map of Canada.

8. Why would steamships such as the *Segwun* be needed a century ago to carry vacationers to their summer homes in Muskoka (Photo 1.36)? Why are steamships no longer needed to reach this vacation land?

9. Figure 1.12 is a map of Ontario's Golden Horseshoe.
a) Locate and label on your map of Canada the Golden Horseshoe cities of Oshawa, Toronto, Hamilton, and St. Catharines.

b) Suggest a reason for calling the area "golden".

10. Photo 1.39 shows Ontario Place, a recreation centre in Toronto.
a) What might be some reasons for choosing Toronto for such a recreation centre?
b) Make a class list of advantages and disadvantages of living in a large city like Toronto.

11. Photos 1.40–1.42 show farms and a farm community in southern Ontario.
a) How can you tell that the farm in Photo 1.40 is in a prosperous farming area?
b) What are the tall structures beside the barns? What do you think is stored in them?
c) Novelists, poets, and artists have often been attracted to pastoral (farmland) scenery. What do you think attracts them? Express your feelings about the farm scenes in Photos 1.40 and 1.41 either by writing a short descriptive paragraph or poem, or by drawing a picture.

12. Photos 1.43 and 1.44 show Niagara Falls and Niagara Gorge.

a) Locate and label Niagara Falls on your outline map of Canada.
b) Why would people come to see Niagara Falls?
c) How does southern Ontario benefit from their visits to the Falls?
d) Why do Canada and the United States share Niagara's water power?
e) Why would both countries have agreed not to take all the water from above the Falls for making electricity?

13. The Great Lakes and St. Lawrence Seaway are profiled in Figure 1.13.
a) On your outline map of Canada, label the Great Lakes, and note their elevations above sea level.
b) Between which two lakes is the difference in elevation greatest?
c) How far below the level of Lake Ontario is Montréal?
d) Before the opening of the Seaway in 1959, ocean-going ships could not sail beyond Montréal. How did the opening of the Seaway affect harbours on the Great Lakes?

QUÉBEC

1. Refer to the photographs of Montréal (Photos 1.50 and 1.51). Why would Montréalers want to save the old part of their city?

2. On your map of Canada, draw the route a ship would take from Montréal to Pangnirtung on Baffin Island. What is the approximate distance by water?

3. In Photo 1.53, a group of Inuit at Pangnirtung watch for the arrival of an airplane.
a) Why would the arrival of an airplane be an important event?
b) In the photograph, what traditional Northern items can you see?

4. Photo 1.57 shows a Québec village on the St. Lawrence River.

In the Prairie Provinces, distant grain elevators tell you that you are approaching a community. What type of building would show you that you were approaching a village in Québec?

5. Photos 1.58–1.60 show views of Québec City.
a) Locate and label Québec City on your map of Canada.
b) Why has the wall around Québec City (Photo 1.60) very few gates?
c) The city gates are narrow and slow down traffic. Why would the city not tear them down so that the streets could be widened?

6. Refer to Figure 1.15.
a) On your map of Canada, locate

and label the Saguenay River and Lac St-Jean.
b) On your outline map, shade and label the North Shore sub-region from the Saguenay River to the community of Havre St-Pierre.
c) On your map, shade and label the Gaspé sub-region.

7. a) On your outline map, locate and label Percé Rock (Photo 1.63).
b) Notable features like Percé Rock often become the subject of legends. Working as a class or in small groups, plan and write a "legend" to explain the appearance of Percé Rock. You might also wish to illustrate your legend.

ATLANTIC PROVINCES

1. Many small Maritime towns are famous for their Lobster Suppers. You are a member of a committee entrusted with planning a Lobster Supper and an hour's entertainment to follow. Meet with other members of the committee to plan a menu, and to arrange for traditional Maritime entertainment. (If you can find "volunteers" in your class, you might provide 20 to 30 minutes of the "live" entertainment planned for the Supper.)

2. Photos 1.67–1.70 show views of Prince Edward Island.
   a) Why do you think many Islanders oppose the plans to build a causeway between P.E.I. and the mainland?
   b) Suggest three attractions that might bring tourists to Prince Edward Island.

3. On your map of Canada, label Nova Scotia, the Bay of Fundy, Halifax, and Cape Breton Island (Figure 1.17).

4. Photos 1.77–1.79 show views of Newfoundland.
   a) Why is the very narrow entrance to the harbour at Tilting an advantage (Photo 1.77)?
   b) On your map of Canada, locate and label St. John's and Cape Spear.
   c) Use a globe or an atlas to determine the distance from Cape Spear (Photo 1.79) to Ireland. How does this trans-Atlantic distance compare with the length of the Trans-Canada Highway?

Chapter Two

The Natural Environment

Our Changing World

Over thousands and even millions of years, Canada's natural environment changed very slowly. Small changes in one part of the environment caused small changes in other parts. In the more recent past, when Canada's Native peoples controlled the land, they adapted themselves to nature and made only slight changes in the environment. In fact, their communities had neither the numbers of people nor the technologies to transform the natural world.

Noticeable changes in Canada's natural environment began when large numbers of people arrived from other lands. The pace of change quickened as Canada's population grew. By the beginning of the 1900s, modern technologies were helping the Canadian people to bring about rapid and often alarming changes.

Modern technologies have damaged our natural environment. Can modern technologies repair the damage? Perhaps a more important question is: ''How much do we need to know about our natural environment before we can take the proper steps to preserve it?''

Mount Robson, a peak in the Rocky Mountains

CANADA'S LANDSCAPE

Canada's natural environment is made up of a number of interrelated parts. The parts contain many different sorts of landforms spread over many thousands of square kilometres. In our vast land climate also varies from region to region, and differences of climate produce various kinds of vegetation. Before we can understand how the parts of the Canadian environment relate to one another, we need to know about the parts themselves. Only then can we begin to understand how people might work in harmony with their natural surroundings.

*Above the flat land of the open prairie, the sky looks immense. Here and there the grassland is dotted by a small shallow pond, or **slough**.*

LANDFORMS

The photographs in this chapter of mountains and plains show differences in the shape of the land. A landform may be shaped by the solid rock that lies beneath its surface. Or such forces as water, wind, and ice may cause particles of rock to scrape and sculpt the surface of the land. This process of wearing down the surface is called *erosion*. In time, particles moved by erosion are dropped, or deposited. This process, called *deposition*, builds up the surface of the land. Both erosion and deposition help to shape most landforms.

A large area of the earth's surface that has similar landforms is called a *landform region*, or *physiographic region*. Canada can be divided into eight physiographic regions (Figure 2.1, page 40).

Using Figure 2.1, design a table to record Canada's landform regions. In the first column, list all the provinces and territories. In the second, name the physiographic region or regions in which each is located.

CANADIAN SHIELD

The oldest and largest physiographic region in Canada is the Canadian Shield. It has acted as a large rugged barrier between eastern and western Canada; exposed ancient rock can be seen throughout this region. The Shield contains valuable resources, such as forests that support the pulp and paper industry, and metallic minerals that are worth mining.

The Canadian Shield contains the oldest rock in Canada. Some scientists have reckoned that some of it dates back about 4000 million years! Much of the Canadian Shield was formed by the cooling and hardening of molten rock. The *igneous rock* that results from this process is very hard. A common igneous rock in the Shield is granite. Some tombstones and monuments are made of pink or grey granite. Some igneous rock was changed by pressure and heat into *metamorphic rock*, which may contain minerals important to industry.

For hundreds of millions of years, a series of large mountain systems formed on the Shield; each group of mountains was slowly levelled by the forces of erosion; then others were built up and worn down in their turn.

This great rock outcrop on the north shore of Lake Superior is part of the Shield.

The cycle repeated itself several times in different parts of the Shield. For the last 500 million years, however, the Shield has been a fairly stable mass. The hard rock erodes so slowly that the surface of the Shield has changed only a little over that period of time.

Today the surface of the Shield consists mainly of rounded hills of rock. A multitude of lakes fill the many small hollows carved out by the Ice Ages. Streams seem to run in all directions as one lake simply spills over into the next. The Canadian Shield is by far the largest of our country's physiographic regions. It covers half of Canada's mainland, yet is home to only 10 percent of the nation's people.

Part of the Canadian Shield is exposed at the bottom of the Grand Canyon in Arizona.

1. Using Figure 2.1, describe the location and size of the Canadian Shield.
2. Describe the landscape in the photos of the Canadian Shield.
3. The Canadian Shield has been called a barrier between eastern and western Canada. Explain why it can be called a barrier.
4. Many Canadian artists have painted the powerful landscape of the Canadian Shield. Try to find a copy of such a painting to show to your class. Be prepared to tell the artist's name and two other facts about him or her.
5. Why does the Canadian Shield contain important minerals?

INTERIOR PLAINS

To the west of the Canadian Shield lies a region of plains and rolling hills, the Interior Plains (Figure 2.1). The general surface of this region takes its form from the flat layers of rock that underlie it. The gently rolling landform aids agriculture, and the oil, natural gas, and coal found in some of

The Haliburton district in Ontario, with its rocky hills and lakes, also has landforms typical of the Canadian Shield.

Lakes of meltwater from the last Ice Age formed this flat plain.

A meltwater valley in southwestern Saskatchewan marks the course of an ancient river.

the underlying rock provide a rich source of energy.

Rock materials eroded from the Canadian Shield over several hundred million years were deposited in shallow seas around the Shield area. Close to shore, the deposits were coarse materials such as sand. As the deposits piled up, they compressed the sand underneath and cemented it into rock called *sandstone*. Finer material, clay, was deposited some distance from the shore and remained suspended in the water for a longer time. Clay compressed into rock is called *shale*. As the seas evaporated, lime that had been dissolved in the water was left behind, like scale in a teakettle. This lime, together with the shell remains of sea animals, formed *limestone*. Sandstone, shale, and limestone are types of *sedimentary rock*. Sedimentary rocks are formed of eroded rock particles that have been deposited and compressed. The bedrock of the Interior Plains to the west of the Canadian Shield consists of flat layers of sedimentary rock resting on top of Shield rock.

If you drill deeply enough anywhere in Canada, you will come to Canadian Shield rock.

Some of the shallow seas teemed with tiny shelled sea animals. The organic remains of these creatures were deposited on the seabed, where they provided the chemical material for oil and natural gas. Ancient swamps, inland from these shallow seas, contained many luxuriant plants. As these plants died, their remains formed *peat*, which was later covered by other sediments and compressed into *coal*. Evaporating seas also left behind deposits of salts.

The surface of the Interior Plains region, like the bedrock under it, is much flatter than the Canadian Shield.

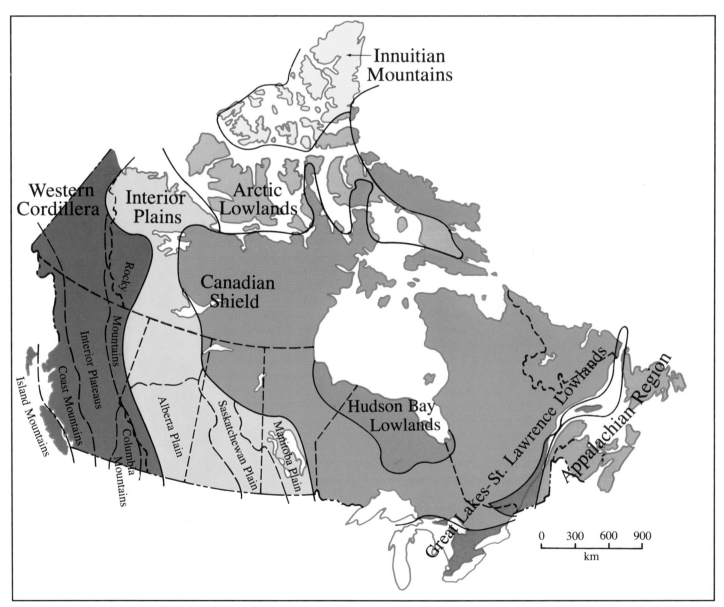

Figure 2.1 *Physiographic Regions of Canada*

Deposits from the last Ice Age left behind a gently rolling plain, but the former bottoms of *glacial meltwater* lakes produced very flat land. Near the end of the last Ice Age, meltwater rivers eroded deep valleys throughout the Interior Plains region. Many of today's rivers still follow these old meltwater valleys.

The Interior Plains region rises towards the west to form three fairly distinct levels from the Manitoba Plain in the east to the Alberta Plain in the west (Figure 2.1).

Earth's plates move at about the speed a fingernail grows.

1. Draw sketches to show how the landscape of the Interior Plains differs from that of the Canadian Shield. Label your sketches.

2. a) Why are oil, natural gas, and coal found in the Interior Plains?
   b) Why are these same minerals not found in the Canadian Shield?

Coal beds that formed in low-lying swamps are now near the tops of mountains in the Rockies.

GREAT LAKES-ST. LAWRENCE LOWLANDS

The Great Lakes-St. Lawrence Lowlands lie between the Canadian Shield and the Appalachian region (Figure 2.1). Though these Lowlands form a much smaller region than the Interior Plains, they share features with the Plains. The Lowlands, too, consist of sedimentary rock lying on the Shield. As the name suggests, the Great Lakes-St. Lawrence Lowlands have two parts; one lies in southern Ontario

and the other mainly in southern Québec. A narrow belt of Shield rock separates the two sections at the eastern end of Lake Ontario. Although the Great Lakes-St. Lawrence region is small, over half of Canada's people live there.

Almost the whole of southern Ontario is covered with ground-up rock material deposited by *glaciers* during the last Ice Age. This gives much of the area the gently rolling landscape shown in the photograph. The only major bedrock feature is the Niagara Escarpment, a cliff or steep slope facing away from southwestern Ontario and running all the way from Niagara Falls to Manitoulin Island (Figure 2.3, page 42). An *escarpment* forms in sedimentary rock that has a dip or slant. Softer layers of rock such as shale erode faster than the harder cap rock of limestone. As the limestone

---

F O C U S

How Did the Canadian Shield Get Its Name?

The earth's surface, or crust, is composed of a number of *plates*. Continental and oceanic crust together make up these plates. About 180 million years ago, the continents of the earth fitted very closely together, like pieces of a jigsaw puzzle. Over time, the plates shifted, causing the continents to separate from one another. The movement of continental plates, called *continental drift*, continues to the present time. The arrows on the second map of Figure 2.2 show the present direction of continental drift. North America is still moving very slowly away from Europe. The third map predicts the position of the continents 50 million years from now.

Each of the continental plates has a core of ancient hard rock known as a shield. In North America, this rock is called the Canadian Shield because the part of it that is exposed to view lies mainly in Canada.

1. Refer to the third map in Figure 2.2. On this prediction map, what has happened to the following continents/country?
   a) North and South America
   b) Australia
   c) eastern Africa and the west coast of the United States

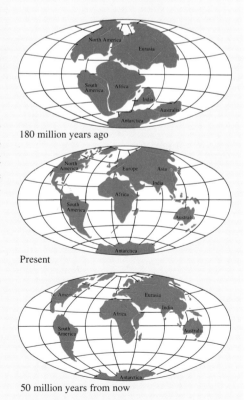

180 million years ago

Present

50 million years from now

Figure 2.2 *Continental Drift*

is undercut, pieces of it break off, forming a cliff.

The Niagara Escarpment resulted from erosion of the alternate layers of softer and harder sedimentary rock that dip gently toward the southwest.

Toward the end of the last Ice Age, the Montréal Plain of southern Québec was formed from deposits in an inland sea. A number of hills, called the Monteregian Hills, rise abruptly out of the Montréal Plain; most of them form a row running eastward from Montréal. These hills were formed over millions of years. First, molten rock from beneath the earth's surface melted some of the sedimentary rock near the surface and absorbed it. As the molten rock intruded into the sedimentary rock, it cooled and became very hard. Then millions of years of erosion wore down the softer sedimentary rock from around the harder igneous rock, leaving the harder rock as hills (Figure 2.4).

1. How does the gently rolling landscape of southern Ontario differ from the landscape of the Canadian Shield?
2. Why is the Ontario government trying to preserve the natural beauty of the Niagara Escarpment?
3. Suggest one action the government might take to protect the Escarpment.

WESTERN CORDILLERA

The western edge of Canada contains the highest and youngest mountains in the country. Here steep slopes make farming difficult, and high mountain ranges form barriers to transportation.

This Western Cordillera region (Figure 2.1) lies along a line dividing two plates. As the North American plate moves slowly westward, it slides over the Pacific plate, which is forced down under it. This downward movement, in turn, lifts the western edge of the North American plate, which is

The long ridges in this landscape show the direction of the ice movement in the last Ice Age.

The steep cliff face of the Niagara Escarpment, part of the bedrock of the region, is a striking feature of southern Ontario's landscape.

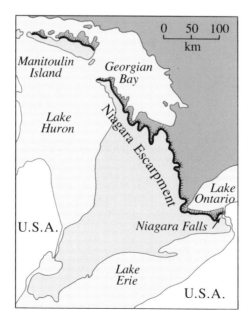

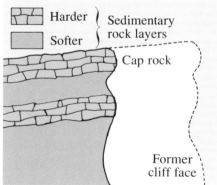

Figure 2.3 **The Niagara Escarpment**
Of what use is the escarpment to the people of Ontario? Why would an escarpment not form if all of the rock was of the same hardness, or if the rock did not have a dip?

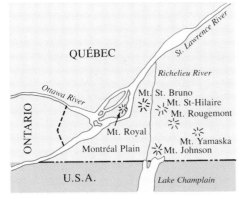

Mont St-Hilaire is one of the Monteregian Hills that rise abruptly out of the Montréal Plain.

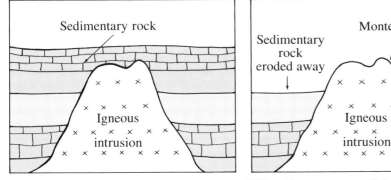

Figure 2.4 **Formation of the Monteregian Hills** *How can you tell from the diagram that the intruding rock did not push upward as a solid but instead melted its way into the layers of sedimentary rock?*

formed of sedimentary rock, and makes it buckle. The buckled plate folds and cracks, or faults, into mountains (Figure 2.5). This process of

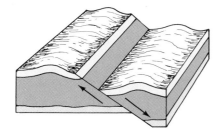

Faulting of Sedimentary Rock

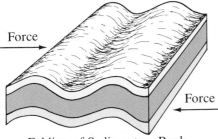

Folding of Sedimentary Rock

folding and faulting continues in different parts of the region.

Mountain-building forces also acted on the sedimentary rock layers of the western edge of the Interior Plains. As mountains were being raised, running water and glaciers cut down into the rock, eroding it and

giving the mountains their jagged appearance.

Sudden movement of plates against each other causes *earthquakes*. Most earthquakes in Canada take place near the west coast, which lies along the edge of the Pacific and North American plates.

The Rocky Mountains, which make up the east side of the Cordillera region, include some of the highest peaks in Canada. The youth of the Rockies is part of the reason for their spectacular appearance. The Rockies are not old enough to have been worn down by erosion. They began to form relatively recently, some 70 million years ago.

To the west, a deep valley known as the Rocky Mountain Trench

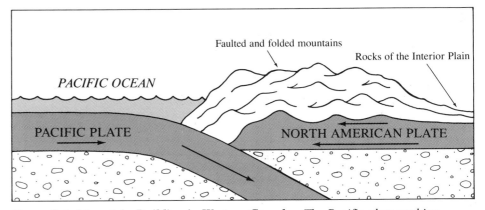

Figure 2.5 **Mountain Building in Western Canada** *The Pacific plate pushing under the North American plate has built the mountains of Western Canada. Earthquakes along the plate boundaries are common. Why would sedimentary rock fold and fault much more easily than the igneous rock of the Canadian Shield?*

43

separates the Rockies from the older Columbia Mountains, which are made up of a series of mountain systems separated by trenches (Figure 2.6). Much of the central part of the Western Cordillera region consists of level areas called plateaus that are deeply cut by rivers and former glaciers. Near the Pacific coast the landscape again becomes mountainous, with the Coast Ranges on the mainland and the Island Mountains offshore (Figure 2.1).

In the interior of British Columbia are a number of long north-south valleys called trenches. The best known of these is the Okanagan Valley (Figure 2.6).

---

1. Why is the highest mountain region in Canada located in the western part of the country?

2. a) Why is east-west transportation across this mountain region so difficult?
   b) By what means has this mountain barrier to transportation been overcome?

3. When explorer Alexander Mackenzie reached the Pacific Ocean, he carved on a rock: "Alex Mackenzie from Canada by land 1793". What makes this inscription memorable?

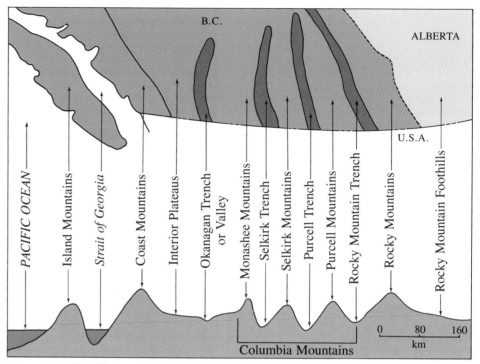

Figure 2.6 *The Western Cordillera   The Western Cordillera consists of a number of distinct and separate mountain systems. Some people refer to all of the mountains as the Rocky Mountains. Why is this incorrect?*

Mountain glaciers from the Coast Mountains carved out deep valleys that ran down to the Pacific coast. These valleys now form narrow inlets called fiords.

Rivers and glaciers carved valleys into the plateaus of the Western Cordillera.

The Okanagan Valley is a trench in the Fraser Plateau.

Earthquakes and the Richter Scale

Most of the world's earthquakes occur along the boundaries between plates of the earth's crust. The strongest earthquakes occur where plates are moving towards each other or are sliding sideways against each other. Friction between the plates keeps them from moving until considerable pressure builds up. Then the plates move in sudden bursts, causing the earth's surface to vibrate like a released spring.

The strength of earthquakes is often given a number on the Richter Scale, but this scale can be very confusing. For each increase of one on the scale, the height of the jagged line on the seismograph printout increases 10 times. However, the actual energy released at the centre of the earthquake is 30 times that of the preceding number. For example, an earthquake measuring 4 on the Richter Scale is 30 times more powerful than one measuring 3.

Richter Scale

Earthquake Strength	Description
1	Detected only by instruments called seismographs
2	Barely felt even at centre of quake
3	Felt by a few people in tall buildings
4	Felt as vibrations like those from a passing truck
5	Frightening to most people: furniture moves; some walls crack
6	Frightening to everyone: damages poorly built buildings
7	Cause of general panic; cracks in ground; damage to most structures Cause of landslides, broken dams, ruptured pipes
8	Generally destructive: few buildings left; public service lines out, bridges collapsed
9 +	Totally destructive: little left standing; obvious changes in the shape of land surfaces.

1. Why is an earthquake with a Richter Scale strength of 4 hardly noticed when one with a strength of 5 frightens most people?
2. Why do you think the west coast of Canada has many earthquakes, while the Canadian Shield has very few?

APPALACHIAN REGION

The Appalachians form a region of rounded hills and plateaus in eastern Canada (Figure 2.1). This older mountain system illustrates how the forces of erosion can change a landscape over a long period of time. In some areas of the Appalachian region the land is too steep to farm, but natural resources support forestry, fishing, and a little mining.

As long ago as 400 million years, mountain building began along what is now the east side of North America. At that time, our continent was still attached to Europe (Figure 2.2). This explains why the Appalachian region of North America and the highlands of Britain and Scandinavia are similar in some ways. In both continents, mountain building occurred more than once, followed by periods of erosion. Finally, the land was lifted up to form a plateau-like structure. Rivers cut valleys into the plateau to form a landscape that ranges from rounded hills to small mountains. The region's larger valleys, such as the Annapolis Valley in Nova Scotia, contain good farmland.

Both sedimentary and igneous rock occur in the Appalachian region.

Much of the region was so badly folded and faulted that mining is difficult.

On a map, the eastern edge of North America seems to come to an end where the land meets the ocean. Actually, the edge of the North American continent lies under the water, some distance from shore. This slightly submerged **continental shelf** has important fishing areas. The shelf also contains deposits of oil and natural gas.

<hr>

1. a) The Appalachians are an old mountain region. The Western Cordillera is made up of newer mountains. Draw sketches to illustrate the differences between the two regions.
   b) Suggest reasons for the difference between the two landscapes.
2. How does the structure of the Appalachian region differ from that of the Canadian Shield?

Rugged mountains in the Gaspé Peninsula section of the Appalachian region

Rounded hills and valleys in the southern Québec section of the Appalachian region

Folded rock in the Gaspé area of the Appalachian region

HUDSON BAY LOWLANDS

The Hudson Bay Lowlands (Figure 2.1) are made up of flat layers of sedimentary rock resting on older Shield rock. Like the Montréal Plain, the Hudson Bay Lowlands owe their very flat surface to deposits from a sea. Near the end of the last Ice Age, Hudson Bay covered much of this Lowlands area.

ARCTIC LOWLANDS

The Arctic Lowlands (Figure 2.1) also consist of layers of sedimentary rock resting on the Shield foundation. The Arctic Lowlands are located mainly among the islands of the far North. Like the Interior Plains, the Arctic Lowlands contain major deposits of coal, oil, and natural gas.

INNUITIAN MOUNTAINS

Canada's extreme North consists of high mountains and plateaus called the Innuitian Mountains (Figure 2.1). They look more like the mountains of the Western Cordillera than like other mountainous areas of Canada. The long distance of this region from southern Canada and the extremely cold weather there have made any search for minerals very difficult.

---

1. Why are the Hudson Bay Lowlands, the Arctic Lowlands, and the Innuitian Mountains less well known to most Canadians than Canada's other regions?
2. Draw and label a cross-section diagram of Canada from west to east. Your diagram should be similar to Figure 2.6. Show the Western Cordillera, Interior Plains, Canadian Shield, Great Lakes-St. Lawrence Lowlands, and Appalachian region.

The last Ice Age arrived in the Arctic from the south.

THE ICE AGES

Imagine almost all of Canada covered by sheets of slowly moving ice up to 3 km thick! How could it happen?

Glaciers develop if more snow falls during the coldest period of the year than melts away during the warmest period. If this pattern continues year after year, the snow accumulates. The mass of the upper layers compresses the snow beneath so that it re-crystallizes into glacier ice. This ice differs from ordinary frozen water because it can flow, ever so slowly, along the ground. In time, the mass of the accumulated ice layers pressing down causes the glacier ice to ooze outward in all directions. Glaciers have formed and spread in this way on our continent at least four times during the last million years.

The last *continental glaciers* formed some 70 000 years ago in areas east and west of Hudson Bay (Figure 2.7). Glacier ice moving west out of the Hudson Bay area met glaciers oozing out of the mountains of the Western Cordillera. Ice moving towards the east pushed out into the Atlantic Ocean, where it would break off as huge icebergs. The exact extent of the glacier's northward movement into the Arctic is not known. Glacier ice moving southward covered all of southern Canada and part of the northern United States. The more intense sun along the southern edge of the glacier sometimes melted the edge as quickly as it advanced. For thousands of years, the edge advanced and melted back a number of times as North America's climate cooled and warmed.

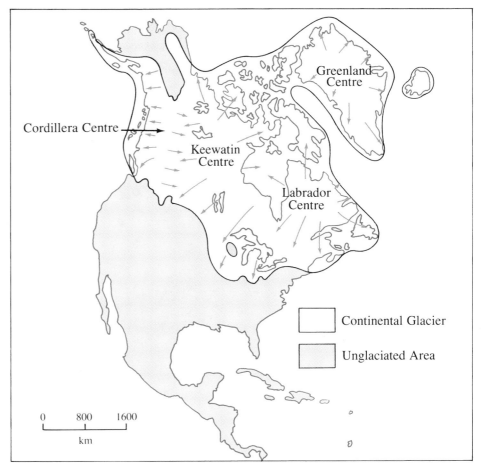

Figure 2.7 *Continental Glaciation in North America* As the map shows, the last Ice Age did not spread out from the polar regions. Why do you think parts of the Yukon and Alaska were not glaciated? Why did the continental glacier extend farther south in eastern North America?

A warming trend started about 14 000 years ago. The glacier ice started to melt back more rapidly than new ice advanced. Canada was slowly uncovered (Figure 2.8). Except for parts of the Innuitian Mountains and the higher elevations of the Western Cordillera, the last Ice Age came to an end about 6000 years ago.

The last Ice Age gave Canada's surface a brand new face. As the ice moved, it tore rock materials loose. These materials, in turn, acted as scrapers and grinders on the surface over which they moved. Exposed bedrock often shows the scratchs, or *striations*, made by rock carried in moving ice. As the ice melted, the rock materials carried in the ice were deposited. This process covered the land with a fresh layer of ground-up rock.

Where the ice edge of a glacier melted back at about the same rate as the ice advanced, rock materials in the ice were deposited in hilly ridges called *moraines*. Moraines are composed of a mixture of materials ranging from boulders to clay.

Drumlins are oval-shaped hills formed of materials deposited by moving ice. The steeper side of a drumlin points in the direction from which the ice moved.

Gravel deposits in meltwater tunnels in stationary ice formed steep-sided ridges. These ridges are called *eskers*.

On the Interior Plains and the Great Lakes-St. Lawrence Lowlands, the softer sedimentary rock materials

Greenland is still covered by a thick sheet of glacier ice that oozes outward and breaks off to form icebergs along the coast.

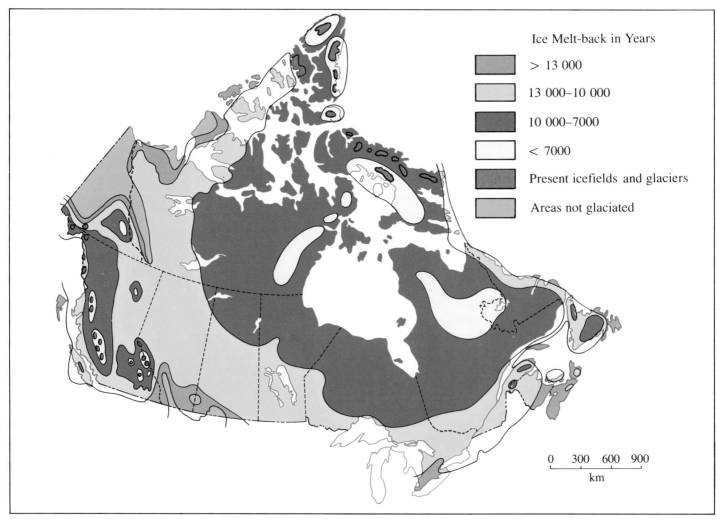

Ice Melt-back in Years

> 13 000

13 000–10 000

10 000–7000

< 7000

Present icefields and glaciers

Areas not glaciated

0   300   600   900
km

Figure 2.8 *Ice Melt-Back at the End of the Ice Age*   *This map shows the position of the ice edges 13 000, 10 000, and 7000 years ago. As the ice melted back, which parts of Canada were uncovered first? Where was the largest remaining ice sheet 7000 years ago?*

were ripped loose, ground up, and much later deposited again.

In some areas of sedimentary rock, glaciers scraped most of the soil away, exposing bedrock. Where the ice melted back at a fairly steady rate, glacial deposits formed a flat landscape called a *till plain*. Although a till plain contains some stones, most of it is made up of sand, silt, and clay.

On the Canadian Shield, loose and soft rock materials were not as plentiful, and much of the area was simply scraped bare. The glacier also gouged out many hollows on the Shield. When the hollows filled with water, thousands of lakes were formed. In many parts of Canada, such as southern Manitoba and Northern Ontario, large meltwater lakes covered the land. The sediment left when the lakes disappeared formed today's flat clay plains.

Large boulders of rock that are different from the rock of an area where they are found appear in much of Canada. Such boulders are known as *erratics* or *erratic blocks*.

As the ice moved over the land, plant life was destroyed, and animals migrated away from the ice edge. As the climate became warmer and the ice melted back, living creatures once more began to occupy the land. Vegetation gradually returned, replenishing the soil and making it possible for animals to survive.

The Work of Continental Glaciers

Striations

Moraine

Drumlins

Esker

Till plain

This limestone plain lies in Ontario's Bruce Peninsula.

An erratic block. This boulder of Shield rock rests on top of sedimentary rock on the Bruce Peninsula.

1. Explain how glacier ice differs from ordinary frozen water.
2. Consult the Glossary to find a definition of each of the captions of the photos showing the work of continental glaciers. Draw up a chart in your notebook that lists, defines, and illustrates these terms.
3. Draw sketches of three landforms created by glaciation. Base your drawings on the photos of the work of continental glaciers in this book and in reference books.
4. In what ways did the last Ice Age change the surface of Canada?

LOCAL STUDY

1. a) In which physiographic region of Canada do you live?
   b) Draw some sketches of landforms in your area that are typical of the region.
2. a) In what ways have people in your area made use of the landforms?
   b) What problems, if any, have the landforms caused people in your area?
3. Look in the area where you live for evidence of past continental glaciation. Take a photo or sketch a diagram, and use it to explain to your class how continental glaciation was responsible for what you found.

CLIMATE

This part of Chapter Two tells more about the climate of Canada and its influence on vegetation and soil. So far we have been focusing on Canada's physiographic regions, but Canada can also be divided into other natural regions, according to climate, vegetation, and soil.

WEATHER AND CLIMATE

Weather consists of the temperature, *precipitation*, wind, cloud cover, and humidity for any given time in any given place. The day-to-day weather in all parts of Canada is very changeable. The weather in a particular place on a certain date may also vary greatly from year to year. In Canada a weather record is broken somewhere almost every day.

Canada's weather is recorded daily at a number of weather stations across the country. These stations use special equipment to make accurate records of a number of factors that relate to weather.

Every weather station in Canada keeps temperature-measuring instruments in a Stevenson screen. It is a vented white box supported above the ground on posts. Within the box are two horizontal thermometers that record current temperature, as well as the highest and lowest temperatures reached since the last reading. The liquid in the thermometer tube moves small metal markers; the markers remain at the highest and lowest temperatures. A magnet is used to move the markers back each time a weather person records the temperatures. There are also two vertical thermometers inside the box; these are used to record the amount of moisture in the air.

Wind vanes and anemometers show wind direction and wind force. The wind vane has a pointer and a fin to show the direction the wind is blowing from. The anemometer has rotating cups to show the wind force.

The sunshine recorder is a glass sphere that concentrates the sunlight to a small point on a cardboard chart. The concentrated sunlight burns holes into the chart.

Small amounts of rain cannot be measured accurately without a rain gauge. The hole into which the rainwater flows is one-tenth the size of the large opening at the top of the gauge. A graduated tube of the same diameter as the small hole extends down inside the container.

On a windy day in winter, weather persons find it hard to decide whether snow has fallen from a cloud or has blown up from the ground nearby. Snow gauges are designed to measure only the snow that has actually fallen.

At a Weather Station

A Stevenson screen

Inside a Stevenson screen

Rain gauge

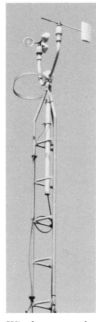

Wind vane and anemometer

Snow gauge

Sunshine recorder

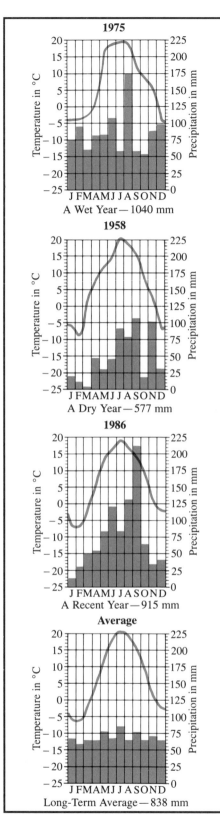

1975

Temperature in °C / Precipitation in mm

J FMAMJ J A SOND
A Wet Year — 1040 mm

1958

Temperature in °C / Precipitation in mm

J FMAMJ J A SOND
A Dry Year — 577 mm

1986

Temperature in °C / Precipitation in mm

J FMAMJ J A SOND
A Recent Year — 915 mm

Average

Temperature in °C / Precipitation in mm

J FMAMJ J A SOND
Long-Term Average — 838 mm

Figure 2.9 *Climographs: Waterloo-Guelph Airport*
How does the precipitation bar graph on the last climograph compare with the other three precipitation bar graphs? How does the temperature line graph compare with the other three line graphs?

Climate is the average weather over many years. The two most important ingredients of climate are temperature and precipitation. One way to illustrate the climate of a place is to make a climograph, drawing bars to show average monthly precipitation and a line to show average monthly temperatures. You can see in Figure 2.9 that even the average weather for any single year may differ greatly from the average over many years. Figure 2.9 shows four graphs for the Waterloo-Guelph Airport. The first three record climate in three separate years, and the fourth records average data collected over many years. In 1975, there was more precipitation than usual. By contrast, 1958 was a dry year. And 1986 was unusual in that most of the precipitation fell during the middle part of the year.

---

1. a) Why do the first three graphs in Figure 2.9 differ from one another?
b) Why does the fourth graph differ from the other three, which are part of the average it records?
c) Explain why climographs cannot be used to predict next year's weather.

AIR MASSES

One of the important factors that affects daily weather is the *air mass* covering an area. Figure 2.10 shows the air masses that influence Canada's weather. In Canada's far North, the air is usually cold and dry. If this air mass moves into southern Canada, it brings with it unseasonably cold, dry weather. The Gulf of Mexico and the Caribbean areas have warm, moist air. When this air mass moves into Canada, it brings unseasonably warm, humid weather. Air masses from the Pacific bring mild, damp weather to the west coast. In crossing the Cordilleran region, a Pacific air mass is dried and warmed; it therefore brings with it pleasantly warm and dry weather (Figure 2.10). Often eastern Canada experiences an "Indian Summer" in the fall resulting from an invasion of Pacific air after an arctic air mass has passed through.

Refer to Figure 2.10.
1. Why is it that the weather on Canada's west coast is neither very hot in the summer nor very cold in the winter?
2. During what season does Canada experience most invasions of Arctic air? of tropical air?

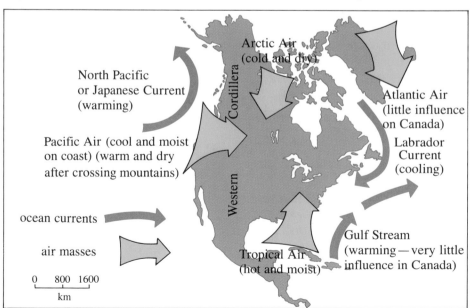

North Pacific or Japanese Current (warming)

Arctic Air (cold and dry)

Atlantic Air (little influence on Canada)

Cordillera

Pacific Air (cool and moist on coast) (warm and dry after crossing mountains)

Labrador Current (cooling)

Western

ocean currents

air masses

0   800   1600
km

Tropical Air (hot and moist)

Gulf Stream (warming — very little influence in Canada)

Figure 2.10 *Air Masses and Ocean Currents*   *Ocean currents can warm or cool an area but only if air moves onshore over the water.*

PRECIPITATION

Precipitation can occur only if air rises and cools. If the air cools enough, the lower temperature causes the invisible water vapour that the air contains to condense into tiny droplets. First clouds form, and if cooling continues, the droplets combine into rain drops.

Precipitation on the west coast is heavy because air masses rise and cool as they move up the west sides of mountain slopes. On the east side of the mountains, Pacific air falls and warms, and thus becomes drier. The drier side of the mountains is said to be in a *rain shadow* (Figure 2.11).

Precipitation can also occur if a warmer and lighter air mass rises up over colder and heavier air. This often happens when warm, moist air from the south is forced to rise by the cold, dry air from the north. The line of contact between two such air masses is called a *front*. The rising air along the front causes *low pressure*. Low-pressure disturbances, or storms, form along the front. They move west to east along it, becoming stronger toward eastern Canada. This is why precipitation increases toward the east coast (Figure 2.12, page 54).

The path of these storms and their west-to-east movement results from the flow of the *jet stream* (Figure 2.13). The jet stream is a narrow "river" of air moving from west to east in the upper atmosphere. It travels at speeds greater than 100 km/h, at about the altitude used by commercial airplanes. Because of this eastward flow of air, Atlantic air masses seldom invade North America (Figure 2.10).

---

1. Refer to Figure 2.13 for help in answering the following questions:
   a) Why would southern Canada often have long periods of hot weather in summer and long periods of cold weather in winter?
   b) Where would the jet stream often be located in spring and fall?
   c) Why would spring and fall in southern Canada have the most changeable weather?
2. Clip weather maps from your local newspaper for a period of at least three days, and observe the direction in which weather patterns have moved.
3. What circumstances cause precipitation?
4. Draw a diagram to show how precipitation can result when warm, moist air meets cold, dry air.

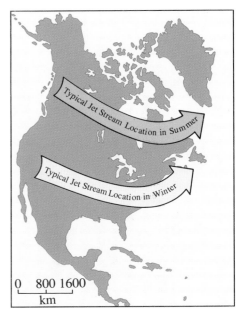

Figure 2.13 *Winter and Summer Jet Stream Locations* *Jet streams tend to control the direction in which low-pressure storms move. How could the jet stream affect westward flying aircraft? eastward flying aircraft?*

Precipitation is measured in two units: rainfall is measured in millimetres; snowfall is measured in centimetres because each centimetre of snow contains one millimetre of water.

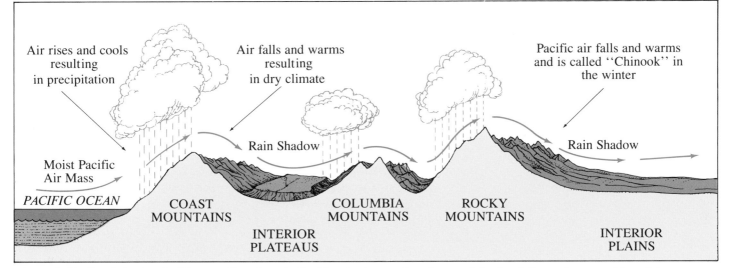

Figure 2.11 *Precipitation in Western Canada* *As Pacific air rises and cools, precipitation falls on the west sides of the mountain systems. Why are the eastern sides of the mountains dry?*

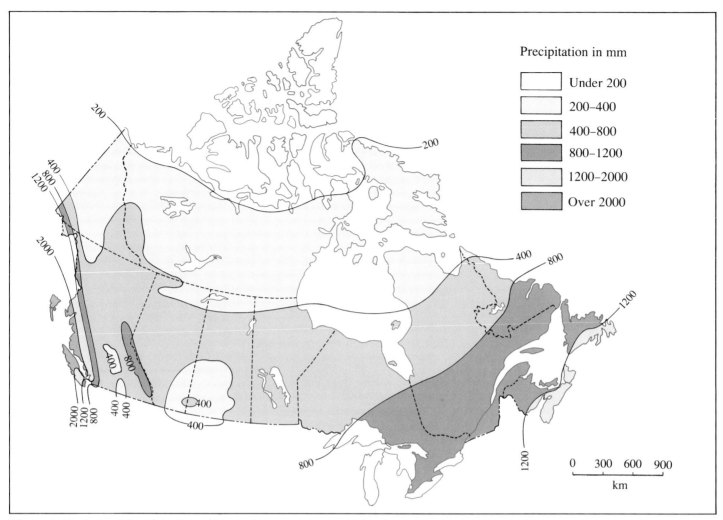

Figure 2.12 *Annual Precipitation* *Why is the west coast so wet? Why are the interior of British Columbia and parts of the Prairie Provinces dry? Why does the east coast of Canada have more precipitation than the interior?*

TEMPERATURE

Isotherms are lines marked on a map to join places with the same average temperature. Even a quick glance at the isotherms on the January and July temperature maps (Figures 2.14 and 2.15) will show major differences in temperature between one part of Canada and another. For example, temperatures become colder towards the North. But if latitude were the only factor affecting temperature, the isotherms would run east-west, parallel to the lines of latitude.

Large bodies of water can influence temperature because water maintains its heat or cold much longer than land. But bodies of water influence temperature only if air masses are moving towards the shore. The west coast has an onshore movement of air masses.

For this reason it has milder winters and cooler summers than it otherwise would. A warm Pacific current (Figure 2.10) helps to make west coast winters even milder. In contrast, Canada's east coast has an offshore flow of air masses and a cold ocean current, and so the ocean has little moderating effect there.

The interior of large land masses heats and cools more quickly than bodies of water. This produces hot summers and cold winters. Such a climate is called a *continental climate*. Much of the interior of Canada has a continental climate, with great differences in temperature between summer and winter.

Although Hudson Bay is a large body of water, it has no moderating influence on winter temperatures in

the lands surrounding it. It freezes over in the winter, when it might be expected to have a warming influence on the surrounding land. In the summer, the Bay has a chilling effect on the land around it.

The difference in the heating and cooling properties of water and land help to explain some of the curves and twists of the isotherms of the temperature maps (Figures 2.14 and 2.15).

---

1. Refer to Figure 2.16 (page 56) to answer the following questions:
   a) In what ways do the temperatures on the Vancouver graph differ from those on the Medicine Hat graph? Explain these differences. How does the precipitation differ? Why?

b) How does the amount of precipitation change as you move from Winnipeg to Toronto to Québec City? Why?

c) Describe and explain the differences in temperature between Winnipeg and Resolute.

d) Using what you have learned in this chapter, try to explain the small amount of precipitation in Resolute.

2. a) Hudson Bay is sometimes called "Canada's Refrigerator". In what way would this name apply? In which season would it apply most?

b) How do you think the climate of central Canada would change if Hudson Bay were not there?

> **The hottest temperature ever recorded in Canada was 45°C, on 5 July 1937 at Midale and Yellow Grass, Saskatchewan. The coldest temperature ever recorded was −63°C on 3 February 1947, at Snag in the Yukon.**

L O C A L   S T U D Y

1. a) As part of a class project, obtain monthly climate information for your area for the past 10 years from your nearest weather station or weather observation post.

b) Calculate the 10-year average for temperature for each month, and plot the data as a line on a climograph.

c) Calculate the average monthly precipitation over the 10-year period, and plot the data as bars on a climograph.

d) Which years differed from the average?

2. Find out from the staff of the weather station or observation post if the average climate in your area over the last 10 years has changed from the previous 10 or 20 years.

3. From what direction does most of the weather in your area come? Why?

4. What are the main factors that determine the climate in your area?

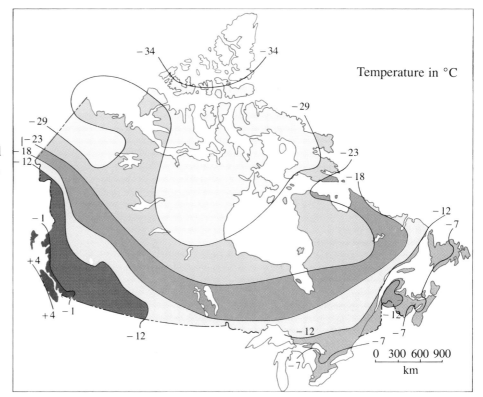

Figure 2.14 *January Isotherms* In the Western Cordillera region, most of the isotherms have been left out because too many would be needed to show the differences in temperature between valley bottoms and mountain tops. Why is the west coast warmer than the east coast in January? Suggest why the isotherms in central Canada curve southward in January.

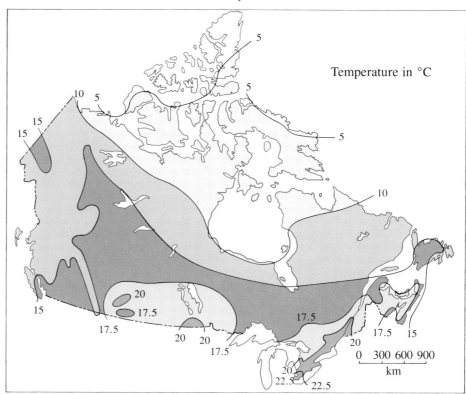

Figure 2.15 *July Isotherms* As in Figure 2.14, most of the isotherms in the Western Cordillera region have been left out. Why does the 10°C isotherm west of Hudson Bay in central Canada curve northwards in July?

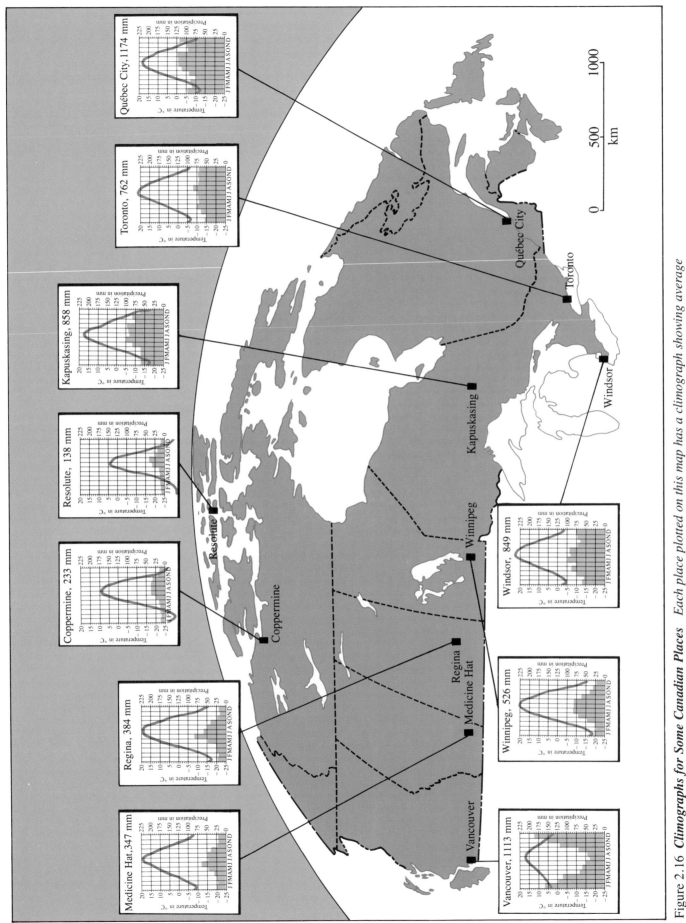

Figure 2.16 *Climographs for Some Canadian Places* Each place plotted on this map has a climograph showing average monthly temperature and precipitation. Which place has the warmest winter? the hottest summer? the highest precipitation? the lowest precipitation?

Human Bodies and Temperature

Our bodies are poor thermometers. The temperature outside often "feels" quite different to us from the temperature reading on a thermometer. The temperature that our bodies seem to feel is called *sensible temperature*.

Wind Chill

On a windy day the air feels colder than the temperature the thermometer shows. This is because the moving air takes heat away from our body surfaces, but wind blowing on a thermometer does not make the recorded temperature drop.

Wind chill is the chilling effect on the human body of strong winds combined with cool temperatures. To be comfortable or even to survive, the most important fact to know is not the temperature but the wind-chill reading. Exposed human skin will start to freeze at a temperature of −25°C. In a wind of 20 km/h, skin will start to freeze at only −15°C. Though the temperature is −15°C, the wind-chill temperature is −25°C.

The wind-chill chart shows the temperature recorded on a thermometer and the sensible temperature that our body would feel at different wind speeds. For example, when the temperature is −10°C and the wind is blowing at 40 km/h, we feel as cold as we would at a temperature of −27°C on a day with no wind.

Humidex

In the summer, the sensible temperature is often much warmer than the thermometer reading indicates. On a

hot day or when we exert ourselves, our body temperature wants to rise, but perspiration comes to the rescue. Our bodies are cooled by the evaporation of perspiration. Using a fan can speed up evaporation, which in turn speeds up cooling. On a humid day, evaporation is much slower, and our bodies feel much warmer. For this reason, warm temperatures in a dry area feel much more comfortable than the same temperatures in a humid area.

Using a complicated formula, weather forecasters calculate the *humidex* on hot humid days and give the information to the news media. The humidex reading is like the sensible temperature: it represents what your body feels, not the temperature recorded on the thermometer. You would be better off to choose your summer outdoor activities according to the humidex reading than according to the actual temperature.

Humidex information can help us lower heating costs in the winter. If we increase the humidity in our home in winter, temperatures seem warmer than in a dry house.

Wind-Chill Chart

Wind Speed (km/h)	Actual Temperature (°C)								
	0	−5	−10	−15	−20	−25	−30	−35	
10	−2	−7	−12	−17	−22	−27	−32	−38	Wind-
20	−7	−13	−19	−25	−31	−37	−43	−50	Chill
30	−11	−17	−24	−31	−37	−44	−50	−57	Temps
40	−13	−20	−27	−34	−41	−48	−55	−62	(°C)
50	−15	−22	−29	−36	−44	−51	−58	−66	
60	−16	−23	−31	−38	−45	−53	−60	−68	

1. Use the table above to find the wind chill temperature in each of the following situations.

Wind Speed (km/h)	Actual Temperature (°C)
a) 30	−20
b) 50	−15
c) 60	−5

2. a) Why should your outer layer of winter clothing be windproof if you go outside on a cold, windy day?
b) Why would a motorcycle driver travelling at 80 km/h be more affected by wind chill than a hiker in the same area?

3. Why would higher humidity in your home in the winter make the temperature feel warmer to you?

4. In summer, air conditioners that cool the air also remove moisture from it. Why would the lower humidity make you feel more comfortable?

Carbon Dioxide and Climate

During the past century, the development of industry and the growth of human population have increased the amount of carbon dioxide in the atmosphere. Most of this increase has resulted from the burning of fossil fuels such as coal, oil, and natural gas. Forests consume carbon dioxide through the process of *photosynthesis*. The destruction of forests has allowed more carbon dioxide to build up in the earth's atmosphere. The amount of carbon dioxide in the air is now increasing at the rate of three percent a decade.

As the carbon dioxide in the atmosphere increases, the climate grows warmer. Energy from the sun reaches us mainly in the form of light. When sunlight strikes an object on the earth, some of the light energy is converted into heat energy. From year to year, a fairly close balance exists between the energy coming from the sun and the energy radiated back by the earth or stored in plants by photosynthesis. This balance is upset if the air contains too much carbon dioxide, which works like a greenhouse in trapping some of the heat. The carbon dioxide allows the light energy of the sun to penetrate but holds back some of the heat energy from the earth that would otherwise be radiated into space. This "greenhouse effect" could warm temperatures by as much as 3°C (up to 10°C in the Arctic) in the next 50 to 75 years.

Climate changes in the past have taken place over thousands of years. Scientists use fossil records to construct a model of past climate changes and their effect on our world. On the basis of this model, scientists then make predictions about the effects of the more rapid changes that result from increased amounts of carbon dioxide.

A warming trend could be both beneficial and harmful to Canadians. A longer *growing season* could permit farming in areas farther north. But warmer temperatures would produce more drought in southern Canada. A larger amount of carbon dioxide would increase photosynthesis, producing greater crop yields and quicker growth of newly planted forest. The Great Lakes would not freeze over in winter, and so the shipping season would be longer. On the other hand, the lowering of water levels in the Great Lakes would make shipping channels shallower. A decrease in snow in southern Ontario would shorten the skiing season. Buildings would require less heat in winter, but in summer, especially in southern Canada, the use of air conditioners would increase. In the Arctic there would be less polar ice, and ships such as oil tankers might be used more. Massive melting of the Arctic ice would raise sea levels, which could flood parts of seacoast cities.

To plan wisely for the future, scientists must study climate trends carefully. Unfortunately, changes in climate are difficult to predict accurately. In the near future, people might reduce carbon dioxide emissions by conserving fuel or using it more efficiently, thus reversing the warming trend. Some events, both natural and human, could even cause the climate to cool. Volcanic eruptions or industrial pollution might significantly increase the tiny particles of material in the upper atmosphere. These particles lessen the amount of light energy received from the sun, while allowing the heat energy on the earth to radiate back into space. The effect of such a change would be a cooler climate.

Most natural changes in climate take place over thousands of years. But if human activity brings about a more rapid change, you may experience a climate change during your lifetime.

1. Draw a diagram that shows how the "greenhouse effect" works.
2. a) On a two-column chart, list the benefits to be obtained from a warmer climate in Canada. List the harmful effects of a warmer climate, as well.
   b) Using information from the two lists, debate the proposition: "Resolved that Canadians should reduce carbon dioxide emissions into the atmosphere."

Photosynthesis

LEAVES

Leaves carry out the following processes:

Photosynthesis

The word equation shows what happens in the green chlorophyll of leaves.

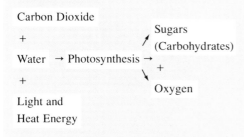

In most plants, photosynthesis requires a temperature of at least 5.6°C and works best at about 30°C.

Respiration

All living cells require energy. Respiration is the process by which that energy is provided when oxygen burns fuels such as glucose (sugar). This is the word equation for respiration.

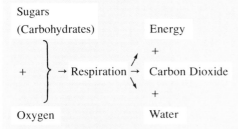

Transpiration

Water that carries dissolved minerals from the roots to the rest of the plant evaporates in the leaves. This process of evaporation cools the plant on a hot day.

ROOTS

Roots absorb water containing traces of dissolved minerals for plant cells to use. Therefore soil nutrients must

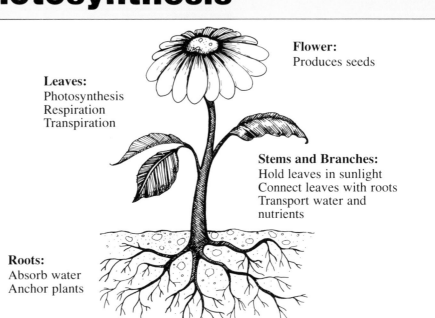

Leaves:
Photosynthesis
Respiration
Transpiration

Flower:
Produces seeds

Stems and Branches:
Hold leaves in sunlight
Connect leaves with roots
Transport water and nutrients

Roots:
Absorb water
Anchor plants

Figure 2.17 *How a Plant Works*

be water-soluble to be useful to a plant. Roots also anchor plants in the soil.

STEMS AND BRANCHES

Stems and branches hold leaves into sunlight. They also connect leaves with the plant's roots. They transport water and dissolved nutrients to the leaves and other parts of the plant.

FLOWERS

Flowers use a great deal of energy as they produce the seeds of future plants.

Referring to Figure 2.17, answer the following questions.

1. a) During what part of a 24-hour day does photosynthesis take place?
   b) Study the word equations for photosynthesis and respiration. How do the two processes relate to each other?

2. a) Why do plants grow more quickly on a warm day?
   b) Why does almost no photosynthesis take place during the winter?

3. a) In what two ways do all animals depend on plants?
   b) Why do most plants not require animals for survival?

4. What do you think often causes the stems of house plants to lean towards a window?

5. a) Why must nutrients in the soil be water soluble before they are useful to plants?
   b) How do you think a potted house plant is able to grow so large without the soil in the pot appearing to go down?

6. a) Give more than one reason why plants need water.
   b) What process in the leaves causes them to wilt if the soil becomes too dry?
   c) People transplanting young plants often damage the roots. Why is it wise to snip off a few leaves of newly transplanted plants and give them extra water?

VEGETATION

Plants make possible the survival of all living things. The green parts of plants draw energy from the sun to convert the simple raw materials of carbon dioxide, water, and minerals into organic compounds. These compounds, mainly carbohydrates, contain stored energy. The process that produces them in plants is called photosynthesis. Almost the entire plant is made up of the products of photosynthesis rather than of materials drawn from the soil.

Plants use the carbohydrates manufactured during photosynthesis to produce more plant cells. Animals that eat the plants convert the food into energy and materials to build their bodies. The animals that prey on other animals obtain carbohydrates from the flesh they eat and use them as fuel to energize their bodies. Without carbohydrates all animals would die.

In the process of photosynthesis, plants release oxygen into the atmosphere. Oxygen is required by all living things, including plants.

The type of vegetation that grows in an area depends on climate. One aspect of climate that helps to determine the type of vegetation is precipitation. Two others are the length of the growing season (Figure 2.18) and the length of the *frost-free period* (Figure 2.19). The growing season is made up of the number of days that have average temperatures of 5.6°C or higher. The frost-free period is the number of days between the last "killing frost" of spring and the first one of autumn. The total growing season includes warm days before the last frost in spring and after the first frost in fall. The number of growing season days in a year is therefore usually larger than the number of frost-free days in the frost-free period.

The frost-free period varies with altitude, as well as with latitude. In the Western Cordillera, for instance, the number of frost-free days varies from

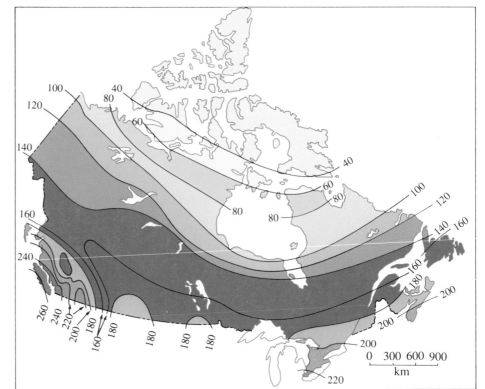

Figure 2.18 *Average Annual Growing Season Days Above 5.6°C* Lines on the map join places with the same number of days averaging over 5.6°C. Which region of Canada has the largest number of days with an average temperature over 5.6°C? Why?

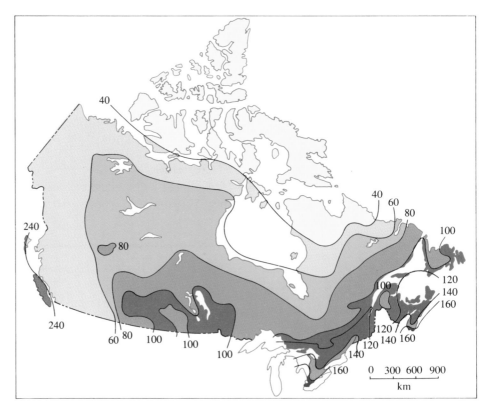

Figure 2.19 *Average Annual Frost-Free Period* The lines on this map join places that average the same number of frost-free days between the last frost in spring and the first frost in fall. For any part of Canada, how does the number of frost-free days compare with the number of growing season days? Why?

60

140 in the valleys to zero on the mountain tops.

To express the total energy available to plants during the growing season, *growing degree days* are used. Plants need a temperature of at least 5.6°C to grow. Each day the average temperature is recorded. If the average temperature for a day exceeds 5.6°C by 1°C, that day is recorded as one growing degree day. If a day averages 2°C above the basic temperature required for growth, it counts as two growing degree days, and so on. An average temperature of 21.6°C would equal 16 growing degree days. The total for all the days in the year is the number of annual growing degree days. This total becomes an important measure in farming. For instance, over 2000 growing degree days a year are needed to grow corn successfully (Figure 2.20). Therefore the highest numbers of growing degree days provide the best temperatures from the farmers' point of view.

1. Make a general statement comparing the growing season and the frost-free period shown in Figures 2.18 and 2.19.
2. Which do you think would be a better guide for farmers: the number of growing degree days shown in Figure 2.20 or the frost-free period shown in Figure 2.19? Explain.

NATURAL VEGETATION

Figure 2.21 (page 62) shows the vegetation of Canada as it existed when the Native peoples occupied the land. They did little to disturb the vegetation that had grown here naturally for centuries. Settlers from Europe, however, brought about major changes.

In some parts of southern Canada, large amounts of the original forest were removed to create farmland and space for homes and communities. People ploughed the grasslands of the prairies and converted them to grainfields. Forest industries cut down trees for lumber and pulp and paper. Only in the unsettled parts of the country and in Northern Canada can you find vegetation as it appeared before the arrival of people from other lands. The mixture of plants that grows undisturbed by people is called *natural vegetation*.

1. Refer to the natural vegetation map of Canada (Figure 2.21) and the annual precipitation map (Figure 2.12). In southern Canada, what type of natural vegetation grows if the annual precipitation is over 400 mm? under 400 mm?
2. a) What is the most obvious reason for the lack of trees in Canada's far North?
b) How does this reason relate to the southward dip of the northern limit of the forest around Hudson Bay?
c) What isotherm on the July temperature map in Figure 2.15 lies approximately along the tree line?

SOILS

As the continental glaciers melted, the ice and its meltwater deposited fresh layers of ground-up rock materials on the land's surface. These became the *parent material* in which topsoil-forming processes took place. At first, this parent material was the same pale colour from the surface downwards for many metres. Only after plant growth began did the surface begin to change. The plants helped to form humus, and topsoil began to accumulate.

HOW HUMUS IS FORMED

Dead vegetation that falls to the ground begins to decompose. Water moves some of the smaller plant remains down between the ground-up rock particles. Over a long period of time, the upper few centimetres of the parent material begin to darken as the plant material continues to penetrate downward. This decomposing plant

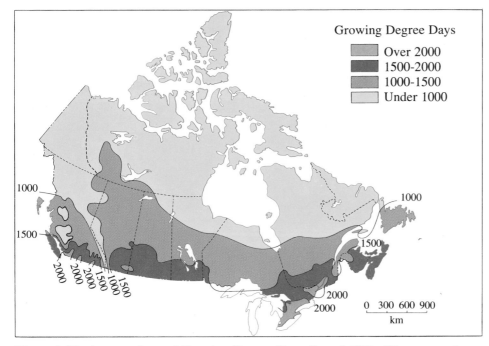

Figure 2.20 *Average Annual Growing Degree Days Over 5.6°C* *What parts of Canada have the best average temperatures for farming?*

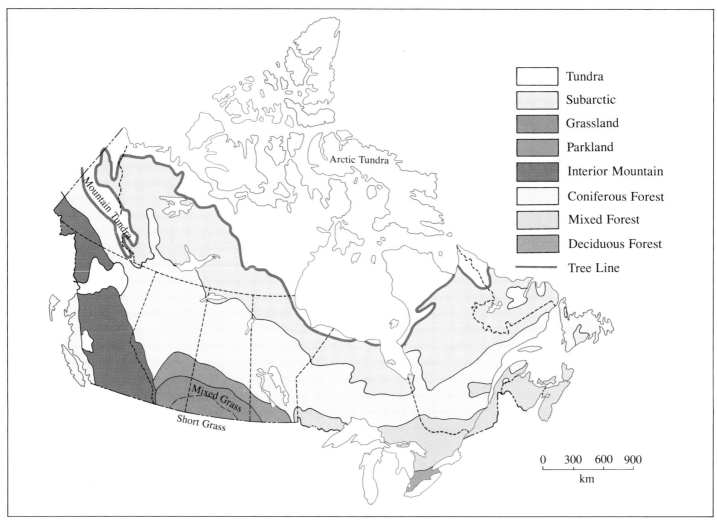

Figure 2.21 *Natural Vegetation Regions of Canada*

material, which may be enriched by the droppings and bodily remains of animals, is called *humus*.

In time some of the humus decomposes enough to become soluble in water. At this stage, the nutrients in the humus can be absorbed by plant roots. The upper part of the parent material that contains the humus is called *topsoil*. The oldest, and therefore the most water-soluble, humus is located near the bottom of the topsoil layer.

Humus decomposition is aided by a variety of living organisms including earthworms. Earthworms feed on dead plant material in the topsoil. The material passes through the worms' digestive systems, returning to the soil where plants then use it. As much as

forty tonnes of soil per hectare may pass through earthworms each year.

Most soil-making organisms work best in warm, humid conditions. However, almost all of them require air that is found in the tiny passages between the soil particles. Humus that is saturated with water decomposes very slowly. On rainy days, earthworms stop their soil-making activities and come to the surface for air.

Topsoil formation is a very slow process. In forested areas only 15 to 25 cm of topsoil have formed over the past 10 000 to 12 000 years since the ice melted away from southern Canada. In grassland areas much more humus has been added, because grass dies every year. Here topsoil with a thickness of 60 to 120 cm is common.

OTHER SOIL-FORMING PROCESSES

Besides humus accumulation there are two other processes that can take place in topsoil. In those parts of Canada with a moist climate, rain water soaks down into the topsoil. It dissolves part of the water-soluble humus and minerals so that plants can use them. However, if the rainfall is heavy, some of the water dissolves the nutrients and carries them away from the plants' roots to lower depths in the parent material. From here the water and nutrients make their way to springs and streams. This process is called *leaching*. Leaching takes place mainly at the bottom of the humus layer, where the nutrients are most soluble. Leaching water stains the parent material below the topsoil layer. This second layer is called **subsoil** (Figure 2.22).

In drier parts of Canada, ground water, carrying dissolved salts and minerals, moves upward through the soil in the same way that water moves up into a paper towel, or coffee moves up into a sugar cube. This process is called **capillary action**. Near the surface the ground water evaporates, leaving salts and minerals behind in the soil. In extreme situations, salts that accumulate in the topsoil harm plants. In dry areas, the subsoil is often stained and cemented together by ground water minerals (Figure 2.23).

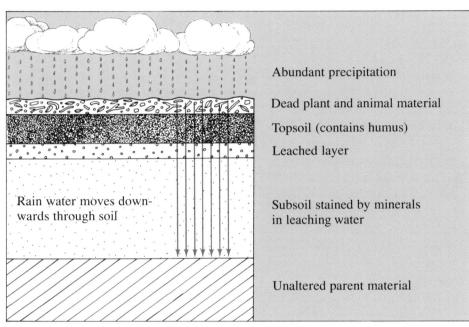

Abundant precipitation

Dead plant and animal material

Topsoil (contains humus)

Leached layer

Rain water moves downwards through soil

Subsoil stained by minerals in leaching water

Unaltered parent material

Figure 2.22 *Cross Section of Moist Climate Soil*   *Why does leaching take place mainly at the bottom of the topsoil layer?*

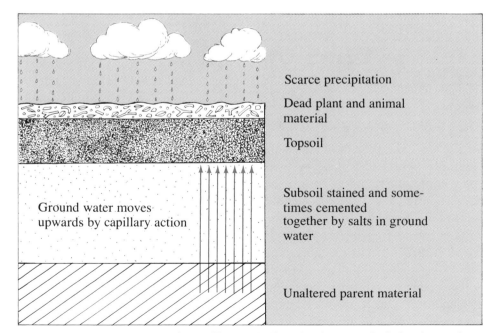

Scarce precipitation

Dead plant and animal material

Topsoil

Ground water moves upwards by capillary action

Subsoil stained and sometimes cemented together by salts in ground water

Unaltered parent material

Figure 2.23 *Cross Section of Dry Climate Soil*   *Why does very little leaching take place in dry climate soils?*

1. Why has Canada's present topsoil formed only since the last Ice Age?
2. Draw and label a diagram similar to Figure 2.22, to show the same cross section as it might have appeared at the end of the last Ice Age.
3. a) What soil-building process is stopped when land is cleared for farming?
   b) In a moist area what process in the soil continues after land is cleared?
   c) What finally happens to land that is farmed continuously? How can farmers prevent this?
4. How can new topsoil be produced? How long does it take?

SOIL TEXTURE

The earth materials left behind by the last Ice Age range in size from boulders to clay. The names given to this ground-up rock of various sizes are as follows:

- gravel–particles over 2 mm in diameter
- sand–particles 2.0 to 0.05 mm in diameter
- silt–particles 0.05 to 0.002 mm in diameter
- clay–particles less than 0.002 mm in diameter

The formation of topsoil depends largely on the particle size of the parent material. If the soil is sandy, rain water drains down through it too quickly. If the soil is mainly clay, rain water often sits on top of it in puddles and soaks in very slowly. To grow most plants, the topsoil should allow water to drain through it at a moderate rate. Farmers prefer a mixture of sand, silt, and clay. This kind of soil is called **loam**.

Bring to class some soil from your area, enough to fill a container 30 cm x 30 cm x 30 cm.

1. Place a small amount of the soil in the bottom of a jar. Fill the jar

with water, shake well, and let the materials settle. What does this experiment tell you about the composition of the soil in your area?

2. a) To the rest of the soil in the large container begin to add composting such as household garbage scraps (but no fat or animal matter), leaves, and grass cuttings. Add about two dozen earthworms. Lightly water the soil about once a week. You will also need to add composting about once a week. Watch what changes take place in the soil over the next three weeks. On a page in your notebook record your observations. Remember to return the earthworms to their natural habitat when you are finished.
b) After about three weeks plant some fast-growing seeds in the soil. Record the date of planting, how and when you water the soil, and the growth rate of the plants.
c) Try to find out how earthworms help to create good growing soil.

speed to escape predators. Sharp incisor teeth help beavers to cut down trees. Gophers dash to underground burrows to escape hawks.

---

1. Bring pictures of animals to make a class bulletin board display. Choose each picture for its value in illustrating how the animal is adapted for survival. Write captions to point out adaptive characteristics.
2. The following animal species have already become extinct in Canada: swift fox, great auk, Labrador duck, passenger pigeon, timber rattlesnake, paddlefish, and blue walleye. Other species are on the brink of extinction, mostly because of human hunting, fishing, gathering, destruction of habitat, and pollution. Such endangered species include sea otters, whooping cranes, whales, Vancouver Island marmots, and eastern cougars.

   Choose one endangered species in Canada, and do library research to find out the causes of its diminishing numbers. What could be done to preserve the species?

study that investigates these relationships is called *ecology*. An area in which all the living and non-living parts relate to one another is called an *ecosystem*. An ecosystem can be as small as a classroom aquarium or as large as Canada's Arctic region. One ecosystem is distinguished from another mainly on the basis of natural vegetation. Differences in types of vegetation, in turn, result from differences in climate.

---

1. a) Working in small groups, draw a diagram to show how several parts of an ecosystem depend on other parts.
b) Find pictures or make sketches to illustrate your diagram.
2. a) Choose one of the parts of the ecosystem you have put together, and tell how people might disturb it.
b) How might the disturbance you have described cause changes in other parts of the ecosystem?
c) Repeat a) and b), using another part of the ecosystem.

WILDLIFE

Every vegetation region provides a home for animal life (including birds, reptiles, and fish) that lives in a close relationship with other living things in the area. Animals called *herbivores* live by eating plants. Among the herbivores are squirrels, deer, rabbits, gophers, mice, and beavers. The herbivores become, in turn, the prey of meat-eating animals known as *carnivores*. Carnivores include wolves, foxes, cougars, and birds of prey such as hawks and owls. Those meat-eating creatures that search out their prey are also known as *predators*.

Most animals are specially adapted for survival in their *environment*. Rabbits have keen hearing and high

ECOSYSTEMS OF CANADA

WHAT IS AN ECOSYSTEM?

So far we have been looking at the landforms, climate, vegetation, soil, and wildlife of a region as factors that have nothing to do with one another. But to talk about one of these factors without considering at least one of the others is difficult. For example, vegetation depends on climate and soil. Soil depends on climate, vegetation, and landforms. In recent years, people have learned that in any one part of the world, almost every feature depends on all other features. The

DECIDUOUS FOREST ECOSYSTEM

The *deciduous* forest ecosystem is located in the southernmost part of Canada. Southern Ontario juts southward into the United States. Its situation makes the region more like the eastern United States in climate and vegetation than like the rest of Canada.

---

1. Locate the deciduous forest region on the natural vegetation map (Figure 2.21).
2. On an outline map of Canada, shade in the deciduous forest ecosystem. Title the map Canadian Ecosystems. You will use this ecosystem map again.

A deciduous forest in southern Ontario.
Most of the trees in this forest are beech and maple.

Climate
The climate maps in this chapter give information about the climate of the deciduous forest ecosystem. The following activity will help you organize that information.

Windsor, Ontario, is in the deciduous forest region. Although climate varies somewhat within this ecosystem, the climate data for Windsor can be used as an example of deciduous forest climate.

Use the Windsor climograph in Figure 2.16 and the other climate maps that include the Windsor area to estimate Windsor's climate data. On a full page in your notebook, prepare a chart with the following headings:

- Ecosystem
- Average Annual Precipitation
- Average January Temperature
- Average July Temperature
- Average Number of Growing Season Days
- Average Frost-Free Period
- Average Growing Degree Days

Arrange these headings down the left side of the page, leaving space on the right for four columns of ecosystems. In the first column, headed Deciduous Forest Ecosystem, record the Windsor data. You will be using this chart again later to add information about other ecosystems.

Natural Vegetation
The photograph shows a typical deciduous forest in southern Ontario during mid-spring. Because the leaves of these trees are broad and thin, they capture a great deal of sunlight for photosynthesis. Many trees will have over 100 000 leaves with a total surface area of several classroom floors.

The delicate leaves cannot survive the winter freeze-up. Therefore, each autumn, the trees drop their leaves. Most deciduous trees require at least five warm months with an average temperature of 10°C or more to survive the winter without leaves.

The sugars (carbohydrates) manufactured by leaves in the summer are stored in the roots and trunk of the dormant tree in the winter. In the spring, the sap starts to run to provide the buds with the material to grow new leaves.

Trees in the deciduous forest ecosystem include maple, beech, oak, ash, and hickory. The southern part of the region has some trees, such as the tulip tree, that are usually found only farther south in the United States. The deciduous forest vegetation invaded from the south after the last Ice Age.

1. Prepare a class bulletin-board display of leaves of the deciduous trees common in your area. The leaves may be either natural or drawn and coloured by class members. Label each leaf.
   If there are photographers in your class, they might add photos of the various trees represented by the leaves you have used.
2. Why do deciduous trees drop their leaves in the fall?
3. a) In the autumn after the leaves have changed colour or dropped, why would warm growing season days not help a tree to grow?
   b) Why would warm growing season days in early spring not help a tree to grow?
4. Which of the following statistics would best show the true length of the growing season for deciduous trees: number of growing season days or frost-free period? Why?

Soil
The vegetation that began to grow in southern Ontario after the last Ice Age helped form new topsoil. Much of the soil parent material in which this

The autumn trees owe their beautiful colours to a breakdown of chlorophyll with falling temperatures and less daylight. The removal of the green chlorophyll frees the other colours it was masking and reveals the bright red, orange, and yellow leaves of fall.

growth took place was loam. Most of the mixture of ground-up rock was deposited directly from the ice. Water also deposited some parent material. Near the shores of former and deeper Great Lakes, deposits of clay left behind flat clay plains. The *deltas* of some meltwater rivers formed sand plains, such as the Norfolk Sand Plain on the north shore of Lake Erie.

For the last few thousand years, deciduous trees have dropped their leaves each year, providing raw material for humus. Decomposed dead trees and animals added to the humus in the topsoil. However, leaching carried a portion of the water-soluble humus away to lower depths. As a result, the amount of topsoil that formed was only about 15 to 25 cm thick. Figure 2.24 shows a simple cross-section view of forest soils in southern Ontario.

1. After several thousand years of topsoil formation since the last Ice Age, the topsoil in southern Ontario was still quite thin even before farmers began to use it. Explain why.
2. Because of its texture, much of the soil in southern Ontario is classified as the best farming soil in Canada. However, judged by humus accumulation, this soil can be classified as soil likely to be harmed or even destroyed by farming. Explain how both classifications can be valid.
3. a) What soil problem would farmers have on clay plains? on sand plains?
   b) Which kind of soil—clay or sand—poses the most problems in an abnormally wet year? in an abnormally dry year? Why?

Wildlife

Most of southern Ontario's deciduous forest region has been cleared for farming. Almost none of the original forest remains. Many farms, however, have woodlots with younger trees in them. These woodlots are generally too small to support the large number of animal and plant species found in an undisturbed, deciduous forest ecosystem. The most heavily farmed areas have the fewest trees and therefore the fewest bird species. The resulting increase in insect population has damaged farm crops.

People have destroyed the larger carnivores such as wolves and cougars in the mistaken belief that they are very dangerous. As a result, populations of the animals they prey on, such as rabbits, mice, and other rodents, have increased. These rodents, in turn, consume farmers' crops.

Some animals have adapted to city life. Our garbage is attractive to skunks, raccoons, and an ever-increasing population of gulls. The droppings of gulls and Canada geese have helped to pollute some of our inland bodies of water.

1. a) Although much of the deer population moved northward as the forests were cleared, parts of southern Ontario may sometimes still be overpopulated with deer. What reason might there be for an increase in the number of deer?
   b) What problems do you think would be created by a surplus of deer in southern Ontario?
   c) How might the deer population be controlled?
2. a) Groundhogs like open fields and pastures. They dig holes in the fields to make their homes. How might this activity create a problem for farmers?
   b) The natural enemies of groundhogs are foxes, wolves, and lynxes. Suggest how human actions have led to an increase in groundhog population in southern Ontario.
3. The location of the eyes in an animal's head help determine how well it survives in its environment.
   Think of some predators and the animals they prey on. By means of a sketch or a description, point out the difference in the position of their eyes. Suggest a reason for this difference.

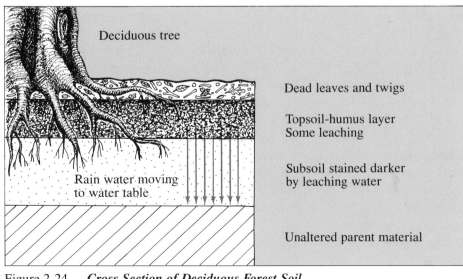

Figure 2.24   *Cross Section of Deciduous Forest Soil*

Human Impact

Destruction of forests by people changed the balances in the original deciduous forest ecosystem. People also drained many of the natural *wetlands* in southern Ontario and converted them to farmland. Wetlands and forests are natural reservoirs of rain water. They act as big sponges, absorbing water from precipitation. They then release the water slowly to streams throughout the year. Open fields, on the other hand, allow rapid water run-off. This rapid run-off erodes precious topsoil and causes sudden changes in stream flow.

To rid the farmland of damaging insects and weeds, farmers use chemical sprays. Chemical fertilizers are used to replace nutrients lost from the topsoil. Some of these chemicals find their way into our ground water and streams. This process creates concerns about the purity of our drinking water. A similar problem can result from the disposal of industrial wastes.

---

1. How might each of the following actions reduce the problems created by people in the deciduous forest region?
   a) Enlarging the farm woodlots
   b) Replanting trees on the poorer farmland
   c) Preserving the remaining wetlands
2. a) In a farming area, why are streams brown after a heavy rain?
   b) What layer of soil is partly removed from a field by every rapid run-off of water?
   c) Why must farmers try to prevent this loss?
3. Working with other students in your class, draw a mural showing a deciduous forest ecosystem. Show vegetation, wildlife, and soil. Using your ecosystem diagrams (page 64, activity 1) to help you organize your ideas, try to think of ways to show how various parts of the ecosystem relate to one another. Extend the mural to show the results of actions by people.

CONIFEROUS FOREST ECOSYSTEM

The *coniferous* forest ecosystem covers a broad band across mid-Canada from the Atlantic coast to the Western Cordillera. Sometimes this coniferous forest of the North is called the *boreal* forest.

---

1. Locate the coniferous forest region on the natural vegetation map (Figure 2.21).
2. Shade in the coniferous forest ecosystem on your Canadian Ecosystems map.

Climate

The following activity will help you organize information about the coniferous forest region to develop an idea of its climate.

---

1. The coniferous forest ecosystem is much larger than the deciduous forest area. Great variations of climate occur within this larger ecosystem. The climate of Kapuskasing, Ontario, represents the climate in the central part of the coniferous forest ecosystem.

   Use the Kapuskasing climograph in Figure 2.16 and the climate maps in this chapter to estimate data for the Kapuskasing area. Enter the information on your ecosystem chart in the column for the coniferous forest ecosystem.
2. a) For each feature of climate on the chart, tell how the climate of the coniferous forest ecosystem differs from that of the deciduous forest.
   b) Suggest a reason for each difference.

Natural Vegetation

Much of the coniferous forest has a short growing season (one to three months with an average temperature above 10°C). Most deciduous trees could not survive the long winters following such a short growing period. Coniferous trees of the boreal forest, however, are specially adapted to the climate of the region in a number of ways:

- They keep their needle-like leaves year round. This permits photosynthesis to take place on any warm days before or after the regular growing season.

Topsoil (dark) has been eroded from the slopes and deposited on the lower land.

- The pitch or sap of the evergreens acts like an anti-freeze, which helps the needles to resist freezing.
- The narrow leaves and flexible branches of the trees help them to shed snow.
- These trees require less energy for leaf building than do deciduous trees. As the coniferous tree grows, only the ends of the branches produce new needles.
- The narrow leaves help to reduce water loss by evaporation. This water conservation is important in the drier northern and western sections of the region.
- The trees are sometimes called "upside-down trees" because their branches spread out at the bottom rather than at the top. This cone shape helps expose more of the needles to the sun for photosynthesis.

White and black spruce, and balsam fir grow in these northern forests, but most trees in the coniferous forest region are spruce. Jack pines grow in after a fire. Two hardy deciduous trees found in parts of the coniferous forests are birch and aspen. They can tolerate a short growing season and a very cold winter.

---

1. On a full page in your notebook, draw a sketch of a coniferous tree and of a deciduous tree.
   a) On the coniferous tree label the features that help it to survive in a cold climate with a short growing season.
   b) On the deciduous tree label the features that hinder its survival in such a climate.
2. Canada's Native peoples developed special uses for many species of trees. Try to discover how they used some particular species.
   Make a class collection of legends, traditions, or poems relating to their use of trees.

A coniferous forest in Northern Ontario.   The bog in the foreground is overgrown mainly with sphagnum moss and lacks the nutrients to grow trees.

Without forest fires, jack pines would become extinct. Jack pine cones release their seeds only after the heat of a fire.

One conifer behaves like a deciduous broadleaf tree: the tamarack or larch sheds its needles in winter.

Soil

Since coniferous trees drop only a few dead needles and some lower branches, humus beneath them accumulates very slowly. Furthermore, the tough skins of the needles and a natural preservative in needles and branches help to slow down decomposition. Cool temperatures and a lack of soil organisms, such as earthworms, also slow down the formation of humus.

As a result, what little humus becomes water soluble is easily leached away by snow-melt water and rain. This thorough leaching makes the bottom of the topsoil layer almost white in colour. Figure 2.25 shows a simple cross section of coniferous forest soil.

Much of the coniferous forest grows on the Canadian Shield. Here parent material for soil was removed from some areas by the last Ice Age. Outcrops of bare rock appear in many places. The ice also gouged out many small hollows and long grooves in the rock. These now hold water and account for the many lakes on the Shield.

Often, shore vegetation grows out into the lakes, and some even floats on the water. Each year the shore and

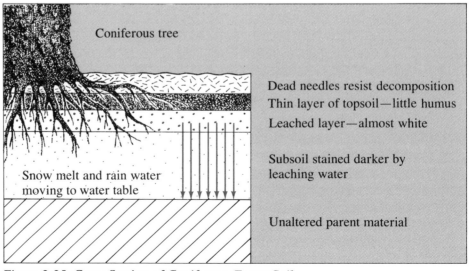

Figure 2.25 *Cross Section of Coniferous Forest Soil*

water plants add dead plant material to the lakes. The rotting vegetation uses up oxygen in the lake water. As the stagnant lakes become more oxygen starved and acidic, only *sphagnum moss* can grow well. It finally takes over the lake as a thick mass of floating vegetation called a *quaking bog*. Layer upon layer of dead sphagnum moss becomes peat, which absorbs water like a huge sponge. Sponge-like peat bogs are called *muskeg*.

Muskeg in the coniferous forest region. Shore vegetation is growing out into the lake in the background of this photo. The foreground shows a quaking bog. A beaver dam created the lake in the middle.

Not all muskeg in the coniferous forest has a lake beginning. Muskeg can form wherever there is more precipitation than evaporation in a poorly drained landscape. Sphagnum moss is poor material for soil because it lacks water-soluble nutrients. For this reason few trees grow on it.

The photograph shows some of the stages by which lakes fill in to form muskeg.

1. Explain why soils in a coniferous forest region would be infertile for farming.
2. Draw a series of three sketches to show the formation of muskeg.

3. Suggest some of the problems that people would face when building roads and communities in areas of muskeg.
4. Why is it easier to transport logs from the coniferous forest in winter than in summer?

Wildlife

In the colder climate of the coniferous forest region there is a smaller variety of trees than in the deciduous forest region. For this reason there is also a smaller variety of animals.

The largest *mammal* in the coniferous forest region is the moose. Its stilt-like legs allow the moose to wander through wetlands to find summer food. In the winter, a moose can also walk through deep snow to search for plant materials such as fir twigs and aspen branches.

White-tailed deer prefer to feed on the shrubs and aspen that grow in a burnt-over area after a forest fire. In the winter they have great difficulty walking in deep snow. Often the deer trample down an area of deep snow to form a "deer yard". Unable to eat balsam fir as the moose do, white-tailed deer depend on the bark and branch tips of aspen in the winter.

When food is scarce, deer often starve. The timber wolf helps to control deer population by selecting the weaker animals for food.

Some animals, such as squirrels and beaver, are food hoarders. In the summer, squirrels gather food for the winter, such as seeds from cones. Beavers cut down aspen for food. They store the branches by sticking them into the bottom of ponds near the underwater entrances to their lodges. Beavers build dams to create ponds in which to build their lodges. They also use the pond to float to their lodges the aspen branches on which they feed.

The moose feeds in wetlands in summer.

A beaver dam and pond

Other animals have made special adaptations that help them to survive. The snowshoe hare has tufted feet to help it keep on top of the snow. In the winter, the snowshoe hare turns white for camouflage.

Insects in their *larva* stage, such as the spruce budworm, can destroy large numbers of trees. Others, such as the black-fly and mosquito, make life miserable for mammals (including people). Millions of insect-eating birds, called warblers, migrate into the coniferous forest each spring. They consume enormous numbers of insects to feed their young and to build up their bodies for the long flight south in the autumn. Insecticide sprays are sometimes used to poison the insects. The same chemicals can also poison birds. Even if the birds survive the insecticide, the reduction in insects will cause a drop in bird population. When bird populations are reduced, the results can be disastrous, as insect populations greatly increase.

> The bite of the tiny black-fly may prove more serious than that of the larger mosquito. The mosquito sips your blood through a tube it inserts in your skin. The black-fly chews a hole and laps the blood. Black-fly bites are therefore more open to infection.

1. What would happen to the parts of the coniferous forest ecosystem if the wolf populations were reduced?
2. Spruce budworms have destroyed many trees in the coniferous forest region. Suggest why it is hard to control the spruce budworm populations.

Human Impact
In contrast to the deciduous forest region, little agricultural settlement has taken place in the coniferous forest region. It is largely through forestry and mining that humans have made an impact on the coniferous ecosystem. Large sections of forest have been cut down to supply the pulp and paper industry. Fires also destroy large areas of forest. Careless smokers and campers have added to the numbers of natural fires caused by lightning.

Replanting has not kept pace with forest destruction. Herbicides are used to control the growth of broad-leaved plants, shrubs, and *saplings* while new coniferous trees are starting to grow. This practice reduces food for deer.

Chemicals from pulp and paper mills must be treated before being released into streams. Accidental spills can be devastating to fish life. Chemicals are used in the processing of mineral ore, and their release into the natural environment can be very damaging.

1. a) In what ways would forest fires be harmful to a coniferous forest ecosystem?
   b) How might forest fires be beneficial to parts of that ecosystem?
2. Suggest why people should replant forests that have been cut down, rather than just letting them regrow naturally.
3. Some forest fires are caused by people's carelessness. Design a poster and a slogan to encourage people to help prevent forest fires.

TUNDRA ECOSYSTEM
The *tundra* ecosystem is located mainly in Canada's far North. It includes all the Arctic islands and sweeps south on the mainland in a large arc around the shores of Hudson Bay. There is tundra at the higher elevations of the Western Cordillera, as well; it is called alpine tundra.

1. Locate the tundra region on the natural vegetation map (Figure 2.21).
2. Shade in the tundra ecosystem on your ecosystem map.

Climate
The following activity will help you organize information about the climate of the tundra ecosystem.

1. a) Use Coppermine, N.W.T., to represent the tundra ecosystem as you used Windsor and Kapuskasing as examples of their ecosystems. Estimate the data for Coppermine from the climograph in Figure 2.16 and the climate maps in this chapter.
   b) Enter the information on your chart in the column for the tundra ecosystem.
2. a) For each aspect of climate on the chart, tell how the climate of the tundra ecosystem differs from that of the coniferous forest.
   b) Suggest a reason for each difference.

> Pingos, found mostly on the Tuktoyaktuk Peninsula, are volcano-shaped hills with an ice core formed by the upward pressure of freezing water. Nearly 1500 pingos have been located so far, ranging in height up to 50 m.

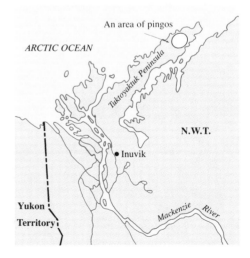

Natural Vegetation

The growing season in the tundra eco-system is very short. No month has an average temperature of over 10°C. Winters are long, windy, and bitterly cold. Only specially adapted plants can survive. Plants must leaf, flower, and produce seed within a few weeks. Cool summer temperatures and low sun angle slow photosynthesis. On the other hand, long daylight hours (up to 24 hours north of the Arctic Circle) in the summer allow photosynthesis to take place over a long time each day.

Some plants break up their growth cycle over two years and produce seed every other year. Other plants produce seed only if the summer is longer and warmer than usual. Almost all plants in the tundra are **perennials**. This gives them a head start at the beginning of each growing season. All plant life remains close to the ground to gain maximum warmth and to protect itself from the chilling winds.

Tundra vegetation consists of small flowering plants, mosses, and **lichens**. In a few protected areas, dwarf trees can be found. Creeping birch and dwarf willow only a few centimetres high might be over a century old. Growth is so slow that a microscope is needed to see a tree's growth rings.

Tundra vegetation: flowers, mosses, and lichens.   The low tundra plants flower briefly in July at Auyuittuq National Park on Baffin Island.

1. Why do plants grow slowly in the tundra region?
2. In what ways are plants adapted to the tundra climate?

Soil

The extremely cold winter in the tundra regions causes the water in the soil parent material to freeze to great depths. In the short summer, only a few centimetres of soil near the surface thaw. The permanently frozen soil below is called **permafrost**. Permafrost prevents water from draining downward in the summer. As a result, the surface soil becomes liquid muck covered by a mat of vegetation (Figure 2.26).

There is almost no humus. Decay of the sparse plant material is slowed by cool temperatures, water-saturated soil, and lack of soil organisms. If the surface of the land is disturbed, recovery can take centuries because plants grow back very slowly.

1. Why would tundra soils be of little use for agriculture?
2. What problems would land vehicles have in travelling on the tundra?

Decay of all kinds is very slow in the tundra region. In 1984 and 1986, for instance, bodies and clothing of members of the Franklin expedition who were buried in shallow graves during the winter of 1846 were found well preserved.

Low tundra vegetation

Little humus—some peat

Frozen in winter—water-logged in summer

Permafrost

Figure 2.26 *Cross Section of Tundra Soil*

Wildlife

To survive in the tundra, land animals such as musk-ox and arctic fox are protected from the fierce cold by thick hair or fur. An insulating layer of body fat also helps them maintain their body temperature. Their legs are often quite short and are sometimes protected by extra fur. Most tundra animals can stand lower temperatures in their legs and feet than can other animals.

Seals and walruses are adapted for life in the sea. Their flippers help them swim as they search for fish. Polar bears, the largest predators of the tundra, also need to be good swimmers. They prey on seals.

Some animals live in the tundra only during the warmer part of the year. Each spring multitudes of sea and shore birds migrate to the tundra to nest. They fly south again before winter sets in. Large herds of barren-ground caribou come to the tundra each summer to feed on the vegetation. As winter approaches, they move southward to the forest.

The harsh climate of the tundra region reduces the variety of plant and animal species. For this reason, *food chains* are shorter and simpler than in other regions of the country. Any disturbance in one part of a tundra food chain can change much of the whole ecosystem. The interdependence among living things in the region is so delicately balanced that the tundra ecosystem is the most fragile in Canada.

The lemming provides one example of interdependence in the tundra. Lemmings are small rodents that play an important part in regulating the populations of other tundra animals. Female lemmings can give birth to 10 young ones every month from April to September. The large numbers of lemmings provide food for predators such as foxes, wolves, bears, owls, and hawks, whose populations also increase when lemmings are plentiful. Every three or four years, overcrowding of lemmings takes its toll. At

The polar bear eats fish and smaller animals, some of which feed on tundra vegetation.

times, countless lemmings migrate across the tundra, eating up the vegetation as they go. This creates a food shortage for caribou. The lemmings even swim across rivers and ponds in search of living space. Unfortunately, they cannot tell the difference between small and large bodies of water. Many lemmings drown at sea or in large lakes. The overcrowding of the lemmings also causes diseases to spread more rapidly throughout their population. The crash in lemming population, in turn, reduces the predator population. Gradually the lemmings begin to increase once more, and the cycle starts again.

---

1. Draw a simple sketch to illustrate one food chain in the tundra ecosystem.
2. In paragraphs or by making a list of points, describe what would happen to other parts of the tundra ecosystem if all the lemmings died.

Human Impact

In the past, the cold climate of the tundra region made the area very unattractive to Europeans. The *Inuit*, however, have lived on the tundra for

The arctic hare feeds on tundra vegetation.

several thousand years. Their survival depended on the animal life in the tundra region. If the Inuit disturbed the balance between parts of the tundra ecosystem, the consequences could be disastrous for them. For example, over-hunting could lead to starvation. Over the years, the Inuit who survived were those who least disturbed the ecosystem.

The events of European history changed the way many Inuit related to their environment. Early explorers, looking for the northwest passage to Asia, were followed by whalers and fur traders. The newcomers persuaded many Inuit to change their traditional way of life. The Inuit began to hunt animals for fur rather than for food.

Exploratory drilling for oil in a permafrost area. The machine drills holes into the permafrost. The pipes are then put into the holes, where they freeze in place.

In return, the traders offered them modern weapons, clothing, and food. But in adapting to this new way of life, the Inuit came to be at the mercy of changes in the animal populations and the successive fads of fashion. They also contracted European diseases.

Today many Inuit are caught between the old way of life and the new. They have few opportunities to make an adequate living in modern white society, yet they are rapidly losing the skills that helped them to survive in the past.

In the last half of the 20th century, discoveries of oil and natural gas in the Arctic have brought more southern Canadians and their technologies to that region. Many people believe that the impact of these new developments is not well enough understood to prevent damage to the Arctic's fragile environment.

1. Why was it important for the earlier Inuit not to kill more animals than necessary for survival?
2. Debate the resolution: ''Modern development in the tundra region has benefited the Inuit.''

3. Modern people have had some problems building settlements in the tundra region. Suggest the problems that would result from each of the following situations:
   a) The warmth from a heated building starts to melt the permafrost under it.
   b) Heated oil is pumped through pipelines to southern markets.
   c) Garbage and sewage are left to decompose naturally.

GRASSLAND ECOSYSTEM

The grassland region of Canada is located in the southern part of the Prairie Provinces. Grasslands are often called *prairies*.

1. Locate the grassland region on the natural vegetation map (Figure 2.21).
2. Shade in the grassland ecosystem on your ecosystem map.

Climate

The following activity will help you organize information about the climate of the grasslands ecosystem.

1. Use Regina, Saskatchewan, to represent the grassland ecosystem. Estimate the data for Regina from the climograph in Figure 2.16 and the climate maps in this chapter. Enter the information on your chart in the column for the grassland ecosystem.
2. How is the climate of the grassland ecosystem like that of the deciduous forest region? How is it different?
3. How is the climate of the grassland ecosystem like that of the coniferous forest region? How is it different?

Natural Vegetation

The climate of the grassland ecosystem is too dry and variable for most trees to survive. The figures for average precipitation on the grasslands are deceiving. They result from periods of wet years followed by periods of dry years, mixed in with a few average ones. No predictable pattern exists. Only a few trees, such as aspen, can survive the years of drought.

Grass, on the other hand, adapts well to variations in moisture. During dry periods, it simply dies off as it does each winter. The spark of life remains in the root system until weather conditions are more favourable. New green grass sprouts from below as moisture increases or when temperatures warm in the spring. Proportionately, grass also has a much bigger root system than most plants. Roots can extend to depths of several metres to search out ground water.

The intertwining root systems of many grass plants form an almost impenetrable layer called a *sod mat*. The sod mat is very important because it absorbs and holds moisture. This layer also holds the topsoil in place, preventing it from blowing away in the strong prairie winds.

In the driest areas, the grass is much shorter. Drought-resistant plants such as sagebrush also grow in these areas.

(See the photo of prairie grassland on page 38.)

Throughout the prairies grow flowering shrubs and plants of many kinds. Several varieties of aspen grow in the places where moisture is most plentiful, such as along rivers and in valley bottoms.

---

1. Why can grass withstand drought conditions better than trees?
2. Why do you think the early farmers on the grasslands were called "sod busters"? What was the first use the European settlers made of the prairie sod? (You will find the answer—and possibly a picture—in Canadian history books.)
3. What problems might be caused by removing the grass cover and sod mat?

Soil

Because grass dies each year, a great deal of humus develops in grassland soils, and there is very little leaching to carry away the water-soluble part of the humus. The result is thick and very fertile topsoil. In areas of tallest grass, the topsoil is black.

During periods of dry weather, ground water, containing dissolved salts, actually moves upward through the soil. Near the surface the water evaporates, leaving the salts behind in the soil. A concentration of salts in the soil can harm some plants. Figure 2.27 shows a cross-section view of grassland soil.

Throughout much of the grassland region are millions of ponds, called *sloughs*. A slough is a small depression in the glacial deposits that goes below the *water table* of the surrounding land. Some sloughs fill with water from snow melt in the spring and gradually dry out during the summer through evaporation. Pond vegetation adds plant material to the bottom of the sloughs, making them rich in nutrients.

---

1. Why would grassland soils need less fertilizer than forest soils when they are farmed?
2. Why is too much capillary action harmful to farming?
3. What would happen to the water level in a slough if the water table in the surrounding land went down? went up?

Wildlife

People have changed the grasslands so much that it is difficult to imagine what they looked like over a century ago. In those days, over 50 million bison (sometimes termed 'buffalo') roamed the grasslands of North America. These animals were well suited to the grassland environment. Their heads were built close to the ground for easy grazing, and their continual movement prevented overgrazing. Besides the bison there were 50- to 100 million pronghorn antelope. They did not compete with the bison for grazing land because they ate mainly sagebrush and other shrubs.

Large populations of plant-eating rodents lived in underground burrows. These included gophers, ground squirrels, and prairie dogs. A variety of carnivores helped to keep the populations of these herbivores in check. Among the predators were wolves, grizzly bears, cougars, and coyotes, as well as hawks and eagles. Over eight million sloughs in the grasslands make excellent homes for waterfowl. Although these ponds have no fish, they provide water and contain plant foods that ducks enjoy.

The bison is well suited to the grasslands and cold climate of the western prairies.

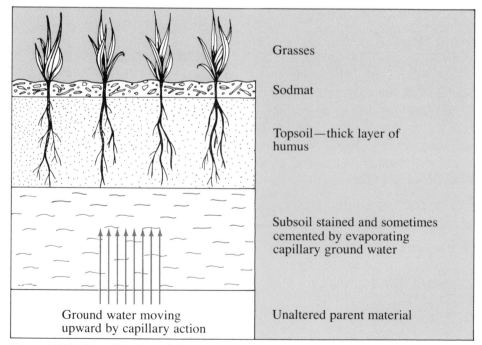

Figure 2.27 *Cross Section of Grassland Soil*

- Grasses
- Sodmat
- Topsoil—thick layer of humus
- Subsoil stained and sometimes cemented by evaporating capillary ground water
- Unaltered parent material
- Ground water moving upward by capillary action

1. Why did pronghorn antelope and bison not compete for food?
2. What change do you think would occur if the number of predators in a grassland ecosystem were reduced?

Human Impact

As people settled on the prairies and removed the prairie sod, they changed the grassland region considerably. The bison, the quarry of ruthless hunters, were wiped out by 1890. The present herds, maintained in national parks, originated mainly from a few remaining animals in the United States. Bison were simply not compatible with grain farming and cattle ranching. Pronghorns almost suffered the same fate, but they are now tolerated because they do not eat the grass needed by cattle.

Except for the coyote, the former carnivores of the grasslands were wiped out. People have tried to wipe out the wily coyote as well. A reduction in coyote numbers leads to an increase in the population of Richardson's ground squirrels. These rodents, often wrongly called gophers, eat grain crops.

Ploughing the land for farming has also altered the ecosystem. Soil formerly held in place by the sod mat was exposed by ploughing to the strong prairie winds. In the dry years of the 1930s, large quantities of topsoil were simply blown away. Only by using special cropping methods and planting *windbreaks* have farmers been able to reduce wind erosion.

Sloughs in farmers' fields (see the photo on page 38) make farming more difficult. Many sloughs on the prairies have been drained and converted into farmland. Waterfowl that migrate between southern and northern parts of North America use the prairie sloughs as feeding and resting places. Other waterfowl live on the sloughs all summer. Eliminating sloughs endangers North American waterfowl populations.

1. Prepare a chart to show how people have affected the grassland ecosystem. Use these headings:
- People's Actions
- How These Actions Altered the Ecosystem
- Suggestions for Reducing the Impact on the Ecosystem
2. Why are sloughs a problem for prairie farmers? Why should they not be drained?

MOUNTAIN ECOSYSTEMS

Canada's mountain ecosystems are located in the Western Cordillera (Figure 2.1). The differences in altitude in the region result in great variations of climate, vegetation, and wildlife. In fact, the Western Cordillera contains several ecosystems.

Climate

Climate maps of the Western Cordillera are much more complex than climate maps of other parts of Canada. Temperatures at the bottom of mountain valleys are warmer than those on the mountain slopes, and many mountain tops remain frozen all year. Temperature drops by up to 1°C for each 150 m rise in altitude. In southern British Columbia, climbing from a valley floor to the top of a tall mountain takes a hiker through as many climate regions as does travelling from the southern prairies to the northern Arctic.

Precipitation also varies greatly within the region. West-facing slopes receive the heaviest precipitation. The valleys on the east-facing slopes are often in rain shadows (Figure 2.11).

1. On your ecosystem map, shade in the Western Cordillera region and label it ''Mountain Ecosystems''.
2. Why do the west sides of the Canadian Cordillera mountain ranges have more precipitation than the east sides?

Pronghorn antelope feed mainly on sagebrush and other shrubs.

Natural Vegetation

Natural vegetation also changes with altitude (Figure 2.28). As mountain slopes rise, the temperature drops. Trees growing in the cooler air and thinner soil need less moisture. The dry climate of some interior valleys results in grasslands like the dry parts of the prairies. Part way up the slope, drought-resistant ponderosa pines dot the landscape. Higher still, other conifers cover the slopes with unbroken forest. On the higher slopes, temperatures are lower, and so there is less evaporation and more moisture for the trees. These woods look like the coniferous forest of central Canada, except that the trees belong to different species. Engelmann spruce replaces white and black spruce. Lodgepole pine appears in place of jack pine. Alpine fir substitutes for balsam fir. Above the *tree line* are only scrub trees and bushes, and alpine tundra with its summer show of flowers. In fact, as in the Interior Plains region, there are two tree lines: trees will not grow below the lower tree line because the climate is too dry, or above the upper because the climate is too cold. The tops of taller mountains, like the coldest parts of the Arctic, remain covered with snow all year.

The moister west side of the region near the coast has the tallest trees. These species include Douglas fir, western hemlock, and western red cedar. Because of their large size, they are used by sawmills to make building materials.

1. Why are dying trees good for a forest ecosystem?
2. In what ways is a climb up a mountain slope similar to a journey from the U.S. border of the southern prairies to Canada's extreme North? Why?

Soil

The soils in the mountain region resemble those in the other ecosystems, but there is one major difference. So much of the land is sloping that materials often move downhill, leaving the soils thinner and stonier. The steepest slopes have no soil at all.

1. Why do mountain regions have a variety of soil types?
2. Why is farming less important in mountain ecosystems than in Canada's other ecosystems?

Wildlife

Animal life also varies with altitude. Some sure-footed animals, such as mountain goats and bighorn sheep, are specially adapted to roam about on the steep slopes. A number of animals, such as deer, elk, and bighorn sheep, sometimes move up and down the mountain side, according to the seasons. They move to higher levels in summer and return to the valley bottoms in winter.

Why does each level of a mountain slope have its own kinds of animals?

Bighorn sheep

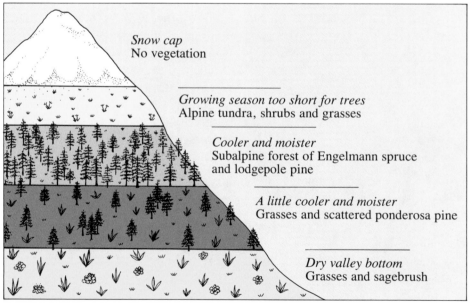

Snow cap
No vegetation

Growing season too short for trees
Alpine tundra, shrubs and grasses

Cooler and moister
Subalpine forest of Engelmann spruce and lodgepole pine

A little cooler and moister
Grasses and scattered ponderosa pine

Dry valley bottom
Grasses and sagebrush

Figure 2.28 *Vegetation in Mountain Areas* (*Read levels from bottom up.*)

Alpine Vegetation

A west coast forest in a natural state.   Here dead trees are in various stages of decay, and enough have fallen to allow sunlight to reach the forest floor. Young trees will soon refill this forest opening.

Fireweed in a burnt-over area. Fireweed is one of the first plants to start growing again after a forest fire. Next will come shrubs and perhaps aspen. Finally, coniferous trees will re-establish themselves.

Drought-resistant ponderosa pines need less moisture than do other species.

Alpine meadows.   At the upper tree line in mountain areas, alpine meadows grow flowering plants like those of the tundra.

Permanent snow and alpine tundra high in the mountains. Above the tree line, only a few hardy tundra plants can grow, and large areas have no vegetation at all.

Human Impact

A large proportion of the mountain region cannot be used for human settlement. For this reason, much of the region appears as untouched wilderness. But this appearance can be deceiving.

The main human impact occurs in the valleys. Here are concentrated the effects of pollutants such as sewage, garbage, and industrial wastes. In the past, constructing roads and railways and establishing mines and settlements in the valleys increased the number of forest fires that swept up the treed slopes. Even today careless campers and forestry machine operators cause fires. The most noticeable sign of human activity is the large number of cut-over areas of forest, where trees have been removed for lumber industries.

Even the mountain national parks, where the natural environment is being preserved, can be over-used by people. Large numbers of mountain hikers trample the vegetation. Garbage and animal-people encounters create a problem for wildlife. Alpine ski operations clear trees for ski runs and build villages on the mountain slopes. This leads to erosion and problems in disposing of sewage.

---

1. a) What problem could result from cutting down trees on steep mountain slopes?
   b) Why is replanting trees more difficult in the mountain region than in Canada's coniferous forest region?
2. Why should the number of mountain hikers be restricted, particularly in the alpine tundra areas?

CANADA'S OTHER ECOSYSTEMS

If you check the size and location of the five ecosystems discussed so far, you will notice that they do not cover all of Canada. Between them are *transition zones* where one region gradually blends into the next. Transition zones contain a mix of natural vegetation, soils, and wildlife found in their neighbouring regions.

Between the deciduous forest ecosystem and the coniferous forest ecosystem is an area of mixed forest. On the southern edge of this mixed forest

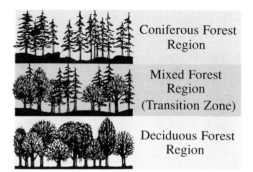

Coniferous Forest Region

Mixed Forest Region (Transition Zone)

Deciduous Forest Region

L O C A L S T U D Y

1. a) In which ecozone do you live?
   b) In what ways are the ecozones around you the same as or different from yours?
2. One way to learn more about your community is to construct a model or *diorama*, or to paint a mural of the area. Discuss in class the best way of carrying out such a project, given the choice of materials and space you have. As you review this chapter, choose the type of project you prefer and begin work on it. If you live in a city or town, plan to include some of the outlying area. If you live in the country, plan to include the nearest town.

   Imagine what the land in your area was like before it was settled. At this point include in your project only those geographic elements that occur naturally (e.g., hills, valleys, lakes, rivers). As you work through later chapters, you will add other elements to your project.

© King Features Syndicate

3. a) Make a list of the plants in the area where you live that would be typical of your natural vegetation region.
   b) What plants that are not typical of your vegetation region have people introduced? In what ways are these plants not typical?
   c) What are some of the more common wild animals in your ecozone? How are several of these wild animals adapted to your ecozone?
4. a) Dig a small hole in the ground near your home, and measure the thickness of the topsoil.
   b) Does this sample give you a true picture of farmland soil in your area? Explain.
   c) The following activity should help you discover the type of soil texture in your area.

   Add a cupful of subsoil, or parent material, to a large jar of water. Shake the jar thoroughly, and then let it stand for 24 hours to allow the materials to settle. Observe the different bands of the soil materials: sand, silt, and clay. About what proportion is there of each?

area, the woods contain more deciduous than coniferous trees; on the northern edge, they contain more coniferous than deciduous trees.

Between the grassland and the coniferous forest is *parkland*, an area of tall grasses and groves of aspen trees. Between the coniferous forest and the tundra is an area of stunted trees and barrens.

On your ecosystem map, shade in and label the transition zones.

CANADA'S FIFTEEN ECOZONES

Statistics Canada provides Canadians with up-to-date information about many aspects of Canada, including the environment. Until recently, most of the information has related to political areas, such as provinces. But natural regions of the environment have boundaries quite different from the political ones (Figure 2.29). For example, Ontario includes parts of *three* major ecosystems and two transition zones. Each of these areas stretches into neighbouring provinces, as well. Environmental information about a province as a whole can therefore be misleading.

In the early 1980s, Environment Canada and Statistics Canada, in partnership, designed a new system for giving information. Because there is such a variety of ecosystems and transition zones, Environment Canada divided Canada into 15 smaller ecological regions that they have called ecozones.

The boundaries of the ecozones were drawn according to physiography, climate, vegetation, and soil surface materials. Since people interact with the environment, human activities were also considered. For years to come, information about Canada's environment will be gathered and published in relation to the 15 ecozones. Canadians will know the environmental conditions in each ecozone and will be able to detect problems that need to be corrected.

Refer to the ecozone map (Figure 2.29). Choose any three ecozone boundaries and tell why you think each boundary was chosen.

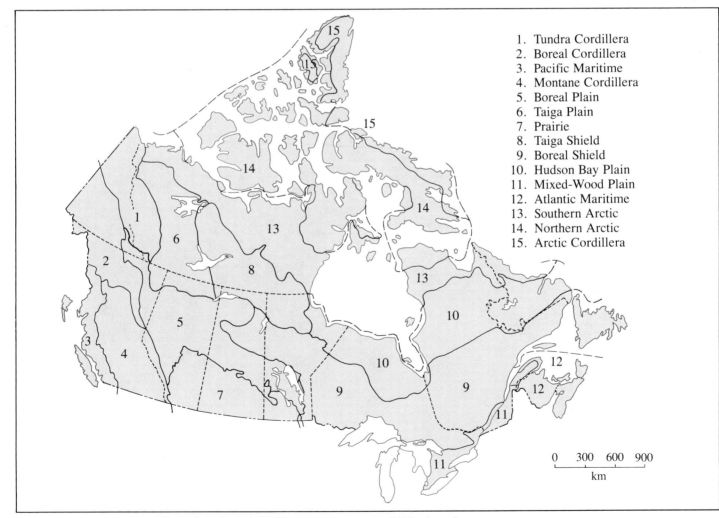

1. Tundra Cordillera
2. Boreal Cordillera
3. Pacific Maritime
4. Montane Cordillera
5. Boreal Plain
6. Taiga Plain
7. Prairie
8. Taiga Shield
9. Boreal Shield
10. Hudson Bay Plain
11. Mixed-Wood Plain
12. Atlantic Maritime
13. Southern Arctic
14. Northern Arctic
15. Arctic Cordillera

0 300 600 900
km

Figure 2.29 *Ecozones of Canada*   *Canada's 15 ecozones were established on the basis of physiography, climate, vegetation, and soil surface materials.*

Remote Sensing

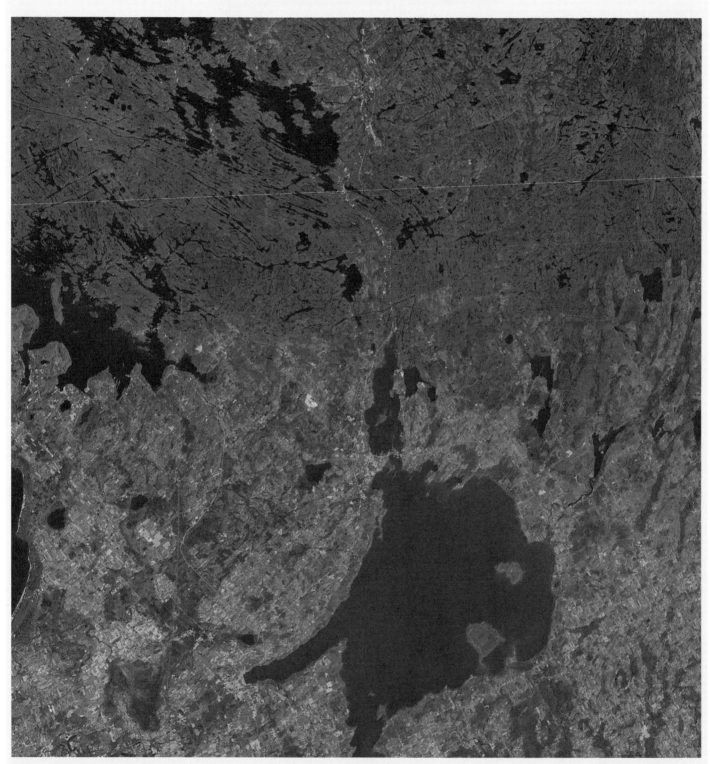

Figure 2.30 *Landsat Image from Space*   *This Landsat image shows an important regional boundary near Lake Simcoe, Ontario. What ecozone boundary appears on the image? What physiographic boundary is located in the same place? Draw a sketch map of the area shown in the image, and draw and label the boundary. Use arrows to show the direction of ice movement in the northern part of the image.*

What Is Remote Sensing?

The illustration in Figure 2.30 is neither a map nor a photograph. It is an image developed from information "sensed" by a spaceship called a satellite. Because the satellite is far away in space, the process that furnishes its information about the earth is called remote sensing.

The first remote sensing satellite was launched by the United States in 1972. It was originally known as ERTS 1 (Earth Resources Technology Satellite One) but was later renamed Landsat 1 (Land Satellite One). Since then, each new Landsat has been better than the one before. The latest Landsat satellites can detect areas on the earth as small as 30 m². Another type of satellite, known as SPOT, was launched by France in 1986. It can detect areas as small as 10 m². Canada's own remote sensing satellite, called Radarsat will be operative by 1994. Its new radar technology will enable it to collect data through cloud cover.

How Does It Work?

A Landsat satellite flies at a height of about 900 km in an orbit that passes close to the North and South Poles. Instruments on board the orbiting satellite sense reflections from the earth's surface below (Figure 2.31). The rotation of the earth across the path of the satellite causes the reflections to come in strips or swaths. The whole surface of the earth is covered by a series of swaths that the satellite completes every 18 days.

On the satellite an instrument called a scanner records the brightness of the light reflected from the section of the earth directly below. The scanner does not take photographs. It senses reflected sunlight in four wavelengths that are colours and converts the sensations to numbers. It then transmits the numbers to receiving stations on earth.

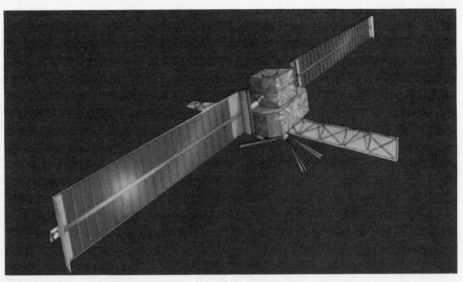

Radarsat, a Canadian satellite to be launched in 1994

Geographers and other scientists use computers to process the numbers into images. A single image requires the processing of millions of numbers. The scientists also change the colours by computer to make the images more useful for their purposes. The colours of these images are not intended to be realistic. For example, a forest may be represented by green, but it is just as likely to be represented by red. The correct interpretation of a satellite image is therefore not obvious.

Of What Use Is It?

By means of remote sensing, scientists can see broad patterns of both landscape and land use. They can also measure changes in the land, for a new image of the same area can be made every 18 days.

Combined with the interpretation of air photos and maps, remote sensing has many applications. Here are a few:

- Taking inventory of forest resources
- Discovering and monitoring forest fires
- Determining rock structure and types
- Observing the movement of pollutants in bodies of water
- Measuring the rate of urban growth
- Mapping land uses in remote parts of the world

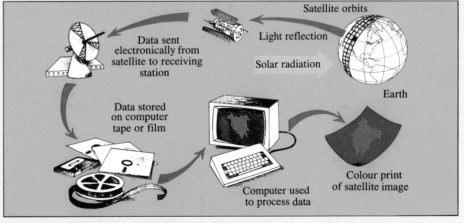

Figure 2.31 *Remote Sensing Equipment*

CANADA'S NATIONAL PARKS

In 1885, after the discovery of hot springs near Banff, the Canadian government decided to set aside a portion of the Rocky Mountains for public use and enjoyment. Over the next 10 years, five more mountain areas were made unavailable for "sale, settlement or squatting". Within a few years all of these areas became national parks. Since the beginning of the 20th century, a number of other parts of Canada have been set aside as national parks (Figure 2.32).

At first, it was mainly areas of scenic beauty that were chosen for parks. As people learned more about ecology, however, more of the parkland was set aside to represent special environments in Canada, both terrestrial and marine.

As part of background information, Parks Canada Policy (1983) states:

Canadians live in a land rich in natural beauty. The shores of three oceans, the Great Lakes, mountains, prairies, thousands of lakes and rivers, forests and tundra—these along with the flora (plants) and fauna (animals) are some of the natural treasures we have inherited . . . For centuries this landscape was affected mainly by natural forces. But more recently, with the advent of an agricultural and then an industrial society, human activities have been altering the natural environment at an accelerating pace.

Parks Canada's objective for National Parks is:

To protect for all time representative natural areas of Canadian significance in a system of national parks and to encourage public understanding, appreciation and enjoyment of this natural heritage so as to leave it unimpaired for future generations.

1. List some of the ways that the National Parks background information reflects what you have learned in this chapter.
2. Parks Canada has made it known that its objective is to encourage the public to enjoy the national parks and at the same time to leave these parks unimpaired for future generations.
a) In what ways do the two ideas conflict with each other?
b) How do you think the government should deal with this conflict?

WHAT LIES AHEAD?

More and more emissions of carbon dioxide are heating up our climate; soil is eroding at an alarming rate; plant and animal species are disappearing; industrial wastes are polluting air, land, and water. Some people think that our living planet is doomed. Yet people have a clearer understanding of environmental inter-relationships than at any earlier time in history. We study and measure human impact on the environment. We continue to improve methods of correcting the mistakes of the past. Have we the will to insist that governments, industries, and the public take the necessary steps to preserve Canada's delicate ecosystems for future generations?

REVIEW QUESTIONS

1. Prepare an eight-column chart with the following headings: Ecozone, Physiographic Region, Jan. Temp., July Temp., Annual Precip., Natural Vegetation, Soil.

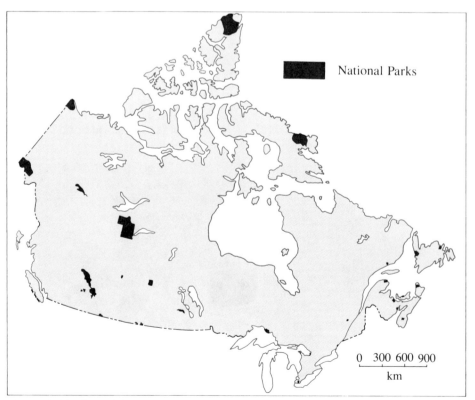

National Parks

0 300 600 900
km

Figure 2.32 *Canada's National Parks*

Pukaskwa National Park

Use the information in this chapter and the ecozone map of Figure 2.29 to fill in as much of the chart as you can.

2. a) Refer to the map of Canada showing national parks (Figure 2.32) and the map of ecozones (Figure 2.29). Make a list of Canada's national parks and tell in what ecozone each is located.

b) Choose an ecozone that has no national park. As a member of a small ''local'' committee, write a letter to Parks Canada describing what you think a national park could show about the area.

3. a) Along with the other members of your class, collect newspaper and magazine clippings dealing with environmental concerns in Canada. Display them on your classroom bulletin board.

b) Illustrate each article with a sketch, or describe the effects on the environment referred to in each.

c) Suggest possible solutions for the environmental concerns expressed in the news articles.

Chapter Three

Economic Development, Settlement, and Population

Hewers of Wood and Drawers of Water?

''Canada is a nation of hewers of wood and drawers of water.'' This statement has often been made, in both speech and writing. Discuss it in class. What does it mean? Give examples of present-day occupations that might be compared to hewing wood and drawing water. Give examples of Canadian occupations that disprove this quotation.

This modern painting shows Captain James Cook of the British Royal Navy meeting with Indians on the island later called Vancouver Island. Captain Cook landed there in 1778.

NATURAL RESOURCES AND RESOURCE DEVELOPMENT

This chapter tells how Canadians have developed **natural resources** since the earliest of times. Natural resources include those parts of the natural environment that people find useful. Water, soil, plants, animals, fish, minerals, and energy sources such as waterfalls are all natural resources. Even climate may be seen as a natural resource. **Resource development** evolves from the human use of natural resources.

For thousands of years before Europeans came to North America, Native peoples had used natural resources to obtain food, clothing, and shelter. They collected seeds, fruits, and nuts; fished, hunted, and trapped animals; and some groups planted and harvested crops.

Some of the Native peoples lived in highly organized societies that carried on a thriving trade with people belonging to other Native cultures. One such group was the Iroquoian-speaking Hurons living on the southern shores of Georgian Bay. They traded surplus corn, tobacco, and fish nets in return for dried fish, meat, furs, and clothing. When Europeans arrived in what is now Canada and realized the wealth of furs and other resources the land supplied, trade entered a whole new phase.

The Europeans who came to Canada exported vast amounts of fish, furs, timber, minerals, and farm products to other countries, mostly in Europe. In return, they imported supplies and manufactured goods from Europe. This trading economy became the foundation of Canada's economic development. It also had a lasting effect on our country's settlement patterns.

Before you begin to study early resource development across Canada, see what you can find out about early resource development in your own area. First, make a list of the kinds of work done by early inhabitants of your area. The list should give you topics for your project. To tell your local story, you will need to use many different sources such as history books, historical atlases, old newspapers, museums, art galleries, historical societies, and special collections in libraries. A different group of students might do research on each topic. Some groups may wish to make posters, paintings, or drawings to illustrate the information they gather. The following questions may help guide your investigation.

1. What natural resources were the Native people of your area using for food, shelter, and transportation when Europeans arrived? Describe or illustrate the equipment they used to hunt, trap, fish, and collect food. Describe or illustrate how they made useful items from natural resources.

2. What natural resources in your area did early European settlers use? Describe the equipment they used for making useful items from these resources. What did they learn from the Native peoples about local resources and how to use them? What crops and methods of using resources did the pioneers from Europe introduce into Canada?

3. How did contact with Europeans affect the Native economy in your area?

4. New settlers needed to be alert to the natural resources in their region. What evidence can you find today of some of the resources they would have observed?

   Collect photos, or make sketches, of some of the animals and vegetation in your area. Use the pictures to create a "Fauna and Flora" display in your classroom. Use a large loose-leaf notebook to begin a "Nature Observation Journal" where you can write down throughout the year the mammals, birds, wildflowers, and trees that you see, and any comments you can make about them. Add as many sketches as you can.

5. How long did it take the settlers of your area to produce *surplus* products that could be exported to other regions of Canada or to other countries? What products were the first to be exported from your area? List some products that were exported in later years. Roughly when did the people of your area begin to *process* resources before exporting them? (Sawing logs into lumber or milling wheat into flour are examples of processing resources.)

6. How did the development of resources in your area influence the location of villages, towns, and transportation routes? Search historical sources to find out whether any village in your area began because of the development of one particular resource but later expanded because of the development of other resources.

7. Visit a pioneer village in your area. If there is no such local village, visit a mill or other historic site of pioneer days. Find out all you can about a craft or skill used in pioneer days, and make a presentation about it to the class. If you can demonstrate the craft or skill, show the class how it is done. If this is not possible, try to bring photos or sketches to illustrate your presentation.

NATIVE PEOPLES AND RESOURCES

Native peoples lived in what is now Canada for thousands of years before Europeans first arrived. Contacts made before Columbus' voyages, such as visits by Norsemen, had little effect on the Native peoples' way of life. When Columbus sighted and later explored the Caribbean islands, he thought he had reached the East Indies. For this reason he called the Natives "Indians", and the name stuck. Indeed, it is the term used in Canada's revised *Constitution Act, 1982*.

In Canada, the word "Indian" has a legal definition, given in the *Indian Act* of 1876. Canadians who have been registered as Indians by the federal government are known as *status Indians*.

The Native peoples of the far North were first called Eskimos by Algonquin Indians, their "neighbours" to the south, but they dislike that name and never use it. They call themselves Inuit. The Inuit of the western Arctic use the name Inuvialuit, and those of northern Québec-Labrador, Innu.

The way the Native peoples of Canada adapted to their environment and used natural resources to provide the necessities of life varied greatly from region to region. The culture and technology developed in each region depended mainly on the climate and the kind of resources available. Early Native societies in Canada may be classified according to the regions they inhabited: Pacific Coast, Plateau, Plains, Subarctic, Arctic, and Eastern Woodlands (Figure 3.1).

PACIFIC COAST

The Pacific coastal area was rich in sea resources. The Indians of the Pacific coast region ate mostly fish (herring, smelt, halibut, and salmon) and sea mammals (whales, seals, sea lions, porpoises, and sea otter) (Figures 2.1 and 3.1). Of these foods, salmon was the most important. During the *spawning* runs, the Indians speared and netted large numbers of salmon. When they caught more salmon than they could eat at one time, they cured the extra fish by smoking or sun-drying to preserve them for later use.

The dense rain forest of the Pacific coast provided wood and bark for building shelters, carving dugout canoes, and making many household utensils such as boxes, baskets, bowls, and dishes. The Pacific Coast Natives became expert carvers as the intricate

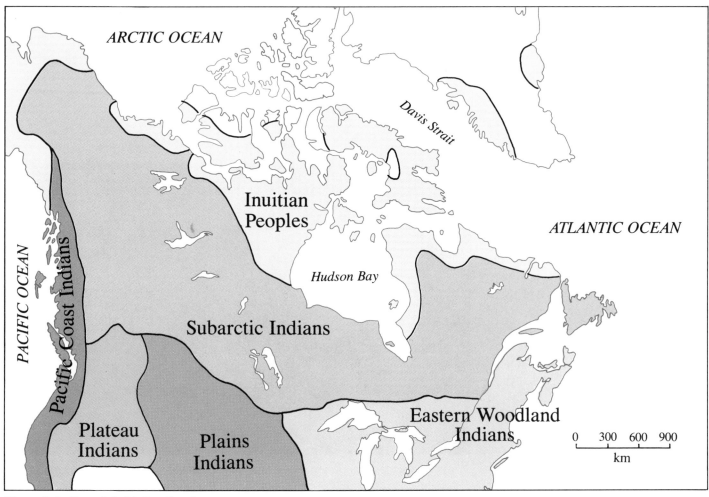

Figure 3.1 *Canada's Native Peoples*

designs of their totem poles show. These peoples usually lived in villages located in sheltered coves or on channels near a river mouth. Because the mountain barriers separated one group from another, the Coast Indians developed as many as 19 different languages.

PLATEAU

The Plateau Indians of British Columbia lived in the central part of the Western Cordillera region (Figures 2.1 and 3.1). Bounded by high mountains on both east and west, the Plateau country has hot, dry summers and cold winters. Its uplands are wooded, and the valleys are grasslands.

The dress, customs, and religion of the Plateau Indians were a blend of the practices of the Pacific Coast tribes and the Plains peoples. Because the Plateau peoples occupied the grassland in the valleys, their way of life was more like that of the peoples of the Plains. For food they depended on animals (mostly deer) and birds. They also caught fish (mostly salmon) in the streams and lakes of the valleys.

The Plateau Indians spent only part of the year in their villages. When food supplies ran low, they made long journeys to hunt animals.

PLAINS

The groups that made up the Plains Indians occupied a vast triangular grassland region that extended from the Rocky Mountains on the west to the coniferous forests on the north and east (Figures 2.1 and 3.1). This region had a continental climate of short, dry, hot summers and long, very cold winters. Its resources included deer, antelope, and bison (commonly called buffalo).

The bison ranged the vast grasslands in their millions. They were the Plains peoples' most important natural resource. The Plains Indians used the bison's hide for clothing, bedding,

tent covers, and shields. They carved the bison's horns into utensils, and made thread and bow strings from their sinews. The flesh of the bison provided most of their meat supply.

The Plains Indians did not live in villages. Instead, they were **nomads** who moved camp from place to place as they followed the migrating bison herds. They usually hunted in groups of 50 to 100 persons, including women and older children. Groups of this size were needed to handle a bison drive. Before Europeans brought the horse to the Americas, the Plains peoples hunted on foot. The most efficient way to kill the bison in those days was to chase them into an enclosure or drive them over a cliff.

The Spanish conquerors of Mexico and Peru brought the horse to the Americas in the 1500s. By the mid-1700s, wild horses ranged as far north as the Canadian Plains, where the Natives learned to capture them and break them for riding. Mounted on horseback, the Native hunters learned to kill the bison even more efficiently. They would surround a bison herd, and then hurl spears and shoot arrows to kill hundreds of the panicked animals. The Plains peoples also used

The famous Canadian artist Emily Carr painted this great brooding totem pole carved by Haida Indians of the Queen Charlotte Islands. The artist called this painting "Skidigate" after the village where it stood.

Plains Indians hunting bison. This watercolour, painted in 1867, shows mounted Indians driving bison over a cliff. Why did the Plains Indians adopt this method of killing bison? (Look at the painting for evidence.)

The Nootka woman in this photo was a traditional gatherer of the bark of the great red cedars of the Pacific coast. The photo was taken about 1915. What evidence does it show of the ways in which the Nootka Indians used the bark they gathered?

horses to pull their *travois*. Horses replaced dogs for this labour because a horse could pull five times as heavy a load as a dog and could travel twice as far in a day.

The use of horses made important changes in the way of life of the Plains Indians. Mounted hunters could pursue bison much farther from camp. Extending the hunting range increased the available food supply. The people could therefore stay in one camp for a much longer time. Using the horse as a draft animal, they could also carry much bigger loads from one camp to another. Because they could transport more goods, they began to keep extra suits of decorated clothing, extra robes to wear in winter, and an extra supply of dried meat.

SUBARCTIC

The Native peoples of the Subarctic occupied a vast forested territory of the Canadian Shield from Alaska on the west to Labrador on the east (Figures 2.1 and 3.1). The northern boundary of the Subarctic peoples' territory was the tree line. These peoples depended on forest resources for survival during the long, cold winters. The forest provided both shelter and the animal life they needed for food and clothing. The moose and the caribou were as important to the Subarctic peoples as the bison were to the peoples of the Plains.

In winter the Subarctic Indians lived in small bands of about 25 to 30 people who were related by family ties. These bands would scatter across the land in search of food. They might not see people of another band until the beginning of spring. In summer, several hunting bands would settle in one camp, which was usually pitched by a river or lake that provided good fishing.

ARCTIC

The Inuit were a Native people who lived north of the tree line, on the Arctic tundra (Figures 2.21 and 3.1). For eight months of the year, the Arctic tundra is covered with snow, and the waters are nearly all frozen. Because of the long, harsh winters, the tundra region supports little vegetation and few animal species. The Inuit developed a technology and a way of life to suit this environment. They learned how to survive the harsh winters and even how to live reasonably well off the land.

An Inuit father and son hunting seal. Inuit children learn the skills they need for survival by watching and imitating their parents. What are some advantages of this way of learning?

This photo was taken at Fort Whoop-Up in 1881. It shows a Blood Indian woman with her horse-drawn travois. What changes did the horse-drawn travois make in the way of life of the Plains Indians?

In 1821, 15-year-old Peter Rindisbacher travelled with his family from Switzerland to York Factory on Hudson Bay. On the way he painted this picture of a Labrador Innu paddling his kayak. As the Rindisbacher family made the long voyage by canoe from Fort York to the Red River Colony, Peter painted pictures of the Hudson Bay Company's fur forts along the way. His pictures are the only visual record of those forts that still exists.

The **nomadic** Inuit followed the seasonal migration of animals such as caribou, walrus, and seals. They lived in snow houses called igloos during the winter and in tents made of caribou skins during the summer. For transportation they used dog sleds in winter and boats called **kayaks** in summer. The Inuit response to their environment showed imagination. They developed techniques for hunting and fishing, including ways to hunt whales; they invented ways to make use of all parts of an animal for food, clothing, or shelter.

EASTERN WOODLANDS
The Indians of the Eastern Woodlands occupied the forested region south of the Subarctic. The Woodlands extended from the Plains on the west to the Atlantic Ocean on the east.

The Indians in the northern part of the Eastern Woodlands followed a way of life much like that of the Indians who lived in the Subarctic. They obtained most of their food by hunting and fishing. During the winter they separated into family groups to hunt deer, elk, bear, and beaver. They travelled by birch-bark canoe in summer and on snowshoes in winter.

In the southerly region of the Eastern Woodlands (southern Ontario), the lifestyle of the Indians was very different. The Iroquoian-speaking peoples who lived in this region planted crops to add to the food they obtained by hunting and fishing. Corn, which the Indians of Mexico had cultivated for over 3000 years, was introduced to the Natives of southern Ontario about A.D. 500. By the time Europeans arrived, over 1000 years later, the Indians of southern Ontario were growing corn, beans, squash, and sunflowers. They used wooden implements to cultivate the

Iroquoian women cultivating their crops

crops and sometimes fish for fertilizer. They came to depend on their crops for about eighty percent of their food. When they no longer had to rely on hunting game and collecting wild forms of food, they were able to establish permanent villages. The population of a typical village ranged from about 100 to 2000 people. Groups of from 10 to 30 families lived in dwellings called **longhouses**. A longhouse was made by covering a framework of wooden poles with bark. Each village of longhouses was surrounded by a *palisade* to protect the villagers against enemies.

In Iroquoian society, women planted, cultivated, and harvested the crops. The men hunted, fished, and defended the village.

---

1. In which regions of Canada were the early Native peoples mostly nomadic? Why did they have to follow this pattern of living?
2. In which regions did the early Native peoples build permanent villages? Explain what made permanent villages possible in each region.
3. How did the use of horses change the way of life of the Plains Indians?
4. How, in general, did the natural environment and the resources available affect the way of life of Canada's Native peoples?
5. Construct a diorama of early Native life in your area. Show the type of economy practised by the peoples, and include activities or items that show their respect for the natural environment.

NEW SETTLERS AND CANADA'S RESOURCES

From the 1500s, European explorers were looking for a way to reach the Orient by travelling westward. In their quest, they reached the land we now call Canada. They began to explore its eastern shoreline and followed waterways inland, hoping to find a passage to Cathay (China). In Canada, instead of the gold, silk, and spices of the Orient that they were seeking, they found other natural resources. First, they discovered abundant fish and forests. Inland they found fur-bearing animals, land suitable for farming and as

time went on, minerals. Each type of resource exported to Europe was shipped almost in its natural state. Little processing was done in Canada. The way the early Europeans in Canada developed and exported these resources set patterns for the growth, economic development, and settlement of our country.

FISH

The early explorers, such as John Cabot and Jacques Cartier, reported that the waters bordering the northern portion of North America were teeming with fish. During the 1500s, British, French, Spanish, and Portuguese ships sailed regularly to the fishing grounds off the east coast of North America (Figure 3.2). The fishers were attracted by the plentiful supply of codfish that were easily caught in the shallow waters southeast of Newfoundland. It was profitable to transport the cod from the New World to Europe, where fish were in great demand. The Europeans depended heavily on fish for protein and for a meat substitute on Fridays and other special religious days of fasting declared by the Roman Catholic Church.

The cod had to be preserved soon after it was caught to prevent it from spoiling. Since artificial refrigeration had not been invented, other methods of preserving food had to be used. The French, Spanish, and Portuguese fishers packed the cod in salt on board their ships. Salt was cheap in their home countries because evaporation of sea water from shallow ponds produced large amounts.

In Britain salt was expensive. The cool, cloudy weather there slowed evaporation and prevented the British from producing salt in quantity. For this reason, the British method of preserving cod used as little salt as possible. The crews gave the fish a light salting and then dried them outdoors along the shores of Newfoundland. At first they simply spread the cod on rocks to dry, but later they built wooden platforms called *flakes*. The dried fish produced by this method of preserving was not valued as highly as the moister fresh-salted cod, but it was still in demand. The British drying process required workers to spend periods of time on shore. Even so, in the early days of the fishery the harsh winters discouraged shore workers from settling permanently in the New World.

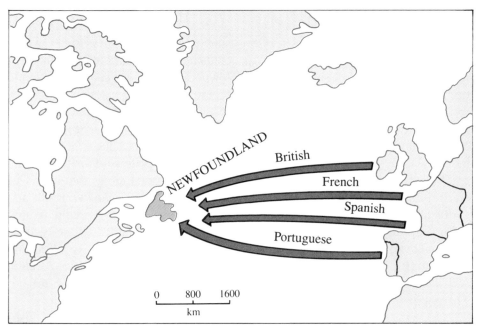

Figure 3.2 *Route of European Fishing Boats to Newfoundland*

Cod drying on flakes. The traditional method of drying cod has been handed down by generations of Newfoundland fisherfolk.

Many Newfoundland outports, like this one, have survived for centuries.

Later, from the 1600s to the 1800s, Europeans founded permanent settlements called **outports** in many protected harbours along the Newfoundland coast. By the 1850s, there were more than 600 outports in Newfoundland; each outport housed about five to ten families. The houses were close to the shore and the wharf where the fish were cleaned. The surrounding forest provided wood for the buildings and for fuel. The soil in some areas was fertile enough to grow vegetables, but all other supplies had to be brought by ship. **Commercial farming** was out of the question because the land would not support enough grain and livestock. In Newfoundland, permanent settlement depended entirely on the fishing industry.

The earliest fishing settlements were built in Newfoundland during the 1700s and 1800s. Many more fishing villages sprang up along the shores of what are now Nova Scotia, New Brunswick, Prince Edward Island, and the Gaspé Peninsula of Québec. The population of the Atlantic fishing villages grew as new markets for dried fish were found. One of these new

markets was the West Indies, where more and more slaves were being kept to work on the sugar cane plantations. Dried cod kept well and made cheap food for the slaves. This cod market helped complete the Atlantic trading triangle connecting Europe, North America, and the West Indies (Figure 3.3).

Some of Newfoundland's original fishing villages have been abandoned as the fishing industry has adopted modern methods. Other villages have adapted to the changing times. Many of the small coastal communities still found along the shores of the Atlantic region owe their existence to fishing. But except for St. John's, few major cities have developed from the original fishing settlements.

The same pattern of fishing settlements developed along the shores of British Columbia in the late 1800s and early 1900s. Although many fishing villages were established, only two, Vancouver and Victoria, became major port cities. As in the Atlantic region, the fishing industry did not lead to settlement of the interior.

In the 20th century, a major fish-processing industry grew up, based on

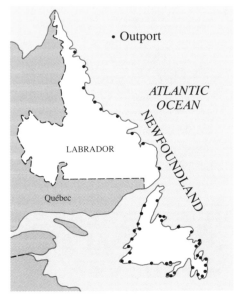

the canning or freezing and packaging of fish products. On the east coast the transportation needs of the fishing industry led to shipbuilding and to a shipping industry.

Fishing is important in Canada's economic history because it was fish that lured Europeans to the New World in large numbers. As they settled here, the Europeans learned about other valuable resources in North America.

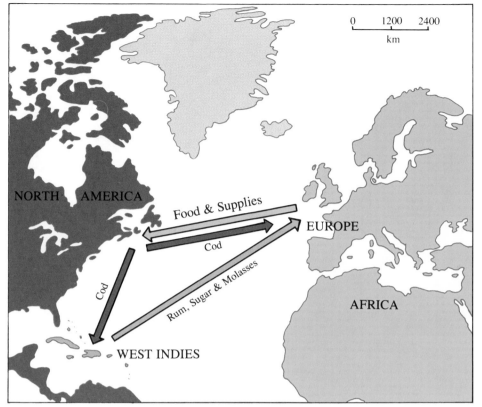

Figure 3.3 *North Atlantic Trading Triangle in the 1700s*

Fishing is still an important industry in Canada. The fishing industry contributes about twelve percent of the value of all commodity-producing industries in the Atlantic Provinces. Along the Atlantic coast, about a thousand communities still depend totally on fishing for their livelihood. Although the value of fish production is high in British Columbia, the fishing industry is not as important to the economy of that province as it is to the economy of the Atlantic Provinces.

1. Explain how the British method of curing cod led to permanent settlements in the New World.
2. Explain why most of the Atlantic coast fishing *outports* did not grow into larger settlements.
3. Why did the early fishing industry not lead to the settlement of Canada's interior?
4. Over the last three centuries, St. John's, Newfoundland, has grown from a tiny fishing port to become

a major city. Working in small groups, prepare a "Civic History" of St. John's. Illustrate the "History" with photos or sketches. As your final "Chapter", develop an overview of the city today, including its most important industries.

FURS

The fur trade, unlike the cod fishery, was based on a luxury item. The furs most in demand were beaver pelts. At first the pelts themselves were worn as furs, but later they were processed into felt to make the broad-brimmed hats that became fashionable in Europe (Figure 3.4). Perhaps one reason for their popularity was that they were almost waterproof. No other material was as good as the underwool of beaver pelts for making felt. Later on, fur coats became popular for women, and this fashion increased the

demand for other furs such as fox, muskrat, mink, and ermine.

Fewer Europeans took part in the fur trade than worked in the cod fishery. The Europeans were the organizers of the fur-trading business, and they provided the money to build forts and fur-trading posts. They themselves did not trap the fur-bearing animals. They bought the furs and shipped them home to be manufactured into clothing.

The success of this fur trade depended on the Native peoples. Indians trapped and skinned the animals, cured the pelts, and took them to the fur-trading posts. There they traded their furs for the goods available, such as muskets, gun powder, shot, blankets, knives, a variety of metal tools, and liquor. Some Indians specialized in trapping beaver to the neglect of hunting for food; they depended on the fur-trading posts for most of their supplies. When the beaver in an area were nearly all harvested, the Indians could not collect enough furs to trade for the food they needed, and hardship often resulted.

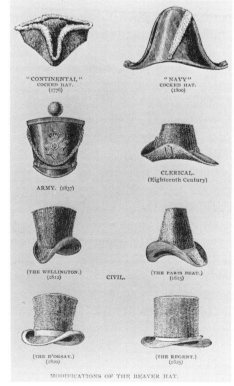

Figure 3.4 *Fashionable Beaver Hats*

93

By the mid-1800s, when the European demand for furs fell, the Indians were no longer able to pay for European goods by bartering furs. By this time, they had come to rely on certain goods from Europe. Some of them had even come to depend for their food on trading furs. Many had lost the knowledge and skills they needed to make use of the resources around them as their ancestors had done before the fur-trading boom.

Although very few Inuit were involved in the early fur trade, they, too, have suffered ups and downs as the demand for furs has fluctuated. In the early 1900s, they came to depend on money from the sale of furs for buying supplies. To obtain furs, they had moved from their traditional hunting and fishing areas to areas where the highly desired white fox was available. Their standard of living improved, but only as long as the market lasted for white fox and other furs. In the economic depression of the 1930s, the demand for furs dropped sharply. The Inuit who sold furs for a living suddenly found themselves without income. Like some Indians before them, these Inuit lost their ability and desire to live off the land. Even worse, they had moved to areas that did not have enough animals and fish to support them.

The problem of "boom and bust" in the fur industry is still with Natives today. Organizations in both Europe and North America have mounted campaigns to stop cruelty to wild animals. They have focused much of their criticism on the killing of young seals off the east coast of Canada. They have also convinced many people that it is wrong to wear furs because to trap any animal is cruel. As a result of these campaigns, the demand for furs has dropped. Many Native families have found themselves without money to buy essential items. They cannot even maintain the snowmobiles they now use for hunting.

Colin Fraser, trader at Fort Chipewyan in the 1890s, sorts a fortune in fox, beaver, mink, and other precious furs. How were the furs packaged for shipping?

LOCAL STUDY

For thousands of years before Europeans first came to the New World, the Native peoples of Canada had obtained much or most of their food by hunting and fishing. They became very skillful hunters because their lives often depended on their success. And much of their success depended on their skill at tracking animals over plains and through forests.

Wild animals still roam through all parts of Canada, in the towns and cities, as well as in the countryside. Why not try your skill at tracking some animals in your community?—not to kill but to observe and to learn to recognize their various tracks.

Figure 3.5 shows a number of animal tracks. Study them carefully; then try sketching them from memory. Remember that the shapes of the marks and the spaces between them are both good clues to learning to recognize the tracks.

When you think that you can recognize the tracks of the animals you are most likely to note in your community, you might go for a walk with friends or family to see what tracks you can observe. Winter is probably the best time for finding tracks, but tracking is possible in other seasons, too, if the ground is soft or muddy.

If you would like to make a record of the tracks that you observe, take along a sketch pad and pencils, or else materials to make a cast of the tracks.

If you decide to make sketches of the tracks you find, you might mount the sketches in your "Nature Observation Journal" (page 86).

If you wish to make a cast, you will need the following items:

- an empty bottle with a spray top
- a small amount of salt
- cold water
- a stick or twig for stirring
- paper clips
- newspaper (to wrap your cast)
- plaster of paris (from a hardware store)
- a small plastic margarine container
- cardboard strips, 3 cm x 40 cm
- hairpins or extra paper clips (for hanging the cast later)

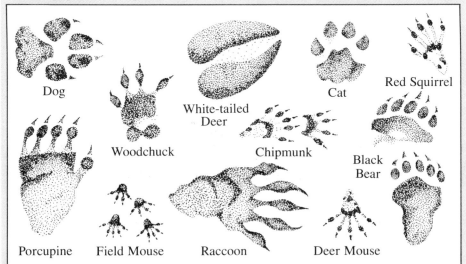

Figure 3.5 *Animal Tracks*

Then follow these steps:
1. Find a clear track. Use the spray bottle to mist the track with a thin layer of water.
2. While the track freezes, use the cardboard strip and paper clips to form a collar that completely encircles the track and leaves a space of one to two centimetres around it.
3. Mix the plaster of paris according to the directions on the container, using two parts of plaster to one part of water. If the day is very cold, add a pinch of salt to help the plaster set faster. Work quickly. Stir well, and tap the container to release air bubbles. Add more plaster or water until the mixture is like a thin cake batter.
4. Carefully pour the plaster into the cardboard collar, leaving a space of about 0.5 cm at the top.
5. Smooth the surface of the plaster with your stick. If you wish to hang your cast later, insert the wire "hanger" when the plaster has partly set.
6. The cast should set in about 20 to 30 minutes. When it has set, wrap it carefully in newspaper to carry it home.

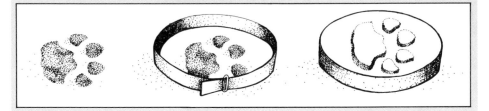

THE EFFECT ON SETTLEMENT

The fur trade in North America roused keen competition between the British and French. In 1606, the French, led by Samuel de Champlain (Canada's first geographer) and Pierre de Monts, built a fur-trading fort at Port Royal (now Annapolis Royal, Nova Scotia). The site was well protected, with fertile soils and a moderate climate, but it had serious disadvantages. Most serious was its location. Port Royal gave only limited access to the rich store of furs in the interior of the country. The barrier of the nearby Appalachian Mountains was too close, and the entrance to the continent at the mouth of the St. Lawrence River was too far away. In 1608, after only two years, Champlain and de Monts decided to move their small colony from Port Royal to a site that was to become Québec City (Figure 3.6, page 97).

The new site proved to be a much better location. It was at the end of the fur-trade route for most of the interior of the continent. The traders carried the furs eastward by way of water routes and then shipped them down the St. Lawrence River for transport to Europe (Figure 3.7, page 97).

Montréal, founded in 1642, became the major fur-trading centre of the northern part of the continent. Over the years, the French fur-trading companies made headquarters there. Each company operated by virtue of a licence from the King of France for fur trading in North America.

To counter the Montréal-based French fur traders, the British founded the Hudson's Bay Company, and built a ring of fur-trading forts around the shores of Hudson and James bays. From these forts they penetrated Canada's interior, establishing fur-trading posts as far inland as the Mackenzie and Saskatchewan rivers. As they advanced into the interior, the French and British fur traders came into conflict. They often clashed in armed skirmishes and raided each other's trading posts. In 1763, Britain obtained all of French Canada, and between 1783 and 1784, a group mostly made up of Scots founded the Northwest Company. The new company operated out of Montréal to compete against the Hudson's Bay Company. In 1821, the Hudson's Bay Company absorbed its rival and gained a *monopoly* of the North American fur trade.

The fur-trade competition had extended fur trading right across the continent. The chief factor that determined which areas the fur trade would expand into was physical geography. The terrain, climate, and vegetation of an area affected both the quantity and the quality of its furs. In general, fur-bearing animals were to be found throughout the forest regions of North America. But the better-quality furs were found in the more northerly areas because in the colder winters the animals produced thicker coats. In pursuit of the best furs, traders pushed

Native infant mortality in Canada is twice the national average, and life expectancy among the Native population is still 10 years less than the national average.

north and west looking for new fur resources. By good fortune, the general alignment of great waterways led the explorers in these directions. Since the most efficient means of transportation was the canoe (and later the **York boat**), rivers and lakes also became the trade routes (Figure 3.7). Notable water systems included the Great Lakes-St. Lawrence River-Saskatchewan River route and the long courses of the Mackenzie and

Columbia rivers. Large freighter canoes were used to transport goods and company personnel over the trade routes.

The fur trade opened up Canada for future resource development and settlement. In extending the trade, explorers discovered and charted the waterways that would later be used to transport goods and people not employed by the trading companies. They also discovered other resources,

Samuel de Champlain, Canada's first geographer

Birchbark freighter canoes on Lake Superior. Frances Ann Hopkins, wife of a Hudson Bay Company's administrator, painted this picture in 1869. Mrs. Hopkins accompanied her husband on many business trips into Canada's interior. Here she shows herself seated in the middle of the canoe in the foreground.

such as stands of timber suitable for cutting and fertile farmland.

The effect of the fur trade on settlement was limited in one important way: the fur trade did not lead to large settlements in the interior. On average, a trading post employed only 10 to 15 people. These employees were traders, not trappers. Most trading posts consisted of little more than a few simple log buildings that served basic functions. They housed the people and stored food and supplies (for staff use and for trading with Native hunters) and, of course, furs. The locations of the trading posts were fixed by practical factors. A good location would provide plenty of fur-bearing animals; Natives who were willing to trap and trade; water for transportation; an adequate supply of game, fish, and wood; and a site for a vegetable garden.

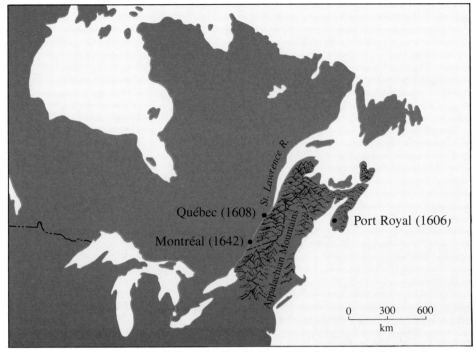

Figure 3.6 *The First French Forts in North America* Samuel de Champlain, explorer, geographer, and statesman, established the first French settlements in North America at Port Royal and Québec City.

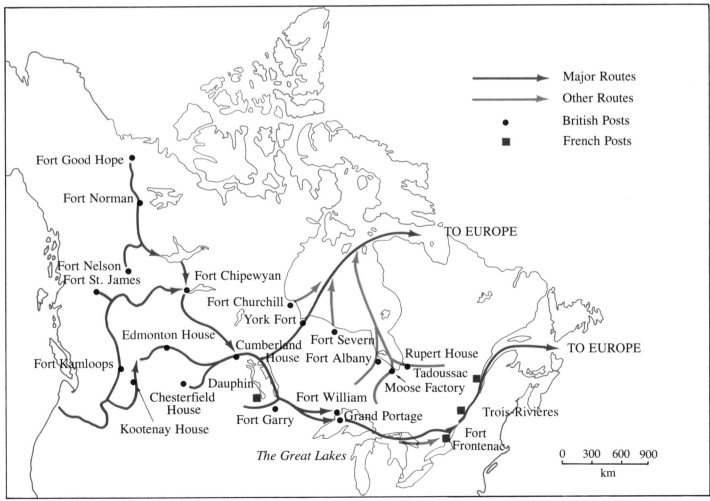

Figure 3.7 *Fur-Trade Posts and Routes*

Plan of a Fur Post

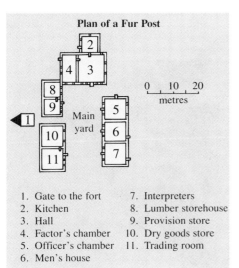

0   10   20
metres

1. Gate to the fort
2. Kitchen
3. Hall
4. Factor's chamber
5. Officer's chamber
6. Men's house
7. Interpreters
8. Lumber storehouse
9. Provision store
10. Dry goods store
11. Trading room

The fur-trading companies discouraged settlers from coming to develop the land because farming would destroy the natural habitat of fur-bearing animals. Only in the Red River Valley, in what is now Manitoba, was there much farming to supply food for the fur traders.

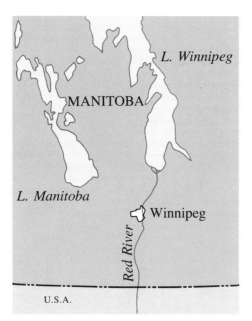

In short, the fur trade did not lead to great population increases or large settlements across the country. It fostered the growth of only one city: Montréal, the *gateway* city of the northern part of North America.

All the furs were brought to Montréal, where they were stored, sold, and then loaded onto ships. The fur traders bought their equipment and supplies in Montréal. The fur trade led to many other economic activities that promoted Montréal's growth.

The Canadian fur trade declined considerably in the late 1800s. Today the value of wild fur pelts in Canada is about $70 million a year. The industry is still an important source of income for the people who live in northern areas.

---

1. a) You are a fur trader living in 1800. You have been instructed to plan a route to transport furs from Fort Norman, in the Northwestern Territory, to Montréal. Using an atlas as a guide, make a sketch map of the route you would follow. Label all the rivers and lakes you would use.

b) Prepare a menu for one day's meals en route. (Remember that the *voyageurs* will be working hard paddling and portaging, and that they will need to eat heartily. Remember, too, that there will be no refrigerator and no stove—only an open fire, an iron frying pan, and an iron soup kettle.) List the ingredients for the meals you have planned.

2. Your class is divided into fishers and fur traders. Each group will prepare a presentation on the effects of "their" early industry on the exploration, settlement, and economic development of Canada.

3. Select a fur-trading post shown in Figure 3.7 or on an atlas map. Discover its story, and tell your class about it in a one- or two-minute presentation. You should consider the following information:
- location and description
- founders of the post
- reasons for its choice as a site for a post
- its present population (if it still exists)
- one further fact about it (past or present)

(*The Canadian Encyclopedia* is an excellent resource for this exercise.)

After studying the likely impact on Native peoples of a proposed pipeline, Justice Thomas Berger said of the Inuit: "The remarkable thing is that despite attempts to make them into people like us, they have remained themselves."

FORESTS

When the fur traders penetrated the northern part of North America, they found forests that seemed endless. Trees covered the southern two-thirds of what is now Canada, except on the grasslands of the western plains. Over the years, Canadian forests have provided five types of products for export: logs cut from trunks of tall pine trees; squared timbers *hewed* from the pine logs; sawn lumber (planks and boards); wood pulp and paper; and plywood, chipboard, and particle board (Figure 3.8). Each successive product in the preceding list results from more processing that increases the value of the product.

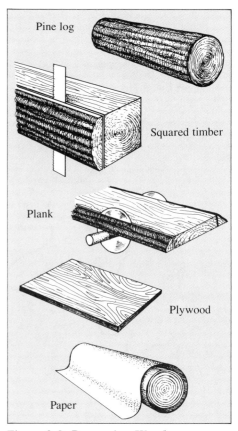

Figure 3.8 *Processing Wood*

This increase of value through a manufacturing process is called *value added*. When processing adds more value to a commodity that will be exported, more money is brought into the producing country, and usually more employment is created. The sixth stage in wood processing is the production of finished manufactured goods, such as furniture. The furniture industry has been important in Ontario and Québec, but furniture has never become a major Canadian export.

Until the 1820s, the demand for Canadian timber came mainly from Britain. As a maritime nation depending on overseas trade, Britain required masts, timbers, and planks for its naval and merchant ships. The demand was so great that Britain used not only its own forests but also those of other countries. Lumber for ships was imported from countries bordering the Baltic Sea, and tall timbers for masts were brought from the Thirteen Colonies in America (Figure 3.9). After the rebellion of the Thirteen Colonies (the American Revolution), Britain relied more on timber from colonies farther north, from the region now called Atlantic Canada.

The British demand for Canadian timber increased rapidly after 1807, when the Napoleonic Wars cut off Britain's supplies of wood from Scandinavia. Later, free trade between the British colonies and the United States, which began in the 1820s, led to large exports of lumber from Britain's "Canadian" colonies to the United States. The West Indies also provided a good market for lumber and barrel staves. Lesser amounts of lumber were needed for the Canadian shipbuilding industry, for building houses and barns, and even for the textile industry, which used wooden spools.

The forest industry in the Canadian colonies was especially important to New Brunswick. At first, large timbers were shipped overseas from the Saint John River area. When the lower areas of the major rivers were cleared of forests, sawmills were built farther up the Saint John and other rivers such as the Miramichi and the Restigouche. Early sawmills were always located where a stream could be harnessed for water power. Small villages sprang up around these sawmills. When the forest was cleared, the villages became ghost towns. Only in areas where there was good farmland did villages survive or grow. The forest industry did foster the growth of Saint John, but only because nearly all the New Brunswick timber was exported through that port city.

In the Great Lakes-St. Lawrence Lowlands, lumbering was only a temporary activity; farming followed as

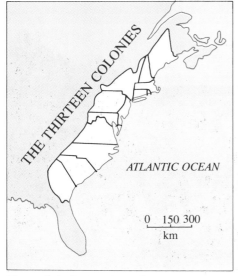

Figure 3.9 **Britain's "Thirteen Colonies" in North America became independent in 1783.**

British merchant ships with wooden hulls and tall masts crossed the Atlantic Ocean carrying all sorts of cargo. The ship shown here is a replica of the Nonsuch, *the first trading vessel sent out by the Hudson's Bay Company. The modern* Nonsuch, *which has actually sailed in Atlantic, Great Lakes, and Pacific waters, can now be seen in Winnipeg's Museum of Man and Nature.*

not practise conservation or reforestation, the supply of white pine in North America was so great that it met the demands of the world lumber market for about 100 years!

The giant white pines were all but cleared from the Great Lakes-St. Lawrence Lowlands by the end of the 1800s. The lumbering industry then moved to the nearby Canadian Shield. Here the best white pine trees were quickly cut, and then smaller softwood trees were used for sawn lumber. They included the jack pine, spruce, fir, and tamarack, softwood trees that grow everywhere on the Canadian Shield, much farther north than the limits of the white pine. By this time pulp and paper were in demand, and the smaller species of trees were well suited to the manufacture of these products.

In the second half of the 20th century, new lumber products became popular. Two such products were

soon as the timber was cleared. Nobody gave a thought to conservation or reforestation because most people saw the forest as a barrier to settlement and economic growth. If a supply of wood should be needed in the future, there was always more forest farther north and west. Logging in the Great Lakes region was limited at first to areas close to the shores of the lakes. Later, railways opened the whole interior to the lumbering industry. When the surrounding land began to be farmed, *grist mills* were built near the sawmills, on rivers and streams where there was water power. Small villages grew up around the mills, and many of these villages grew into towns and cities as farming and manufacturing expanded.

The chief tree harvested, prized both here and abroad for house- or shipbuilding, was the white pine. This tree was found throughout the Atlantic Provinces, the Great Lakes-St. Lawrence Lowlands, and the southern edge of the Canadian Shield (Figure 3.10). It also grew throughout the northeastern United States, providing that country with its own supply of pine lumber until about the 1820s. The white pine grows to a height of sixty to seventy-five metres on fertile soils, and its trunk can reach a diameter of more than 1.5 m. In an age that did

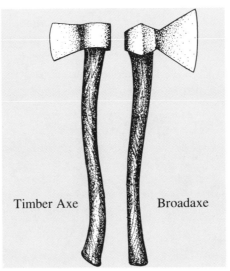

Before the 1870s, Canadian loggers used only axes on even the largest trees: a timber axe to fell the tree and remove the bark and outside wood, and a broadaxe to hew the logs.

The white pine was the most valuable tree in eastern Canada.

A water-powered sawmill. Why was water power so important in Canada's early days?

chipboard and particle board. Manufacturers of these products could use a variety of trees and even the waste products of other lumbering operations.

The forest industries gave rise to many communities in Northern Ontario. Throughout the Canadian Shield, sawmills and pulp and paper mills became the nuclei of many towns. The mills were always located on a waterway and had access to a road or railway. Mill towns were not built in places suitable for manufacturing or in the midst of good farmland. The best sites for mills were not good sites for cities. In contrast to towns in the Great Lakes-St. Lawrence Lowlands, none of the towns in the Shield grew into large cities. A few Shield lumbering towns grew larger when mining activity created more jobs.

In British Columbia, the forest industry did not develop on a large scale until the 1850s, when prospectors who were unable to find minerals turned to the vast forest resources to make a living. The construction of the Canadian Pacific Railway (CPR) in the 1880s expanded the forest industry. It created a demand for lumber for railroad ties, bridges, and stations. The CPR also transported lumber to eastern markets. The industry's greatest asset, however, was the quality of the trees themselves. The huge size of the Douglas fir, the sitka spruce, and the red cedar, and the high quality of their wood, soon made British Columbia lumber popular all over the world. Widespread use of plywood, which required large trees, increased the demand for British Columbia's forest products.

The lumbering industry in British Columbia brought into being many small coastal villages, but the most growth took place in the large port city of Vancouver. Later in the 1800s, lumbering spread into the interior of British Columbia. As in the Canadian Shield, lumbering resulted in many settlements that remained small unless other resources were found in the area to support their growth.

The early forest industries had an indirect effect on the growth of Canada. In the heyday of lumber exports to Britain, many transport ships were required to carry bulky cargoes of lumber across the Atlantic. Ship owners were often faced with the problem of finding a cargo for a ship that would otherwise return empty to Canada. In the circumstances, the ship owners were willing to transport cargo at very low rates. One available cargo was people. Ship captains offered to take passengers to Canada for as little as fifteen shillings (about $3) a head, which was one-fifth the cost of transportation to an American port. As a result, hundreds of thousands of British immigrants (mostly Scots and Irish) came to Canada in the early 1800s.

The forest industry has remained very important to Canada's economy right up to the present. It employs over 40 000 Canadians and contributes greatly to the export trade.

1. List the five types of forest products mentioned on page 98.
a) What size of trees were required for each product?
b) What kinds of trees were required for each product?
c) Comment on the amount of processing required for each product. Explain how processing of raw materials creates more jobs and wealth in Canada.
d) To which countries were most of these products exported?
e) How do you think the development of steam power and iron hulls for ships affected the Canadian forest industry?
f) How would the development of the new wood products indirectly increase the supply of forest resources?
2. How did the development of forest resources influence Canada's settlement pattern? Comment on the number, size, location, and growth of villages, towns, and cities affected by the forest industry.

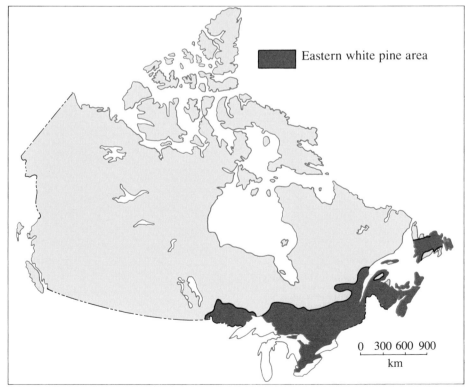

Eastern white pine area

0 300 600 900
km

Figure 3.10 *The Original Extent of the Eastern White Pine*

MINERALS

Mining in Canada began on a very small scale. In the early 1800s, a few small mines provided the minerals needed for local markets. Later, coal for export was mined in Nova Scotia and on Vancouver Island, and asbestos was exported from Québec.

In the late 1800s, the great railroad-building boom led to the discovery and use of new mineral resources in remote parts of Canada. The railroads made it possible to transport these minerals to market. At the same time, the demand for minerals was growing rapidly in the industrializing Western world. As a result of all of these factors, mining activity in Canada grew rapidly in the 1900s. By 1950, Canada had become one of the world's leading exporters of minerals. It was the largest producer of nickel, and ranked second as a producer of gold and zinc, and fourth as a producer of copper and lead. Like the resources discussed earlier in this chapter, most minerals were exported after very little processing.

Most mineral development in Canada occurred far away from settled agricultural areas and major cities. In these remote areas the development of mineral resources, like the development of fishing and lumbering, usually led to the growth of small settlements. The economic growth and population increase that resulted from mining show up in the large established cities in southern Canada but not in the mining communities farther north. The headquarters of mining companies are in the big cities, as are the industries that refine minerals and fabricate metals. While cities in southern Canada expand, the mining towns themselves often decline over time and even die. As mines are exhausted, the mining operation moves on, perhaps to develop another town elsewhere.

The mining industry had more impact on economic development and settlement patterns in the Canadian Shield than in any other region of Canada. In the Shield region the opening

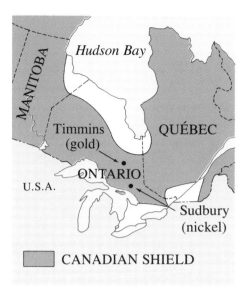

CANADIAN SHIELD

of mines depended heavily on the building of transportation systems, particularly railroads. At first, mines were opened only in the southern part of the Shield, where railroads and highways had been built for other reasons. Later, after the CPR was completed across Northern Ontario in 1884, mining companies began to develop resources such as the nickel and copper ores in the Sudbury area. After the Second World War (post 1945), mining promoters built railroads northward into the Shield for the specific purpose of opening mines. Notable examples are the railroads built to Lynn Lake, Manitoba, in 1953, and to Schefferville, Québec, in 1954. Sometimes mining led to the growth of cities such as Sudbury and Timmins, but most mining communities remained small. Populations of these towns have risen and fallen with the rise and fall in demand for certain minerals.

Montréal, Toronto, and Winnipeg have gained more than other Canadian cities from mining activities. These cities are the chief financial, transportation, and supply centres for the Canadian Shield.

The discovery of gold led to settlement in the area that is now British Columbia. During the Cariboo Gold Rush of 1861, thousands of people

The INCO stack in Sudbury, Ontario. What is one advantage of this mine's very tall smokestack? What is one disadvantage?

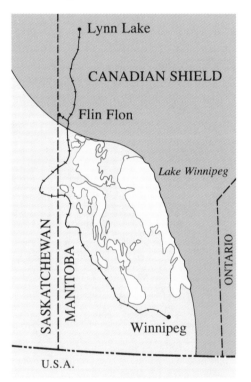

spread into the interior of that province-to-be. Only a few prospectors "struck it rich", while most went home penniless. When the gold rush ended, about 10 000 people stayed in the colony as permanent settlers. The Province of British Columbia was formed as a result of this settlement.

Later, rich deposits of other minerals such as coal, lead, and zinc led to the founding of small mining towns throughout the interior of the province. These towns remained small, since most of the population growth that resulted from mining took place in Vancouver.

The oil and gas industry of Alberta is an example of a recent major mineral development boom in Canada. Exploration and drilling for oil and gas, refining of petroleum products, and the related petrochemical industry led to rapid economic growth in Alberta between 1960 and 1980. Alberta's population also grew, and as happened when mines were opened up elsewhere, the province's largest cities—Edmonton and Calgary—grew most. When the growth rate of these two cities slowed down in the 1980s, it was not because the mineral resource was running out, but because a rapid decline began in the world demand and price for oil.

1. Why did mining not lead to the development of large towns throughout Canada's undeveloped regions?
2. Is a mining town or a forest-product town more likely to become a ghost town? Explain your answer.
3. Choose one of the mining towns listed below. (Each member of the class should choose a different town.) Using an atlas and *The Canadian Encyclopedia* as sources of information, prepare a brief oral report for your class. Your report should include the following information about the town you choose:
- physiographic region in which the town is located
- province in which the town is located
- mineral(s) mined there
- recent population figure
- population growth pattern

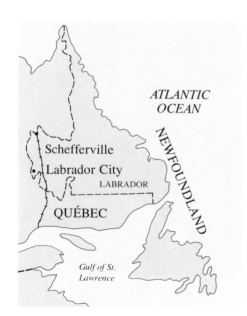

The mining town of Nelson, British Columbia, in 1896.   A copper and lead smelter operated in Nelson from 1896 to 1907.

- one or two details about the history of the mine's or town's development
- why mining has ceased (if applicable)

Choose one of: Buchans, Bathurst, Glace Bay, Lac Allard, Labrador City, Schefferville, Gagnon, Asbestos, Chibougamau, Noranda, Kirkland Lake, Sudbury, Elliot Lake, Manitouwadge, Thompson, Esterhazy, Kimberley, Trail, Turner Valley, Leduc, Pembina, Fort McMurray, Pine Point, Yellowknife, Anvil, Keno Hill, Uranium City, Rankin Inlet.

4. As a class, make a collection of pictures of Canadian mining towns that illustrate some of the information you have presented. Add maps and sketches. Mount your collection as a bulletin board display. Then try to form some general conclusions about mining towns.

FARMLAND

Where good agricultural land was available, most Canadian pioneers supported themselves and their families by farming. The farmers soon required services such as sawmills, grist mills, blacksmith shops, and general stores. As a result, in the centre of each agricultural area, a village grew up. The growing farm communities produced larger and larger *surpluses*. The farmers sent some of their surplus products to nearby towns for processing into various foodstuffs. As time went on, they sent other farm produce, such as apples and wheat, to Europe. This exporting of farm produce created business for port cities.

The general store and Post Office at Campbellton, Ontario. What evidence can you find in this photo that this village store served a farming community?

A traditional mixed farm in Ontario. What is the tall structure in the centre of the photo? What was it used for? What evidence is there that this house and barn were fairly new when this photo was taken?

The machinery and supplies required by the farm industry made it possible to build factories and open stores in the towns and cities. In these ways agriculture stimulated growth and economic development over entire regions. Farming brought about the founding of a network of villages, towns, and cities, and the construction of connecting roads and railroads.

In the Atlantic region, farming has always been of secondary importance. The only farm products ever exported in quantity from the region were apples grown in the Annapolis Valley and potatoes grown in New Brunswick and Prince Edward Island.

In southern Ontario, farming brought about economic development and population growth. It also influenced the settlement pattern of villages and towns. During the 1800s, the Ontario farm economy depended on the export of wheat. Toward the end of the century, *mixed farming* was introduced. By then most farmers had a mix of livestock that included cattle and hogs, and occasionally sheep, laying hens, and poultry. They grew their own feed grain (mostly oats and barley) and hay, and they set aside enough land to pasture their cattle during the summer. Farmers would sow one field of *winter wheat* for a cash crop, but most of their income came from the sale of animal products: cheddar cheese, for instance, was sold in large volume to Britain.

Mixed farming required many supplies and services: a good road network, livestock markets, meat packers, machinery, fertilizer, bankers, insurance agents, and veterinarians. Many of these supplies and services had to be close by, and so a whole network of villages, towns, and cities grew up to provide them.

On the prairies, the expansion of farming required thousands of kilometres of roads and railways. The CPR was completed as far west as Winnipeg in 1865, but pioneers did not move west in large numbers to farm at that time. The most serious problem for prairie farmers then was that the growing season was too short for their varieties of wheat. This problem vanished early in the 1900s, with the development of Red Fife and Marquis wheat. These new varieties were *spring wheat*, which could ripen during a short growing season and did not have to withstand winter. This hard grain

Palliser's Triangle, Canada's most important grain-growing region, is named after Captain John Palliser, whose report to the British government in 1857 declared the region unfit for farming or settlement.

Palliser's Triangle

stored well and made excellent bread flour. As a result, Canadian prairie wheat became a popular export, particularly to Europe.

By the beginning of the 1900s, when most of the good farmland in the United States was settled, settlers began pouring into the Canadian prairies to take up wheat farming. Some came from the eastern part of Canada, but most came directly from Europe. Between 1901 and 1931, the area of prairie land sown in wheat increased from one million hectares to 10 million hectares, and the population increased five fold (Table 3.1). By 1931, wheat made up 40 percent of Canada's total exports.

During the early part of the 20th century, wheat was the driving force of the economy of the Prairie Provinces. Farmers poured into the region, and these wheat growers created a demand for more services and supplies, which led to many more jobs in the towns and villages.

Although wheat was king, other farming activities also expanded in the Prairie Provinces. In the drier regions, settlers used vast areas for cattle ranching. In the more humid regions, farmers turned to mixed farming, which included the growing of wheat, oats, and barley, and the raising of cattle and hogs.

The railroad branch lines, needed to transport grain, joined settlements like beads on a string (Figure 3.11, page 107). Each village had its characteristic grain elevator. The need for rails and railroad cars led to the growth of steel and other manufacturing industries in Ontario. The demand for repair and maintenance of railway cars created jobs in major cities such as Winnipeg. As in Ontario, the demand for many kinds of supplies and services led to a network of settlements of various sizes.

In British Columbia, farming affected settlement little, except in the lower Fraser Valley near Vancouver (Figure 3.12, page 107) and in some

Table 3.1 *Population and Area Planted in Wheat in the Prairie Provinces, 1901 to 1931*

Year	Population	Area in Wheat (ha)
1901	419 500	1 009 500
1911	1 328 100	4 043 100
1921	1 950 100	7 847 000
1931	2 353 500	10 354 700

Source: Compiled from Canadian census data

Prairie Farming in Earlier Days

Stooking was hot, heavy work! The sheaves of ripe grain had to be firmly balanced upright with their heads together so that they would shed rain, and so that the kernels would become hard and dry enough for threshing.

*This photo, taken in 1899, shows Doukhobor women **winnowing**. After the cut grain was **flailed**, the winnowers would shovel it into a sturdy frame with a sieve-like bottom, and then shake the frame. The heavy kernels of grain would fall to the ground, and the light chaff would blow away.*

Threshing required many hands. Neighbours would band together to form a "threshing gang" that visited the farmsteads in turn. Here one farmer (right) pitchforks a sheaf of grain into the hopper of the threshing machine. The straw piles up in the foreground. The kernels of grain, stripped from the husks, pour into the wagon in front of the threshing machine. This photo was taken about 1915. What kind of machinery would today's farmers use to harvest their grain?

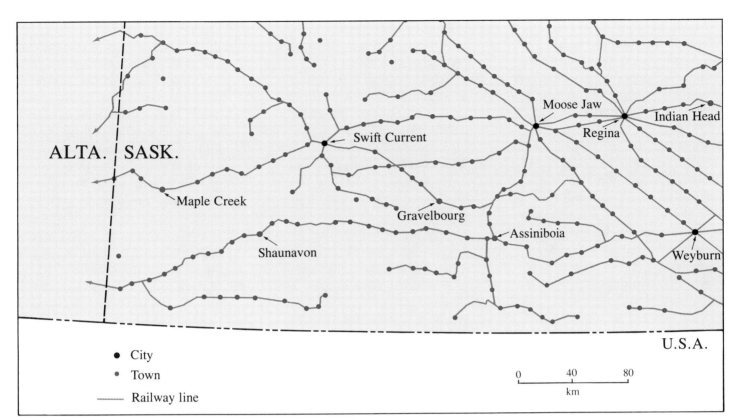

Figure 3.11 *Railroad Lines and Towns in Southern Saskatchewan*

of the interior valleys such as the Okanagan (Figure 3.13). In most parts of the province, farming only supplemented other economic activities.

The agricultural industry has had a lasting effect on the settlement pattern of Canada. Wherever there is good farmland, a dense network of villages, towns, and cities has grown up. Although farming today supports fewer Canadians than it did earlier in this century, the industry is still very important to Canada's economy.

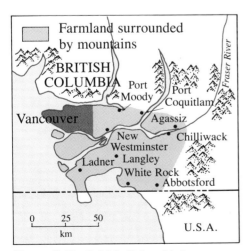

Figure 3.12 *British Columbia's Lower Fraser Valley*

1. a) Draw a line graph showing the changes in population and the changes in area sown in wheat between 1901 and 1931. Place the years on the *x* axis. On the *y* axis, let 1 cm equal 1 000 000 units.

   b) Describe the slope of the population and wheat lines. Did population or wheat production grow more rapidly? (The steeper the slope, the more rapid the growth.) What do you suppose was happening to farm sizes during this period? How does the change in farm size reflect the relation between area farmed and population shown in Table 3.1?

2. Nellie McClung, a well-known Canadian author of the early 1900s, moved with her family from Chatsworth, Ontario, to

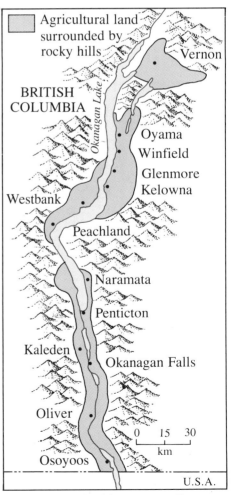

Figure 3.13 *The Okanagan Valley*

107

Manitoba when she was six years old. In her autobiography, *Clearing in the West*, she tells the story of her family's journey and their early years on their Manitoba homestead.

From this book or another Canadian author's book about growing up on the prairies, choose an anecdote that you enjoy and read it to your class.

Some other Canadian authors whose books you might use are:

- W.O. Mitchell: *Who Has Seen the Wind? Jake and the Kid*
- Max Braithwaite: *Why Shoot the Teacher?*
- Pauline Johnson: *The Moccasin Maker*
- Margaret Laurence: *A Bird in the House*

3. The population of southern Ontario was also growing rapidly during the first 30 years of the 20th century. How do you think prairie wheat production helped Ontario's population to grow?

4. Why are so many of the settlements shown in Figure 3.11 located on railroads?

5. a) What means of transportation do you think farmers used in the first quarter of the 20th century to take grain to market and bring supplies to the farm? Try to find some photos or illustrations to support your answer.
b) About how far could a horse walk in an hour?
c) How do the answers to questions a) and b) help you explain why settlements were established so close to one another?

6. a) About how far can a modern farmer travel by truck in an hour? How does your answer help to explain why fewer grain elevators are needed today than in the early 1900s?
b) If only one elevator were needed between Moose Jaw and Weyburn, in which village do you think it would be located? If all but one elevator in this area were closed down, what do you suppose would happen to the other villages?

7. Suggest geographical reasons for the smaller number of railroads and settlements in the southwest corner of Saskatchewan than in other parts of the province.

8. Why did the agricultural industry lead to the founding of more villages and towns and the development of a denser network of railroads and roads than did the fishing, fur, forestry, or mining industries?

9. In what way did the agricultural industry stimulate the growth of the manufacturing industry?

10. Make a general statement about the effect of the development of natural resources on the size and distribution of Canadian villages, towns, and cities. Explain why areas with good farmland have become the most densely populated.

Grain elevators in Kamsack, Saskatchewan

LARGE-SCALE RESOURCE DEVELOPMENT AND NATIVE PEOPLES

Before the Europeans came, as we saw in Chapter Two, Canada's Native peoples had a natural resource base that had changed very little over thousands of years. These peoples believed that the land, water, and air belonged to everyone, including past and future generations. They cut only as many trees as they needed for their immediate use or to clear small patches of forest for planting crops. They made use of all parts of the animals they killed. When game became scarce in one area, they moved to another. This movement allowed wildlife species to reach their natural levels again in the old location.

The Europeans had a different attitude about resources and the natural environment. They seemed to believe that Canada's resources were unlimited. They would clear all the trees from a large tract of land and then move on to a new forest area and clear it. When a section of forest was cleared, wild animal and bird life disappeared, and many streams and lakes were ruined for fishing. European hunters shot so much game that many species became very scarce, and some became extinct. Hunters were often wasteful, killing more game than they could use. For example, they killed thousands of bison, often using only the animals' tongues and hides, while leaving the rest of the carcasses to rot. Farmers on the prairies broke up the sod that had protected the soil for thousands of years. Serious soil erosion resulted.

As Canada's European population grew, more and more land was

The bison, Canada's largest land mammal, was also one of the most numerous animals in North America. About 50 million bison lived on the prairies in 1800. By 1885, the bison was nearly extinct.

A Native worker in the power plant at Cominco's Polaris lead-zinc mine

required for resource development. The resource frontier was constantly rolled back, reducing the area where Indians could make a living in their traditional ways. Under great pressure from the advance of European culture and development, various Indian peoples signed treaties that turned over great tracts of land to the Canadian government. In return, the Indians were given small areas of land reserved for them alone. These *reserves* were not always good farmland, and they were too small to support the traditional Indian lifestyle. Today about 375 000 status Indians live on reserves. Another 800 000 Native persons, *Métis*, and Inuit live off the reserves. These people are scattered all across Canada (Figure 3.14). In general, their opportunities have been limited, and their standard of living is far below the Canadian average.

The method of developing resources in Canada is still causing social and economic problems for some Native people. Resource development jobs usually require the family's provider to leave home or to move the whole family to unfamiliar surroundings. When a provider is laid off, the whole family suffers great stress. Hopes for a higher standard of living are dashed. The providers, unemployed through no fault of their own, believe that they have failed their families. It is hard for proud people

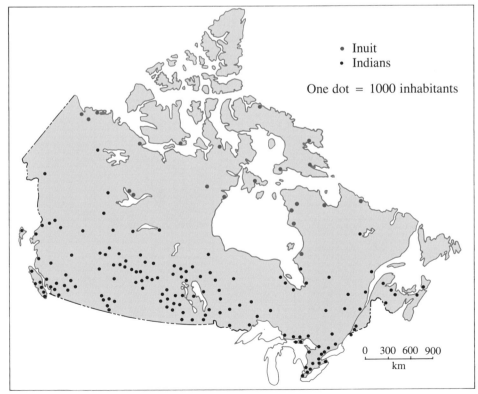

- Inuit
- Indians

One dot = 1000 inhabitants

0   300 600 900
km

Figure 3.14 *Distribution of Indians and Inuit in Canada*

who were once self-sufficient, to lose control of the resources that made them independent and to become dependent on government welfare cheques.

The future development of oil and gas resources in the Arctic may cause similar problems for Canada's Native people. There will be jobs for them during the construction phase. But when that phase is over, many Natives may lose their jobs and again have to search for other means of supporting themselves or depend on government welfare.

GROWTH OF MANUFACTURING

The early settlement and growth of Canada depended on developing and exporting natural resources. After Confederation, more than half of the labour force was working in farming, lumbering, fishing, and mining. Lumber, fish, coal, and farm produce were exported to Europe, the United States, the West Indies, and other countries. Toward the end of the 1800s, manufacturing became important to Canada's economy. Manufacturing was based mostly on the country's own natural resources. The resources were processed or refined and turned into the manufactured goods needed by the resource industries and the growing population.

Government encouragement stimulated manufacturing. The National Policy of 1878 promoted the building of transportation systems. By 1890, the Canadian Pacific Railway was completed from Saint John to Vancouver. In the early 1920s, several other railroads united to form another coast-to-coast line, the Canadian National Railways. Many branch lines were built throughout the settled part of the country. The high demand for steel rails and railway cars greatly stimulated the iron and steel industry and

metal manufacturing companies.

The National Policy also placed *tariffs* on the import of manufactured goods. This tariff policy protected Canadian manufacturers from having to compete against products that could be made more cheaply in other countries. It also encouraged many U.S. companies to build branch manufacturing plants in Canada so that they could supply the Canadian market without paying a tariff.

Two world wars (the First World War, 1914–1918 and the Second World War, 1939–1945) created a high demand for all kinds of war equipment such as ships, tanks, airplanes, and guns. The Canadian iron and steel industry and other related manufacturing industries grew rapidly during these wars, especially in southern Ontario and Québec. These regions had special advantages. They were close to:
- the manufacturing belt of the United States
- the forest and mineral resources of the Canadian Shield
- the cheap transportation of the Great Lakes-St. Lawrence waterway

They possessed:
- readily available water power
- an abundant supply of fresh water
- excellent farmland

Because the manufacturing industry grew rapidly in the Great Lakes-St. Lawrence Lowlands, that region's towns and cities also grew rapidly. Growth caused more growth. Manufacturing companies wanted to locate in towns and cities where other firms

could provide the supplies and services they needed. The companies created work, which attracted people, and so increased the size of the cities. The large, growing cities, in turn, attracted manufacturers by expanding the market for products and attracting a work force with various skills. By the middle of the 1900s, the steady expansion had developed the urban-industrial heartland of Canada in southern Ontario and Québec. In 1951, this heartland had 62 percent of Canada's population and 78 percent of its manufacturing employment (Table 3.2).

The general pattern of industrial and urban development established by mid-century continues to the present. In 1986, the heartland had 62 percent of the country's population, as well as 75 percent of its manufacturing employment (Table 3.2). The slight decline of employment in manufacturing was offset by an increase in employment in the *service industries*.

Today, Canada's economy and the creation of jobs depend more and more on the service industries and the "high tech" (high technology) industries such as the manufacture of electronic equipment and computer information systems. Service industries do not actually produce goods; they provide personal, legal, medical, and financial services, as well as education and entertainment. Both high tech industry and specialized services are attracted to large cities. The trend toward service industries has reinforced the economic importance of the heartland of Canada.

Table 3.2 *Population and Manufacturing Employment across Canada*

	% of Population		% of Manufacturing Employment	
	1951	1986	1951	1986
Ontario	33	36	45	48
Québec	29	26	33	27
Rest of Canada	38	38	22	25
Total	100	100	100	100

Source: Compiled from Canadian census data

1. Construct two circle graphs. In the first one, show the proportion of Canada's population in Ontario, Québec, and the rest of Canada, in 1986. In the other, show the proportion of Canadians employed in manufacturing in Ontario, Québec, and other parts of Canada, in 1986.

2. Calculate a Manufacturing Concentration Index for each of Ontario, Québec, and the rest of Canada for 1951 and 1986. Calculation method:

$$\text{Index} = \frac{\text{\% of 1951 manufacturing employment in } x}{\text{\% of 1951 population in } x}$$

(Let x represent in turn Ontario, Québec, and the rest of Canada.)

A manufacturing concentration index of 1.0 is average for the country. The higher the index is above 1.0, the greater the manufacturing concentration; the lower the index is below 1.0, the lower the manufacturing concentration.

3. Using data in Table 3.2, make a general statement about the concentration of Canada's manufacturing industry.

4. Construct a large classroom chart with headings as shown below. For each natural resource name a product or several products under each of the three headings across the top of the chart. The example for farmland illustrates the idea.

Natural Resource	Unprocessed	Processed or Refined	Manufactured
Farmland	wheat	flour	bread
Fish			
Furs			
Forests			
Minerals			

5. Why are more jobs created in Canada when natural resources are processed, refined, or manufactured into finished products rather than exported unprocessed?

6. Why are manufacturing industries attracted to large cities where a number of manufacturing industries are already based? If possible, provide examples from your local area.

THE SERVICE INDUSTRIES

People's jobs can be divided into three basic categories of industry called *economic sectors*: primary (resource development), secondary (manufacturing), and tertiary (services). Examples of these different economic sectors are given in Table 3.3.

Table 3.4 (page 112) shows how the proportion of the various economic sectors that make up Canada's labour force has changed since the beginning of the 20th century. In 1901, more than 40 percent of Canadian workers were employed in primary industry. By 1971, this figure had decreased to less than 10 percent. The percentage of workers in secondary industry has remained steadier. The greatest growth in employment since 1900 has been in the tertiary or service industries. For every job created by developing a natural resource or setting up a new factory, several more service jobs are created.

One of Canada's fastest-growing service industries is tourism. Both Canadian and foreign travellers spend hundreds of millions of dollars each year on accommodation, food, recreation, and entertainment. By 1986, the tourist industry was providing employment for more than 10 percent of Canada's total labour force. Each year, it brings more foreign money into Canada than does the export of Canadian wheat. Some geographers have predicted that by the year 2000, tourism will be one of the most important single economic activities in Canada.

Table 3.3 *Economic Sectors*

Economic Sector	Sample Industry	Sample Economic Activity
Primary (developing natural resources)	agriculture fishing forestry mining	wheat farming cod fishing logging gold mining
Secondary (transforming raw materials into new products)	food processing mineral refining manufacturing	milling wheat refining crude oil into oil and gasoline building automobiles
Tertiary (providing services)	commerce finance transportation communications education health care personal services community services tourism	wholesaling and retailing banking trucking radio and television newcasting teaching nursing hair styling fire fighting operating a motel

Table 3.4 *Canada's Labour Force by Economic Sector*

Year	Primary Industry (%)	Secondary Industry (%)	Tertiary Industry (%)
1901	44	20	36
1911	42	16	42
1921	40	16	44
1931	37	17	46
1941	30	20	50
1951	20	23	57
1961	15	21	64
1971	8	26	66
1981	7	26	67
1986	6	25	69

Source: Compiled from Canadian census data, 1901 to 1986

1. Table 3.3 shows only a few examples of industries and economic activities in the three economic sectors. Brainstorm with your classmates to add as many more examples as you can.

2. a) Many of Canada's Community Colleges offer courses for people who wish to work in the service industries. Working in small groups, try to find out what courses or training programs are available in your area for any three of the jobs identified in Table 3.3 or your expanded list. Jot down any information you can find about these courses.
b) Prepare a two- or three-minute report for your class on the information you have gathered.

3. Draw a multiple line graph showing the changes in the percentage of Canada's labour force in each economic sector. Describe the slope of the line representing each sector.

4. Suggest how advances in technology tend to reduce the number of people employed in primary and secondary industries. Give some examples.

5. Which employment sector do you think will show most growth in the next 10 years? Give reasons for your answer.

6. As a population becomes more prosperous, service industries become more important as a source of jobs. Why does this change take place?

SETTLEMENT AND POPULATION

We have been looking at the way different economic activities affected the early settlement and development of Canada. We are now going to consider the settlement patterns that resulted and the nature of the population across our country.

SETTLEMENT BY PATCHES

Early intensive settlement depended on farmland. Since good farmland is located in widely scattered patches, it can be said that Canada was settled in patches (Figure 3.15). One Canadian geographer has described this pattern of settlement in patches as follows:

The fundamental line of the Canadian land is the southern edge of the Canadian Shield. It is our boundary between the wilderness and the garden.

Its location meant that in an age when most people depended on agriculture, there could not be a continuous expansion of settlement across the land. Settlement proceeded in patches. One patch would fill up, and then people would emigrate, south to the United States more often than west, because the next Canadian patch of good land was far away and across a major barrier.

For the Newfoundland outports the barrier was rocky wilderness; for the Saint John and Annapolis valleys, hills and forests; for lowland Québec, the Canadian Shield and anglophone Ontario; for southern Ontario, the lakes and the Shield; for the western plains, the Rocky Mountains and the Shield; for settled British Columbia, everywhere mountains. Thus different patches were settled at different times by different people from different European countries. Occasionally Europeans who first settled in the United States joined the Europeans who came directly from Europe. The country did not expand westward from an Atlantic beginning; it was settled patch by patch from Europe.

—Cole Harris,
"Within the Fantastic Frontier: A Geographer's Thoughts on Canadian Unity" (Adapted)

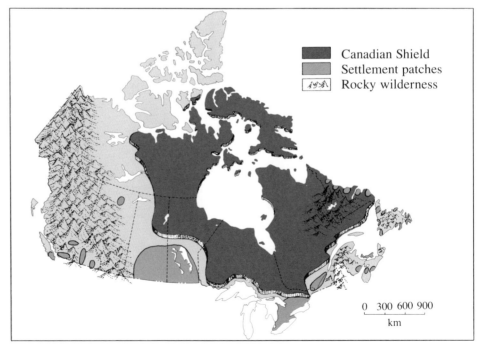

Figure 3.15 *Patches of Settlement Across Canada*

Settlement Patterns in Canada

Peggy's Cove, Nova Scotia.
Along Canada's Atlantic coasts, small
fishing villages grew up where coves and
inlets offered sheltered harbours for
small craft.

The typical settlement pattern in the southern regions of
rural Ontario was a grid of roads bordered by farmsteads,
with villages at the crossroads.

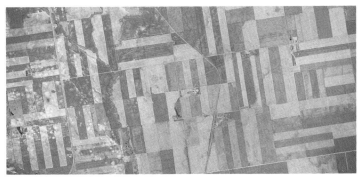

Settlement patterns on the prairies were fixed by the grid pattern
that the early surveyors used to mark out the land. In this
satellite image, pink and red colours represent green vegetation
such as grass and grain in fields. Alternating strips of unplanted
cropland appear as blues or greens. Clusters of farm buildings
are strung out along intersecting rural roads (white lines). A
small prairie village is built beside the railway line that curves
across a flat landscape.

These long lots bordering the St.Lawrence River are
typical of an early settlement pattern in Québec. Why
was it important to Québec's early settlers to occupy
land with a river frontage?

In the mountain areas of British Columbia,
most settlement took place in the valleys.

113

This patches pattern of settlement has had a profound influence on Canadian society. The people in each patch had few connections with the people in the next patch. They were more likely to have relatives in the United States than in another part of Canada. Each patch developed its own culture and way of life. Its people were able to retain the culture and customs of their European roots. Canada developed into a multicultural country with many different customs and lifestyles. The patches development also encouraged Canadians to feel loyal to their local area and to form no strong attachments to other parts of the country. Some of Canada's problems in developing a unified country and a feeling of Canadian nationalism may stem from this pattern of early settlement. It certainly made the building of trans-Canada railroads an essential task in the early years of the country's history. Later, trans-Canada airlines, highways, and telecommunication systems became necessary to link together the population patches and encourage national unity.

The Canadian pattern of patches settlement contrasts with the pattern of settlement of the United States. There, people settled first along the Atlantic seaboard; they moved westward as the land filled up, travelling through the Appalachians to the vast interior plains. The various inland groups lived together, blended their cultures, and were assimilated as English-speaking Americans. The flow of people from Europe and the east coast to the interior continued for several decades. In contrast to Canadian settlers, American pioneers advanced continuously westward. Once across the Appalachians, the settlers faced no major barriers until they reached the Rocky Mountains and the great deserts of the southwest. As an area filled up, people would move on to the one just beyond, keeping in touch with the settlement they had left. Through this process, Americans lost some of their European heritage, but they developed a greater feeling of unity and nationalism than did settlers in Canada.

---

1. Make a large sketch map of Canada. Show the barriers in the Canadian landscape that required settlement by patches rather than encouraging a continuous east-west flow. In the settlement patches, record the date when settlers new to Canada founded their settlements.
2. While the settlement patterns of Québec farms and prairie farms look very different at first glance, they have a common factor. Compare these two patterns of settlement, and explain their similarities and differences.
3. Using at least three of the patches mentioned in the quotation, find evidence to confirm or refute Harris's claim that different patches of Canada were settled at different times by different people from different European countries.

4. Early Canadian immigrants often named their new villages and towns after places in their home country. Because of this custom, place names may suggest the origin of the early settlers of an area. Review the patches mentioned in the "Settlement by Patches" quotation, and with the help of an atlas, use place-name clues to name one ethnic group among the early settlers for each patch. Try to find some place names that commemorate Canada's Native heritage. If possible, find out the origin or meaning of these place names.

POPULATION DISTRIBUTION

Resource development, as we have seen, influenced the early settlement pattern in Canada. Later the manufacturing and service industries reinforced the established pattern. This later population pattern can be mapped in several different ways.

---

1. Using the statistics in Table 3.5, plot on a map of Canada the population density for each province and territory. Use three colours to distinguish areas of sparse, medium, and dense population.
2. Compare your map with Figure 3.16. What are the main differences between the figure and your map as sources of information about population density?
3. In Figure 3.17 (page 117), the population density of southern Ontario has been mapped by means of the same technique that you used to prepare your map of Canada (question 1). This map differs from yours in two important ways. First, the scale of this map is large enough to show differences from one part of the

LOCAL STUDY

1. Prepare a case study of the area in which you live to test Cole Harris's statement about settlement by patches. You will need to find or make maps and photographs to illustrate your study. When you have assembled your material, display it on your class bulletin board.
2. Interview a parent, grandparent, or other family member who can tell you when and why your family settled in the area where you now live. Working backward from yourself, construct a family tree. Make a "Family Album" to keep pictures, stories, and treasures of your family's history.

region to another. Secondly, the units for which statistics were provided are small enough to show those differences.

a) In how many census divisions is the population density greater than the average density for the province?

b) In how many is it less than average?

c) In how many is it the same?

4. Look at Figure 3.16 or an atlas map that shows distribution of population in Canada. Compare the population map with maps showing the following:

a) physiography

b) length of growing season

c) closeness of large American cities

How might each of the above factors have affected Canada's population density? Give an example to support your opinion.

5. After studying these maps, state how, in general, a map's scale relates to the amount of detail that the map shows.

6. Figure 3.17A (page 117) shows the distribution of population density in the census division of Ontario's Frontenac County. In this map, the scale is large enough to map by census subdivisions. How was Figure 3.17 misleading about the population density of Frontenac County?

7. To the model, diorama, or mural which you began in Chapter Two, add some houses to represent the earliest settlement. Then add buildings to represent industries and businesses.

ETHNIC ORIGINS

Table 3.6 (page 118) shows clearly that Canada is a multicultural country. About one-half of Canadians descend from one of the two founding nations, the French and the British. At the time of Canada's first census (1871), about 50 percent of the population was British, and 31 percent was French. Now British Canadians and French Canadians make up only 25 percent each of Canada's population. This decline resulted from a decrease in the number of immigrants coming to Canada from Britain and France, and an increase in the number coming from other countries.

In 1986, the rank order of ethnic origins among Canadians, after the British and French, was as follows: German, Italian, Ukrainian, Native Indian or Inuit, Dutch, Chinese, Scandinavian, Polish, Portuguese, Hungarian, Czech and Slovak, Austrian, Belgian, Japanese, and Russian. In the 1970s and 1980s, more people began coming to Canada from Southeast Asian countries. As Table 3.6 shows, these ethnic groups are unevenly distributed across Canada.

Table 3.5 *Population and Area by Province and Territory*

Province/Territory	Population	Land Area (km²)
Newfoundland	568 000	371 700
Prince Edward Island	126 700	5 700
Nova Scotia	873 200	52 800
New Brunswick	710 400	72 100
Québec	6 540 300	1 350 600
Ontario	9 113 500	891 200
Manitoba	1 071 200	548 400
Saskatchewan	1 010 200	570 700
Alberta	2 375 300	644 400
British Columbia	2 889 200	929 700
Yukon	23 500	479 000
Northwest Territories	52 200	3 293 000
Canada	25 354 100	9 215 400

Source: Compiled from Canadian census data, 1986.

Note: Numbers are simplified by rounding to the nearest 100 people and the nearest 100 km² of land area, excluding water.

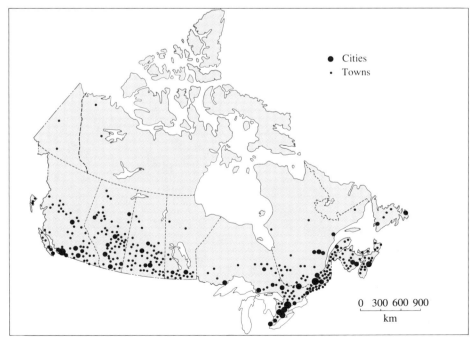

Figure 3.16 *Distribution of Population in Canada, 1986*

115

Settlement Barriers

*A Newfoundland outport nestles against a rocky backdrop.
The rocky barrier rising behind this village might provide welcome
shelter in bad weather. Would it have any disadvantage?
Explain your answer.*

*Vancouver is bounded by the Coast Mountains
to the north and the ocean to the west.*

*A prairie farmstead in the lee of the Rocky Mountains.
Compare this settlement pattern with the one illustrated by
the Newfoundland outport. How is it similar?
How is it different?*

Toronto's Chinatown.   This streetscape shows the vitality and colour of an urban Chinese community.

Ethnic groups have tended to settle in "colonies". Ukrainians have been attracted to the prairies, where the land and climate are similar to those of their homeland. Many Dutch have settled on the fertile flat farmland in the extreme southwestern part of Ontario, where they can practise intensive farming by growing fruit and vegetables the way they did in the Netherlands. Many Chinese, Portuguese, Greeks, and Italians have settled in particular sections of large cities such as Toronto.

Because immigrants from different countries have tended to settle in groups, they have created distinctive

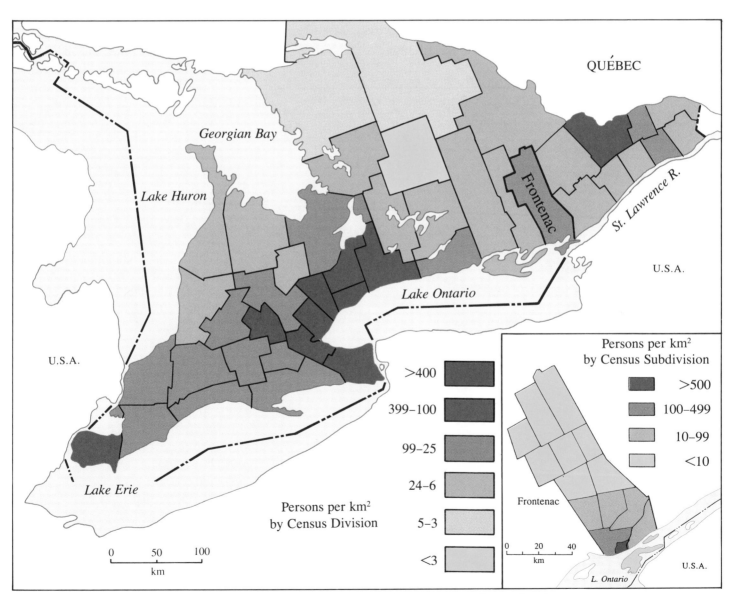

Figures 3.17 and 3.17A *Population Density in Southern Ontario and in Frontenac County* (inset)

117

landscapes in different parts of Canada. In the countryside, they have brought particular methods of surveying land, building fences, and laying out farmsteads, as well as distinctive architectural styles of barns and houses. In the towns and cities, they have affirmed their backgrounds by store signs, the names of streets, the architecture of churches, and ethnic specialty food stores and social clubs. The language, speech, accents, dress, and customs of the ethnic neighbourhoods offer striking examples of Canada's cultural diversity.

This cultural diversity among its people gives Canada a unique character. It is officially a bilingual country, but it is also a multicultural country. The cultural diversity of Canada makes our society rich and interesting, but it also poses some problems. Ethnic groups with different values can clash. Some groups believe that they lack equal opportunity with other groups. The differences and confrontations between English-speaking Canadians and French-speaking Canadians are well known. Tensions exist between other ethnic groups, as well. Caucasians in Canada do not always welcome people who have a different racial background. Immigrants of other races often believe that discrimination works against them in Canada's job market. To counter harmful prejudice, the federal and provincial governments have passed legislation aimed at providing job opportunities to all Canadians, regardless of race, colour, or ethnic origin.

1. a) Rank Canada's ethnic groups (Table 3.6) in descending order, according to their proportion of the total population.
b) Which of Canada's provinces or territories has the highest percentage of people descended from people of a single ethnic origin?
c) Which province or territory has the highest percentage of people descended from Native peoples?
d) Which province or territory has the highest percentage of people of Asian origin? Suggest an explanation for this circumstance.
2. In seven of the provinces and Territories listed in Table 3.6, there are more descendants of people from "other European countries" than from France. Name them.
3. Make a survey of the ethnic origins of members of your class. Construct a circle graph from this data, using the same categories as those used in Table 3.6. Make a general statement about your findings.

You might wish to organize a class "Heritage Day" and ask the members of each ethnic group represented to prepare a five-minute presentation of *one* aspect of their culture that they would like to share with the class. They might choose to share, for instance: a traditional legend, poem, or song; a traditional recipe; information about a national festival; examples of traditional art; pictures or examples of traditional costume.
4. Draw circle graphs on an outline map of Canada to show the percentage distribution of ethnic groups in each province and territory according to the statistics provided in Table 3.6. Make the size of each circle proportional to the total population of each political unit.

Table 3.6 *Canadians' Ethnic Origins by Province and Territory* (%)

Ethnic Origin	Can.	Nfld.	P.E.I.	N.S.	N.B.	Qué.	Ont.
British	25.1	79.8	47.4	48.3	35.8	5.0	32.4
French	24.2	2.1	8.9	6.1	33.1	77.7	5.0
Other European	14.5	0.5	2.0	4.8	1.6	5.6	18.9
Asian	4.8	0.4	0.6	1.0	0.5	3.0	6.3
African	0.7	0.01	0.1	0.9	0.1	0.6	1.2
Latin American	0.1	0.0	0.01	0.01	0.01	0.2	0.1
Multiple Origins	27.6	16.6	40.8	38.0	28.1	6.9	33.9
Native People	3.3	0.7	0.3	0.7	0.6	0.8	0.6
Others	0.6	0.04	0.1	0.2	0.1	0.3	0.7

Ethnic Origin	Man.	Sask.	Alta.	B.C.	Yukon	N.W.T.
British	21.4	22.3	25.3	30.6	23.0	13.5
French	5.3	3.4	3.3	2.4	3.3	2.9
Other European	26.5	26.9	21.7	16.9	11.4	5.4
Asian	4.92	1.7	5.5	8.8	1.2	1.3
African	0.4	0.1	0.3	0.2	0.04	0.2
Latin American	0.1	0.1	0.2	0.1	0.1	0.04
Multiple Origins	35.1	39.3	40.6	38.2	50.0	23.1
Native People	5.3	5.6	2.2	2.2	14.1	52.2
Others	1.1	0.7	0.9	0.7	2.0	1.3

Source: Calculated from Canadian census data, 1986
Note: Totals may not add up to 100 percent because of the rounding off of numbers to the nearest tenth percentage point.

5. By multiplying the percentage in Table 3.6 by the total population figure in Table 3.5, you can calculate the number of people of any given ethnic origin in each territory. For three of the following items a) to h), rank the three provinces that have the most people of the given ethnic origin.
   a) British
   b) French
   c) European other than British or French
   d) Asian
   e) African
   f) Latin American
   g) Native
   h) Multiple

WHAT LIES AHEAD?

Canada has many policy choices to make that will affect our country's future. These choices will shape Canada's economic development, population growth, and settlement pattern. The following items suggest a few options. You need not decide which choices are better or what compromises might be worked out. Simply by reading the contrasting pairs you will realize the difficulties facing Canada's policy makers of the next few decades.

1. Canadians should concentrate on developing primary industry and exporting raw materials because Canada has the advantage of a much greater supply of natural resources than have most countries.

   OR

   Canada should stop exporting unprocessed raw materials and concentrate on the manufacturing and service industries, which create more jobs for Canadians.

2. Too much of Canada's population and economic activity is concentrated in a few large cities. Canada should adopt policies that would encourage the growth of small towns and the creation of new cities in the more remote areas of the country.

   OR

   Large cities and major towns have grown because they have advantageous locations. No government should interfere with the natural evolution of this settlement pattern. Small towns and villages with poor locations should be allowed, even encouraged, to disappear.

3. The government should encourage the growth of Canada's population by both natural increase and much more immigration because we need a much larger home market for our industries.

   OR

   We should limit population growth because a large population tends to destroy the quality of our natural environment and therefore downgrades the quality of life.

4. As a wealthy country, Canada could afford to throw its doors wide open to immigrants. We should admit much larger numbers of refugees and underprivileged people from all over the world.

   OR

   Canada should be selective in choosing immigrants. The government should admit only people who can fill current job vacancies in Canada and who will fit readily into Canadian society.

REVIEW QUESTIONS

1. Turn to the beginning of this chapter and answer the questions in the section "Hewers of Wood and Drawers of Water".
2. Listing both similarities and differences, compare the ways Native people and European settlers used Canada's resources.
3. How did the development of each of the following major natural resources affect Canada's settlement pattern? As development of these resources proceeded, which had the greatest effect on the settlement pattern?
   a) trees
   b) fish
   c) minerals
   d) farmland
4. Explain why the percentage of Canada's labour force in the primary sector has decreased substantially since the early part of the 20th century.
5. Do you think that the population distribution pattern in Canada will change much in the next 50 years? Give reasons for your answer.
6. Hold a classroom debate on one of the policy choices in the section "What Lies Ahead?"

Chapter Four

Canada's Evolving Political Geography

Canada: A Mistake in Political Geography?

"Canada is a nation despite its geography" is a statement often quoted. What do you think it means? Do you agree? Explain why or why not.

Queen Elizabeth II signs the patriation document of Canada's Constitution while then Prime Minister, the Right Honourable Pierre Trudeau looks on.

O CANADA!

What's in a name? One possible origin of the name "Canada" is the Huron-Iroquois word "Kanata", which means a village or settlement. Jacques Cartier used the name for the area around Stadacona, the future site of Québec City. Cartier had heard two of his guides, sons of the Chief of Stadacona, use the word to refer to their village. "Canada" was later used as a synonym for New France, which included all French possessions along the St. Lawrence River and the Great Lakes. After the British conquest of New France, the name "Québec" was used for a while instead of Canada. The name "Canada" was restored after 1791, when Britain divided Québec into the provinces of Upper Canada and Lower Canada. Later, in 1841, Britain reunited the two provinces to form the single Province of Canada. Although Canada was a united province from 1841 to 1867, the people of the day continued to use the names "Upper Canada" and "Lower Canada". Some people in the Atlantic Provinces still refer to Ontario as "Upper Canada", and Ontario's professional society of lawyers is still called the Law Society of Upper Canada.

THE POLITICAL MAP OF CANADA

In this chapter we consider how the political geography of Canada has evolved. To understand the process, we need to form a mental picture of the political map of Canada as it is today (Figure 4.1). The following activities will help sharpen that image.

1. On a political outline map of Canada:
   - Label the chief political units (provinces and territories) and their capital cities.
   - Make each political unit a different colour.
   - Draw a 1 cm-wide blue border around all of Canada's coastline, including offshore islands. Colour the Great Lakes blue, as well.
   - Label the parallels of latitude by tens from 50°N to 90°N.
   - Label the meridians of longitude by tens from 50°W to 140°W.
2. The capital city of a political unit is the place where its government is located. The capital is not always the largest city in a territory or province. Consult an atlas to learn in which Canadian provinces and territories there are cities with a population larger than that of the capital. Mark and label these larger cities on your outline map of Canada.
3. Working in small groups, prepare a classroom display. Each group will make a coloured sketch or painting of the flag of one province or territory. Write a brief account of what the flag tells you about the area's history and/or geography. Arrange the flags and written accounts on a bulletin board. (See *The Canadian Encyclopedia* under the names of the provinces.)

In 1857, Queen Victoria selected Ottawa (then called Bytown) as the capital of the United Province of Canada.

Canada's Parliament Buildings, Ottawa

4. On a blank sheet of paper make a freehand drawing of the political map of Canada, complete with provinces, territories and capital cities. The following guidelines may be helpful:

Outline

Start by drawing the outline of a simplified map of Canada, using straight lines as much as possible.

Above Québec's National Assembly building flies the flag of La Belle Province.

Shapes

Draw only the main shapes. Ignore all the little capes and bays along the coastline, and outline the basic shapes only.

Look for striking shapes. For example, Québec-Labrador looks like a dog's head, with New Brunswick and the Gaspé Peninsula forming the dog's lower jaw. One can imagine that the islands in the Gulf of St. Lawrence are pieces of food that the dog is about to eat.

Pay particular attention to the shape and direction of the shoreline in the Maritime Provinces; note that Nova Scotia's Atlantic shoreline runs more east-west than north-south.

Proportions

Notice the proportions of the provinces and territories that make up Canada. The four western provinces are all roughly the same size; the western edge of Lake Superior is approximately the midpoint between the east and west coasts; the distance from the southern tip of Ontario to the North Pole is about the same as the distance between Canada's east and west coasts; Saskatchewan measures about twice as far north to south as it does east to west.

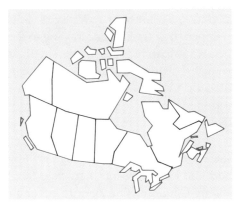

Canada has the second-longest coastline of any country in the world.

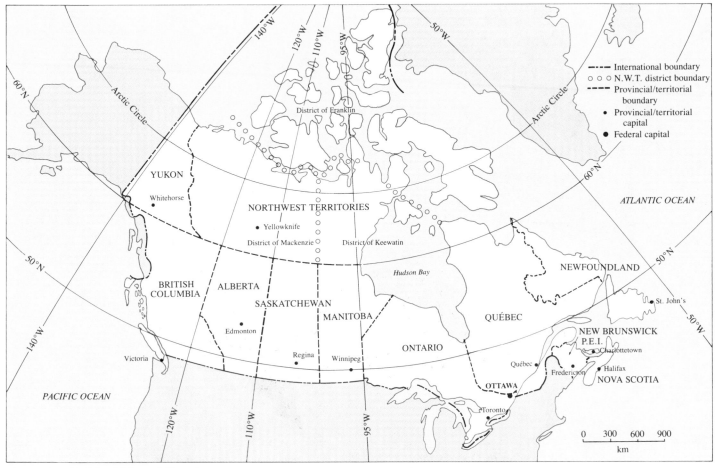

Figure 4.1 *Political Map of Canada*

NATIVE POLITICAL GEOGRAPHY

When Europeans first arrived in what is now Canada, as we noted in Chapter Three, the land had been occupied and used by Native peoples for thousands of years. In that chapter we identified different groups of Natives and mapped their territory according to the geographical regions in which they lived. Canada's Native peoples can also be grouped and their territory mapped according to the language they speak (Figure 4.2).

When the first Europeans came, there were 10 Indian language groups and one Eskimo-Aleut language family in Canada. The people of each Native language family occupied a particular region of the country as Figure 4.2 shows. In other words, there was a Native political geography in Canada before the French and British began colonizing the country and fighting for its political control.

The family groups of Native languages were as different from one another as a European language such as German is from an Asiatic language such as Chinese. Eight of the eleven language families each included several distinctive languages. For example, the Algonquian language family

> During the Mackenzie Valley Pipeline Inquiry, Tommy Kakfwi, a Dene from the Northwest Territories, told Judge Thomas Berger: "I think people would find it funny today if I went across to Europe and planted a flag saying, 'I claim this land for the Dene.' "

included subgroups such as the Blackfoot, Cree, Micmac, and Ojibwa. There were several Eskimo-Aleut languages, of which only one, the **Inuktitut**, was spoken by the Inuit, who live in the Canadian Arctic. Other language "families" were actually a single unique language, such as the Haida spoken on the west coast.

Some of the Native language subgroups divided themselves further into tribes and even further into bands. Each tribe had a grand chief, and each band had a chief and a general fishing and hunting territory. The tribe defended its territory against invasion by any other tribe (Figure 4.3).

The Iroquoian-speaking people, who occupied the Great Lakes-St. Lawrence Lowlands, were divided into many tribes. Five of these tribes that originally occupied northern New

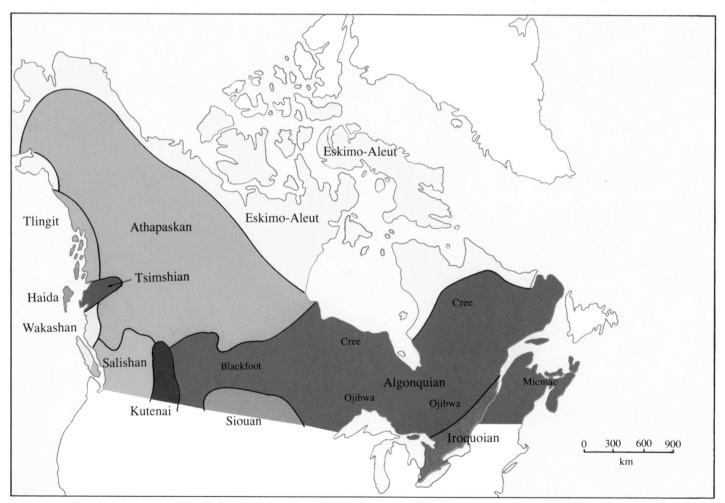

Figure 4.2 *Native Language Families in Canada about 1500–1800* *This map shows some distinctive languages of the Algonquian language family. Cree, Ojibwa, and Micmac are still spoken in Canada.*

York State formed a *confederacy* called the League of Five Nations or the League of the Iroquois. Later, when a sixth tribe joined, the confederacy became known as the Six Nations. Each tribe sent members to a governing council. Generally, the confederacy of Iroquoian tribes is simply called the Iroquois.

1. Referring to Figure 4.3, answer the following questions:
   a) In what language is the legend that explains this drawing? What does this suggest?
   b) The artist has described area C as "Piazza". What would this area have been used for?
   c) Building D is described as "Casa del Re Agouhana": The House of King Agouhana. Why would the artist have called Agouhana a king? What term would we use instead? Is one term preferable to the other? If so, why? What would be the best term of all? Why?

What important information does this give about all the buildings shown in the drawing?

2. Make a class list containing all the information you can find in this drawing about the country, the Native people and their way of life, and the relations between the new arrivals from France and the Mohawks at Hochelaga.

EUROPEAN INTERVENTION

The Beothuk of the Island of Newfoundland were among the first Native people to come in contact with Europeans. Because the Europeans did not try to learn anything about the Beothuk, we know almost nothing of their language. We do not even know for certain if it was a language distinct from the languages of the other mainland groups. (Some scholars think that it belonged to the Algonquian family of languages.) The numbers of Beothuk quickly declined soon after the Europeans arrived. Some Beothuk the Europeans killed outright, while others died from European diseases to which they had no resistance. The last Beothuk died in 1829.

During the 1600s, the British had settled the Atlantic seaboard of what is now the United States. They soon began to trade guns and other supplies to the Iroquois in return for furs. Iroquoian tribes attacked their neighbours to gain control of the supply of furs. They attacked and dispersed the Hurons (an Iroquoian-speaking group that lived around the upper part of Lake Huron) and conquered several other neighbouring tribes. They also attacked Algonquins in the St. Lawrence Valley. The French traded with, and provided guns to, many of the tribes who were enemies of the Iroquois. Because the French supported their rivals, the Iroquois considered them enemies. As a direct result, the Iroquois fought the French. As an indirect result, the Iroquois supported the British efforts to crush the French and gain control of North America. After the British won Canada from the French, the Iroquois helped to repel American invasions of Canada. The Iroquois took an active part in the battles that laid the foundations for the modern political geography of Canada.

Huronia, the region lying north of Barrie, Ontario, was once the home of the Huron Indians. Today it is a tourist region, containing Huron archeological sites and a museum at Midland.

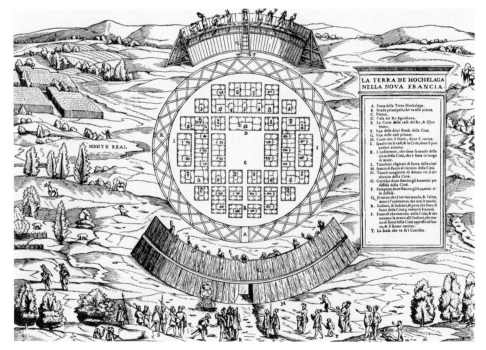

Figure 4.3 *Hochelaga, 1535* *When Jacques Cartier reached the large island in the great (St. Lawrence) river where Montréal now stands, he found a group of about 1500 Indians living in a well-organized community.*

THE FRENCH-BRITISH STRUGGLE

During the same period, the long-standing hostility and fighting between France and Britain in Europe spilled over into North America. The French and British fought about the fisheries in the Atlantic Ocean and the fur trade in the interior of the continent. At issue was control of the vast North American territory.

By 1700, the French had built a network of fur-trading posts and forts that gave them control over the St. Lawrence Valley, the Great Lakes Lowlands, and the entire Mississippi Valley to the Gulf of Mexico. The waterways of the Mississippi, the Great Lakes, and the St. Lawrence became the major transportation corridor for the fur trade. The French expanded the fur trade northward and westward from their strategic central position (Figure 4.4).

The British trade route inland through the Appalachian Mountains led to conflict with the French fur traders. The British had established fur-trading posts around James Bay, and when their northern traders moved southward, they, too, confronted the French. Their best trading route for furs collected in the vast area northwest of the Great Lakes was through the St. Lawrence waterway, which was under French control. The French had clearly outmanoeuvred the British in the struggle for power in North America.

Early in the 1700s, Britain made some gains in its struggle with France for colonies in North America. By the Treaty of Utrecht, one of the treaties ending a war in Europe, France, in 1713, officially recognized British control over Nova Scotia (except for Cape Breton Island) and the vast Hudson's Bay Company territory called Rupert's Land. One situation remained unchanged by this treaty:

France retained its strategic control of the interior of the continent from the Gulf of St. Lawrence to the Gulf of Mexico. The territories still under dispute gave an excuse for French and British to fight whenever they met (Figure 4.5).

BRITAIN AND THE ACADIANS

When Britain took over Nova Scotia, most of the settlers already there were French speaking. These people were known as Acadians. The Acadians wanted to keep their own culture. They also wanted to remain neutral in any fighting between the British and the French. Through several decades of British rule, the Acadians prospered, and their numbers grew rapidly. But because they would not swear an oath of loyalty to the British crown or fight in the British army, the British thought that they were a threat. In 1755, the British governor of Nova Scotia decided to send the Acadians into exile. He deported some 10 000 men, women, and children. But even after the Acadians were taken to various other British North American colonies, they kept their sense of themselves as an independent community. In the several decades that followed, large numbers returned to their former homeland. Most of the returning Acadians settled in the area now

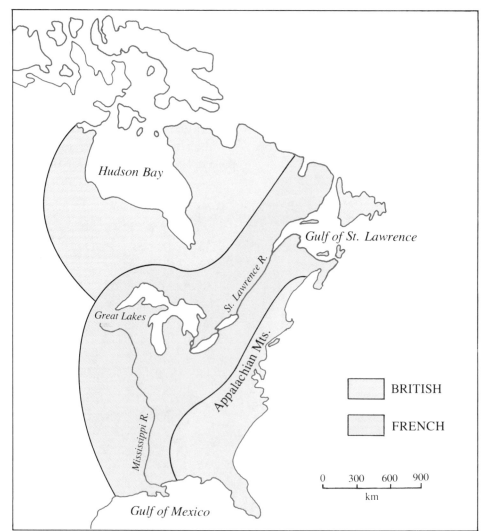

Figure 4.4 *French and British Territories, about 1700* The French controlled the waterways of the continent's interior from the Gulf of St. Lawrence to the Gulf of Mexico.

Acadians wait on the beach to be taken to the ships that will transport them to a strange country. What clues can you find in this picture of the problems that expulsion caused the Acadians?

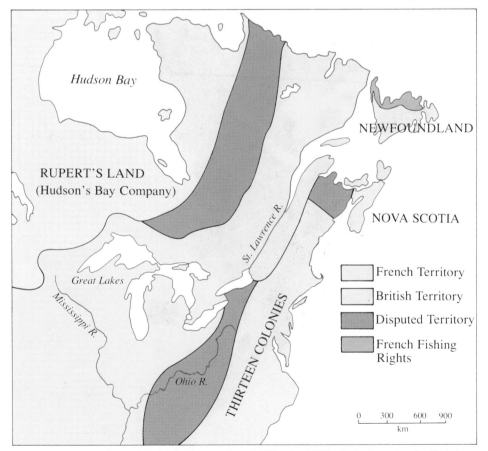

Figure 4.5 ***French and British Territories, 1713*** *In 1713, Britain gained official control over Nova Scotia and Rupert's Land.*

known as New Brunswick. Today about 40 percent of New Brunswick's population is descended from those early French Acadians.

A ROYAL PROCLAMATION

After the Seven Years War (1756–1763) between France and Britain, all of New France, except for the islands of St. Pierre and Miquelon, was turned over to Britain. France also retained the right for its fishers to dry their catches along the north shore of Newfoundland. The Royal Proclamation of 1763 established the land rights of Native peoples in Britain's North American territories. The "Proclamation Line" marked off the lands reserved as "Indian hunting grounds" from those that could be opened to settlement (Figure 4.6, page 128). The Royal Proclamation promised the Natives within the "Indian Territory" that Britain would purchase, not take by force, any land needed for settlers.

As a document, the Royal Proclamation had flaws. For example, it did not identify the precise western boundary of the "reserved lands", nor did it refer to the Maritime Provinces. Because its wording was very vague, arguments arose about which lands had been recognized as belonging to the Native peoples. To clarify the situation, a number of treaties were signed by Native groups and *the Crown*.

BRITAIN AND NEW FRANCE

When the British gained political control over New France, they re-named the territory "Québec". ("Québec", like "Canada", is an Indian word. Québec means "where the river narrows".) In 1774, Britain passed the *Quebec Act*, which was meant to ensure that Québec would not support the rebelling Thirteen Colonies in what is now the United States. The *Quebec Act* extended the boundaries of Québec beyond the junction of the Mississippi and Ohio rivers to include the upper Mississippi Valley (Figure 4.7). It also gave the French a number of rights and privileges. They were granted the right to keep their language and customs, and to use their own civil law in the courts. The *seigneurial system* of land holding would continue, and their Roman Catholic Church was to have special privileges. The *Quebec Act* did much to help the French in Québec remain a distinct cultural community. Politically, New France had been conquered, but culturally, its people remained independent. The French-speaking people of Québec still keep this sense of cultural independence.

The American Revolutionary War began soon after the *Quebec Act* was passed. The leaders of Québec society (the landholders, or *seigneurs,* and the clergy) remained loyal to Britain and encouraged the French Canadians to join the British troops in repelling American invasions. When the war ended, the Thirteen Colonies had gained their independence as the United States of America, and a new border had to be drawn for Québec. By the Treaty of Paris, which brought the war to an end, the Great Lakes became the southwest boundary of Québec (Figure 4.8) and France's fishing rights were shifted to the western shore of Newfoundland. In the following years, thousands of United Empire Loyalists (those people of the Thirteen Colonies who had remained loyal to Britain) fled the United States. Some of them went to Nova Scotia, which included what is now New Brunswick, but even larger numbers settled in the southwestern part of Québec (now Ontario). So many English-speaking Loyalists came to Québec that in 1791, Britain decided to divide it into the provinces of Upper Canada (Ontario) and Lower Canada (Québec) (Figure 4.9, page 130). By this time New Brunswick had become a colony separate from Nova Scotia. Living in a separate political unit helped the French to retain their culture and their sense of independence.

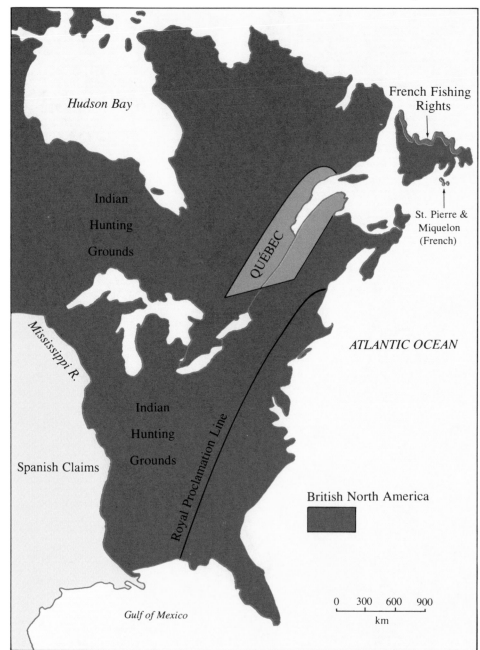

Figure 4.6 *British North America after the Seven Years' War and the Royal Proclamation of 1763*

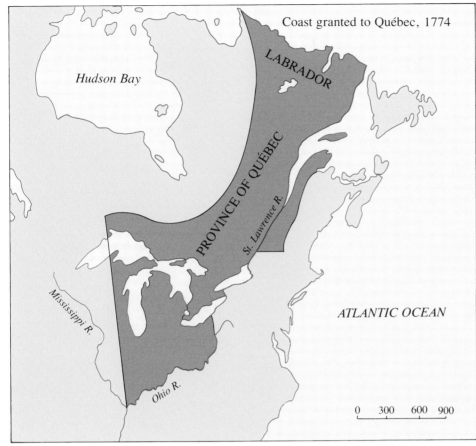

Figure 4.7 *The Province of Québec after the* **Quebec Act, 1774**

1. Look up the words "strategy" and "strategic" in your dictionary. What was the strategic advantage of the French position in North America about 1700?

2. Compare the British conquerors' treatment of the French-speaking Acadians with their treatment of the French-speaking people of Québec. Why do you think the British treated the two groups differently?

3. Canadian historians tend to call the conflict between Britain and the Thirteen Colonies the American Revolution. American historians usually call it the American War of Independence. Suggest a reason for this difference in terms.

4. Following are two scenarios that suggest what might have happened if there had been no *Quebec Act*. Choose the scenario you think most likely, or else make up one of your own. Explain the reason for your choice.

a) Without the *Quebec Act*, the French in Québec would not have remained loyal to Britain. The United States would have conquered Québec, and Canada as we know it today would never have been created.

b) Without the *Quebec Act*, the French in Québec would have been **assimilated** into the British society there. Québec would not have become a province with claims of special status. Canada would not have become officially bilingual.

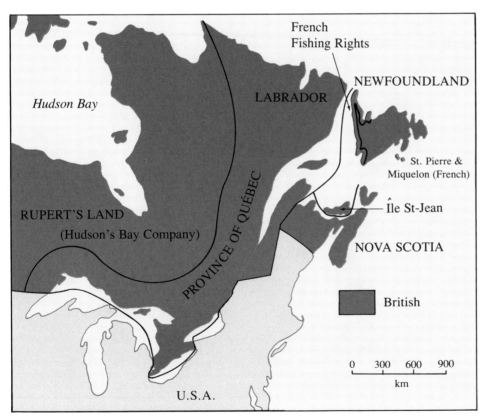

Figure 4.8 *British North America, 1783*

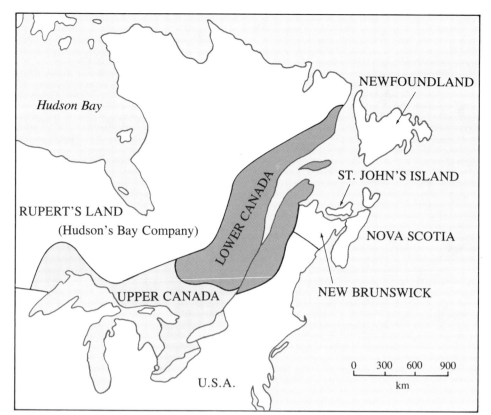

Figure 4.9 *The British Colonies in North America, 1791*

Kahnawake Reserve near Montréal. The men of this reserve are internationally renowned for their skill as high steel-construction workers.

A 1987 study comparing housing on Indian reserves with off-reserve housing showed that:
1. **The proportion of reserve houses needing repairs (23 percent) was three times as high as that of off-reserve houses.**
2. **The proportion of overcrowded houses was 10 times higher on reserves than off reserves.**

TREATIES AND RESERVES

All the treaties signed between the British government and Canada's Native peoples after 1850 required the Indians to give up title to their land. In return, the Natives were to receive land reserves, annual payments, and the right to hunt and fish on unoccupied Crown lands. Rights promised to the Native peoples in these treaties and in previous agreements made during the French régime were confirmed by the *Indian Act*, 1876, and the Canadian *Constitution Act, 1982*. The *Indian Act* stated that only status Indians (that is, Indians registered by Canada's federal government) had the right to live on Indian reserves. A community of status Indians living on one or more reserves is known as a band. At present, about 375 000 status Indians are living on approximately 22 000 reserves in Canada.

Areas set aside for Indians are called reservations in the United States. In Canada their proper name is reserves.

LIFE ON THE RESERVES

Most Indians living on reserves are not well off. Some of Canada's poorest families are found on these reserves. The roots of this poverty may often be traced to the type of land granted to the Natives. The Native peoples who had been *nomadic* hunters, fishers, and trappers were restricted to reserves where there was little wildlife. Quite often the land was not suitable for farming. Reserves were often located in isolated areas where opportunities for employment are few. It is difficult to establish successful industries in these remote areas. The reserve Indians have not usually had the opportunity to develop the skills required to do the few jobs that open up. Often these jobs relate to the construction phase of a resource development project that lasts only for a short time. The following accounts of the Westbank and Grassy Narrows Indian bands show the best and worst conditions on Canada's Indian reserves.

Housing on a northern Indian reserve. The climate in this area is harsh, with short summers and very long, cold winters. What does this picture suggest about the housing on this reserve? In your view, what are the most urgent needs for improvement in the housing in this community?

A Tale of Two Bands

I. Grassy Narrows, Ontario

For almost 20 years, Grassy Narrows (Figure 4.10) has symbolized all that is wrong on Canadian Indian reserves. The 700 Ojibwa living in this remote village 90 kilometres northwest of Kenora, Ontario, have seen their community devastated by the actions of outsiders.

Grassy Narrows' tragedy began in 1965, when the federal government, with the best of intentions, relocated the band members to a new, specially created village connected to Kenora by a logging road. The new village offered the people of Grassy Narrows reasonable housing, a reserve school, regular medical attention, electricity, piped water, and a sewage system. The move was intended to improve the band's lot by bringing its people out of isolation and opening the way for integration into the non-Indian world.

Although the new village was only eight kilometres from the band's traditional habitat, the effect of the move was profound. Previously, the people of Grassy Narrows had lived scattered across the islands and peninsulas of the English-Wabigoon rivers system. They trapped, fished, grew vegetables, harvested wild rice and berries . . . Although they were poor, they had a strong stable community.

The new government-created community removed them from their familiar lifestyle. The new land proved too rocky to grow vegetables. Living in homes tucked neatly together in rows was alien to them. They were cut off from their traditional land and suddenly connected to non-Native civilization by road.

Almost overnight, the community of Grassy Narrows began to collapse . . .

Wife beating, child abuse, suicide, violence, murder, and rape became common: this among a people who had cherished each community member, had doted on its children, and had looked to its elder members as a source of wisdom.

Alcoholism became rampant. Many adults and even children regularly drank themselves unconscious. When the liquor ran out, they turned to sniffing gasoline fumes—a deadly means of "getting high" which killed many band members.

As the band struggled unsuccessfully to adapt to a new way of life, it was dealt another terrible blow. In 1970, it was discovered that the English-Wabigoon river system was polluted . . .

The more fortunate band members were not . . . severely poisoned, but the contamination of the river system further distanced them from their traditional life. No longer could they earn a living fishing or acting as guides for the tourists who had travelled from all over the world to fish for the area's famous pike and pickerel.

. . . By the mid-1970s almost 100% of the adults were on welfare . . .

By the end of the 1970s, almost 75% of reserve deaths resulted from violence. Before the relocation, 91% of all deaths were from natural causes . . .

Life at Grassy Narrows promised little for the future, but in 1984 a flicker of hope appeared. Out of the despair emerged a strengthening resolve among the people to create a viable community. By a vote, the people banned liquor from the reserve. A crisis centre was set up, and it dramatically reduced the suicide rate.

Most important of all, in December 1985, the band negotiated $8.7 million from the federal and provincial governments in compensation for the mercury poisoning. This money has been used to establish a non-profit economic and social development corporation and an investment corporation. Both will provide jobs by encouraging a forestry industry and re-vitalizing tourism.

It is still early in the recovery process, but the people of Grassy Narrows now have hope for the future.

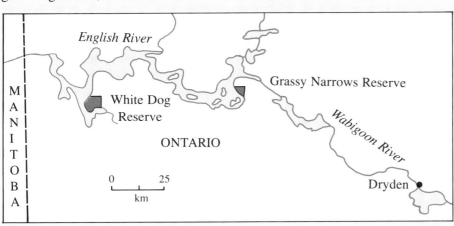

Figure 4.10 *Grassy Narrows Reserve*

II. Westbank, British Columbia

In 1975, the Westbank Indian Band, situated on 930 hectares of land across Lake Okanagan from Kelowna, B.C., was foundering. Most band members lived in poverty; housing was little more than shacks; alcohol-related deaths were common; broken families abounded; education levels were low and murders occasional. Most of the band was on welfare. A badly managed housing development venture had run up a debt of $2 million: nearly $12 000 for every one of the then 170 band members. The band administration was thinking about declaring bankruptcy.

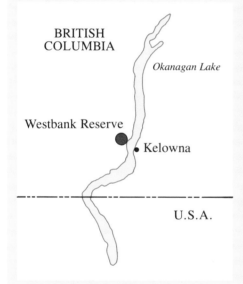

Westbank's was a familiar story to this point; then it took a new twist. For the first time in Canada, an Indian band decided to improve its social and economic lot, not by seeking government handouts, but by launching an aggressive business- and land-development campaign. The programs have resulted in the creation of one of Canada's richest Indian bands. In ten years, the lifestyle of Westbank's people was totally transformed.

The election to Chief of self-made millionaire Ron Derrickson, in

1975, was the start of Westbank's recovery. Mr. Derrickson and a core of band members applied to the band's affairs everything they had learned from their success in the non-Native-dominated business world.

Through the Westbank Indian Band Development Corporation, they created an executive-class housing subdivision for non-Natives working in Kelowna. In the first year, the Corporation earned several million dollars profit, paid off the band's debt, and began a program of growth that has made it a major economic force in the Okanagan Valley . . .

Nearly all band members are employed within the band's more than 42 businesses. The average salary paid a member working for the band is about $18 000 a year. Few band members are now on welfare. Westbank also boasts 25 millionaires among its current population of 242 members.

Alcohol abuse is no longer a major problem. The band's large population of children is finishing school, and increasing numbers are going on to university. Violence among family members is almost unheard of, and family life is good.

Throughout the late-1970s and early-1980s, the band has risen to achieve one of the highest standards of living of any band in Canada . . .

The people of Westbank have entered into the non-Native-dominated world and have done well within its structures. Rather than striving to maintain their own society separate from that of the non-Natives, they have adapted the strongest points of the dominant culture to their own. In this way, the traditional values of Indian society have been maintained without hindering the people's ability to function in the modern world . . .

The band's self-reliant approach

to development has little in common with the government's view of how living standards should be improved on reserves. The Department of Indian and Northern Affairs has usually encouraged, intentionally or not, dependence on government for financial support and services.

In 1985, Ron Derrickson did not seek re-election as Chief, and Brian Eli succeeded him. Mr. Eli and the new band council have pledged to continue Westbank's economic and social program . . .

—Mark Zuehlke,
"A Tale of Two Bands" (Adapted)

1. Working in small groups, prepare for a "press conference" to explain the situation in Grassy Narrows. Some groups will represent "the press", and some will represent the Band Council and people of Grassy Narrows.

    The press will prepare questions about the move to Grassy Narrows, how it affected the Native people there, and how problems developed.

    The people of the Community will plan their response to the questions they expect to be asked.

    If you can, tape the "conference" and play the tape back to the whole class. Would you change any parts on a second taping? If so, why?

2. a) Compare the life of the people in Grassy Narrows with that of the people in Westbank. In a class discussion, name five factors that led to prosperity on the Westbank Reserve and to poverty and social disaster on the Grassy Narrows Reserve. Consider the following points in your discussion:
   - location of the reserve in relation to urban development
   - natural resources available

- government intervention or assistance
- leadership within the band
- opportunities for participating in the ''non-Native-dominated business world''
   b) Make a general statement to account for Westbank Reserve's success.

3. Would you advise people on other reserves to use Westbank Reserve as a model for their own development? Explain your reason.
4. Why is it unfair to draw a general conclusion based on only one or two examples?
5. Do you agree or disagree with the statement in the Westbank story that ''the traditional values of Indian society have been maintained''? Be prepared to explain your answer.

The Champagne/Aishihik Indian Band in the Yukon provides computer word processing and other office services for businesses in Whitehorse.

LOCAL STUDY

As a class, make a study of the Indian reserve closest to your community. Try to find answers to the following questions:
a) When was the reserve established?
b) To which language group do the Indians belong?
c) How many members has the Band?
d) How much land belongs to the reserve?
e) What proportion of the land is good for agriculture?
f) What other natural resources does the reserve contain?
g) How do the residents on the reserve make a living?
h) How is the Band organized to administer itself?
i) Does the school program on the reserve differ from yours? If so, how?
j) Compare the standard of living and way of life of the young people on the reserve with your own.

To find the information you need, you might arrange a class visit to the reserve, or invite the Chief of the Band to visit your school. Write a letter to the Department of Indian and Northern Affairs, Ottawa. To obtain information about education on the reserve, write a letter to your provincial Department/Ministry of Education. Arrange through the principal of the school on the reserve to write a letter to one of the classes, telling them about your school and its program, and asking about theirs.

NATIVE LAND CLAIMS

The many Indian treaties and the agreements about reserves apply only to a small proportion of Canada's Native people. The rights and land claims of some status and non-status Indians and of large numbers of *Métis* and Inuit have not been settled. These Native peoples have been trying for years to get legal possession of lands and recognition of rights that they never sold or exchanged by treaty.

The search for oil and gas and hydro-electricity in the Canadian North has led to conflicts between developers and Native people. Since the 1960s, Native people have been very active in making land claims. They claim that they own the land, and that any development must be negotiated with them. They have formed various political organizations to fight their case. One of these organizations, the Assembly of First Nations, represents status Indians, including 90 percent of the Indian chiefs across Canada. Another, the Native Council of Canada, represents non-status Indians and Métis outside the Prairie Provinces. A third organization, the Métis

COPE stands for Committee for Original People's Entitlement. In 1984, COPE negotiated an agreement with the federal government that gives the Inuvialuit of the Mackenzie Delta title to 91 000 km² of land.

National Council, represents prairie Métis, and a fourth, the Inuit Committee on National Issues, or Inuit Tapirisat of Canada, represents all Inuit groups.

MÉTIS LAND CLAIMS

The Métis who occupied the plains of western Canada (Figure 4.11, page 134) are one group whose land claims were never settled by treaty. These people are descendants of European traders and settlers and their Native wives. In the years when traders and explorers were moving into the plains, the Métis were renowned for their knowledge of the land and for the life skills they excelled in practising in difficult territory. In the second half of the 19th century, the Canadian government refused to give them clear title to their land. When government surveyors began to map the Red River Valley, ignoring the Métis land claims, their leader Louis Riel and other Métis seized Upper Fort Garry, the main Hudson's Bay Company post in the region; they held it until the new federal government agreed to negotiate with them. The negotiations after this Red River Rebellion (1869–1870) led to the formation of the Province of Manitoba and a government promise to grant more than 500 000 hectares of land to the Métis. The government did not keep this promise. Instead, it gave to the Canadian Pacific Railway much of the land that it had promised to the Métis.

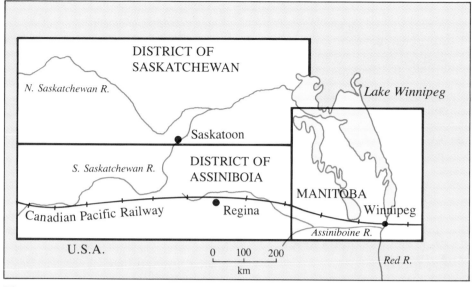

Figure 4.11 *Métis Country in the 1880s*

At the same time, settlers began to pour onto the prairies, turning the Métis hunting grounds into farmland. In deep frustration, the Métis took up arms under the leadership of Louis Riel and Gabriel Dumont. They fought against the Canadian troops in what is known as the North-West Rebellion (1885). The Métis lost the skirmishes, and Riel was hanged.

The Métis did not give up their fight for land. In Alberta they succeeded in obtaining 500 000 ha, where 4000 Métis still live in a string of settlements across the northern part of the province. In 1989, Alberta granted the Métis official title to these lands. Elsewhere, the Métis were not successful. But they continue to negotiate for settlement of their land claims.

In 1974, the federal Department of Indian Affairs and Northern Development (now the Department of Indian and Northern Affairs) set up a special office to settle Native claims.

In 1990, the Dene and Métis of the western Arctic made a land claim settlement with the federal government. The agreement gives about eighteen percent of the land in the region to the Dene and Métis. It also gives them subsurface mineral rights on 10 000 km², and a cash *compensation* of $500 million to be paid over a period of 20 years.

The office was reorganized in 1985, to handle "comprehensive" land claims. These claims are based on Native rights and involve the traditional use of land by large tribal groups in British Columbia and the North. They are negotiated under the Department's self-government program. The government also provided funds to help Native groups research their claims and obtain legal advice in presenting them.

1. You and your class are a Native council that represents all Native groups in Canada. The council's task is to prepare a brief to the federal government supporting Native land claims. As a class, make a list of the points you will include in the brief. The following questions may give you some ideas.
a) How long have the Natives occupied the land which they are now claiming?
b) How long ago did Europeans "discover" North America?
c) Does "discovery" of land already occupied by Native peoples mean that the land then belongs to the "discoverers"?
d) How important is the land to Natives for making a living?

e) What will happen to the way of life of the Natives if they lose their land claim?
f) Compare the way Canada's Native peoples treated the land and its resources with the way that European and other immigrants treated them.
2. Check past and current issues of newspapers and magazines for information about Native rights and land claims. Collect the articles in a loose-leaf binder or file folder for your classroom use.

CANADA'S GROWTH TO NATIONHOOD

In 1867, the *British North America (B.N.A.) Act* created the provinces of Ontario and Québec by dividing the United Province of Canada, and brought the new provinces into union with Nova Scotia and New Brunswick. In this way, the *B.N.A. Act*,

The Prime Minister of Canada, the 10 provincial premiers, and leaders of Native organizations attended the Constitutional Conference on Native Rights, in March 1987. Here the House of Commons stands to pray with Native leaders just before the Conference opens. Though the issues of Native rights were thoroughly discussed, the government took no immediate action.

which is now known as the *Constitution Act, 1867*, formed a **confederation** of colonies called the Dominion of Canada. The term 'Dominion' has fallen into disuse, but we have kept the name Canada.

GEOGRAPHY AND CONFEDERATION

After the American Revolution, the British Colonies in what is now Canada came to depend more on one another. Upper Canada (Ontario) and Lower Canada (Québec) needed access to ice-free seaports. The Maritimes wanted closer commercial ties with the Canadas. By the 1860s, the lumber trade in the Maritimes was declining, as wooden sailing ships were being replaced by metal steamships. Both New Brunswick and Nova Scotia hoped that closer links with the Canadas, including a railroad, would bring prosperity. Merchants and bankers in Saint John and Halifax had visions of their cities becoming the commercial centres of British North America.

Upper and Lower Canada already depended on each other economically. Montréal financiers invested in the Welland and St. Lawrence canals so that products from Upper Canada would move through the Great Lakes and the St. Lawrence River to Montréal instead of through the Erie Canal to New York. Montréal merchants also favoured construction of a railroad to the Maritimes, in the hope that Montréal would become the commercial centre of British North America.

Many railroads were built in the mid-1800s. The Grand Trunk Railway was built from Sarnia to Montréal, where it connected with a railroad to Portland, Maine. The Great Western Railway connected Toronto, Hamilton, and Windsor. In the Maritimes, railroads joined Halifax to Sydney and Saint John (Figure 4.12).

The railroad-building boom was good for the economy of the colonies. Payments for construction materials and the wages paid to workers put a large amount of money into circulation. Operation of the trains created hundreds of railway jobs and a demand for coal, wood, and other supplies. Railways meant that farmers

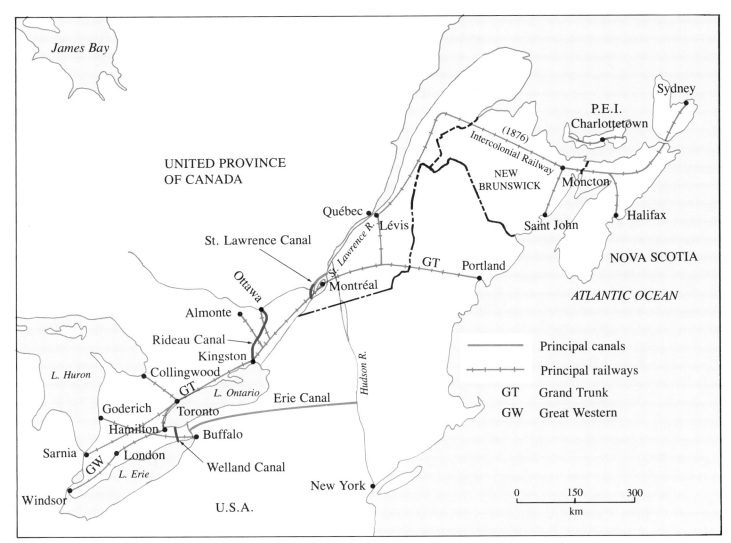

Figure 4.12 *Early Canals and Railways in the United Province of Canada and in the Maritime Colonies*

The Rideau Canal at Bytown in 1840. How did Bytown get its name? What is it called today?

and manufacturers could send their products to more distant places. A railroad through a town brought growth: the building of factories and stores, and population increase.

Because railways could operate all year round, they overcame the disadvantages of transport by rivers, lakes, and canals, which were closed by winter freeze-ups. The Grand Trunk and Great Western railways could carry products from both Upper Canada and the American Midwest to the port of Montréal in summer and to Portland, Maine, in winter. What was missing by 1860 was a railway connection between the United Province of Canada and the Atlantic Maritime colonies. The idea was growing that some kind of union of the colonies would help to finance an intercolonial railway that in time would make the colonies more prosperous.

Troubled relations with the United States made the idea of closer ties among the British North American colonies more appealing. The United States had threatened to end free trade

with the colonies. This change would seriously damage the economy of the colonies because the United States was their biggest export market for grain and lumber. Several times, too, the United States had threatened to invade Canada and take it by force. The United Province of Canada became convinced that its survival depended on some form of union with the Maritime colonies. Britain also favoured a union of the colonies so that they could all share some of the military cost of their protection.

1. It has been claimed that "Confederation (1867) was achieved mainly because of the British colonies' fear of the United States." Do you agree? What is your reason?
2. In point form, list the ways in which the pre-Confederation British colonies came to depend economically on one another after the American Revolutionary War.

CANADA: A RESULT OF COMPROMISE

The *Constitution Act, 1867,* joined Ontario, Québec, New Brunswick, and Nova Scotia in a confederation of provinces (Figure 4.13). The four provinces agreed on its terms only after much debate in their individual legislatures.

Of all the British colonies in North America, the people of Ontario supported union by the greatest majority. They thought that union would hasten western expansion, which would be good for the economy of Ontario. They also saw union as a way of halting the domination of Canada by the French of Québec.

Opinion in Québec was divided. Business people in Montréal thought union promised their city great prosperity. But some French Canadians thought that they would be a minority in a larger Canada and would lose influence.

The Atlantic colonies opposed union most strongly. Newfoundland and Prince Edward Island decided not to join the union. Many folk in New Brunswick and Nova Scotia opposed the idea. Some opposed it through fear of high taxes, others because they believed that a small province would have little influence in the new Canada. Some thought that the Atlantic colonies would be better off to strengthen ties with the United States, which was much more accessible to them than was Ontario or Québec.

Without compromise, Confederation would never have taken place. Ontario wanted a single, central government that would run the whole country without any provincial governments. The other three colonies would join the union only if there were to be a federal government and four provincial governments. Canada was to be a confederation of provinces, and provincial governments were to have certain powers that they believed they needed, in their view to retain their identity and protect the customs of their people. Finally, Ontario accepted the idea of a federal system with one central government and a separate government for each of the provinces.

---

1. The percentage of people supporting Confederation was higher in Ontario than in the other colonies. Why was this so?
2. Why were many people in the Atlantic colonies less than enthusiastic about Confederation?
3. Which province made the greatest compromises in negotiating the form of government for the new country?
4. Of Canada's original four provinces, which one do you think prospered most as a result of Confederation?

Canada became the third country in the world to adopt a federal system of government, after the United States of America and Switzerland. Today more than half the people in the world live in countries that have a federal government.

DIVISION OF POWERS

Canada's parliamentary system was modelled on that of the United Kingdom. The federal system of Canadian government, however, was influenced by the form of government in the United States.

A federal system has two levels of government; each is given specific powers and functions. The central government in a federal system is referred to as the federal government. The *Constitution Act, 1867* gave the federal government control over all areas where there was both a national and a provincial interest. These areas included navigation, fisheries, the money system, public debt, Indian territories, immigration, and defence. The provincial governments were given control over resources, education, health services, business, industry, transportation, and municipal institutions.

The "Fathers of Confederation" believed that the central government of the United States was too weak, and

that this weakness had led to the Civil War. For this reason they included a clause in the *Constitution Act, 1867* that gave all residual powers (i.e., all powers that had not been specifically assigned) to the federal government. This *Act* included a "Peace, Order and Good Government" clause, which said that in cases of national emergency, the federal government could take on whatever powers were necessary to solve the problem.

The federal government was also granted more power than the provinces to collect taxes. This provision became a source of federal-provincial conflict in the years that followed. During the Great Depression of the 1930s, hundreds of thousands of unemployed Canadians lacked enough income to feed their families. The costs of *welfare* were the responsibility of the provincial governments, but they did not have enough tax income to provide the relief needed. Some provinces were close to bankruptcy before a federal-provincial agreement

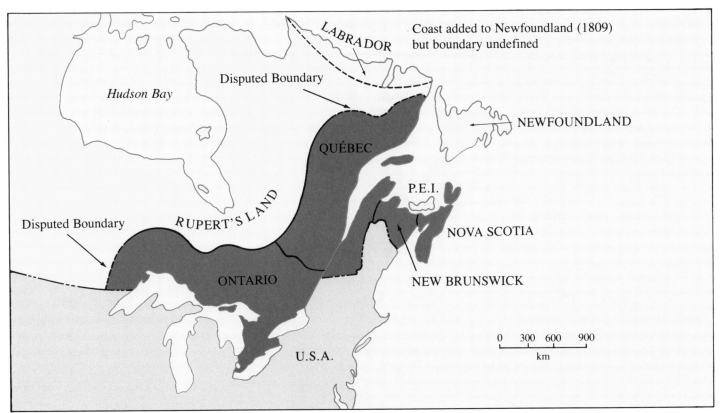

Figure 4.13 *The Dominion of Canada, 1867* *The Provinces of Ontario and Québec were much smaller in 1867 than they are today.*

The Canadian Charter of Rights and Freedoms

Part I of the *Constitution Act, 1982,* includes a Charter that guarantees the following rights and freedoms to every Canadian citizen and permanent resident:

1. Freedom of conscience and religion
2. Freedom of the press and other media of communication
3. Freedom of peaceful assembly
4. Right to enter, remain in, or leave Canada
5. Right to live and work in any place in Canada
6. Right not to be arbitrarily detained or imprisoned
7. Right to be presumed innocent until proven guilty
8. Right of a person who does not understand or speak the language of court proceedings to have an interpreter
9. Right to equal benefit of the law without discrimination based on race, national or ethnic origin, colour, religion, sex, age, or mental or physical disability
10. Right to use either English or French in the Canadian Parliament or in courts established by Parliament
11. Right to communicate with or receive services from the Government of Canada in either English or French
12. Right to receive primary and secondary school education in English or French in any province, provided that there is a sufficient number of children in the minority language groups.

The Charter provides that anyone whose rights or freedoms have been denied may apply to a court for justice.[1]

---

1. a) Many persons and groups of people have tested the Charter of Rights in the courts. Bring the story of one test case to class. (See past and current issues of major newspapers and a Canadian news magazine.)
   b) Collect all the articles in a loose-leaf binder or file folder for class reference.
   c) Through a class discussion, prepare an index for the collection by grouping types of cases that seem similar.
2. How might the Charter of Rights apply to the following situations?
   - A French-speaking person in Ontario receives a parking violation ticket written in English only.
   - A teacher is dismissed because she or he is an atheist.
   - A company refuses to hire a person because of his or her ethnic origin.
   - A provincial government hires only people who are already residents of the province.
   - A company refuses to employ the most capable applicant for a job because she is female.
   - An employee of a firm refuses to retire at the age of 65.

[1]This is a summary only, and the statements have been greatly simplified. For the complete text, see "Constitution Act, 1982", in *The Canadian Encyclopedia.*

was reached to transfer federal tax money to the provinces on the basis of need. Debate still goes on today about the fairness of the transfer of taxes from the federal government to the provinces.

The *Constitution Act, 1867* made it possible for the federal and provincial governments, acting together, to make changes in the constitution. Over the years, constitutional amendments have been made to the division of powers between the federal and provincial governments. Serious debates have always taken place between the federal government and the provincial governments before these amendments were made. Before 1982, any amendments to the Constitution had to be approved by the British Parliament, although approval was always given routinely, without any debate.

Major amendments to the Canadian Constitution were made in 1982, when the Constitution was **patriated**. At that time, the name of the *B.N.A. Act* was changed to the *Constitution Act, 1867.* The Canadian Constitution is now known as the *Constitution Acts, 1867 to 1982.* Included in the *Constitution Act, 1982,* was the *Canadian Charter of Rights and Freedoms,* and a new formula for making future amendments without approval of the British Parliament. The new formula required agreement of the federal government and seven provinces that together represent 50 percent of Canada's people.

The changes in the Constitution were agreed on only after prolonged and heated debate. Most of the provinces objected to the Charter of Rights because they thought it would further limit their powers. Representatives of the federal government and the provinces made enough compromises to achieve agreement among nine provincial premiers and the Prime Minister. They accepted the new Constitution. One province did not. The Premier of Québec, René Lévesque, refused to approve the new Constitution because it gave Québec no special status and no vet on future constitutional amendments.

In the years following the patriation of the Constitution, the federal and Québec governments continued to discuss the changes required to persuade Québec to accept the document. Québec made five conditions:

1. Québec must be recognized as a "distinct society".
2. Québec must have a veto on future constitutional changes.
3. Québec must share in the selection of Supreme Court judges.
4. Québec must have some power over immigration to the province.
5. Québec must be compensated by the federal government if it should decide to opt out of any future federal-provincial shared-cost program. (Medicare is an example of a shared-cost program.)

In 1987, all 10 provincial premiers met with the Prime Minister of Canada at a government retreat called Meech Lake, to discuss Québec's terms for accepting the Constitution. Together they worked out an agreement called the Meech Lake Accord. The nine other provinces agreed to Québec's conditions, provided that each of them be given most of the same powers that Québec would enjoy. Exceptions included the provisions that three of the nine Supreme Court justices would be chosen from Québec, and that only Québec would be recognized as a "distinct society" within Canada.

The federal government and the provinces were unable to reach a unanimous agreement to ratify the Meech Lake Accord by the 1990 deadline set in 1987. The Accord was meant to secure Québec's signature to the Constitution. At the same time, it would have weakened the federal government and given more power to the provinces. By its terms, any change affecting Canada's institutions would have required consent of the federal government and all the provinces. Such changes might include both innovations in the House of Commons, the Senate, and the Supreme Court of Canada, and also the creation of new provinces. The Accord would have allowed all provinces to opt out of federal-provincial shared-cost programs. It would have granted provinces the right to prepare a list of candidates from which all appointments to the Senate and the Supreme Court of Canada would have had to be made. Finally, all provinces would have gained the right to negotiate immigration agreements with the federal government to limit the number of immigrants they would accept.

---

1. a) Name one way in which Canada's system of government resembles the British and American models and one way in which it differs.
   b) What advantages might there be in a federal system of government such as ours? What disadvantages?
2. If you were negotiating the division of powers between federal and provincial governments, which powers would you give to each level of government? Explain your reasons.

CANADA EXPANDS

The Fathers of Confederation made it clear in the *Constitution Act, 1867* that other British North American colonies were welcome to join Canada in the future. In 1870, Canada bought Rupert's Land from the Hudson's Bay Company and took over the rest of the Northwest Territory from Britain. A small part of this vast territory became the Province of Manitoba, which included the agricultural colony along the Red River. British Columbia joined Canada in 1871, enticed by the promise of a railroad to connect the west coast with eastern Canada. Prince Edward Island followed in 1873. The Provinces of Alberta and

Liberal M.P.s in the House of Commons applaud Prime Minister Pierre Trudeau. The Prime Minister had just signed an accord with the provincial premiers that led to the 1982 talks on the Constitution.

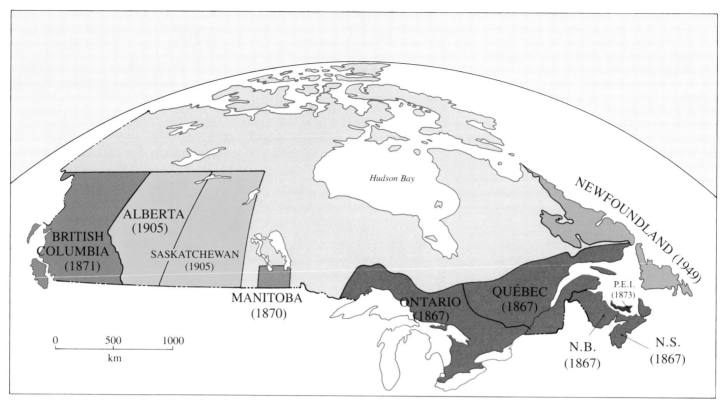

Figure 4.14 *An Expanding Canada* *Canada expanded as more provinces joined Confederation.*

Saskatchewan were created in 1905, as wheat farmers flooded onto the prairies. The goal of creating a country that stretched "from sea to sea" had been achieved (Figure 4.14).

Some boundary adjustments were still needed. In 1912, the boundaries of Manitoba, Ontario, and Québec were extended to the shores of Hudson Bay. In 1927, the boundary between Labrador and Québec was legally established, though Québec has never accepted the decision. Finally, in 1949, Newfoundland (which includes both the island of that name and Labrador) became Canada's tenth province.

The Yukon Territory and the Northwest Territories have only a limited amount of self-government. They are controlled mainly by the federal government. Division of the Northwest Territories to create new provinces in the North remains a possibility for the future.

---

1. a) The Atlantic Provinces voted to join Canada only by narrow margins, and some people from this region believe that they would now be better off if they had joined the United States instead. Suggest reasons for this view.
b) If opinion in your class is sharply divided, organize a debate: "Resolved that the Atlantic Provinces have gained more from entering Confederation than they would have gained from joining the United States".
2. Draw a map of Canada to show how the country would appear if the Atlantic Provinces had joined the United States.
3. Name two ways in which the people of the Atlantic Provinces might find themselves worse off if they belonged to the United States. Name two ways in which they might be better off.

CANADA BECOMES AN INDEPENDENT NATION

For about half a century after Confederation, Canada was not an independent nation. The Canadian government ran its own internal affairs, but Britain managed all Canada's foreign affairs. Britain declared war on Canada's behalf, represented Canada at international conferences, and negotiated with the United States on Canadian-U.S. boundary disputes. It was only at the end of the First World War that Canada started to sign treaties with other countries and to attend international conferences. The *Statute of Westminster, 1931*, declared that Canada was a fully independent nation within the British Commonwealth of Nations.

Formal links remained between Britain and Canada after the passing of the *Statute of Westminster*, and some still exist. The Queen of England is Queen of Canada. Until the Canadian *Citizenship Act* was passed in 1947, Canadians had the rights and privileges of British citizens: for example, Canadians could use the services of British Embassies in foreign countries. Until 1964, Britain's Union Jack was also Canada's official flag. The red ensign, with the Union

Figure 4.15 *Canada's Flags, Past and Present* (from left): *Union Jack, Red Ensign, Maple Leaf*

Jack in the upper left corner and the Canadian coat of arms on the fly, was often flown in Canada, but it was not Canada's official flag. In 1965, Canada officially adopted the maple leaf flag. The British national anthem, ''God Save the King (Queen)'' was Canada's national anthem until ''O Canada'' was officially designated our national anthem some years later (Figure 4.15). In 1982, our Constitution was patriated to Canada, and we obtained the right to make constitutional changes without reference to Britain's parliament.

This slow evolution to nationhood, with continuing links with the United Kingdom, has produced a Canada that is quite different from the United States. The United States broke away from the mother country and became an independent nation immediately after the Revolutionary War. As a result, it developed a form of government and other official institutions quite different from those of Britain.

1. a) Working in small groups, find three examples of significant ways that Canadian government, institutions, or official attitudes differ from those of the United States.
   b) Working as a class draw up a blackboard chart to summarize your findings and compare the two countries.
2. Give three examples of links that Canada still retains with Britain.

FOCUS

New Provinces in the North?

The Yukon and the Northwest Territories elect governments called assemblies, but these assemblies have less authority than the provincial legislatures. An assembly lacks the right to choose the head of government in a territory. Instead, the federal government appoints a commission to lead the government, and this commission reports to the federal Department of Indian and Northern Affairs. The federal government, not the assemblies, controls natural resources and directs environmental protection. The Territories do not share in most of the joint federal-provincial programs. They are more like colonies than provinces.

Many residents of these Territories believe that their regions should become provinces, with the same rights and responsibilities as other provinces. If the Territories are to become provinces, some serious problems will need to be overcome. Some of these problems are discussed below.

Cost
The Territories could not afford to become provinces under existing federal-provincial arrangements. The existing provinces would have to allow the federal government to provide special financial assistance to the new northern provinces.

Location of Boundary Line
The present boundaries between the Districts of Mackenzie, Franklin, and Keewatin (Figure 4.1) are unacceptable to the people of the Northwest Territories. The Inuit of the eastern Arctic want political control over their territory, which they call Nunavut. The Dene Nation, the Inuvialuit (western Inuit), and the Métis want political control over the

141

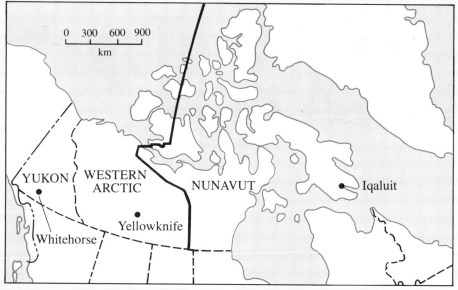

Figure 4.16 *The Proposed Dividing Line for the Northwest Territories* Iqaluit (formerly Frobisher Bay) is the proposed capital of Nunavut.

western Arctic, which as yet has no official name. (In the news media, the western Arctic is sometimes called Denendeh, but that name implies, wrongly, that only the Dene people live there.)

In 1982, the residents of the Northwest Territories voted in favour of dividing the area into two political units. The leaders of Nunavut and the western Arctic have agreed on the location of the boundary line (Figure 4.16). Iqaluit (formerly Frobisher Bay) is the proposed capital of Nunavut.

The residents of the Northwest Territories must vote in favour of this boundary line before it can become official. The target date for official division of the Territories is October 1991, after the settling of all outstanding land claims.

In 1990, Canada's federal government and the Inuit of Nunavut concluded a land claim agreement that gives the Inuit 350 000 km² and $612 million in compensation.

Protection of Minority Groups

The rights of minority groups in all the Territories must be protected. Most of the people living in Nunavut are Inuit, but there is a minority of Métis and non-Natives. In the western Arctic, non-Natives are in the majority, and the Métis and Inuvialuit are concerned that the non-Natives might dominate their government.

Federal Land Claims Priority

The federal government has stated that Native land claims must be settled before any decision is made to divide the Northwest Territories. Settling land claims may take a long time.

Constitutional Amendment

To create new provinces, after the land claims and boundary issues are settled, the *Constitution Act, 1982* must be amended. By the terms of the Meech Lake Accord, an amendment of the *Constitution Act* would require agreement of all 10 provinces.

Serious problems block the forming of provinces in the Northwest

Territories. It seems likely that it will take many years to solve all these problems.

The Yukon is closer to becoming a province. It already has a greater degree of self-government and an agreement about its boundary. The Yukon might become a province by about the end of the 20th century.

You will find the following sources helpful for answering the questions asked below: *The Canadian Encyclopedia*, a Canadian atlas, the most recent *Canada Year Book* or *Canada Handbook*.

1. On an outline map of the Yukon and the Northwest Territories, mark the following:
   a) the capital cities of the Yukon and Northwest Territories
   b) the Districts of Mackenzie, Franklin, and Keewatin, and the boundaries that separate them
   c) the tree line
   d) Indian and Inuit population (Figure 3.14)
   e) the 12 largest settlements
2. Compare the areas of the Yukon and the Northwest Territories with the area of Québec, Canada's largest province. Draw a diagrammatic map, using shapes and colours to illustrate your findings.
3. Compare the total populations of the Yukon and the Northwest Territories with the population of Prince Edward Island, Canada's smallest province. Make a bar graph to illustrate your findings.
4. a) The mix of ethnic origins of the people of the Northwest Territories is as follows: Dene, 18 percent; Inuit, 34 percent; Métis and non-Natives, 48 percent. Use a bar graph to record this information.
   b) In which part of the Northwest Territories does the largest proportion of each group live?

Newfoundland, Canada's Tenth Province

In the late 1500s, Britain claimed the island of Newfoundland. In the 1600s, France laid claim to the same island. There followed many years of conflict between Britain and France over the control of Newfoundland. The struggle over the island ended with the end of the Seven Years' War, in 1763. In that year, Newfoundland came under British control, but the French were given fishing rights along the north shore; they kept these rights until 1904. The islands of St. Pierre and Miquelon remained under French control.

By the mid-1800s, Newfoundland's government was both representative and responsible. Newfoundland sent delegates to all the Confederation conferences but chose not to unite with Canada in 1867. Newfoundland had done most of its business with Europe, the West Indies, and Brazil rather than with British North America. Besides, Newfoundland Catholics feared that a union with "Protestant Ontario" might limit their freedom to fund their own schools. Irish Catholics were fearful that Confederation might cause problems similar to those created by the union between England and Ireland. For these reasons, talk of trade with the west and of a nation that spanned the continent did not attract Newfoundlanders.

The Great Depression of the 1930s dealt Newfoundland a severe economic blow. The colony lost many of its traditional markets for its fish, and for its forest and mineral products. Prices for raw materials plummeted. By 1932/33, about one-quarter of the population was on government relief. The government was facing bankruptcy. At this point Newfoundland gave up its representative government and allowed itself to be controlled again by Britain. The British government appointed a governor and six commissioners to manage Newfoundland.

During the Second World War (1939–1945), the high demand for raw materials and defence spending by Canada and the United States greatly improved Newfoundland's economy. After the war Britain, faced with serious post-war economic problems, decided that it was time for Newfoundland to govern itself again. Newfoundlanders hotly debated whether to become a self-governing colony again or to join Canada. In 1949, under the leadership of Joseph Smallwood, Newfoundland voted by a narrow margin to become Canada's tenth province.

You will find the following sources helpful for answering the questions below: *The Canadian Encyclopedia*, a Canadian atlas, the *Canada Year Book* or the *Canada Handbook*.

1. Compare Newfoundland's area of land and fresh water with that of Canada's largest and smallest provinces.
2. Compare the size of Newfoundland's population with the size of the population in:
   a) the province with the most people
   b) the province with the fewest people
3. Compare the gross domestic product of Newfoundland with that of Prince Edward Island and Ontario.
4. Draw up a three-column chart that illustrates your findings. Head the columns:
   Newfoundland | P.E.I. | Ontario

The long-standing dispute between Canada and France over fishing and mineral rights in the sea off Newfoundland arose from France's ownership of St. Pierre and Miquelon. These islands are the last remaining possessions of France in North America.

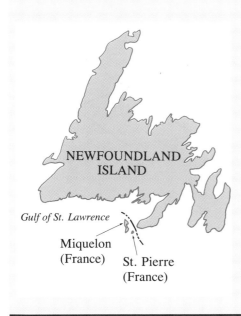

NEWFOUNDLAND ISLAND

Gulf of St. Lawrence

Miquelon (France)   St. Pierre (France)

DIVISIVE FACTORS

Over the years that have passed since Confederation, Canadians have not found it easy to weld their country into a unified nation. They have had to deal with many divisive factors. These factors are discussed below.

SETTLEMENT PATTERNS

Because of its physical geography, Canada was settled in patches or islands of usable land. Each patch (or region) was settled at a different time, by a different group of people. Each region developed a different kind of economy. The people in these regions often had more social, cultural, and trade connections with a neighbouring area in the United States than they had with any other region in Canada. The Canadian regions were separated by long distances and usually by geographical barriers such as mountains, rocky terrain, and bodies of water.

ECONOMIC DEVELOPMENT PATTERNS

Decline in the Maritimes' Economies

Manufacturers in the Maritimes thought that the Intercolonial Railway (1876) and the *National Policy* (1878) would open up the markets of Ontario and Québec to their products. This did not happen. Instead, the Maritime manufacturing industry lost out to competition from larger-scale and more efficient new industries in Ontario and Québec. Economically, the Maritime Provinces never did catch up with Québec and Ontario, which developed into what became known as the industrial heartland of Canada. This difference in prosperity between the Maritimes and central Canada has been an important cause of division in Canada ever since Confederation. As we have noted, some Maritimers believe that they would have been better off not to have joined the Canadian union. (Figure 4.17 compares the average family income in the Atlantic region with that of other regions over a 35-year period.)

Economic Problems of the Prairie Provinces

The combination of a major economic depression and severe drought in the 1930s led to serious economic problems right across the country. Many farmers in the Prairie Provinces abandoned their land, and large numbers of people could not find jobs. Thousands lived on welfare, and many depended on the *soup kitchens* for food. The Prairie Provinces, like Atlantic Canada, are often at an economic disadvantage. Compared with residents of Ontario and Québec, people living on the prairies must pay higher prices for goods manufactured in central Canada. If they buy imported goods instead of Canadian products, they must often pay a price inflated by a protective tariff.

Conflicts about Control of Resources

The Canadian Constitution gives the provinces control over resources, with some important exceptions. The federal government may regulate

The "Dirty Thirties" brought a combination of severe drought, damaging dust storms, and the effects of a worldwide depression. It hit many prairie farm families so badly that they had to abandon their land.

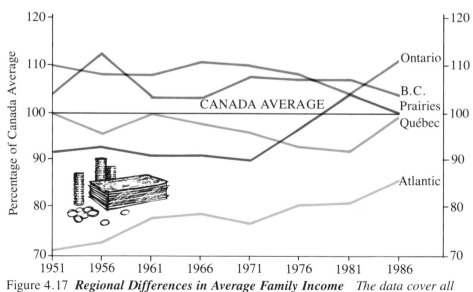

Figure 4.17 ***Regional Differences in Average Family Income*** *The data cover all family income, including salaries, wages, investment income, Family Allowances, and pensions.*

resource industries by paying them subsidies, taxing them, or establishing prices for their products. It claims that this control is in the national interest. The province whose resource industry is being regulated often believes that the federal action is *not* in its interest. Bitter disputes often result. Such a dispute occurred in 1980 between Alberta and the federal government, when Ottawa placed several taxes on the petroleum industry and kept the price of oil in Canada well below world levels.

Inadequate Provincial Income

Ever since Confederation, the provinces have claimed that they do not receive enough income to provide their residents with adequate services. Although the provinces receive grants from the federal government, they always contend that they need more income. The federal government insists that it cannot afford to provide more. In recent years the tax-sharing issue has become more acute. While the provinces' expenses for education, health, and social services have been increasing rapidly, the federal government has been lowering payments to provinces because of the need to reduce the national debt.

Regionalism and Separatism

Canada's pattern of settlement and resource development, as well as its political structure, has reinforced the sense of separateness that Canadians in each region feel. It has strengthened the various groups' belief that they possess an identity and set of concerns different from those of Canadians in other regions. The development of a distinct identity in a region, based on shared territory, economy, and culture, is called *regionalism*. If regionalism becomes strong enough, it is expressed in a movement that favours independence from the larger political unit. A region's urge for political independence is called *separatism*.

Separatist Movements

As a result of regional and provincial grievances, political groups have sometimes advocated that a particular province (or group of provinces) separate from Canada to become an independent nation.

The first serious separatist movement in Canada arose in Nova Scotia shortly after Confederation. The leaders of the movement believed that Nova Scotia's economy had suffered because of its union with Canada. In a provincial election, the anti-Confederates won 36 out of 38 seats, but Britain would not allow Nova Scotia to separate from Canada. Since that time, serious doubts have often been expressed about the wisdom of Nova Scotia's joining Confederation, but Nova Scotia has never again tried to withdraw from Canada.

The strongest separatist movement has emerged in Québec. The French-speaking *Québécois* have not forgotten that they were once a conquered people. For a long time they considered themselves at a disadvantage in their own province. Because of language barriers, they were not able to participate as equals with the English in Québec's economic development. For many years, even though French was an official language, *francophone* Canadians could not obtain high executive positions in Québec's businesses and industries, which were dominated by *anglophone* Canadians. French was not really the language of commerce in Québec.

By the 1960s, other developments seemed to threaten French Québec. French families there were beginning to have fewer children, and most immigrants to Québec were learning English instead of French. It looked as though, if those trends were to continue, the French language and culture would finally disappear. A number of political groups who shared a concern for the loss of French language and culture formed a political party called the Parti Québécois. The major policy of the Parti Québécois was to have Québec become a separate country, independent of Canada in most ways.

The separatists' idea came closer to

This soup kitchen in Montréal was typical of the food relief provided for unemployed men across the country. There was never really enough "to go around", and other men begged from door to door or offered to do a day's chores in return for a meal.

reality when the Parti Québécois won a provincial election in 1976. Although the new government wanted political independence (sovereignty) for Québec, it wanted to retain economic association with the rest of Canada; this arrangement would include free trade with Canada and a common currency system. The Parti Québécois called this form of semi-independence *sovereignty association*. In 1980, it took its proposal to the people of Québec. The proposal, voted on by *referendum*, was defeated, and the Parti Québécois then abandoned sovereignty association as a party policy.

The policy of the Liberal government, which was elected in 1986, was to keep Québec as a distinct society within Canada. To help protect the French language and culture, the government passed a law (Bill 101) which forbids the use of English on street signs and store fronts. Québec language law also requires that the children of immigrants, including people who move to Québec from other parts of Canada, send their children to French-language schools. The new law was hotly debated by two factions: separatists who believed that without such a measure, French would become a forgotten language in Québec; and supporters of a united Canada who believed that French and English could and should co-exist peacefully in the province. The anglophone population of Québec has bitterly opposed the Bill's language restrictions.

A separatist movement arose in western Canada in the early 1980s. The chief reason was dissatisfaction with the federal government's regulation of the petroleum industry. A Western Concept party was formed, but only one member of the new party was elected to a provincial legislature (in Alberta). Differences of opinion within the Western Concept party and better relations between the federal government and the western provinces have sharply reduced the popularity of western separatism.

La loi 101/Bill 101? Oui et Non! *Québec's Bill 101 outlawed the bilingual signs that had been a notable feature of Montréal.*

1. Refer to Figure 4.17, and then explain:
   a) why families in the Atlantic region have a lower average income than families in other regions of Canada;
   b) why the average family income in Ontario and Québec increased between 1981 and 1986.
2. Make up one other question about the information presented in Figure 4.17. Hold a ''quiz'' session to give the class a chance to ask and answer the questions.
3. Regionalism has often been considered a threat to Canadian unity. Do you agree or disagree with this view? Give an example to support your answer.
4. Name two problems that the separation of Québec from Canada would create for the rest of the country. Name two problems it might create for Québec.
5. To show your community's growth since its beginning, add more houses to the model that you began in Chapter Two. The new buildings should represent the population to about 1970. Add government buildings, schools, and other public buildings.

UNIFYING FACTORS

Although many factors have tended to pull Canada apart, others have united Canadians. Some unifying factors have been historical events, and others have been policies and programs developed by the federal government. Many of these policies and programs were designed to strengthen the economies of the poorer provinces. We shall examine some of these policies and programs.

FEAR OF THE UNITED STATES

Fear that individual colonies would be taken over by the United States was one of the reasons for Canadian Confederation and for Canada's later expansion from sea to sea. In the early years, the U.S. threat was a direct military one. In recent years, the threat has been American economic and cultural domination. Americans have invested much capital in Canadian resource industries. Branch plants of U.S. companies make up a large proportion of Canada's manufacturing industry. Besides, about three-quarters of Canada's foreign trade takes place with the United States. The fear of U.S. domination of the Canadian economy has heightened strong nationalist feelings among Canadians.

TRANSPORTATION AND COMMUNICATIONS

From the very beginning of European settlement, transportation was a key factor in linking the various parts of Canada. The promise of railroads helped persuade many of the provinces to join Confederation. Railways were considered so important to Canada that when early railroad companies ran into financial trouble, the federal government took them over and united them to form the Canadian National Railways. The federal government also gave financial aid to the second trans-Canada line, the Canadian Pacific Railway. Until nearly the end of the 1980s, the Canadian government followed a policy of subsidizing rail transportation because it considered this policy to be in the national interest.

Many other transportation facilities have helped overcome Canada's vast distances. These facilities include the St. Lawrence Seaway, the Trans-Canada Highway, two trans-Canada airlines, and oil and gas pipelines from western to eastern Canada. Major communication systems also link different parts of the country. Spanning Canada are the Canadian Broadcasting Corporation (radio and television), telephone and telegraph communications, and computer communication systems. Mail service reaches every community in Canada, and major national magazines and newspapers add to the country-wide flow of information. To help Canadian magazines compete against foreign journals, Canada Post delivers them at a special low rate.

The Trans-Canada Highway is the longest paved road in the world. It stretches 7700 km between St. John's, Nfld., and Victoria, B.C.

All these transportation and communication links help to unify Canada. The federal government subsidizes many of these services. The money collected from taxpayers to cover this cost is one of the prices Canadians must pay for national unity.

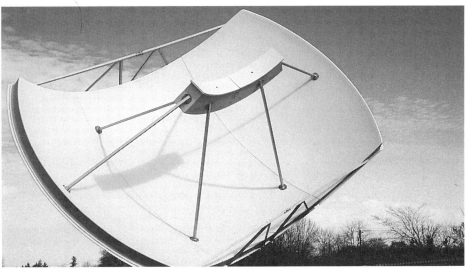

A satellite dish

TARIFFS AND SUBSIDIES

Shortly after Confederation, Canada established a high-tariff policy to protect the country's infant manufacturing industry. Over a hundred years later, Canada's manufacturing industry is still protected by a tariff. This protection has benefited the country's industrial **heartland**, but not the **hinterland**, where the economy depends more on the export of natural resources. To help the "have-not" sections of the country, the federal government has paid large subsidies to the major resource industries such as agriculture, forestry, fisheries, and mining.

SOCIAL WELFARE PROGRAMS

Canada has developed a whole series of national social welfare programs to help people in need. These programs include Family Allowances, the Canada Pension Plan, Old Age Security Pension, the Unemployment Insurance program, the Canadian Job Strategy Programs, and the National Health Insurance program. Although these programs apply all across Canada, they are most valuable in provinces where the economy is not strong: where average incomes are lower, and more people are unemployed and living in poverty.

FEDERAL/PROVINCIAL TAX SHARING

A series of federal-provincial conferences has worked out major tax-sharing agreements to help the provinces meet their obligations under Canada's Constitution. In addition, "equalization" grants to some of the less wealthy provinces help to bring their level of services (including education and health care) up to the Canadian national average. In the Atlantic Provinces, in some years, these equalization grants have made up almost half the provincial income. Without these tax-sharing agreements and equalization grants, Canada would probably have split into several units. A country where there are great differences of prosperity from one region to another is not likely to survive.

SPECIAL REGIONAL DEVELOPMENT PROGRAMS

In spite of the policies and programs described above, some parts of Canada have continued to be better off than others (Figure 4.17). Over the years, the federal and provincial governments have co-operated in putting together many special development programs to reduce these **regional economic disparities**. Some government enterprises, such as the *Agricultural Rural Development Act* (ARDA) passed in 1961, were intended to help rural people make better use of their resources. ARDA helped farmers to increase the size of their land holdings, and to practise soil-conservation measures. It also helped the forest and fishing industries to become more efficient.

Another set of government programs provided grants and tax incentives to encourage industries to locate in areas where incomes were low and the rate of unemployment was high. A federal government department called the Department of Regional Economic Expansion (DREE) was created in 1969 to co-ordinate all regional development programs. In 1983, the functions of the Department of Industry and Trade were added to DREE, and it became known as the Department of Regional and Industrial Expansion (DRIE).

DREE and DRIE spent hundreds of millions of dollars on regional development programs. Some Canadians think that the money was well spent, and that without these programs the income gap between the rich and the poor provinces would be even wider. Others think that the money spent has not helped much to reduce regional disparities; they believe that most of this money was used to hire government employees in Ottawa and to provide profits for industry. In 1988, the federal government disbanded DRIE. The regional development programs were divided among other government departments, and separate programs were set up in co-operation with each of the provinces. In the Atlantic region, one of Canada's neediest areas, a special agency known as the Atlantic Canada Opportunities Agency (ACOA) was created to administer development programs. The federal government promised that ACOA would distribute more than $1000 million in a five-year period.

The problem of regional disparities has not been easy to solve because these differences have deep roots in Canada's history and geography. Most people who have studied the problem agree that the gap between the rich and poor provinces would have been even greater if there had been no government regional development programs.

Television weather maps are provided by Telidon, a communications system that was developed in Canada and sold around the world.

1. Review the unifying factors noted in the preceding section, and add another factor if you can. Rank the factors in descending order of importance. Be prepared to support your top choices.
2. Debate one of the following statements:
   a) In Canada, unifying factors are more powerful than divisive factors.
   b) Canada never became a completely independent nation: it merely replaced British influence with American influence.
3. The news media often say that Canada is experiencing an "identity crisis". In a class discussion, decide what this term means. Do you agree that it is difficult for Canada to establish an identity separate from that of the United States? Give reasons to support your answer.

LOCAL GOVERNMENT

All of Canada's provinces are divided into municipalities administered by some form of local government. Since municipalities are the responsibility of the provincial governments, local government organization varies slightly from province to province. All provinces have established regulations for organizing local governments for cities and towns. Some provinces have also divided their territory into counties and regional municipalities; the counties are further subdivided into townships.

Every level of municipality has its own governing council. At the lower (or local) level of city, town, or township, the council is elected by the direct votes of citizens. At the upper level of the county or the regional municipality, the council is usually selected from the members of the councils at the lower level.

All municipalities have the power to collect property taxes. They also receive grants from the provincial government, which in turn receives grants from the federal government.

F O C U S

Local Government in Ontario

A southern Ontario county usually contains at least one city, a number of towns and villages, and several rural townships (Figure 4.18). A city or town has an elected mayor and council. Each township has an elected reeve and council who govern the rural area, including the villages. A town or township sends its mayor or *reeve* and one other councillor to a county council. The county council is responsible for services affecting all municipalities in the county except the city. The city does not send a representative to the county council. Although the city is located in the county, it is politically separate from the county.

In areas where cities have spilled across township and even county boundaries, regional municipalities have been created (Figure 4.18). In a regional municipality each town is joined with its surrounding township to form a new municipality, or local level of government. All the municipalities, including the city, send representatives to the regional municipal council. Each local municipality administers local services. The regional municipality is responsible for services that affect the whole region, such as water supply, sewage disposal, regional roads, and police. One of the most important functions of a regional municipal government is to plan growth, land uses, and services for the whole region.

A metropolitan municipality, such as Metropolitan Toronto, is a type of regional municipality in which all member municipalities are cities. By contrast, Winnipeg, Manitoba, and its surrounding suburbs have been amalgamated into one large city, Metropolitan Winnipeg.

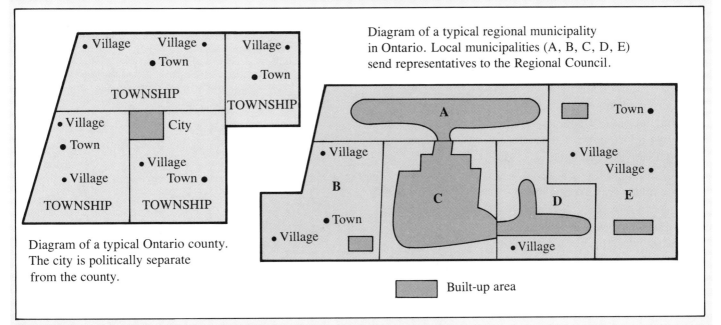

Diagram of a typical Ontario county. The city is politically separate from the county.

Diagram of a typical regional municipality in Ontario. Local municipalities (A, B, C, D, E) send representatives to the Regional Council.

Built-up area

Figure 4.18 *Types of Local Government Organization in Ontario*

Each level of municipality is responsible for providing specific services.

Besides the units of government already discussed, there are many special-purpose government organizations. For example, *school boards* run the school systems in most provinces. They are responsible for building schools, hiring teachers, establishing courses of study, and asking the local municipality to raise the amount of money required to balance their budget. School-board members, often called trustees, are elected by adult residents of the community.

Other special-purpose agencies include *planning boards*, public utility commissions, and *conservation authorities*. Each of these agencies has particular responsibilities specified by Acts passed by the provincial legislature.

This whole arrangement sounds very complex. It is! Perhaps the following activity will help make it clearer.

1. Working in groups and using as an example the chart set up below, complete the information for the public services and facilities listed at the end of this question. You will likely think of other items to add to this list.

Your parents may be able to give you some information to help you carry out this activity. You might find out other facts by phoning particular government agencies or departments listed in the telephone directory. (To avoid over-using busy telephone lines, arrange to have one class member *only* phone a given agency or department. Before you call, write down your questions in order of importance, and number them. Use the corresponding numbers when you jot down notes about the answers so that later you can report accurately to your class.)

List of Services or Facilities

- community colleges
- universities
- local streets
- major highways
- secondary highways
- tertiary (or side) roads
- neighbourhood park
- conservation area
- camping park
- wilderness area
- sidewalks
- street lights
- police force
- fire protection
- libraries
- sports facilities
- pet licensing
- garbage disposal
- sewage treatment
- water supply
- toxic waste disposal
- health and medical insurance
- food protection laws
- environmental protection
- manpower training and placement
- unemployment insurance
- family allowance
- old age security pensions
- coast guard service
- defence
- ports
- airports
- weather forecasting service
- auto licensing
- passports
- immigration services
- courts for criminal offences
- courts for civil offences
- hospitals
- local jails
- penitentiaries

Some of Canada's Public Services/Facilities

Service or Facility	Public Agency or Level of Government Providing Service	How Elected or Appointed	Source of Finances
Public education	School Board	Elected by residents	Property taxes collected by municipality; provincial government grants

Municipal fire departments provide a vital service.

2. All the services provided by governments and public agencies must be funded by taxes.
a) Working as a class, list 10 different taxes that Canadian citizens pay and the level of government to which they are paid. Which of these taxes are hidden?
b) How much is the municipal tax on a house that would sell for about $250 000 in your municipality?
c) How much provincial sales tax must be paid on a $100 purchase in your province?
3. a) Invite to your class an administrator or worker in any local government or service group to hold a ''press conference''. Ask your guest to explain the responsibilities of the job. Find out ahead of time what decisions your guest has to make that affect you and your classmates. During the press conference, ask how these decisions are made.
b) Write a class letter to thank your guest for attending the ''press conference''. Summarize in your letter what you learned from the conference, and what action, if any, you are planning to take as a result.

GOVERNMENT IN CONFLICT
There are often conflicts between levels of local government, and between local governments and senior governments (provincial or federal). The following examples show types of conflicts in a regional municipality such as the one shown in Figure 4.18.
1. City C is pressuring the regional municipality to develop a sanitary landfill site in municipality E.
2. The provincial government proposes to widen a highway through a village in municipality B. The widening will require the removal of mature trees on both sides of the village street.

3. The federal government has announced plans to expand an airport just north of municipality A.

---

1. Who would be likely to oppose each of the above proposals?
2. You are a member of a group which supports/opposes *one* of the above proposals. Meet with other members of your group to plan the arguments you will present at a public meeting.
3. Make a brief (three to five minute) presentation of your arguments at the meeting (of your class). Use charts, diagrams, or pictures if these will support your arguments.

L O C A L   S T U D Y

1. Using a diagram, describe the local government organization in your area. Compare this organization with the models shown in Figure 4.18.
2. List the services in your county or region that each level of local government provides.
3. Follow your local news media for stories of conflict between different levels of government in your area. ''Brainstorm'' in class any methods that might be used to resolve such conflicts.

WHAT LIES AHEAD?

Canada's future political geography depends on responses to two questions discussed in this chapter. First, will new provinces be carved out of Canada's North? Secondly, will the Meech Lake Accord or some similar agreement tip the balance of power away from the federal government toward the provincial governments?

If the provincial governments gain more power, Canada will become a loose confederation of provinces. This type of organization has advantages because the provincial governments are closer to the people and know their needs better than is possible for one central government. But the price that must be paid to decentralize government power is to make Canada a less unified nation. Besides, without a strong central (federal) government, the northern Territories are unlikely ever to become provinces.

In which direction do you think Canada should go?

REVIEW QUESTIONS

1. Return to the questions on political geography at the beginning of this chapter. What do you think now of the statement that Canada is a nation despite its geography? Discuss in class any changes of opinion.
2. Comment on the statement: ''The political organization of what is now Canada began long before Europeans arrived in North America.''
3. Working in small groups, describe three of the historical roots of the current problems on some Indian reserves and Native peoples' land claims.
4. Name two geographical factors that moved Canadians toward Confederation in 1867.
5. Explain one way in which Canada is a result of compromise.
6. Comment on the compromises that led to the patriation of Canada's Constitution in 1982.

Chapter Five

Urban Canada

Which is the Real Canada?

Canada is a huge, open country that contains many varieties of landscape. There are Arctic barrens and permafrost; vast coniferous forests; western mountains; broad expanses of fertile prairie farmland; the mineral-rich Canadian Shield, rocky and lake studded; rolling hills clad with deciduous forests in the east; the much-farmed lowlands of the Great Lakes and St. Lawrence River region; and the farms, forests and fisheries of the Atlantic provinces. Most of the country is sparsely populated; the narrow band of settlement close to the U.S. border contains few large cities. Is this the "real" Canada?

Canada is a settled land. Eight out of every 10 Canadians live in or near a corridor of towns and cities along our southern border, and these towns and cities are linked by transportation and communication systems. Most Canadians see a landscape of high-rise office buildings and apartment blocks; suburban factories and housing subdivisions; shopping malls, schools, theatres, and parks; expressways, streets, and sidewalks. Everywhere urban Canadians see automobile traffic, parking lots, and crowds of people on the move. Is this the "real" Canada?

A view of Halifax skyline from the harbour

CANADA TODAY

The real Canada, of course, is a mix of the two contrasting descriptions you have just read. Canada does have huge expanses of wilderness environment and *rural* landscapes. Yet most Canadians now live, work, and play in settlements and not in the open countryside. The landscape most Canadians see every day and the environment that affects their daily lives are *urban*.

People think of Canada as urban because so many Canadians live in large cities. Many of these cities are located close together near the Great Lakes and the St. Lawrence River. The cities in this region, as well as other cities in Canada, are important centres of industry that supply goods and services to all Canadians. Cities served by a dense transportation and communication network become centres that exchange people, goods, services, and ideas with other urban settlements and with the rural areas of Canada. Within each city, as the population grows, different uses of land develop to provide citizens with homes, shops, jobs, and recreation.

1. a) Make a classroom collection of advertisements promoting Canada that appear in popular Canadian and American magazines. What images of Canada are suggested by these advertisements?
b) What percentage of these images emphasizes urban Canada? rural Canada?
c) How do these images compare with the way you see Canada?
2. Using the illustrations you have collected or other sources, make a class collage of Canada's image as you and your classmates see it. You might use an outline map of Canada drawn on (or cut out of) heavy paper as a base for your collage.

AN URBAN NATION

Because over fifty percent of our population lives in cities, towns, or villages, Canada is classified as an urban country. Figure 5.1 shows the areas of the major cities in each province, drawn in proportion to their populations. In all provinces except New Brunswick and Prince Edward Island, more people live in urban areas than in rural areas. (The populations of the Yukon and the Northwest Territories are so small compared with those of the provinces that they are not included in Figure 5.1.)

The name and population of each *Census Metropolitan Area* (CMA) appear in Table 5.1. A Census Metropolitan Area generally includes any city with a population of 100 000 or more, plus the surrounding area within easy commuting distance of work in the city.

A few cities with populations over 100 000 are themselves part of larger nearby CMAs. For example, both Mississauga and Brampton, on the western border of Metropolitan Toronto, are included in the Toronto CMA (Figure 5.2). Indeed, the population for the Toronto CMA includes a large number of suburban communities outside Metropolitan Toronto. In 1986, the population of the City of Toronto was 612 289, while that of Metropolitan Toronto was 2 192 721.

Canada has not always been a country of "urbanites". In earlier days, most Canadians lived in rural areas (Table 5.2) and made their living by

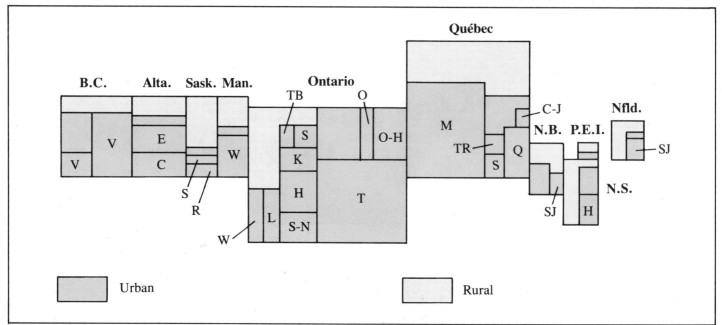

Figure 5.1 *Urban Canada: Area in Proportion to Population* *The initials that appear in the figure stand for the CMAs listed in Table 5.1. Those areas of the figure in which no initials appear represent all other urban areas in the province.*

Source: Adapted from J. & R. Simmons, *Urban Canada*, 1974

Table 5.1 *Canada's Largest Cities (Census Metropolitan Areas)*

City	Population
Toronto	3 427 200
Montréal	2 921 400
Vancouver	1 380 700
Ottawa-Hull	819 300
Edmonton	785 500
Calgary	671 300
Winnipeg	625 300
Québec	603 300
Hamilton	557 000
St. Catharines-Niagara	343 300
London	342 300
Kitchener	311 200
Halifax	296 000
Victoria	255 600
Windsor	254 000
Oshawa	203 500
Saskatoon	200 700
Regina	186 500
St. John's	161 900
Chicoutimi-Jonquière	158 500
Sudbury	148 900
Sherbrooke	130 000
Trois-Rivières	128 900
Thunder Bay	122 200
Saint John	121 300

Source: Compiled from Canadian census data, 1986
Note: The populations given in this table are for Census Metropolitan Areas (CMAs), which generally include satellite communities.

Table 5.2 *Canadians as Urban Dwellers*

Year	Percentage
1871	18.3
1881	23.3
1891	29.8
1901	34.9
1911	41.8
1921	47.4
1931	52.5
1941	55.7
1951	62.4
1961	69.7
1971	76.1
1981	75.8
1986	76.5

Source: The Canadian Encyclopedia, 1988. Compiled from Canadian census data.
Note: Percentages represent the number of Canadians living in villages, towns, and cities.

developing natural resources. It was not until 1931 that more Canadians lived in towns and cities than in rural areas. In 1986, more than three-quarters of Canadians were classified in Canadian census data as urban dwellers.

Even more Canadians are city dwellers than Table 5.2 shows. Many people classified as rural in the census are people who have moved from the cities to a house in the country but commute daily to the city to work.

The view of Canada that most Canadians know best is one of streets and urban buildings. The city pictured here is Winnipeg.

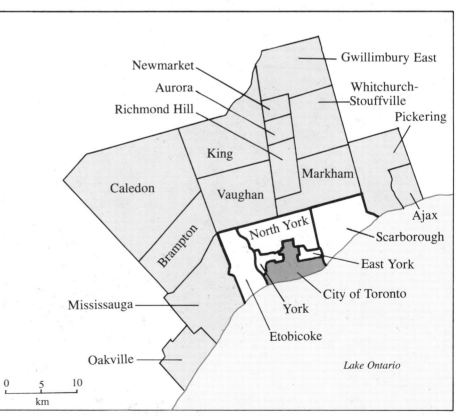

Figure 5.2 *Toronto Census Metropolitan Area* *The Toronto CMA includes all the municipalities shown on this map. Parts of Metropolitan Toronto are bounded by the heavy black line. The City of Toronto is shaded.*

Although these people live in a rural area, they are more urban than rural. They are usually more involved in city life than in the life of the rural community.

Between 1971 and 1986, Canadian census data recorded that about 80 percent of the increases in rural population resulted from city dwellers moving into nearby rural areas. The actual rural farm population decreased over the same period. Only when so many people move into the countryside that 50 percent of an area's population lives in settlements is a rural area reclassified as urban.

In Canada and other countries, urban population has grown rapidly in the 20th century. Three Canadian cities—Toronto, Montréal, and Vancouver—have populations of more than one million people. In the 60 years from 1920 to 1980, the world's urban population increased from 100 million to 1000 million, a ten-fold increase. There are about one hundred cities in the world with populations of one million or more, and 37 of them have populations greater than that of Canada's largest city, Toronto. In the last few decades, the largest cities of the world have grown most. Some of these cities have populations of more than 10 million. In 1986, one city dweller in three lived in a city of one million people or more.

Signs of urban growth that is changing the natural environment appear everywhere in southern Canada. State all the evidence you can see in this photograph of changes to the landscape.

Much of Canada is too rugged, water-covered, or desolate for settlement. Landscapes like this one—which has its own stark beauty—are common in the mountains of British Columbia.

In North America, 1000 million (1 000 000 000) is equal to a billion. In most of the rest of the world, a billion is reckoned at a million million (1 000 000 000 000). Because of the different ways a billion is defined, the word is gradually falling into disuse.

Cities in developed countries receive people who have migrated from countries all over the world. This explains why most large cities are *cosmopolitan*.

Why are the world's largest cities growing so rapidly? One reason is total population growth. The world's population is growing at a rate of about 75 million people a year. This annual growth equals three times Canada's population.

Fewer and fewer people can make a living in rural areas. Machines have replaced workers on farms and in the other *primary industries*. The price of farm products is often so low that many farmers cannot make farming pay. Some give up farming and move into the city.

Many small businesses are started by immigrant entrepreneurs who contribute a great deal to Canada's economy and culture.

People are "pushed" out of the rural areas and "pulled" into the cities. They cannot make a living in rural areas, and they are attracted by the opportunities offered by cities: jobs, shelter, and food.

Unfortunately, when too many people move into the cities too quickly, there are not enough jobs, shelter, and food to go around. Instead of becoming prosperous, many newcomers to the cities live in poverty. Many cities in *developing countries* have large areas of illegal *squatter slums*. The people do not own the land they live on, but they build crude shelters and survive on *relief food* supplies and by means of scavenging and begging. Cities in *developed countries* also have their slums, where people live in substandard housing and are often undernourished.

Not all people who move to the cities fall on hard times. Many find good jobs and can afford good housing. Many become quite successful. In cities all over the world, there are great contrasts between those people who live in wealth and those who live in poverty. Canadian cities are no exception.

The population density of some cities in other countries is many times that of any Canadian city. Examples include Manila, capital of the Philippines, with 42 000 people per km², and Paris, France, with 21 000 people per km². Montréal has only 6000 people per km².

The signs and flags in Toronto's Danforth district show that many Greeks live in this area—and celebrate Greece's Independence Day.

1. a) Using data from an atlas or *The Canadian Encyclopedia*, draw up a chart to show the urban population of the Yukon and Northwest Territories, and the population of their largest (capital) cities. Add to the chart the urban population figures for the province where you live and its largest city.

Use your chart to make a brief statement comparing the urban population in your province and the Territories.

b) According to Figure 5.1, which province has the most CMAs? the fewest? none at all?

c) Which province appears to be most urban? most rural?

2. a) Calculate the percentage of Canada's total population that lives in our 25 CMAs.

b) What percentage of CMA population lives in the three largest CMAs?

3. a) You and a small group of your classmates are members of a committee appointed to choose a "twin city" for a Canadian city listed in Table 5.1. Using an atlas or world almanac, choose a large city in some other country that would make a suitable "twin" (for size, site, and location) of the city of your choice.

b) Draft a letter to the city council of the "twin city" you have chosen. Describe "your" city and explain why you think theirs would be a suitable "twin". (Of course, only a city council can send such a letter.)

4. Using the data from Table 5.2, draw a line graph to show the changing proportions of urban and rural Canadians. Colour the area below the graph line, and label it "Urban". Choose a different colour for the area above the graph line, and label it "Rural".

5. In which decade before 1971 did urban population increase most? In which did it increase least? Suggest reasons.

6. Suggest why the steady increase of urban population and the decrease of rural population began to level off after 1971.

7. To your community model begun in Chapter Two, add more housing to show development since 1970. Add shopping malls, and show examples of all types of transportation facilities: highways, railroads, and airports and harbours if your community has them.

8. a) Some Canadians live in slums. Working in small groups as "Local Housing Committees", collect newspaper articles and other resource material to find out some facts about substandard housing in Canada. (Remember that not all Canada's slums are urban.)

b) Write a brief report, summarizing the information you have collected and making some recommendations for remedying the problem.

Homes like this one on a Vancouver estate show how some wealthy Canadians live.

Canada also has areas of slum housing where some Canadians live at or below the poverty line.

Montréal's Vietnamese

. . . Nguyen, his wife and their five children flew here from Saigon in 1985. "We couldn't live under Communism," Nguyen explains, echoing the feeling of many of Canada's 100 000 Vietnamese. Since the fall of Saigon (now Ho Chi Minh City) to the army of the Socialist Republic of Vietnam (North Vietnam), in April 1975, almost one million citizens of the Republic of Vietnam (South Vietnam) have fled their country.

. . . In Vietnam, Nguyen was an accountant and manager of a textile plant; in Montréal, he has a $5-an-hour job in a furniture factory. When work is available in the garment industry, his wife and eldest daughter can help make ends meet. The family lives in a tiny, sparsely furnished apartment in the city's east end . . .

The Vietnamese community is one of Montréal's newest ethnic groups . . . In a short time these people have built a strong network of organizations to preserve their culture and help new immigrants get settled. Vietnamese doctors, dentists, engineers and other professionals have their own associations . . .

The biggest influx of Southeast Asians—including Vietnamese, Chinese Vietnamese, Cambodians and Laotians—began in late 1978. These were the "boat people", those who escaped their countries in overcrowded boats of dubious seaworthiness, and whose plight aroused so much public sympathy. By the end of 1980, some 5500 new Vietnamese immigrants, sponsored by private groups or churches, had settled in Montréal . . .

There are now some 22 000 Vietnamese in the Montréal area. Toronto's Vietnamese community is about 25 000 strong, and another 50 000

Vietnamese are dispersed across the country, notably in Vancouver, Calgary, Edmonton, and Winnipeg. Many who started in smaller towns have since gravitated to Montréal or Toronto to be closer to friends and jobs.

Le Van Nhung owns the Mai Huong grocery store on Côte des Neiges Road in the heart of a crowded, multi-ethnic neighbourhood. Le was a civil engineer and army captain until the fall of Saigon. He spent three years in re-education camps. After his release, he and his family fled the country aboard a 20-metre boat carrying some 500 people.

The family spent five months in a disease-ridden refugee camp in Malaysia. Eventually they arrived in Montréal, where Le's niece had already been established since 1979. Three years later, they managed to buy their store from a friend.

Running a grocery store in Montréal is a far cry from civil engineering in Vietnam, but Le doesn't mind. "I did forced labour in the camps. I can do anything now, even the heaviest work. The most important thing is to have our freedom. We paid dearly for that."

Vietnamese in Canada have many problems in common with other immigrant groups. The biggest is language . . . Finding jobs to fit their qualifications has been difficult. Some lawyers, teachers and other professionals are working in factories or restaurants. Finding such jobs is not so difficult, and some employers, especially in Montréal's garment industry, prefer to hire Southeast Asians because they are conscientious workers. Vietnamese women have often found work more easily than their husbands. They

possess the dexterity needed to work in garment manufacturing, while the men are at a disadvantage in jobs involving heavy labour because of their generally slight physique.

While the majority of Vietnamese remain less affluent than the average Québecker, their situation has improved in recent years. A few have managed to buy houses or invest in small businesses. With several family members working, they put up with inconveniences, such as cramped living arrangements, to save for what they consider a greater priority — sponsoring relatives to come to Canada . . .

—Janice Hamilton,
"Montréal's Vietnamese" (Adapted)

---

1. Many Vietnamese immigrants faced enormous problems in coming to Canada.
   a) Working in small groups of "Vietnamese", "local newspaper reporters", and "sponsors", conduct a TV interview session to be "taped" for your local station. The reporters will interview the new arrivals and their sponsors. The Vietnamese will describe the problems they faced in reaching Canada and their hopes for their future as Canadians. The sponsors will explain what arrangements they made to welcome the Vietnamese immigrants and help them to start a new life. An anchorperson will introduce the three groups and make certain that each member has a chance to ask or answer a question.
   b) If your class has access to a video camera, make a tape of the interview session.

GROWTH OF URBAN CENTRES

Urban growth begins with the founding of cities, towns, and villages, as discussed in Chapter Three. Expansion of such urban centres, and their final size and shape depend on their location. Location involves two factors: the kind of site occupied and the access to necessary resources such as water, food, power, minerals, and trees. If the site of a settlement is large and flat enough, construction and expansion are easy. A plentiful source of fresh water nearby is important for water supply and waste-water disposal. Other resources must either be available in the region surrounding an urban centre or be readily linked to it by transportation routes. Transportation routes, of course, run both ways, allowing urban centres, especially larger ones, to provide services and manufactured goods to their **tributary areas**.

---

1. In a class brainstorming session, list the features that determined the location of the centre and tributary area of your local community or the one nearest you.
2. Locate Toronto, Montréal, or Vancouver on maps in an atlas or in *The Canadian Encyclopedia*.
   a) Name two site factors that you think have made each city grow.
   b) Which of these cities appear to have the most and least favourable sites for expansion? Explain your choices.
   c) On a large sheet of construction paper draw a map showing one of these cities and the area around it. Show major transportation routes, locations of other nearby cities, and natural resources that serve the **metropolis**. Add sketches or photos to give a "view" of the area. Choose one map of each city to mount on the class bulletin board for display.

d) Which cities seem to have the largest and smallest tributary areas?
3. Compare the site and location of your local community with those of Canada's three largest urban centres. Draw a "pictograph" (a chart showing a city symbol in different sizes) to illustrate the comparison.

CANADA'S HEARTLAND

In the Great Lakes-St. Lawrence Lowlands, cities stretch across an urban region from Windsor to Québec City. These cities are located along early waterways and pioneer roads that have developed into the transportation routes most heavily used today. Because of the large concentration of industries, businesses, and services that it holds, this urban region is called the **heartland** of Canada. It contains 54 percent of Canada's population, almost half the CMAs (Figure 5.3), and 73 percent of the manufacturing employment. Manufacturing has been a major source of growth in this

region, but service industries, such as transportation and communication, now provide almost three times as many jobs as manufacturing. Canada's heartland is only a small part of a larger North American heartland extending south of the Great Lakes into the United States.

URBANIZATION

The most urban parts of the heartland are found in and around Canada's largest cities, Toronto and Montréal (Figure 5.4). A ring of semi-urban **census subdivisions** or municipalities, which are becoming more urbanized, surrounds each of these cities. Other CMAs are located in the urban census subdivisions scattered across the heartland. Some urban sections have grown together to form a continuous urban region; one of these is the area around the western end of Lake Ontario known as the Golden Horseshoe.

Not all of Canada's heartland is urban. There is still much open space, as well as productive farmland. But the effects of **urbanization** are plain throughout most of the region. Even census subdivisions classified as semi-rural and rural are affected by development for urban use.

From the top of Toronto's CN Tower, an observer sees buildings and transportation routes stretching to the horizon along the rim of Lake Ontario.

The construction of larger electric transmission lines, the widening of highways, and the excavation of huge sand and gravel pits show the urban influence on many rural areas. Other marks of urbanization in rural areas are the building of seasonal homes by city people and the development of recreational resorts for summer and winter use.

Nearly forty percent of Canada's two million manufacturing jobs exist because of exports.

Because some of the most productive agricultural land in the country lies in the Great Lakes-St. Lawrence Lowlands region, many Canadians are concerned about the loss of agricultural land to urban building. Much of our best farmland has already been urbanized, and more has been ruined for agricultural use by the indirect effects of urbanization. Geographer Maurice Yeates estimates that another 668 000 hectares in the heartland will be ruined for agricultural production between 1981 and 2001.

Between 1976 and 1981, Canadians converted about one hundred thousand hectares of their rural land (roughly the area of Toronto) to urban uses. Half of this land was prime farmland in Ontario and British Columbia.

1. a) If you live within the map area of Figure 5.4, locate your census subdivision.

b) In which of the four categories or degrees of urbanization does your census subdivision fall?

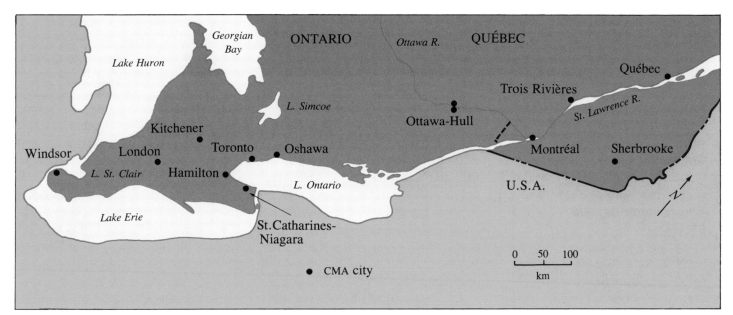

Figure 5.3 *Corridor of CMA Cities*

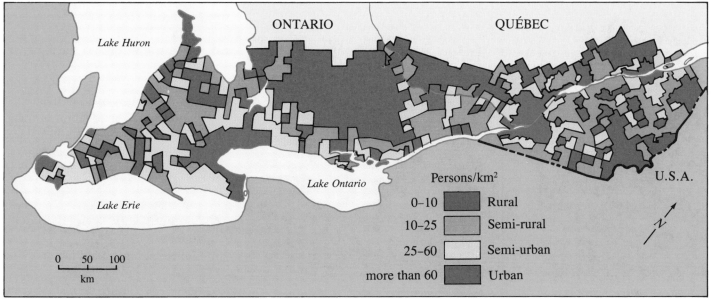

Figure 5.4 *Urbanization in the Heartland*
Source: Yeates, *Land in Canada's Urban Heartland,* 1985

161

c) Divide land area into current population for your census subdivision to calculate its precise population density.

2. a) If you live in a census subdivision outside of Canada's heartland, calculate your subdivision's population density. Using Figure 5.4 categories, calculate the degree of urbanization that your subdivision represents.

b) Make a bar graph to compare the degree of urbanization that your subdivision represents with any three other subdivisions in your area.

3. a) How many CMAs are located in Canada's heartland? (See Table 5.1.)

b) What percentage of Canada's total population lives in these CMAs?

c) Each CMA shown in Figure 5.3 is located in a cluster of urban and semi-urban census subdivisions. Which cluster contains the most CMAs?

4. a) Drawing on the travel experience of all your class members, estimate what percentage of the area of your census subdivision is urban and what is rural.

b) Using the same method, estimate the rural/urban proportion of a nearby census subdivision that is either more urban or more rural than yours.

c) According to the criteria in Figure 5.4, what are the main rural and urban characteristics that make the two census subdivisions different?

MANUFACTURING INDUSTRIES

Not all regions across the heartland support equal amounts of manufacturing. Some cities have a combination of qualities that promote manufacturing. The location of urban centres in relation to other cities and resources often determines the type of *manufacturing industry* that develops in a particular region. Urban centres provide the workers for manufacturing industries and a market for the goods they produce.

Some manufacturing industry is found in all the urban municipalities scattered across the heartland from Windsor to Québec City. Most manufacturing, however, is concentrated in the clusters of urban and semi-urban areas in southwestern Ontario and southern Québec (Figure 5.5). This

concentration shows how the large metropolitan areas of Toronto and Montréal attract industry.

The heaviest concentration of manufacturing in the heartland (and in all of Canada) is found in the Golden Horseshoe (Figure 5.6, page 164). Lately more manufacturing industries have been locating to the west of the *Golden Horseshoe* towards the Kitchener and London areas. Companies are discovering that some of the smaller cities have advantages such as cheaper land, less traffic congestion, and a more pleasant living environment. They find that highways and railroads provide easy access into and out of the Golden Horseshoe market: railway lines and major highways in the region centre on its largest cities. From these cities goods and people move east and west to other parts of the heartland, south to the United States, or north and west to western Canada. Air transportation, too, connects companies in the Golden Horseshoe with markets farther away. The location of Pearson International Airport on the west side of Toronto makes most places in Canada or the world as easy to reach from the cities of southwestern Ontario as from the Golden Horseshoe itself (Figure 5.7). From Kitchener you can drive to Pearson Airport in about 45 minutes, less time than it would take from some parts of eastern Toronto during rush hour.

Why has this heartland region grown to dominate Canada's manufacturing industry? The location of manufacturing industries in the heartland (or any part of Canada) depends on a combination of many factors. Among them is easy access to:

1. raw materials
2. competitively priced power sources
3. skilled and unskilled labour
4. means of transportation
5. parts or semi-manufactured goods from other manufacturing industries

New streets, homes, schools, and factories built around cities like St. Catharines, Ontario, overlie much valuable farmland, which can no longer be used to produce crops.

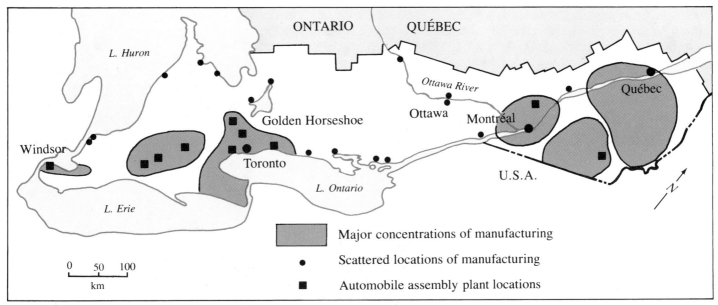

Figure 5.5 *Manufacturing in the Heartland*

Heartland Employment in Some Manufacturing Industries (as % of Canadian employment)

Industry	%
Leather	94
Electrical products	90
Textiles, fabrics, clothing	88
Rubber & plastics	84
Chemicals	81
Transport equipment	80
Furniture & fixtures	78
Machinery	76
Fabricated metals	76
Printing & publishing	71

Source: Adapted from Yeates, *Land in Canada's Urban Heartland*, 1985

6. financial, legal, and other support services
7. markets
8. industrial sites serviced with water
9. an attractive living environment for management and workers
10. investment capital
11. government tax breaks (or concessions) and incentives

The manufacturing industry has played an important part in making the Great Lakes-St. Lawrence Lowlands

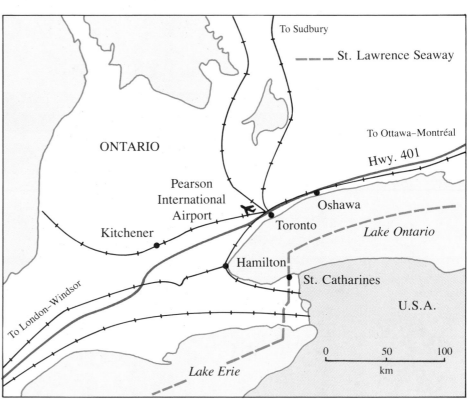

Figure 5.7 *Major Transportation Routes in the Golden Horseshoe*

the most populous and wealthy region of Canada. But the heartland manufacturing industry has its own problems. In the past few years, barriers to world trade have been crumbling, and worldwide markets for manufactured goods have opened up. Developing countries with lower costs of production, particularly lower labour costs, can produce manufactured goods more cheaply than can Canadian plants. Countries such as Japan and Sweden are more advanced than Canada in using robots instead of people to do routine manual labour. They are also ahead in computer-aided manufacturing, where computers that "communicate" with one another co-ordinate the various activities. These computers control all

Figure 5.6 ***Landsat Image of the Golden Horseshoe*** *This satellite image shows the patterns of land use in the Golden Horseshoe area of Ontario, from Toronto Harbour (top) to the Niagara River (lower right). The image was made on May 5, 1987, just after the beginning of the growing season.*

In the urban areas, red represents grass growing in parks, on golf courses, and in other open areas. In the rural areas, red represents fields of pasture, hay, and winter wheat. Light brown represents deciduous trees, including fruit trees, which have not yet come into leaf. Dark brown represents coniferous trees. Various shades of blue represent asphalt and concrete surfaces in cities and towns; in rural areas, blues represent plowed or cultivated fields.

stages of the process from handling orders to production, packaging, shipping, and billing. As a result of these international advances, Canadian manufacturers are finding it hard to compete in world markets, and imports are replacing products made in Canada.

World competition is forcing out of business some older, less efficient industries called **sunset industries**. Other newer or modernizing industries known as **sunrise industries** are becoming more efficient, but in the process they are employing fewer people. People who are laid off are usually unskilled workers. They have problems finding other jobs because the new industries require a larger proportion of skilled workers. Changes like these lead to what may seem an absurd result: much unemployment in the heartland at the same time that its manufacturing industry shows healthy growth.

In the electronics industry, which includes computer and communications **hardware** and **software**, Canada can compete with other nations. The so-called **micro-chip** industry, which is concentrated in the Ottawa area, has captured markets all over the world. Although the electronics industry is highly automated and does not employ large numbers of people, it offers young people a number of new career choices.

In less than 10 years, modern technology has reduced the time it takes to make a locomotive from 16 days to 16 hours.

Industrial computers can be used to communicate ideas for designing, manufacturing, and distributing most products.

Canada also has one of the most efficient iron and steel industries in the world. Steel is a major ingredient of much of the secondary manufacturing industry, particularly the automobile industry.

1. a) Working in small groups, list four products made by *one* group of the manufacturing industries that appear in Figure 5.5. Then find or make some illustrations of the products you have listed. Using this material, prepare a short, colourful brochure to promote sales of these products in other countries.
   b) How does the manufacturer of specific products in the group you have chosen help to produce items in another group? Draw a flow chart to show some linkages that help to explain why many manufacturing industries like to cluster close together in one area.

2. a) Which groups of products shown in Figure 5.5 would be used in automobile manufacturing?
   b) Why would automobile manufacturing be one of the largest employers in the transportation field?

3. Why would the heartland employ a lower percentage of workers to manufacture wood, paper, and food and beverage products than do other parts of Canada? (Facts you learned in Chapter Three about the locations of these resource industries will help you answer this question.)

4. a) Consult an atlas map for help in identifying the following items shown in Figure 5.6: Toronto, Hamilton, St. Catharines, City of Niagara Falls, Niagara Escarpment, Queen Elizabeth Way, Welland Canal, Niagara River, and New York State.
   b) Why is it difficult to find the boundaries of cities on this image?

Some of the manufacturing industries and storage facilities in Toronto's eastern harbour. The harbour shelters shoreline shipping channels and docks from the sometimes rough waters of Lake Ontario. Trucks use the elevated Gardiner Expressway to speed them on their way to distribute manufactured goods quickly throughout southern Ontario.

5. a) You are the president of a company that is planning to build a manufacturing plant. Design a model of an industrial location to find the best site for the new plant. On a page, mark symbols for one location each of raw materials, power, labour force, and main market. Show how far they are from one another by drawing a scale. Mark three possible plant sites (A, B, and C) anywhere on the page. Suppose that the distances between each plant location and the other components are the only cost factors. Measure the distances between each possible plant site and the other components. In your notebook, record the distances on a chart such as this:

	Raw Materials	Power Source	Workers	Market
Site A				
Site B				
Site C				

b) At which site will you build your new plant? (Use your chart to help you make the most profitable choice.)

6. A factory has been losing money on its operation for several years. Management has tried to persuade the federal government to raise tariffs to protect its business from low-priced imports, but so far the government has refused. There are many possible solutions to the factory's problem. Here are a few examples:

- Lower costs by reducing wages and requiring employees to work harder.
- Modernize the factory operation. (This course would mean laying off large numbers of employees, but those who were kept on would be paid as much as they are being paid now.)
- Persuade the government to provide the money to keep the plant operating as it has been.
- Close the plant.

a) You and each of your classmates belong to one of three groups: the shareholders, the employees, and a Conciliation Board. The first two groups will hold private meetings to discuss possible solutions to their problem. Then they will hold a joint meeting to propose the solutions they prefer.

If the two groups cannot reach a satisfactory solution, they will each have an opportunity to meet with the Conciliation Board. When the Conciliation Board has considered both proposals, it will make a recommendation on which both the shareholders and the employees will vote.

b) Suggest three advantages to the whole community of working out an acceptable solution.

SERVICE ACTIVITIES

Although the heartland of Canada is known for its manufacturing, *service industries* (sometimes called tertiary industries) employ more people. For example, more people are employed in colleges and universities than in the iron and steel industry; more people are employed in providing health and social assistance services than work in the automobile industry. In fact, the service industries listed in Table 5.3 employ almost three times as many people in the heartland as does the manufacturing industry. Over 50 percent of the workers in each service industry live in Canada's heartland.

Employment in the service industries has been rising quickly in the last couple of decades. This increase in employment has helped to relieve the slowing down of employment growth in the manufacturing industry. Service activity has helped greatly to keep the heartland prosperous.

In Toronto, more people earn $150 000 a year than do people in Montréal, Vancouver, and Ottawa combined. Twenty-five percent of all Canadian managers and professionals live in Toronto.

1. a) Working in groups, list at least two kinds of business under each major service industry listed in Table 5.3.

b) Survey the members of your class to find out how many people are or might be interested in making a career in the service industries.

If you wish to take a larger sample, organize a poll of all the classes in your grade or in your school.

Table 5.3 *Workers in the Heartland Employed in Service Industries*

Type of Service Industry	% of Heartland Workers Employed by Industry
Retail trade	17.4
Transportation and communication	11.0
Health and social assistance	10.7
Education	9.6
Wholesale trade	9.0
Finance, insurance, and real estate	8.6
Personal services	8.4
Accommodation and food services	8.0
Services to business	6.7
Provincial and local administration	5.8
Federal administration	4.8

Source: Adapted from Yeates, *Land in Canada's Urban Heartland*, 1985

c) Draw up a graph or chart to display the results of your poll.

2. Why do you think so many people in Ottawa-Hull are employed in service industries compared to the numbers employed in manufacturing?

3. a) Service industries tend to group together in or near large urban centres. Suggest two geographic reasons to account for this. Be prepared to share your reasons with your class.

b) List three links between the service industry groups that would influence them to locate close to one another.

4. a) Suppose that you are interested in employment in one of Canada's service industries. Prepare a list of four to six questions that you would like to ask a person employed in that industry before you make a decision.

b) If you have a family member or family friend who is employed in the industry you have chosen, arrange to interview the person, and ask your questions. After the interview, write a brief profile of the job as you understand it.

c) Collect the job profiles your class has written, and arrange them in a loose-leaf notebook for class members to read.

About seventy-five percent of part-time workers are female, and most of these people work in service industries.

Canada's health care services are among the best in the world.

TRANSPORTATION AND COMMUNICATION

A steady flow of people, goods, services, and information links heartland cities. Most links are between metropolitan areas and their surrounding urban centres.

In the past, transportation by water and railroads was very important to the development of the heartland *urban system*. Today, most people and goods (by value) move between cities by road transport. If you have travelled on Ontario's Highway 401 or Québec's Highway 20, you know that these major highways are often jammed with cars and trucks. Figure 5.8 (page 168) shows these highways and the volume of traffic that flows through Canada's heartland. People who commute to work and trucks that move goods account for most of the traffic in and around the CMAs of the

Large numbers of motor vehicles using highways in and around cities like Montréal often create traffic jams, especially during rush hours.

heartland. Some traffic volume is the result of people driving to recreation and vacation sites outside the major cities. Notice the heavy volume of traffic around the two *metropolitan cities* of Toronto and Montréal, and in the Golden Horseshoe, as well as westward into the Kitchener area. Note also the heavy volume of traffic all the way from Windsor to Québec City.

The east-west highway traffic flow is heavy between Toronto and Montréal. The volume of air traffic, too, is heavy between Toronto and Montréal: about 1.5 million airline passengers travel between these two cities each year, almost twice as many people as travel between any other two cities in Canada. The volume of air traffic is also heavy between Edmonton and Calgary, and between Toronto and Ottawa.

For the movement of heavy and bulky cargo like iron ore or grain, water and rail transport are still very important. These transport lines, too, run east and west between Windsor and Québec City. In recent years the use of containers that can easily be moved from ship to train to truck has made water and rail transportation more efficient.

Some other transportation facilities are the pipelines that carry oil and natural gas, and the transmission lines

Mirabel Airport, built on an autoroute northwest of Montréal, handles only international air traffic. Domestic flights use Dorval Airport, which is closer to the heart of the city.

that carry electricity across the whole heartland. These lines provide the heat, power, and light needed to keep an urban system functioning.

Urban centres also need information systems. The heartland is laced with communication networks: postal mail, courier services, telephone, telex, telecomputer, television, radio, trade and news magazines, and daily newspapers. These communication networks make it possible for people in all parts of the heartland (and most of southern Canada) to exchange information with one another constantly.

Transportation and telecommunications provide a vital service for the manufacturing and service industries, as well as for the public. Everywhere they connect places inside the heartland with those in all the other parts of Canada.

---

1. a) Name the two major highways in Ontario and Québec that form a fast, continuous, and direct link from Windsor to Québec City.
   b) According to Figure 5.8, how many thousands of vehicles per day travel over highways along the north shore of eastern Lake Ontario? How does this traffic flow compare with that of the Golden Horseshoe?
   c) List four cities on the main traffic corridor. Do highways radiate toward other parts of the heartland?
   d) Draw a sketch map of southern Ontario and Québec that shows the linking and radiating patterns of two highways in heavily travelled areas.

2. Rush-hour traffic in Toronto has moved at the following speeds: 19 km/h in 1900; 32 km/h in 1935; 27 km/h in 1965; and 19 km/h in 1985.
   a) What was the most important means of transportation in 1900? in 1935?
   b) Suggest reasons why Toronto's rush-hour traffic slowed down between 1935 and 1965. Why did it slow down even more between 1965 and 1985?
   c) What do you think the rush-hour speed is likely to be in the year 2001? Why?
   d) You and several of your classmates are members of a Traffic Commission for your (nearest) urban community.

Identify two areas of serious traffic problems. Develop a map that you might use to show the City Council how these traffic problems might be reduced.

3. a) List six kinds of service jobs for the transportation industry and six for the communications industry.
   b) Create a chart or poster to show how transportation and communications services are useful to *one* of the following manufacturing industries:
   - iron and steel smelting
   - petrochemical refining
   - automobile assembly
   - an industry of your choice

4. There has been a long shutdown of a major transportation network *or* manufacturer *or* service industry.

   Develop a flow chart to show how the shutdown would affect *one* of the following:
   - transportation and communication systems
   - other service industries
   - manufacturing production *and*
   - you personally

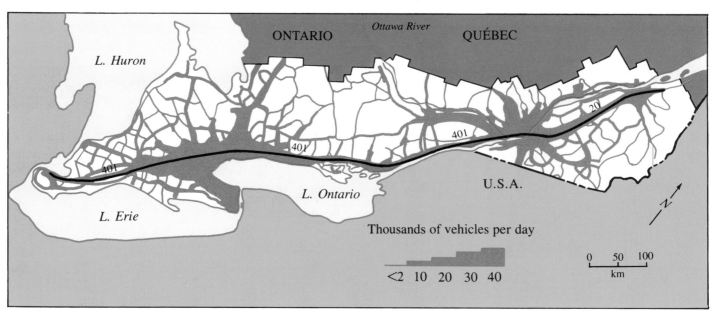

Figure 5.8 *Traffic Volume on Heartland Highways*
Source: Adapted from Yeates, *Land in Canada's Urban Heartland*, 1985

HEARTLAND/ HINTERLAND

Some geographers classify all of Canada beyond the heartland as *hinterland*. This means that in the rest of Canada the setting is more rural, the economy depends more on *primary resources*, and there is less manufacturing. You have read in Chapter Three how the production of minerals, and forest and agricultural products in the hinterland results in the founding of many small settlements but only a few major cities. Many primary resources are transported from the hinterland to Canada's heartland as raw materials or semi-processed goods to be made into finished products. In return, heartland cities send manufactured goods and services back to hinterland centres. For example, heartland cities in southern Ontario-Québec exchange goods with hinterland areas in Canada's northeast and west. As more hinterland resources are developed, cities in the heartland grow.

But this "heartland/hinterland" idea is really too simple. Table 5.4 and the activities that accompany it show that although most Canadian cities are located in the heartland, there are large urban populations in the rest of the country, as well. Cities in some parts of the hinterland are small "heartlands" for their surrounding regions, just as the major cities of the Great Lakes-St. Lawrence Lowlands are a heartland for the rest of Canada. The activities relating to Table 5.4 will help you decide which cities are mini-heartlands in their own regions.

---

1. a) Which two provinces are least urban?
   b) Using your knowledge of geography, explain why the Atlantic provinces are less urban than other regions in Canada.
2. a) On an outline map of Canada, draw a circle in each province in rough proportion to each province's total population. Colour and label the sector of each circle that represents the urban proportion of the population.
   b) Using Table 5.1 and an atlas, locate and label on your map the largest city in each province. Add Charlottetown, P.E.I. (pop. 15 800).
3. a) For each province listed in Table 5.4, calculate the percentage of the urban population that lives in its largest city. Use data from Table 5.1, as well as the population figure for Charlottetown (15 800).
   b) In which provinces does more than 50 percent of the urban population live in the largest city? These cities could be classified as mini-heartlands for the regions around them.

LINKS AMONG SETTLEMENTS

Earlier we considered how transportation and communications networks linked the heartland cities. The linking of central places does not stop at the heartland. In fact, there is more traffic and a heavier flow of communication between Toronto or Montréal and other major cities such as Vancouver, Calgary, and Winnipeg than between Toronto or Montréal and the smaller cities that surround them. People, goods, and information flow from the rural areas to the cities closest to them, from these cities to the nearest metropolis, and then from metropolis to metropolis. Rural areas must use the urban network to link with one another. The movement is from country to city, from city to city, and from city back to country.

Figure 5.9 (page 170) illustrates the flow of people, mail, and high-value goods. Over 50 percent of Canada's air traffic flies on routes between the 15 cities shown on this map. This east-west strip also contains the Trans-Canada Highway, two transcontinental railway lines, and a multitude of communication systems. No wonder that it is sometimes called Canada's "Main Drag"!

---

1. Choose a small village in each of two different provinces. Suppose a person living near one village mails a letter or parcel to someone near the other village. Trace the route that you think the letter would take. You may wish to

---

Table 5.4 *Urban Population by Province*

Province	Total Population*	Urban Population*	% Urban
Ontario	9 113 500	7 469 400	82.0
British Columbia	2 889 200	2 285 000	79.1
Alberta	2 375 300	1 877 800	79.1
Québec	6 540 300	5 089 000	77.8
Manitoba	1 071 200	766 900	71.6
Saskatchewan	1 010 200	620 200	61.4
Newfoundland	568 400	334 700	58.9
Nova Scotia	873 200	471 100	54.0
New Brunswick	710 400	350 300	49.3
Prince Edward Island	126 700	48 300	38.1
Canada	25 354 100	19 352 100	76.3

Source: Compiled from Canadian census data, 1986

*The figures are simplified by rounding to the nearest 100 people; therefore the provincial populations do not add up to the exact Canadian totals.

Note: See Figure 5.1 for a diagrammatic map of the urban part of each Canadian province.

consult with your local post office to verify your suggested route.

2. Check similar routing for a telephone call or a trip by air.

3. a) How does Figure 5.9 show that Toronto and Montréal are the main focal points for east-west flights?
b) What provinces have no major airport on part of Canada's "Main Drag"? Why?

4. a) Using an atlas map, label the most northerly destination for regularly scheduled commercial air flights in each of the following regions: the Yukon, the Northwest Territories, Northern Ontario, and northern Québec.
b) What vital services do flights to Canada's North provide for that region's residents? Why are the services particularly important to these Canadians?

5. a) Using an atlas, draw on an outline map of Canada the routes of the Trans-Canada Highway, Canadian Pacific Railway (CP Rail), and the Canadian National Railways (CN).

b) Compare your map with Figure 5.9. In which parts of Canada do these land routes most closely parallel air routes? least closely?
c) How close do you live to each

trans-Canada transportation route?
d) Name three Canadian cities that seem to be focal points of transportation to other parts of the country.

Via Rail, operated by the Canadian government, provides passenger service across most of the settled parts of southern Canada.

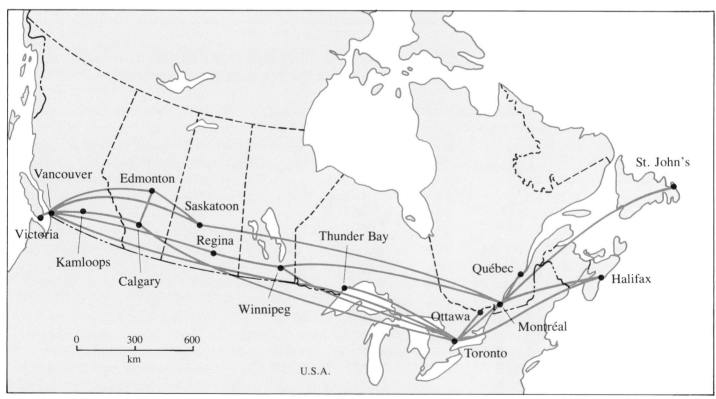

Figure 5.9 *Canada's "Main Drag": Most-Travelled Airline Routes*
Source: Adapted from J. & R. Simmons, *Urban Canada*, 1974

Village Life: A Problem and a Solution

I. Hodgeville, A Dying Village

Hodgeville, Saskatchewan is located about 60 km southeast of Swift Current. At its peak, about 25 years ago, Hodgeville had a population of 420 persons. In 1986, only 284 people still lived there. Only a few service stations and stores survive among the boarded-up buildings along Main Street. In two decades, the village has lost a railway station, an elevator, a lumber yard, a general store, a law office, a barber shop, a pool hall, a hardware store, a television repair shop, and four farm machinery dealerships.

"This town is dying," said a local farmer, who is also a Hodgeville town councillor. "There are hardly any young people left here. More than half the people are pensioners, and lots of them are over 80 years old."

Unless Hodgeville can attract some new industry, it will likely die in another 25 years. It will not be the first Saskatchewan village to disappear. In fact, the survival of Hodgeville in recent decades was largely the result of the decline of nearby villages such as Bateman, St. Boswells, Hallonquist, and Neidpath [Figure 5.10]. Bateman, for example, had a population of 250 in the 1920s, but by 1987 it had only 33 people. Farmers from the Bateman area started to go to Hodgeville for supplies. Before long, they are likely to go to Swift Current instead if Hodgeville's services are reduced further.

Like most agricultural towns and villages in the Prairie Provinces, Hodgeville was born in the early years of this century. Farmers used horses and wagons to transport grain and to obtain supplies, and so a grain elevator and stores needed to be located about every 15 or 20 km along a railroad. Each time an elevator was built, another hamlet was created. Altogether, more than 1500 prairie hamlets, villages, and small towns were created. Now that farmers have trucks, they can travel many kilometres to carry their grain and obtain supplies. Farms have also increased in size, and this means that there are fewer farmers to supply. As a result of this process of change, railroad branch lines are closed and elevators shut down, signalling the beginning of the end for many prairie towns. There are already many ghost towns dotting the prairie landscape; in another 25 years, there will be many more.

—Geoffrey York,
"Hodgeville: A Dying Village" (Adapted)

II. Recipe for Survival: Add Noodles

Mossbank, Saskatchewan (population just under 500) shares with many other prairie towns the problem of surviving loss of transportation services. In the early 1970s, a group of residents pondered the town's problems and prospects. Someone mentioned that oriental noodles were becoming very popular in Canada and wondered why they could not be made in Saskatchewan instead of Japan. After all, Saskatchewan produces an abundance of the ingredients of noodles: wheat flour and Canola oil. Instead of exporting the wheat and Canola and importing noodles, why not make the noodles right in Mossbank?

A company was formed, and money was raised by selling shares to Mossbank residents. When more capital was needed, the company negotiated loans from both the federal and the provincial governments. A small factory was built, and Mossbank began to produce noodles.

But the company soon found itself facing serious financial problems. It had not done enough marketing promotion. It was producing noodles,

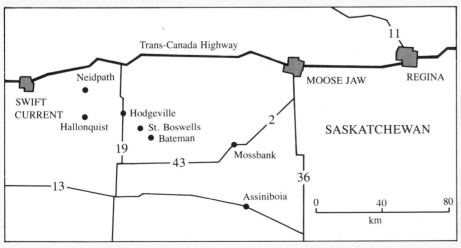

Figure 5.10 *Hodgeville and Mossbank, Saskatchewan*

but it wasn't selling them. The company went bankrupt, and local investors lost their money.

Yet not all was lost. A Winnipeg company bought the noodle factory and established Moss Foods Ltd. which is producing noodles under several different labels. The noodle plant employs 13 people, all Mossbank residents. The business is prospering, and the community hopes that the plant will expand and employ more people.

Mossbank is mainly a service town for the surrounding agricultural area. The local residents hope that the noodle plant will help their community to survive. The recipe for survival is not as simple as the title of this story suggests. It is not possible for all the towns in the Prairie Provinces to survive changing transportation technology (see the description of Hodgeville). All the same, local initiative is a prime ingredient for economic development in any community.

After the noodles emerge from the roller, they are carried on a conveyor belt to the oil cooker. Workers in the Mossbank factory arrange the noodles as they pass along the belt.

---

1. a) Suggest three reasons why some prairie villages such as Hodgeville are disappearing.
   b) Not all declining villages, such as Mossbank, can find a way to survive. Suggest two steps that citizens and government officials might take to help towns survive. If survival is not possible, suggest two things that these same groups might do to ease the social and economic impact on people in dying towns.
2. Compare the facilities and services of Mossbank with a town of about the same size in your region. If there are major differences, try to explain the reasons for them.

Some of the shops and service buildings along the main street of the village of Mossbank, Saskatchewan

Figure 5.11 *Topographic Map of Brampton, Ontario* *The scale of this map is 1:25 000.*

Source: This map is based on information taken from the National Topographic System map sheet number 30M/12f © 1973. Her Majesty the Queen in Right of Canada with permission of Energy, Mines and Resources Canada.

SETTLEMENTS AS SERVICE CENTRES

Every village, town, or city serves not only the people within its boundaries and the rural people around it, but also any centres smaller than itself in the surrounding area. These urban centres offer such facilities as stores, theatres, churches, doctors, lawyers, and services like schools and post offices. Geographers call the services which these central places provide, **central place functions**. Not all central places provide the same range of functions. Generally, the larger the central place, the wider the area it serves, and the greater the selection of services it provides.

Central places and their functions may be ranked in order, from the smallest village to the largest metropolitan centre. People's shopping habits illustrate this order:

- The rural family satisfies its daily needs by shopping in the nearest village. There, too, family members pick up items that they suddenly need or forgot to buy when doing their major weekly shopping.
- Rural residents and villagers go to the nearest town for some weekly grocery shopping.
- Rural people, town residents, and villagers travel to the nearest city, perhaps about once a month, to shop for ''dress'' clothes and sometimes for major household appliances or other expensive goods.
- Most people, including city dwellers, travel to a very large city on a Christmas shopping spree or to browse in a specialty shop for goods they cannot find closer to home.

Use of other services, such as entertainment or medical facilities, follows the same pattern. A person may attend local hockey games every week, but go to see an NHL game in the big city only occasionally. A person who visits the town physician for stitches in a cut finger may go to a specialist in a big city for major surgery.

Leading central places are the cities that provide the most central place functions and that serve the largest hinterlands. These cities draw customers from many hundreds of kilometres to use their financial, legal, and medical services, their specialty shops, and their first-class entertainment centres. Most Canadians who live within four or five hours' driving time of these cities will visit them at least once a year. Many Canadians from all across the country will visit one of the big three—Toronto, Montréal, Vancouver — at least several times in a lifetime.

URBAN ENVIRONMENTS

You have seen that people, goods, and services flow between the different regions of Canada. The same type of flow also takes place within urban centres, and especially in cities. This flow sometimes takes place within small sections of a city and sometimes across a whole city. Wherever the flows start, stop, or cross in a city, many different types of land use develop. Often land in certain parts of a city is used for the same or similar purposes, and all these areas of land use, taken together, form the whole urban environment.

Different types of land use are best shown on a large-scale topographic map. Such a map shows most of the important surface features in urban and rural areas.

Although most Canadians are urbanites, not all Canadians live in cities, and those living in the countryside may be a long distance away from the nearest city. If you do not live in a city, you may find some of the following sources helpful as you answer the questions (below) on land uses:

- a large-scale topographic map (1:25 000) of a city, like the map of Brampton, Ontario, shown in Figure 5.11 (page 173)
- recent aerial photographs that cover parts of a city
- a city street map that you can obtain from a gas station, a tourist booth, an engineering and planning office, or a chamber of commerce
- information from friends or relatives who live in cities
- a city map showing types of land use that you can obtain from municipal offices, a chamber of commerce, or a board of trade
- an extensive class field trip to look at parts of a city

1. a) What two highways cross in the downtown core of Brampton? What are the city street names for these highways?
   b) Name four kinds of stores that are likely to be located in the buildings grouped around this major intersection.
2. Name two purposes for which people might use the buildings along the railway lines that cross each other west of the city core?
3. List three recreation services provided throughout the city.
4. Besides schools, find two additional public services that use land.
5. Identify three urban uses of land in the farmland area beyond the built-up part of Brampton.

NEIGHBOURHOODS

What is a neighbourhood? Every urban dweller in Canada lives in one. Most of us think of a neighbourhood as the familiar part of the city close to our home, but its size seems to expand as we grow from children to young adults. To a young child, the neighbourhood consists only of the nearby homes. Later it might take in an entire city block. As we become more independent, we see our neighbourhood as a city district with special features that distinguish it from other nearby neighbourhoods.

Every neighbourhood has some special features that help to identify it. If you saw photographs of the special features of your neighbourhood, you would recognize it instantly. These features are known as *landmarks*. They might include buildings, parks, monuments, bridges, and natural formations.

A neighbourhood's boundaries are usually formed by a major road, a railway, or a physical feature such as a river. Sometimes its boundaries can be vague and difficult to identify. Often a neighbourhood is considered to be the same size as the local elementary or secondary school district.

After people live in a neighbourhood for several years, they usually become quite familiar and comfortable with it, and they expect that it will always remain about the same. But change must come. Sometimes it comes gradually, like general aging; and sometimes it comes suddenly as when buildings are demolished to make room for new developments.

War memorials, like this one in Charlottetown, P.E.I., are well-known landmarks in many Canadian towns and cities. They were built to honour those who fought in the First and Second World Wars.

Some changes might please most of the people in the neighbourhood, but other changes might make them uncomfortable and angry.

If you live in a city, your neighbourhood and all the others around you combine to make up your city. The land uses that you see near your home are also found in other parts of the city. In the whole city there are many more types of land use than there are in any one neighbourhood, and some types of land use are concentrated in particular parts. Each land use represents a type of city environment with its own special characteristics. In most cities, homes or industries and businesses take up larger areas of land than do recreation facilities, utilities, and means of transportation.

---

1. What makes your neighbourhood different? Think about the route(s) you take to school, and note any features of the neighbourhood that you would mention if you were describing it to a newcomer. If you have a camera, take pictures of these features.

   a) As a class, collect photographs of your neighbourhood from newspapers, tourist bureaus, the Chamber of Commerce. Add to your collection the pictures you have taken yourselves.

   b) Choose from your collection the 10 to 20 pictures that best represent your neighbourhood and tell its story. Write captions for the pictures and create a layout. Hang the pictures as an ''exhibition'' or create a ''brochure'' to promote your neighbourhood.

LAND USES

Residential Land Use

Much of the land in most neighbourhoods has been developed for *residential land use*. People live in many

types of buildings that differ in location, size, design, age, and the number of families that they can accommodate. Not everyone wishes to live in exactly the same kind of home. People's choice of housing might depend on their age, lifestyle, or income; on whether they have children; or on the distance from their work. Some people prefer to live near the downtown core of a city, while others prefer *suburbs* at the outer edges of the city.

More Canadians own their homes than rent. Winnipeg and Vancouver rate among the top 10 world cities for percent of owner-occupied housing (60 percent, including owners of apartment units).

Commercial Land Use

The clothes we wear, the food we eat, the furniture we use, and the electronic equipment that entertains us are bought in various kinds of stores. The land occupied by the stores and other businesses is said to be for *commercial land use*. The commercial buildings in residential neighbourhoods and throughout a city are usually located along or at the intersection of major transportation routes.

Stores spring up in cities along the major routes of *public transportation* vehicles such as streetcars, buses, or other types of *mass transit*. Such commercial growth often becomes an almost continuous row of stores stretching for several kilometres from its starting point in the city centre. Urban geographers call this growth pattern *ribbon development*. In the suburbs, commercial developments are strung out along streets not always served by public transport but accessible by car. Such development is often called a *commercial strip* or *strip plaza*. Some suburban *shopping plazas* are so large that they draw customers from many kilometres around. Such plazas are often called *regional shopping centres*.

Types of Housing

High-rise apartment buildings

Single-family homes

Condominiums in St. John's, Newfoundland

Duplex row houses in Montréal

Commercial buildings in the downtown core of a large city are usually taller than those in other locations. This cluster of tall buildings, usually called the *central business district* or CBD, contains banks and other financial institutions, as well as many business head offices and branches. In the CBD, some types of stores, such as supermarkets, are less plentiful because fewer people live in this part of the city.

Special commercial developments in some large Canadian cities are so innovative that they serve as models for others. In Ottawa, Calgary, and Vancouver, street malls have been established. These pedestrian malls give the public attractive and quiet places to shop in the CBD, free from the noise and risks of automobile traffic. Such malls encourage shoppers to use off-street parking or public transit. In Québec City, Mall St-Roch, a street mall, was roofed over to form an enclosure five blocks long. This and other malls, such as the Eaton Centre in Toronto, are very large. The largest of all is the West Edmonton Mall, which contains over 800 shops, 34 movie theatres, 11 major department stores, and indoor recreation and amusement parks.

Canadians spend almost forty percent of their food dollar on restaurant meals.

1. a) On a map of your (nearest) city, mark and label six locations of commercial land use.
   b) Refer to a city land-use map in your atlas or *The Canadian Encyclopedia*. In groups, each group choosing a different city, draw a sketch map, and label two examples of each of the following types of commercial land use:
   - the CBD
   - ribbon development
   - shopping malls

2. a) With your classmates, construct a chart of information to use for comparing corner stores, strip plazas, regional shopping centres, and the CBD in your (nearest) city. Set up your chart in columns, using the following headings:
   - Types & Value of Goods
   - Most Important (''Anchor'') Store
   - Distance from Home
   - Frequency of Visits
   - Access to Transportation
   b) Write a summary of the characteristics of each type of commercial land use.

3. Commercial development along a major street or road often slows the flow of traffic.
   a) As head of your community's Planning Department, prepare a presentation to your city/town council, proposing a new commercial strip that will be attractive to look at and will not hinder traffic flow. To back up your proposal, you should prepare a brief written description of the new strip, a map locating it, and sketches to show current and proposed land use.

4. If you could redesign one commercial building in your community, what changes would you make? Why?

5. Suggest two advantages of roofing over a shopping street to create an enclosed mall. Suggest two disadvantages.

Industrial Land Use

Almost all Canadian cities have areas of *industrial land use*. Some cities, such as Hamilton, Ontario, with its steel plants, have industries that change natural resources into materials needed in manufacturing. But in most cities industries mainly convert these refined materials into finished goods or into parts that will be assembled into finished goods.

Specialized industries locate in cities that provide unusual advantages. To attract new industries cities often set aside areas of land for the development of planned *industrial parks*. These parks contain one-storey buildings with landscaped front yards and easy access to transportation, water, electricity, natural gas, and sewage facilities.

1. a) Draw a large outline map of the city in which you live or the one nearest you. On your city map, plot and label four industries. Using different colours, indicate the major railway lines, two main roads, water transportation facilities (such as a harbour), and airports.
   b) In general, where are the industrial areas in your city in relation to transportation facilities?
   c) What type of transportation facility is closest to each of the four industries you have chosen? Suggest why each industry was located close to a particular transportation facility.

2. a) Working in small groups, each group on a different city, plot and label on a sketch map two areas of industrial land use and the types of transportation near these areas. You will need to refer to city land-use maps in your atlas or *The Canadian Encyclopedia*.

An industrial park in suburban Winnipeg shows plants on large, well-landscaped lots. Workers use the nearby ring road to commute from residential parts of the city like those seen in the background.

177

Housing: Search for a Roof

Canada's deepening housing crisis takes some of the shine off the excitement and pleasure of city living. For more and more Canadians, it is now impossible to find an affordable home in a city.

The struggle to find an affordable place to live affects all but the rich, who can live wherever they wish. But for others, putting a roof over their heads is a constant worry.

Most desperately in need of housing are the homeless ''street people''; the luckiest of these find a place to sleep overnight in shelters run by relief agencies. And in spite of popular belief, such people are not all down-and-out alcoholics. Many of them are simply unemployed people with no place to go. And for the first time in Canada's history, this group now includes a large number of women.

Next most in need of affordable housing are people on social assistance. Because of the lack of low-cost housing, many of these people are forced to spend up to 70 percent of their income on shelter. (For most people, the cost of housing is usually about 25 percent of income.) Such a major expense leaves them too little money for other necessities, such as food and clothing.

The working poor who pay their own way without any government support are also victims of the shortage of affordable housing. Their earnings from a job that pays the minimum wage or a little more do not go very far these days. These people often spend more than half their incomes on shelter that is generally run-down, as well as rat- and roach-infested.

In many Canadian cities public housing does exist for people in these two groups. But since, for some time, very few new housing units have been built, the wait to get in is measured in years. In the meantime, these people must look for other places to live, and these other places are always more expensive.

For the middle-income group (the group to which most Canadians belong), the housing outlook is a little brighter. For many of these folk, however, the problem is not so much the complete lack of a place to live as the shortage of suitable choices: a conveniently located house or apartment at a reasonable price.

For most families, which often include husbands and wives with full-time jobs, the dream of owning their own home is remaining just that: a dream. In the Toronto area, for example, owning a home inside the city limits is fast becoming a privilege of families with above-average incomes.

As house prices climb each year, the areas with affordable homes get farther away from the downtown core. In fact, nearby suburban subdivisions, which earlier were the traditional places for families buying their first homes, are now full of ''country estates'' intended to attract people earning high incomes. This change has forced younger couples to buy homes farther out of the city, which means that they must spend an hour or more getting to and from work.

—Ken Mark,
''Search for a Roof'' (Adapted)

---

1. In some Canadian communities, house prices and apartment rents are going up; in some, they are going down. What is the trend in your community? Suggest one or more reasons for this trend.

2. If there are public housing projects in your city, who runs one or two of them? Find out how tenants qualify to live there.

3. a) Is a family more likely to have satisfactory accommodation by buying a home? by renting a home?
   b) What do you think are the advantages of buying? of renting?
   c) What do you think are the disadvantages of buying? of renting?

4. Many families renovate houses in the downtown area of cities, often at great cost. Why do you think people would want to live in this part of a city rather than in the suburbs, where houses of the same size might cost less?

5. Working in groups, suggest the type of housing and city location that might be suitable for each of the following:

- a young working couple who enjoy theatre, restaurants, and the excitement of city life
- a student living away from home for six months of the year
- a business executive who works in a downtown office tower
- a disabled person wishing to live alone and be self-sufficient
- a couple with a young family who wish to provide a secure and safe environment for their children
- a family with no car and a small income
- an elderly single person or couple living on a fixed income
- a single person who has just arrived in the city
- a single-parent family in which the parent earns a moderate income

6. Elderly persons with small incomes and limited strength, handicapped persons who work inside or outside their homes, working single parents, young families with small children, and young single persons earning a beginner's salary all need affordable housing.
a) Working in small groups, plan a housing unit for *one* example mentioned above. Target the unit's cost (including land) at 60 percent of the average cost of a comparable housing unit in your area. Remember the special needs of the group you have chosen.
b) Post your housing plans on your classroom bulletin board.

7. In recent years, more city workers have decided to live in small rural communities outside the city. Sugget two advantages you think there would be in living in a rural area and working in a city. Suggest two disadvantages.

8. a) In what type of building do you prefer to live? Why?
b) Briefly interview three other classmates to find out in what types of buildings they prefer to live.

---

b) Check the general statements you made in response to 1. b) and c) (above) against the sketch maps your class groups have made. How well do they match?

3. a) Choose three industrial plants in the planned industrial park nearest to your home or school, and try to find out what each plant manufactures.
b) Describe in a general way the size, type, and variety of manufacturing plants in the industrial park.

Recreational Land Use

Recreational land use in a neighbourhood or city provides different types and sizes of parks, as well as arenas, playgrounds, and other facilities. Other areas of recreational land provide space for theatres, sports stadiums, libraries, and museums, where people enjoy entertainment in their leisure time.

Many groups of young people use local arenas for hockey games and practices. Here a group of young players enjoys an exciting game on the ice.

1. a) On the sketch map you have made of your town/city, show and label the closest recreation facility to your home that you might use for each of the following activities:

- hockey
- swimming
- boating
- tennis
- bowling
- basketball
- golf
- fitness training

b) Which of these facilities are paid for out of tax dollars? Which are privately owned?

2. In every community conflicts arise over the use of some of the land. Suppose that a proposal has been made in your community to convert prime industrial land to a high-density housing development; or to locate a large sports complex close to a quiet residential area; or to trade public waterfront land for an old railway right of way that could be used for a cross-country ski trail. The federal or provincial government, local developers, your local Council, and residents of your community all have an interest in the proposal.
a) Conduct a ''public meeting'' at which ''representatives'' of all these groups have a chance to express their views about the proposal.
b) As a reporter of the local paper present at the public meeting, write a news article that reviews the arguments put forward at the meeting.
c) As the editor of the local paper, write an editorial commenting on the proposal and its likely effects on the community.

Schoolyards and local parks often provide neighbourhood children with playground equipment for exercise and entertainment.

179

Commercial Land Uses

Commercial strip (ribbon) development along a major road offers the driving public easy access to such commercial firms as fast-food outlets, automobile service stations, and supermarkets.

The CBD of a city like Winnipeg is usually located where major roads meet, near the point of original settlement.

Pedestrian street mall in Calgary, Alberta

The submarine amusement area of the indoor West Edmonton Mall attracts people to the shops nearby.

The largest mall in the world, the West Edmonton Mall, draws over forty percent of its shoppers from outside Alberta. It attracts people by its size and the variety of its services.

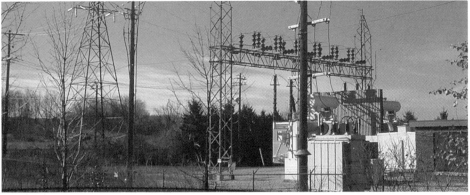

At this transformer station, high-voltage electricity from a nearby generating station is reduced to a lower voltage for municipal use.

UTILITIES

The *utilities* and services that cities provide are often taken for granted. Only on the rare occasion when one of them fails do we suddenly realize how difficult city life would be without them. How would it change your family's life if your home were not supplied with plentiful, clean, safe water? After we pollute water by using it in our homes, it is carried out of our neighbourhood as waste into sewers. In most cities, waste water and sewage are treated before being released back into the environment.

Electricity and natural gas are sources of energy that are distributed to most urban homes in Canada. The electric generating stations are usually within a few hundred kilometres of the town or city they serve, but the source of natural gas is often several thousand kilometres away, and the gas must be piped over great distances. The high voltage of electricity that travels over transmission lines on steel towers is reduced by a *transformer station* before being distributed to various parts of a town or city. Neighbourhood transformers further reduce the voltage for use in our homes. In older neighbourhoods, transformers are attached high up on poles along the street, but in newer subdivisions they are enclosed in metal boxes on the ground.

LOCAL STUDY

1. a) Find out from the public works department the source of water for your (nearest) town/city and the stages it passes through on the way to your home.
   b) On a street map or sketch map, draw and label the following items:
   - the main source of city/town water
   - the water treatment plant, if any, that filters the water and treats it for organisms and chemicals that could harm your health
   - the reservoir or water tower from which water is piped to your home

2. a) How much does the municipality pay for the water it takes from a lake, a river, or a well?
   b) Why, then, does the city charge consumers for the water that is used?

3. On a city/town map, find and mark the location of the sewage treatment plant and the stream or body of water into which the treated wastes are emptied.

4. a) On a map of your town or city, locate and label the major electric transmission lines closest to your home.
   b) Try to trace the route from the main electric transmission lines to your home and plot the route on your map. Show the transformer stations along the route.
   c) What electric generating stations are nearest to your town/city? What kind of generating stations are they?

5. a) In Canadian cities, people produce over 500 kg of garbage per person per year. Where does the city/town take the garbage picked up from your home for disposal?
   b) Mark this location on the map of your municipality, or mark an arrow where it leaves your community.
   c) How could the amount of garbage produced by your municipality be reduced?
   d) Suggest some ways in which your class/school could reduce garbage.

6. a) Mark on your map the fire station nearest your home. How far is it from your home?
   b) Mark the next nearest fire station. What is the approximate radius of the circular area each station seems to serve?

7. List three other services that a municipality provides for its citizens during the year.

8. What comforts and activities in your life would change if the services mentioned above were interrupted?

At this sewage treatment plant in Brantford, Ontario, waste sewer water is treated in the tanks shown here before it is emptied into the nearby Grand River.

181

Where Should Our Taxes Go?

I. City Politics: Sewers Not Circuses

"Dawsonville will never be a world-class city if it doesn't have a domed stadium." That's the sort of remark that civic leaders are making more and more these days. It's called city boosterism, and it comes in many shapes and sizes. Somehow, the belief has got about that if you don't have a domed stadium [or] theme park . . . you're accepting second-class status.

What has happened is that some politicians have forgotten what city government is all about. It's about sewers and street cleaning, garbage collection and policing, land use and housing. Not very exciting stuff. Excitement comes from trying to lure major-league sports to your city, or lobbying for a world's fair.

Today, the most popular item on the shopping lists of many civic leaders is the domed stadium. The boosters always claim that the dome will make money; no doubt about it. The truth is that domed stadiums usually lose money. The biggest and best dome is the 76 000-seat Superdome in New Orleans. It loses about $8 million a year, which is drawn from the deep pockets of Louisiana's taxpayers.

But a domed stadium is a very small affair compared with the granddaddy of events that only really serious city boosters go after: the Summer Olympic Games. Snare that one and you can let your chest swell with pride, secure in the knowledge that yours is now a truly world-class city.

Montréal landed the big one for 1976. Canadians were promised an Olympic Games that would run at a profit. It didn't quite work out that way. The debt was around $1.5 billion, and Montréalers will still be paying it off 18 years after the last race was run . . .

Toronto has decided it wants to be a world-class city, too. It's pitching for the 1996 Summer Olympic Games. The cost of just making the bid is estimated at $6.5 million. But this, according to the boosters, will come back to the city many times over. The Toronto Olympics will chalk up a profit of $56 million and bring a net benefit to southern Ontario of $2 billion. That's the promise. History suggests a different outcome.

Apart from the vast quantities of money that are wasted on spectacular events such as Expo 86 (estimated deficit $300 million) in Vancouver, the real tragedy of boosterism is that it diverts the energies and talents of people. Most cities have limited human resources. These should be applied, first and foremost, to solving human problems. When all the problems are solved, then peoples' energies could be turned to circuses.

But what city doesn't have a problem with the homeless? What city doesn't have old folks who need support services? What city has a good supply of low-cost housing? What city doesn't have pollution problems that need cleaning up? What city has streets that are totally free of crime? . . .

—Rupert J. Taylor,
"Circuses not Sewers" (Adapted)

II. SkyDome: A Family Affair

SkyDome will be a state-of-the-art facility sure to gladden the heart of anyone who has ever been soaked at a baseball game, snowed on at a football game, or half frozen at an outdoor concert. But it will be a good deal more than that. The Dome will be a symbol of civic vitality that is already linked to development and tourism in southern Ontario and will become even more so in years to come.

The Dome was planned to include a 364-room hotel, designed and built right into the north end of its structure, with 70 rooms overlooking the playing field; a three-level entertainment centre featuring indoor golf, computer games, a theatre, fast food outlets, fine restaurants, a health club, and special conference facilities.

So the Dome will draw people by the tens of thousands—to sporting events and concerts, as a tourist attraction unto itself, and as part of a rapidly changing downtown area.

During the construction phase, an estimated $258 million is being added to the province's gross domestic product, and the equivalent of more than 10 000 man-years of employment are being created. Once the stadium is up and running, it will contribute an estimated $326 million annually to the economy of Metropolitan Toronto and an additional $45 million annually to the Province of Ontario. Small wonder both the city and province had little hesitation kicking in $30 million each toward the Dome's $383-million budget.

"There are many benefits that will

grow out of the project," says Bob Hunter, vice-president (operations) of the SkyDome, "but the major impact will be on the number of jobs involved. For a major event we will need 2500 employees, including technicians and people to work in fast food concessions, restaurants, bars, and the hotel and health club."

Since SkyDome has the capacity to function year round, it could play host to a *plethora* of other events, everything from international soccer to tractor pulls to Super-Cross motorcycle racing. Aside from its initial attraction as the world's newest and most spectacular domed stadium, it will have enduring practical appeal as well. Out-of-town fans currently make up about 20 percent of the attendance at a Blue Jays game. SkyDome will make the Jays and the Argos even more attractive. Visitors will know that there will be no such thing as a rained-out game and that they will be comfortable in any weather.

Stadium Corporation officials are already in touch with the organizers of major trade shows and conventions too large for the Metro Convention Centre. The Alcoholics Anonymous convention scheduled for 1995, for example, is expected to attract 60 000 people, and Billy

Graham is planning a tour in the early 1990s. Dome officials have also forged a strong relationship with the management of the Convention Centre, and some events that are usually held there—such as the Home Show and the Toy Show—could spill over into the SkyDome. With this sort of overlap in mind, SkyDome officials plan to build a heated walkway between the two facilities. The close proximity of the structures may also generate inventive new uses for the facilities.

"Look at what happened at the Superdome in New Orleans and the Houston Astrodome," says Bill Duron, president of the Metropolitan Toronto Convention and Visitors Association. "New consumer shows have been created just to take advantage of the space."

The Dome has been touted as the newest and sexiest of many sights that draw people to Toronto. "From the standpoint of tourism," says Duron, "it's not just a stadium. It's a major attraction, and it will lure tourists from all over the world."

— *Financial Times*

1. a) In the Focus article about "city boosterism", what positive points does the author emphasize? In the article about Toronto's SkyDome, what positive points does the author emphasize?
b) How do the points of view of the two authors relate to each other?

2. a) Choose four items from each article that show some concerns authorities must keep in mind in making decisions about funding municipal/provincial projects.
b) You are a member of the provincial government. The municipal government of your province's capital city has applied for help in funding two new projects: construction of an affordable housing project for low-income families and development of a super-marina with facilities for world-class pleasure craft. The provincial budget will allow you to fund only one of these projects.

Form small committees with your "fellow members" to priorize the items you have chosen in part a) above.
c) Considering the priorities you have set, which project will you vote to fund? Be prepared to explain your decision to the press and public.

Of the many services that municipal governments provide for their citizens, garbage collection is perhaps the most visible because it takes place each week. Street cleaning and snow removal take place less often, and a visit from the fire department is a very rare occurrence.

Some large cities are facing a crisis because they have nowhere to put their garbage. One possible solution to this crisis is to incinerate wastes and use the resulting heat energy for industrial fuel.

MOVEMENT OF PEOPLE AND GOODS

The Myth of The North American City is the title of a book written by two Canadians, one an economist and the other a geographer. Authors Goldberg and Mercer claim that Canadian cities are quite different from American cities in several important ways. Canadians cities have:

- 50 percent more automobiles for every city dweller
- 25 percent more kilometres of expressway per person

- double the kilometres of public transit per capita
- more households with children in the centre of cities
- higher rates of immigration to the central city
- more attractive, livelier, and safer downtown areas (more offices, shops, entertainment centres, and people)
- more urban and regional planning
- less urban growth that sprawls out into rural areas

In any large city, people need to

move from their homes to places of work, to schools, to shopping areas, and downtown. This need creates a great demand for different forms of transportation.

Many people who live in the suburbs of large cities work downtown or in some part of the city beyond their own neighbourhood. They generally prefer to travel to work by private automobile. Unfortunately, there are so many motor vehicles in a large city that if they all travelled at the same time, the streets would become completely clogged. City governments try to relieve traffic congestion by building more multi-lane roads with traffic-light controls at major intersections. To find a better solution to traffic problems, "controlled-access" expressways are built with large intricate interchanges that allow the traffic to flow from one expressway to another without interruption.

Nearly three-quarters of the people who travel into downtown Toronto during rush hour come by public transit.

Some people become so frustrated with traffic congestion during rush hours and with the high cost of operating and parking an automobile that they prefer to use public transportation. Almost all cities provide bus service, and some of the larger ones have subways or other forms of rapid transit.

Nearly seventy-five percent of Canadian workers travel to their jobs by automobile (including car pools). Only 15 percent use public transit. The rest travel by other means, including walking.

There seems to be no single ideal way of moving people and goods, but city councillors, planners, and transportation experts have made many suggestions. Often their suggestions conflict. Here are a number of ideas that have been tried or suggested:

- Build more and larger expressways.
- Provide more buses.

An elaborate cloverleaf system of roadways is usually built where the traffic of two expressways meets. Unfortunately, such a system uses up much expensive land and creates waste space.

- Since a rapid transit line or subway can carry as many people as up to 15 lanes of expressway, build more subway lines.
- Provide "bus only" lanes on major roads.
- Stop building expressways, and soon traffic will be so congested that people will start to use public transit.
- Since most cars carry only the driver, encourage car pools by designating one of the expressway lanes for the use of cars carrying three or more passengers.

You have now completed a study of the major land uses, services, and means of transportation found in urban neighbourhoods and urban centres. Each type of land use creates its own unique kind of urban environment. There are also other types of land use that occupy smaller, more scattered sites. These include land used for churches, temples, or synagogues; day-care centres, schools, colleges, or universities; and military facilities, government offices, or service club buildings. These ways of using the land are often grouped together and classified as ***institutional land use***;

institutional properties are usually found scattered throughout the other land-use sections of the city. For example, educational buildings may be located anywhere from the downtown commercial districts, to the older residential neighbourhoods, to the newest suburban areas. Vacant lots and railway lines are also part of the land use of most communities. How well this mixture of land uses fits together in neighbourhoods and across the whole city partly determines the quality of life of the community's citizens.

1. Draw a sketch map to show how, without using a car, you would get from your home to your school, to your favourite shopping mall, and to the downtown core of your city.
2. a) Draw a sketch map to show how one person living in your home gets to work.
   b) Why does that person choose this method of transportation?
   c) What type of transportation do you and your family use most often to visit other parts of the city?

Public Transportation Vehicles

A Toronto streetcar

Light Rapid Transit (LRT) cars, Scarborough, Ontario

A GO transit train, serving Toronto and its satellite communities

Buses in Ottawa

Expressways, parking facilities, and service stations occupy 35 percent more land than that used by all types of public transit in Canada.

The Manitoba Legislature building, where the provincial government meets, is an example of institutional land use and a landmark in downtown Winnipeg.

3. Draw a design for an expressway interchange that would allow two four-lane expressways to cross each other without interrupting the flow of traffic. Make sure that the ramps in your interchange allow drivers coming from all directions to choose a route going in at least two other directions. Your diagram should show which roads go over and which go under the others.

4. a) Suggest three advantages for the people who take city buses to work.

   b) In spite of these advantages, why do some people prefer to use their automobiles?

   c) In your opinion, why do cities not provide frequent regular bus service on many of the streets in large suburban areas?

   d) What problems has a bus on downtown streets during rush hours?

Over 150 old postal, government, military, and bank buildings across Canada are protected by federal legislation as heritage sites.

WHAT LIES AHEAD?

THE URBAN FUTURE

Some geographers try to predict future trends in different matters relating to population characteristics. Although such estimates may not prove accurate, here is a list of what some futurists expect will happen in Canada by the year 2001. Compare these projections with the conditions in the mid-1980s that were described earlier in this chapter.

- Over eighty percent of Canada's 30 million people will live in urban areas.
- The greater Toronto and Montréal regions may each have populations of 6.0 million, followed by Vancouver with 2.0 million.
- The continuing expansion of population in the Windsor to Québec City heartland will occur mostly in the outlying parts of the Toronto CMA and around the smaller cities of southwestern Ontario; urbanization will overtake prime agricultural land at an even faster rate.
- A larger percentage of workers, 58 percent of whom might be female, will have jobs in tertiary services rather than in manufacturing industries; with automation, more work will be done in less time, and the average work week will be shortened to 25 hours.
- Faster, high tech transportation and communication systems should create a better-integrated network for air, highway, and mass transit traffic; existing subway or elevated light rapid transit systems will be expanded, or new ones will be constructed in many cities.
- An aging urban population will require more affordable housing and health care facilities.
- More immigrants will make cities more culturally interesting and cosmopolitan.
- More people will participate in sports and use outdoor recreation facilities as a result of the increased leisure time of both working and retired people.

If only some of these predictions are accurate, it will require careful planning to preserve the present quality of Canadian life in urban Canada.

REVIEW QUESTIONS

1. Why are Canada's population and the world population becoming increasingly urban?

2. Why do so many Canadians live in cities located in the Golden Horseshoe?

3. In your view, could a mini-heartland elsewhere in Canada begin to challenge the importance of the Windsor to Québec City corridor? If so, suggest two changes that might bring this about. Name a region that might offer a challenge, and give reasons for your choice.

4. Can services provide Canadians with even greater opportunities for employment in the future than they do at present? Explain your answer.

5. What transportation and telecommunication networks link the central places strung out along "mainstreet Canada"?

6. Why might transportation and communication links between heartland-hinterland centres become stronger or weaker than those between heartland places?

7. Suggest two advantages of motor vehicles as a means of moving people and goods in large cities. Suggest two disadvantages.

8. Name three different types of housing and locations in cities. Suggest two advantages of these different types and locations. Suggest two disadvantages.

Chapter Six

Water: Uses and Abuses

Surplus or Scarcity?

- ''Canada has more fresh water per capita than any other country''
- ''Canada will face water supply crisis before end of century''

These two headlines appeared in a Canadian newspaper in the same year. How can they both be right?

Montmorency Falls, Québec

A VALUABLE RESOURCE

In this chapter we look at Canada's freshwater resources: what they are and how important they are, and how we have used and abused them.

Water is one of our most valuable resources. All plants, animals, fish, and insects depend on water for their survival. As you answer the following questions, you will see how important water is to human beings.

---

1. Make a list of at least six ways you and your family use water in your home.
2. Tell why water is important to the following undertakings:
   a) livestock farming
   b) growing crops in dry regions
   c) the manufacture of steel, paper, and any two other products
   d) the production of electricity
   e) the transportation of bulky cargoes
   f) commercial and sport fishing
   g) recreational activities
   h) cleanliness
3. Calculate the amount of water that you use at school in one day. Time your drinking and handwashing and record them in a notebook. Record also the number of times that you flush the toilet. As a class measure the amount of water that flows from a fountain and from a sink faucet in 10 seconds. Use these measurements to calculate the amount of water you use every time you drink or wash. Measure also the amount of water used per flush (that is, the amount a toilet tank contains). At the end of the day add together all of the separate amounts that you have recorded. This will give you your total daily school consumption. Calculate how much water the whole class uses in one day. Make a three-

dimensional chart to illustrate the total. You can do this by collecting empty coffee creamers and letting one creamer represent four litres. Think of ways to reduce the amount of water you use.

THE WATER CYCLE

Water that is available for human use is always on the move (Figure 6.1). It falls from clouds as rain or snow on land and sea. Some of the *precipitation* that falls on land runs off. Passing through lakes, streams, and rivers, it finally reaches the ocean. The rest soaks into the ground. Some of the water that goes into the ground remains in the soil and subsoil, where it is used by plants. If there is enough precipitation, some water moves underground through layers of sand and gravel or porous rock to feed

streams and lakes. Some of the underground water percolates deep, where it may remain until someone digs or drills a well to tap this source. If the land is near a seacoast, some of this *ground water* slowly works its way into the ocean.

As soon as precipitation reaches the surface, it starts making its way back up into the atmosphere. Some of it *evaporates* directly from the land and water surface. Plants begin at once to use any water that reaches them. Later they give off vast amounts of moisture into the atmosphere through a process called *transpiration*. The moisture released by evaporation and transpiration forms clouds. The clouds later return the moisture to earth, completing the water cycle.

Human actions often affect the movement of water in the water cycle. When forests are cut, water runs off the land more rapidly, and less water soaks into the ground. Water *run-off* increases even more when we build cities, where rain water quickly runs off roofs and paved surfaces. This

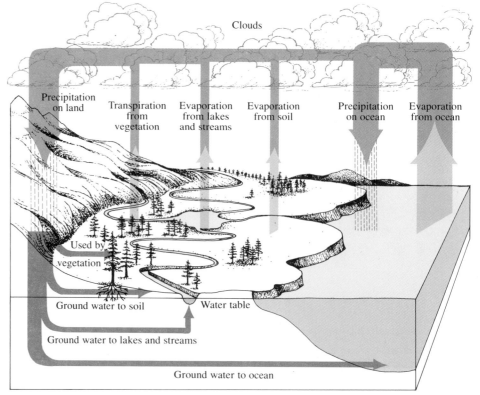

Figure 6.1 *The Water Cycle*

increased run-off often has drastic results. Rapid run-off decreases the supply of ground water for plants, animals, and people. It also causes rivers to flood during wet periods and streams to run dry during droughts. The following activities may make you even more aware of how much our actions alter the water cycle.

1. What happens to precipitation that falls on rooftops, streets, and parking lots? Where does it go from there? Compare its course with what happens to rain that falls on grass or treed areas.

2. Estimate the proportion of your schoolyard that is covered with asphalt or other material that water cannot penetrate. Do the same for the lot on which your home is located, and for a downtown block in your city or town (or the nearest city or town). How do these surfaces limit the amount of water available for human use in each of these areas?

3. From topographic and other maps of the general area where you live, sketch a map of local drainage patterns. Show the location of the main rivers, streams, lakes, and wetlands. Place arrows on all the bodies of water to show the direction in which the water is moving. (Even a lake, which seems to contain still water, actually has some slow movement of water from points where streams flow into it toward the points where other streams flow out.)

4. On the same sketch map, use different colours to show forested areas, parks with trees and grass, farm cropland, and built-up urban areas. Make a rough estimate of the proportion of the total area taken up by each of these kinds of land use. Make a general statement about the ways human activity in your area has interfered with the natural water cycle.

An urban area of high run-off

A rural landscape.   In rural areas much of the rain water soaks into the ground.

CANADA'S WATER RESOURCES

The total amount of water on the earth has remained almost unchanged since the early days of the planet's history. Most of this water is sea water, too salty for our needs. Fresh water makes up less than three percent of all the world's water, and most of that small proportion is not available for human use. Most of the world's fresh water is locked up in polar ice caps or lies deep underground beyond our reach. The available fresh water is stored in lakes and wetlands, and in the ground not far below the surface.

LAKES AND WETLANDS

Canada possesses a very generous share of the world's available fresh water. Though Canada has only *one* percent of the world's population, it has *nine* percent of the fresh surface water supply. Much of this water is stored in lakes and wetlands such as *bogs*, *swamps*, *marshes*, and *sloughs*. These lakes and wetlands cover about twenty percent of Canada's surface. The list of Canadian lakes in Table 6.1 includes only the largest; you will find many thousands more on a large-scale map of Canada.

Table 6.1 *Large Canadian Lakes (Lakes covering more than 2000 km²)*

Lake	Area (km²)
Superior*	84 500
Huron*	63 500
Great Bear	31 400
Great Slave	28 400
Erie*	25 800
Winnipeg	24 400
Ontario*	19 300
Athabasca	7 940
Reindeer	6 640
Nettilling	5 530
Winnipegosis	5 360
Nipigon	4 850
Manitoba	4 630
Lake of the Woods	4 340
Dubawnt	3 830
Amadjuak	3 120
Melville	3 060
Wollaston	2 290
Nueltin	2 280
Mistassini	2 340
Southern Indian	2 250
Michikamau	2 030

Source: The Inquiry on Federal Water Policy, *Currents of Change, Final Report*, 1985
Note: These Great Lakes are shared with the United States.

1. Locate in an atlas the lakes named in Table 6.1. Mark them on an outline map of Canada.
2. On your outline map, mark the southern edge of the Canadian Shield. Which of these lakes lie within (or partly within) the Canadian Shield?
3. Which provinces have none of the lakes listed in Table 6.1? Use your atlas to find the single largest lake in all of these provinces.

RIVER FLOW

Lakes and wetlands are important reservoirs. They store water, but by themselves they are not *renewable resources*. If a lake is drained, it stays dry until it is filled again by rivers that empty into it. For this reason, the number and size of lakes do not provide a good measurement of our renewable water supplies. A much better measurement is river flow.

River flow depends on the amount of water run-off resulting from precipitation. As you would expect, the highest amount of water run-off in Canada occurs in British Columbia, where the precipitation is highest (Figure 6.2). Run-off rates are lowest in the southern prairie region, where there is much less precipitation. In this region there is no run-off at all in many years; the precipitation either evaporates or soaks into the ground. The volume of the river flow in any area is very difficult to measure because it varies from day to day and from month to month. The river flow data provided in Figure 6.3 (page 194) have been obtained by:
a) averaging the daily flows for a month
b) averaging the monthly averages for a year
c) averaging the annual averages for a number of years

1. Why is river flow a better measurement of renewable water supply than the number and size of lakes and wetlands?
2. Compare the map showing run-off (Figure 6.2) with the map in Chapter Two showing precipitation (Figure 2.12). Draw a general conclusion from this comparison.
3. Using an atlas and Figures 6.2 and 6.3, provide the following information:
   a) Name the two river systems in Canada with the largest average annual flow. Which of these two would have the steadiest flow throughout the year? Why?
   b) Name the major tributaries of the Mackenzie River. Trace each tributary to its source. Explain the large volume of flow of the Mackenzie River.
   c) Name the major rivers that drain into the Arctic Ocean and Hudson and James bays. Comment on the density of population in the area drained by these rivers (Figure 3.16). Roughly what proportion of the flow of all the rivers shown in Figure 6.3 do the northern rivers represent?
   d) Name the rivers of British Columbia that drain into the Pacific Ocean. Which ones have their source in Canada but flow through the United States to the ocean? How might an international problem arise from this fact of physical geography?
   e) Name the river that flows through Canada's largest dry region. Where is its source? What tributaries from a nearby river could be diverted into this river to provide more water flow for this dry region?
   f) Name all the rivers that flow into Lake Winnipeg (including some not shown in Figure 6.3). Which of these rivers rise in the United States? Name two activities in the United States that could affect the supply and quality of water in Lake Winnipeg.
   g) Using the scale for river flow in Figure 6.3, calculate the combined average flow of the rivers that empty into James Bay. How does this compare with the flow of the St. Lawrence River at the point where it leaves Lake Ontario?

RELIABILITY OF RIVER FLOW

Figure 6.3 shows the *average* annual river flow. The *actual* amount of flow in any year may vary greatly from the average. In a year of heavy precipitation, the flow will be high. In a year of light precipitation, the flow will be low. River flow varies much more widely in a dry region such as the prairies because precipitation there

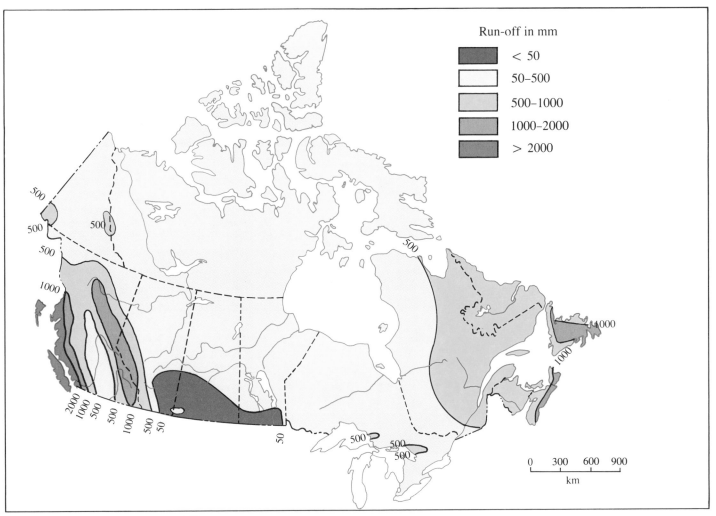

Figure 6.2 *Mean Annual Run-Off*

varies greatly from year to year. Annual flow is most reliable in a region with reliable precipitation from year to year.

A river flow from year to year is more likely to be steady, too, if a **drainage basin** has a number of lakes. In an area without lakes, heavy rain increases river flow immediately, and lack of rain causes rivers to shrink. By contrast, lake areas store vast quantities of water. The water levels of lake reservoirs rise slowly and go down slowly. A rise in the level of lake water will increase the flow of the rivers that depend on that lake; a fall in the lake's water level will decrease river flow. Two years of heavy rain may be needed to raise a lake's level enough to cause a significant increase in water to its rivers. A two-year drought

A spring flood. In spring an overabundance of meltwater causes flooding.

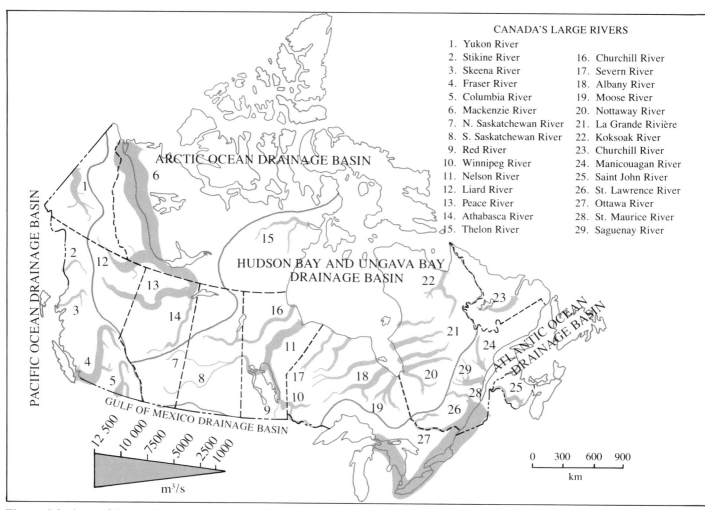

Figure 6.3 *Annual Large-River Flow in Canada*
Source of river flow data: The Inquiry on Federal Water Policy, *Currents of Change, Final Report*, 1985

CANADA'S LARGE RIVERS

1. Yukon River
2. Stikine River
3. Skeena River
4. Fraser River
5. Columbia River
6. Mackenzie River
7. N. Saskatchewan River
8. S. Saskatchewan River
9. Red River
10. Winnipeg River
11. Nelson River
12. Liard River
13. Peace River
14. Athabasca River
15. Thelon River
16. Churchill River
17. Severn River
18. Albany River
19. Moose River
20. Nottaway River
21. La Grande Rivière
22. Koksoak River
23. Churchill River
24. Manicouagan River
25. Saint John River
26. St. Lawrence River
27. Ottawa River
28. St. Maurice River
29. Saguenay River

would be required to lower the lake and cut off river water. The Great Lakes region is an example. Here one dry year will not immediately lower lake levels and reduce river flow. If the dry year happens to be followed by a wet year, the lake levels and the flow of connecting rivers will remain fairly stable. It takes several wet or dry years in a row to make much change in the river flow of the Great Lakes water system.

The changes in river flow from season to season are greater than those that occur from year to year. Some rivers have so much water in the spring that they overflow their banks, but in summer they shrink to a trickle. Such rivers are not a very reliable water source. For this reason the average annual flow data in Figure 6.3 are

not an accurate guide to usable water resources. The data promise more than our rivers deliver. Say, for example, that River A has an annual flow of 12 500 cubic metres per second (m³/s). This figure is based on averages for each of the 12 months. But during the spring months River A's flow was 25 000 m³/s, while in summer it was only 5000 m³/s. The spring floods brought more water than was wanted; the low supply in summer was not enough. The amount of usable water provided by River A throughout the year was certainly less than a steady flow of 12 500 m³/s. Canada's usable water resources, then, are less than the total average annual flow of all its rivers.

The great seasonal fluctuations of Canadian river flow cause two major

A summer trickle. In summer stream flow is often reduced to a trickle.

194

problems: in some seasons, there is too much water; in others, too little. Water accumulates during the winter as snow and ice. In spring, the meltwater surges down the *river channels* and spills out over the *flood plains*. This flooding sometimes damages personal property and may even cause loss of life. In summer, when the need for water is greatest, the rivers are at their lowest level. Our seasonal problems of flooding and drought are partly our own fault. We have increased flooding by clearing the land of forests, by draining wetlands, and by building cities. In doing so, we have interfered with the natural process that created the flood plain over thousands of years. Forests soak up much of the rainfall and slow down the melting of snow in spring. Wetlands store spring run-off water and then release it slowly in the dry summer season. When we cut the forests and drain the swamps, we let the rainfall run off quickly instead of soaking into the ground. We have made matters even worse for ourselves by building many of our cities and towns on the very plains where the flooding occurs. In these cities the rain runs off roofs and asphalt surfaces, and rushes to the rivers through storm sewers, adding to the damage of flood season.

It is clear that people have reduced summer water supply and increased flooding by interfering with the water cycle.

Flood damage.   Because we have built on flood plains, spring flooding can cause a great deal of damage.

A river channel and flood plain.   The flat flood plains along river channels are created by repeated flooding over thousands of years.

1. Explain in your own words why Canada's supply of renewable water resources is not as great as the river flow data in Figure 6.3 suggest.
2. Check back issues of your local newspaper for stories about summer drought and spring floods in your region. Explain why your local area has both floods and drought.
3. a) Observe a local stream or river over the school year, and record the following information:
   - the difference in depth between early spring and late June
   - the number of times it overflowed its channel onto the flood plain
   - variations in the appearance of the water (clear, muddy, algae accumulation)

   b) Make a general statement about the usefulness of the stream/river for water supply.
4. Locate a wetland near you, and construct a scale model of a part of it. To make your model accurate, get information from a local conservation authority, parks commission, or your province's Department of Natural Resources.

GROUND WATER SUPPLY

Below the surface of the earth lies a large amount of water called ground water (Figure 6.4). Ground water comes from precipitation that has soaked through the ground until it reaches the *water table*. All earth materials below the water table are saturated with water. Underground layers of sand or gravel or very porous rock in which water moves freely are called an *aquifer*. Ground water in aquifers supplies wells, and feeds streams and lakes. Water obtained from aquifers is sometimes called spring water. Most rural areas and many towns and cities obtain their water from wells deep enough to be fed by aquifers. About thirty percent of Canada's population uses ground water for domestic purposes.

Ground water has some advantages over surface water. The supply of ground water is more reliable from season to season and year to year. Ground water remains at a constantly cool temperature all year. It is less likely to be polluted than surface water because it is cleansed of many impurities as it soaks through hundreds of feet of soil and rock. One disadvantage of ground water is that it often contains considerable amounts of dissolved minerals such as calcium, magnesium, and iron. These minerals prevent soap from forming suds when the water is used for bathing or for washing dishes. Water that has too many minerals to be used for washing is said to be hard.

Hard water costs users more because softening it is expensive.

In heavily populated areas such as southern Ontario, the ground water supply is gradually being depleted. Every year we pump more water out of the aquifers, and as the water table drops, we drill even deeper wells. At the same time, we have been reducing the amount of *ground water recharge* by clearing forests, draining swamps, using farming methods that increase run-off, and covering land with buildings and asphalt.

Ground water supply is said to be like a bank account: if you withdraw more than you deposit, your balance drops.

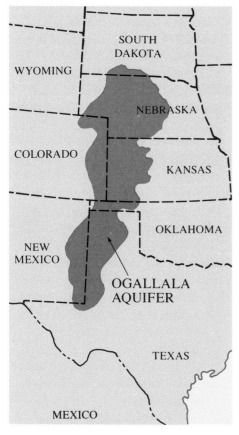

The water in the Ogallala Aquifer, the largest aquifer in the world, is going down. U.S. farmers who need this water for their irrigation think they know the source of a refill. They want to replenish their aquifer with water from the Great Lakes.

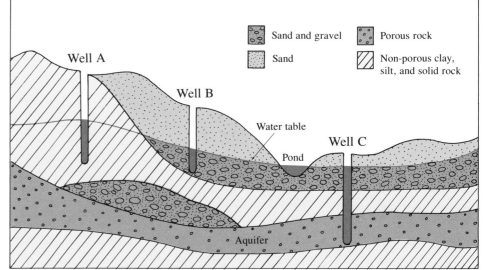

Figure 6.4 *Ground Water Supplies* *Earth materials below the water table are saturated with water, but only the water in an aquifer will flow freely into a well.*

LOCAL STUDY

1. a) If your municipality depends on ground water, write a class letter to municipal officials, asking the following questions:

i) Where are the wells, and how deep are they?

ii) Over the last 10 years, have new wells been drilled farther from the city? Have old wells had to be deepened?

iii) Have farmers complained that the water table has been lowered, and that their wells have gone dry? If so, what has been done to solve this problem?

b) Discuss in class the answers you receive to your questions. Suggest how you think the answers might relate to water supplies and water policy in your community.

Uses of Water

Cooling in nuclear plants

Drinking

Transportation

Irrigation

Fishing

Swimming

1. Consider Figure 6.4 to find answers to the following questions:
   a) Why would Well A not produce water?
   b) If the water table dropped, which would go dry first, Well B or the pond?
   c) If the water table dropped so that Well B became dry, how could the well's water supply be maintained?
   d) Suppose that the water table dropped so much that Well C became dry. Why would deepening the well not solve the problem?
2. Make a chart to show the advantages and disadvantages to a town or city of using ground water and surface water (lakes and rivers) to supply their needs. Which would you prefer for household use? Why?

DIFFERENT KINDS OF WATER USES

People can use water without consuming it (using it up). You do not consume any water by going for a swim in a lake. Nor does transportation by boat consume any water. Even when water is removed (or withdrawn) from a lake or river, it is not always consumed. For example, water that is removed from a lake to use in some industrial cooling process and is then returned to the lake, is not consumed. Swimming, boating, and cooling are considered *non-consumptive* water uses.

Some water drawn from natural sources is actually consumed: that is, less water than was removed (or no water at all) is returned to the source. Such *consumptive* uses of water reduce the water supply for other uses.

Irrigation of farmland is one example of consumptive use of water. Irrigation water removed from a lake or stream soaks into the ground or evaporates, or is used up by growing crops. None of it is returned directly to the original water source so that other uses can be made of it.

Figure 6.5 shows the major uses of withdrawn water in Canada and the proportion consumed in each use. Note that most withdrawn water is used for generating thermal electricity and for manufacturing goods. The highest proportion of consumption—nearly half of all the water consumed—relates to water used for farming. Farming consumes a large amount of water for irrigation. In Canada the relation between the consumptive and non-consumptive uses of water differs greatly from region to region (Table 6.2).

1. List five consumptive uses of water and five non-consumptive uses.
2. Construct a bar graph based on the data in Table 6.2. Use Figure 6.5 as a model. Place the names of the regions along the horizontal axis; place the volumes of water used along the vertical axis. Shade in the portion of each bar that represents the amount of consumed water.

3. a) Explain why Ontario withdraws more water than any other region of Canada. (Clue: consider both population and major economic uses of water.)
   b) Explain why the Prairie Provinces consume more of their available water supply than any other region of Canada. (Clue: consider both amount of precipitation and major uses of water.)
4. For each region in Canada, obtain the most recent population, and calculate the per capita consumption of water and the per capita total withdrawal. How does the rank order of regions change when consumption and withdrawal of water are based on per capita data?

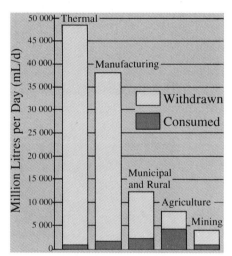

Figure 6.5 *Water Use in Canada*

Table 6.2 *Water Use by Region*

Region	Consumptive Uses (mL/d)*	Non-Consumptive Uses (mL/d)*	Total Withdrawal (mL/d)*
Atlantic	500	14 400	14 900
Québec	1 100	14 500	15 600
Ontario	2 100	53 300	55 400
Prairie Provinces	4 100	12 300	16 400
British Columbia	1 400	8 000	9 400
Total Canada	9 200	102 500	111 700

Source: The Inquiry on Federal Water Policy, *Currents of Change, Final Report*, 1985
*million litres per day

WATER QUALITY

The first European settlers in Canada found plenty of fresh water. The water in streams and lakes was pure enough to drink without treatment. Even in midsummer, streams provided plenty of clean, cool water. Shallow wells or natural springs supplied by a high water table were also a source of pure water. It is no wonder that early settlers thought Canada's supply of pure water was unlimited and would last forever.

What a contrast we find today! Many of our streams and rivers flood their banks in spring, but by midsummer they shrink to trickles of water connecting a few stagnant pools. Most of the water we now have is no longer clean. We have dumped so much sewage and so many chemicals into our rivers and lakes that it is difficult to purify the water enough to drink. Many lakes are so polluted that their beaches are closed for swimming in midsummer. Even some well water is not safe to drink because pollutants have seeped into the ground water.

As Figure 6.5 and Table 6.2 show, much water is withdrawn without being consumed, and it often returns to the original water source. The returned water, however, is not as pure as the water that was withdrawn. Water used for producing thermal electricity or for industrial cooling returns to its source at a much higher temperature and so has a negative effect on fish life. The water returned to its source by industries and municipalities contains a wide variety of pollutants.

There are many kinds of water pollution. Three of the main types, which we shall now consider, are nutrient pollution, toxic chemical pollution, and acid rain.

NUTRIENT POLLUTION

Chemicals such as nitrogen, potash, and phosphorus are found in human waste, animal manure, and artificial fertilizers. For plants, these chemicals are nutrients required for growth. Nutrients are not directly harmful to human beings, but when too many of them get into a water supply, they cause serious pollution problems.

When a lake or stream becomes rich in nutrients, it supports the rapid growth of plants like algae and milfoil weed. As the algae and milfoil die, they settle to the bottom and decay. The process of decay uses up large amounts of oxygen from the water. When the water's oxygen level becomes too low, fish die.

In the 1960s, Canadians became aware that nutrient pollution could seriously harm lakes, even those as large as the Great Lakes. Lake Erie provided a prime example. Along the shores of the lake, the algae grew so thick that people were reluctant to swim or go boating in the water. Many of the more valuable fish species began to die out, and both sport and commercial fishing began to decline. Many people called Lake Erie a dying lake.

Since the 1960s, nutrient pollution in the Great Lakes has been greatly reduced. When phosphorus was found to be a major nutrient pollutant, Canada and the United States co-operated to reduce the amount of phosphorus entering the Great Lakes. Because there are so many more people on the U.S. side of the Great Lakes than there are on the Canadian side, both nations must co-operate to improve the water quality. In both countries governments banned the use of phosphorus in dishwashing and laundry detergents. Senior governments helped municipalities to finance costly sewage treatment plants. As a result, the amount of phosphorus entering the Great Lakes from municipal sources dropped sharply in little more than a decade. In Lake Erie, the amount of phosphorus from municipal sources declined from over 15 000 tonnes a year in 1972 to under 2000 t a year in 1985 (Figure 6.6). Lake Erie is reviving.

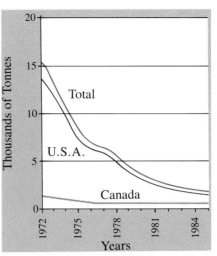

Figure 6.6 *Phosphorus Entering Lake Erie from Municipal Sources* This graph illustrates how pollution can be reduced when governments decide to take joint action.

If the polluting of Lake Ontario stopped tomorrow, the chemicals now in the lake would remain in its water for several decades.

Sport fish are thriving again, the commercial fishing industry is making a comeback, and many beaches have been re-opened for swimming.

Canada has not yet solved the problem of nutrient pollution. Some parts of our country are still discharging much of their municipal sewage, untreated, into lakes and rivers (Table 6.3, page 200). Until the 1980s, Québec dumped most of its sewage, untreated, into the St. Lawrence River. Now, however, Québec has begun a major sewage control program. Still, in the 1990s, only a little over half of Canada's urban population is served by any kind of sewage treatment. Many municipalities provide only ***primary sewage treatment***, which removes only the larger particles and most of the solids suspended in the liquid. The federal and provincial governments are pressuring municipalities to move to ***secondary sewage treatment***, which uses bacteria to "eat" dissolved solids and then removes the bacteria. The ideal is ***tertiary sewage treatment*** or "final effluent polishing''. This process is similar to the treatment of drinking water: it removes all impurities, including toxic chemicals, from sewage.

One serious source of nutrient pollution lies outside the towns and cities: fertilizers used on farms. The crops use up much of the animal manure and artificial fertilizer spread on farmland, but they do not use it all. Streams and lakes also receive large doses in rain run-off. To prevent this pollution will not be easy. It may involve changing the farming practices of hundreds of thousands of farmers.

At least 800 different toxic substances have been identified in the waters of the Great Lakes.

A modern sewage treatment plant in Montréal

Answer the following questions, using the data recorded in Table 6.3.

1. Suggest why the Prairie Provinces have a high percentage of population served by sewage treatment. (Clue: Note prairie river flow.)
2. Which province provides the most sewage treatment for the largest number of people?
3. Why have the governments of Québec not considered it necessary to provide as much sewage treatment as do other provinces? (Clues: Note the volume of flow of the St. Lawrence River at Montréal and the size of the body of water into which that river empties.)
4. How could dumping untreated sewage into the St. Lawrence River affect the shell fish industry of the Maritime Provinces?

TOXIC CHEMICAL POLLUTION

Most of the roughly 100 000 chemicals used in Canada today (a number that rises by about 1000 each year) could pollute our water supply. Of particular concern among chemical pollutants are the *toxic chemicals* discharged into water supplies. These are the chemicals that once taken in by plants or animals, become locked into the *food chain*. For example, toxics such as polychlorinated biphenyls (PCBs) or dioxins might get into the food of small fish; the small fish, in turn, are a food supply for large fish. The more of these small fish a large fish eats, the more the chemical builds up in its flesh. When a person eats the large fish, the chemical it contains is transferred to that person's body. The more fish a person eats, the more that chemical builds up. Some drinking water is also polluted with toxic chemicals. (Most sewage treatment plants do not remove these chemicals.) A mother suckling her infant may be passing on dangerous chemicals that can build up in her baby's body. Recent studies have shown that polluted fish and water taken by the mother may indirectly kill her infant. Mothers' milk was found to contain up to one million times as many PCBs as polluted lake water. Such toxic chemicals can cause cancer and other illnesses, and even immediate death by poisoning.

Modern industry produces large quantities of toxic chemicals. Such chemicals are produced, for example, in oil refineries, mining smelters, and pulp and paper mills. These sources of pollution are easy to trace, and this makes it possible to enforce new laws that order such industries to stop discharging their chemicals into bodies of water.

Table 6.3 *Sewage Treatment Services Across Canada*

Province/Territory	Population Surveyed[a]	% with Sewage Treatment[b]
Alberta	1 852 700	99
Saskatchewan	611 000	99
Manitoba	839 200	95
Prince Edward Island	57 600	95
Yukon Territory	21 900	86
Ontario	7 641 600	84
British Columbia	2 175 800	78
New Brunswick	409 900	61
Northwest Territories	44 000	53
Nova Scotia	536 600	21
Newfoundland	497 000	13
Québec	6 685 400	6
Canada	21 372 700	57

Source: The Inquiry on Federal Water Policy, *Currents of Change, Final Report*, 1985
[a]Excludes village and rural population.
[b]Includes at least one of primary, secondary, or tertiary treatment.

Hamilton's harbour. Heavy industry discharges pollutants into both air and water.

Agricultural pollution. Farmers use toxic chemicals to control crop diseases, insects, and weeds.

A polluted river. This part of the Fraser River estuary is polluted with débris and toxic chemicals.

Hamilton Harbour contains so many toxic chemicals that 40 percent of some fish species in it have cancerous tumours.

To prevent thousands of small industries from discharging toxic chemicals into sewers is a more difficult task. Each industry may discharge only a small amount of chemical pollution, but the total from all industries may be very great. These chemicals are usually more difficult to treat in municipal sewage facilities, and so they enter our streams and lakes. Some industries dump their toxic wastes in *landfill sites* or bury them in the earth. The toxic chemicals disposed of in both these ways seep through the earth into the ground water aquifers. Some provincial governments are providing leak-proof sites where toxic chemicals can be stored and destroyed without damaging the environment. But there are not enough of these waste management sites to hold all the toxic wastes produced.

Farmers and city gardeners are also responsible for toxic chemical pollution. Farmers use chemicals to control crop diseases and insects, and to kill weeds. City dwellers use chemicals on their lawns and gardens. Many of these toxic chemicals are carried by run-off into the streams and lakes that supply our water.

In many parts of Canada, toxic chemical pollution has made fish unsafe to eat and water unsafe to drink. The threat to our water supply is increasing. Modern technology is developing new chemical compounds at a very rapid rate. All of these life-threatening pollutants may some day end up in our water.

A joint Canadian-U.S. committee has discovered approximately 300 landfill sites, toxic waste dumps, and sewers that are leaking deadly chemicals into the Niagara River.

1. Why is toxic chemical pollution a more serious threat to human health than is nutrient pollution?
2. a) How do you think most people dispose of turpentine or other fluids used to clean out paint brushes? If they pour such fluids down a drain, where do the fluids

go? What other toxic substances in a home might be poured down drains?

b) Has your municipality special provision for disposing of toxic household substances? If so, what is it?

c) Design a poster to urge people to dispose of toxic substances safely.

3. Municipal councils claim that it would cost too much to remove all toxic pollutants from municipal sewage. Suggest two long-term costs of *not* removing toxic pollutants from sewage.

NIMBY stands for Not in My Back Yard, meaning close to somebody else's home but not mine. Everybody wants sanitary landfill sites and facilities to dispose of hazardous wastes. Nobody wants to live near them: the NIMBY syndrome.

Canada has no law setting national standards for our drinking water. The provinces, except for Québec, simply have guidelines. Québec has passed the only water standards legislation in the country.

ACID RAIN

Coal- or oil-burning thermal electric plants, smelters, and motor vehicles discharge *sulphur dioxide* (SO_2) and *nitrous oxides* (NO_x) into the air. These pollutants combine with moisture in the atmosphere to form sulphuric and nitrous acids, which fall to earth as acid rain. (Although precipitation in the form of snow may be just as acid, the popular term used by all the news media is 'acid rain'.)

In Canada, most of the sulphur dioxide emissions come from nickel and copper smelters in Northern Ontario and Québec, from iron and steel mills at Sault Ste. Marie and Hamilton, Ontario, and from various thermal electric power plants in southern Ontario. In the United States, the largest source of sulphur dioxide is in the upper Ohio valley (eastern Ohio, northern West Virginia, and western Pennsylvania), where high-sulphur coal is burned in thermal electric plants. In both countries large amounts of nitrous oxides are produced by the exhaust of cars and trucks. The general location of the sources of sulphur dioxide and nitrous oxides in eastern North America is shown in Figure 6.7.

Because of the general direction of storm tracks, most acid rain falls hundreds of kilometres east and north of the source of the pollution (Figure 6.8, page 204). This means that Canada receives acid rain not only from Canadian sources but also from sources in the United States. The greatest damage has been done to the lakes in the Canadian Shield and to some parts of the northeastern United States, where the soil and water are already slightly acid (Figure 6.8). In the late 1980s, an estimated 200 or more lakes in the Muskoka and Haliburton areas of Ontario were too acidic to support fish. Projections suggest that thousands of additional lakes may reach the same state of acidity by the turn of the century. Acid rain is also harming lakes in the Shield portion of Québec, in the Adirondacks and the New England States in the United States, and in parts of the Atlantic Provinces. Lakes in the Great Lakes-St. Lawrence Lowlands are not as much affected because the limestone bedrock tends to neutralize the acid. But farmers in both southern Ontario and Québec claim that acid rain is slowly killing their sugar maples, and so reducing their production of maple syrup.

The problem of acid rain is hard to solve. *Smokestack scrubbers*, needed to prevent the escape of the deadly gases, are expensive. If Ontario Hydro were ordered to stop all emissions of sulphur dioxide, the cost of electricity to Ontario industry and residents would rise sharply. For a mining company, the cost of eliminating sulphur dioxide might increase the cost of production so much that the company would no longer be able to compete in world markets. It might be forced to lay off large numbers of employees. Concerns like these help to explain why governments have been very slow to legislate control of acid rain.

But *not* controlling acid rain is clearly expensive too, even though the

---

L O C A L   S T U D Y

1. Has any beach in your region been closed in recent years because of pollution? What kind of pollution was it? What was the source of the pollution?

2. As a class project, obtain the following information from your municipal engineer or other appropriate municipal officers:

a) What proportion of the municipal sewage in your municipality is given primary, secondary, and tertiary treatment?

b) Sanitary sewers transport human and other wastes to treatment plants before releasing the sewage into a body of water. Storm sewers transport rain water directly into a body of water. Has your municipality a combined sanitary sewage and storm water sewage system? If so, how often is the system overloaded so that raw sewage is discharged directly into a river or lake along with the storm water?

c) If your municipality has a combined system, why does it not replace the system with a modern sewage system that separates the sanitary sewage from storm water?

cost is hard to measure. Acid rain damages forests, lakes and rivers, farm crops, and buildings made of stone. Losses to the farm and forest industries could total hundreds of millions of dollars. To lose the sport fishing done by tourists and Canadians on holiday could cost Canadian businesses millions of dollars each year. To reconstruct buildings damaged by acid rain is expensive.

Awareness of the dangers of acid rain has prompted some government action. In 1985, the Ontario government announced a program that requires all the major producers of acid rain to cut back by 60 percent in sulphur dioxide emissions by 1994. This cutback will reduce the acid rain by 14 percent in the Muskoka and Haliburton regions of Ontario, by 10 percent in Québec, and by four percent in the Maritime Provinces. In the United States it will also benefit the Adirondacks region and the New England States by reducing acid rain there.

Other provinces have also taken action against acid rain. Québec passed regulations to reduce emissions from a mining smelter that was Canada's second-largest single source of sulphur dioxide. These regulations provided for a 50 percent cut in the emissions by the end of 1989. The Atlantic Provinces and the New England States have jointly pledged to

Acid-producing smoke. Smoke from thermal electric plants and smelters contains large amounts of sulphur dioxide.

Automobile exhaust.
Exhaust from automobiles
contains nitrous oxides.

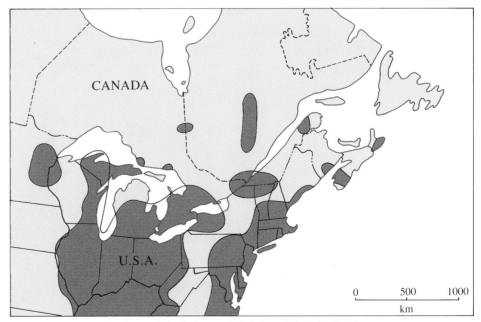

Figure 6.7 *Distribution of Emissions of Sulphur Dioxide (SO$_2$) and Nitrous Oxides (NO$_x$)*

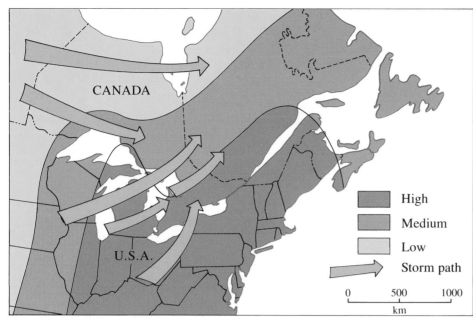

Figure 6.8 *Important Storm Tracks and Distribution of Acid Rain*

reduce sulphur dioxide emissions in their regions by 32 percent, by 1994. The federal government of the United States recently passed a Clean Air Bill which, by the year 2000, will force some of the country's worst offenders to reduce their emissions of sulphur dioxide.

Both Canada and the United States have legislated strict regulations about pollution control devices on automobiles. From 1990, the use of leaded was banned in Canada. This control is helping to reduce lead and nitrous oxide emissions.

Working together, Canada and the United States are studying the effects of acid rain and considering ways of controlling it. They realize that acid rain is a continental problem that cannot be solved in a piecemeal fashion. The solution requires the commitment and co-operation of all governments and all industries in North America. More action is needed—and soon. If we delay taking steps to eliminate acid rain, we may find that our efforts come too late.

---

1. a) Collect articles on acid rain from newspapers and magazines, and keep them in a clipping file in your classroom. On a bulletin board post some articles that deal with jobs lost because of the effects of acid rain.

   b) You with half the members of your class make up a team that represents workers in a factory. The factory is a major contributor to the acid rain problem. The other half of your class makes up a team that represents operators of recreational lodges in areas where lakes are dying from acid rain pollution. Discuss with members of your team the issues involved in trying to bring acid rain emissions under control. How does your team feel about threats to its members' livelihood? Then meet with the other team to try to suggest a solution that would benefit everyone.

2. Why is it impossible to solve the acid rain problem in Canada without the active co-operation of the United States?

3. You are a Senator from the State of Michigan. Why might you oppose legislation that banned the emission of all sulphur dioxide, effective immediately? Consider such questions as:

   a) Who would benefit most from such legislation (Figure 6.8)?

   b) Who would bear most of the costs?

   c) Do you think that Michigan electors would support you in the next election if you voted for the ban?

4. You are the Minister of Environment in the Ontario government. Develop a press release to explain why Ontario Hydro has not been required to put an end to its emission of sulphur dioxide.

5. You are an environmentalist trying to influence your provincial government to legislate against acid rain. What arguments will you use to convince the government that the cost of *not* banning pollution that causes acid rain will be greater in the long run?

6. How could greater use of public transit instead of private automobiles help reduce acid rain?

7. Design a pamphlet that Pollution Probe might use to persuade both the public and the controllers of industries to reduce acid rain.

MANAGING WATER RESOURCES

Canada has vast water resources, but in this land of plenty, serious water shortages exist. Some shortages occur simply because of a lack of water in a given place or at a given time. Others are caused by our polluting existing water supplies, and so making them useless.

From the days of early settlements, the grasslands region of the Prairie Provinces has suffered from periods of water shortage. The farmers were hard hit when little rain fell for a number of years in the 1930s and again in the 1980s. Today, even more water is needed in the developed Prairie Provinces for irrigation projects, agricultural processing, oil refining, and the petrochemical industry. This arid region consumes more water per capita than any other region in Canada. In the future, the demand for water will be even greater, to support such projects as deep-well injection to maintain pumping pressure in dwindling oil fields and oil sands developments.

Even southern Ontario, with its moderate precipitation and the closeness of the Great Lakes, is facing water shortages. Because of the concentration of cities and industries, the supply of useful water has decreased. The water table is being lowered, and the surface waters are being polluted so that municipalities are forced to restrict water use, especially in the dry summer months.

One out of every three people in Canada and one out of every seven in the United States depend on the Great Lakes for their water.

SUPPLY MANAGEMENT

The easiest point at which to start managing the supply of water is the place where the raindrop falls. Remember the statement at the beginning of this chapter that water is always on the move. To make the most use of precipitation, we must slow down its rush to the sea. Farmers do this when they follow such soil conservation practices as rotating crops, maintaining high organic content in the soil, and practising contour cultivating and planting. They do the same when they construct farm ponds and dams on small streams to store water so that it can be used before it escapes. Natural vegetation helps keep water on the land. Forest soils soak up water like a sponge, and wetlands are like reservoirs that release the water gradually.

In Ontario the provincial government has established a Conservation Authority for each *watershed* in the southern part of the province (Figure 6.9). These authorities plant trees,

preserve wetlands and wilderness areas, and build many small dams in the upper reaches of the river tributaries. In some places they have pumped water into gravel beds, where it soaks down and recharges the ground water

supply. They also co-operate with municipalities to prevent further building on the flood plain. And finally, with both federal and provincial aid, they have prevented spring flooding and increased the summer

A prairie slough drying up.   The water level in this slough in Saskatchewan dropped by one metre in the 1980s. Some prairie sloughs have dried up completely because of prolonged drought.

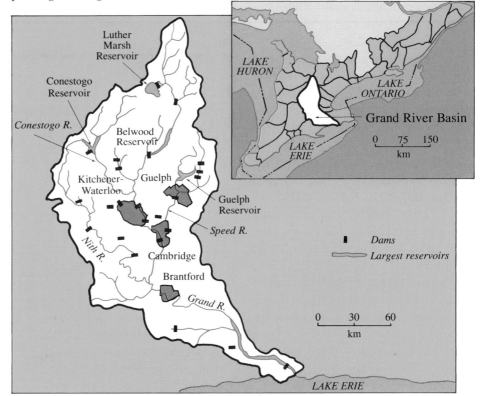

Figure 6.9 (Upper right) *Conservation Authority Watersheds;* (Left) *Control Dams and Reservoirs on the Grand River Watershed*

Conestogo Dam and reservoir on the Grand River, Ontario

stream flow by building large dams on the main river branches above cities.

In other parts of Canada, huge dams collect and store water in the high run-off season and release it when it is needed in the low run-off season. Two such mammoth dams are the Gardiner Dam in Saskatchewan and the LG2 Dam on La Grande Rivière in Québec. (La Grande Rivière project actually involves construction of four dams, LG1–LG4. Three have been built, and the fourth, LG1, will be finished in the 1990s. See Figure 6.10.) There are 51 other dams in Canada with at least as much storage capacity as each of these (Figure 6.11). Most of the largest dams have been constructed to create hydro-electric power. Some of these are also of value for irrigation, municipal water supplies, flood control, and recreation.

1. Using Figure 6.9:
   a) Name three major tributaries of the Grand River.
   b) The primary purpose of the largest reservoirs is to prevent floods. What other uses can be made of these reservoirs?
   c) Suggest why the largest reservoirs were built north of the City of Cambridge. Name the cities that they were built to protect from flooding.
   d) The City of Brantford obtains its water from the Grand River. Explain how the upstream dams help Brantford to obtain enough water in summer.

2. Conservation authorities were established in Ontario to manage water resources. Why have these authorities set up tree planting and soil conservation programs?

3. Use atlases and other reference books to do the following:
   a) For one dam in each of seven provinces shown in Figure 6.11, compose a table listing the name of the dam (or reservoir), the name of the river on which it is located, the body of water into which the river flows, and the major purpose(s) of the dam.
   b) Figure 6.11 shows only the very largest dams in Canada. There are hundreds of other large dams throughout the country, most of them in Newfoundland, Québec, Alberta, and British Columbia. As a class, add to a base map of Canada as many other dams as you can, in addition to those shown in Figure 6.11.

LG2 dam powerhouse (James Bay project) is the largest underground powerhouse in the world.

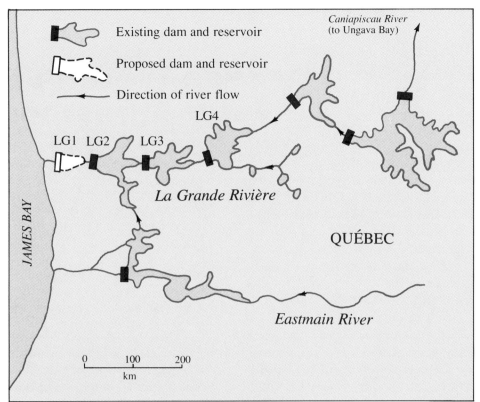

Figure 6.10 *Dams LG1–LG4 on La Grande Rivière*

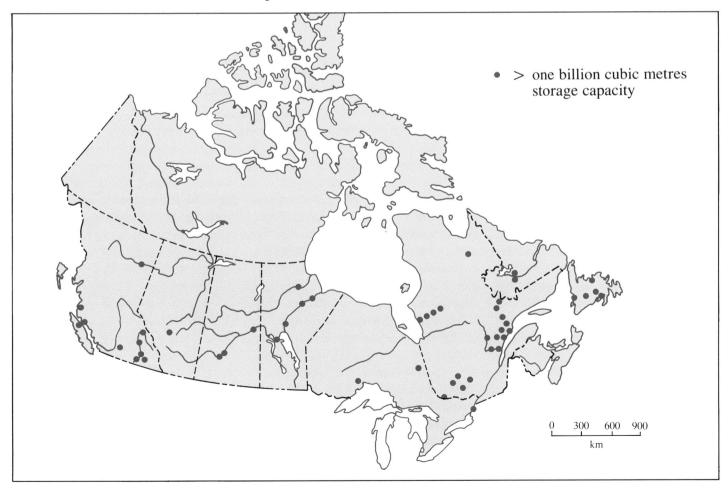

Figure 6.11 *Large Dams in Canada*

Canada-United States Water Agreements

There are several hundred waterways that either cross or mark the boundary between Canada and the United States. These waterways include major rivers such as the Columbia, Yukon, and Saint John, and the entire Great Lakes-St. Lawrence system. To manage these waters, Canada and the United States must work together.

The basic rules for guiding boundary water relations between the two countries were established in the Boundary Waters Treaty of 1909. This treaty includes the following points:

1. The upstream country has control over the use and diversion of water on its side of the boundary. However, the upstream country may not deprive the downstream country of the amount of water needed for established uses.

2. The downstream country may not construct dams that would flood the upstream country.

3. Boundary waters may not be polluted by either country to the degree that they cause injury to users in the other country.

4. Any development that would change the level of water along the boundary must be approved by the International Joint Commission (IJC).

The IJC has six members, three appointed by Canada and three by the United States. It is a kind of court that referees boundary water disputes. It also conducts studies and makes recommendations on questions referred to it by the two governments. It was an IJC study that led to the Great Lakes Water Quality Agreement in 1972, and its renewal in 1978 and 1987. The IJC also took part in the early negotiations for the Columbia River project and the negotiations that prevented Seattle from building a dam which would have flooded the scenic Skagit Valley in British Columbia.

In disputes, Canada is likely to get fairer treatment from the IJC than it might get in political negotiations between the Canadian and U.S. governments. Referring a disagreement to the IJC is like referring to a court of law to settle an argument between a small boy and a giant instead of letting them have a fist fight to see who wins.

WATER TRANSFER

In Canada dams have been used widely for another purpose: to transfer water from one *rivershed* to another. Figure 6.12 shows only a few of the largest transfer projects. All 54 Canadian water transfer projects added together would make a river flow almost equal to that of the St. Lawrence River. The primary use of the largest of these transfers is to produce hydro-electricity (Table 6.4).

There has not yet been any major transfer of water for general use, but there have been some grandiose proposals. One proposal called NAWAPA (North American Water and Power Alliance) would transfer water from the Yukon River to southern Canada, and even as far south as California. To carry out this scheme would be so expensive and would cause so much ecological damage that neither the Canadian nor the U.S. government has ever considered it seriously.

The Prairie Provinces did consider the possibility of transferring water from the Peace and Athabasca rivers (which finally flow into the Arctic Ocean) into the Saskatchewan River, to provide more water for the dry prairie region (Figure 6.13, page 211). This project was called PRIME (Prairie River Improvement Management and Evaluation). A study of the PRIME project disclosed that it would cost too much and do too much damage to the environment.

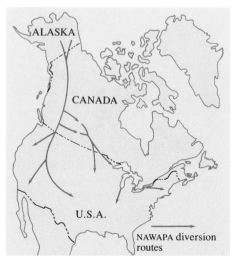

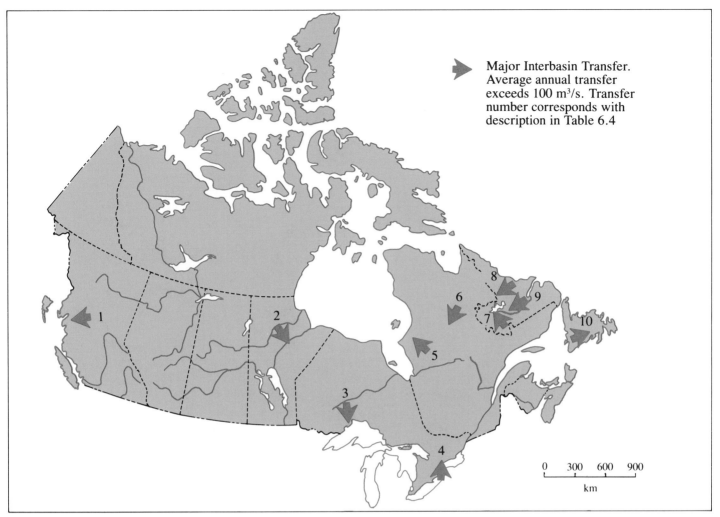

Figure 6.12 **Water Transfers in Canada**

Table 6.4 **Water Transfers in Canada**

No.[a]	Province	Project	Contributing River	Receiving River	Average Annual Transfer (m³/s)	Uses
1	B.C.	Kemano 1	Nechako (Fraser)	Kemano	102	Hydro
2	Man.	Churchill Diversion	Churchill (Southern Indian Lake)	Rat-Burntwood (Nelson)	752	Hydro
3	Ont.		Ogoki (Albany)	L. Nipigon (L. Superior)	120	Hydro
4	Ont.	Welland Canal	Lake Erie	Lake Ontario	250	Hydro/Navigation
5	Qué.	James Bay	Eastmain-Opinaca	La Grande	798	Hydro
6	Qué.	James Bay	Caniapiscau	La Grande	771	Hydro
7	Nfld.	Churchill Falls	Julian-Unknown	Churchill	196	Hydro
8	Nfld.	Churchill Falls	Naskaupi	Churchill	200	Hydro
9	Nfld.	Churchill Falls	Kanairiktok	Churchill	130	Hydro
10	Nfld.	Bay d'Espoir	Victoria, White Bear, Grey, and Salmon	Northwest Brook (Bay d'Espoir)	185	Hydro

[a]Numbers correspond to those in Figure 6.12.

Caribou Drowned at Limestone Falls

In the fall of 1984, about 10 000 caribou drowned at Limestone Falls on the Caniapiscau River, south of Ungava Bay in northern Québec. The caribou had been overwhelmed by an unusually strong current as they tried to swim the river. More than half of the water in the river where the caribou were swept over the falls had been suddenly released from the Caniapiscau reservoir upstream. The reservoir is part of the huge James Bay hydro-electric project in Québec. Its purpose is to divert water from the Caniapiscau and Koksoak rivers into La Grande Rivière. The accident that destroyed the caribou illustrates vividly how dams can damage the natural environment.

UNGAVA BAY

Koksoak River

Mélèzes River

Limestone Falls

Caniapiscau River

QUÉBEC

Caniapiscau Reservoir

Caribou drowned at Limestone Falls, Québec.

A Canadian engineer, Tom Kierans, has proposed a project that would transfer to the Great Lakes much of the water now flowing into James Bay. The water to be transferred would be about one-third of the amount now being discharged from the Great Lakes into the St. Lawrence River. Kierans has suggested that to build a dam across the mouth of James Bay would turn it into a freshwater lake. Its water could then be pumped through a canal that would follow the Harricana River valley until it reached the Ottawa River, and then be diverted into the Great Lakes through Lake Nipissing and the French River. This additional water could be used by Ontario and the States that border the Great Lakes; some of it could also be diverted to the Prairie Provinces and to the midwestern United States. Kierans calls his proposed project the GRAND Canal. GRAND stands for Great Recycling And Northern Development.

Kierans claims that his GRAND proposal offers the following benefits:
1. It would solve municipal water shortages in the Great Lakes region. An adequate water supply would attract more urban and industrial development.
2. It would increase the amount of hydro-electricity produced at

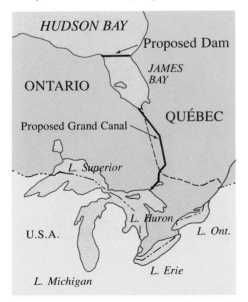

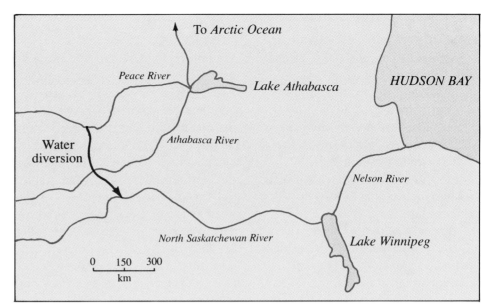

Figure 6.13 *Proposed Diversion of Water into the North Saskatchewan River*

power installations already in place on the Niagara and St. Lawrence rivers.
3. Deeper water in the connecting rivers and canals would allow more shipping tonnage to be moved through the Great Lakes.
4. A greater flow of water through the Great Lakes would give a greater capacity for diluting pollution.
5. Water could be provided for irrigation projects in the Prairie Provinces.
6. Vast quantities of water could be sold to the United States.

A number of serious objections have been raised to the GRAND Canal scheme:
1. Kierans has not assessed the social and economic cost of the environmental change. No study has tried to measure the likely impact of the development. Other major water transfer projects have caused serious environmental damage. The ecology of James Bay, the James Bay coastal zone, and the entire Harricana River would be disrupted. Fish and wildlife habitats would be harmed, causing a loss of food supplies for Native people. Such a massive transfer of water might even change the climate.
2. Pumping the water from James Bay

to Georgian Bay would require huge amounts of electric power. This power would be generated by hydro-electric or nuclear power plants. Both hydro-electric projects and *nuclear reactors* have serious environmental effects.
3. The GRAND Canal scheme would raise the levels of the Great Lakes. The raising of Great Lakes water by even a metre would flood the shoreline, causing damage that might amount to hundreds of millions of dollars.
4. Water transferred to the prairies would be very expensive. Prairie farmers could not afford to use such costly water for irrigation.
5. There is little chance that the United States would buy the water. The transfer cost would make it too expensive to use for irrigation.
6. The estimated cost of the project, approximately $1000 million, is too high. The investment capital would have to be raised by governments that already have problems with budget deficits.
7. Both in the United States and in Canada, other less expensive options are available. These include reducing pollution of existing water supplies and reducing the amount of water used.

1. Debate the following resolution: In the long run, the GRAND Canal project would be beneficial to Canadians.
2. Metropolitan Toronto has considered the possibility of piping water from Georgian Bay. Why would the municipal authorities consider such a project when their city is located on a major lake?
3. Write a brief to the Canadian government outlining options that should be pursued in place of major water transfers.

CONFLICTING DEMANDS

As industry and population increase and create greater demands for water, conflicts arise between different users. One possible conflict is between city and country. A city drills deep wells far out into the country to add to its water supply. The withdrawal of so much water lowers the water table, and farmers' wells go dry. On the other hand, farmers might withdraw river water for irrigation, decreasing the water supply of a city downstream. Conflicts also arise between water uses of fellow townspeople. The discharge of sewage into bodies of water makes them less useful for recreation. The building of a hydro-electric dam may destroy upstream fish habitats.

1. a) From such sources as local and/or national newspapers and journals, find a current example of conflicting water demands.
   b) Briefly describe how the demands in the situation conflict. How was the conflict resolved? If there is still a conflict, what recommendations would you make to resolve it?

FOCUS

No Extra Lake Water for Chicago Sewage

Since 1905, water has been taken out of Lake Michigan via the Chicago Sanitary and Shipping Canal. About 90 000 litres a second flow from Lake Michigan through the canal into the Mississippi River. This water helps to dilute Chicago sewage effluent and other wastes.

Over the years, U.S. interests have tried a number of times to increase the amount of water diverted from Lake Michigan to the Mississippi River. Since Lake Michigan is wholly within the United States, the International Joint Commission has no control over this matter. The U.S. Supreme Court controls the amount of water diversion from Lake Michigan. Because of opposition from both the Government of Canada and the governments of downstream States, all requests to increase diversions from Lake Michigan have been refused.

Chicago Sanitary and Shipping Canal. This canal diverts water from Lake Michigan into the Mississippi River system.

2. Have any rivers in your province been dammed to store water and regulate the stream flow? What reasons did the government(s) give for building the dams? Are these dams being used for all of the stated reasons? Describe one conflict of interest among those who benefit from the dams. The following points about the uses of a dam should help you discover some conflicts:

- *To prevent flooding* the reservoir should be *empty* in late winter, for storing the spring meltwater and rains.
- *To provide water supply* the reservoir should be kept *full* all year.
- *To regulate stream flow* the reservoir should be *empty* in late winter and should gradually be *emptied* during the summer.
- *To provide recreation* the water level in the reservoir should be kept *stable*.

3. To the model which you began in Chapter Two, add examples of the wetlands and water resources of your area, as well as sewage and waste disposal facilities.

Skagit Valley Saved from Flooding

The Skagit River rises in British Columbia but crosses the border into the State of Washington on its way to the Pacific Ocean. The part of the Skagit River Valley that lies in British Columbia is a scenic wilderness area much loved by naturalists and outdoor buffs. It is only about a two-hour drive from Vancouver.

In the 1960s, the British Columbia government signed an agreement with a Seattle power company that would have allowed the company to increase the height of the Ross Dam, just south of the Canadian-U.S.border. The higher dam would have generated more electric power in the United States. It would also have meant the flooding of 2000 ha of the scenic Skagit Valley in British Columbia.

Environmentalists on both sides of the border protested. After many years of debate and many hearings before the International Joint Commission, the two sides reached agreement in 1983. Seattle agreed not to raise the Ross Dam. In return, British Columbia agreed to sell Seattle the same amount of electric power that the higher dam would have generated. The agreement also created a $5 million environmental fund to make the valley more attractive and accessible to the public.

The Skagit Valley story is an example of a group of concerned citizens who succeeded in preventing the destruction of a natural resource. The final outcome benefited everyone.

Skagit River valley

DEMAND MANAGEMENT

Up to the present the managers of water resources in Canada have concentrated on increasing the water supply. They have planted forests and built many small dams to slow down water run-off. They have built large dams to store spring flood water for use in summer. They have diverted rivers to supply water where and when it is needed. They have constructed pipelines to move water from large lakes to cities that have outgrown their original water supply. They have drilled wells ever deeper and farther out into the country to service cities that depend on ground water. In short, they have used the most convenient sources first, and then steadily developed more distant and costly resources as more water was used.

Today, this policy of constantly increasing a supply to meet a growing demand is being questioned. The old approach is becoming too expensive and, at the same time, is often ruining large areas of natural environment. In the 1980s, environmentalists began to ask: Do we really need to use so much water? Can we manage the demand for it? The Inquiry on Federal Water Policy (1985) suggested that there are many ways we can use water more efficiently and avoid waste.

The amount of water we use in our homes can be reduced by many simple measures. We can install a gadget in the toilet tank that will reduce the amount of water used to flush the toilet. We can also install a special shower head that uses less water. We can repair or replace all leaky faucets. In industry, we can recycle water several times before discharging it.

Water resource specialists have suggested that the best way to reduce the use of water is to increase its price. At present most Canadians think of water as a free commodity. Municipal water charges cover only a part of the cost of obtaining, treating, and transporting the water. If the price of the water charged by municipalities to household and industrial users were increased, say, 10 times, the amount of water used would decline abruptly. People would find many ways to reduce their use of water just as they found ways to reduce their use of oil when prices rose rapidly in the late 1970s and early 1980s.

> **A human being requires only two litres of water a day to survive. The average Canadian uses 7100 litres per day.**

1. a) If the climate warmed up and the southern portion of the prairies became too dry for grain crops, where in Canada do you think we should try to grow more grain?
   b) The problem of drought referred to in part a) might be solved in two ways:
   i) Move water to the farms in the drought area.
   ii) Move the farming to an area where water is plentiful.
   Which solution do you think would cost more? Consider social and environmental costs, as well as economic costs.
2. If you have a water meter, find out how much water your family uses in a year. How much water is this per person per day?
3. Suppose that the cost of water were as high as the cost of energy (say, $1000–$2000 a year). In what ways do you think you and your family could reduce the amount of water you use?
4. Owners of single-family houses or the caretakers of apartment buildings and condominiums usually water the grass regularly in the summer. Is all this watering necessary? When grass turns brown in the summer, is it dead? Suggest some kinds of vegetation other than grass that might be appropriate in a front or back yard.
5. Place a stopper in the bathtub outlet to measure how much water you use in taking a shower. Compare this amount with what you use in taking a bath. Estimate the number of litres saved by whichever method is more conserving. Multiply the number of estimated litres by the number of showers or baths you take in a year to find how much water you might save by using the more conserving method. Estimate how much water would be saved if 10 households in your municipality used the most conserving method of bathing.

WHAT LIES AHEAD?

Water, water, everywhere
Nor any drop to drink.

The verse quoted was first written of a sailor drifting in the middle of an ocean, surrounded by water that was too salty to drink. If past trends continue into the future, the same quotation might one day be applied to southern Ontario, which is surrounded by freshwater lakes that contain water too polluted to drink.

REVIEW QUESTIONS

1. Turn back to the contradictory headlines at the beginning of this chapter and discuss with your classmates how both could be right.

2. Hold a class "think tank" to find specific examples of how human interference with the water cycle leads to many of our water resource problems. Make a chart to record your findings.

3. Explain why the number and size of our lakes and the average annual flow of our rivers are not accurate indicators of the amount of fresh water available to Canadians.

4. Why is southern Ontario running short of ground water?

5. Explain the difference between the consumptive and the non-consumptive uses of water. Give two examples of each. Which Canadian region consumes the most water per capita? Why?

6. Name three kinds of water pollution. In the long run, which do you think is the most harmful to human beings? Which one will be the most difficult to control? Why?

7. Explain why Canada must have the co-operation of the United States to solve all three kinds of water pollution problems described in this chapter.

8. What is the difference between "supply management" and "demand management" of water? Give one example of each. In the long run, which type of management do you think will be the more effective? Why?

9. Why do you think the Canadian government has not encouraged grandiose water diversion schemes such as NAWAPA and the GRAND Canal?

10. Why must the management of water resources be integrated with the management of other renewable resources, and with urban and regional planning?

Chapter Seven

Fish and Fisheries

To Fish or not to Fish?

- The government restricts fishing in order to safeguard future fish supplies or protect public health.
- Fisheries workers claim that they make less income when limits are put on fish catches, and some therefore catch more fish than the official limits allow.

How would you view limits on catches if you fished for a living? How would you respond to such limits?

The fishing dock at Port Edward, B.C.

FISH: A RENEWABLE RESOURCE

Fish that inhabit Canada's oceans, lakes, and rivers are an abundant natural resource, and fishing is Canada's oldest industry. Figure 7.1 illustrates cod fishing in early Canada. This engraving, published in 1718, was drawn from a tiny illustration inset in a map of North America published in 1698. It shows how the cod fishers dressed (A), the type of hook and line they used (B), their method of fishing (C), and their manner of drying the cod, as well as other details.

Both sea and freshwater species of fish are caught as a food source by Native people and by other Canadians who make a living selling fish. But human interference with parts of the environment is now having a negative effect on the size and the health of some fish. To ensure larger catches in the future, fisheries workers in government and industry are looking for better ways to manage fish resources. This is important, for fish are a renewable resource only if they are managed wisely.

USES OF FISH

Fish are important to Canadians in many ways. Besides providing a part of our food supply, fish are used to make many consumer and industrial products. Fish are an important item of trade: Canada is one of the world

People spend money on equipment and supplies in the local communities where they live or visit to fish.

leaders in volume of fish exported to other countries. Many Canadians enjoy fishing as recreation in all seasons of the year.

Fish inhabit the ocean waters off the coasts of Canada, and the inland lakes and rivers. In this vast area, only a few regions provide enough marketable fish to support *commercial fishing*. In most areas fishing is recreational and is known as *sport fishing*. Both commercial and sport fishing industries are important to their communities.

Although fish resources are widespread across Canada, most of the fish catch is sold for export and not for Canadian consumption. Many Native Canadians depend on fresh and dried fish as a staple part of their diet. For the rest of Canadians, fish competes for sales with other types of meat. Our fish must also compete for sale with the fish products imported from other countries. In some cases, government regulations restrict the catches of fish Canadians like to eat. Some low-value species of fish and the waste parts of fish processed for food are made into a variety of fertilizers, medicines, animal fodder, and chemicals.

Despite the great quantity of fish available in Canada, Canadians eat little of it compared with meats. Yet the demand for fish to export sustains a Canadian fishing industry. The fishery, in turn, helps to support many different industries in Canadian ports, especially along our east and west coasts.

Canada catches only two percent of the fish taken from world oceans but ranks first among all countries in volume of fish exports.

Canada's seafood exports are worth about four times as much as the imports. Most of the imports are shellfish such as shrimp and crab species that do not thrive in Canadian waters.

A View of a Stage & also of ye manner of Fishing for, Curing & Drying Cod at NEW FOUND LAND. A. The Habit of ye Fishermen. B. The Line. C. The manner of Fishing. D. The Dressers of ye Fish. E. The Trough into which they throw ye Cod when Dressed. F. Salt Boxes. G. The manner of Carrying ye Cod. H. The Cleansing ye Cod. I. A Press to extract ye Oyl from ye Cods Livers. K. Casks to receive ye water & Blood that comes from ye Livers. L. Another Cask to receive the Oyl. M. The manner of Drying ye Cod.

Figure 7.1 *Cod Fishing in Early Canada*

Hold a classroom survey on local fish and fishing by collecting answers to the following questions. When your survey is complete, you might prepare a poster to illustrate the results.

1. a) Where are the most successful fishing places in your region?
b) How far away is the closest fishing spot in your region? the farthest fishing spot?
c) Are these spots used for commercial or sport fishing?

2. a) If you fish for sport, where do you buy the equipment you use for fishing: boat, fishing rod, line, tackle, special clothing, and bait?
b) List three ways in which these expenditures help some people to make a living.

3. a) How many students in your class have visited a fishing port or resort?
b) Name three local facilities located in these communities that would serve sport fishers.

c) How do you think tourist visits help the economy of fishing resorts? Give two examples.

4. How many times a month do you eat fish and fish products? Calculate the class average. Include meals eaten at home, at school, or in a restaurant.

5. a) Assuming 0.2 kilograms a serving, calculate the kilograms of fish the average person in your class will eat in a year. Compare this amount with Canada's average annual consumption of fish, which stands at about 9.0 kg per person.
b) In fish consumption, does your class meet the national average, or is it above or below that average?
c) What reasons might explain your answer?

6. The average Canadian eats about eight times as much red meat (e.g., pork, beef, and lamb) and poultry as fish. How does your class average compare?

7. Working with a partner, prepare either a poster or a one-minute radio "spot" to encourage Canadians to eat more fish.

8. a) As a class, list all the ways you can in which the fishery helps to support other Canadian industries.
b) Working in small groups, prepare a chart to illustrate some of the links between an active fishing industry and a healthy regional economy.

LOCAL STUDY

1. a) Some parts of Canada have private fishing places where people can pay to fish. Is there such a facility in your area? If so, where?
b) Find out how the fish are raised, and how long it takes to produce fish large enough to catch for eating.

2. Obtain a copy of the fishing regulations for your province or territory. (Write a class letter to your provincial Ministry/Department of Fisheries, or visit a local licensing office or sporting goods store.)
a) In your local area, what are the rules about the season in which you may catch any two species of fish? How many of these fish is an angler allowed to catch? What is the minimum size of the fish that may be caught and eaten?
b) In some areas there are restrictions on the number of fish an angler may catch and eat. Is there any such restriction in your area?
c) Suggest reasons for these government rules and regulations.

3. a) Check your kitchen shelves and freezer for canned or frozen fish products. (Don't forget to check the pet food tins!) List the products you find. From what region were these products obtained?
b) Do most of these fish products come from your local area, other parts of Canada, or outside the country?
c) What percentage are saltwater fish products? What percentage are freshwater?

4. Make a general statement about the sources of fresh, frozen, and canned fish available in your local area.

THE FISH FOOD CHAIN

Most of the conditions that make for the greatest numbers of fish are found near coastlines and shorelines. In these waters both surface-feeding and bottom-feeding fish thrive in a complex food web, along with a variety of tough-shelled animals called *crustaceans* (or shellfish).

Like plants on land (as shown in Chapter Two), plants in oceans, lakes, and rivers use sunlight to manufacture food for growth, in the process of photosynthesis. Sunlight for this process penetrates water up to a depth of about two hundred metres. Microscopic aquatic plants called *phytoplankton* consume *nutrients* from this water layer. The phytoplankton is eaten by tiny aquatic animals in the water called *zooplankton*. These minute plants and animals, or *plankton*, provide food for small fish and for crustaceans. The small fish and crustaceans provide food for large fish, which in turn provide food for still larger fish, animals, and humans. This process is known as the fish food chain (Figure 7.2, page 220). The fish food chain in oceans, lakes, and rivers is built like a pyramid, from a broad base of millions of small plankton to a sharp peak with larger but fewer fish and mammals.

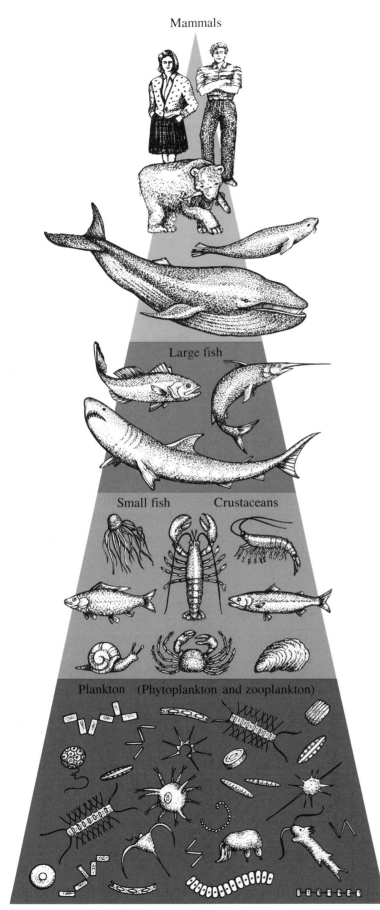

Mammals

Large fish

Small fish   Crustaceans

Plankton   (Phytoplankton and zooplankton)

Figure 7.2 *The Fish Food Chain*

1. The chart below shows how much aquatic life is consumed from the food chain (Figure 7.2) to produce 1.0 kg of added mass in fish such as the mackerel.

Mass consumed	*Mass increase*
500 kg phytoplankton	100 kg zooplankton
100 kg zooplankton	10 kg herring
10 kg herring	1.0 kg mackerel

To increase its mass by 10 kg, how many kilograms of herring would a mackerel have to consume? How many kilograms of zooplankton and of phytoplankton would have been consumed to feed it?

2. If humans need to eat about 10 kg of large fish like mackerel to increase their mass by 1.0 kg, how many kilograms of each of the two kinds of plankton would be used from the fish food chain to provide this increase?

3. State your general conclusions about the importance of a healthy fish food chain in producing valuable fish resources.

Fish are more efficient flesh producers than livestock. For example, catfish raised in freshwater ponds increase their mass by 1.0 kg for every 1.5 kg of grain they eat. To increase their mass by the same amount, chickens need 2.0 kg of feed, pigs 3.0 kg, and beef 6.0 kg.

FISH HABITATS

Whether fish live in oceans or in lakes and rivers, they depend on the other living things in the water, or *aquatic environment*, that they inhabit.

1. a) Do the best fishing places in your local area contain sea fish or freshwater fish?
   b) Name the most common species of fish caught there.
2. What water and site conditions do you think make the best fishing spots?

ATLANTIC MARINE ENVIRONMENT

Atlantic Canada, with its large islands and peninsulas, possesses ideal conditions for an abundance of fish. The coastline is long and indented with the bays and estuaries that create a great many wetlands (Figure 7.3). A maximum amount of sunlight for plant growth is able to penetrate the shallow water above fish banks located on the wide continental shelf offshore. The waters of the warm Gulf and cold Labrador ocean currents mix together to attract many different species of fish.

Since plankton grow and multiply only to a depth of 200 m, most fish feed in the shallow waters of the **continental shelf** (Figure 7.3), and these waters are the important ocean fish areas. The rivers emptying into the sea carry nutrients to the ocean bottom on raised parts of the continental shelf called **banks**. The meeting of cold and warm ocean currents in these areas keeps the water stirred up and spreads through it the nutrients on which plankton feed.

Masses of algae, a type of phytoplankton, grow or bloom in open water. Algae provide a habitat for the zooplankton on which some fish feed.

Sedges, cattails, and shrubs in the wetlands along this shoreline provide an ideal habitat for young fish.

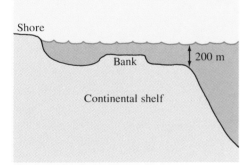

The **estuaries**, or wide mouths of rivers that empty into the sea, are also important areas for fish. In these estuaries the water is shallow, and is constantly mixed by river flow and tides. Marsh vegetation that grows along low-lying ocean coastlines (and lake shorelines) traps an abundance of nutrients. These **wetlands** provide a safe environment for many aquatic animals in the fish food chain.

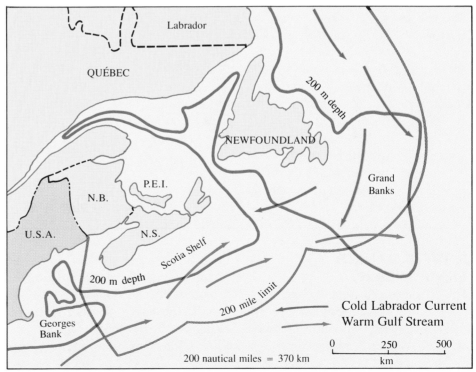

Figure 7.3 ***Atlantic Fishing Areas*** *By international agreement, Canada manages fish within 200 nautical miles (370 km) of our coastline.*

221

Dividing Georges Bank

Georges Bank, off the southern coast of Nova Scotia, produces more fish than the famous Grand Banks. Because the water on Georges Bank is very shallow, there is maximum sunlight penetration for producing plankton. The Bay of Fundy tides move large amounts of nutrients to Georges Bank. The circular ocean currents transport the nutrients to areas where they are available to the plankton. Menaces to fishing, such as dogfish sharks, which can destroy fish nets and greatly reduce catches, are not as common on Georges Bank as in some other areas.

It is little wonder that both Canadian and American fishing industries highly prize such a rich fishing location. For a long time, Canada claimed the eastern half of Georges Bank, and the United States claimed the whole of it. Canada made its claim because the Nova Scotia and New Brunswick fishing fleets had fished there for centuries. The United States based its claim on a deep undersea channel that forms a natural dividing line between continental shelves. For a number of years, Americans fished in the area claimed by Canada. When it appeared that the dispute might result in violence, the Canadian and U.S. governments submitted the problem to the World Court.

In 1984, the World Court established an official boundary line at a point midway in the overlapping claims of Canada and the United States. The Canadian zone is much smaller than the American, but the Canadian area has much more valuable fish resources (Figure 7.4).

The fish, of course, do not respect this artificial boundary. Many groundfish winter in the U.S. zone and spawn in the Canadian zone. Unless the two countries negotiate a fisheries agreement that includes catch quotas, the fish could be seriously over-harvested.

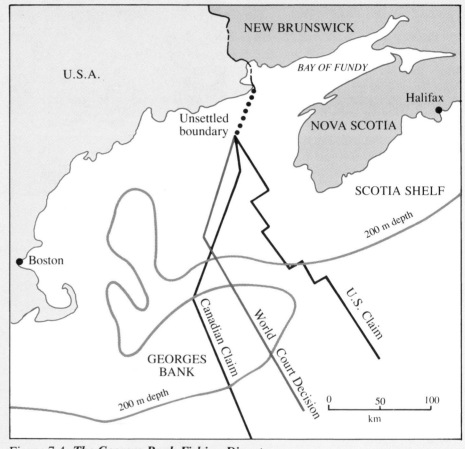

Figure 7.4 *The Georges Bank Fishing Dispute*

PACIFIC MARINE ENVIRONMENT

The ocean, or marine environment, on the Pacific coast differs from that of Atlantic Canada. The continental shelf off British Columbia is narrower than the shelf along Canada's east coast; it is generally less than forty-five kilometres wide. It contains no banks, but the shallow water that surrounds the hundreds of small islands hugging the coastline provides a suitable habitat for fish resources. Farther offshore, Vancouver Island and the Queen Charlotte Islands provide shelter from severe Pacific Ocean storms for the waterways next to the mainland (Figure 7.5).

Many rivers from the Coast Mountains empty into the ocean, or more often into the long, narrow inlets known as fiords, carved by glacial ice. Estuaries at these river mouths serve as nutrient traps, depositing riverborne organic and inorganic materials in sea-bottom sediments. The enriched food supply attracts a great deal of marine life, including waterfowl.

One of the most important features of the coastal waterway is called a *sill*. Sills are underwater ridges deposited by glaciers; they create shallow depths at the entrances to many inlets, fiords, and straits. Although the restricted flow across these sills creates some *deoxygenated water*, it also provides warmer and more uniform surface temperatures throughout the year. As a result, plankton has a longer growing season in which to serve as food and develop fish resources. Sills also provide habitats with a slow water circulation. Shellfish such as oysters prefer a slow circulation because it does not sweep away the floating larvae on which they feed.

The special features of the inshore waters on the west coast help to create a Pacific marine environment for fish resources that, despite notable differences, is generally similar to the fishing banks farther out to sea on the broader Atlantic continental shelf.

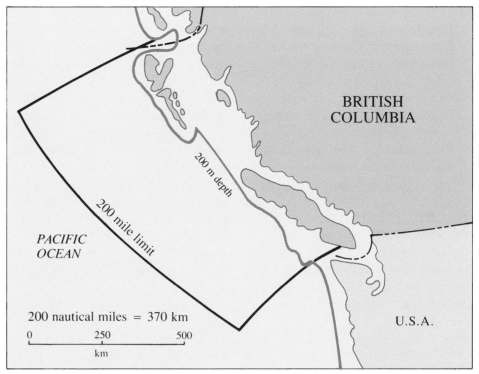

Figure 7.5 *Pacific Fishing Areas*

Many water channels and islands along the Pacific coast, such as these in the Queen Charlotte Islands, provide fish with an excellent marine environment.

1. When you have read about the Pacific marine environment, suggest two ways in which the fish habitats of the Pacific and Atlantic coasts are alike. Suggest two ways in which they are different.
2. Compare Figures 7.3 and 7.5.
   a) Along which coast—west or east—is the area of the continental shelf greater?
   b) Suggest an explanation for the difference in size.
3. a) What deep river estuary on the Atlantic coast separates the Scotian Shelf from the Grand Banks?
   b) Which province has the longest coastal area inside this estuary?
4. a) On a base map of British Columbia, mark and name the larger rivers with estuaries along the Pacific coast.
   b) Suggest why the Pacific continental shelf has no fish banks.
5. Where is there a part of the continental shelf lying outside Canada's 200 mile (370 km) limit? (See an atlas for another section of shelf, called the Flemish Cap, to the east of the Grand Banks.)
6. Which coast do you think has more favourable conditions for fish? Support your answer with evidence.
7. a) Make a chart to rank the following countries according to the length of their coastline: Canada, the United States, Norway, France, and Germany. Where does Canada rank?
   b) What might one advantage be in having a long coastline?

8. a) Using an atlas and what you have learned about the factors that make for productive fish areas, outline on a world map three ocean zones that you think are likely to be high in fish resources.
b) How do Canada's fish areas compare in size with those you have marked in other parts of the world? How important do you think this is for Canada? Explain.

ARCTIC MARINE ENVIRONMENT

On the Arctic and North Atlantic Oceans, as well as on freshwater surfaces in winter, ice forms and reduces the distance that sunlight penetrates into the water. Besides making the water colder, the lack of sunshine limits the quantities of phytoplankton and zooplankton.

When sea water freezes, the ice it forms contains less salt than the unfrozen water beneath it. The water coming from melted sea ice is fresh.

In summer the meltwater in the Arctic produces a layer of fresh water over the deeper salt water. Because fresh water is less dense, it floats on top of the salt water with very little mixing. This stable layer of fresh water reduces upwelling (a vertical exchange of water), thus reducing the supply of nutrients in the upper layer of water.

The Arctic rivers pour large amounts of sediment containing nutrients into the ocean (Figure 7.6). The Mackenzie River, for example, carries a plume of brown water some hundreds of kilometres into the Beaufort Sea.

In winter, constant upwelling occurs in a few areas and prevents **pack ice** from building up; this increases the photosynthesis of plankton. Scientists call these unusual areas **polynyas**. Figure 7.6 shows their scattered locations in the Arctic. Ocean currents paralleling the shoreline (known as **shore leads**) transport nutrients from river mouths to these areas. The shore leads are not completely ice free all winter, but they are areas where the first open water appears in spring. Because polynyas and shore leads have a thinner ice cover and are rich in nutrients, they have larger fish populations than do waters farther out to sea. The fish provide feeding areas for mammals in the food chain, such as walrus, seals, and polar bears. Many of these feeding areas lie close to shipping channels, where accidents could cause environmental damage to the food chain.

---

1. a) Using an atlas, mark and label on an outline map of the Canadian Arctic, the following ocean features:
- permanent polar ice in the Arctic Ocean and Beaufort Sea
- the southern edge of pack ice in fall
- the direction of ocean currents in the Arctic Ocean, Davis Strait, and Hudson Bay
- the 200-m edge of the continental shelf

b) Which parts of the Arctic are most free of ice during the year? least free?

c) By comparing the map you have drawn with Figure 7.6, what relationships can you find between the locations of rivers, ocean currents, shore leads, and polynyas?

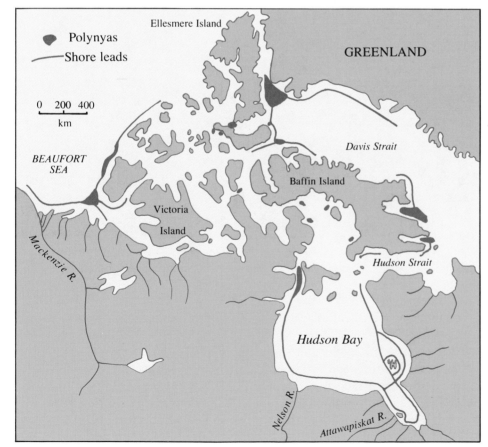

Figure 7.6 *Major Arctic Sealife Areas*

A polar bear searches for fish or seals along a shore lead in Arctic pack ice.

2. Which polynyas and shore leads appear likely to face the greatest environmental impact from future resource developments in the Arctic?

3. How does the Arctic compare with the Atlantic and Pacific coasts of Canada in area of continental shelf?

4. The thickness of winter ice and the concentration of silt in water affect the supply of plankton available for fish. Suggest reasons.

Arctic Whales

After 300 years of commercial whaling, the Arctic is the last refuge for many whale species. Whales are the largest animals in the fish food chain. Many species of whale live in Canadian waters. Scientists divide them into two classes: those with teeth and those without. Narwhals and beluga whales belong to the first group. The bowhead whale belongs to the second (Figure 7.7).

Narwhals are easily identified because of their tapered tusk, which sometimes grows to be two hundred centimetres long. Canadian narwhals are widely distributed across the eastern Arctic waters. Their total population is about 10 000. Scientists believe that they are over-hunted, and that their numbers are decreasing, but there is not enough reliable information to be sure about this.

The beluga whale inhabits both the eastern and western Arctic, as well as Hudson and James bays. Harvesting of beluga whales has now been reduced to about one-half the numbers taken in the 1950s and 1960s. Scientists believe that the current harvest is about equal to the number of beluga whales being born.

The bowhead whale inhabits the eastern Arctic Ocean, the Bering Sea, and the Beaufort Sea. This whale almost became extinct in the eastern Arctic in the early 1900s. Since then, it has been protected from commercial harvesting, and the present eastern stock is estimated to number a few hundred animals. The Bering-Beaufort stock has been reduced from 18 000 in the mid-1800s to between 1000 and 2000 in the 1980s.

The traditional Inuit used all of the whale. They ate the flesh and the internal organs. They used the baleen and bones to make buildings, furniture, and tools. The oil was a source of heat and light.

Europeans were more wasteful. At first they used the oil extracted from blubber to make soap and to fuel lamps. Later they used it in paints and as a lubricant. From baleen, particularly the baleen of the bowhead whale, they made a wide range of products including buggy whips, skirt hoops, umbrellas, carriage wheels, corset stays, and fishing rods. But although the oil and baleen were used, the rest of the carcass was discarded. Using only part of the carcass was very wasteful and led to a sharp decrease in the number of whales; and so, when the Canadian government asserted sovereignty over the Arctic islands before 1900, it began to issue whaling licences. Government controls and a decreasing demand for whale products have helped to stabilize Arctic whale populations in the 20th century.

Baleen is a flexible bone-like substance that hangs in strips from the roof of the mouth of some species of whales. The most important whale for the production of baleen was the bowhead. A single bowhead whale might produce over 700 strips of baleen.

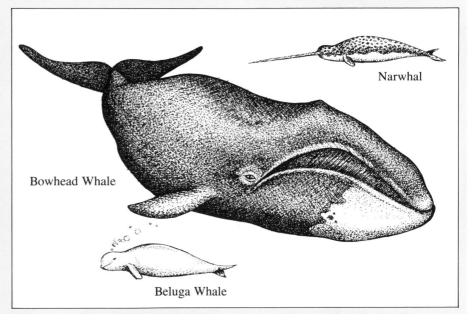

Narwhal

Bowhead Whale

Beluga Whale

Figure 7.7 *Some Whales of Canada* *Whales and fish in Figures 7.7–7.9 are not drawn to scale.*

FRESHWATER ENVIRONMENT

The most important freshwater fish areas are located in the shallow shore waters of the large lakes listed in Table 6.1, especially near the mouths of rivers.

Fish in lakes and rivers do well under roughly the same aquatic conditions as fish in the oceans. The basic need is the building of a strong food chain. A large food supply makes both salt- and freshwater fish reserves plentiful and healthy.

1. a) From Chapter Six you learned that about twenty percent of Canada's total area is covered by fresh water. Which province or territory has the largest percentage of its area covered by fresh water?
   b) Besides the Great Lakes listed in Table 6.1, identify some of the large lakes that likely contain a plentiful supply of fish.
2. Use library sources to discover the most favourable aquatic conditions for establishing a plentiful supply of freshwater fish species.

VARIETY OF FISH RESOURCES

SEA FISH

Sea fish are divided into four different types according to their physical characteristics and the part of the marine environment each occupies (Figure 7.8).

Groundfish is a collective term used to describe fish that feed near the ocean floor. The most important species of groundfish are cod, haddock, flounder, sole, pollock, and halibut. All of these species are harvested extensively from the banks of the east coast. Halibut is also important in the Pacific fishery.

Pelagic fish usually feed near the surface, often in large schools. The chief pelagic species include herring, mackerel, capelin, and tuna. All of these species are important in the Atlantic fishery; herring is also important in the Pacific fishery.

Anadromous fish spend their adult life at sea and migrate to streams and lakes to *spawn* in the same place where they were hatched. Salmon are the most important anadromous fish. Less important are the alewife and smelt. Salmon are the most important fish in the Pacific fishery. Salmon are also native to the east coast, and there is an Arctic variety called char, the only fish harvested in large numbers in the Arctic Ocean. Arctic char reproduce very slowly—they do not spawn until they are 12 years old—and so they can easily be over-fished.

Mackerel are a type of pelagic fish caught off the coast of Nova Scotia's Cape Breton Island.

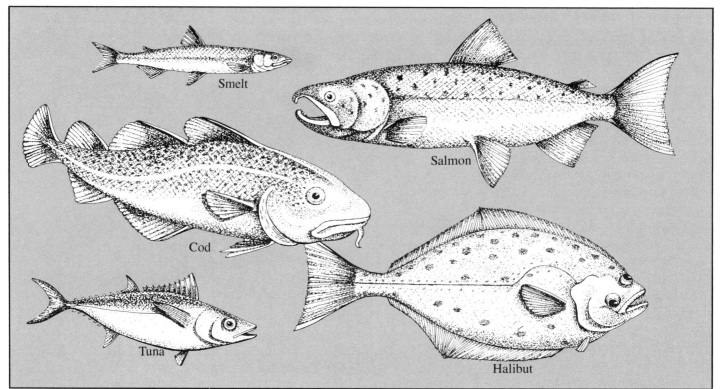

Figure 7.8 *Sea Fish*

As you know, crustaceans are shellfish. On the Atlantic coast, the main species caught are lobster, scallop, shrimp, crab, squid, and clam. On the Pacific coast, the important species are geoduck, oyster, crab, clam, shrimp, and abalone.

1. a) Using an atlas or reference book, map the locations along the east and west coasts of Canada of three species of sea fish (including crustaceans) mentioned in the preceding section.
   b) To which type of sea fish do these species on each coast belong?
   c) Does the east or west coast produce the greater amount of sea fish? Refer to Figures 7.3 and 7.5, and give reasons for your answer.
2. a) Using a library reference, find and mark on a map of Canada the major salmon spawning rivers that drain into the Pacific, Atlantic, and Arctic oceans.

b) Which coast has the most salmon spawning rivers?
c) Up which river do salmon migrate farthest to spawn? Suggest why.

At high tide, schools of herring swim into the shallow water of New Brunswick's Bay of Fundy and are trapped in **weirs**.

Salmon and the Fraser Delta

Salmon are anadromous: they migrate to the place they hatched to spawn. Adult salmon, heading for the upper Fraser River to spawn, spend time in the waters of the Fraser delta. When the young salmon are on their way to the sea, they again spend time feeding in the marshes of the Fraser delta. Biologists believe that the periods of time salmon spend in these waters are very important to their development.

The area around the Fraser delta, with its mild climate and deep rich soils, is excellent for farming. But flooding from tides and spring runoff made it necessary to build dykes and drain the lower-lying land. The result has been a loss of about seventy percent of the original delta marshlands.

The land in the Fraser delta area has also been used for urban development. Port facilities, especially, have destroyed large amounts of delta marsh. Both urban and agricultural land uses have polluted the delta waters.

All in all, human use of the land around the Fraser delta poses a serious threat to the salmon fishery of British Columbia.

Lobster

Oyster

Shrimp

Clam

Scallop

Blue crab

Shellfish

FRESHWATER FISH

Lakes and rivers in the interior of Canada contain many species of freshwater fish (Figure 7.9) but only a few crustaceans, which are of no commercial value. Fish are most plentiful in the larger lakes (listed in Table 6.1). High-value fish species in the Great Lakes include lake sturgeon, splake, American eel, coho salmon, yellow perch, lake trout, rainbow trout, cisco, whitefish, and crappie. There are also many lower-value species such as alewife, white perch, carp, smelt, and suckers. In the Prairie Provinces, the most valuable of all commercial and recreational fish species is the walleye. Whitefish, pike, and carp are also fished commercially in prairie waters.

At one time sturgeon were so plentiful in the Great Lakes that they were burned as fuel on steam ships. Now only a few lakes and rivers in Northern Ontario contain sturgeon, a fish so primitive that it is sometimes called a living fossil.

1. How are the species and the locations of freshwater fish similar to those of saltwater fish? How are they different?
2. Divide your class into two groups: fishery workers and land-use planners. Debate the issue: Resolved that the estuary wetlands on the outskirts of our community should be developed for industrial and commercial uses.
3. Arrange to make a class visit to a fish hatchery, fish farm, or fish processing plant if there are any in your area.
   a) Before you go, develop a class list of questions to ask about the facility you will visit.
   b) When you return, write a brief ''article'' for a local newspaper, giving an account of your trip and information about your findings.
   c) As a class, write a letter of thanks to the facility you have visited. Comment on the highlights of your visit.
4. Draw a poster of a pond showing various elements of a food chain.

Include these items: aquatic plants, crayfish, diving beetle, dragonfly nymph, frog, muskrat, northern pike, otter, and sunfish.

Splake is a cross between speckled trout and lake trout. It is used to stock parts of Lake Huron.

CHANGES AFFECTING FISH RESOURCES

Any natural development or human interference that upsets the balance in the fish food chain affects fish resources. Figure 7.10 shows various types of such occurrences. Most result from human activity. Fish resources increase or decrease with changes in two factors: the quality of the water and the variety of the life in it, which is known as its *biotic composition*. Fish, crustaceans, and other aquatic creatures face many threats to their

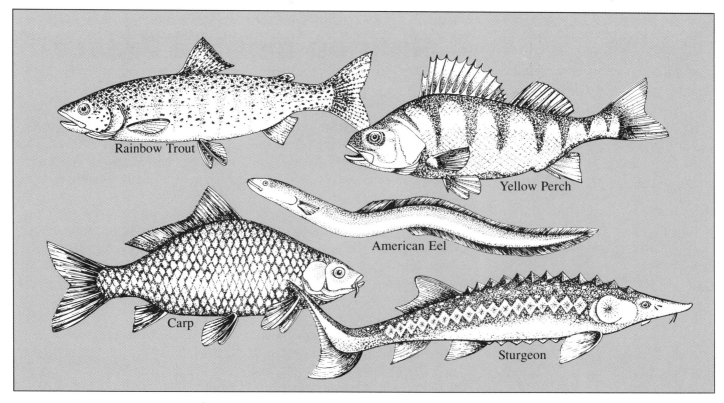

Rainbow Trout

Yellow Perch

American Eel

Carp

Sturgeon

environment. Some kinds of fish will not be able to adapt to changes in their environment and will die out.

The amount of marketable fish in the food chain depends on the species put into and taken out of the fish environment, as well as on the stability of the environment itself. The range of fish resources (or the biotic composition of rivers, lakes, and oceans) is affected by physical changes in the environment, harvesting, and management of fish. See Figure 7.10 for these and other factors that affect fish resources.

WATER QUALITY

Acid rain, chemical nutrients, and toxic wastes all have separate effects on water quality, but collectively their effect on fish resources is even more serious. Chapter Six describes each type of pollutant in more detail. The following text sums up the combined effect of these pollutants on fish resources.

Acid rain is the pollutant that causes the most serious effects in the Canadian Shield and the Appalachian region, where the water is already naturally acidic, mostly because the area lacks limestone. Hundreds of lakes in the Canadian Shield are already too acidic for freshwater fish to survive in them, and many more will become "dead" lakes if we cannot reduce acid rain in the future. Increased acidity is also a serious threat to the spawning of anadromous fish, such as Atlantic salmon, in smaller inland lakes or rivers.

When too many chemical nutrients are added to the water of lakes and rivers, growth of algae, or *eutrophication*, becomes rampant. Decaying algae use up oxygen so that many fish cannot survive. Eutrophication has been most serious in the Great Lakes, where large amounts of phosphorous enter the lakes from municipal sewers and farm fields. Now, because of regulations governing waste disposal, this process has become much slower.

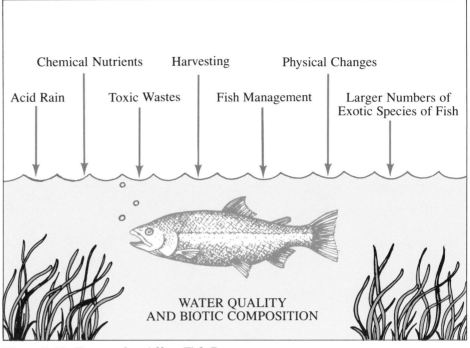

Figure 7.10 *Factors that Affect Fish Resources*

Chemicals in toxic wastes are taken in by the phytoplankton and zooplankton at the bottom of the fish food chain. Since a very large fish consumes the equivalent of many tonnes of plankton before it is fully grown, it accumulates large amounts of toxic chemicals in its body. These toxic chemicals are not excreted, but are stored in the body of the fish. If people eat too much toxic fish, they may become seriously ill or even die. Figure 7.11 (page 230) shows in map form the recommended amounts of fish that most adults may safely eat. The fish consumption levels shown on this map are averages. Persons eating larger portions, whole fish, or older fish should eat less than the amounts suggested. Children and young women are advised to eat only fish that are unrestricted.

One of the most serious cases of toxic poisoning in Canada occurred on the Grassy Narrows and White Dog Indian Reserves in northwestern Ontario. (See "A Tale of Two Bands" page 131.) A pulp and paper mill at Dryden dumped mercury into the Wabigoon-English river system for a number of years. The fish in these waters became highly toxic with mercury. The local Indians, who depended on the fish for much of their food, began to feel the effects of mercury poisoning. The Ontario government intervened, but the consequences were already very damaging. Even though the pulp and paper mill stopped discharging mercury into the river, the fish from these waters will not, for many years, be fit to eat.

Water quality is generally better for fish along Canada's coastlines than in interior bodies of fresh water. Oceans have less concentrated sources of pollutants and a larger volume of water to dilute pollution. But the possibility of oil spills from tanker ships and the offshore drilling rigs on the east coast and in the Arctic Ocean (Figure 7.12, page 230) remains a constant threat.

Red tide is the popular name for discoloured sea water caused by a population explosion of organisms that give off a toxic substance fatal to much marine life. The dumping of human sewage into warm summer water may trigger red tides.

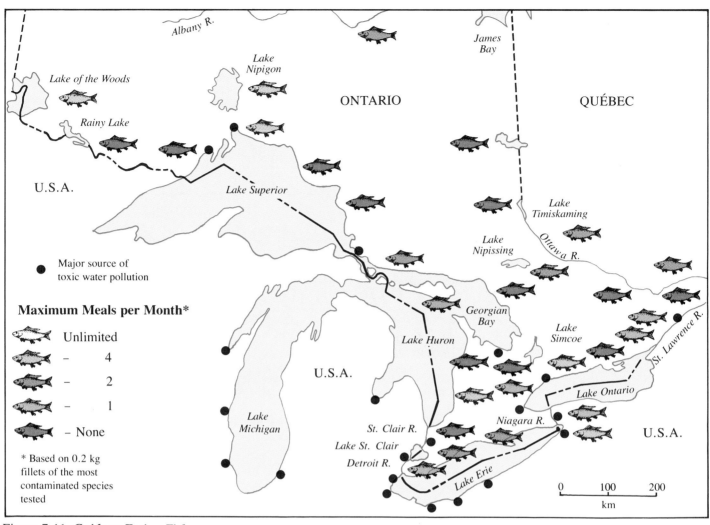

Figure 7.11 *Guide to Eating Fish from the Great Lakes region*

Major source of
toxic water pollution

Maximum Meals per Month*

Unlimited

– 4

– 2

– 1

– None

* Based on 0.2 kg
fillets of the most
contaminated species
tested

Atlantic fishery workers want a guarantee of compensation for loss of catch from oil pollution when the Hibernia oil field on the Grand Banks is developed.

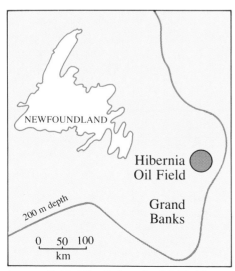

Figure 7.12 *The Hibernia Oil Field*

1. a) Name a source of each of the following contaminants of fish waters: acid rain, chemical nutrients, and toxic wastes.

b) Brainstorm the effects of any local sources of pollution on fish resources from past to present.

2. a) Name two Ontario lakes and rivers in which the fish are seriously contaminated. Name two in which the fish are suitable to eat.

b) In which parts of the Great Lakes are the most areas of pollution found? the fewest areas?

c) How do you think toxic pollution in Lake Michigan and on the U.S. side of the lower Great Lakes is able to contaminate fish in Ontario waters?

d) Why might the fish in Lake Ontario be more contaminated

from toxic build-up than those in Lake Huron? (Consider the flow and volume of water within the Great Lakes as shown in Figure 6.3.)

3. In Chapter Six you were asked to construct a model of a thriving wetland. Now construct a similar model of a dying wetland. Prepare a chart showing the factors that led to the area's decline.

Fish die in polluted lakes and rivers from lack of oxygen, scarcity of food, or a high level of toxic chemicals in the water.

230

HUMAN ACTIVITIES

Many human activities create physical changes in the environment of fish. Building dams can prevent fish from reaching upstream spawning grounds. Dredging sand and gravel from lakes and streams also ruins spawning beds. Draining wetlands along shorelines destroys the feeding grounds of certain fish at various stages of their life cycle. Large water-diversion projects disrupt spawning places by changing the pattern of erosion and the deposit of sediments. Cutting forests, draining swamps, and practising poor farming methods have reduced the summer flow of streams and warmed their water.

In the mid-1970s, one of Canada's biggest water transfer projects spelled disaster for a large, commercial, freshwater whitefish industry in northern Manitoba. Behind a low dam built across the Churchill River, water from Southern Indian Lake was diverted southward into the Nelson River drainage basin to generate hydro-

Wetlands on the Canadian shore of Lake Ontario have decreased by 50 percent since the time of early settlers.

electricity (Figure 7.13). The lake level also rose 3.0 m to flood over 400 km² of land and increase the size of an already large lake by 20 percent. A small Indian settlement had to relocate, and fish habitat was severely damaged.

Fish stocks in the area may never be what they once were because the

More than 500 000 t of sediment are deposited each year in the bottom of Dauphin Lake, Manitoba. These layers of sediment are burying the gravel beds that fish use for spawning.

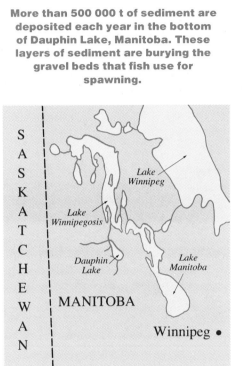

water level of Southern Indian Lake is unstable, since it is made to rise or fall according to the demand for hydro power. When a lake level fluctuates, the shoreline never stays in one place long enough for a fish habitat to develop.

Fish ladders let migrating fish by-pass obstacles in river channels. Obstacles might be bridge footings, dams, or waterfalls and rapids.

Atlantic salmon almost became extinct in Lake Ontario in the 1800s, but not because of over-fishing. The spawning beds were devastated by excessive run-off and silting from the clearing of forest land for farming.

When shorelines are eroded and the sediment is deposited elsewhere, fish habitats may be destroyed. Sedimentation may be a natural process as it is occurring here in a soil slump along the bank of a Yukon river in flood. But too much sedimentation may occur when people make changes to land surfaces.

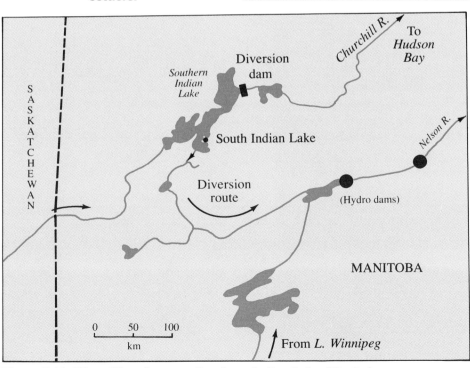

Figure 7.13 *Water Diversion near Southern Indian Lake, Manitoba*

231

EXOTICS

The term *exotics*, refers to non-native species of fish introduced into a new habitat either on purpose or by accident. Exotics can be harmful or beneficial. The sea lamprey is an example of a harmful exotic species. This species made its way into Lake Ontario over a hundred years ago, either up the St. Lawrence River or through the Erie Canal. With the building of the Welland Canal, it was able to migrate into other Great Lakes (Figure 4.12). The sea lamprey feeds on live fish by rasping a hole in the flesh and sucking the blood and body fluids. Even if the fish does not die immediately after the attack, its chances of long survival are greatly reduced. By the 1950s, the sea lamprey had ruined the lake trout and whitefish fishing industries. The development and use of a chemical lampricide now controls the numbers of this parasite.

The rainbow trout is an example of an exotic species beneficial to the fishing industry. It was transplanted from British Columbia and is now reproducing very successfully in the Great Lakes. Several kinds of salmon have also been successfully introduced to the Great Lakes. Because they are large and good ''fighters'' with an appealing taste, rainbow trout and salmon are highly valued for sport fishing.

HARVESTING

The harvesting of fish to maintain a balance in the food chain is a difficult task. If environmental conditions are right, fish stocks can be harvested at certain levels without destroying the fish resource. In other words, enough fish are reproduced each year to replace those harvested. This level of harvesting is known as the *sustainable development* of fish resources. If the number of fish harvested is greater than the number reproduced, this over-harvesting gradually reduces the supply of fish.

If Canadians, in the future, are to enjoy sport fishing in all parts of our country, we must all work to protect fish habitats.

Fish are often called a *common-property resource*. This means that like air, fish belong to everybody. Since they move from one area to another, no one government has responsibility for their management. In general, fishers have little incentive to conserve the resource, and the result is often over-harvesting.

The plight of the Atlantic salmon is a good example of what can happen to a common-property resource. Salmon spawn in the headwaters of many Canadian rivers that flow into the Atlantic Ocean. The young salmon then swim out to sea, where they grow into adults before returning to the same stream where they were hatched.

In the process of this life cycle, the salmon pass through waters where they can be caught by fishers of many different countries. The main salmon feeding grounds are off the coast of Greenland, where a large Danish fishing fleet operates. For many years, Europeans, Japanese, Americans, and Canadians harvested salmon along Canada's east coast. Then the catch of Atlantic salmon began to decline. Biologists feared that the salmon resource might be completely destroyed unless something was done to reverse over-harvesting.

As a result, Canada severely restricted salmon fishing in Atlantic waters and obtained an agreement from Denmark that its fishers would limit their salmon catch. The salmon are gradually increasing in numbers, but many years will pass before there are as many as there were in the early part of this century.

Seals and Fisheries

Some fisheries people blame an over-abundance of Atlantic seals for the decline of fish harvests and want to be allowed to harvest seals. The more seals, they believe, the fewer fish are left for Atlantic fishing crews to harvest. For example, one researcher estimated for a Royal Commission that grey seals off Sable Island consume 100 000 t of fish each year, an amount greater than the size of the catch made by fishing boats from the surrounding area.

Other researchers argue, however, that of the fish eaten by seals, very few would be harvested commercially. Most of these fish, they believe, are non-commercial varieties, and the estimated 100 000 t represent the total consumption of all fish eaten by grey seals in that area.

Fishers also complain that seals are host to parasites called seal worms or cod worms. The worms mature inside seals and produce eggs that are released in the seals' excrement. As bottom feeders, young cod eat the eggs; the eggs then hatch into worms that burrow into their flesh. Mature cod infected with seal worms have a lower market value and require more expensive processing than healthy cod.

Marine biologists reply to these complaints that the so-called seal worms are hosted not only by most seal species but also by at least 25 species of fish, as well as many intermediate hosts. Therefore, reducing the numbers of seals would not resolve the problem of worm infestation.

limit to 200 nautical miles (370 km) offshore. Our government took this step in order to manage most of the valuable continental shelf fishing grounds shown in Figures 7.3 and 7.5. Within these waters, by international agreement, Canada licenses fishing and manages catch quotas. As a result, the Canadian share of the cod catch greatly increased. Overall, the total catch of cod has risen slightly over its low point in 1977 and 1978, though it is still only about one-third of what it was in 1968. Sometimes, however, other countries refuse to accept Canada's territorial claims, and their refusal leads to boundary disputes over fishing rights. (See "Dividing Georges Bank", page 222 and "St. Pierre and Miquelon Fishing Dispute", page 234.)

Cod is one of the most migratory fish species. Many cod winter in the warmer waters of the Gulf of St. Lawrence and in spring move to the Scotian Shelf or Grand Banks to spawn. The cod also move north to south along the coast, as well as inshore and offshore, following the available plankton throughout the year.

FISH MANAGEMENT

Fish management tries to regulate the composition and harvesting of fish resources. The cod fishery in Canadian Atlantic waters provides a good example of fish management. Total *landings* of cod by all countries peaked in 1968. Figure 7.14 records

the importance of fish management for the eight years leading up to 1977 and the eight years following. At that time, Canada had no control over fish resources beyond a 12 nautical-mile limit, and fishing by foreign fleets began to deplete the codfish stock. The annual catch declined in 1969 and continued to decline into the 1970s.

In 1977, Canada extended our territorial water boundary and fishing

Our federal government determines the *total allowable catch* (TAC) for scarce seafish resources taken in Canadian coastal waters. The TAC is based on an estimate of the number of fish that can be caught without lowering the overall fish population. A

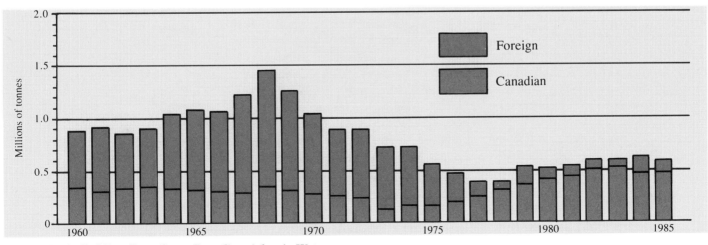

Figure 7.14 *Cod Landings from Canadian Atlantic Waters*

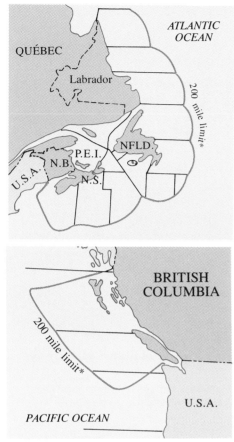

An inland fish hatchery on Vancouver Island. Young salmon are raised in the winding channel built beside this river. When they are mature enough, they are released to begin their journey to the sea.

different catch **quota** is set each year for each of the sectors into which the Atlantic and Pacific fish management zones are divided. The provincial governments are responsible for freshwater fish resources. Besides setting catch quotas, the provincial and federal governments place restrictions on fishing seasons, the size of fish taken, and methods of fishing.

Fisheries research officers work to improve fish habitats and fish species. If spawning beds and feeding grounds are upgraded, they yield more fish. Young fish raised in hatcheries are used to stock lakes and rivers. Scientists produce **hybrid** fish by crossbreeding similar species, and they develop new types of fish through **biotechnology**.

With the help of subsidies provided by federal and provincial governments, five east-coast fishing companies were able to consolidate into two "super-companies", one based in Newfoundland and the other in Nova Scotia. This action made these new

St. Pierre and Miquelon Fishing Dispute

The Treaty of Paris, struck in 1763, gave almost all of France's possessions in North America to Britain. There were two exceptions. Fishing boats from France retained the right to land on part of the shores of Newfoundland to dry their fish and to obtain supplies; and the islands of St. Pierre and Miquelon continued to belong to France. French rights on the shores of Newfoundland were later terminated by negotiation, but St. Pierre and Miquelon still belong to France.

In 1978, a year after Canada had declared a 200 nautical mile (370 km) fishing zone, France claimed a similar zone around the islands of St. Pierre and Miquelon. This meant that trawlers from St. Pierre and Miquelon, as well as from France, would be able to fish in this zone without regarding Canada's fishing regulations. Obviously, both coun-

tries cannot control the same area. The two countries have agreed to settle the dispute by negotiation. If Canada and France cannot reach a long-term agreement, the issue may have to go to the World Court for resolution as did the Georges Bank dispute.

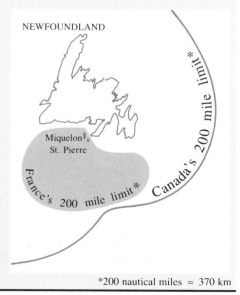

*200 nautical miles = 370 km

companies more efficient so that they could better compete with the fishing fleets from foreign countries. But the small independent operators could not compete with the larger companies. Small-boat crews complained that the larger **trawlers** catch fish at a faster rate than they can. This means that catch quotas are reached much earlier than they used to be, closing the fishing season for everyone.

Though the Atlantic cod catch had increased slightly in the late 1970s, in the late 1980s, scientists reported that cod stocks off eastern Newfoundland were seriously depleted because some European nations were over-fishing outside Canada's 200-mile (370 km) limit. As a result, Canada had to lower cod quotas for Canadian fishers. This change increased unemployment and caused hardship in many coastal communities.

On the west coast, too many people were fishing for too few fish. The federal government brought in a system of fishing boat quotas. The system worked for those who received a licence to fish, but it forced some fishery workers out of business.

Government policies that protect fish resources do not always satisfy the people who fish. Just what role government should play in the fishing industry is a matter of much debate. Fishery workers tend to resist government intervention, yet without government involvement, the resource on which the industry is based would likely not survive.

The management of fish resources involves more than just fish and water. It must be concerned with matters as diverse as urban development and practices of the agricultural, forest, mining, and manufacturing industries, as well as the siting of hydro-electric dams. It is clear that the management of fish resources requires the co-operation of all levels of government, many different industries, and even countries, as well as individual fishery workers.

A trawler can fish more efficiently and faster over a larger area of sea than can smaller fishing boats that operate closer to shore.

Biotechnology has produced a new hybrid type of fish that is two-thirds Atlantic salmon and one-third arctic char. This fish grows faster than salmon raised in captivity. Gourmet restaurants prefer it because it tastes like char.

1. After studying Figure 7.14, describe the general trend in the total landings of cod between 1960 and 1968, between 1968 and 1977, and between 1977 and 1983. Explain the reasons behind the trends.

2. Describe the trends in the Canadian proportion of the total cod landings. Explain why the Canadian proportion increased so dramatically between 1973 and the mid-1980s.

3. The life of Atlantic fishers has never been an easy one, but despite its hardships, the fishers have developed a pride in the work they do and a sense of fun that often masks the real dangers they must often face. Their folk songs give many strong messages about their life and work.
a) Try to find records or tapes of folk songs from the Atlantic region that you can listen to in class. Why do you think many of these songs have choruses?
b) Do these songs help you to understand the work and workers of the fisheries better? Give examples.
c) As a class or in small groups, write a verse (that you might set to music) about a small fishing boat that makes a big catch.

4. a) Draw up a three-column chart that lists the factors you think affect the quantity of fish life.
b) Use the second and third columns to explain why each factor influences the quantity or the quality of fish resources.

5. Which factors mentioned in question 4 do you think have:
a) the most serious effects on fish resources? the least serious effects?
b) a greater influence on saltwater stocks? on freshwater stocks? on local fish stocks?

Government regulations to protect fish from over-harvesting sometimes conflict with the rights of Canadian Indians to unlimited fishing.

FISHING INDUSTRIES

Sea fisheries flourish on Canada's Atlantic and Pacific coasts. Freshwater fisheries are located on a few large lakes scattered across the interior of the country. In all these regions, the fishing industry is vital for employment and for the money it brings into the local economy.

IMPORTANCE OF THE FISHING INDUSTRIES

The fish catch gives employment not only to persons on fishing boats but also to many persons ashore. Workers in fish-processing plants total 50 percent of the number employed on boats. The value of processed fish is double the value of *fish landings*. People in hundreds of fishing ports work at service jobs that provide equipment and supplies for the fishing industry.

Because Canadians eat so little fish, the fishing industry depends on Canada's export trade to sell most of the catch. More than half of Canada's fish exports are shipped to the United States. The next most important markets are Western Europe and Japan.

The fishing industry is very important to Canada's coastal provinces. Ocean fisheries account for over ninety percent of the total value of the annual commercial fish catch (Table 7.1). The largest catch of sea fish, by value, comes from the east coast, and the balance comes from British Columbia. Most of the freshwater and Arctic fish landings are from a few, small, widely scattered fisheries.

A Canadian company is marketing artificial crab sticks, a substitute for a Japanese delicacy called *surimi*. The crab sticks are made from small, unsalable cod (or other less marketable species).

Table 7.1 *Value of Fish Landings by Fishery* ($000 000[a])

Newfoundland	168	
Nova Scotia	300	
Prince Edward Island	40	
New Brunswick	76	
Québec	66	
Atlantic		650
Pacific (B.C.)		250
Freshwater and Arctic		50
Total		950

Source: Data taken from *Monthly Statistical Review*, Fisheries and Oceans Canada

Note: The Atlantic and Pacific fish landings include some freshwater species. Québec fish landings are reckoned as part of the Atlantic region's because most of the catch is sea fish. [a]Three-year averages for the mid-1980s

1. a) How much greater is the value of Atlantic fish landings than that of Pacific fish landings?
   b) Suggest reasons for the difference (Figures 7.3 and 7.5).

OCEAN FISHERIES

Maritime fishing takes place off all three of Canada's seacoasts. The greatest concentration of fishing activity is in the Atlantic and Pacific oceans. In the Arctic, there is a very small number of commercial, recreational, and Inuit fisheries.

Along the Atlantic coast, there are about a thousand communities that depend wholly or mostly on the fishery. Most of these communities are small villages with fewer than 500 people. Some larger places benefit indirectly from fish-processing plants and shipbuilding facilities. In Nova Scotia, processing plants are concentrated along the south coast from Digby to Lunenburg. In New Brunswick, Shediac and Caraquet are the principal fish-processing areas (Figure 7.15). In Newfoundland, Québec, and Prince Edward Island, most of the fish-packing plants are scattered in smaller settlements along the entire coast.

About 70 000 people work at fishing or fish processing in the Atlantic provinces. There are thousands of fishing boats and over 300 processing

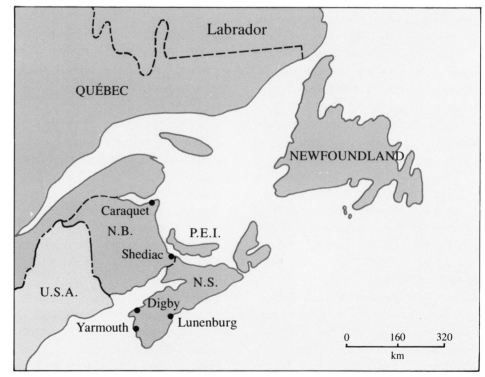

Figure 7.15 *Centres of the Atlantic Fishing Industry*

plants. In Newfoundland, fishing, including fish processing, is the major industry, providing work for about fifteen percent of the province's total labour force.

The Atlantic fishery is divided into two types of fishing. The *inshore fishery* uses small boats and operates within 20 km of the coast. The *offshore fishery* operates farther out to sea and uses larger vessels, mostly trawlers. Offshore trawlers are owned by large companies or village co-operatives that operate their own processing plants. The inshore boat crews complain that the offshore trawlers catch the fish before they can get close to shore. Most of the inshore owners cannot afford to buy big boats or expensive fishing equipment, and they must sell their catch to the large companies. More than half the people who fish inshore make only part of their living from fishing. Some have other part-time or full-time jobs. Others depend on unemployment insurance to support their families during the fishery's off-season.

Only the roe, or eggs, of most of the herring caught in Nova Scotia is used; the rest of the fish is discarded. The Canadian Institute for Fish Technology is studying the possible use of ground herring to make "herring hotdogs" or luncheon meats.

Fish-plant workers prepare herring for market in this Nova Scotia processing plant.

In the Atlantic fishery, cod, lobster, scallop, crab, and herring are the most valuable species harvested. These types of sea fish are caught by a variety of fishing methods: weirs, gill nets, longlines, trawl lines, traps, and drag nets. Although Newfoundland's catch leads the Atlantic Provinces in volume, Nova Scotia's leads in value because of the large shellfish catch (Table 7.1).

A 15 m inshore fishing boat costs up to $250 000, plus $500 a day for fuel and bait. The larger offshore fishing boats cost much more. Factory trawlers that catch, process, and refrigerate or freeze fish on board cost several million dollars.

Small inshore fishing boats like this one are used to catch lobsters. The baited traps, called lobster pots, are lowered to the shallow sea bottom.

Fishing is one of the most dangerous of all occupations. Besides the dangers of the work itself, boat crews face many natural hazards such as fog, ice, and storms.

F O C U S

Factory Freezer Trawler Joins the Atlantic Fleet

Canada's first factory freezer ship began fishing off the east coast in the mid-1980s. It was granted one of three new federal licenses to fish offshore from Newfoundland in a $7.5 million, used, West German trawler. Its home port is Lunenburg, Nova Scotia.

Freezer trawlers can stay at sea for as long as it takes to process and quick-freeze a full catch. Foreign countries have been using factory freezer trawlers to fish for over 40 years, but until recently, the federal authorities would not permit freezer trawlers to operate out of Canadian ports. The government was concerned that the trawlers might lower the fish catch of smaller fishing boats and eliminate jobs in fish-processing plants on shore.

Now with fish quotas in place, factory trawlers are not as likely to reduce the catch of other kinds of fishing vessels. In fact, the trawlers may take more of the under-fished species such as turbot and pollock. Although some Lunenburg plant jobs may disappear, the income from the large crew of the factory freezer trawler will inject extra millions of dollars into the local community.

The major advantage of using factory freezer trawlers for fishing is the opportunity such a trawler offers to capture more specialty markets with a higher-quality product. Fast-frozen fish bring top prices. For example, frozen cod is considered a superior product because it will cut into the thinner slices preferred in many North American and European restaurants. The Japanese prefer to buy fast-frozen redfish, also known as ocean perch, because of its superior colour and taste.

In the future, more factory freezer trawlers may provide technological improvement that will give the east-coast fishing industry a more stable economy.

The Pacific fishery employs about twenty thousand boat-crew and fish-processing workers. Most of the fish-processing plants are located near Vancouver and at Prince Rupert, though a few plants are scattered in small coastal villages.

Most fishing takes place close to shore because of the narrow continental shelf along the west coast. Most of the boats used are relatively small. They are larger than small boats used by the Atlantic inshore fishery but smaller than the Atlantic offshore trawlers. The Pacific boats are usually well equipped with modern fishing gear. Purse seining and trolling are the most common fishing methods. The average income of Pacific fishery workers is higher than that of the Atlantic fishery workers because of the high value of salmon. For this reason, not as many Pacific fishery workers need to hold other jobs to make a living.

Salmon is by far the most important catch along the Pacific coast. Sockeye salmon is the most valuable, followed in order by coho, chinook, chum, and pink salmon. Herring and halibut are also commercially fished, as are cod, ocean perch, and shellfish species.

Working in small groups, prepare a ''TV spot'' report to give to your class. Base your report on answers to one of the following questions. To find these answers you will need to refer to library references and other textbooks.

When you have written your report, which might include a brief ''interview'' with people in the industry, you will need to collect or make illustrations to make it suitable for a TV presentation.

1. a) What are the chief fishing methods used in ocean fisheries to catch groundfish, pelagic or anadromous fish, and crustaceans (shellfish)?
b) Which fishing methods are used in the inshore and the offshore Atlantic fisheries?
c) How do offshore fishing boats preserve their fish catch until their return to port?

2. a) How does a fish-packing plant process the fish catch?
b) List five products made from processed fish.
c) What happens to fish wastes and low-value species in a fish-processing plant?
3. Name two differences in fishing and fish-processing methods between the Atlantic and Pacific fisheries.

INLAND FISHERIES
The commercial fishery on Canada's lakes (Figure 7.16) employs about nine thousand boat-crew and fish-processing workers. Lake Erie provides over half the freshwater catch, while a series of large lakes as far northwest as Great Slave Lake yields much smaller tonnages.

Most freshwater fishing takes place close to shorelines of lakes, where the best feeding and spawning habitats for fish are found. The fishing boats ride low in the water to make the handling of fish nets easier. They are much the same size as Pacific fishing boats, but smaller than offshore Atlantic boats and larger than those of the inshore Atlantic fishery.

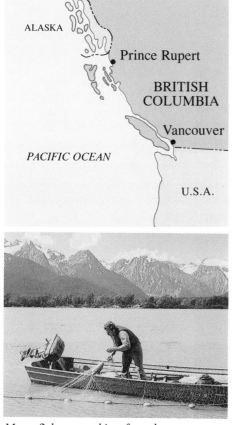

Many fishers working from large or small boats along British Columbia's coast use gill nets to catch Pacific salmon.

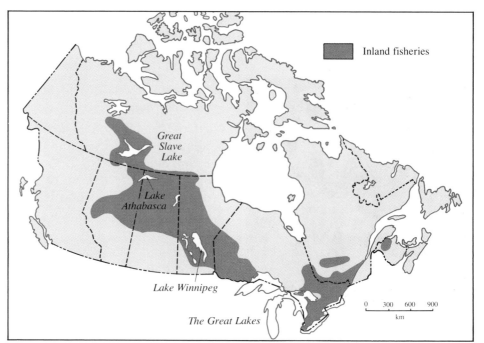

Figure 7.16 **Areas of Canada's Inland Fishery**

238

Lake Erie fishing boats are built to protect workers from cold temperatures, rain, or snow, and lake ice conditions.

The leading fish species caught, by volume, are smelt, walleye, and whitefish. Yellow perch bring the highest value per tonne of all species harvested. Fishing boats operate out of a few small lake harbours with facilities to process the catch. Most of the catch is sold fresh or frozen to restaurants, stores, and fish markets in the United States because Canadians eat so little freshwater fish.

It is estimated that recreational or sport fishing for freshwater species in Canada yields almost twice as much fish as the commercial fishery. Anglers prefer such species as trout, pike, bass, and salmon. Sport fishing, in winter as well as summer, helps the tourist industry and the economy of many communities across Canada.

1. Which provinces and territories appear to have no commercial freshwater fishing other than for salmon?
2. Name two ways in which freshwater fishing and fish-processing methods differ from those in the ocean fisheries.

Snowmobiles tow huts on sleds to the best offshore locations for ice fishing.

WHAT LIES AHEAD?
IS FISH FARMING A SOLUTION?

As we have seen in this chapter, many human activities threaten Canada's fish resources. In some parts of the world, fish farming provides an alternative supply of fish to eat. About fifteen percent of the total world fish production comes from fish farming. This means of food production is most common in Asia, where water-covered rice paddies are stocked with fish to provide additional protein in the diet of the people. In southern Ontario, too, trout farms have become fairly important supplies to restaurants that serve this fish.

In Canada, the federal and provincial governments have been hatching fish to stock the lakes and streams in areas where fish have been seriously reduced. Recently, some people have been raising fish in ponds, to sell as

food or to provide sport fishing for a fee. Some companies raise Atlantic salmon and tuna in cages in the Bay of Fundy or enclose Pacific salmon in bays along the coast of British Columbia. The salmon in this controlled environment grow to full size faster than they do under natural conditions. In Prince Edward Island, another company produces market-sized lobster in temperature-controlled feeding tanks.

Overall, Canada's commercial fish farming is not very important when compared to the production of the entire fishing industry. But if our natural fish resources decline as much in the next century as they have done in the current century, fish farming may be the wave of the future.

REVIEW QUESTIONS

1. Since Canada has such vast water areas, why are its fish resources limited?
2. How can pollution, exotic species, and harvesting methods put our fishing grounds under stress?
3. Besides fish products, name two further benefits that the fishing industry provides for Canadians.
4. How could fish farming and better fish management increase the supply of fish to meet our future needs?

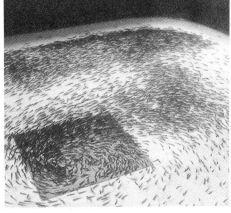

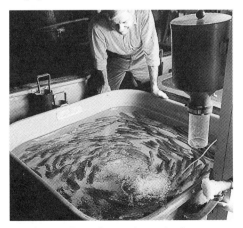

West coast salmon and some species of fish in Atlantic Canada are intensively managed from birth to harvest in fish-farming operations.

Chapter Eight

Forests and Forestry

Forests Unlimited!

■ Canada has more forest resources per person than any other country in the world.

■ The Canadian forest industry may have a timber shortage early in the next century.

How can both these statements be true?

Lumbermen in a B.C. forest about 1900. The two men who have just completed the undercut are standing on the springboard from which they worked. Next they will make the back cut with a two-man saw. The tree will fall in the direction of the undercut.

A RENEWABLE RESOURCE?

Forests, like fish, have been important to our country from the days of its earliest inhabitants. To the first explorers and settlers from Europe, as you read in Chapter Three, the forests were both awesome and beneficial. Today forests provide more kinds of products and benefits to Canadians than do fish. Indeed, forest products make up a larger part of our export trade than do the combined exports of farm, fish, and mineral products. Forest industries create many more jobs than does fishing in hundreds of communities across Canada.

In some ways, forest and fish resources are remarkably alike. Both are renewable resources, and if managed wisely, they can produce abundant harvests year after year. Both forest and fish industries have a history of over-harvesting and of harvesting in harmful ways that hinder or prevent the resource from renewing itself. Fish and trees alike are threatened by competition for the land or water they need. Just as power dams and offshore oil wells compete for use of the fish environment, so mines, parks, and farms compete for forest land. Unless our forest and fish resources are better managed, Canada could face shortages in the future.

DISTRIBUTION OF FOREST LAND

Trees are the most common type of natural vegetation in the Canadian landscape. A natural vegetation map (Figure 2.21 or an atlas map) shows the distribution of forests across Canada from our southern border to the northern tree line. Most of Canada's ecozones (Figure 2.29) are forested.

Forest land can be divided into two types: productive forest land and unproductive forest land. Productive forest land is land that can produce, on 10 percent or more of its area, trees with a trunk diameter of at least ten centimetres. Trees of this size are useful for commercial purposes. The parts of Canada that provide the greatest volumes of **commercial forest** have the largest land areas of productive forest, as well as much precipitation and warmer annual temperatures.

Timber grows fastest on the Pacific coast and in the mixed forest region of southern Ontario, but the largest area of productive forest in Canada is in Québec.

1. From the data in Table 8.1, calculate:
   a) the percentage of Canada's total land area that is forested
   b) the percentage of Canada's total forest land that is productive.
2. About how many times larger is Canada's productive forest land area than its agricultural land area?
3. State your general conclusions about the amount of productive forest land in Canada compared to the amount of land included in all the other land uses mentioned in Table 8.1.

FOREST SPECIES

Forest species can be classified as belonging to one of two main groups: **deciduous** trees and **coniferous** trees. In Canada's major forested regions, there are more species of coniferous trees than of deciduous trees, and the coniferous trees provide a greater volume of wood (Table 8.2). The greatest volume of **conifers** is in British Columbia, while Ontario and Québec produce most of Canada's deciduous timber.

Many coniferous and deciduous trees have shapes that are easily identified. As you read about different species of trees in this chapter, you might refer to a guide to trees that shows their typical shapes.

Table 8.2 *Canadian Forest Volume by Species*
(000 000 m³)

Conifers

Spruce	7 146	
Jack and lodgepole pine	4 087	
Balsam fir	2 827	
Hemlock	1 278	
Cedar	885	
Douglas fir	696	
Other coniferous	915	
Total coniferous		17 834

Deciduous

Poplar (aspen)	2 979	
Birch	1 124	
Maple	652	
Other deciduous	565	
Total deciduous		5 320
Total Forest Volume		23 154

Source: Data from Forestry Canada, 1986
Note: Forest volume includes only trees with a trunk diameter of 10 cm or greater, less the stump and top.

Table 8.1 *Area of Forest and Other Land Uses in Canada*
(000 km²)

Productive forest land	2 433	
Unproductive forest land	2 096	
Total forest land		4 529
Agricultural land		730
Other non-forest land		3 952
Total land area		9 211

Source: Data from Forestry Canada, 1986
Note: "Other non-forest land" is treeless land unsuitable for farming; it includes tundra, ice-covered areas, grassland, and rocky areas above the tree line.

Canada has 31 native species of conifers. Nine are pines, five are spruce and five fir, three larch and three hemlock, two cedar and two juniper, and one is cypress and one yew.

1. a) About how many times greater is the total volume of coniferous timber than the total volume of deciduous timber?
b) Where does the leading deciduous species rank as compared to species of coniferous trees?
2. a) Make a class list of as many different species of spruce and cedar as you can.
b) Name four species of trees in the ''Other coniferous'' category in Table 8.2.
c) Why is the white pine tree, used in pioneer times, not listed? (Clue: check Chapter Three.)
d) Name four trees that belong to the ''Other deciduous'' class listed in Table 8.2.
3. a) Using Chapter Two and other reference sources, find where four of the major commercial tree species listed in Table 8.2 grow in Canada.
b) On a sketch map of Canada, plot and label these species.
c) Which conifers are native to British Columbia? to eastern Canada?
d) Which of these coniferous species grow the fastest and become the largest trees?

THREATS TO OUR FORESTS

In all regions, forests face a variety of hazards that threaten their productivity. Anything that reduces the growth rate of trees damages forest resources. The chief threats to Canada's forests are illustrated in Figure 8.1. Some of these dangers are natural and have

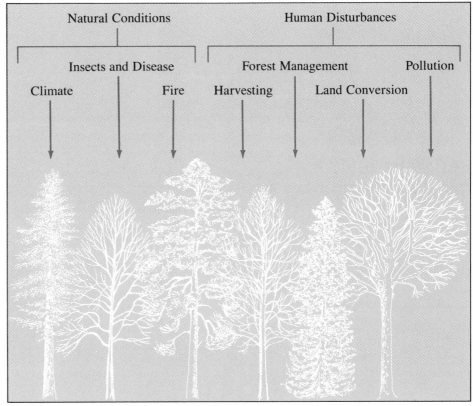

Natural Conditions   Human Disturbances

Insects and Disease   Forest Management   Pollution

Climate   Fire   Harvesting   Land Conversion

Figure 8.1 *Destructive Effects on Trees*

1. a) In your local area, recall or look for damage to trees caused by the following natural hazards:
i) winter and summer storms
ii) accidental fires started by people or by lightning
iii) disease and harmful insects
iv) air pollution
b) Which of these natural hazards damage trees most often? cause the greatest amount of damage? are the easiest to control?
2. a) What types of land use replace woodlots and forested areas in your city or town, or on farms in your area?
b) What benefits do local residents lose when land is converted from woodland to other uses?
3. Tree resources in some urban and rural areas are managed and cut under the direction of a Department/Ministry of Forestry.
a) If there are any such managed woodlots in your area, try to arrange a visit to one.
b) How successful do these management and harvesting methods seem in maintaining a healthy forested environment?
4. Plant a tree or shrub in a vacant lot at or near your school. Use a species that is native to your area. Be sure to get permission first, from your school board and from the owner of the lot.
Before you plant the tree/shrub, draw a plan of the area where you will plant it. Discuss in class the points you will need to consider in choosing the best place for planting. (Don't forget that trees and shrubs *grow*.) Mark the planting site on your plan.

always been present. Others are caused or increased by human activity. These dangers fall into two classes: natural hazards and human disturbances. Not all species of trees are able to adapt to environmental changes, and some do not survive under altered conditions.

NATURAL HAZARDS

Natural hazards such as storms, extremes of weather, insects, disease, and fire have serious effects on forest resources. Figure 8.1 and the following text outline how natural hazards may harm the forest environment.

Extremes of weather affect forests in many ways. A period of time when precipitation is much below average is harmful to trees. It can slow their growth and weaken them, making them more liable to disease. On the other hand, above-average precipitation for a period of years harms trees that cannot tolerate much moisture. Violent windstorms sometimes uproot large areas of trees. Unusually warm periods in early spring kill conifers in certain areas, such as the eastern edge of the Rocky Mountains. Here the sudden warmth and sunlight increase transpiration, and the still-frozen ground cannot supply the moisture to replace the moisture the trees lose by this process. As a result the needles dry out, and the trees die. Severe thunderstorms often ignite forest fires.

Insects and disease can be a menace to our forests. Insects often **defoliate** trees, and then the weakened trees are attacked by disease. Insects and disease infest every forested area, but they do not usually damage the trees severely. Forests where there are only one or two species of trees and where all the trees are about the same age are most likely to suffer from insect and disease epidemics. The most severe insect damage occurs in the forests of Ontario, Québec, and New Brunswick. In these provinces, in the mid-1980s, insects were defoliating between 20 000 and 30 000 ha of forest each year.

By far the most serious pest in eastern Canadian forests is the spruce budworm. This insect kills coniferous trees by eating their needles (Figure 8.2); it prefers the tender needles near the ends of the branches. The damaged needles turn yellow and fall to the ground. The damage caused by the spruce budworm accounts for over one-third of the timber losses from insect and disease attacks in all of Canada. Despite this insect's name, its favourite food is the balsam fir. Spruce budworm epidemics are cyclical: that is, years of heavy infestation are followed by years with almost no budworm damage (Figure 8.3). The damage from annual budworm attacks is limited by an increase in natural predators such as birds. Over the years, however, the area of forest land infested by the spruce budworm has increased.

The spruce budworm may be the most destructive single pest to attack Canadian forests, but other insects combine with diseases to cause even more tree damage.

---

1. a) According to Figure 8.3, roughly how many times larger is the area of spruce budworm infestation at each successive peak year of 1915, 1945, and 1975?
   b) Estimate when the next severe spruce budworm attack may take place.
2. a) Suggest why the spruce budworm infestations have become more widespread over the years.
   b) Why would insects and disease cause more damage to forests where the trees are of one species and all about the same age?

Ontario and Québec contain more than eighty-five percent of Canada's trees that are defoliated, dead, or dying from insect and disease attack.

Mountain pine beetle infestation

BRITISH COLUMBIA

Strong winds often blow down trees with weak root systems, especially those around the edges of cleared forest patches.

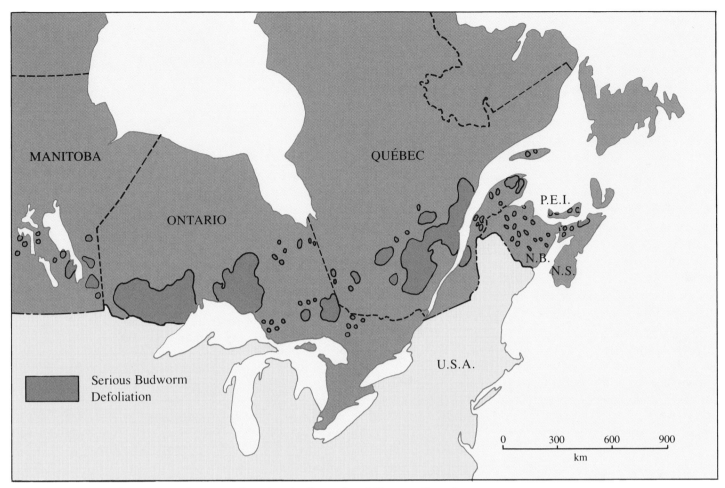

Figure 8.2 *Areas of Spruce Budworm Infestation in Central and Eastern Canada*

The mountain pine beetle is active largely in the Montane Cordillera ecozone in British Columbia, where it destroys the larger pines. Pine beetle infestations, like those of the spruce budworm, are cyclical, with rising peaks. In the mid-1970s, the mountain pine beetle was killing only 40- to 50 million trees a year; before the end of the 1980s, its annual toll was 180- to 200 million trees.

The gypsy moth is a relative newcomer to Canada from the northeastern United States. It did not become a forest menace in Canada until the 1980s, when it began to spread very rapidly in eastern Canada. Its favourite food is the leaves of deciduous trees. The gypsy moth may be a greater threat to forests than the spruce budworm. It feeds on a greater number of tree species, can lay more eggs, and can kill a conifer faster.

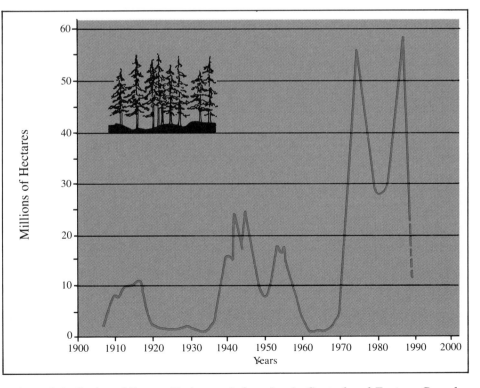

Figure 8.3 *Cycles of Spruce Budworm Infestation in Central and Eastern Canada*

The forest tent caterpillar does most of its damage in the hardwood forests of eastern Canada. Operating on a 10- to 12-year cycle, it infests most deciduous trees, including poplar, maple, oak, ash, and birch.

Dutch elm disease, which is spread by insects, has killed most elm trees from Nova Scotia to Manitoba in less than 50 years (Figure 8.4). The loss of these stately trees has greatly changed the appearance of both urban and rural landscapes, particularly in the Mixed-Wood Plain and Atlantic Maritime ecozones. Fortunately, a few elms survived the rapid spread of this disease, and a new generation of these beautiful trees is beginning to grow up in Canada.

Insects and disease have caused great destruction in forests, and so scientists have tried to control them. So far there is no general agreement on the best method. One approach is to spray infested forests with chemicals, but this method causes several problems. Rain washes the toxic chemicals into streams, where they work their way through the fish food chain to affect people. The chemicals kill not only the harmful insects but also others that prey on them. Through the food chain, the toxic spray that poisons insects also poisons insect-eating birds, and this reduces the numbers of birds that could help to control insect populations. The bad effects of chemical sprays make their use undesirable. Another objection to such sprays is that over time they become ineffective: some insects and diseases develop an immunity to pesticides.

An alternative to spraying toxic chemicals is to spray a biological insecticide like **Bacillus thuringiensis** (Bt). Bt is a kind of stomach poison

These elm trees are among the survivors of Dutch elm disease in central and eastern Canada. When they shed their leaves in winter for protection against the cold, the graceful shape of their trunk and branches stands out clearly against the sky.

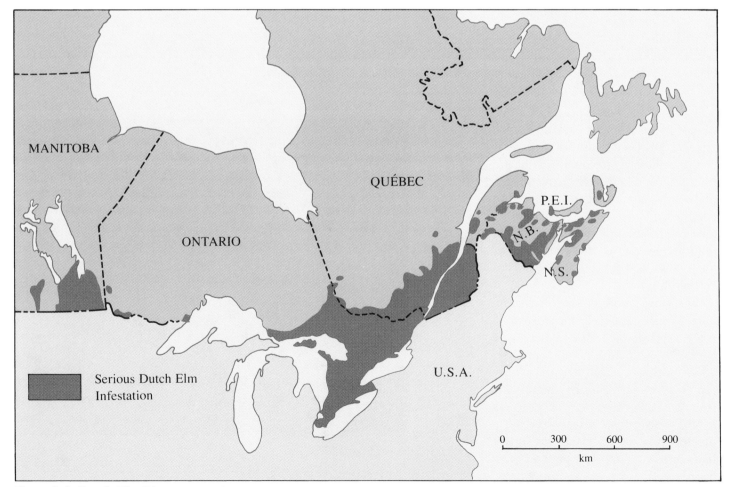

MANITOBA

QUÉBEC

P.E.I.

ONTARIO

N.B.

N.S.

U.S.A.

■ Serious Dutch Elm Infestation

0   300   600   900
km

Figure 8.4 **Dutch Elm Disease** *Dutch elm disease destroyed many of Canada's most beautiful trees.*

that affects only the spruce budworm. It has no effect on other insects, birds, earthworms, or people. But it is an expensive spray, and it is only effective in ideal weather conditions. A better option is to find a natural predator to control insect populations. Canadian scientists are experimenting with a tiny wasp that lays its eggs on the spruce budworm and kills it. The best option is to reforest with trees that are more resistant to budworms or any other insects and diseases. But this is a long-term solution that would take 50 to 100 years to accomplish.

To be effective, Bt must be sprayed when there is weak sunlight or none; little dew; no chance of rain; and the budworms are in their peak eating period.

Budworms (inset) *have defoliated and killed the spruce trees in this Ontario forest, but left other species untouched.*

Aircraft spray chemicals on the most severely infested areas of commercial forest to help reduce damage caused by insects and disease.

One of the most dramatic and destructive natural hazards that threaten a forest is fire. Forest fires destroy not only timber but also natural beauty, recreational environments, and wildlife habitat. Lightning causes over eighty percent of the fires that damage forests. The remaining fires are caused by human activity, and many of these result from the carelessness of people enjoying recreation in the forest. The fires caused by humans are often the most destructive because they usually start in southern areas, where timber is more abundant and the forest has the greatest recreational value. In northern or mountainous regions, too, fire may be especially destructive because here the soil is thin, and repeated fires can ruin it for further forest growth.

The satellite image shown in Figure 8.5 records widespread forest fires. The reddish tones represent forest cover, and the dark irregular shapes are lakes. The bluish-grey haze in the upper part of the figure was caused by the extensive forest fires burning at the time when this image was recorded.

Fires cause tremendous damage to our forests, but they can be helpful as well as harmful. **Foresters**, debating the effects of forest fires, have stressed their long-term benefits. For example, periodic fires give our northern forests their enduring vigour and many different types of plants and animals. Some species of trees, such as the jack pine, need fires to regenerate. Only after a fire, do jack pine cones release seed to produce new trees. After a long period of time without fire, mature stands of jack pines die off, and the forest is taken over by various species of spruce. In some areas, foresters purposely set fires and burn forests to regenerate the kind of forest they want.

Forest fires caused by lightning burn 10 times the area of fires caused by human beings. Lightning may strike remote spots, where fires take longer to detect and are harder to suppress.

Fires instantly change forest ecosystems.

The amount of damage caused by fire in a forest area shows on images recorded by remote sensing satellites. These images also show the types of trees growing in a forest, the volume of harvestable timber, and the damage caused by insects and disease.

Young jack pine trees grow from the seeds released during a forest fire 16 years earlier.

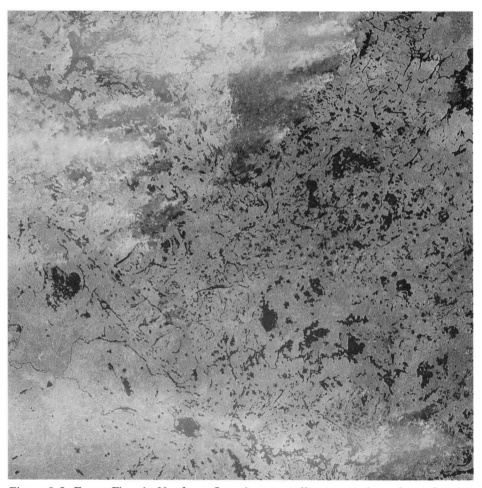
Figure 8.5 *Forest Fires in Northern Ontario* *A satellite image shows forest fires in Northern Ontario (centred on 50°00′N, 95°00′W).*

A mixed forest, southwest of Ottawa, in early fall

Sugar maples in eastern Canada seem to be the trees most likely to be damaged by acid rain.

After a forest fire, many different flowers, shrubs, and trees start to grow. This growth provides variety in the forest ecosystem. Regrowth in burned-over areas provides habitat and food for more kinds of birds and animals than a mature forest of very few species can support. Different kinds of species in a forest lead to a more stable ecology. If one species is attacked by disease or insects, the whole forest ecosystem is not destroyed because other species are there to take the victim's place in the food chain.

Natural hazards affect all forested parts of Canada at one time or another, but the forests of Ontario, Québec, and British Columbia appear to suffer most often and most severely from adverse effects of weather, insects, disease, and fire.

> The average annual loss of forest caused by fire, insects, and disease is greater than the annual amount of forest harvested.

1. Locate the area shown in Figure 8.5 on an atlas map. About how far is this area from the Manitoba border? How far is it north of Kenora?
2. In which physiographic region is this area located (Figure 2.1)?

3. What kind of forest grows here (Figure 2.21)?
4. Images obtained at later dates would show the amount of forest destroyed by fire. How could this kind of information be used in managing forest resources?

HUMAN DISTURBANCES

Human beings interfere with the natural development of Canadian woodland in many ways. Air and water pollution, conversion of land to other uses, methods of tree harvesting, and techniques of woodland management all have serious effects on forests. The areas that suffer most from this human interference are the same parts of Canada most affected by natural hazards: Ontario, Québec, and British Columbia.

The direct effects of air pollution can be seen downwind from smelters used in mining and from other industries that release large volumes of sulphur dioxide and other pollutants into the air. In the centre of some of those pollution zones, only bare rock and soil remain. As far as twenty-five kilometres downwind from the sources, a viewer can see dead and dying trees. Taller smoke stacks, built to solve local problems, simply spread the pollutants over a much broader area. But such local "hot spots" of air pollution

> The recent manufacture of equipment to control pollutants such as those that produce acid rain has generated over 100 000 new jobs and billions of dollars worth of economic activity.

may soon become things of the past as the government imposes new regulations to lower toxic emissions.

Many people consider acid rain a threat to our forests, especially in eastern Canada. But others argue that the destructive effects of acid rain are exaggerated. Some scientists believe that acid rain is killing many trees directly. They cite as evidence the ***dieback*** of sugar maples in southern Ontario and Québec (Figure 8.6, page 250), which has been progressing rapidly in recent years. Other scientists claim that no proof exists that acid rain is the sole cause of such tree losses. They believe that other factors such as old age, disease, insects, and even thin soils have weakened the trees. In other words, they think that acid rain contributes to the death only of those trees that are least fit to survive.

249

The exact effect of acid rain on our forest resources will not be known for many years. In the meantime, foresters recommend that forests be managed in a way that keeps trees as healthy as possible, to give them a better chance of surviving the damage of both acid rain and forest pests.

Land conversion often wipes out forests. As parts of Canada were settled, huge tracts of forest land were cleared to make way for agriculture. By now, most of the good farmland is already under production, and so little forest is being cleared for farming. In fact, in some areas, marginal farmland is being abandoned and turned back to forest.

But the conversion of land to other uses still takes large amounts of forest land out of production. Dams, built to generate hydro-electric power or transfer water, cause floods in forest areas. Cities expand into forested land. Highways, railroads, pipelines, electric transmission lines, and *seismic* lines for petroleum exploration cut wide swathes through Canada's forests. Most mine sites are located in the forest. In some areas, cattle grazing in the forest slows or prevents the regeneration of trees. Trees cannot usually be harvested from forested land that is set aside as national parks or wildlife preserves.

The harvesting of trees itself disturbs the natural forest ecosystem. Removing only certain species changes the proportions of kinds of trees in the forest. Similarly, removing trees of a certain age changes the proportions of old and young trees in the forest. Harvesting large quantities of trees reduces the amount of humus in the forest soil, and this change hampers regeneration. If the rate of harvesting is higher than the rate of regeneration, forest resources will diminish. To maintain forest resources at the current level, timber lost in logging and from other causes must be balanced by new tree growth.

All logging does not have the same effect on forests. Different kinds of harvesting produce different effects. The method of harvesting most commonly used is *clearcutting*. In clearcutting, all the trees are cut; no mature trees remain to re-seed the area. Clearcutting on steep slopes causes serious soil erosion. This means that the regeneration of a stand of commercial timber will take longer than it would if another method of harvesting were used.

Environmentalists often urge governments to prohibit logging in

Patches of cleared land in the valley and on the hillside of this Nova Scotia farm are surrounded by forest.

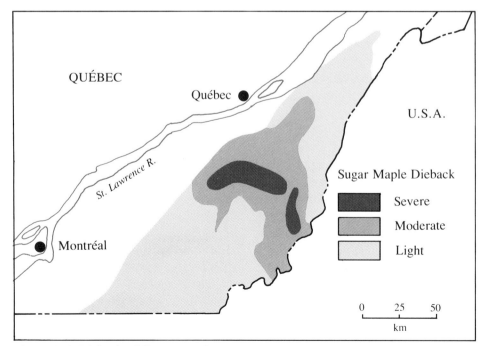

QUÉBEC

Québec ●

U.S.A.

St. Lawrence R.

Montréal ●

Sugar Maple Dieback

■ Severe

■ Moderate

□ Light

0   25   50

km

Figure 8.6 *Dieback of Sugar Maple in Québec*

A small patch of clearcut coniferous forest on the thin rocky soil of the Canadian Shield in Northern Ontario. Trucks use the logging road to haul the cut timber to a nearby mill.

World Deforestation

In some other parts of the world, tree harvesting causes more severe forest losses than it does in Canada. In South America and Southeast Asia, for example, the harvesting of tropical rain forests, which are located on or near the equator, is a major cause of **deforestation** (Figure 8.7). In these areas, the expanding population wants wood for fuel or export and cleared land on which to grow food. Large forest tracts are logged each year by both clearcutting and full-tree logging. Scientists believe that this wholesale destruction of the forests is also wiping out many plant and animal species. The loss of rain forest habitat is reducing the numbers of some of the tropical plants used to make prescription drugs. It is also reducing the numbers of migratory birds that visit Canada and other countries. Deforestation of tropical regions may also be intensifying the greenhouse effect and causing major changes in world climate.

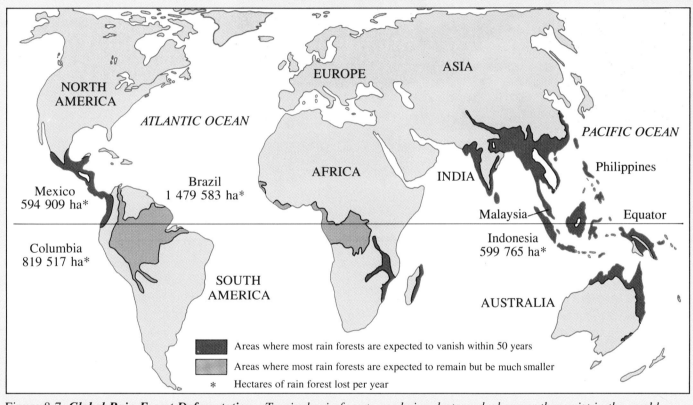

Figure 8.7 **Global Rain Forest Deforestation** *Tropical rain forests are being destroyed wherever they exist in the world.*

national and provincial parks. They want these forests to remain in a natural state. They say that old trees should be permitted to die and fall to provide nutrients for the young trees that replace them.

Specialists in forestry often argue that they can improve on nature. By proper management, they say, the forest can be kept young and vigorous. Foresters claim that as unmanaged forests grow old, large numbers of trees die and create a fire hazard. Forest fires are followed by the growth of less desirable species of trees. It is better, they argue to harvest trees before a forest reaches the age of decline. A forest managed in this way can provide useful wood products and recreation for an unlimited time.

A satellite image can preserve a useful record of forest operations. In the one shown here (Figure 8.8, page 252), dark green stands for coniferous forests and light green for deciduous trees and shrubs. The small, irregularly shaped, pink patches indicate recent clearcutting. The patches of light green show where a second growth of shrubs and small trees is reclaiming cut-over areas. The logging roads appear as pink lines.

When clearcutting is combined with **full-tree logging**, the harmful effect on the forest is even greater. In full-tree logging, the whole tree is

251

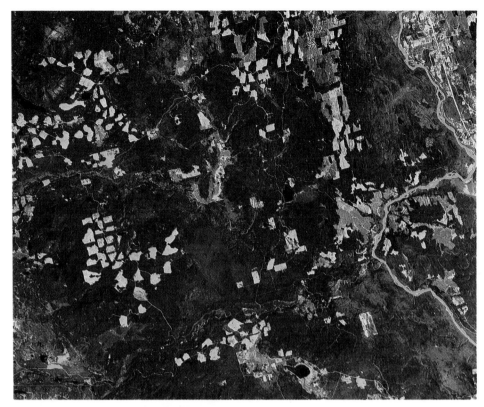

Figure 8.8 ***Clearcutting in British Columbia's Forests*** *A satellite image shows forest operations near Vanderhoof, in the interior of British Columbia (centred on 54°05'N, 123°76'W).*

hauled to a central location to be de-limbed. Because the trees are not topped and de-limbed where they were growing, the forest soil is not replenished with nutrients from the decaying limbs, branches, and twigs. Full-tree logging was introduced as a new harvesting method about 1970, and by the mid-1980s, it was used for about 20 percent of the logging in Canada.

1. Locate on an atlas map the area shown in Figure 8.8. What is the river on the right side of the image (the thick, pink, meandering line)?
2. Why would clearcutting in many small patches instead of in one large section of equal area be less damaging to the environment?
3. The satellite image shown in Figure 8.8 was taken in the month of June. Why would an image taken in January be much less useful?

Loggers now leave a border of trees around lakes and along rivers, the better to protect the habitat of fish and other wildlife that depend on water resources.

Less wasteful methods of harvesting could reduce damage to Canadian forests. Instead of clearcutting, loggers might leave a number of trees to provide seeds for regeneration; or they might cut down trees in strips and patches, leaving nearby uncut sections of seed trees. (Figure 8.9 is a satellite image of an area clearcut in patches. The dark green is coniferous forest, the light green, deciduous forest. Both the irregular light pink patches at the lower left and the much larger dark pink patches at the lower right

For every dollar received for timber, only about half a cent is spent on forest regeneration. This neglect, not overcutting, is the main reason why Canada's forest is decreasing.

represent clearcut sections. The light pink areas along the shore and inland parallel to it are farm fields and settlements.) But the options to clearcutting yield less profit, and they are not widely used.

1. Locate on an atlas map the image shown in Figure 8.9. Name the body of water at the top of the image and the city near the centre.
2. Compare this forest-cutting pattern in New Brunswick with the one in British Columbia shown in Figure 8.8. Why would clearcutting in New Brunswick cause less soil erosion than clearcutting in British Columbia?

Logging companies do not own most of the forested land where they cut trees, and so they have little incentive to improve their methods of tree harvesting. Most of the ***crown land*** they lease is owned by the provincial governments, which collect taxes for all the timber cut. The more timber cut, the more taxes paid to the government, and so governments, like private companies, do not always make the best harvesting methods their top priority.

Each provincial government sets an ***annual allowable cut*** for the volume of timber that logging companies may harvest each year. In recent years, the logging in most provinces has totalled less than the annual allowable cut, yet the volume of accessible commercial timber is shrinking. Perhaps government timber quotas and agreements with forest companies should be set lower to allow forests to ***regenerate***.

The managing of forests can be considered a kind of farming called ***silviculture***. Forest managers or tree farmers select superior trees to provide the best possible seeds for ***seedling*** production. The farmers grow the improved seedlings in ***nurseries*** and use them to regenerate the harvested

Strip logging in this deciduous forest of colourful fall trees is a form of clear-cutting. The strips of trees left uncut provide better natural seeding for the cleared areas and reduce soil erosion.

Figure 8.9 ***Logging Patterns in New Brunswick*** *A satellite image shows an area in northeast New Brunswick (centred on 47°70′N, 66°23′W).*

forest. Sometimes they cultivate the floor of the harvested forest to improve growing conditions for the planted seedlings. During the early stages of *reforestation*, the tree farmers thin their crop to get rid of weak or unwanted trees and make space for healthy trees of preferred species. Sometimes they use *herbicides* to control weeds and grasses that rob young seedlings of water, light, and space for growth. If necessary, they provide fertilizer for the young trees to give them all the nutrients they need for rapid growth.

Canada has had a poor record in forest management over the years. Scandinavian countries, for example, produce three to four times as much wood per hectare as does Canada. The situation in Canada actually seems to be getting worse. Increasing wood shortages in most areas have forced loggers to harvest trees far from processing plants. In some cases, wood is being hauled as far as 600 km for processing. Some 30 million hectares of harvested forest land require replanting. Of the total forest resources of Canada, only a small part is being managed according to the best methods known.

1. a) As a member of a small group, help to research one of the following topics. When your group has researched the topic, prepare a report to make to your whole class.
   i) methods of fighting forest fires
   ii) acid rain damage to sugar maples in Ontario and Québec
   iii) the impact on forest resources of the James Bay project in Québec or the Bennett Dam in British Columbia
   iv) infestation of Canadian forest by an exotic forest pest or disease
   v) new technologies in silviculture that make timber land more productive
   vi) a dispute between loggers and environmentalists over an area of forest with a sensitive ecology
   b) Suggest a practical solution for one type of hazard to forest resources noted in part a). What governments, agencies, industries, and other organizations would likely be involved in implementing the solutions you have suggested?

2. a) What kinds of hazard do you think would reduce the quantity of timber in an area more than the quality?
   b) What kinds of hazard are likely to have long-term effects on forest resources?
   c) Explain why you made the choices you did in parts a) and b).

USING OUR FORESTS

Forests are important to Canada because of the benefits trees provide to ecosystems across the country. Trees conserve soil and water resources. Our forests even affect our climate and help to protect our natural environment. Forests also provide a habitat for wild animals and birds. They create a recreational environment for people who wish to hike, camp, take photographs, draw or paint, and observe wildlife. Our economy, too, benefits from the productive use of forests, which creates jobs and provides raw materials for hundreds of wood and paper products that are found in homes, schools, workplaces, and recreational facilities.

Canadian forests have always provided some firewood for heating purposes. When oil prices rose during the 1970s, many people began to use wood stoves, fireplaces, and even wood-burning furnaces to heat their homes. This change of fuel created a great demand for firewood, particularly in areas around towns and cities. Some farmers who had neglected their woodlots for years began to cut trees for firewood.

1. a) Brainstorm with your class to list as many uses of forests as you can.
   b) Make a chart under the following headings, showing all the uses of forests you have listed: Wood Products, Paper Products, Recreational, Environmental, Other.

2. If there is a forested area in your local region, explain how it contributes to the forest uses you have listed.

Ninety-four percent of Canada's timber is located on crown land owned by the federal or provincial governments.

On steep, clearcut slopes in British Columbia, a tangle of branches, stumps, and unused logs helps protect seedlings from harsh weather and soil erosion.

FIREWOOD

Deciduous trees provide the best firewood because, as *hardwoods*, they burn "cleaner" (i.e., more completely, producing less black smoke and leaving less ash) and provide more heat than coniferous trees, or *softwoods*. The softwood from conifers may be used as fuel, but it does not provide as much heat nor burn as cleanly. When only softwoods are burned in a fireplace, the chimney must be cleaned more often. The most popular firewood in eastern Canada is maple, but other trees such as beech and birch are also burned. Poplar (aspen) trees do not make as good firewood as other deciduous trees.

CHRISTMAS TREES

One forest product we might overlook is Christmas trees. Some Christmas trees, such as spruce, balsam fir, Douglas fir, and hemlock, are cut from natural forests. Others, particularly the Scots pine, are specially grown on plantations. The growers prune these trees each year to produce trees of the same height and shape. After seven to ten years these uniform trees are ready to ship to markets in North America. The uniformity of the trees makes it easier for the growers to cut, wrap, and ship them to market.

After the trees are cut, the area where they have grown is replanted with seedlings. About five million Christmas trees are cut in Canada each year. About half of these trees are exported to the United States. Nova Scotia is the province that exports the most Christmas trees.

---

1. Survey the members of your class to find out how many of your families use natural Christmas trees.
   a) What do you think are the advantages of natural Christmas trees? the disadvantages?
   b) What do you think are the advantages of artificial Christmas trees? the disadvantages?

Cut wood is stored and used for campfires, fireplaces, and stoves or furnaces in many Canadian homes and cottages.

Christmas trees ready for shipping to North American markets

LOCAL STUDY

1. Conduct a survey in your class about the use of wood as fuel in your neighbourhood:
   a) Estimate what percentage of the heating fuel in your homes is wood.
   b) In your neighbourhood is wood burned in i) fireplaces, ii) stoves, or iii) furnaces?
   c) What species of trees are most commonly used as fuel for the heating devices used in your area?
   d) What is the difference in price between the different species used?
   e) Try to find out:
   i) where local firewood dealers obtain their wood supply
   ii) how many families burn artificial firelogs made from pressed sawdust
   iii) whether any local industries burn waste wood or logs.

2. How much does your community depend on local firewood supplies? Explain the reasons behind your findings.

3. To the model of your community that you began in Chapter Two, add examples of woodlots and wooded recreational areas.

c) What are the most popular species used as natural Christmas trees in your homes?

d) Why, in your opinion, are these species more popular than others?

2. a) Where in Canada are Christmas trees grown on plantations?

b) Where in your local area can you go to cut your own Christmas tree?

3. What do you think are the advantages to Christmas tree dealers of harvesting trees from forests rather than plantations? the disadvantages?

MAPLE SYRUP

Maple syrup is another forest product that we might overlook. It is produced from sugar maples growing in deciduous forests or mixed forests in southeastern Canada. In the early spring, when the sap begins to flow up into the branches of the maples, from winter storage in the roots, syrup makers drive *spiles* into the trunks of the trees. The sweet, colourless sap of the sugar maple runs through the spiles into buckets or plastic tubing, in which it is carried to a sugar house for processing. When this sap is boiled down, much of the moisture evaporates, leaving a sweet syrup with a distinctive maple flavour. If maple syrup is boiled down even more, it turns into maple toffee and finally into maple sugar.

Each year Canada produces about $30 million worth of maple syrup products. Over ninety percent of these products are made in the Province of Québec; the rest comes from Ontario, New Brunswick, and Nova Scotia. But Québec has lately been producing less maple syrup because of dieback in the sugar maples.

Thirty to fifty litres of sap from sugar maple trees produce one litre of maple syrup.

FORESTS OF COMMERCIAL VALUE

Canada has an abundance of trees, but while all forest land is useful, not all of it has commercial value. That is to say, not all of Canada's forested land provides forest products. Figures recording the area of forest land in Canada with trees large enough to harvest (productive forest land) were given in Table 8.1. Even on this land not all the large trees are worth harvesting. Some are too difficult to get to or too far away from markets to have commercial value.

In fact, timber in commercial volume grows in only a few regions in the southern part of the country. British Columbia leads all provinces in volume of timber, with softwoods from many large, fast-growing, coniferous species. Ontario and Québec lead in hardwood timber from deciduous trees; they also produce a large quantity of softwood from conifers.

Collecting sap to make maple syrup

The South Moresby Forest Struggle

South Moresby is the name for the southern part of the Queen Charlotte Islands, which lie 100 km off British Columbia's Pacific coast. This moist, warm, mountainous area contains some of the oldest and largest coniferous trees in Canada. Several rare and unusual plants and animals live in these forests. Mudslides and gully erosion also occur in this area as a result of violent thunderstorms, frequent earthquakes, and logging activity.

The first Europeans to visit South Moresby harvested some of its timber resources (as well as furs, salmon, and minerals). They introduced deer, which browsed on young cedar trees, reducing replacement timber. The Haida Indians used the region's resources in traditional ways to satisfy their basic need of food and shelter. They used the large trees to make special items such as dugout canoes and totem poles. The arrival of the Europeans brought a change. The Haida began to hunt, trap, and log for the newcomers. In

time many Haida died from small pox, a contagious import from Europe; others left the Queen Charlotte Islands for the mainland. The development of logging on the steep slopes and the damming of some of the streams destroyed the habitat of wildlife such as salmon, abalone, and geoduck.

In the early 20th century, loggers in the Queen Charlottes ignored South Moresby because its timber stands were smaller and harder to reach than others available. South Moresby forests became more attractive to logging companies in the mid-1970s as there came to be a shortage of mature timber on the B.C. mainland. The Haida objected to this

logging because the area being logged was their ancestral home. Environmentalists also protested because the logging was destroying the beauty of the landscape.

In the late 1980s, the government of British Columbia and the federal government reached an agreement on the use of this land. South Moresby is now a Park Reserve which will not become a National Park until Haida Indian land claims are settled. The federal government paid British Columbia millions of dollars to compensate logging companies for loss of timber revenue from their cancelled land leases and to relocate loggers who had lost their jobs.

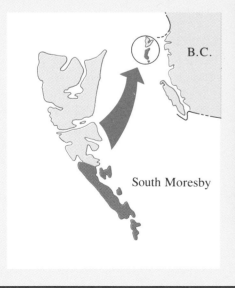

Large, mature trees grow close together on the productive forest land in South Moresby.

Table 8.3 *Commercial Forest Volume by Province and Territory* (000 000 m³)

Newfoundland	525
Nova Scotia	244
Prince Edward Island	26
New Brunswick	571
Québec	4 225
Ontario	3 529
Manitoba	680
Saskatchewan	905
Alberta	2 656
British Columbia	8 867
Yukon	480
Northwest Territories	446
Canada	23 154

Source: Data from Canadian Forestry Service, 1986

Note: Forest volume in this table represents cubic metres of timber from usable trees in areas where it pays to harvest logs and move them to market.

Fifty percent of the trees growing in Canada cannot be harvested because they are protected in parks, located in swamps or on steep slopes, or are too small and hard to reach for logging.

1. Using the data in Table 8.3, rank the provinces and territories according to their volume of commercial forest.

2. a) The Northwest Territories contain about one-third of Canada's total land area. Why, then, is the commercial forest volume in the Territories so small?
   b) Why is Alberta's forest volume greater than those of Manitoba and Saskatchewan combined?
   c) Québec has the largest area of forest land of all Canada's provinces, but British Columbia has the greatest commercial forest volume. Explain the reason.

3. In which provinces would there be enough commercial timber to support large forest industries?

THE FOREST INDUSTRY

The forest industry is one of Canada's most important industries. Forest products account for about fifteen percent of all goods manufactured in Canada. One of 10 Canadian workers has a job in the forest industry, which is the country's largest employer after government. Each job in the woods provides another job in a local forest community and another somewhere else in the Canadian economy. More than three hundred communities across Canada depend on the forest industry for their prosperity. In British Columbia, wood processing makes the largest contribution to the economy. In Northern Ontario, Québec, and New Brunswick, pulp and paper manufacturing is a mainstay for employment and income. Many people are employed in the industry itself, and the trucking and railway companies that transport the paper products also employ more workers than they could without the business the forest industry gives them.

Canada produces about ten percent of the world's forest products. Both the United States and the Soviet Union produce more, but Canada exports the most. Nearly thirty percent of all forest products that enter the world market come from Canada. Our best customers for export sales are the United States, Europe, and Japan. We export 90 percent of our newsprint, 70 percent of our lumber, and 60 percent of our pulp.

The forest industry can be divided into three main sub-industries: logging, general wood processing, and pulp and paper manufacturing. Logging, or tree harvesting, provides the raw materials used by the other two industries all across Canada.

LOGGING

The logging, or *roundwood*, industry produces logs for many kinds of wood industries, as well as pulpwood and wood chips for the pulp and paper industry. About sixty percent of logs become processed wood products, and 30 percent becomes paper. The industry also produces telephone poles, railway ties, fence posts, and *pilings* for bridge supports, mine tunnel props, and shoreline breakwalls. These uses account for about nine percent of the logs cut in Canada. Only one percent is used for firewood.

This paper mill in Bathurst, N.B. creates jobs for many people living in the city and its surrounding region.

Large rolls of unfinished paper or newsprint are loaded aboard an ocean freighter for export.

Canada's more than one thousand logging companies employ nearly fifty thousand workers in specialized jobs. Forest engineers plan the tree harvest from laying out and building local logging roads to advising on the best method for getting the timber. Fallers use mechanical felling machines or chain saws to cut, de-limb, and top the trees. Machine operators haul the logs to the road by *skidding* or *yarding*. Full-tree harvesters cut, trim, stack, and haul timber out of the bush faster than is possible by means of other logging methods. These machines are most efficient in forests where trees of the same species grow on gently sloping land east of the Rockies. Drivers of special flat-bed logging trucks transport most logs from forest to mill. Graders sort the logs either before or after this trip. (Sometimes, for especially long trips, logs travel by rail.) In British Columbia, logs are floated through coastal waters in rafts called *booms* or on barges; in eastern Canada, logs are often floated down rivers and collected in booms near the mill sites.

Tugboats tow log booms to a sawmill in British Columbia's Fraser estuary. In the foreground is a barge that collects sawdust and other wood waste used in a nearby pulp and paper mill.

1. Design a flow chart to diagram stages in the logging process from forest to mill.
2. a) In which natural vegetation area of Canada are most hardwood trees logged?
   b) Name two ways in which these deciduous logs are used.
3. Why do Québec and Ontario have more logging companies than British Columbia, where most Canadian timber is cut?
4. The logging industry, like the fishery, has its folk songs. Try to find some of these songs on records or tapes, and play them in class. Plan and draw a class mural or series of sketches based on the songs that illustrates the way of life of some early loggers.

WOOD PROCESSING

Canada's many wood industries fall into two groups: the primary and secondary wood industries. The primary wood industries make lumber products that require little processing; they operate sawmills and *planing mills*, shingle mills, and *veneer* and *plywood* mills. The secondary wood industries operate millwork plants that manufacture products such as flooring, matches, equipment handles, baskets, boxes, doors, window frames, coffins, kitchen cabinets, bathroom vanities, furniture, and charcoal. Some of these plants make particle board and waferboard from sawdust and wood chip wastes that are produced by the mills of both primary and secondary wood industries.

Sawmills and other wood-processing plants use about half of the logs cut in Canada; the balance is used by the pulp and paper industry. About 1300 sawmills are scattered across Canada's commercial forest belt. Most large-capacity sawmills are located in British Columbia, which produces 70 percent of Canada's lumber. These mills manufacture expensive finished lumber and veneers from the high-grade timber of Douglas fir, sitka spruce, and western red cedar trees. From western hemlock and lodgepole pine, they produce construction-grade lumber.

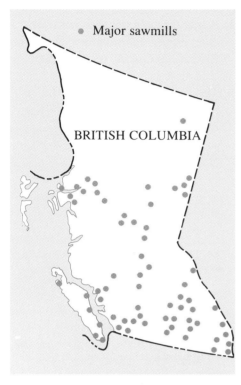

● Major sawmills

BRITISH COLUMBIA

A new hybrid poplar tree planted in southern Ontario can grow large enough in 10 years to be used to make waferboard that is better and cheaper than the plywood usually used in the construction industry.

Forest companies save money today by using wastes such as bark, sawdust, shavings, chips, edgings, and slabs for fuel to produce steam power in mills. This recycling also saves the cost of waste disposal.

PULP AND PAPER

Among Canadian manufacturing industries, the pulp and paper industry stands first in number of employees, value of salaries paid, and value added in the manufacturing process. This industry provides over 150 000 jobs in forests and mills, and creates many other jobs in the manufacture and distribution of thousands of paper products.

Pulp and paper mills make pulp from wood and then turn it into paper or cardboard. The paper products manufactured from pulp include cardboard boxes, wax paper, facial tissues, toilet paper, newsprint, and the many grades of paper used to make books, photographs, posters, and stationery.

The wood pulp is made from lower grades of coniferous trees of all kinds. Black spruce, jack pine, and hemlock are the species preferred for making newsprint.

About seventy companies operating 150 mills make up Canada's pulp and paper industry. Some mills manufacture only pulp, others only paper. Most make both pulp and paper. Several companies produce lumber, shipping containers, packages, bags, and chemicals.

Most of Canada's pulp and paper mills are located close to large supplies of timber, fresh water, and hydro power. Québec, Ontario, and British Columbia provide the sites for most of these mills (Table 8.4). The highest concentration of pulp and paper mills in the country is found in Québec along the St. Lawrence, Ottawa, St. Maurice, and Saguenay rivers (Figure 8.10). While some of the wood pulp used to make paper in British Columbia comes from the industry's waste chips, in most parts of Canada, pulp is produced from specially cut logs.

Paper is manufactured in several stages. The first stage is the making of pulp. Logs used to make the pulp must first be de-barked (Figure 8.11, page 262). The machinery that takes off the bark uses either great revolving drums or powerful streams of water for this process. Then the logs (or wood chips) go for pulping, a process that separates the wood fibres. Pulping may be done mechanically or chemically, and both methods are used in Canada: 60 percent of Canada's wood pulp is made by chemical processing and 40 percent by mechanical processing. Mechanical pulping shreds the wood with grindstones or rotating discs. In chemical pulping the fibres are separated by cooking the logs in a

Wood pulp is used to make cellulose, which is used, in turn, to produce rayon, cellophane, celluloid, some textiles, and hundreds of other manufactured products.

A full-tree harvester in northwestern Ontario

special solution in a huge pressure cooker. The wood pulp is then screened to remove large particles, and it may be further purified by bleaching. Many types of paper are made from a mixture of chemically and mechanically produced wood pulps. Only special kinds of paper require added chemicals or dyes.

Table 8.4 *Pulp and Paper Mills by Region*

Atlantic	18
Québec	57
Ontario	36
Prairies	7
British Columbia	24
Canada	142

Source: Data from Canadian Pulp and Paper Association, 1986
Note: Over half the mills produce both pulp and paper; the rest are divided about equally between pulp production and paper making.

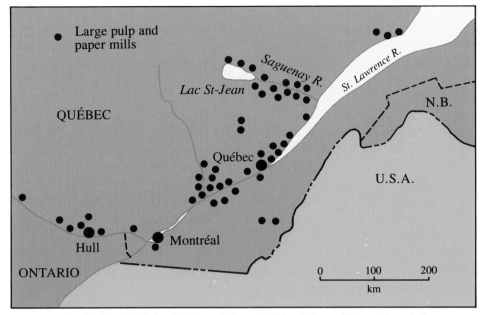

Figure 8.10 *Québec's Major Pulp and Paper Mills* *Most mills are found close to large supplies of timber, fresh water, and hydro power. Most of the mills between Montréal and Québec City are located on the St. Maurice River, a tributary of the St. Lawrence.*

Pulp And Paper Pollution

You can always tell when you are near a pulp and paper mill—by the smell. Foul-smelling sulphur and other air pollutants from a pulp and paper mill are irritating, but they are not the mill's worst product. The waste water that mills discharge into nearby rivers and lakes does far more damage to the environment. The clean water becomes clogged with waste solids (bark, chips, fibres) and polluted with toxic chemicals from the paper-making process. It turns an ugly brown and becomes harmful to humans, and to fish and other wildlife.

During the first half of the 20th century, people thought that the huge volumes of water in streams and lakes could safely dilute the pollutants. Canadians considered their supply of fresh water inexhaustible. But by the 1960s, many people had adopted a different view. As concern for the environment grew, the federal and provincial governments passed legislation requiring the industry to clean up pollution and gave grants to help with the cost. The pulp and paper industry, in turn, began to take serious measures to reduce pollution.

Now pulp and paper companies use bark-reclaiming equipment and filters to remove bark and other solids from waste water. They recycle water in their plants to reduce the volume of waste water that needs treatment. They remove chemicals from the effluent, or waste water run-off, in aerated ponds before discharging it. Sometimes they recover these chemicals and use them again. The pulp and paper industry is also taking steps to reduce air pollution. Here the possibilities are limited. It is possible to remove solid materials from the air, but nobody has discovered a way to eliminate the stink from the chemical pulping process.

Pollution control measures in the pulp and paper industry have been reasonably successful. Between 1960 and 1990, the amount of pollution from pulp and paper mills has been reduced by about eighty percent. This reduction may represent the best standard that can be achieved, for further improvement is likely to be difficult and much more costly.

The wet pulp is poured in a thin mixture onto an endless moving belt of wire screen. As the screen moves along, the water drains away, causing small bits of the wood fibre to mat together like wet felt. This continuous, matted sheet of pulp moves through press rollers and heated drying cylinders to remove the last traces of moisture. Finally, it is ironed by heavy rollers and becomes smooth paper. On high-speed machinery, pulp may take only 10 seconds to go from the wire screen stage to finished paper.

Some paper mills use rag fibres or recycled paper instead of wood pulp as their raw materials, but the general process is the same. The material is shredded into fibres and then matted into paper.

High-quality mushrooms grow three times as fast in wood-cellulose waste from B.C. pulp mills as do mushrooms grown in other dead organic matter.

To create the many different kinds of paper we use each day requires occasional use of other processes. Sometimes a coating of clay or another binder is used to make the paper's finish more glossy. Some paper may be coated with wax to make it waterproof. But most paper is produced by the basic paper-making process described in this section.

1. Although British Columbia has Canada's largest commercial forest by volume (Table 8.3), it ranks only third in number of pulp and paper mills. Suggest the reason.

2. a) What proportion of the total number of pulp and paper mills in Canada is in Québec and Ontario?
b) Suggest a reason why there are so many more mills in central Canada than in other regions of the country.
c) In which ecozones are most of the mills in these provinces located? (See Figure 2.29.)

3. After consulting an atlas, describe and explain the locations of pulp and paper mills in the Prairie Provinces and in Atlantic Canada.

4. To make small amounts of paper by hand is fairly simple. Yet quite beautiful paper can be made with little equipment. Try making your own sample of paper.

Equipment you will need:
- Large mixing bowl
- Food blender
- Large shallow tray
- Wooden frame—a sturdy old picture frame will do—with fine wire mesh. (This frame must sit flat within the tray.)
- Absorbent cloths
- Electric iron

Materials you will need:
- Hot water
- Powdered starch
- Uncoated scrap paper torn into small pieces (Stationery, construction paper, craft paper, brown wrapping paper, and watercolour paper are all suitable, but do not use more than 25 percent newsprint.)

Optional:
- Vegetable matter (potato, carrot, cornstalks, grasses and straw, dried flower leaves or stalks, and many other garden products). Besides vegetable matter you may also use clothes dryer lint and wasp nests—but make sure there are no wasps in or around them.
- Food colouring or natural dyes

Method:
Pour a litre of hot water into a large bowl. Add five millilitres of powdered starch and about two hundred millilitres of paper scraps. Soak overnight. Put the pulp into a food blender (about one-half at a time) and blend for 10 to 20 seconds, or until the mixture is a creamy colour. (If the

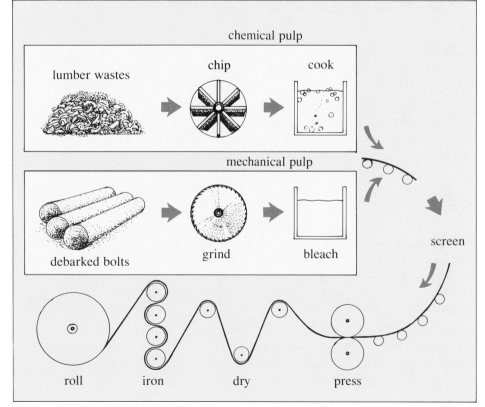

Figure 8.11 *The Pulp- and Paper-Making Process*

mixture turns grey, it has been blended too long.) Place the shallow tray beneath the framed screen, and pour the mixture onto the screen. Lift the framed screen above the tray, and shake it lightly to allow the excess water to run off. Turn the screen over so that the sheet of paper that has formed falls flat onto an absorbent cloth. Place another absorbent cloth over the sheet and press to squeeze out as much water as you can. Iron the sheet with a warm (not hot) iron and hang to dry.

5. Every society has its "culture heroes and heroines": men and women who have won "name and fame", and whose exploits make good stories.

The tales of the mythical giant lumberjack Paul Bunyan were first told in print in an American newspaper and have become a part of the American folk tradition. However, according to *The Canadian Encyclopedia*, "a Canadian origin has often been claimed." The Bunyan mythology may have originated in the French Canadian folk lore of Jean Bonhomme or in the legends of Glooscap. Try to find tales of Paul Bunyan, and choose one to read in class.
a) What does the tale tell about an early lumberjack's ambitions and problems?
b) Write your own Paul Bunyan "tall tale" to read in class.

WHAT LIES AHEAD?

FUTURE TREE FARMING
Trees, like other plants, grow much more quickly on better soil. In Canada the land with the best soil has been cleared of forests to produce farm crops. As a result, most of our remaining forests are growing on relatively poor soil.

Southern Ontario has an environment favourable to tree growth. Its soils are good to excellent for forests. The growing season is long, and precipitation is adequate. Of all Canadian regions, southern Ontario is best suited for growing deciduous trees. Here land planted in trees would match some of the most productive forest land in the country.

The value of large tree farms in southern Ontario would be tremendous, both commercially and in other ways. Hardwood from maple, oak, walnut, and other deciduous trees is scarce and brings a high price. One mature black walnut tree may be worth as much as $2000. An increase in forested land in southern Ontario would also have very positive environmental effects. The forests would reduce water run-off, erosion, spring floods, and the summer dry-up of streams. Trees would expand the habitat for wildlife and birds.

Trees planted and managed in plantations would probably take 50 or more years to reach maturity for harvest. Investors are seldom willing to wait that long. Government subsidies to growers might be required to help get such a project started. But if, in a century or two, food production was needed more than forest products, the land could be cleared of trees and returned to agriculture. The soil would be far more fertile after having been in forest for a hundred years or more.

REVIEW QUESTIONS

1. Since Canada has such vast forest areas, why do we say that our country's tree resources are limited?
2. a) Explain how natural hazards, pollution, and harvesting can put our forest lands under stress.
b) Describe some actions that have been taken to relieve some of this stress.
3. What benefits, besides wood products, does the forest industry provide for Canadians?
4. Why is most of our country's lumber produced in western Canada, and most pulp and paper in central and eastern Canada?

Coniferous seedlings (from a greenhouse nursery) are transplanted in rows in a field on this tree farm belonging to the Government of Ontario.

Chapter Nine

Farmland and Farming

How Can It Be?

■ Millions of Sahel (sub-Sahara) Africans are starving, while some Canadian farmers have a surplus of products they cannot sell.

■ Canada produces more of some farm products than the market requires, but many people are worried about the threats to our farmland caused by soil erosion and increasing urbanization.

Modern combines harvest wheat on the prairies.

THE VALUE OF FARMING

The agricultural industry, which we usually call farming, is very important to Canada. In fact, in one way or another, all Canadians depend on farming. Farming provides an income for large numbers of people, not all of them farmers. Many of these people work in industries based on farm products, while others produce machinery and supplies that farmers need.

Just as Canadians depend on farming, farming depends on Canada's supply of agricultural land. Farmland is therefore an important resource.

Like fish and forests, farmland can also be a renewable resource. In the long run, the land's value to us will depend on how well we manage it. If we manage our farmland well, it can produce forever. If we mismanage it, within a generation we may destroy both the farmland and the industry based on it. A look at Canada's farmland and how it is used may show which road we seem to be taking.

CANADA'S FARM PRODUCTS

Whether we live on a farm, in a village or town, or in a large city, we depend on farms to provide much of what we need. Many of us do not realize how much we depend on farms and farmers. Some Canadian farm products are processed and packaged in such a way that we do not recognize their farm origin. Many other farm products come from outside Canada. It is safe to say that at every meal we eat or drink some food produced on Canadian farms (Figure 9.1), and that we regularly use Canadian non-food farm products, as well.

1. How often do you use Canadian farm products in your home? To find out, construct a table that lists Farm Products (column 1), Processed Products (column 2), and notes how often they are used (column 3). Head column 3 as follows:

Frequency of Use		
Often	Occasionally	Rarely

When the tables have been completed, work in small groups to compare results. Each group might work on one category of farm products to find out how often each item is used, on average, in the homes of class members: often (at least once a week), occasionally (once a

Figure 9.1 *Canada's farmers produce many foods in all four of the basic foods groups recommended for a healthful diet in Canada's Food Guide.*

month), or rarely (once or twice a year).

You may have to check the list of ingredients in many packaged food products to identify the farm products they contain. For example, one hot cereal on the market contains four Canadian-grown grains, and your favourite cookies may contain both oatmeal and wheat flour. The first column lists the general farm product groups and some specific crops used to make the processed products; the second column lists examples of the processed products.

2. a) As a class make a list of farm products grown for sale on farms within one hundred kilometres of your school.
b) Working in pairs or small groups, design a poster to advertise local farm products and a slogan to promote their use.

3. a) Plan three meals for a family of four for one day. Make a grocery list of all ingredients that you will need. From newspaper advertisements, establish prices for the ingredients, and calculate the cost of each meal.

What is the total cost of all three meals? What is the cost per person? Record your data on a chart. Compare your findings with those of other students in your class.
b) Find out the source of each product on your menus. List the products that are produced from plants and those that are produced from animals.

What percentage of the food for your menus comes directly from plants? from animals?

Where do the foods originate? Are they grown or raised locally? imported from other provinces? imported from foreign countries?

Make another chart to record the sources of the food on your menus.

THE IMPORTANCE OF FARMING IN CANADA

Farming has been important to Canada since pioneer days. At first, each family's farm provided no more than enough for the household. Soon, however, the farm dwellers were selling surplus products to people in the nearby villages and towns. The money earned from sales of produce provided the farmers with supplies and implements that increased farm production. The increase provided a surplus of agricultural products that was then shipped to other countries. Today about thirty-five percent of Canada's agricultural production is exported. These farm exports, valued at about $8000 million a year, aid Canada's balance of trade with other countries.

Farming also promoted economic development in Canada and helped establish settlement patterns (Chapter Three). Every area with climate and land suitable for farming became densely settled. The farms, villages, towns, and cities were all interconnected by a complex network of transportation routes. A map of Canada that highlights the areas of highest population density (such as Figure 3.16) also shows the most productive agricultural areas of the country: the valleys and coastal lowlands of the Atlantic Provinces, the Great Lakes-St. Lawrence Lowlands, the western prairies, and some valleys in British Columbia.

This relation between agricultural land and dense population is no accident. Farming produces plant and animal products that must be processed, packaged, and distributed for sale. These activities take place in towns and cities. Farmers require many items of machinery and equipment, as well as many services. All of these goods and services come from towns and cities. We can see more clearly how farming and towns or cities depend on each other when we consider what supplies and services the agricultural industry needs.

The businesses and industries needed to process, package, and distribute farm products include:
- flour mills
- bakeries
- cookie factories
- fruit and vegetable canneries
- food freezing plants
- dairy plants
- cheese factories
- ice-cream factories
- meat-packing plants
- breakfast cereal factories
- grocery wholesaling companies
- grocery stores
- tanneries
- glue factories
- woollen mills
- sugar-beet refineries

All of these facilities are located in towns and cities.

The following farm machinery, equipment, and supplies come from towns and cities:
- tractors
- trucks
- wagons
- ploughs
- disks and cultivators
- seed drills
- mowers
- combines
- hay balers
- corn harvesters
- corn cutters
- grain storage bins
- grain grinders
- artificial fertilizer
- fuel
- weed and insect killers (insecticides, herbicides, and fungicides)
- miscellaneous tools and hardware items

The average Canadian farmer produces enough food to feed about ninety people.

Farms require the services of many people to keep their equipment running; to protect their property, livestock, and crops; and generally to manage their business. These people, who usually have their offices in towns or cities, include:

- veterinarians
- horticulturalists
- soil scientists
- electricians
- mechanics
- welders
- accountants
- bankers
- insurance brokers
- computer programmers
- truckers

The lists you have just read show that although only about five percent of the Canadian work force is employed on farms, many other people have jobs that depend on farming. For example, a farmer who buys a tractor helps to create jobs in an iron mine, a steel mill, a tractor parts factory, a tractor assembly plant, a rubber tire factory, an advertising agency, a trucking business, a farm implement dealership, and the bank that finances the purchase.

One Canadian job in ten depends on agriculture or agriculture-related industries.

1. Poll the members of your class to discover how many members of your families have jobs that depend directly or indirectly on the agriculture industry.
2. Develop a poster that shows the various types of farm machinery, equipment, and supplies that come from cities. To find illustrations, look through news magazines, farm magazines and newspapers, hardware catalogues, brochures from fall fairs or agricultural exhibitions, and advertising material available from farm machinery and supply companies.

3. Add to your model from Chapter Two examples of farm buildings, cultivated fields, undeveloped lots, and public land in your area.

CANADA'S AGRICULTURAL LAND RESOURCES

A country's agricultural land resources depend on the nature of its terrain, the quality of its soil, and the nature of its climate. Canada has a huge land area, but how much of this area has the right combination of slope, soil, and climate to qualify as agricultural land?

THE EXTENT OF CANADA'S AGRICULTURAL LAND

Canada is a large country, but only a small part of it is suitable for farming. Terrain and climate limit the amount of Canada's productive land. In the northern half of our country the summers are too short to grow farm crops, and the winters are too cold for livestock such as cattle, hogs, or poultry. In the Western Cordillera, only a few valleys contain land level enough to cultivate for crops. Some of the lower mountain slopes may be used for grazing cattle, but the higher mountains are too steep and rocky for any kind of agriculture. In the Atlantic region, the low mountains and hills restrict farming to the coastal lowlands and major valleys. The southern portion of the Canadian Shield, which has a growing season long enough to raise farm crops, has only a few large patches of land suitable for farming; the rest is too hilly, rocky, or swampy. Only the Great Lakes-St. Lawrence Lowlands and the grassland region of the Interior Plains have extensive

areas of agricultural land. To sum up, only 13 percent of Canada's land area is suitable for any kind of agricultural production.

Most farm crops require 100 frost-free days to mature. They also need a warm summer (17.5°C or warmer in July) and plentiful moisture (a minimum annual precipitation of about 400 mm). Besides this, they need fairly level land and deep soil.

1. On an outline map of Canada:
   a) Use horizontal lines to mark the areas that have an average of 100 or more frost-free days (Figure 2.19).
   b) Use vertical lines to mark the areas that have an average July temperature of 17.5°C or higher (Figure 2.15).
   c) Use diagonal lines to mark the areas that have average annual precipitation of 400 mm or more (Figure 2.12).
   d) Colour lightly the areas where horizontal, vertical, and diagonal lines overlap. This coloured area shows where farming can be carried out in Canada.
2. Review the landform section of Chapter Two, and then explain why large parts of the Atlantic region, the Canadian Shield, and the Western Cordillera cannot be farmed, even though the climate is suitable.
3. The Peace River Valley is the most northerly agricultural area in Canada. At such a northerly latitude, there are more summer daylight hours than in southern Canada. How does the longer period of daylight help compensate for the short frost-free season of the Peace River Valley (Figure 2.19)?
4. Suggest why most of the Rocky Mountain foothills and the Interior Plateau of British Columbia are used for grazing cattle instead of growing crops.

THE QUALITY OF CANADA'S AGRICULTURAL LAND

Not all of Canada's agricultural land is being farmed. Some farmland is occupied by cities, highways, railroads, or industries. Other land that could be farmed is being used to grow forests. Some land is not farmed because it cannot produce enough to provide a living for farmers. In some of Canada's more northerly districts, for example, such as the Peace River Valley and the Clay Belts of Northern Ontario and Québec, farming has not proved profitable because early fall frosts have often destroyed crops. Over the last 30 to 40 years, many people have abandoned their farms in these northern areas. In the Atlantic region, much of the potential farmland lies in scattered patches that are too small for modern farming.

Canada's Land Inventory (CLI) Classification

Early settlers found out the hard way, by trial and error, which parts of Canada's land were best for farming. Today, Canada Land Inventory (CLI) maps provide such information. The CLI maps classify land according to its suitability for agriculture (Figure 9.2). They divide the land into seven categories according to its value for crop production (Table 9.1).

Land in the first three categories (CLI 1, 2, 3; Figure 9.2) ranges from good to excellent (Table 9.2, page 270). It will not only grow more of a given crop but will also grow a greater variety of crops than will land in lower categories. This good-to-excellent land is easier and more profitable to farm. Class 4 land has limitations that would prevent most people from making a living by farming it. Class 5 land can be cultivated and planted in grass or clover for hay or pasture, but it is not suitable for grain or other farm crops. Class 6 land has too many limitations—it is usually too steep or stony—to be cultivated and is suitable only for grazing. Class 7 land, or wildland, is not useful for any agricultural purpose.

The CLI is based mainly on such factors as soil and slope of the land. Only the most extreme of other factors that affect the suitability of the land for agriculture are considered. For

Table 9.1 *CLI Agricultural Land Classes*

Class	Percentage of Total Area	Description	Limitations[a]
1	0.5	Excellent	None
2	1.8	Very Good	Minor
3	2.9	Good	Moderate
4	2.8	Fair	Severe
5	3.7	Poor	Suitable only for hay or pasture
6	2.0	Very Poor	Suitable only for grazing
7	86.3	Wildland	No agricultural use

Source: Adapted from Simpson-Lewis, and others, *Canada's Special Resource Lands*, Map Folio No. 4

[a]Limitations include low water-holding capacity, excess water, stoniness, low fertility, steepness of slope, and adverse climate.

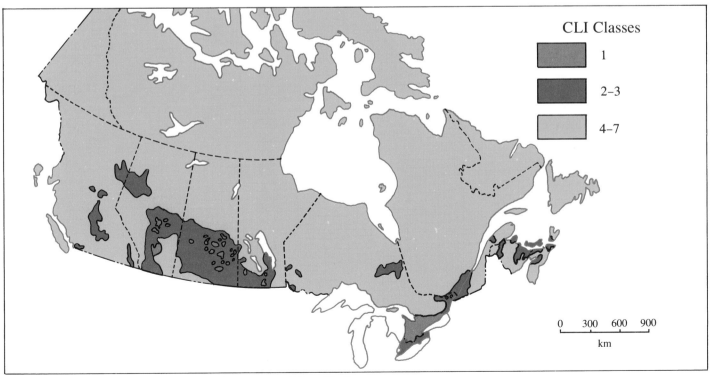

Figure 9.2 *Canada's Agricultural Land Resources (Classified)*

example, if the precipitation was too low to support any crops, climate would be considered a factor. As Chapter Two states, climatic factors such as amount of annual precipitation, length of frost-free season, and summer heat vary greatly across Canada. Because of the differences in climatic factors, patches of land with the same CLI classification but in different parts of the country can produce very different crop yields. For example, Class 3 land in southern Ontario or southwestern British Columbia could produce more than twice as much grain per hectare as Class 3 land in Saskatchewan.

Table 9.2 *Good-To-Excellent Agricultural Land in Canada by Province*

Provinces	CLI Classes 1–3 Land as Percentage of Total Area
Newfoundland[a]	0.0
Prince Edward Island	0.9
Nova Scotia	2.5
New Brunswick	2.9
Québec	4.8
Ontario	15.8
Manitoba	11.2
Saskatchewan	35.4
Alberta	23.3
British Columbia	3.2
Canada	100.0

Source: Adapted from Simpson-Lewis, and others, *Canada's Special Resource Lands*, Map Folio No. 4
[a]Newfoundland has 5500 ha of Class 3 land, which is less than one-tenth of one percent of Canada's total area.

1. a) What percentage of Canada's land surface falls in CLI Classes 1–3 (excellent to good)?
   b) The area of Canada not suitable for agriculture is classified as wildland (Class 7) by the CLI. What use is made of this land?
2. a) Rank the provinces from highest to lowest according to how much good agricultural land (CLI Classes 1–3) each contains (see Table 9.2).
   b) The Prairie Provinces are all about the same size. Why has Manitoba much less Class 1–3 land than Alberta and Saskatchewan?

FARMING AS AN INDUSTRY

We may not think of farmers as businesspersons involved in an industry, but they are. We also tend to think that all farmers do exactly the same job, but all farming is not the same. Canada's agricultural industry is made up of several types of farming, depending on the kind of land resources available.

TYPES OF FARMING

The physical factors of climate and land place limits on what farmers can grow. Many other economic factors affect their decisions about which crops they will grow, and what livestock they will raise, if any. Farmers must decide which farm products they can produce and transport to market most profitably. Some farmers must also decide whether they can make more money by growing crops to sell for cash or by growing feed for livestock and then selling the livestock. Government *subsidies* may encourage farmers to produce certain products. Farmers who live near cities often produce fruit, vegetables, and milk because it is easy to transport these perishable products to the urban market. If economic conditions change, some farmers may have to change their type of farming.

Table 9.3 *Leading Provinces[a] For Some Farm Products*

Beef Cattle	%		Dairy Products	%		Hogs	%
Alta.	39		Qué.	40		Qué.	35
Sask.	27		Ont.	31		Ont.	32
Man./Ont.	11		Alta.	9		Alta.	12
Sheep	**%**		**Poultry[b]**	**%**		**Tree Fruit**	**%**
Ont.	31		Ont.	37		Ont.	44
Alta.	25		Qué.	24		B.C.	25
Qué.	14		B.C.	10		Qué.	19
Small Fruit[c]	**%**		**Vegetables**	**%**		**Potatoes**	**%**
Ont.	36		Ont.	53		P.E.I.	23
N.S.	19		Qué.	28		N.B.	20
B.C.	18		B.C.	7		Qué.	16
Oats/Barley/Rye	**%**		**Wheat**	**%**		**Corn**	**%**
Alta.	44		Sask.	63		Ont.	74
Sask.	29		Alta.	22		Qué.	16
Man.	16		Man.	13		Man.	7
Oilseeds[d]	**%**		**Hay**	**%**			
Sask.	36		Alta.	27			
Man.	32		Ont.	20			
Alta.	31		Qué.	19			

Source: Calculated from Statistics Canada data
[a]Provincial rank as a percentage of Canadian total for each farm product value
[b]Poultry: chickens, ducks, geese, turkeys
[c]Small fruit: strawberries, raspberries, currants and others
[d]Oilseeds: Canola, sunflower seeds, flaxseed

Table 9.3 shows the importance of different kinds of farming in different parts of Canada. It shows which provinces are the largest producers of the farm products listed. It also shows that some provinces produce specialty crops including the tree fruit, small fruit, and vegetables grown in Ontario, and the potatoes grown in Prince Edward Island, New Brunswick, and Québec.

The types of farming in Canada form complex patterns, since farmers raise many combinations of crops and livestock and produce scores of different farm products. Figure 9.3 gives a very general picture of types of farming across Canada. The categories in the legend include only the major agricultural activities. An area mapped as a single type of farming may also produce other crops and livestock. In the wheat belt, other grain crops are also grown, and many cattle graze on the open range. The mix of crops and livestock differs from one region to another. For example, in the dairy and grain category, the grain grown in Manitoba is mostly wheat, in southern Ontario mostly corn, and in the Atlantic region, mostly oats and barley.

---

1. According to Table 9.3:
   a) Which province produces the largest number of farm products (commodities)? Explain why it is the leader in each case.
   b) For which commodities do three provinces produce 90 percent or more of the Canadian total?
   c) For which commodities does a single province produce 50 percent or more of the Canadian total?
2. a) Which two areas of Canada produce the greatest variety of crops? Why?
   b) Which part of the prairie region do you think would have the least variety in farm activities? Explain your reasoning.
3. Suppose that there are two 1000 ha farms available to you at the same price. One is in the wheat belt of Saskatchewan; the other is in the mixed farming area in southern Manitoba. Which one would you

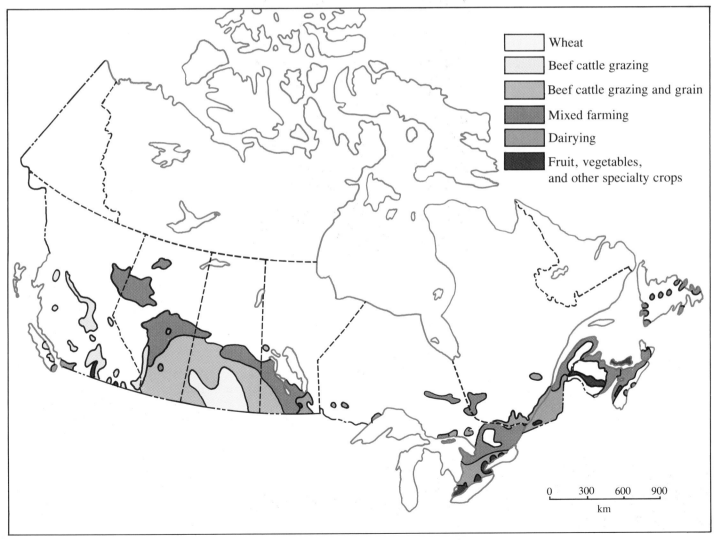

	Wheat
	Beef cattle grazing
	Beef cattle grazing and grain
	Mixed farming
	Dairying
	Fruit, vegetables, and other specialty crops

Figure 9.3 *Types of Farming in Canada*

choose? In giving reasons for your choice consider:

- soil
- annual precipitation
- variety of crops that could be grown
- possible differences in yield of crops
- access to a large urban market

British Columbia

Vancouver and Victoria provide large urban markets for such items as milk and many kinds of fruits and vegetables. Therefore in the areas about the cities, there is much dairy farming and *market gardening*. The long growing season and mild winter make it possible for growers to produce a wider variety of crops than in any other place in Canada. Raspberries, strawberries, and boysenberries are grown in large quantities. This area also produces large crops of flowers and flower bulbs, and many of these are shipped across Canada.

In the Interior Plateau region of British Columbia, great herds of beef cattle graze, as well as some sheep. The ranches are huge: none is less than a thousand hectares, and some are several hundred thousand hectares in extent. Ranchers usually own their grassland and rent additional **timber range** from the provincial government. In winter they keep their cattle in the valley bottom, where they feed them hay and grain when the grass runs out. In spring the animals graze the lower slopes, where the first grass appears. As the season goes on, herders move the cattle farther up the slopes, where late new grass is available. By midsummer they are grazing timber range. Ranchers who also have sheep sometimes herd them higher up than cattle, to alpine meadows above the tree line. In the fall, all the livestock is gradually moved down the slope again.

A few of the southern interior valleys of British Columbia produce a number of tree fruits and other fruit crops. Because the climate here is dry,

Market gardening in British Columbia

the farms must be irrigated. The most important of these valleys is the Okanagan Valley. It produces over ninety percent of the province's tree fruits and all of its grapes. About seventy-five percent of the Okanagan tree fruit area is used to grow apples. Other tree fruits produced in the Okanagan include pears, plums, cherries, peaches, and apricots. Of all Canada's provinces, British Columbia is second only to Ontario in producing tree fruits.

The Prairie Provinces

The three Prairie Provinces lead all Canada's provinces in producing beef cattle, wheat, other grain (oats, barley, rye), and oilseeds (Table 9.3). Alberta is also one of the top three Canadian provinces in producing hay, sheep, hogs, and dairy products.

In the wheat zone of the Prairie Provinces, other grain crops are grown, and there is much cattle grazing. Similarly, in the areas of beef cattle grazing, grain growing, or mixed farming, wheat is also an important crop. Oilseeds are grown throughout the prairie region except in the dry southwestern corner of Saskatchewan. Sheep graze in the Rocky Mountain foothills; they are less common in the grain and the beef-cattle grazing zones.

Orchards in the Okanagan Valley

Wheat growing on the prairies

The prairie region is rightly famous for its production of wheat. It produces 90 percent of Canada's wheat. The wheat is planted early in the spring and grows rapidly, nursed along by the cool wet weather and long days of spring and early summer. In the dry heat of summer the wheat ripens, and the kernels dry out and harden. The relatively dry climate helps produce a high-quality **hard wheat** for bread flour and a high-quality **durum wheat** for pasta. It also has a negative effect: the yield of wheat per hectare on the prairies is very low compared to that in a more humid region such as the Great Lakes-St. Lawrence Lowlands. The prairie wheat farmers make up for the low yield by farming very large areas. It is common for a wheat farmer to own two or three **sections** of land.

The demand for Canola and sunflowers has increased with the growing concern for eating healthful foods. People prefer food products such as cooking oil, margarine, salad dressing, and shortening made from sunflower or Canola oil instead of from animal fats or coconut oil. In recent years prairie farmers have responded to the new demand by growing more oilseed. The increase in Canola planting has been dramatic. In the 1960s, Canola was a relatively insignificant crop. By the late 1980s, prairie farmers were planting close to three million hectares of Canola each year.

Figure 9.4 *A Landsat Image of the Alberta-Montana Border* *Note the contrast between the uncultivated range land in Alberta* (top) *and the intensive crop farming in Montana.*

A cattle ranch in southern Alberta

Canola in blossom. Canola is an important oilseed crop on the prairies.

Sunflowers in bloom. Prairie farmers are growing more of this oilseed crop.

273

Types of Farmland

Good farmland (CLI Class 2) planted in apple orchard

Poor farmland (CLI Class 5) suitable only for hay or pasture

Wildland (CLI Class 7) of no use for farming

Ontario and Québec

Ontario and Québec are leaders in the production of a wide range of farm commodities (Table 9.3). Most of their farm products come from the Great Lakes-St. Lawrence Lowlands, a region with long, warm summers, adequate precipitation, level land, and fertile soils. This region produces a wide variety of crops. Its farmers enjoy a ready market for their goods in the dense network of cities and towns nearby.

This close urban market is most valuable to producers of perishables such as milk or fruits and vegetables. The large dairy farming areas owe their existence to this market rather than to any climate or soil conditions. The heaviest concentration of dairy farming is therefore closest to the two largest cities, Toronto and Montréal (Figure 9.3). In the dairy regions of Ontario and Québec, the largest crop grown is corn. (See shaded area of the sketch for the corn belt in southern Ontario.) In southern Ontario the corn is grown for grain; in southern Québec it is grown mostly for fodder, which is chopped up and stored in silos. In both Ontario and Québec, the "dairying areas" also produce hay, oats, barley, and **winter wheat**. These crops are fed to dairy cattle and hogs, beef cattle, poultry, and laying hens. Of course, these dairy-farming areas do not limit their production to dairy products. They produce so many different crops and types of livestock that they might just as rightly be classed as areas of mixed farming with a dairy emphasis.

The mixed farming areas in southern Ontario and Québec resemble the dairying areas with their mixture of crops and livestock. The major differences are more raising of beef cattle and the lack of a corn crop. The three largest crops are hay, oats, and barley.

A great many special crops, including various kinds of fruits and vegetables, are grown in the Great Lakes-St. Lawrence Lowlands. Soybeans and white beans are also important cash crops in southwestern Ontario. Kent and Essex counties, in the extreme southwest corner of Ontario, produce large vegetable crops that are trucked to most cities in southwestern Ontario. The early springs and warm summers of these counties produce such large amounts of fruits and vegetables that many are canned or frozen and then distributed all across Canada. The Holland Marsh is another important producer of vegetables, most of which go to Toronto's fresh food market.

The Norfolk sand plain along the north shore of Lake Erie provides a long frost-free season in most years. But the sandy soil does not hold enough moisture for most farm crops. Farmers here are now looking for other crops to replace the tobacco plants grown in former years. A few farmers are experimenting with growing peanuts on this sandy soil.

In southern Ontario, tree fruit growing is concentrated along the shores of Lake Ontario and Georgian Bay. The closeness of the lakes moderates the winters and delays spring blossoming until after the threat of frost is over. The south Georgian Bay district is the largest producer of apples in the province. The Niagara Fruit Belt, between Hamilton and the Niagara River, is famous for its grapes, peaches, pears, cherries, and plums.

Mechanical cherry picker on an orchard farm in southern Ontario

A market garden in Holland Marsh

F O C U S

Growing Peanuts in Ontario

Peanuts grow in Ontario. Peanuts are a crop that likes sandy soil and a long, warm, growing season. Ontario peanuts are sweeter and better tasting than peanuts grown in the United States, and they do not have aflatoxin, a mould linked with cancer. In recent years some southern Ontario farmers have considered growing peanuts.

But switching from other crops to peanuts is not simple. The peanut plants grown in Ontario do not yield as many peanuts per hectare as those grown in the United States. Ontario peanuts therefore cost more to produce. American peanut growers have another advantage: their government subsidizes peanut growing very heavily. As a result, U.S. peanuts sell in Toronto for about half the price of Ontario peanuts. Only a few people are willing to pay twice as much for the higher-quality product. It seems likely that the Ontario peanut industry will remain small.

Harvesting peanuts on sandy soils near Lake Erie

The Holland Marsh, which produces a large share of Ontario's vegetables, has lost an inch of organic soil a year since it was drained in 1930.

Varieties of Farming in Southern Ontario

A crop of corn in southern Ontario.
The corn is fed to livestock.

A southern Ontario farm with a variety of crops

Hogs on a southern Ontario farm

A corn crib and silos.   The corn cobs are stored in a well-ventilated crib.
Green corn stalks are chopped up and stored in silos (background).
This fodder is called ensilage.

Cattle on a southern Ontario farm

In Québec, there are important orchard districts within an 80 km radius of Montréal. The winters here are colder than they are in Ontario, and so apple trees—and only the hardier varieties—are the only fruit trees to survive. The orchards are planted on slopes to help drain away cold air, but every few years a severe winter reduces the crop of apples and kills a number of apple trees.

Picking apples on a Québec orchard farm

A potato field in Prince Edward Island. Seed potatoes from P.E.I. are sold all over North America.

Atlantic Provinces

Farming in the Atlantic Provinces is restricted in two ways. The agricultural land resource is limited, and the local market for farm products is small. Most of the mixed farming area is composed of small farms (under 100 ha). The farmers grow hay, oats, and barley, raise small herds of cattle and hogs, and keep small flocks of laying hens. Many of these farmers have difficulty supporting their families from farm proceeds, and must find off-farm work in the mining, lumbering, or fishing industries. Some of the farmers consider themselves fishers who live on a farm. Near the cities, a few farmers specialize in dairy cattle to supply fresh milk to the urban market.

There are several specialty crop areas in the Atlantic Provinces. In New Brunswick, the Saint John Valley is important for its production of potatoes and apples. The Annapolis Valley of Nova Scotia is well known for its apple production, but it also produces vegetables, poultry, and eggs. In Prince Edward Island, the most important crop is potatoes. The high quality of P.E.I. potatoes has created a demand for them as *seed potatoes* all over North America. P.E.I. farmers grow potatoes as their chief cash crop, but they also grow hay, oats, and barley, and raise cattle, hogs, and poultry.

Newfoundland has less agricultural production than any other province, because of its short, cool summers and its lack of farmland. It produces only a small part of the food it needs. The largest farming areas are near St. John's, where vegetables, beef, and milk are produced for the urban market. The island contains large areas of bog that could be drained for farmland. The cost, however, would be higher than the cost of importing produce from outside the province.

Canada exports more seed potatoes than any other country except the Netherlands.

ECONOMIC CONCERNS OF FARMERS

Canada's agricultural industry has had serious problems for several decades. One of the chief problems for farmers is that production costs have risen faster than prices for farm commodities. At the same time, Canadian farmers face growing competition from the exports of other countries. In response to these and other problems, the government and the farmers themselves have adopted various measures to help Canadian agriculture survive. Some of these measures have had a negative effect on the agricultural resource base.

THE COST-PRICE SQUEEZE

For some years, the costs of production on farms have been rising faster than prices for farm produce. Such a situation is termed a 'cost-price squeeze'.

Since the 1970s, farm costs have been rising rapidly. The increase of world prices for oil from $4 a barrel in the early 1970s to almost $40 a barrel in the early 1980s had a severe impact on farm production costs. Higher oil prices meant higher prices for lubricating oil, gasoline, diesel fuel, and many chemicals that farmers use in large volume. The costs of land, building construction, tractors, trucks, and other farm machinery also shot up. Farmers had to pay more for farm help, as well, to match the big wage increases being awarded to labourers in other industries.

To meet their expenses farmers often had to borrow money. When the Bank of Canada set a high interest rate on borrowed money, another farm cost went up. For example, when

Between 1980 and 1987, more than 3200 Canadian farmers went bankrupt, an average of more than one a day.

interest rates rose from 7 percent to 14 percent, the interest costs on a loan or mortgage of $500 000 rose from $35 000 a year to $70 000 a year.

The prices paid for farm produce have not kept pace with the farmer's rising costs. Prices for farm commodities have remained relatively stable, some have increased only slightly, and some have declined. Grain is an example of a farm commodity that has

decreased in price since the 1970s. The reason for that lies outside Canada.

GLOBAL COMPETITION

Because Canada produces large amounts of high-quality grain and has a relatively small population, it is one of the world's largest grain exporters. The value of Canada's export of grain (mostly wheat and wheat flour) is

---

F O C U S

Down and Out on the Farm

Saddled with debts and threatened by bankruptcy, Dale Frombach has little to show for 22 years of labour on his once-sprawling grain farm 35 km northeast of Regina. Since last fall's harvest, he has sold 2400 [971 ha] of his 3200 acres [1295 ha], and last month he disposed of more than half his equipment—including a combine and a four-wheel drive tractor—at an auction that drew 500 onlookers. Then, as Frombach prepared last week to seed a crop of wheat and barley on his remaining acreage, grain prices plummeted by an average of 18 percent. The 47-year-old farmer struggled to conceal his concern for his future—and the future of his wife and three daughters. "After a while, you become immune to the fact that you are going to suffer another blow," Frombach said. "But I tell you this: if I lose once more, farming will be history for me."

Many of Canada's 145 000 grain farmers shared Frombach's anguished lament. Charles Mayer, minister of state for the Canadian Wheat Board, had recently announced that the guaranteed prices paid to grain growers would shortly

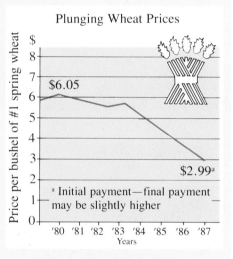

Plunging Wheat Prices

Price per bushel of #1 spring wheat

$6.05 ... $2.99[a]

[a] Initial payment—final payment may be slightly higher

Years '80 '81 '82 '83 '84 '85 '86 '87

be slashed by 15- to 25 percent. That decline had followed a drop of 19- to 26 percent in the preceding year—and had brought the price of a bushel of No. 1 red spring wheat down to $2.99, an 11-year low. Indeed, when inflation is taken into account, grain prices were at their lowest level since the Depression. As a result, for the first time in Canadian history, federal assistance to Prairie grain farmers would be almost as large as their total revenues from grain sales—an estimated $4 billion . . .

— Mary Janigan,
Maclean's, May 1987

more than twice the value of all of Canada's other agricultural exports put together.

It is very difficult to find export markets for Canadian grain year after year. A number of other countries produce much more grain than does Canada (Table 9.4), and also have huge surpluses for export. The United States, for example, produces about ten times as much grain as Canada and accounts for almost half of all world exports. Both Australia and Argentina, like Canada, have small populations, so they are able to export large quantities of grain. Western Europe, which used to buy large amounts of Canadian grain, now grows more grain than it can use and is looking for export markets.

Table 9.4 *Annual World Grain Production*

Producing Country or Region	Millions of Tonnes per Year[a]
U.S.A.	217
Western Europe	91
China	88
U.S.S.R.	87
Eastern Europe	68
India	31
Canada	24
Brazil	22
Argentina	18
South Africa	7
Australia	7
Others	96
Total	756

Source: Calculated from Statistics Canada data
[a]Average production for five-year period 1981–85. Grains included in this table are corn, wheat, oats, barley, and rye, but *not* rice.

1. a) Group the countries and regions in Table 9.4 by continent.
   b) In which continent did you place the U.S.S.R.? Why?
2. Which two continents produce the most grain?

Most of Canada's grain exports go to the Soviet Union, China, and a number of developing countries in Africa and Asia. Exports to the Soviet Union and China vary from year to year because their own crop yields go up and down with changes in growing conditions. Some developing countries, such as India and Pakistan, have produced much more grain in recent years by using improved varieties of seed, more fertilizer, and better farming methods. India now produces more grain than Canada, and in some years exports grain. Some developing countries need more grain to feed their populations, but they lack the money (or credit) to buy Canadian grain.

Canada's toughest competition for grain exports has come from two international giants, the *European Economic Community* (EEC) and the United States of America. For many years, the EEC has given its farmers large subsidies. Because the EEC farmers received these large payments from their governments, they were able to sell grain on the world market at less than the true cost of production. To meet this competition, the United States increased its subsidies to grain growers so that they could compete with the EEC farmers. To help Canadian farmers compete on the world grain market, the federal government has also increased subsidies to grain growers. In the late 1980s, these subsidies amounted to several thousands of millions of dollars a year. To try to obtain an agreement to reduce farm subsidies, Canada has arranged talks with the EEC and the United States. It is not likely, however, that farm subsidies will be reduced a great deal for at least another decade.

Despite the keen competition, Canada has succeeded over the years in constantly increasing its wheat exports (Table 9.5). Our second- and third-ranking agricultural exports are oil-seeds and meat products. We export less of other farm products such as dairy products, fruit, and vegetables.

Indeed, Canada has been importing these products in increasing quantities, and Canadian production of some of them has actually been declining. Of all farm crops except grain, Canada imports more in value than it exports.

Table 9.5 *Canada's Wheat Exports 1955–1984*

5-Year Average	Total Wheat Exports (tonnes)
1955–59	6 833 000
1960–64	9 402 000
1965–69	10 834 000
1970–74	12 392 000
1975–79	12 748 000
1980–84	17 510 000

Source: Calculated from Statistics Canada data

A large new market for Canadian grain may be on the horizon. Ethanol, which can be used instead of lead to improve gasoline, is made from grain.

1. Draw a line graph showing Canada's wheat exports between 1955 and 1984. Place the years on the *x* axis and the millions of tonnes on the *y* axis.
2. a) Wheat exports often rise or fall rapidly from one year to another. Why?
   b) What is the advantage of presenting wheat export statistics in five-year averages instead of annually?
3. How do a high price for oil and high interest rates increase Canadian farm production costs?
4. Why is Canada able to export more grain than China, the U.S.S.R., or India, even though these countries produce more grain than Canada?
5. In order to export farm products to some Southeast Asian country, Canada might have to agree to permit that country to export a

certain amount of textiles and clothing to Canada. Why might a labourer in the Canadian textile industry disapprove of such an agreement?

6. How do you think Canada's climate relates to the large quantities of fruits and vegetables our country imports?

The food that developing nations export to Canada is worth more than the food that Canada exports to the developing nations.

FARMERS' RESPONSES TO THE COST-PRICE SQUEEZE

Farmers have adopted various measures to help them continue to operate profitably in the face of an ever-tightening cost-price squeeze. Their choices include the following seven possibilities.

1. Increase Size

If a farm family is able to operate a 1000 ha farm with the same type of equipment that is used for a 500 ha farm, its cost of production per hectare is lower. This method of reducing costs is called *economy of scale*. The larger the operation, the lower the cost of production per unit.

The average size of a Canadian farm has doubled since 1951 (Table 9.6). As some farmers have retired or decided to cease farming, neighbouring farmers have bought up the land to enlarge their holdings. Farmers who could not afford to buy have rented such land to enlarge their farm operations without making large capital investments.

Farmers have also increased the size of their livestock operations. In 1951, a flock of 1000 laying hens was considered large; today flocks of several hundred thousand are common.

2. Specialize

Canadian farmers are specializing more and more in growing fewer kinds of crops and raising fewer kinds of livestock. Even in mixed farming areas, many farmers are concentrating on one or two crops and specializing in one kind of livestock. Specializing helps them to be more efficient in their operation, by cutting costs of production.

3. Mechanize

To cut labour costs, farmers have mechanized every possible farm operation. Machines are used to milk cows, feed hogs, clean manure out of stables, and even pick fruit. Computers are used to help organize the farm operation and to keep financial records. Without mechanization, Canadian farmers could not have increased the size of their operations as much as they have done.

4. Increase Yields

Canadian farmers have increased farm yields in a number of ways. They have:
- improved the breeds of livestock and the varieties of crops
- used more artificial fertilizer
- used more chemicals to control weeds, insects, and disease
- improved farm management

5. Organize Marketing Boards

If farmers across Canada produce more of a certain commodity than can be sold, the price of that commodity will fall. It is impossible for individual farmers to decide in advance whether too much or too little of a commodity is going to be produced in a given year. In order to help farmers to manage collectively the supply of farm products, the federal and provincial governments have passed legislation that permits farmers to organize *marketing boards*.

There are marketing boards for commodities such as eggs, poultry, hogs, certain fruit crops, and wheat. Each marketing board estimates the demand for the particular commodity and then tells the farmers how much each of them is permitted to produce. The amount a farmer is permitted to produce is called a *quota*. If the demand goes up, each farmer's quota is increased; if the demand goes down, the quota is decreased. This procedure is called *supply management*. By controlling the amount of a product that goes to market, the marketing board helps make a farmer's income more secure. In some cases, a *floor price* is established. If the commodity sells at a price lower than the floor price, the federal and/or provincial governments subsidize the farmers up to the floor price.

The Canadian Wheat Board is a special kind of marketing board set up to market prairie grain. It not only

Table 9.6 *Average Farm Size By Province*

Province	Average Farm Size (ha)				
	1951	1961	1971	1981	1986
Newfoundland	9	13	24	49	56
Prince Edward Island	44	53	69	90	96
Nova Scotia	55	72	89	92	97
New Brunswick	53	76	99	108	115
Québec	51	60	71	79	88
Ontario	56	62	68	73	78
Manitoba	137	170	220	259	283
Saskatchewan	223	278	342	385	419
Alberta	213	261	320	329	358
British Columbia	72	91	128	109	127
Canada	113	145	187	207	231

Source: Compiled from Canadian Census data

This freighter is being loaded with Canadian wheat for export.

assigns quotas, but also sells the grain for the farmers. At the beginning of each year, the Wheat Board estimates the world demand for grain and sets a floor price for each grain crop. The farmers are paid this floor price when they deliver the grain to the grain elevators. If the Wheat Board later receives more than the floor price, the board passes on the extra to the farmers. If the Wheat Board receives less than the floor price, the federal government makes up the loss.

6. Form Corporations

Several farmers have sometimes grouped together to form legal corporations. The corporation is run like a business enterprise. Each farmer has shares in the corporation and also receives a salary from it. Any corporation profits are distributed to the shareholders in the form of dividends. By pooling their capital, the farmers are able to achieve certain economies of scale. For example, farming individually, each would have bought a combine, but with a corporation, all use one large combine bought for the whole group.

7. Integrate Vertically

Most farm products are processed, packaged, stored, and moved many times before they end up on the shelves of a food store. When a single company handles production, processing, and distribution, the arrangement is called *vertical integration*. Vertical integration allows a company to obtain profits from every step of the operation and to operate on a large enough scale to take advantage of economy of scale.

Vertical integration is usually arranged not by farmers, but by some large company that handles farm products. Farmers sometimes sell their farms to the integrated company and receive a salary to produce farm products for the company. Some farmers remain owners of their farms but raise livestock or grow crops that belong to the company. The farmers receive a fee for their work.

---

1. a) Using Table 9.6, rank the provinces from first to last according to the average size of their farms in 1986. From your knowledge of physical geography, explain why the Prairie Provinces have the largest farms and Newfoundland the smallest.
b) Explain why farm sizes have been increasing all across Canada.
2. Why are farmers not able to solve their economic problems simply by employing economy of scale and becoming more efficient?
3. a) If marketing boards were abolished, what do you think would happen to the price of food produced in Canada?
b) What do you think would happen to Canadian imports and exports of agricultural products? Explain your reasoning.
4. Large integrated companies claim that vertical integration benefits the consumer because it leads to lower prices for food products. Small-scale farmers claim that

vertical integration provides unfair competition to farmers. Working in small groups of ''company executives'' and ''farmers'', prepare a debate based on these claims.

THREATS TO AGRICULTURAL LAND

A country's agricultural industry is based on its agricultural land resources. Threats to these resources are therefore threats to the industry. We must now look at two serious threats to Canada's agricultural land.

DESTRUCTION OF THE SOIL

''Canada is facing the most serious agricultural crisis in its history, and unless action is taken quickly, this country will lose a major portion of its agricultural capability . . . We are clearly in danger of squandering the very soil resource on which our agricultural industry depends.''
—*Soil at Risk: Canada's Eroding Future*, Committee report of the Senate of Canada

Government estimates say that Canadian farmers lose more than one billion dollars of income a year through soil erosion.

Only the top portion of the land known as topsoil is a valuable agricultural resource. It is considered a *renewable resource* because it can be used over and over to produce crops if it is managed properly. If topsoil is managed poorly, it may be totally destroyed. The Senate report quoted above provides a great deal of evidence that we are managing our soil resources very poorly indeed.

Soil erosion by wind and water is a natural process. Soil erosion caused by the actions of people is another matter. In Canada people have increased soil erosion by what they have done to the land. From the day the first trees were cleared for farms in eastern Canada or the sod was turned over by ploughs on the prairies, soil erosion became a problem in Canada. The problem has become much worse with the changing agricultural practices of recent years.

Eastern Canada

In eastern Canada, until the 1950s or thereabouts, most of the agricultural industry was made up of small mixed farms. These farms produced a number of crops such as oats, barley, wheat, and hay, and included pasture fields, as well. Such crops, with their masses of roots and vegetation tend to reduce soil erosion.

Each farm had only one or two fields of *row crops* such as corn or beans. Row crops are planted in rows with enough space between them to let farmers cultivate the plants all through the growing season. While this spacing makes it easier to cultivate the plants, it also allows more soil erosion to take place. Farmers, aware of this danger, did not usually plant row crops in the same field two years in a row. They rotated all their crops from field to field.

The rotation of crops had beneficial results. The vegetation that was plowed under, and roots of the hay and pasture grass added organic matter to the soil. The manure from the livestock, mixed with grain straw that was used as bedding for the animals in the barn, also added organic matter, as well as fertilizer. Soil that is rich in organic matter lets rain soak into the ground, and there is less run-off to carry away topsoil.

When farmers practised crop rotation, any field was likely to be used for livestock pasture, and livestock fields had to be fenced. For this reason, the eastern mixed farms had many fences. Fence rows, with their sod, shrubs, and trees, acted as barriers that reduced the erosion of

topsoil by both wind and water. Fence rows, woodlots, and farmstead orchards also provided nesting sites and habitats for birds. A high bird population helped to keep insect numbers in check without the use of pesticides, which would later poison the land.

Although some soil erosion took place on small mixed farms, the problem became much worse when farmers began to increase the size of their farms, specialize in a few crops, and mechanize their operations. As we know, farmers made these adjustments to meet the challenge of the cost-price squeeze.

In their efforts to achieve economy of scale, farmers have not only increased the sizes of the farms, but have also taken down fences to create large fields in which they use huge tractors and equipment. These changes promote erosion. Most of the fence rows that once slowed erosion have disappeared. The heavy machinery used in the large fields compacts the soil, restricting the development of plant roots.

To gain more cropland, farmers have cut down woodlots and drained swamps. These changes have speeded the movement of water from the land, and this process increases erosion and

decreases the supply of moisture in summer.

Some farmers have willfully ignored what is best for the soil. They know, for example, that plowing and planting crops across a slope *(contour farming)* instead of up-and-down the slope helps to prevent soil erosion. When contour farming is practised, each plough furrow and crop row acts as a miniature dam, slowing down the movement of water. With large fields and heavy equipment, however, contour farming requires more time and fuel than does plowing in straight rows. Many fields have therefore been

Soil erosion in southern Ontario. Much of the topsoil of these sandy slopes has been eroded.

Contour farming

plowed and planted from one end to the other, regardless of slope.

The change to larger farms and fields brought with it crop specialization. Specialization can be seen in the row crops of corn and soybeans that are the most common crops in southwestern Ontario, and the rows of potatoes that fill the fields in New Brunswick and Prince Edward Island. Planting row crops, as we know, increases soil erosion. Specialization that requires farmers to plant the same crop in the same field for many years in succession makes the problem worse.

Farmers specializing in row crops often have no livestock. They therefore have no pastures that are fertilized naturally nor barns containing manure to spread on the fields and improve the soil. As the fertility of the soil drops, farmers must use more artificial fertilizer to keep crop yields high. Some of this chemical fertilizer is carried away by run-off water to pollute streams and lakes.

The rate at which Canadian topsoil is disappearing is a matter for concern. Scientists have estimated that in Ontario 1.3 million tonnes of topsoil are washed from farmland each year, and in New Brunswick, topsoil to a depth of 12 cm was lost in 20 years.

In southwestern Ontario, soil erosion has reduced corn yields by 30 to 40 percent.

The Prairies

In the prairie lands of western Canada, the chief cause of soil erosion ever since pioneer days has been wind. Wind erosion was made worse by the dryland farming practice of *summer-fallowing*. Summer-fallowing builds up soil moisture between cropping years, but the repeated cultivation in the summer fallow year drastically increases wind erosion.

When the prairies were being settled in the early 1900s, the climate was wetter than usual. Farmers kept pushing grain growing farther and farther into the driest part of the prairies. In 1917, a period of serious drought began; it lasted into the early 1930s. Crops failed, and thousands of farms were abandoned. The dried out soils, which had been stripped of the protection of their natural vegetation, were exposed to the wind. The topsoil of hundreds of thousands of hectares was seriously eroded. Some areas were totally stripped of topsoil. Dust from blowing topsoil was sometimes so thick that the sun was blotted out as though a heavy cloud had passed over. During this period of drought, the prairie was appropriately called the dust bowl.

Parched land and wind erosion of topsoil in the prairies.   Wind has eroded this prairie land, and topsoil has accumulated along the snow fence.

On plowed fields the bare soil lies open to erosion by wind and water.

The Government of Canada took steps to counter the erosion of the west. In 1935, the federal government passed the *Prairie Farm Rehabilitation Act* (PFRA). In co-operation with the provincial governments, an educational program was developed on how to reduce wind erosion; funds were provided to help with a number of conservation projects. Farmers were encouraged to plant their crops in strips across the path of prevailing winds. This technique is called **strip cropping**. Instead of plowing, farmers began using a **disk-packer** which left the soil packed down with some stubble trash on the surface to reduce wind erosion. Many trees were planted along the edges of fields to provide windbreaks. The government also bought about 800 000 ha of the most seriously eroded land, took it out of grain production, and seeded it to grass for permanent community pastures.

Following the worst years of the dust bowl, there was a general

Disking in the prairies in the 1920s. Why did this kind of cultivation lead to serious soil erosion?

No-till seeding on the prairie. Since the land is not cultivated before seeding, no-till seeding helps to prevent soil erosion.

Strip cropping in the prairies. Planting strips across the path of prevailing winds slows down wind erosion of the soil. Farmers often alternate crops and summer fallow.

increase in precipitation. When there was a dry year, the new conservation practices helped to protect the soil from wind erosion. Then the tightening cost-price squeeze brought a disastrous change. Farmers again expanded their holdings into the drier areas, and they neglected conservation projects. Some very dry years in the late 1970s and during the 1980s caused serious wind erosion. Now farmers are again being urged to follow sound

Farmers use large amounts of chemical herbicides to control weeds.

Salt deposits on the surface of a prairie farm

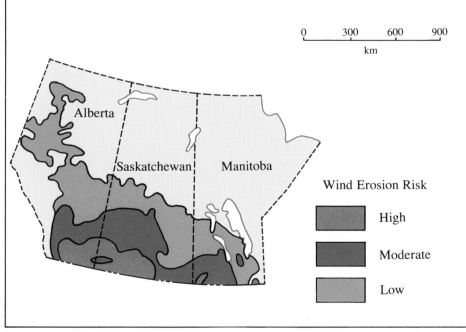

Figure 9.5 *Wind Erosion Risk in the Prairie Provinces*

conservation practices to protect Canada's resource of prairie agricultural land.

Sound conservation practices include a new technique called ***no-till cropping***. When this technique is practised, the land is not tilled (cultivated) in advance of sowing. The stubble is left on the field to protect it from wind erosion between fall harvest and spring seeding. The seeding is done with an implement that loosens the soil just enough to cover the seed. One disadvantage of no-till cropping is that more herbicides must be used to control the weeds.

Some farmers are now using a system of summer fallow without cultivation. They control weeds by several applications of herbicides during the growing season. This use of herbicides is more expensive than

cultivating the fallow land. What is worse, the use of large amounts of chemicals endangers the farmers' health and pollutes the land.

Another conservation practice is called ***continuous cropping***. Instead of leaving some of the land in summer fallow, the farmer plants crops in all the fields every year but rotates the crops often. For example, a field may be sown with wheat one year, barley the next, and Canola the next. Crop rotation seems to help control the weeds and takes fewer nutrients from the soil.

Wind erosion does not have the same effect on all parts of the prairie region. The areas most eroded by wind lie in southwestern Saskatchewan and southeastern Alberta, the driest part of the prairies (Figure 9.5). These areas are also exposed to many high winds, including the warm, dry chinook winds that blow out of the mountains in late winter and early spring. Wind erosion is not as serious in the less arid areas of the prairies because there the soils remain more moist, the winds are less severe, and less land lies in summer fallow. The least wind erosion occurs in the parkland area because it has more trees and shrubs, and because mixed farming is practised there. Mixed farming includes many fields of hay or seeded pasture that protect the soil from wind erosion.

All prairie soil problems do not result from erosion. Irrigation, too, can cause a problem called ***salinization***. Prairie soils contain large quantities of salts. When water enters the ground in large doses, it dissolves the salts and carries them down to the water table. As the water table rises, water moves laterally, carrying the salts with it. The water then collects in low-lying areas and later evaporates. The evaporated water leaves behind white salt deposits, ruining the area for cropping. This process of salinization affects about 810 000 ha of prairie farmland.

Who's to Blame?

The description of farmers' actions in the account of soil erosion is not meant to lay the entire blame for the problem on farmers. Consumers must share the blame because of their demand for cheap food. Canadians spend a smaller proportion of their income on food than do the people of most other countries. The various levels of government—our elected representatives—have not given priority to the problem of soil erosion. Provincial and federal government policies and programs have stressed the opposite concern. They have encouraged farmers to produce more food at lower costs. Their technical and financial help to farmers has been aimed at increasing efficient production, not at conserving the land. Farmers who have tried to make their land as productive as possible, even at the cost of erosion of that land, seem to be simply carrying out the wishes of the Canadian public.

FOCUS

Soil Erosion out of Control in Southern Alberta

Suddenly, visibility was almost obliterated. It had been a bright, sunny afternoon in April, but now the car's headlights could barely define the highway leading to Pincher Creek in southern Alberta. It was like driving through a blinding snowstorm except that the air was hot, dry and gritty. It was a soil blizzard.

I stopped the car and got out. Unrelenting 80-kilometre-per-hour winds whipped soil into my face. Through teary and stinging eyes, I noted the extent of the erosion: earth had drifted a metre deep along snow fences; plants were being sheared off at the surface by the wind's sandblasting action; and ditches, gullies, sloughs and streams were being choked by tonnes of topsoil. Overhead, a yellow-brown cloud covered the land for hundreds of kilometres around.

Spring is usually a time of optimism on the Prairies, but the weather—not to mention declining grain prices—in southern Alberta this year has brought anything but. It has been hot, windy and extremely dry (as it has been every spring since 1982). The massive dust storms are reminiscent of the Dirty Thirties, when dry summers and high winds, combined with poor farming practices, turned the western Prairies into a dust bowl.

Early in 1986, soil specialists had warned that many farms in southern Alberta would suffer serious wind erosion. Indeed, by year's end, winds had carried away at least five million tonnes of topsoil from 400 000 hectares . . . of farmland. In some places the loss was shocking. Some cultivated fields in the Pincher Creek area were eroded to a depth of as much as 50 centimetres—[a serious] loss when you consider that three centimetres of topsoil represent 100 to 300 years of weathered rock.

Many people may not perceive soil loss as a serious problem. After all, soil is all around us—there's too much of it to worry about losing some. However, by losing the top layer, we lose agricultural productivity. Topsoil is the cream. It is the thin fertile layer that contains billions of micro-organisms—fungi, bacteria and other single-celled creatures—which convert dead plants to the organic matter necessary for plant growth. A teaspoonful can contain 50 million of these micro-organisms.

Topsoil also has the best aeration and soil structure, due to plant root action and the burrowing of animals and insects which mixes and loosens soil particles. As a result, topsoil holds moisture long after the rains have stopped, and its exposure to direct sunlight produces temperatures necessary for plant germination.

When the top layer of earth is removed, only lower-quality subsoil remains. It lacks organic matter and has poor aeration, moisture infiltration and structure. As a result, it can't support healthy plant growth.

It took 10 000 years for prairie topsoils to form, and yet in less than 100 years, man's short-sighed farmland management has depleted nearly half the original organic matter, and has greatly accelerated erosion. The land is washing away in spring rains and snowmelt, and blowing away on the winds. It is being lost a great deal faster than it can be replaced naturally.

What has gone wrong? How did we allow our soil resources to get into such a mess?

— Malcolm Stark,
Canadian Geographic, 1987

1. Why does small-scale mixed farming cause less soil erosion than large-scale specialized farming?
2. Why have many farmers in eastern Canada (particularly in southwestern Ontario and southeastern Québec) changed from small mixed farms to large specialized farms?
3. Why do row crops and summer fallow lead to soil erosion?
4. If you owned a section of land in southwestern Saskatchewan, what conservation methods would you practise to preserve your topsoil?
5. Why would farmers grow grain in the drier parts of the prairies when, from a soil conservation point of view, this land would be better left in grass for cattle to graze?
6. Create a bumper sticker to promote the protection of valuable farm resources. Choose as a topic either the promotion of topsoil conservation or the preservation of wetlands.

The average Canadian family spends less than 16 percent of its total income on food.

URBANIZATION OF AGRICULTURAL LAND

Because cities and farms depend on one another, most of Canada's urban population is located on Canada's best agricultural land. The land in and around Canada's 25 metropolitan areas includes 60 percent of the country's CLI Class 1 land, 30 percent of Class 2 land, and 20 percent of Class 3 land. In southern Ontario a high proportion of the land is in one of these classes. This region also contains Canada's most dense urban network. From the top of the CN Tower in Toronto, an observer can see an estimated 37 percent of Canada's CLI Class 1 land!

Urban expansion into the farm community creates a number of serious problems:

- rising land prices encourage farmers to sell off parcels of land and discourage them from increasing the size of their farms to make them more economic operations;
- municipalities increase land taxes on farms to help pay the costs of providing services to urbanites;
- weeds and insects spread to farms from neighbouring non-farm properties where the pests are not controlled;
- farmers suffer more losses from vandalism, theft, and trespassing;
- increased use of ground water for residential and industrial purposes lowers the water table and causes farmers' wells to go dry;
- increased traffic makes it difficult for farmers to move equipment on the roads;
- greater amounts of salt on roads damage adjacent crops;
- increased air pollution from industries damages crops over many square kilometres. For example, pollutants from industries in Windsor, Detroit, Port Huron, and Sarnia have caused a blight on beans, corn, tobacco, and vegetable crops over a large area of southwestern Ontario.

LOCAL STUDY

1. A local radio station has decided to prepare and broadcast a special program on farms and farming in your area. You are a member of a small "committee" that will make a study of local farms to find information that will be used in this broadcast. Consider the following questions and try to find answers for as many as you can. Try to arrange to interview a staff member of a local agricultural college or government office. (You might get permission to "tape" the interview for use in your "broadcast".)
a) What different types of farms operate in your area? How do the different types vary in size?
b) How much money would a person have to raise to buy and equip each type of farm? At current interest rates, what annual interest costs would a bank charge the farmer on that amount of money?
c) What agricultural crops are grown in the region, and what kinds of livestock are raised?
d) What problems relating to urban growth affect farmers in your region?
2. As a result of this Local Study, one of the members of your "Committee" has decided to take up farming. As a group, advise this person as she or he decides on the following points:
a) Which of the following factors would you consider important if you were deciding on the type of farming you would do? Rank them in order from most important to least important.
- advantages or limits relating to climate
- type of soil
- closeness to market
- local, national, and world demand for products
- profit rating (high? moderate? low?)
- availability of money to establish a specific type of farming
b) What major pieces of machinery or equipment would you need on your farm?
c) What conservation measures would you plan to practise to prevent soil erosion?

Low-density housing subdividison on CLI Class 1 farmland

A more serious long-term problem for Canada as a whole is the loss of farmland to urban expansion. Suburban expansion of the major cities located on our best farmland is destroying valuable agricultural resources each year. Beyond the suburbs, scattered low-density urban development spreads out for many more kilometres. This expansion spreads the harmful effects of urbanization on agriculture far beyond the edge of the city. These effects extend to 80 km from the centre of our metropolitan urban areas.

Farmland is often taken out of production many years before it is needed for urban development. Some geographers have estimated that for every hectare of farmland used for urban purposes, at least another hectare is ruined for agriculture. The best land is built on first. When agricultural land in a range of CLI classes is available, developers prefer to use land from Classes 1–3.

Individual farmers sometimes benefit from urban growth. A larger urban population creates a greater demand for farm products and provides a wide range of services for the surrounding farmers. When cities expand into the country, farmers are able to sell their land at a high price. Land slated for future urban development is often rented to the farmers around the city at reasonable rates.

The over-all effect of urban expansion on farming remains harmful. It is not possible to have urban growth without some loss of farmland, but the impact could be reduced. Smaller areas of good to excellent farmland could be used for urbanization. Our cities could be built more compactly with higher population densities. Low-density urban sprawl could be halted. When different classes of farmland are available, development could be directed onto the poorer soils. To achieve these aims we would need more effective urban and regional planning than any province has produced so far.

1. a) On an outline map of Canada, mark and lightly shade all agricultural land included in Canada's CLI Classes 1–3 (Figure 9.2).

   b) On the same map, mark (but do not name) 10 of Canada's Census Metropolitan Areas (Table 5.1).

   c) How many of these metropolitan areas are on Classes 1–3 agricultural land?

   d) Assume that the effects of urban development on agricultural land extend as far as 80 km from the centre of each metropolitan area. Calculate the total area of Classes 1–3 agricultural land affected by the 10 metropolitan areas you have marked.

2. A proposal has been made to develop 1000 ha of Class 1 agricultural land at the edge of a major Canadian city. You are one of the following persons:

   - a farmer in the designated 1000 ha who is at retirement age and has no children who wish to farm
   - a young farmer whose land borders the designated 1000 ha and who wishes to expand his farm to achieve economy of scale
   - the owner of a local construction company
   - a merchant in the city
   - a land-use planning consultant representing a citizen's action group

   Meet with the other persons in your situation, and discuss the view you will adopt about developing this land. Then present your case to your whole class. When all the groups have had a chance to explain their position, hold a general discussion on the issue.

3. News stories about controversies over urbanization of agricultural land break all across Canada every year. Keep a class file of such items reported in the news media in your region.

TENDER FRUIT CROPS: A CASE STUDY

If Canada's land resources are limited for general farm crops, the land to grow specialty crops is even more limited. Specialty crops need particular soil and climate. This applies particularly to the *tender fruit crops* grown in the Niagara Fruit Belt, Kent and Essex counties in Ontario, and in British Columbia's Okanagan Valley.

ENVIRONMENTAL NEEDS

Apricots, peaches, nectarines, and sweet cherries are called tender fruits because they do not stand up well to the cold. Some grapes are also considered tender fruit. They are the European *vinifera* grapes and *hybrid* grapes used to make high-quality wines. Native *labrusca* grapes, on the other hand, are considered hardy, not tender, fruit. Apples, pears, sour cherries, and plums are hardy fruits, too. They can survive much colder temperatures than the tender fruits.

Tender fruit crops prefer the following environmental conditions:

- winters cold enough to make the trees and vines go dormant, but not cold enough to injure the dormant fruiting buds (i.e., no temperature below $-24°C$)
- in spring, no freezing temperatures after the blossoms emerge
- during the blossom period, calm sunny weather so that bees will be active
- summers long and warm-to-hot, with plenty of sunshine
- during the growing season, moderate rains, but during harvest and in the fall, relatively dry weather to prevent the trees and vines from growing too much, while hardening them for winter
- in winter a constant snow cover to protect the roots
- no windstorms or hail
- a sloping site with no depressions that create frost pockets
- well-drained soil, preferably a sandy loam

GROWING AREAS

Only three small areas in Canada meet most of these conditions for growing tender fruits: in southern Ontario, Kent and Essex counties and the Niagara Fruit Belt; and in British Columbia, the Okanagan Valley.

Of these three fruit-growing areas, the Okanagan Valley has the most sunshine and the warmest summers. Unfortunately for farmers, it also has frequent low temperatures in winter that injure the trees, and frost in spring that damages the blossoms. The annual precipitation is low, but irrigation provides enough water for the fruit. Grapes, apples, pears, sour cherries, and plums are grown throughout the valley. The least hardy crops (apricots, peaches, and sweet cherries) are limited to the southern half of the valley, where the winters are not as cold. Apples are the most important crop of the Okanagan Valley, and apple orchards make up about two-thirds of the total fruit-growing area.

In the Kent-Essex area tender tree crops sometimes suffer from winter injury to roots because of lack of snow cover. Often, too, the blossoms open before the last spring frost, and crop losses follow. Many peaches once grew in the area, but the orchards were reduced because of frequent frost injury. Vinifera and hybrid grapes, which are slightly hardier than peaches, have spread over a much larger area in recent years. Only time will tell whether grape production will be successful in the long term in this region.

The Niagara Fruit Belt comes closest of all Canadian locations to meeting all slope, soil, and climate needs for tender fruits. For this reason the Niagara Fruit Belt is a very special agricultural land resource. It is one of the best tender-fruit growing areas in all of North America. For example, the risk of frost damage to peach blossoms here is less than half the risk in the "peach" state of Georgia. The Niagara Fruit Belt also has large areas of deep, well-drained, sandy soils that are ideal for growing tender fruit crops.

The Niagara Fruit Belt has a number of locational factors that make it attractive for various kinds of industry and for urban development as well. It is located in Canada's urban heartland. It provides an environment that many people like as a site for residential subdivisions and individual country homes. For these reasons a great deal of urban development has occurred there in the last few decades. If past trends of urban development of Niagara fruitland continue, it is only a matter of time until all of this valuable agricultural resource will be destroyed.

1. a) What major transportation facilities serve the northern part of the Niagara region?
b) What cities does the Queen Elizabeth Way (QEW) connect?
c) Describe the location of the QEW (Figure 9.7) in relation to the tender fruit soils (Figure 9.6).
d) Explain how the QEW has helped people to live in the country and work in a city.
e) Why would a four-lane highway attract industry?
f) What kinds of industries would be attracted by railroads? by a major shipping waterway?

2. Describe the pattern of urban growth shown in Figure 9.6. Why do people prefer sandy loam to heavy clay as soil on which to build a home?

3. a) Draw a sketch map to show the location of the Niagara Fruit Belt. Base your map on Figures 9.6, 9.7 (page 292), and 9.8 (page 292).

b) Approximately how long and how wide is the Niagara Fruit Belt? Calculate its area.

4. On Figure 9.7, note the hill around Fonthill. How high is it? The hill consists of sands and gravels. This composition makes the hill good for fruit growing and valuable, too, strictly for its content. Fruit growers and sand and gravel companies are competing for the use of this land. Who do you think will win? Why?

5. Name the lake to the north of the Niagara Fruit Belt.
a) How does the lake affect cold air masses in winter? How does this effect benefit fruit crops?
b) How does the presence of the lake delay the opening of fruit blossoms in the spring? How does the delay help protect fruit crops from spring frost damage?

Ontario's Kent and Essex counties produce more than half the tomatoes grown in Canada.

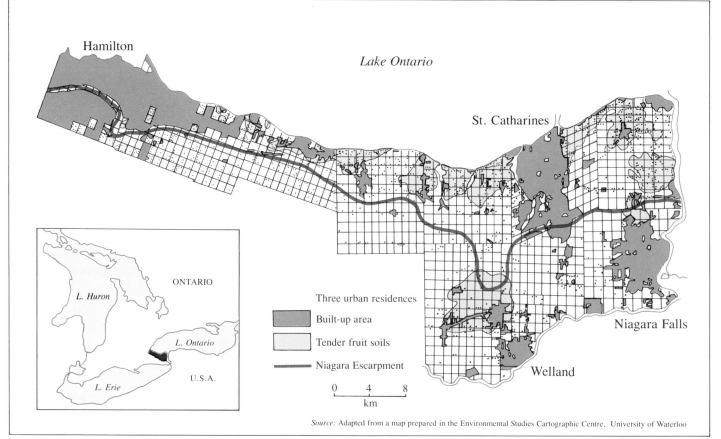

Figure 9.6 *Urban Sprawl in the Niagara Fruit Belt*

FRUIT GROWERS' PROBLEMS

The fruit-growing industry faces the threat of the urbanization of land resources and many of the other problems facing all farmers. At the top of the list of other problems is the cost-price squeeze. The costs of machinery, chemicals, fertilizer, and borrowing money have risen faster than the price of fruit.

Foreign competition has held down the prices of fruit produced in Canada. Because the same kinds of fruit ripen earlier in the season in the United States, much of the Canadian demand for fresh fruit is met before Canadian harvest time. Lower demand reduces the price for fresh fruit by the time Canadian produce reaches the market.

Over the years, most Canadian canneries have been bought by American companies. Many of these U.S.-owned canning factories have been closed because companies achieve economy of scale by using large canneries in the United States to supply the Canadian market. Canned peaches are a good example: in the 1960s imported canned peaches supplied only 20 percent of the Canadian market; by the 1980s, imports had risen to over eighty percent.

Farmers may manage the supply of some farm commodities so as to regulate the price of these commodities. Fruit growing does not lend itself to such managing. Trees and vines do not begin to produce until at least five

Sorting cherries

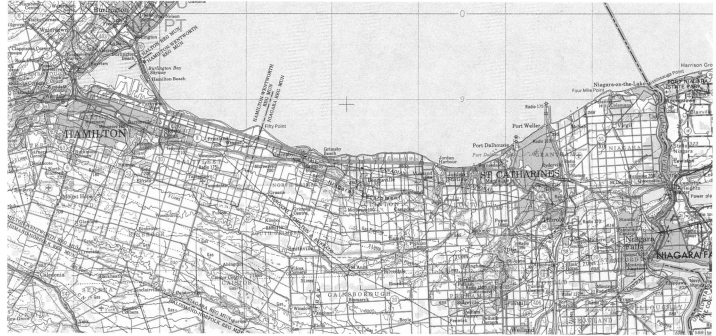

Figure 9.7 *The Niagara Fruit Belt* *The scale of this map is 1:250 000.*

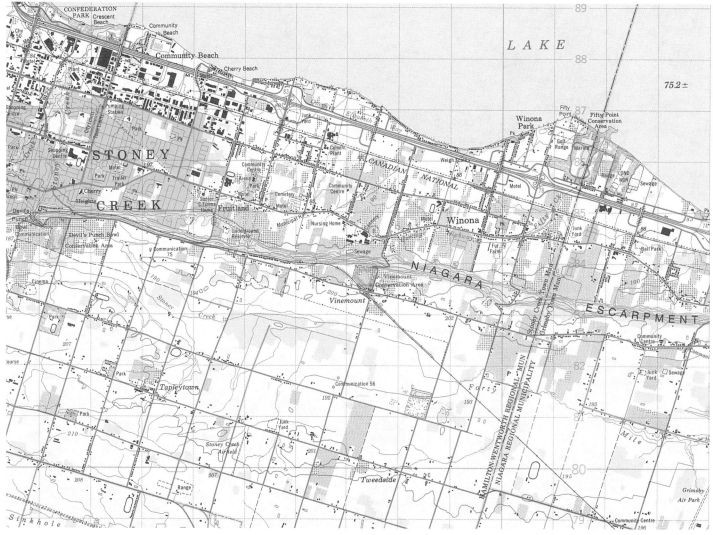

Figure 9.8 *Section of the Niagara Fruit Belt* *The scale of this map is 1:50 000.*

years after they have been planted. Growers cannot make year-by-year adjustments in the amount of fruit they grow. The yearly fluctuations in their production depend on the weather, over which no one has control.

WILL CANADA'S FRUITLANDS DISAPPEAR?

Urban development and poor financial returns to the growers threaten to destroy Canada's tender-fruit lands. In the Niagara Fruit Belt, the area of land used for fruit growing decreased by about 6000 ha between 1951 and 1988, a decrease of about 32 percent (Table 9.7). During the same period, fruit-growing land in the Okanagan Valley decreased by about 2000 ha or 14 percent.

To protect the fruitlands in Ontario, the provincial government re-organized local governments into the Regional Municipality of Niagara. Regional Niagara has an Official Plan, zoning by-laws, and a policy that restricts the sale of farm lots for urban housing. A boundary placed around each city sets the limit of allowable urban development. This urban boundary is supposed to be permanent. It could be changed at some point in the future, but not without a public hearing at which citizens would be invited to express their opinions.

In British Columbia, the provincial government has set up agricultural land reserves to prevent urban development on the defined areas. All the Okanagan fruitland has been defined as an agricultural land reserve. But the boundaries of these reserved areas can be changed if pressure is put on the government to change them. Citizens opposed to such destruction of a unique agricultural resource would then have to make their position very clear to the government.

Table 9.7 *Areas in Tree Fruits and Grapes in Niagara Fruit Belt*

Fruits	1951 (ha)	1989 (ha)	Change 1951–1989	
			(ha)	(%)
Peaches	5 700	2 900	− 2 800	− 49
Cherries	1 700	500	− 1 200	− 71
Pears	2 300	900	− 1 400	− 60
Plums	1 900	500	− 1 400	− 74
Apples	800	900	+ 100	+ 13
Grapes	8 300	6 200	− 2 100	− 25
Total	20 700	11 900	− 8 800	− 42

Source: 1951 data from Canadian census; 1989 data from Ontario Ministry of Agriculture and Food. Data rounded to the nearest 100 ha.

Note: As a result of the Canada–U.S. Free Trade Agreement, a federal-provincial subsidy program was set up to help Ontario grape growers phase out the growing of more than 3000 ha of grapes over a five-year period, beginning in 1989.

Picking strawberries on a southern Ontario farm

1. Explain why Canadian fruit growers have been losing the Canadian market.
2. If the 1951 to 1988 trend shown in Table 9.7 continues, by what year will peaches cease to be grown in the Niagara Fruit Belt?
3. Send a letter to the Preservation of Agricultural Lands Society (PALS) asking for the most recent information about the condition of the Niagara fruit-growing industry and the results of efforts to preserve fruitland from urban development. (See Suggested Readings for the society's address. PALS prefers only one request from each school.)
4. Debate the resolution: "In the long run, Canadians would be better off if we allowed the Niagara Fruit Belt to become urbanized and imported our soft fruit."

WHAT LIES AHEAD?

THE WAY TO THE DESERT

Research has led some geographers to the following conclusion: "If Canadian agricultural trends continue, by the end of the next century Canada will have turned the prairies into a desert and will have covered most of the country's specialty croplands with asphalt." The current plight of the sub-Sahara nations illustrates the position that Canada would then be in. These African countries overused their agricultural resources to the point where the land could not renew itself. A lengthy drought then turned it into a desert. The Canadian prairies almost became a desert during the "dust bowl" era of the 1930s. Another cycle of prairie drought began in the early 1980s. Cities have already expanded over large areas of Canada's best agricultural land. Will Canadians learn from the events of other times and other places?

Only foresight and careful planning can save Canada's valuable agricultural land.

REVIEW QUESTIONS

1. Why is the agricultural industry important to all Canadians, both urban and rural?

2. Why do the areas of Canada with the most productive agricultural land also contain most of the country's urban population?

3. Write a letter to a pen pal who lives in another country. Explain why Canadians, in spite of Canada's large size and small population, are concerned about what is happening to the country's agricultural land resources.

4. List the factors that farmers must consider before choosing to take up a particular type of farming.

5. Suppose that the Consumers Association of Canada sent the following resolution to the Canadian government: ''It would be in the best long-term interests of Canadians to abolish all farm marketing boards and farm subsidies.''
   a) Discuss in class the ''pros and cons'' of this resolution.
   b) After the discussion, hold a secret ballot on the issue.

6. Why do some farmers consider urban growth an advantage, while others consider it a threat?

7. Why has there been so much concern in Canada that the Niagara fruitlands are threatened by urbanization?

8. What problems have fruit growers in common with other farmers in Canada?

Chapter Ten

Minerals and Energy

Wealth from the Earth

■ The value of minerals mined in Canada is less than that of minerals mined in some other countries, yet our country is the largest exporter of minerals in the world.

■ Canada uses much less total energy than some other countries, but our energy consumption per person is the highest of any nation.

Both these statements are true, though each contains a *paradox*, or apparent contradiction. How can this be?

An oil rig burning off gas, off the Atlantic coast

MINERALS: A NON-RENEWABLE RESOURCE

The earth's rocky crust is largely made up of a mixture of **minerals**. All minerals have specific chemical and physical characteristics, but only a few are extracted from the ground for our use. Most minerals are solid inorganic substances, like salt. Some, such as coal and **petroleum**, develop from plant and animal material trapped in the rock. Minerals form in different types of rock as deposits; some of these deposits are very valuable. A section of rock containing a valuable mineral deposit is often referred to as **ore** or an ore body.

We have been looking at some of Canada's renewable resources: water, fish, forests, and farmland. If we manage such resources properly, they will continually renew themselves. Mineral resources, on the other hand, are **non-renewable**. When we mine and use minerals, they are gone forever unless we recycle them. The natural processes that created our minerals millions of years ago work too slowly to replace minerals as quickly as we consume them.

Our bodies require nine mineral elements but only in small amounts. These minerals are iron, iodine, copper, fluorine, manganese, zinc, selenium, chromium, and cobalt.

MINERALS IN OUR LIVES

Mineral use can be clearly seen in almost every aspect of our lives. Household appliances, heavy-duty machines, transportation equipment, and hundreds of metal gadgets come from minerals such as iron, which is made into steel. Other uses of minerals are less obvious.

Fertilizer containing the minerals potash and phosphorus helps grow wheat, from which flour is made to bake into bread. Machinery and equipment made from iron and other minerals are used to sow and harvest the wheat, to transport it by train, truck, or ship, and to process it into flour.

Clothing made from synthetic textiles such as nylon, dacron, and Orlon comes directly from either coal or petroleum, which are both minerals.

Houses, apartment buildings, industrial buildings, and schools all contain large quantities of minerals: cement and concrete blocks; bricks and stone; copper in water pipes and electrical wiring; zinc in heating ducts; gypsum in wallboard or dry wall; steel beams and nails; and asphalt shingles and tar paper. Even the glass in windows is made from the minerals quartz and nepheline syenite.

It is plain that there are minerals in the steel used to make automobiles, trucks, trains, and airplanes. But the fuel, rubber, and plastic in these transportation machines also come from a mineral: petroleum. Petroleum also helps make highway travel possible by providing not only the fuel but also the pavement made of **asphalt**, a mixture of crushed rock and a refined **crude oil** product.

Much of Canada's electrical power depends on minerals. Electricity can be produced by burning coal or petroleum products, or by using uranium in **nuclear reactors**. When hydro-electric power is produced from fast-flowing water, it is developed and transmitted by **turbines**, generators, and transmission lines made from minerals such as nickel, aluminum, and copper.

Nepheline syenite is used in making glass and in the finish of bathtubs, china, and pottery. Only three countries produce this valuable mineral: Norway, the Soviet Union, and Canada (in mines at Blue Mountain near Peterborough, Ontario, Figure 10.1).

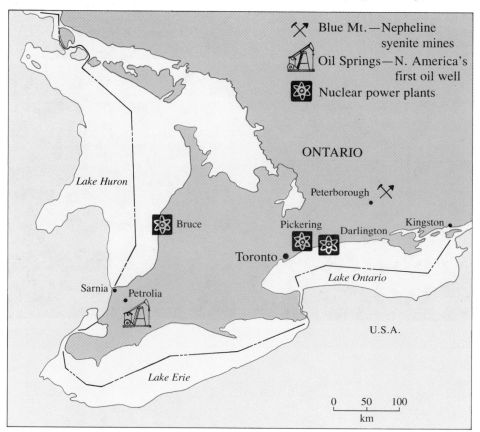

Figure 10.1 *Some Mineral Locations in Southern Ontario*

1. Iron, when smelted into steel, is widely used in the manufacture of machinery and transportation equipment because of its hardness and strength. Name the special characteristics of four other minerals that make them well suited to their use.

2. a) List six activities you engage in every day that involve the use of minerals.

b) Develop a class list of daily activities that involve the use of minerals.

c) Make a class list of any daily activities that are not related to minerals.

3. Make a general statement about the importance of minerals in our lives.

A thin layer of gold in the windshields of jet aircraft blocks out the sun's rays and provides a conductor for electrically de-icing the aircrafts' windshields.

Streets, vehicles, and buildings such as Toronto's Royal Bank Plaza, with its gold windows, are made from many kinds of minerals. Their power, heat, and light also come from minerals.

TYPES OF MINERALS

Minerals may be classified in different ways. For our study we will group them in three basic categories: ***metallics***, ***non-metallics***, ***fossil fuels***. Following is a brief description of some of the important minerals found in each mineral class.

METALLICS

Metallics are usually hard, shiny, heavy, and easy to shape. Most metallic minerals are ***base metals***, but some, such as gold and silver, are ***precious metals***.

Iron is one of the most useful of all metals (Figure 10.2, page 300). It is the basic ingredient for making steel, which has thousands of uses in our industrialized society. To make steel harder, rust-resistant, and stainless, the iron is mixed with other metals such as nickel, molybdenum, and cadmium. The mixture that results is called an ***alloy***.

Copper is soft for a metal and is easy to shape. It was therefore one of the earliest metals to be used for making tools and implements. Copper bends easily without breaking, and is an excellent conductor of heat and electricity. Copper combined with tin forms a stronger, shiny, yellowish-brown alloy called bronze.

The most common use of zinc is to protect steel. Steel, coated or ***galvanized*** with zinc, resists rust. Galvanized steel is used for roofing and in certain parts of automobiles. When zinc is alloyed with copper, it forms brass, a metal with a high sheen which is often used for ornaments.

Gold has traditionally had a special value as a precious metal. Because it is easily moulded, resists corrosion, and readily conducts heat, gold has many uses today in electronics, the chemical and space industries, and the fields of optics and nuclear energy.

Uranium is different from other metallics in that it is radioactive. It is obtained from the minerals brannerite, uraninite, and pitchblende. Its radio-activity makes it useful in nuclear reactors, colour television sets, and cancer-treatment equipment.

Only a small amount of iron (A), copper (B), and nickel in these ore samples is valuable; the rest of the material is waste rock.

Molybdenum, known as moly, is produced in the interior of British Columbia. Molybdenum steel is light and strong. It is useful for oil or gas pipelines, and it is being used more and more in cars.

NON-METALLICS

Non-metallics generally have a duller lustre, are lighter in colour and weight, and break apart more easily than metallic minerals. A typical non-metallic is salt, which is made up of sodium and chlorine. The most common industrial use for non-metallics is in the manufacture of chemicals. Potash, or potassium chloride, is similar to salt. Growing plants need potash, and it is an important ingredient in artificial fertilizer.

In the Western Cordillera and the Appalachian region, the mountains contain some sedimentary rocks in which a few non-metallic minerals occur. One of these minerals is asbestos.

One group of non-metallics is structural minerals, which are used in constructing buildings, roads, and other projects.

Cement is produced by burning a mixture of ground limestone, silicon, alumina (aluminum oxide), and iron

A number system on fertilizer bags tells the proportion of the different chemicals in the contents: for example, 10-6-4. The first number refers to the proportion of nitrogen, the second to the proportion of phosphate (derived from phosphorus), and the third to the proportion of potash that are combined to make the fertilizer.

oxide to which is added another non-metallic mineral, gypsum. When cement is mixed with water and sand or gravel, it becomes a hard, strong material called concrete. Large amounts of concrete are used in the construction of factories, office buildings, houses, sidewalks, bridges, and dams.

Sand, gravel, and crushed stone, materials called *aggregate*, are widely used in the construction industry. Aggregate is added to concrete and asphalt to pave roads. Because it provides good drainage, aggregate is used as fill around buildings and as a foundation for highways and railroads. Limestone and sandstone are cut into blocks and used in the construction of buildings. All these materials are

In ancient times, salt was a very highly valued mineral. It was even used as currency in those countries where scarcity made it costly.

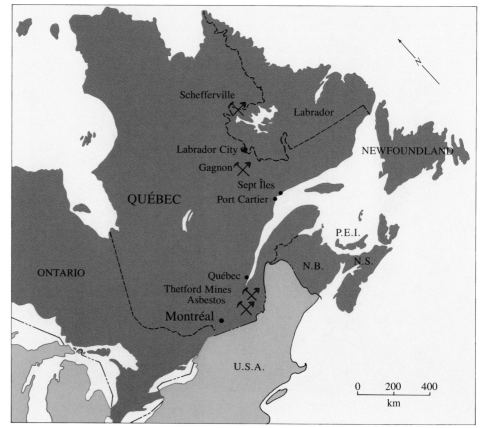

Figure 10.2 *Some Mineral Resources in Québec*

bulky, heavy, and low cost, and so they are usually mined from areas close to the places where they are needed for construction.

The fibrous texture of the non-metallic mineral asbestos is a unique mineral characteristic.

FOSSIL FUELS

Fossil fuels come from the remains of aquatic plants and animals buried underground. The fossil fuel minerals are petroleum or crude oil, coal, natural gas, and natural gas liquids such as propane and butane. These fuels power our transportation systems and help produce electricity or melt down other minerals. Fossil fuels also supply raw materials for the *petrochemical* industry, which produces a wide variety of products such as asphalt, grease, lubricating oils, paints, detergents, plastics, fertilizers, drugs, and perfumes.

The fuel minerals are compounds of hydrogen and carbon known as *hydrocarbons*. Hydrocarbons contain various amounts of sulphur and other impurities that affect their properties. For example, light and medium crude oils (often termed conventional crudes) have a high hydrogen-to-carbon ratio and flow readily at normal

air temperatures. Heavy crude oil has a high sulphur content, is thick and sticky, and does not flow easily. Heavy oil is sometimes found mixed with sand particles. This oil-sand mixture is called oil sands; sometimes, too, it is referred to as tar sands. Natural gas can be sour or sweet, depending on the amount of sulphur it contains. It burns cleaner than the fuels refined from crude oil.

Coal is divided into four grades: anthracite, bituminous coal, sub-bituminous coal, and lignite. Figure 10.3 shows some of the differences. The fuel burned to heat water to provide steam pressure in most industrial plants is either lignite or sub-bituminous coal. Bituminous coal is sometimes used to produce electric power because it burns cleaner, producing less air pollution because of its high carbon and low sulphur content. Most bituminous coal is burned to produce *coke* for melting iron ore in the steel industry. Anthracite coal is blended with bituminous coal to make higher-quality coke and to produce chemicals such as ammonia.

Hard coal burns cleaner and hotter than soft coal because it is more tightly packed. The pressures that formed it underground were greater than those that formed soft coal.

1. a) Which of the three types of mineral resources are found in your local area? In what form are they found?
b) Describe one way in which these minerals are used locally or beyond your region.
c) Speaking generally, how much does your community depend on other parts of Canada to supply mineral fuels and building materials?

Coal Type	Carbon Content	Hardness	Heating Value	Sulphur Content	Pollution from Burning
Anthracite	High	Hard	High	Low	Low
Bituminous Coal					
Sub-bituminous Coal					
Lignite	Low	Soft	Low	High	High

Figure 10.3 *Types of Coal*

2. a) Draw up a three-column chart that lists all the minerals mentioned in this section of the text according to their type.

b) Of all the minerals listed on your chart, which type do you think is most common in Canada?

c) How are metallic minerals different from non-metallics? from fossil fuels? Name two ways in which each of the three types of minerals is used. Name one way in which each type is used differently from the other two.

3. a) Write a brief definition of any six of the following materials: bronze, galvanized steel, cement, brass, potash, aggregate, hydrocarbon, and lignite.

b) Which of these materials are pure minerals (not alloys)?

4. Using Figure 10.3 and the section on fossil fuels, describe the qualities and uses of either bituminous or sub-bituminous coal.

5. Explain why coal might be classified as either a fossil fuel or a non-metallic mineral, and uranium as either a metallic mineral or a mineral fuel.

6. Make a class "collection" of metals.

a) If you have room in your classroom to display a collection of (small) metal objects, arrange and label them as a display.

b) You might prefer to collect pictures or drawings of metal used in various ways. If so, write captions for your "collection" that describe the metals and list their chief uses. Mount your collection in a file folder or loose-leaf notebook and keep it as a classroom resource.

LOCATION OF MINERALS

The location of mineral resources in a country depends on the location of the ore-bearing rocks. A review of the first part of Chapter Two will help you understand the processes that have formed the rock that now contains mineral deposits. Figure 10.4 shows that most of our metallic minerals are located in the Canadian Shield, the Western Cordillera, and the Appalachian region. These regions contain large masses of igneous rocks formed by underground volcanic activity. When sections of the earth's crust fold and fault, the intense heat and pressure that is created change some igneous rocks into metamorphic rocks. Metamorphic rocks often have bands, or veins, of one or two minerals. If the

---

Our Fossil Fuel Savings Account

The coal that we extract and use today started to form 300- to 400 million years ago. Vast forests of living plants and trees captured an immeasurable quantity of incoming solar radiation and stored it in their tissues.

Over many ages, thousands of generations of plants and trees lived and died. When they died, they deposited their lifetime's accumulation of stored energy on the earth's surface, layer upon layer upon layer.

As more time passed, layers of clays and sands and silts were deposited on top of the decaying vegetation. As each new layer was added, the pressure on the bottom layers increased.

Much later still, the earth's surface underwent upheavals, bendings, and foldings. The pressures on the layers of buried vegetation increased more and more and more.

The coal we mine today is the product of those deposits and pressures. When we take it from the ground, we are withdrawing from an energy savings account that was opened hundreds of millions of years ago.

The oil and gas we drill for today began to form 70- to 200 million years ago. The oceans and seas of the earth were then home to a multitude of microscopic animals and plants. During their lifetime, they stored energy in their bodies.

As the ages passed, thousands of generations of sea life lived and died. When these forms of life died, they drifted slowly to the sea floor, where they mixed with sand, clay, and silt.

Over time, thousands of metres of sediments built up on these ancient ocean floors. With every metre added to the top, the pressure on the bottom levels increased. After a very long time, through bacterial action, chemical processes, pressure, and heat, the original materials changed into droplets of oil and bubbles of natural gas surrounded by rock. Finally, through movements of the earth's crust, some of these changed materials were concentrated in "traps".

These "traps" are our deposits of oil and natural gas. When we extract them, we are withdrawing from an energy savings account that was opened approximately one hundred million years ago.

—*Current*, February 1981

mineral concentration is large enough, the ore body will be worth mining.

Non-metallic and fossil fuel minerals come from the sedimentary rocks formed at the bottom of ancient seas and swamps. Rivers deposit sediments in the sea, forming a thick bed on the ocean floor. The bottom layers of sediment are pressed into rock by the weight of the sediment above them. For example, deeply buried sand turns into sandstone, and deeply buried clay into shale. Much later, when the sedimentary rocks formed in this way appear above sea level, they begin to break down. During an ice age, glaciers erode their surface. In a postglacial period, rivers flowing from lakes continue to erode them. The shale and sandstone become loose clay and sand again, and are washed back into the sea.

Other sedimentary rocks are formed in somewhat different ways. Salt, potash, and gypsum form from the layers of precipitate left when the warm shallow sea water near ancient ocean shorelines evaporates. Limestone forms from the lime in the shells of millions of sea animals that died and sank to the bottom.

Some tiny plant and animal life that sinks to the ocean floor is later buried in large, dish-shaped areas called sedimentary **basins**. Here, under the intense heat and pressure of overlying rock, their remains "cook" to form

The United Nations Convention on the Law of the Sea intends to guarantee that the people of all nations will get a fair share of the mineral resources under the oceans that cover 70 percent of the earth.

The irregular veins in this metamorphic rock show how heat and pressure can form valuable bodies of ore from the minerals in igneous rock.

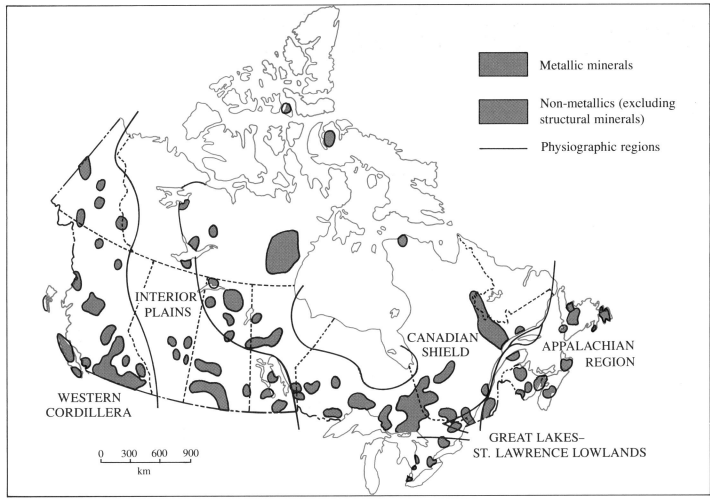

Figure 10.4 *Major Areas of Metallic and Non-Metallic Minerals*

The layers or seams of coal exposed in this B.C. mine represent concentrated masses of ancient vegetation trapped in sedimentary rock.

crude oil and natural gas (Figure 10.5). Coal forms in the parts of sedimentary basins where forest swamps once surrounded ancient seas.

Coal forms from the tree, shrub, and fern vegetation buried in ancient swamps. At first, this vegetable matter becomes peat, much like the peat moss used to condition garden soils. The weight of overlying layers of sediment and sedimentary rock presses the peat into solid lignite or sub-bituminous coal. If sedimentary rocks in the region fold into mountains, an increase in pressure results and produces bituminous and anthracite grades of coal (Figure 10.5).

Not surprisingly, non-metallic and fossil fuel minerals are usually located in the physiographic regions with the most sedimentary rock. In Canada, the Interior Plains contain the largest deposits of crude oil, natural gas, and potash, as well as those of lignite and sub-bituminous coal. The Great Lakes-St. Lawrence Lowlands region has some oil and gas, as well as salt and gypsum. The sedimentary basins off Canada's east coast and in the Arctic also contain oil and gas. The sedimentary rock of mountains in the Western Cordillera and the Appalachian region contain large quantities of bituminous coal.

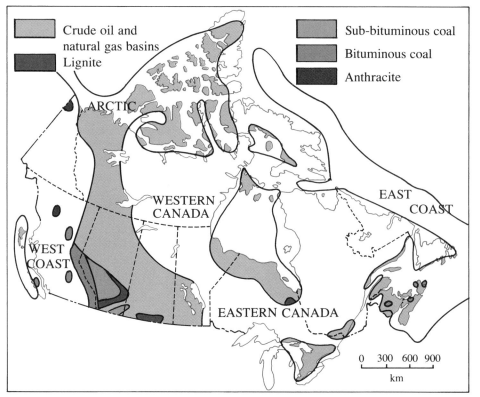

Figure 10.5 **Major Land and Underwater Areas of Fossil Fuel Minerals**

1. a) Are there minerals in the area where you live? If so, draw a sketch map of your area. Label the physiographic region. Mark the approximate location of up to three minerals.
   b) How were these minerals formed?
   c) Are these minerals found in other parts of Canada? If so, where?
2. a) Which province appears to include the largest area of metallic minerals in the Canadian Shield?
   b) Name the physiographic regions containing the most

non-metallic and fossil fuel minerals. Why are they found here?

c) After the Interior Plains and Great Lakes-St. Lawrence Lowlands, which region has the most non-metallics?

3. Summarize three different ways minerals can form on the sea bottom.

4. a) Which province has the largest area containing sub-bituminous coal?

b) What physiographic region has the most bituminous and anthracite coal? Why?

c) Which physiographic region contains the lignite coal of Northern Ontario?

d) Which physiographic region completely lacks fossil fuels?

5. Suggest why the northern parts of Canada might hold more mineral wealth than Figures 10.4 and 10.5 show.

Only one in a thousand exploration drill holes leads to a producing mine.

Geologists, like this one exploring on Ellesmere Island, N.W.T., can tell if a discovery site is worth exploring further.

MINERAL RESERVES

All rocks contain minerals, but only a few locations contain enough high-quality minerals to be worth mining. Mining companies look into a number of factors before they decide what mineral deposits to mine.

Minerals are found in rock formations by professional prospectors, by geological survey teams, and even by amateur *geologists*. The minerals they find can only be considered resources if we have the technology to take them out of the bedrock, process them, and turn them into useful products. Resources represent possible wealth. But the resources will yield wealth only if they can be sold at a price greater than the cost of getting them to market. If it is worthwhile to develop a mineral discovery, the resource becomes a mineral reserve.

Canadian mining companies will not extract a mineral unless they can make a profit by doing so. Many factors affect that profit. These factors include the production costs of mining, processing, and transporting the mineral to market; they also include the price of the mineral on the world market. World supply of a mineral determines its market value: the smaller the supply of the mineral available in the world, the greater its value. If the costs of production are greater than the market value of a mineral, it is uneconomic to mine that mineral. If the market value of a mineral is greater than its production costs, it is economic to mine the mineral. Because of these factors, lower-grade minerals are sometimes more valuable to mining companies than is richer ore.

A country's mineral reserves fluctuate from year to year. They increase or decrease as a result of new discoveries, improved technology, changing costs of production, rising and falling market prices, and the amount of ore mined.

New discoveries can increase Canada's mineral reserve and prolong mining activity. If no new discoveries are made, mining can totally deplete the mineral reserve. New technology may increase the mineral reserve by making it possible to extract more mineral from a given body of ore. On the other hand, new technology may decrease a mineral reserve by developing a substitute product. If the substitute product is less expensive, the price of the mineral it replaces will fall; it might even fall to a point below the cost of production. When production costs increase or when prices fall, only the richest mineral deposits can be mined profitably, and the mineral reserve decreases.

When mineral reserves become scarce, the price of the ore increases, and this development makes mining the mineral resource more profitable. In the long run, of course, the result would be the complete disappearance of the mined mineral. Table 10.1 (page 306) shows how mining depletes mineral reserves.

305

Table 10.1 *Some Mineral Reserves*

Mineral	Reserves (000 tonnes)	Annual Depletion (000 tonnes)	Years Left
Coal	8 750 000	53 170	165
Iron ore	4 521 000	49 550	91
Zinc	29 436	911	
Copper	16 831	691	
Lead	10 119	269	
Nickel	8 304	160	
Molybdenum	550	18	
Uranium	185	8	
Silver	34	1	

Source: Human Activity and the Environment (Environment Canada, 1986)
Note: This table shows the estimated amount of reserves for coal and some metallic minerals. Canada has even greater reserves of non-metallics because they are more abundant than metallics. Crude oil and natural gas are excluded because the amount of these minerals represented by offshore discoveries is unknown.

1. Table 10.1 projects the number of years that Canada's reserve of coal and iron ore is likely to last. (These calculations assume that no new mineral discoveries become reserves and that the annual rate of mining does not change.) Use the data given for the other minerals to project how long their reserve is likely to last.

2. How might each of the following factors affect the reserve life of a mineral?
   a) an increase in the price of the mineral
   b) a decrease in the price of the mineral
   c) a decrease in the cost of production
   d) development of a new technology that makes it possible to mine lower-grade ores
   e) development of a new technology that finds an inexpensive substitute for the mineral
   f) new mineral discoveries

3. a) Someone has said ''Resources are not; they become.'' What does this statement mean?
   b) When does a mineral resource become a reserve?

Hemlo Gold

When news leaks out that a mineral has been discovered, prospectors and all sorts of people usually rush to make mining claims. The Hemlo Gold Rush in Northern Ontario was different: a long time passed between the discovery of the ore and development of the mine. A prospector first discovered gold on the site in 1869, and the first test holes were drilled in 1931.

Gold usually comes in solid veins through the rock or as loose lumps of precious metal called nuggets, but at Hemlo the gold is less obvious. It appears as tiny yellow specks scattered throughout low-grade ore. To

One of the new underground mining sites at the Hemlo gold strike, in a heavily forested part of the Canadian Shield. Settling ponds in the background store mine and mill tailings.

mine such ore is costly. For that reason Hemlo was not developed until 1980, when the world price of gold increased, and such a mine could make a worthwhile profit. Then detailed exploration began. A great deal of test drilling finally showed that Hemlo contained more gold ore than any other known site in Canada.

Mining began at Hemlo in 1985. When Hemlo is fully developed it will be the largest gold mining operation in the world.

Hemlo is a railway stop on the Canadian Pacific Railway. It lies north of Lake Superior and close to the Trans-Canada Highway, which is built over part of the ore body. It is not far from the towns of Marathon, Manitouwadge, and White River (Figure 10.6). The population of these towns is expected to double by the early 1990s.

Rapid growth brings economic gain, but it also brings environmental challenges. In 1984 and 1985, public hearings were held in Marathon to give people a chance to express their concerns about some of the expected changes. Large amounts of water must be used in the milling process. The Hemlo mine will produce a lot of *tailings* because it takes four tonnes of Hemlo ore to produce one ounce[1] of gold. Huge *settling ponds* will be needed to dispose of these tailings. The mining company plans to remove cyanide and metals from waste water in the settling ponds, but this water will still not be pure enough to drink. A small valley will be dammed to contain any seepage from the settling ponds. Mill waste water will not be discharged into a nearby river that supplies an Indian band with its water; instead it will be piped into another river farther away.

[1]The international measurements standard for gold is not metric. One troy ounce (1.2 ounces, avoirdupois) is equal to 23.3 g.

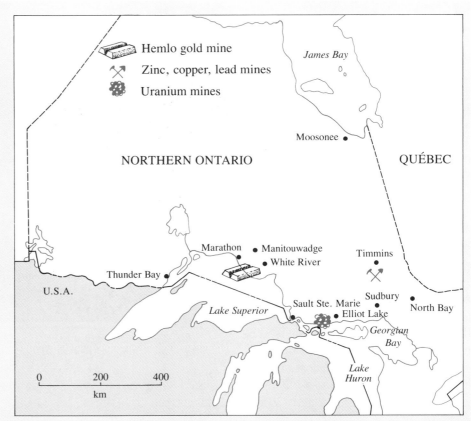

Figure 10.6 *Some Mineral Resources in Northern Ontario*

1. a) If you could obtain a high-paying job at the Hemlo mine (or some other new mining development), would you be willing to move there? Before you answer, consider the changes in your lifestyle that such a move would bring.
b) Discuss your decision with a classmate who has made a different decision.

2. People in a community have many different opinions about the benefits and problems of rapid growth.
a) You are an adult resident in your community. You may be the mayor, a store owner, a retired citizen, a single parent, a police officer, a social worker, a teacher, a doctor, a nurse, a member of the clergy, a city/town planner, a life-insurance agent, or any other resident you wish.
b) Write down your views about the effects you would expect from rapid growth in your area.
c) Ask some of the "residents" to read their statements.
d) Decide by "referendum" whether your "community" favours or opposes rapid growth.

3. As "editor" of your local paper, write an editorial that summarizes the pros and cons of rapid growth in your area.

4. You are a member of a group of local volunteers wishing to help your community to meet the challenge of rapid growth. Suggest three things that might be done to help people living in or moving to your rapidly growing community.

MINERAL PRODUCTION

Canada is one of the leading producers of minerals in the world. We mine 60 different minerals, and we rank third in non-fuel mineral production. Besides the minerals listed in Table 10.2, Canada leads the world in the production of nepheline syenite, is second in the production of potash, titanium, sulphur, and gypsum; third in aluminum and platinum; fourth in cobalt; fifth in salt; and sixth in iron ore.

Because our population is so small, we use only some of the minerals we produce. We export the rest to more than 100 countries. Canada is the world's largest exporter of minerals and mineral products. Minerals make up one-fifth of the value of our total exports. Canada exports more zinc, asbestos, potash, sulphur, and nepheline syenite than does any other country.

Because Canada exports about eighty percent of its mineral products, world competition and prices greatly affect our mining industry. For example, strong competition for iron ore markets by Brazil, Australia, and West Africa led to the closing of iron ore mines at Schefferville, Québec (Figure 10.2) in the early 1980s. The richest ores of Schefferville had been

Coal mined in western Canada is exported to Japan and other Pacific countries through Roberts Bank, a special offshore port facility near Vancouver.

depleted, and the mining company could not sell iron ore at prices that could compete with those of other countries. Later another mine and its *concentrating plant* at Gagnon, Québec, were also closed. Hundreds of miners were laid off work and had to leave their homes. Schefferville and Gagnon became ghost towns (Figure 10.2).

> **By value, about 60 percent of Canada's mineral production consists of fuels, 25 percent consists of metals, and 5 percent consists of non-metallics.**

Although mining occurs all across Canada, it is more important in both value and volume to some parts of the country than to others (Table 10.3). Alberta produces more total mineral value than all other parts of Canada combined, because of its large fossil fuels production. As a result, minerals make up about half the value of Alberta's gross provincial product. Ontario ranks second in total mineral production, but first in non-fuel minerals such as gold, silver, salt, sand, gravel, and stone. Most aggregate mining occurs in the Great Lakes-St. Lawrence Lowlands because this heavily urbanized region requires so much construction.

---

1. a) What type of mineral includes all the examples listed in Table 10.2, except asbestos?
   b) Explain why Canada ranks high among world producers of this type of mineral.
2. South Africa produces over half of the world's gold. How might socio-political events in South Africa affect the production of gold in Canada?

Table 10.2 *Share of World Production of Some Canadian Minerals*

Mineral	% of World Production	World Rank
Uranium	30	1
Zinc	20	1
Nickel	20	2
Asbestos	20	2
Molybdenum	15	4
Silver	13	5
Copper	10	4
Lead	9	4
Gold	4	3

Source: Compiled from Statistics Canada data, 1986
Note: Canada's percentages of world mineral production may vary from year to year because of changes in market conditions or supply schedules. As a result, Canada's world rank for these minerals might alter slightly.

Table 10.3 *Mineral Production by Province and Territory*

Province/Territory	As a % of Total Canadian Value	As a % of Gross Provincial Product[1]
Newfoundland	2	18
Prince Edward Island	< 1	< 1
Nova Scotia	1	3
New Brunswick	1	8
Québec	7	2
Ontario	14	3
Manitoba	2	5
Saskatchewan	8	22
Alberta	52	50
British Columbia	10	8
Yukon and Northwest Territories	2	3

Source: Statistics Canada data, 1986

Note: All mineral types are included in the calculations. The percentages may vary slightly from year to year because of changes in the market conditions for mineral production.

[1]Gross Provincial Product is the value of all goods and services produced in the province or territory within a given period.

1. Why are Alberta, Ontario, and British Columbia Canada's leading producers of minerals? (Consider the size of these provinces and their geology [Figures 10.4 and 10.5], as well as their physiography [Chapter Two].)

2. a) Name the mineral that accounts for most of the value of the mining production in five of the following provinces or territories: Alberta, Newfoundland, Nova Scotia, Saskatchewan, the Yukon and Northwest Territories, and Manitoba.

   b) Draw up a chart that lists each mineral you have named in a) under one of the three general types of minerals described earlier in this chapter.

   c) Add a column to your chart to show the physiographic region in which each mineral is mined.

3. In which parts of Ontario are gold, silver and aggregate mined? Explain why these minerals are located there.

British Columbia, the third-largest mineral producer, mines the most copper and coal of any Canadian province or territory. Other leading producers of specific minerals are Newfoundland for iron ore, Nova Scotia for gypsum, Québec for asbestos, Saskatchewan for potash, and the Northwest Territories for lead-zinc ore. Manitoba's production of nickel is second only to that of Ontario, and New Brunswick mines the third-largest value of lead and zinc in Canada. Mineral value is low in Prince Edward Island because sand and gravel are the only minerals mined there.

About 95 percent of the asbestos produced in Canada is exported. We also export 90 percent of our sulphur and 85 percent of our uranium.

The mining industry employs over 375 000 people in mining, processing, and manufacturing minerals and mineral products. In some parts of the country, it is the largest employer. All regions of Canada gain benefits from the income earned by workers in mining operations, and from the purchase of goods and services by the mining industry. For example, about half of

LOCAL STUDY

As a class, make an environmental assessment of a mining operation in your area. (See ''Mining and the Environment'', page 311.) Since almost all communities have some sand and gravel excavation nearby, the following questions are related to that industry. If you choose a different kind of mining operation, you will have to change some of the questions.

Some sources of information you might use include a local newspaper, interviews with a local municipal planner and a mining company official, and publications by your province's Department of Mines.

1. a) Draw a sketch map locating the sand and gravel pits closest to your school.

   b) What uses were made of this land before it was mined?

2. a) Is there a former sand or gravel pit near your community?

   b) What use has been made of the land since the aggregate was removed?

3. a) Where is the aggregate from your area used?

   b) If all the pits in your area were to close, how far would local sand and gravel trucks have to go to reach the nearest source of aggregate?

4. Environmental problems sometimes arise when companies excavate sand and gravel.

   a) Provide an example of such a problem.

   b) Suggest a solution to the problem you have stated.

5. Public controversies sometimes arise over proposals for new sand and gravel pits or expansion of old pits, or because of the dangers of abandoned pits. Try to find out if there has been such a controversy in your area. If there has, write a short article about it for a ''local newspaper''.

all railway freight revenue in Canada comes from fees charged to move raw and processed minerals.

The list of supplies and equipment used by mining companies is very long: it includes chemicals, explosives, rubber belting, steel cables, electrical wiring, ore crushers, pumps, trucks, and much more highly specialized equipment. Many Canadian manufacturing plants owe their existence to mining. Canadians design and manufacture mining and exploration equipment that is sold around the world. Mining also creates office jobs in Canada's cities, where the headquarters of other mining companies are located.

A Planned Mining Town

At one time, new towns grew up around mining sites in a haphazard way. There was no control over land uses or quality of buildings. As a result, a ''shack town'' often developed.

Later, mining companies financed, built, and owned the new town associated with a mine, but the ''company town'' led to problems between the mining company and their employees. People resented the fact that their employer was associated with every aspect of their lives. They took no interest in governing the town or maintaining the community's services.

More recently mining companies have worked with the provincial governments, other private businesses, and their employees to build a planned town governed by the citizens who live there.

The town of Thompson in northern Manitoba serves as an example of this modern approach to setting up mining towns (Figure 10.7). Thompson was built when rich nickel ores were found and developed by the International Nickel Co. (INCO) Ltd. Thompson was planned and developed with the help of the Manitoba government and the mine's employees. A local government was established, with a council elected by the residents. The mining company paid for the building of schools, hospitals, recreation centres, streets, and sewers. Then they turned the facilities over to the municipality to administer.

The original community was planned with a town core that contained a shopping plaza, a school, a hospital, a recreation centre, and other services. Modern subdivisions of houses and townhouses surrounded the core section. This arrangement gave everybody easy access to services. Later, a second, separate, core area was built without the careful planning of surrounding land uses. Nevertheless, everyone agrees that Thompson is much better as a place to live than the company towns of earlier days.

As the company develops new mines thirty or forty kilometres away from Thompson, it provides commuter transportation to these new mines, instead of building new towns at the sites. This policy has made Thompson the centre of a broad region of mining activity. It should ensure a much longer life for Thompson than mining communities usually enjoy. When a town depends on a single mine, it is likely to become a ghost town if the mine closes.

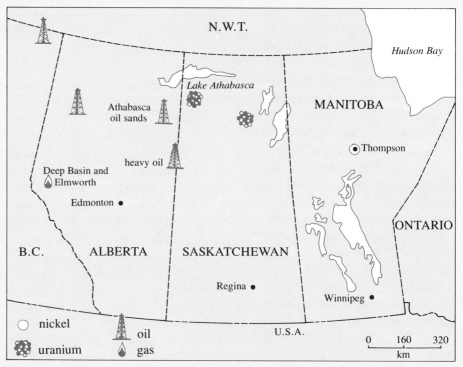

Figure 10.7 *Some Mineral Resources in the Prairie Provinces*

MINING AND THE ENVIRONMENT

In this chapter, mining refers both to the digging of solid minerals from the bedrock and to the extraction of crude oil and natural gas by drilling. Most mines are set in rural areas, often in almost unspoiled country. A mine or well, with its waste materials, its mill or pumps, its noise and dust, makes a stark contrast to the beauty and quiet of the surrounding scene. There is no escaping the fact that mining has a negative effect on the environment.

STAGES IN THE MINING PROCESS

Mining activity usually follows the order of events shown in Figure 10.8. The events fall into three main stages: pre-production, production, and post-production. All three stages affect the environment. Figure 10.8 outlines the steps taken at each stage of the mining process.

PRE-PRODUCTION

The pre-production stage of mining may be going on at as many as 500 to 800 exploration sites in different parts of Canada each year (not counting drilling for oil and gas). But only a few of these sites are developed.

In the beginning, *exploration* has almost no effect on the environment. The work begins with studying maps and taking air photos. But later exploration involves constructing access roads, digging trenches, clearing vegetation to lay **seismic** lines, setting off seismic explosions, and drilling test holes. Major exploration projects require construction of a base camp. All these activities have a harmful effect on the vegetation, soils, and wildlife in the area.

Ecological damage is most likely to

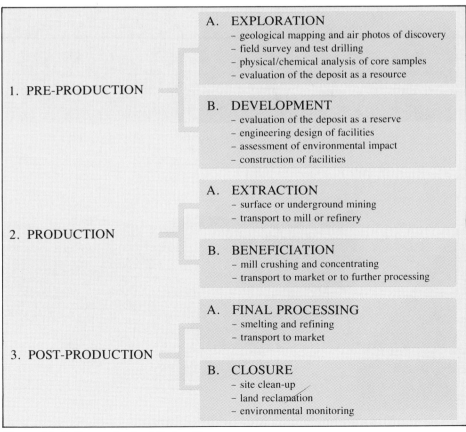

Seismic testing

Sedimentary rock layers

occur in areas with a sensitive environment. Canada's tundra is one such environment. If tundra vegetation is disturbed, the permafrost melts, creating a scar on the landscape that takes decades to heal. Wild animals and birds in the Arctic and sub-Arctic have only a short time each year in which to mate and then produce and rear their young. If they are disturbed during this period, a whole generation can be wiped out.

Regulations passed by our federal and provincial governments help reduce the negative effects on the environment of mining exploration. These rules apply to all three stages of mining activity, including post-production. For example, they limit exploration to times when it will least affect the reproduction of wildlife. After exploration they require companies to restore the environment to its natural state.

The *development* of a mine site requires much disturbance of the earth's surface. Workers use heavy equipment for many tasks, including the building of roads and railway lines. They often excavate streams to get gravel for the road beds, and this process damages fish habitats. They build settling ponds to hold mine wastes and sometimes pipelines to

1. PRE-PRODUCTION

A. EXPLORATION
- geological mapping and air photos of discovery
- field survey and test drilling
- physical/chemical analysis of core samples
- evaluation of the deposit as a resource

B. DEVELOPMENT
- evaluation of the deposit as a reserve
- engineering design of facilities
- assessment of environmental impact
- construction of facilities

2. PRODUCTION

A. EXTRACTION
- surface or underground mining
- transport to mill or refinery

B. BENEFICIATION
- mill crushing and concentrating
- transport to market or to further processing

3. POST-PRODUCTION

A. FINAL PROCESSING
- smelting and refining
- transport to market

B. CLOSURE
- site clean-up
- land reclamation
- environmental monitoring

Figure 10.8 *Stages in the Mining Process*

transport the unwanted rock materials (tailings). Their greatest construction project, putting up buildings, extends in remote areas to the creation of whole towns.

To reduce damage to the environment during mine development, federal and provincial governments require an **environmental impact assessment** before they give permission to proceed with the project. This assessment is made to investigate the possible effects of mining on air, water, soil, and wildlife in a given area. The experts who make the assessment also recommend methods of developing the project that will cause as little damage to the environment as possible. An assessment may take two to three years to complete. Mining companies complain about the delay and the higher cost of production to meet imposed standards at a time when there is stiff international competition for mineral markets.

On average, the opening of a mine is the result of eight years' exploration and two years' development.

PRODUCTION

In the *production* stage of mining (Figure 10.8), mineral reserves are mined and processed into products or into materials needed to make other products.

Extraction is the act of taking a mineral out of the earth. There are two types of extraction techniques: surface and underground. In Canada surface mining is most common. It is the method used to extract about 60 percent of our coal, 40 percent of metals, and 80 percent of non-metallic minerals. A company sometimes uses surface mining at first, and then goes underground when the cost of removing the **overburden** (the overlying soil and rock) becomes too high. The two chief methods of surface extraction are **strip mining** and **open-pit mining** (Figure 10.9).

Strip mining works best where a mineral lies in fairly horizontal layers close to the earth's surface. It is the most common method of mining coal

An open pit coal mine in the Rocky Mountains of southern British Columbia

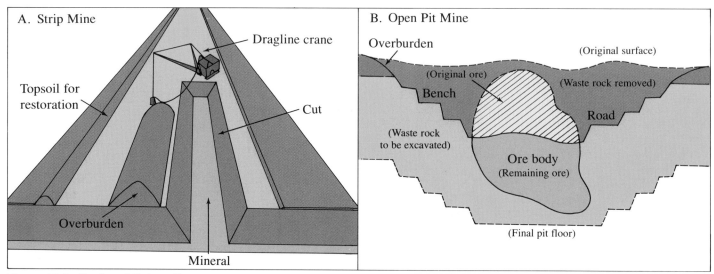

Figure 10.9 *Surface Mining: Strip Mining* (A) *and Open-Pit Mining* (B)

in western Canada. A dragline crane makes a trench, called a cut, exposing the coal (Figure 10.9A). When all the coal is removed from one cut, the crane makes another, and the stockpiled overburden is dumped into the first cut. Strip mining causes minimal environmental damage if the land is reclaimed by replacing the topsoil and re-planting vegetation.

Open-pit mining is used mainly to extract irregularly shaped deposits of minerals that lie near the surface. Open pit mines are often more than one thousand metres in diameter and 100 to 200 m deep. The pit is cut into solid rock in a series of terraces or steps called *benches*. Spiralling benches are used as roads by trucks hauling the minerals. (The walls of sand and gravel pits do not usually have benches, because they are made of loose rock materials.) The area of the pit must be much larger than the ore body so that miners can reach all of the deposit without the sides collapsing (Figure 10.9B). Pit operations usually remove three to four tonnes of waste for every tonne of mineral

extracted. Sometimes *reclamation* is done after the mineral is depleted, but most pit mines leave as their legacy a deep hole that mars the landscape. Reclaiming a pit involves either filling it in or redeveloping it for other land uses.

Underground mining is most useful when a mineral lies deep beneath the earth's surface. This method is used to extract about 60 percent of the metals, 40 percent of coal, 20 percent of non-metallics, and all of the crude oil and natural gas extracted in Canada (except for the oil sands). The exact kind of underground mine depends on the type of mineral and the rock formation enclosing it. Most underground mines have a vertical *shaft* containing hoisting cables. From the shaft horizontal *tunnels* lead to the *stope* where the ore body is extracted (Figure 10.10A). Underground mining does far less damage to the environment than does surface mining. The best operations keep the waste rock below, disposing of it in empty stopes, instead of sending it up the shaft and piling it on the surface.

This nickel drill is operating in the INCO mine at Sudbury, Ontario.

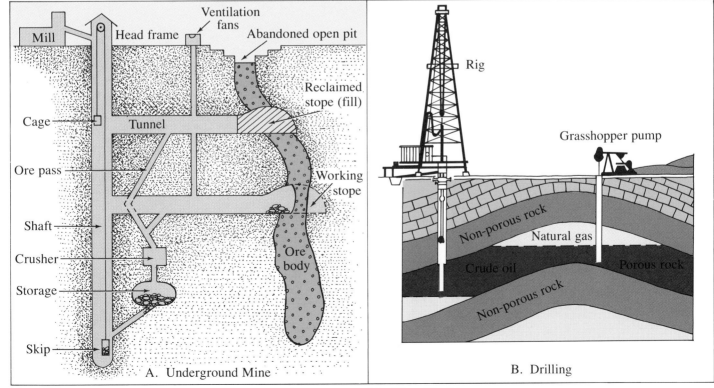

Figure 10.10 *Underground Mining: Underground Mine* (A) *and Drilling Rig* (B)

Extraction of crude oil and natural gas is a form of underground mining that also does minimal site damage. Rigs drill small bore holes through non-porous rock into porous sedimentary rock that contains trapped oil and gas (Figure 10.10B, page 313). Pumps and valves direct the oil and gas up through pipes and into buried pipelines that lead to the *refinery*.

Beneficiation is a process of crushing and grinding both metallic and non-metallic minerals to separate the unwanted tailings from the valuable ore. This process, which takes place in the mill at the mine site, uses large amounts of water. The waste water from the process is stored in ponds to allow the particles of solid tailings to settle out. Many mines recirculate treated water from the settling ponds back to the mill for re-use.

In time, settling ponds fill up with tailings, and the waste has to be moved to another site, or else a new settling pond has to be dug. Sometimes the chemicals and minerals from tailings are washed into streams and lakes by rainwater. In such cases, the wastes from the beneficiation process can have a very serious effect on the environment.

A drilling rig operating on Alberta's heavy oil sands

The most modern smelter in the world processes zinc, copper, and lead for Kidd Creek Mines near Timmins, Ontario. It is almost pollution free (Figure 10.6).

. . . and another in the rigorous conditions of the Arctic pack ice on the Beaufort Sea.

Aggregate and Environment

The most common mining done across Canada is extracting sand and gravel, crushed rock, and building stone. (These materials are known as aggregate.) Because aggregate is bulky and expensive to transport, companies usually mine it near towns and cities, where the demand for it is high. Companies that mine aggregate often come into conflict with the local people about land use and changes to the environment.

Sometimes the land above layers of sand and gravel is also good for farming. At other times the land's surface has features that give it a high value for recreation and housing. Municipal governments might try to restrict the opening and expansion of sand and gravel pits on such land. These restrictions would force the mining companies to locate farther from cities or even to go out of business. If they located farther from the cities, they would have to charge more for the aggregate in order to cover greater transportation costs.

Sand and gravel pits are not pretty sights. In fact, most people consider them eyesores. People also dislike gravel pits because the excavation process is unpleasant. It is noisy and dusty; it also creates heavy truck traffic. The amount of land disturbed or left abandoned by the aggregate industry in Canada is at least as great as the amount of land disturbed by all other forms of mining put together. No wonder that citizens and municipalities have had many conflicts with aggregate mining companies that sometimes lead to expensive legal battles!

In Ontario, where most of Canada's aggregate mining takes place, the government has passed a good deal of legislation, and mining companies have taken action, to reduce such conflicts. The province requires municipal governments, in planning future growth, to identify and protect aggregate resources. Before opening a new pit, a mining company must present a plan to the municipality for approval, showing how the mining will proceed and how the land will be reclaimed. During the mining operation, the company must screen the site from public view with barriers of earth and trees. The operation must proceed by stages. As soon as mining is completed in one section, the area must be restored, complete with topsoil, so that it can be returned to its original use or put to some other desirable use. If the proper reclamation practices are followed, farmland can be productive after sand and gravel have been removed from a site. Excavated sand and gravel pits also make excellent golf courses, parks with ponds for fishing or swimming, or housing subdivisions.

A large sand and gravel pit operation in southwestern Ontario

POST-PRODUCTION

In the *post-production* stage of mining (Figure 10.8), final processing makes some minerals into useful products.

After beneficiation, the concentrated ore of metallic minerals is taken to a **smelter** or a refinery for further *processing*. Smelters (furnaces that reach very high temperatures) reduce ore **concentrates** into metals. Refineries remove all remaining impurities so that the metal is ready for commercial use. Smelters and refineries may be located near a mine, but they are usually hundreds or even thousands of kilometres away.

Smelting and refining often cause serious pollution. Waste rock called **slag** is dumped in heaps on mine property, and fumes from smokestacks go into the air. Because many minerals contain sulphur, smelters and refineries are major contributors to acid rain.

In this processing plant in northeastern British Columbia, coal from a nearby mine is crushed into fine particles, washed, and dried for shipment.

In Canada, from 10 to 15 percent of the total capital spent in any new mining operation goes for environmental protection.

CLOSURE

The last stage in the life of all mines and wells is *closure*. A mine or well is closed when deposits have been exhausted or the operation can no longer compete economically with other producers. But the closing of a mine may not end environmental pollution. Unless the mine operators clean up the area and reclaim contaminated soil, open pits, waste rock dumps, and settling ponds, the environment will suffer.

In the early days of mining, mining companies did no clean-up at all. Since the 1970s, federal and provincial

On land reclaimed at the site of a mined-out coal deposit, a fine crop of wheat is growing.

regulations have required these companies to do everything possible to clean up and reclaim the disturbed land. Reclamation plans start as soon as a mine begins operation. If environmentally sound methods of disposing of wastes are used from the beginning, clean-up and reclamation will be much easier when the mine closes. The costs of reclamation in Canada are now considered part of the costs of mining.

---

1. a) What type of mining is used to extract minerals in your area?
   b) Is there a former mine site close to your community? If so, have its owners tried to reclaim it for other land uses? If they have, how effective have they been in repairing environmental damage?
   c) As a class, suggest some ideas for reclaiming a mine site.
   d) Working in small "committees", draw up plans for an abandoned mine site that would make it a useful (and attractive) area in or near your community.
2. Define the following mining terms: tailings, bench, overburden, seismic test, beneficiation, slag, stope, smelter, and milling.
3. You are a geologist working for a mining company. After a field trip to investigate a new mine site, you will recommend that the company use surface mining or underground mining for the new operation. On what points will you base your recommendation?
4. Which part of the mining process shown in Figure 10.8 do you think causes most environmental damage? Give evidence to support your answer.

More than half the energy that provides transportation in Canada is used by passenger cars. Trucks use another 31 percent. Railways and mass transit systems use a total of only 6 percent of Canada's energy resources.

ENERGY: A RENEWABLE OR NON-RENEWABLE RESOURCE?

Energy is very important to the economy and lifestyle of Canadians. It provides heat, light, and power. In various forms it operates appliances, machinery, and equipment, from household tools to factories and tractor trailers. Most of our energy in this century has come from non-renewable mineral fuels. Some of these fuels are becoming scarce and costly. As a result, scientists are studying other sources of renewable energy to try to secure our energy future.

Of the energy Canada needs, about 75 percent comes from fossil fuels, 20 percent from hydro or nuclear electricity, and the rest from renewable energy forms such as the burning of wood or organic wastes. Figure 10.11 shows that Canada consumes more total energy per person than does any other country. The following activity indicates some of the factors affecting energy use.

1. Referring to an atlas, make a chart that ranks the following countries, listed in Figure 10.11, from largest to smallest, first by area, and then by population density: Australia, Canada, Norway, United Kingdom, United States, U.S.S.R.
2. a) How does Canada rank in land area compared with the other countries listed on your chart?
   b) How does size relate to a country's energy consumption?
   c) Why, then, would the U.S.S.R. use less energy per capita than Canada?
3. a) How does Canada rank in density of population compared with the other countries?
   b) Why do countries with a low-density population like Canada's use more energy than some countries with a higher-density population?
4. Countries with a high standard of living, such as Canada, consume a large amount of energy.
   a) Explain how a high standard of living causes high levels of energy consumption.
   b) The standard of living in the United States is also high, but Americans consume less energy per capita than Canadians. Why?

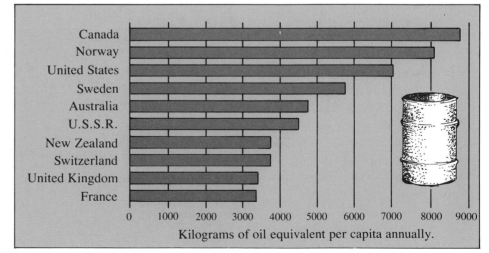

Figure 10.11 *Energy Consumption in Some Countries*[1]

[1]In making comparisons, the use of all types of energy is calculated in terms of oil in kilograms. Usually each form of energy has its own unit of measurement such as barrels for oil, cubic metres (m³) for natural gas, tonnes (t) for coal, and watts (W) for electricity.

5. Norway has the second-highest per capita energy consumption. Describe similarities between Canada and Norway that might account for high per capita energy consumption.
6. Suggest why Canada uses more energy per capita than any other country in the world.

The first successful oil well in North America was drilled in 1858, at Oil Springs, a small place in southwestern Ontario near Petrolia (Figure 10.1).

L O C A L   S T U D Y

Within your class, take a survey to discover the following:
1. What proportion of your homes are heated with fuel oil? natural gas? electricity?
2. What is the most common energy source at home for heating household water? for cooking?
3. What changes of energy source have been made in your homes during the last 10 years? Why?
4. What energy-saving actions has your family taken at home?
5. a) How many families have changed to smaller automobiles within the last 10 years?
   b) How do smaller automobiles save energy? (Consider: amount of material in the automobile, the amount of gasoline consumed per kilometre, and the reduced size of parking spaces.)
6. a) On what type of energy do your homes depend most?
   b) In your opinion, why is this the most common source of home energy in your district?
   c) Why have Canadians been trying to conserve more energy in recent years?

FOSSIL FUELS

Fossil fuels provide energy in the form of natural gas or natural gas liquids and the different types of coal, as well as refined oil products such as gasoline, kerosene, diesel fuel, furnace fuel, and liquid petroleum gases.

The first crude oil in Canada was produced in southwestern Ontario over a century ago. Today almost all Canadian crude oil comes from the basin in western Canada (Figure 10.5), far from the industrial heartland of the Great Lakes-St. Lawrence Lowlands, where most of the oil is needed. Oil companies have been forced to build costly pipelines to carry the oil from western Canada to the central Canadian market (Figure 10.12).

Canada's first long-distance oil pipeline (10 cm diameter) was built during the Second World War (1939–1945), between the oil wells at Norman Wells, Northwest Territories, and a refinery at Whitehorse, Yukon.

The heavy costs of transporting oil explain why the pipeline has not been extended beyond Montréal to the Maritimes. Until offshore oil reserves like Hibernia are developed, Atlantic Canada must depend wholly on imported crude oil. At the same time, the development of fields such as Hibernia

Sections of oil pipe are welded together, cleaned, and wrapped before the pipeline is buried in the trench dug across a farm field.

depend on the price that the oil will bring. This price depends, in turn, on world supply and demand. In 1960, the chief oil-supplying countries formed the Organization of Petroleum Exporting Countries (OPEC) to control the price of world oil. From 1972 to 1982, under the influence of OPEC, world prices for crude oil sky-rocketed from $4 a barrel to about $40 a barrel. At that price, it was worthwhile to explore further Canada's crude oil resources in the Hibernia oil field off the east coast of Newfoundland, and in the Arctic. In the late 1980s, when oil prices dropped below $20 a barrel, plans for developing Hibernia oil were put on hold. But in

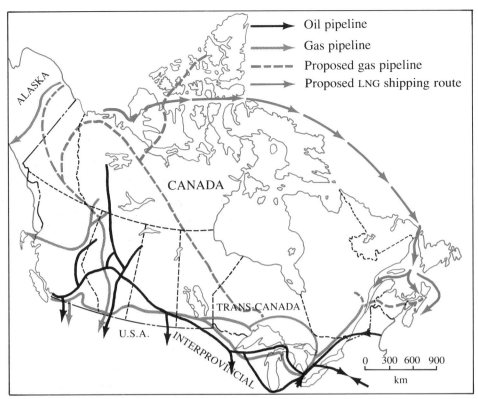

Crude oil pumped from Edmonton to Toronto through the Interprovincial pipeline takes about two days to make the journey.

Figure 10.12 ***Oil and Gas Transportation*** *Compare this map with the natural gas and crude oil basins of Figure 10.5 to see where pipelines originate.*

A dragline crane piles oil sands at one of the Athabasca strip mines.

1990, a political crisis in the Middle East sent the price of oil to $30 a barrel. The Canadian government then announced that development of the Hibernia oilfield would proceed.

During the 1980s, projects were also under way to develop the vast oil sands of western Canada. Because oil sands are found at or near the surface, they are excavated by strip mining. The mined material is then heated to extract the crude oil. The treated oil is piped to Edmonton, Canada's oil capital, for refining. It is not known whether present technology can extract the oil from deeper oil sands. Some heavy oil from deposits along the Alberta-Saskatchewan border is now being tapped by means of special drill and pump methods that heat the oil underground to make it flow more easily.

Experts say that the Athabasca oil sands in northern Alberta contain 175 times as much oil as all the world's conventional reserves, but today's technology can recover less than one percent of it (Figure 10.7).

Canada has huge reserves of natural gas, which are found in the same sedimentary basins as crude oil. It is estimated that the reserves in western Canada will last well into the 21st century. These reserve estimates do not include the known natural gas resources in the Arctic and in the Ventura gas field off the east coast of Nova Scotia. Nor do they include the natural gas found at great depths in the deep basin of west central Alberta (Figure 10.7).

Natural gas is piped from western Canada to the west coast and as far east as Québec City (Figure 10.12). Western Canada exports natural gas to the United States, while central and eastern Canada import some natural gas from the United States. The cost of transporting natural gas is greater than the cost of transporting oil,

Natural gas from the Peace River District is processed at this refinery in Fort St. John in northeastern British Columbia before it is piped to market in southern Canada.

whether the gas goes through pipelines or, in the form of *liquified natural gas* (LNG), by ship. As a result, projects to develop offshore natural gas in eastern Canada and bring it ashore are still only proposals.

Canada has very large coal reserves (Table 10.1). Most of these reserves lie in or near the Rocky Mountains of Alberta and British Columbia. This area provides close to half of Canada's coal production, followed by the Maritime Provinces. Like Canada's petroleum resources, coal resources are located far from the industrial heartland (Figure 10.5).

East Coast Oil and Gas

Since the 1960s, about 200 wells have been drilled off Canada's east coast. These test wells suggest that a large amount of natural gas lies deep in sedimentary rock layers under the ocean. The discovery of Canada's largest amount of natural gas was made in the early 1970s, when the Ventura field was found near Sable Island, off the coast of Nova Scotia. Development of this field has been put off because of the large world reserves and low prices of natural gas.

In 1979, the Hibernia oil field was discovered about 300 km east of St. John's, Newfoundland. It has proved to be a large field, and production is scheduled to begin sometime in the 1990s. Developing an oil field at sea is not as easy as developing one on land. In this east coast field, the ocean floor is about 200 m below the surface of the water. Severe storms and giant icebergs often move through the area, creating dangerous working conditions. In the early 1980s, the Ocean Ranger drilling rig capsized in a bad storm, and the whole crew was lost. These hazards have made it necessary to build a concrete production platform on the ocean floor. The platform is hollow, providing space for storing oil until it is moved to market by shuttle tanker ships.

The Canadian and Newfoundland governments both claimed ownership of the Hibernia field. Under Canada's Constitution, offshore resources belong to the federal government, but provincial governments also have claims. Production plans for Hibernia did not proceed until the federal government signed a special agreement with Newfoundland. This agreement permits Newfoundland to collect royalties and other taxes from the oil companies involved. Newfoundland will also benefit in other ways. Thousands of jobs will be created during the construction phase. More jobs will be created indirectly as Newfoundland's economy improves.

As test drilling continues, and the oil and gas industry develops, parts of eastern Canada should become more prosperous.

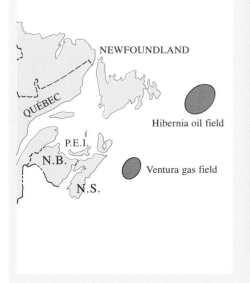

A tugboat tows a semi-submersible rig for offshore oil drilling in Hibernia.

Ontario is one of Canada's largest consumers of coal. About two-thirds of the coal it buys is used for producing electricity and the rest for steel making. Little of this coal comes from Canadian sources. Ontario imports most of it from Virginia, West Virginia, and Pennsylvania. The higher-quality coal from these states can be bought and shipped to Ontario by railway and lake freighter, at a lower cost than coal from the more distant Canadian sources. The amount of coal Ontario imports from the United States is usually about equal to the amount Canada exports to Japan, Korea, Western Europe, and Brazil.

Prairie coal is more expensive than U.S. coal because it contains more water. Its weight must be reduced by drying, before the coal is shipped in covered railway cars to protect it from rain or snow.

1. a) Figure 10.12 shows the Interprovincial oil pipeline from western Canada to southern Ontario that was built in the late 1950s. Why did it cost less to build it through the U.S.A., south of the Great Lakes, than through Canada?

b) The Trans-Canada natural gas pipeline, built in the 1960s, runs east from Calgary, Canada's natural gas capital, passes north of the Great Lakes, and ends in eastern Canada. Why did it cost more to build than the Interprovincial oil pipeline?

(Before you answer these questions, consider the effect of Canada's physiographic regions [Chapter Two] on pipeline construction.)

2. a) In 1973, OPEC decided to cut the amount of oil its members would produce. What effect had this decision on world oil prices?

b) When world oil prices rose rapidly in the 1970s, Canadian oil companies made huge profits, and the Canadian government imposed

A power shovel loads western coal into a 200-t diesel-electric truck.

controls on oil prices. As a result, the Canadian prices for oil stayed well below the world level. Why did this result in reduced oil exploration and development in Canada?

c) By the early 1980s, a world economic recession and energy conservation program reduced the demand for oil. OPEC members could not agree to cut back on oil production. How do you think these events affected world oil prices?

3. a) How do coal, oil, and gas deposits show what the climate of the Canadian Arctic was like in prehistoric times?

b) Why do you think development of petroleum resources in the Canadian Arctic slowed down in the late 1980s?

c) Why did the price of oil rise when Iraq invaded Kuwait in 1990?

4. Debate *one* of the following issues:

a) When Arctic natural gas is developed, it should travel to southern markets by pipelines rather than by LNG tanker ships.

b) Because Canada has larger reserves of natural gas than it has of oil, we should use much more gas.

5. How did each of the following developments affect coal production?

a) the expansion of railway transportation up to the 1950s

b) the conversion of railway engines from steam to diesel in the 1950s

c) the higher prices of oil in the 1970s

6. a) Why does Canada import coal when it has huge undeveloped reserves in western Canada?

b) Why does Canada export large quantities of coal to Japan?

ELECTRICITY

Over thirty percent of the energy consumed in Canada is used to produce electricity. Most electricity is generated as hydro or *hydraulic power* from fast-flowing water (Figure 10.13). Hydro-electricity is a renewable energy resource. It is also one of the least polluting energy sources. But producing hydro-electricity causes severe damage to the environment by flooding land and changing natural water levels behind dams or in water-transfer projects (Chapter Six).

Hydro-electricity is becoming a smaller and smaller proportion of all the electricity produced. The most suitable hydro sites in southern Canada are already in production, and so provincial utility companies must turn to thermal or nuclear power to meet the growing demand for electricity.

Thermal electricity can be generated from any fossil fuel mineral. The generating plant burns fossil fuels to

Coal from the nearby storage piles fuels this thermal electric plant at Nanticoke, Ontario. Coal must be stockpiled to last through the winter, when ice prevents shipping on the Great Lakes-St. Lawrence Seaway.

boil water for steam. Pressurized steam turns the turbines that spin the generators. Most thermal electric stations burn coal because it is less expensive than natural gas or fuel oil. This saves money at the cost of the environment. The burning coal produces large amounts of sulphur, which indirectly causes damage in eastern Canada from acid rain and snow.

Canada has about fifteen percent of the total installed hydro-electric generating capacity in the world.

Nuclear generating stations in Canada now produce as much electricity as do thermal plants (Figure 10.13). Canada has some advantages that might lead us to rely on nuclear energy in the future. Canadian scientists have developed a sophisticated nuclear power technology by which small amounts of uranium can produce large amounts of electricity. The process works in much the same way as does the process of generating thermal electricity. The only real difference is the

fuel used to produce nuclear power: the radioactive mineral uranium. Because small quantities of uranium produce a great deal of power, it costs little to transport the fuel for nuclear power plants in Ontario, New Brunswick, and Québec from Elliot Lake, Ontario and the mines in northern Saskatchewan (Figures. 10.6 and 10.7). However, it costs a great deal to build reactors.

The large amount of nuclear electricity produced in Ontario comes from reactors located beside Lakes Huron and Ontario (Figure 10.1). Nuclear plants like these pose a serious threat to the environment. The melt-down in a nuclear plant at Chernobyl, U.S.S.R., in 1985, shows that accidents can happen. Such accidents discharge radioactive liquids and dust that contaminate soil, water, air, and all living things for hundreds of kilometres around. Canadian officials claim that Canada's CANDU nuclear system is the safest in the world. They say that Canadian nuclear plants have safeguards that would prevent accidents like the one at Chernobyl.

Another issue concerns the deep burial of used uranium fuel in Canadian Shield rock. Scientists are still unsure whether this proposed practice is or is not completely safe.

---

1. a) According to Figure 10.13, in what year was the most hydro-electricity generated in Canada? the most nuclear energy?
b) What is the estimated percentage of each type of electricity that will be produced in Canada in the year 2000?

2. a) Which provinces do you think have the most favourable physiography to lead Canada in hydro-electric production?
b) Which provinces, because they lack good hydro sites, would depend most on thermal or nuclear electricity?
c) Which provinces are likely to use the most bituminous coal to operate their thermal electric plants?

3. You are a member of a small committee preparing a "futures study" for your community. Your committee will prepare a chart on *one* of three types of electricity: hydro, thermal, or nuclear.
a) First, try to find answers for the following questions:
i) Where is the plant that produces electricity for your community?
ii) How far is this plant from your community?
iii) What type of energy source does this plant use?
iv) How long is this source of energy likely to last?
v) Does the plant's production damage the environment? If so, how?
b) When you have found the answers to these questions, enter them on your chart under the following heads:
Electric Power Plant Serving _____ *
- Location
- Distance from _____ *
*Your community.

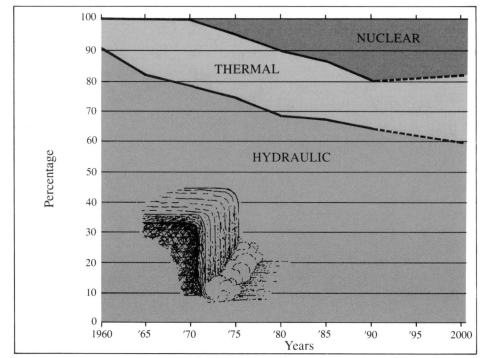

*Figure 10.13 **Generating Electric Power**[1]*
[1]Dash lines represent data estimated by the National Energy Board.

- Energy Source
- "Lifetime" of Source
- Damage to Environment

c) When all the charts are complete, discuss the data you have collected, and then choose by vote the type of electrical energy you will recommend be adopted by your community.

4. To your model begun in Chapter Two, add examples of typical sources of minerals and energy in your area, such as mines and quarries, utilities, and dams.

ALTERNATIVE SOURCES

Canada has energy options for the future besides those that we use today. For example, we could convert more motor vehicles to propane or natural gas and burn peat deposits in thermal electric plants. But these primary forms of energy are non-renewable and do not really offer an alternative. A better option might be to turn to renewable energy such as wind and *solar power*. Today's wind generators can quite efficiently produce small amounts of electricity for individual users. Energy from the sun heats rooms, warms water, and provides a store of electricity in special battery cells.

Other possible sources of energy are plant and animal wastes. They store *biomass* energy provided by living organisms that consume and store solar energy. Canada has vast areas of non-commercial forests that could be logged for energy. Livestock wastes from farms would be another source of energy, but we might do better to leave them as a rich natural fertilizer for our agricultural land. Human wastes and garbage are another possible source of biomass. The organic material provides biomass, which

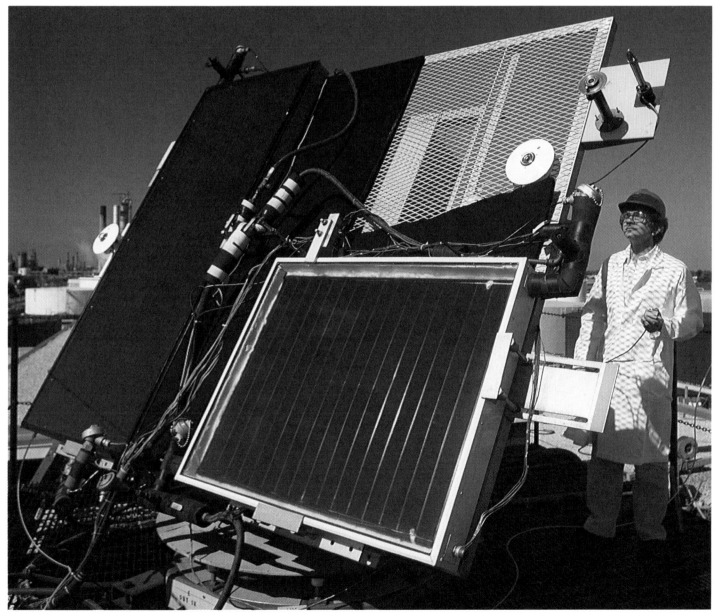

A roof solar panel helps to reduce the cost of heating this building.

could be used to produce a fuel gas called methane. Anything that will burn might be sent to incinerators, which could generate steam heat for industry.

Another energy source is the ocean: the action of the tides, or **tidal power**. Electricity can be generated from the twice-daily change of the tides at favourable sites along the coast. The Bay of Fundy between Nova Scotia and New Brunswick has great possibilities for tidal electricity, because of the extreme rise and fall of the water. A small experimental tidal plant now operates there.

The earth itself is a source of energy: **geothermal** energy radiates from its core. Hot springs and bubbling mud holes often indicate the location of geothermal activity near the surface. Though only a few such sites exist in Canada, scattered throughout the western mountains, heat pumps can be used much more widely. Heat pumps can warm houses in winter and cool them in summer by using the heat and coolness stored in the ground at a depth of about 1.3 m.

All of these alternative energy forms exist in Canada, distributed unevenly across the country. At present they produce only low-output energy. This energy is useful for local areas, but it is difficult to store and deliver long distances to market. Most of them need to be carefully assessed to learn what effect their use would have on the environment. There is also a need for better technology to adapt them to full use as energy resources.

---

1. Write a brief definition of the following energy-related terms: solar, geothermal, tidal, methane, and biomass.
2. How do alternative or secondary energy sources differ from primary ones?
3. You have been transported to the year 2100. You are now a member of a well-known newspaper reporting team.

The world's reserves of crude oil are dwindling rapidly. The price of oil has climbed to $50 a barrel. With other members of your team, list the pros and cons of replacing crude oil as a source of energy with *one* of the following secondary sources: tidal, solar, wind, geothermal or biomass energy. For the secondary energy source on which your team is working consider the following:
- size of reserves
- availability in Canada
- locations of prime users
- ways energy is used
- costs of developing the new technology needed
- effect on the environment of development and use
- difficulty of converting from old energy source
- effect on the environment of transportation

This experimental power plant at Annapolis Royal, N.S., uses the large daily rise and fall of the Bay of Fundy's tides to generate electricity.

WHAT LIES AHEAD?

Minerals, including those used for energy, are non-renewable resources. Someday supplies will run out, and we shall have to find an alternative resource. If that resource is another mineral, then it, too, will one day be depleted. There seem to be limits to the large-scale use of renewable energy sources. Since the mining, processing, transporting, and use of minerals damage the environment, should Canada aim to become a *conserver society* in the future?

A CONSERVER SOCIETY

What does being a conserver society mean? It means reducing consumption, opposing waste and pollution, and recycling used materials. How would the lifestyles of Canadians change if we adopted the standards of a conserver society? Notable differences from present-day Canada would include:

- smaller, more energy-efficient housing units
- fewer single-family houses on lots, and more apartments and town-houses
- more densely populated urban communities
- smaller, more efficient automobiles
- greater use of public transportation
- higher-quality products that would last longer
- elimination of throw-away gadgets

- recycling of empty containers made from metal, glass, and plastic, or of used appliances and machinery
- elimination of unnecessary packaging
- recycling of all household garbage
- using waste as fuel
- more conservation of energy
- greater use of renewable energy

What do you think it would be like to live in a conserver community? What features would make life safer and more pleasant? What features would you find disappointing or difficult?

---

1. As a class, draw up by-laws for a conserver community that has decided to make lifestyle changes noted in the preceding list.
2. a) Demonstrate ways of conserving energy in your home or your school. Prepare a poster with a cut-away model of a house or school building showing areas where energy could be conserved.
   or
   b) Make a cut-away model from cardboard cartons and magazine illustrations, and use it for the same purpose.
3. Select a secondary energy source (e.g., solar heat) and prepare a diorama showing how it works. Could this energy source have a commercial use?

Garbage trucks pick up and sort household waste from boxes like this one, used in a recycling program.

REVIEW QUESTIONS

1. Make a chart that shows three ways that each type of mineral—metallic, non-metallic, and fossil fuel—is used in our society.
2. a) Explain the natural processes that form the three types of minerals in rock.
   b) Name the types of minerals located in each of Canada's major physiographic regions.
3. Develop a flow chart to show the way a mineral's rating changes from deposit to resource and then to reserve.
4. a) Create a bar graph to show the percentage of world production mined in Canada of the following minerals: uranium, nickel, zinc, copper, gold, silver. (See Table 10.2 for data.)
   b) Which Canadian province produces the greatest quantity of fossil fuels? of metallic minerals?
5. List three different types of mining. Describe the damage to the environment that each type causes.
6. a) Why are supplies of Arctic and east coast natural gas not being used at present?
   b) Why does Canada import and export about the same amounts of coal?
7. Draw a line graph to show the trends in Canada's generating of electricity: a) in the past, b) in the present, and c) projected into the future.
8. What alternative (secondary) sources of energy could help secure Canada's energy future?
9. Suggest eight ways in which your lifestyle would change if suddenly no more minerals were available.
10. Do you think that Canada is likely to become a conserver society?

Chapter Eleven

Canada And The World

Believe It Or Not!

Canadians who eat imported frogs' legs help increase the threat of malaria to the population of Bangladesh. (You will find the explanation for this strange but true statement later in this chapter.)

Queen Elizabeth II and heads of the Commonwealth governments posed for this photograph before attending a dinner at the Commonwealth Conference in Vancouver, B.C., 1987.

A GLOBAL VIEW

WHERE IN THE WORLD IS CANADA?

You will see Canada's location in the world most plainly by using a globe. Try viewing Canada's location by looking at a globe from the positions shown in Figure 11.1. You will find that different aspects of Canada's world location come into focus as you view the globe from different positions.

CANADA IS A NORTH AMERICAN COUNTRY

Canada occupies the northern half of North America.

1. Name Canada's North American neighbours.
2. In which of these countries is English the language chiefly used?
3. How many of Canada's Metropolitan Areas (Table 5.1) are located within one hundred kilometres of the U. S. border?

CANADA IS AN ATLANTIC COUNTRY

Canada's eastern seaboard looks out on the North Atlantic Ocean.

1. Name Canada's neighbours that border the North Atlantic Ocean. (Include countries with access to the Atlantic via the Baltic and Mediterranean seas.)
2. The St. Lawrence River is on a *great circle route* between Western Europe and the heartland of Canada.
   a) Compare the distance between Montréal, Québec, and Liverpool, England, with that between New York and Liverpool.
   b) Compare the distance between Montréal and Liverpool with that between St. John's, Newfoundland, and Vancouver.

c) Make a general statement about distances across the North Atlantic compared with distances across North America.
3. From former times to the present, with which two European countries has Canada had the closest ties?

CANADA IS A PACIFIC COUNTRY

Canada's western seaboard looks out on the Pacific Ocean. The countries that border the Pacific Ocean are often called Pacific Rim countries. Pacific Rim countries on the western side of the Pacific include: Japan, South Korea, Thailand, Singapore, Malaysia, the Philippines, Indonesia, Hong Kong, Taiwan, the Peoples' Republic of China, Australia, and New Zealand. (The Soviet Union is not considered a Pacific Rim country because most of its population is in Europe and its economic focus is European.)

1. Using a globe, locate the 12 Pacific Rim countries.
2. In a recent atlas (or a World Almanac), find the size of the population in each of these 12 Pacific Rim countries.

CANADA IS AN ARCTIC COUNTRY

Large areas of Canada's land and water lie north of the Arctic Circle.

1. Measure the distance between Ellesmere Island, Canada, and Severnaya Zemlya, U.S.S.R. Compare this distance with the distance between Montréal and Winnipeg.
2. Explain why many flights to Europe from western Canada and the United States follow routes over the Canadian Arctic.
3. Explain why the United States and Canada have located radar stations across northern Canada to detect approaching aircraft or missiles.

THE GLOBAL VILLAGE

A famous Canadian scholar, Marshall McLuhan, once said that the world was a "global village".

To understand what McLuhan meant, we need to know what it is like to live in a village. A village is a small, tightly knit community. Everyone knows everyone else. Everyone knows what everyone else is doing. Everyone is affected by what happens to one person. Everyone helps those in need.

Technology in communications and transportation has made the world smaller so that citizens of the earth are like dwellers in a village. When something happens on the other side of the world, we see the action that night on television and read about it in the next day's newspaper. When there is a famine in Ethiopia or an earthquake in Chile, the whole world hears about it and can respond to the calamity with help. A war in the Middle East that threatens oil supplies raises the price of oil in Canada, and this rise, in turn, affects the budget of every Canadian family. Even in the natural environment, what happens in one part of the world can have an impact around the globe. For example, the cutting of vast areas of tropical forest can affect world climate. A nuclear accident in the Soviet Union (or in any other country) can contaminate food supplies around the world.

Canada's Global Connections

Canada has various types of connections with other nations. One such connection was related to an outcry from several countries against the Canadian seal hunt off the east coast of Canada. Canadians killed young harp seals for their furs. Pictures of this activity were shown on television in Britain and several other European countries. A public campaign was mounted to stop the sealing operation, which some people considered cruel. Europeans stopped buying Canadian furs. The results in Canada were

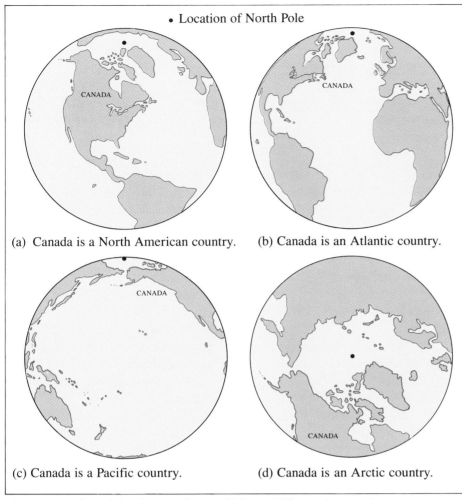

• Location of North Pole

(a) Canada is a North American country.

(b) Canada is an Atlantic country.

(c) Canada is a Pacific country.

(d) Canada is an Arctic country.

Figure 11.1 **Canada's Place in the World from Different Perspectives**

serious. The Canadian east coast sealing industry disappeared, and many Canadian sealers had to apply for unemployment insurance and welfare. A sudden drop in the price of furs caused Native people in the Arctic serious loss of income. Many Natives had to rely on welfare payments to survive.

In another instance, there was a serious drought in the Sahel (sub-Sahara) region of Africa. (See the sketch of the Sahel on page 264.) Dramatic pictures of starving children were shown on Canadian television. The Canadian government quickly responded with aid. It established a "Fund for Africa" and promised that it would match donations from individual Canadians; it set aside $15 million for the purpose. Canadians responded generously. The government increased its allocation to $30 million to match private donations. Non-government organizations (e.g., CARE, OXFAM-Canada, Canadian Hunger Foundation) formed a **coalition** called "Africa Emergency Aid", to help meet this crisis. On average, two out of every three Canadian families made donations to help the suffering people in the Sahel.

Many European women stopped buying fur coats because of the opposition to the seal hunt.

This parched and cracked land shows how serious drought in the Sahel can be.

We Live in the Global Village, Here and Now

Our country has a high international reputation. Canada has taken initiatives for better international understanding—notably since World War II. But even before that. We have a cosmopolitan population, drawn from all the major racial strains on the face of the planet. Yet individual Canadians still tend, too often, to look inward, to their own narrow community or group or region. We cannot afford to do that any more. We live in the global village. It's here. It's now. It's time we got to know our neighbours in it and established fruitful exchange with them.

—Camile A. Dagenais,
as quoted by Export Canada

1. Review earlier chapters of this book to find examples of ways in which events in other parts of the world have affected Canada as follows:
a) From the early history of Canada's economic development, cite an example of the effect on Canada of changing foreign demand for a natural resource (Chapter Three).
b) Summarize briefly how the following wars affected Canada's political evolution (Chapter Four):
i) the British-French wars of the 1700s
ii) the British-American war (American Revolution)
iii) the two World Wars
c) Political revolutions often create refugees. How can such a revolution in another country affect Canadian cities?
d) Explain why Canada must obtain the co-operation of the United States in order to solve the problems of acid rain and pollution of the Great Lakes (Chapter Six).
e) Canada is trying to conserve ocean fish resources (Chapter Seven). How might Canada's efforts affect relations with other countries?
f) How can actions of the U.S. government affect the income of Canadians working in the forest industry (Chapter Eight)?
g) Describe how *subsidies* to farmers in Europe have increased income taxes in Canada (Chapter Nine).
h) Explain how wars and threats of wars in the Middle East result in higher prices for gasoline at Canadian service stations (Chapter Ten).

2. Read the Dagenais quotation in the Focus "We Live in the Global Village, Here and Now". From past issues of Canadian news magazines or other periodicals, or from the clipping files of your local library, give examples of the following:
a) Canadians treating people in a faraway land as though they were neighbours
b) Canadians "looking inward"

A Canadian ambassador in Ethiopia

CANADA AND THE POLITICAL WORLD

Canada has connections with many countries all over the world. Many of these connections are non-political: that is, they do not directly involve governments. However, there are also many official political connections between the Government of Canada and the governments of other countries. The Canadian government has a Department of External Affairs to help carry out all the official business that arises between Canada and other countries. Canada also has officials called **ambassadors**, who work in offices called **embassies** in many capital cities around the world. Foreign countries, in turn, establish embassies in Canada. Official communications between Canada and other countries are exchanged through these embassies.

Canada belongs to many international organizations. Some of these are informal groups based on common interests such as the Commonwealth and Francophonie. Others are formal world-wide organizations such as the United Nations and its agencies. Still others are groups of countries which have signed common defence treaties. In this chapter we discuss only a few of the many international organizations to which Canada belongs.

THE COMMONWEALTH

Since the 1930s, Canada has been a member of the Commonwealth, which at that time was beginning to grow out of the British Empire. The Commonwealth is made up of 49 countries, all of which used to be British colonies (Figure 11.2). Over the years, as the colonies became independent nations, most of them joined the Commonwealth. The monarch of the United Kingdom is also the monarch of some of these countries, such as Canada, Australia, and New Zealand. In these countries, the monarch is represented by a governor-general. Other countries do not recognize the British monarch as the head of their state, but they do recognize the monarchy as a symbol of the Commonwealth.

The Commonwealth is a kind of international association of former British colonies. It gives people from all around the world, of different races, languages, and political viewpoints, chances to get together, exchange views, and co-operate in solving international problems. The Commonwealth Fund for Technical Co-operation is the chief foreign aid organization of the Commonwealth. Canada provides more than forty percent of the Fund's budget. Besides giving economic assistance to developing countries, the Fund provides money for cultural exchange among Commonwealth countries. It also provides Commonwealth scholarship programs that help university students in one Commonwealth country to study in another. The Commonwealth Games allow athletes from Commonwealth countries around the world to compete with one another in athletic events and team games.

The multi-racial composition of the Commonwealth has often led to bitter differences of opinion within the organization. Pressure from Canada led to the withdrawal of South Africa from the Commonwealth in 1961, because of that country's **apartheid** policy of separating different racial groups.

In 1986, Prime Minister Mulroney of Canada led the Commonwealth in imposing **economic sanctions** against South Africa because of that country's apartheid policy. Some Commonwealth countries, including Britain,

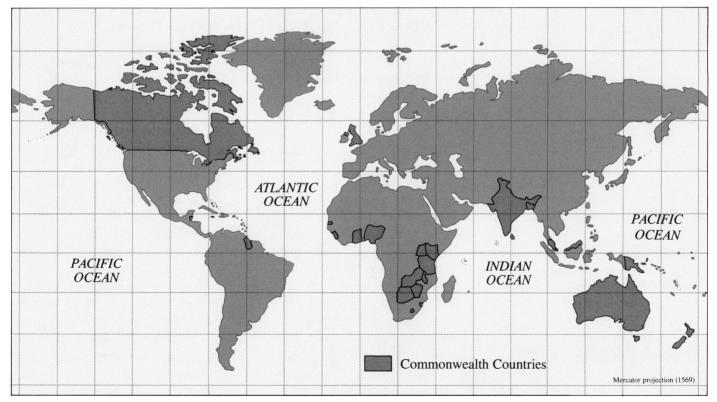

Figure 11.2 *The Commonwealth This map is an example of the traditional Mercator projection.*

The heads of Commonwealth governments attending a Commonwealth Conference in Vancouver, B.C., in 1987

did not agree with this action. They argued that economic sanctions would hurt rather than help South African blacks. The history of the Commonwealth had shown that it is not necessary for all members always to agree with one another in order for an international organization to survive and be useful.

Members of the Commonwealth make up 40 percent of the population of the developing world.

FRANCOPHONIE

Francophonie is the name given to an international organization of French-speaking countries (Figure 11.3). This organization has a much shorter history than the Commonwealth. It was formed in 1970. Its purpose is to promote international communication and co-operation among French-speaking nations. It emphasizes culture, education, and technology.

Francophonie has over 30 members. Most of its members are former colonies of France that became independent nations after the Second

World War (1939–1945).

Canada has been active in Francophonie since its beginning. Two provinces, Québec and New Brunswick, also have the status of participating governments. In 1982, Canada's Prime Minister Trudeau summed up the reason why Canada participates in Francophonie: "We cannot remain indifferent to anything that contributes to unity or that builds bridges between peoples." A large portion of Canada's annual foreign aid goes to Francophonie countries.

---

1. a) Locate the following Commonwealth and Francophonie countries in an atlas. List the countries by continent.

   Commonwealth: Antigua and Barbuda, Australia, Bahamas, Bangladesh, Barbados, Belize, Botswana, Canada, Cyprus, Dominica, Fiji, The Gambia, Ghana, Grenada, Guyana, India, Jamaica, Kenya, Kiribati, Lesotho, Malawi, Malaysia, Maldives, Malta, Mauritius, Nauru, New Zealand, Nigeria,

Papua New Guinea, St. Kitts and Nevis (St. Christopher), St. Lucia, St. Vincent, Seychelles, Sierra Leone, Singapore, Solomon Islands, Sri Lanka, Swaziland, Tanzania, Tonga, Trinidad and Tobago, Tuvalu, Uganda, United Kingdom, Vanuatu, Western Samoa, Zambia, Zimbabwe.

   Francophonie: Belgium, Benin, Burkina Faso [Upper Volta], Burundi, Canada, Central African Republic, Comoros, Congo, Djibouti, Dominica, France, Gabon, Guinea, Guinea-Bissau, Haiti, Ivory Coast, Laos, Lebanon, Luxembourg, Mali, Mauritania, Morocco, Niger, Rwanda, St. Lucia, and Senegal.

   b) Which continent has the most Commonwealth countries? Which has the most Francophonie countries? Why do you think this is so?

2. There are about 160 independent countries in the world. Approximately what percentage of the world's countries belong to either the Commonwealth or Francophonie?

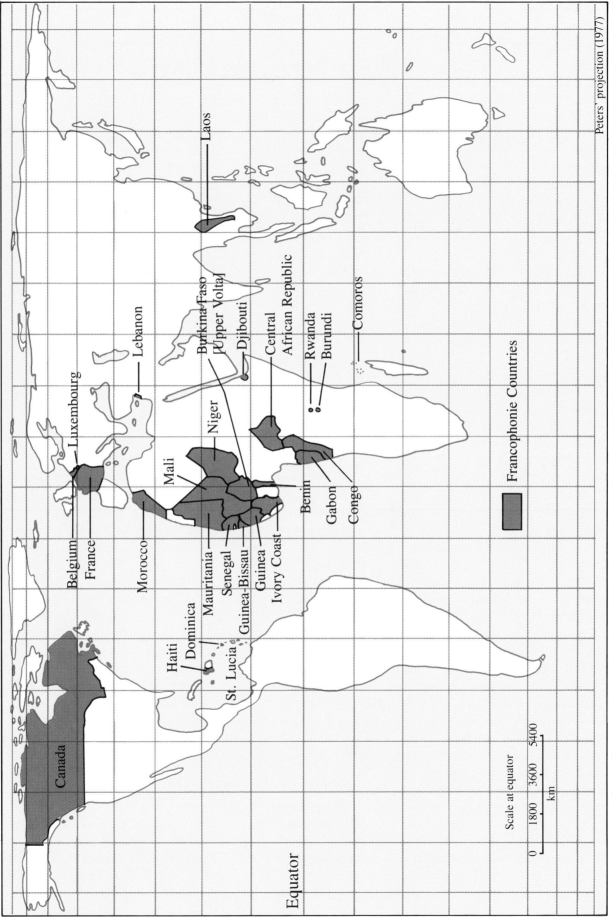

Figure 11.3 **Francophonie Countries** *This map is an example of the Peter's projection.*

Map Projections

The Earth is almost a perfect sphere. The way a sphere or globe is drawn on a flat surface is called a projection. **Map projections** are bound to be distorted in one way or another: for example, think of spreading and stretching out flat the peel of an orange on which you had drawn a map of the world.

Different projections are designed for different purposes; they distort sizes, shapes, relative locations, directions, and distances in different ways. Mercator's projection is probably the best known. It was developed in the 1500s to help sailors navigate at sea, but today Mercator maps are often used as a reference base on which to put any kind of geographical information, even when some other projection would serve the purpose better.

Mercator's projection has a special property: it maintains the true direction of any one point in relation to another; for example, a line drawn diagonally on the map at an angle of 45° to the equator always points northeast or northwest. Mercator's projection also reproduces shapes fairly faithfully. But the price paid is that distances and areas are both magnified towards the poles so that Greenland, for example, looks much bigger than it really is in relation to, say, Africa or China. The distortion increases towards the poles. As a result of this distortion, a Mercator map gives a false impression of the shortest distance between points on the earth's surface.

Some people have suggested that Mercator's projection promotes a Europe-centred view of the world because Europe is in the centre of

the top half of the map and is disproportionately large. Other European influences have had a similar effect on traditional maps. Placing the North Pole at the top (rather than the bottom or either side) dates back to the Ancient Greeks. Measuring longitude from the Greenwich meridian so that London is usually in the middle of a map comes from the period when Britain "ruled the waves".

A much newer projection called Peters' projection was designed to "correct the Europe-centred image of the world as projected by Mercator".[1] It is an "equal-area" projection: that is, regions on the globe which are equal in land (or sea) area are represented by equal areas on the map. Peters' projection also preserves the North-South and East-West directions. But other directions and, more important, distances and shapes, are quite badly distorted. For example, near the equator, the land appears to be elongated in a North-South direction, and near the poles it is stretched in an East-West direction.

Peters' projection still shows the North Pole at the top and the Greenwich meridian down the middle! But perhaps the very fact that Peters' projection "looks funny" draws attention to the **developing countries** presented in "their actual central position".[1]

—*Third World Atlas*, (Adapted)

---

1. a) Using a soft marking pencil or felt pen, draw lines on a large orange or a grapefruit to represent the lines of latitude and longitude on a globe.

b) Peel the orange, removing as much skin as possible in one piece. (You will find it easier to do this if you first roll the fruit on a hard surface, while keeping some pressure on it with your hand.) Describe the problems of trying to stretch the orange or grapefruit peel onto a flat surface.

c) What happened to the lines of latitude and longitude when you flattened the peel?

d) What does this experience tell you about the problems of turning the globe into a flat map?

2. The best symbol of the earth is a globe. Compare the Mercator projection (Figure 11.2) and the Peters' projection (Figure 11.3) with a globe.

a) Which projection shows shapes closest to those on the globe?

b) Which projection shows most accurately the relative size of different countries? (A quick check: Canada appears about the same size as Brazil on a globe. Compare the sizes of the two countries on the two projections.)

3. a) Originally, what was the chief purpose of the Mercator projection?

b) Why was it useful for this purpose?

c) Why might the Mercator projection seem to promote a Europe-centred view of the world?

4. Peters' projection was designed to correct the Europe-centred view of the world shown in the Mercator projection.

a) In what ways has Peters succeeded in doing this?

b) In what ways is the Peters' projection still Europe-centred?

[1]From a poster published by Christian Aid, London, England

THE UNITED NATIONS

Canada has been a member and a strong supporter of the United Nations (UN) since it was founded in 1945. The United Nations has 159 member countries. It includes large countries such as the United States of America, the Union of Soviet Socialist Republics, the Peoples' Republic of China, and Japan; none of these are members of the Commonwealth or Francophonie. The United Nations is the most universal of all international organizations.

The United Nations was organized after the Second World War, mainly as a peace-keeping body. Its members have settled some disagreements through discussion and compromise. In other disputes the UN has had to send in armed peace-keeping forces to prevent war. Canada has contributed armed forces and equipment to several UN peace-keeping projects in such faraway places as Israel, Egypt, Korea, Laos, Kampuchea (Cambodia), Vietnam, Congo, Cyprus, and the Iraq-Iran border (Figure 11.4).

In recent years, the United Nations has worked to reduce social and economic problems such as poverty, hunger, disease, illiteracy, and threats to the environment. Canada has contributed generously to a large number of the agencies that the UN has established to tackle these problems.

The UN agency that Canadians perhaps know best is the United Nations International Children's Emergency Fund (UNICEF), which has been operating since 1946. The unwieldy name was later changed to the United Nations International Children's

In front of the UN building fly flags of the many nations represented in the organization. Canada is a founding member of the UN.

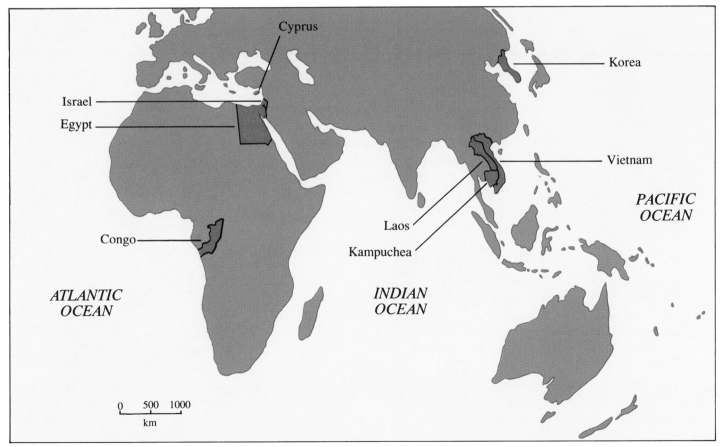

Figure 11.4 *Canada has provided armed forces to UN peace-keeping missions in a number of different countries.*

Fund, but the organization is still known as UNICEF by millions of people around the world. This agency helps governments of developing countries to set up centres to care for needy children and mothers. It provides funds to buy food, medicine, and books for children in more than 100 countries. UNICEF helps needy children around the world, and in turn is supported by well-off children around the world. Many Canadian schools have programs to raise funds for UNICEF. The best known of these is the Halloween collection.

It takes a large amount of money to finance the United Nations' many agencies and programs. The UN headquarters in New York alone has 11 000 people on the payroll. Canada is one of the few countries that pays its full dues and does so on time. Some countries, such as the United States and the Soviet Union, withhold money from the UN because they do not approve of certain UN projects or programs. Other countries, such as Brazil and Argentina, fall behind in their contributions because they are near bankruptcy themselves. Because many countries are not paying their full dues, the UN is facing a financial crisis. A recent special report on UN financing, written by Maurice Strong of Canada and Prince Aga Khan of Pakistan, argues that with greater efficiency and less waste, the UN could carry out its present programs with a budget cut of 20 to 25 percent.

Although most Canadian help to needy countries is given through international organizations, Canada also has an independent foreign-aid program. This program is run through a government agency called the Canadian International Development Agency (CIDA). CIDA's programs help developing countries by providing technology and equipment to build roads and dams, and to increase agricultural production. CIDA also helps young people from developing countries to attend Canadian universities and colleges.

CUSO is an acronym for Canadian University Students Overseas. This organization, supported by government and private funding, recruits Canadians with university training to go to developing countries to teach people the skills that they need to raise their standard of living.

Consult an encyclopedia or other reference book for the full names and the general responsibilities of the following United Nation's agencies: FAO, IMF, UNESCO, UNRRA, WHO.

F O C U S

Canada and the Suez Crisis

The Suez Canal provides an important shipping route between Western Europe and the Middle and Far East. In 1956, Egypt seized the Suez Canal, which the British-French Suez Canal Company had operated since 1869. Israel invaded Egypt, and Britain and France bombed the Suez Canal area.

The Canadian government opposed the use of force in solving problems such as the ownership and control of the Suez Canal. Canada's Secretary of State for External Affairs, Lester B. Pearson, proposed that the United Nations establish an international force to stop hostilities in the Suez area. A Canadian, General E.M.L. Burns, was named commander of a UN Emergency Force that was sent to Egypt to supervise a cease-fire until an agreement about Suez Canal ownership could be negotiated.

Pearson was awarded the 1957 Nobel Peace Prize for his peace-making efforts through the United Nations.

Lester Pearson won the 1957 Nobel Peace Prize for his peace-making efforts through the United Nations.

Canadians Give Foreign Aid

Besides giving foreign aid through UN agencies and CIDA, Canadians provide assistance to foreign countries through a large number of non-governmental organizations (NGOs). Following is a selection of only a few foreign-aid projects undertaken by Canadian NGOs in Africa:

CARE Canada teaches people in Sudan how to care for seedlings.

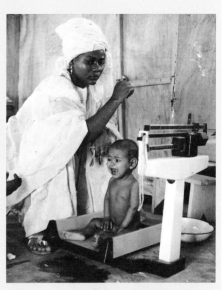

World Vision Canada provides health education and immunization against disease in Mauritania.

Aid Destination	Donor Organization	Nature of Aid
Ethiopia	World University Service	Supporting the Ethiopian Airlift; supplying food and medicine; establishing health clinics
Ethiopia and Sudan	Christian Children's Fund of Canada	Supplying emergency food, medicine, transport
Ghana	World Vision Canada	Participating in nutrition and health programs for 70 villages
Kenya	Canadian Hunger Foundation	Digging wells & installing pumps
Lesotho	PLENTY Canada	Conducting an educational program in nutrition & agriculture
Mali	World Relief Canada	Purchasing trucks to transport food gifts
Mauritania	World Vision Canada	Providing health education & immunization
Mozambique	OXFAM-Canada	Providing tools & materials for building houses; supplying ploughs & tools for farming
Niger	Society of International Missionaries (Canada)	Supplying funds & materials for drilling wells & reforesting denuded areas
Senegal	Canadian Hunger Foundation	Drilling wells; providing pumps; purchasing seeds & tools for crop planting
Somalia	African Medical and Research Foundation	Educating families about nutrition & health
Sudan	CARE Canada	Conducting reforestation & agricultural improvement programs

1. Locate five African countries that receive aid from Canada, and label them on an outline map of Africa.
2. Which of these receiving countries are members of the Commonwealth? members of Francophonie? (Figures 11.2 and 11.3).
3. "If you give a man a fish, you feed him for a day; if you provide him with fishing equipment, you feed him for life." Which of the aid projects described above gave people a "fish"? Which gave them "fishing equipment"?

Canadian foreign aid helps train Bangladesh women to work in textile factories. At the same time, Canada has a quota on the amount of Bangladesh clothing that can be imported into Canada.

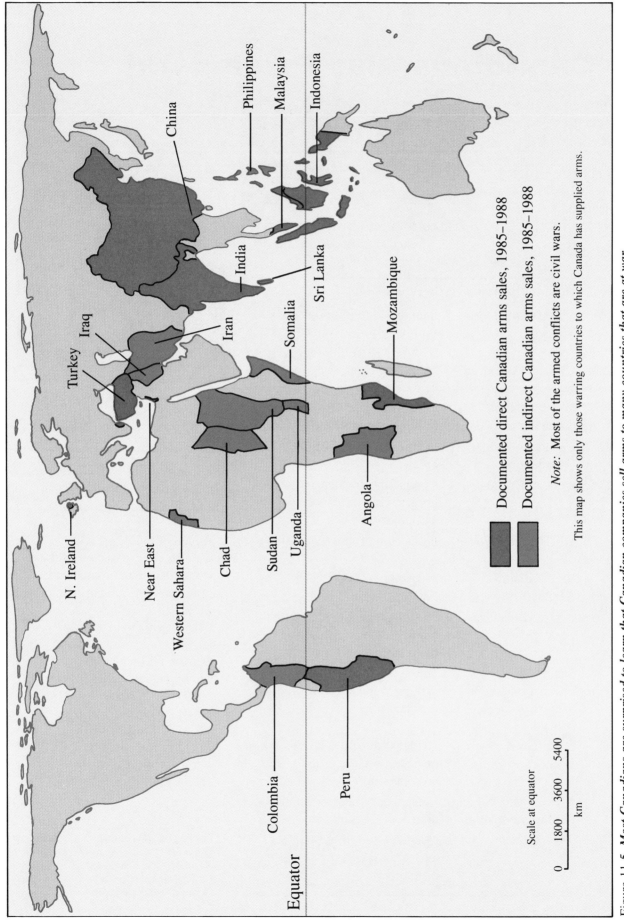

Figure 11.5 *Most Canadians are surprised to learn that Canadian companies sell arms to many countries that are at war.*

Canada and Armed Conflicts

Most of the world knows about Canada's leadership in peace-keeping and its aid to developing countries. It is not so well known that Canadian companies supply military goods to many countries that are at war (Figure 11.5). Canadian military goods have gone directly to about half of these countries at war. While Canada has not shipped military goods directly to the other half, Canadian components have been sold to the military industries of other supplier countries.

Some Canadians believe that our government should not permit Canadian companies to sell military goods directly or indirectly to countries at war. Do you think that all Canadians would agree with such a policy? Why or why not? What do you think Canada should do about supplying countries with arms?

together in a military alliance called the North Atlantic Treaty Organization (NATO) (Figure 11.6).

Under NATO, both Canada and the United States have stationed armed forces in Western Europe. Canadian and U.S. armed forces were sent to Europe in 1950, when many people feared that the Soviet Union might attack at a time when the war-shattered European countries could not defend themselves. Today the Soviet Union is no longer seen as an enemy, and relations between Eastern and Western Europe have improved. The end of the Cold War means that NATO must reassess its role. As well, Canadians will likely apply more pressure on their government to bring the Canadian forces home from Europe.

NORTH ATLANTIC TREATY ORGANIZATION (NATO)

After the Second World War (1939–1945), the Soviet Union created a buffer of Communist-controlled nations in Eastern Europe to ensure that Western European countries would not attack it again. The countries of Western Europe were afraid that the Soviet Union might try to extend its influence all the way to the Atlantic. In response to this fear, Canada, the United States, the United Kingdom, and a group of Western European countries joined

1. What do you think has been the chief contribution of NATO?
2. What effect do you think the end of the ''Cold War'' will have on NATO?

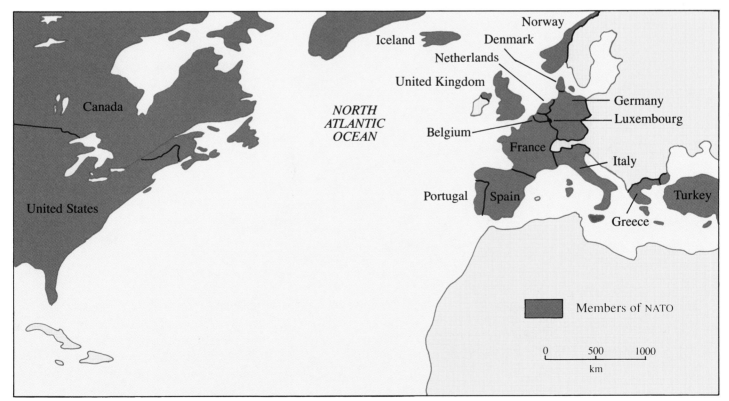

Figure 11.6 *Canada is a member of NATO.*

NORTH AMERICAN AEROSPACE DEFENCE COMMAND (NORAD)

After the Second World War, the Canadian and American governments believed that they must protect their countries from a possible air attack, via the Arctic, by the Soviet Union. In the 1950s, the first two countries signed the North American Air Defence (NORAD) Agreement (later renamed the North American Aerospace Defence Command) and built a line of radar stations across northern Canada called the Distant Early Warning (DEW) line. Because of new technology in long-range bombers and intercontinental ballistic missiles (ICBMs), some of the DEW line sites have been updated. Canada and the United States are co-operating in building a new North Warning System (NWS) composed of both long-range and short-range radar stations across Canada's Arctic (Figure 11.7). These stations can detect aircraft, missiles, or satellites approaching Canada from the north. Data from the radar stations are routed through a control centre at North Bay by way of a series of satellites. The overall NORAD control centre is located at Colorado Springs, Colorado.

Three new sites at Yellowknife, Iqaluit (Frobisher Bay), and Kuujjuaq (Fort Chimo) have been chosen as air bases from which Canadian and American fighter planes could intercept hostile bombers or missiles. The area north of the NWS will be patrolled by U.S. aircraft based in Alaska and Greenland. Some critics claim that the new radar line should be built along the outer northern edge of the Arctic archipelago. A more northerly warning line would provide an earlier alert. Other critics believe that the U.S.S.R. is no longer a military threat to North America, and that the North Early Warning System should be abandoned.

The NORAD centre at North Bay is under about two hundred metres of Canadian Shield granite rock.

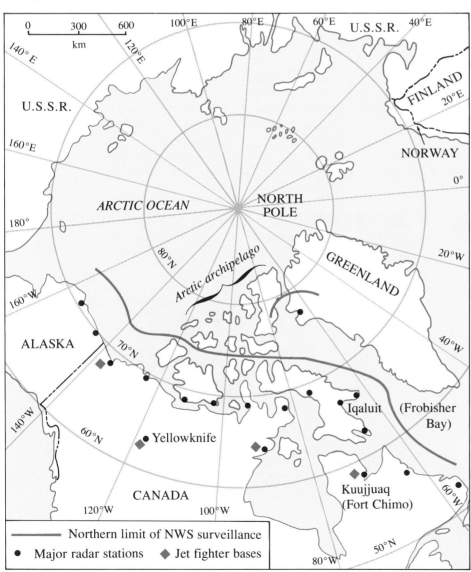

Figure 11.7 **North Warning System** *Canada and the United States built the North Warning System to detect aircraft, missiles, or satellites approaching Canada from the north.*

Following are two contradictory statements relating to Canada's defence policy. Your class represents two "political parties", one supporting the first statement, and the other supporting the second statement.

Stage a parliamentary debate in which the two parties present their own viewpoints:

Party "A"—Canada is so large and underpopulated that it cannot afford to protect itself with an adequate army, navy, and air force. Because of this weakness and because of its global location, Canada should support NATO and NORAD more strongly.

Party "B"—Since Canada is internationally respected for its peace-keeping role and its foreign aid, it should reduce its armed forces, get out of NATO and NORAD, and increase its spending on foreign aid.

CANADA AND THE TRADE WORLD

CANADA IS A TRADING NATION

Canada has always been a great trading nation. In the early days, the growth of Canada's economy depended on the export of large amounts of natural resources: fish, furs, minerals, and forest and farm products (Chapter Three).

At first, Canadians exported their natural resources as raw materials without any processing. Then came a period when some of the raw materials were *processed* before they were exported. Logs from the forests were *fabricated* into timber for ships; iron ore was *smelted* into iron and steel products; steel was *manufactured* into farm implements; wheat was *milled* into flour. Over the years, Canada has exported a smaller percentage of raw materials and a higher percentage of processed, fabricated, and manufactured goods. By the 1980s, almost eighty percent of Canada's exports were processed, fabricated, or manufactured products (Table 11.1).

In recent years Canada has exported more automobiles and automobile parts than any other product. It has increased its exports of other goods, too, including high-technology products. Canadian-made portable electric transformers and electric train engines are marketed world wide. Canadian telephone systems have been installed in many different countries. CANDU nuclear reactors, developed in Canada, have been built in South America and India.

Canada also imports many types of goods. Manufactured goods have always made up the largest proportion of Canadian imports (Table 11.1).

Canadians buy imported products for a number of reasons. We import some products (e.g., citrus fruits and spices) because we cannot produce them. We import other products because some Canadians are rich enough to buy them (e.g., French perfume, Mercedes Benz cars from Germany). We import still other products because the selling country has specialized in that product and can make it at a lower cost or produce a better quality than we can (e.g., South Korean clothing, Italian shoes).

A Canadian subway car for export

French perfume is imported into Canada.

Table 11.1 *Canadian Imports and Exports by Commodity Groups (Types of Goods)*

Commodity Groups	Imports (%)	Exports (%)
Processed food, feed, beverages, tobacco	4.5	4.5
Raw materials	9.8	21.0
Fabricated materials	18.2	32.0
Manufactured products	65.9	41.8
Others	1.6	0.7
Total	100.0	100.0

Source: Data from Statistics Canada, three-year average dollar values, 1983–1985
Note: Processed food is ready to be eaten by humans. Feed is products that domestic animals eat. Raw materials (e.g., iron ore) have not been processed or refined in any way. Fabricated materials (e.g., a slab of steel) have had some processing. A manufactured product (e.g., a jack-knife) is ready to use.

1. Draw two circle graphs, one showing Canada's imports by commodity groups, and one showing Canada's exports by commodity groups.
2. Make a chart to show 10 raw materials and 10 fabricated materials that Canada exports. Use the following headings: Fish; Forest Products; Farm Products; Mineral Products. (You will find examples in Chapters Seven to Ten.)
3. List six imported products that your family has bought in recent years. In which commodity group of Table 11.1 do they fall?

TRADE BARRIERS

Have you or other members of your family recently bought any of the following products: jogging shoes, bicycle, skis, shirt, radio, television set, automobile? If so, you were directly affected by Canada's international trade policy. You paid more for the article because Canada has set up barriers to discourage the import of these goods in order to protect the Canadian manufacturing industry.

If a Canadian industry cannot produce a certain product at as low a cost as another country, Canada usually places a *tariff* on the import of that product. The tariff raises the price of the foreign product so that Canadian producers can compete. Buyers pay a higher price for the product than they would if there were no tariff. For example, a pair of cross country skis might sell for $100 in Austria. A Canadian tariff of $30, plus transportation costs, raises the price in Canada to $150. At this price, Canadian ski manufacturers can compete with the Austrian manufacturer, and so more Canadians may buy Canadian-made skis. This tariff helps Canadian ski makers but costs Canadian buyers money. It also reduces the Austrian ski maker's export sales.

Most countries of the world use tariff barriers to protect their own industries. Tariff barriers discourage countries from specializing in producing goods that they can manufacture most cheaply. To avoid the disadvantage of facing trade barriers on one type of goods, a country must produce smaller amounts of many types of goods. This means that trade barriers prevent countries from benefiting from a trade advantage they might have over other countries if they specialized in producing only the types of goods they could manufacture at a lower cost than other nations.

There are also non-tariff barriers that discourage trade just as much as tariffs. These include:

- **Customs clearance procedures** that slow the movement of imports. For example, Canada used to have *customs clearance procedures* that held up for months the clearing of Japanese automobiles through the port of Vancouver. As a result, some Canadians got tired of waiting for Japanese cars and bought Canadian or American cars instead.
- **Subsidies** paid to producers. For example, the Québec government pays high subsidies to farmers who produce maple syrup. As a result, Québec producers can sell maple syrup at lower prices in the United States than can American producers.
- **Government procurement policies**. Some governments have "buy at home" policies. For example, an

Canada Customs officials check to see that Canadians returning from other countries do not import taxable goods without paying a tariff.

American State that needs road-building equipment, might have a rule that permits it to buy the equipment only from an American company. This rule would prevent Canadian companies from competing to sell the equipment it manufactures to that State. Canadian provinces also have *government procurement policies* to prevent American companies, and sometimes other Canadian provinces, from competing in Canada.

- **Embargoes and quotas**. Sometimes countries set an *embargo* on a certain product. This means that there can be absolutely no import of that product. A *quota* does not go that far. It only limits the quantity of a certain product that can be imported. Canada, for instance, has had a quota for many years on the number of shoes that can be imported into Canada.
- **Devaluing currency**. Sometimes a country purposely *devalues* its money. If Canada were to do that, the Canadian dollar would buy less in other countries. At the same time, other countries could buy more cheaply from Canada. The net result would be to reduce Canadian imports and increase Canadian exports.

Tariff barriers and non-tariff barriers reduce world trade. Most countries agree that trade is a good thing, yet almost every country has set up some trade barriers to protect its own industries.

To get rid of trade barriers, a large number of countries must agree to cooperate. The General Agreement on Tariffs and Trade (GATT) has made a strong effort in this direction. About ninety countries have signed GATT. Since GATT's beginning, in 1947, many tariff barriers have been reduced. However, GATT has been less successful in reducing non-tariff barriers.

Because international trade is very important to the Canadian economy,

Canada has always been a strong supporter of GATT. The success of GATT in lowering tariffs around the world has benefited Canada. But sometimes GATT makes rulings that Canada does not like. In 1988, for example, GATT ruled that Ontario must stop levying an extra handling charge on imported wines because this charge had the same effect as a tariff. In the same year, GATT decided that British Columbia was breaking international rules by requiring all fish caught off its coast to be landed and processed in the province. Canadian industries suffered from both of these GATT rulings.

CANADIAN WORLD TRADING PATTERNS

Because Canada was explored and colonized by Europeans, almost all its early trade was with European countries across the Atlantic. After the British Conquest (Chapter Four), most of Canada's trade was with the United Kingdom. Canada exported raw materials to Britain and imported manufactured goods and supplies in return. British Empire (later Commonwealth) trade preferences encouraged trade between the colonies and the mother country.

Gradually, during the 1900s, Commonwealth trade preferences became fewer. After the United Kingdom joined the European Economic Community (EEC), Canada lost many of its traditional British markets and had to look elsewhere for export markets (Figure 11.8).

For a number of reasons Canada's trade with the United States has grown very rapidly in the latter part of the 20th century. By the 1980s, from 70 to 75 percent of Canada's exports and imports were made with the United States (Figure 11.9, page 346).

In recent years, Canada has been trading more and more with countries of the Pacific Rim. Japan, in particular, is now Canada's second-largest trading partner. Japan produces many high-quality manufactured products such as automobiles, radios, television sets, and other electronic appliances that are in high demand in Canada. Most of Canada's exports to Japan are raw materials from mines, forests, and farms (Figure 11.10, page 346). Most of Canada's exports to Japan are shipped before processing and so do not create as many jobs in Canada as they would if they were processed here.

By the 1970s, Japan was selling so many automobiles to Canadians that the Canadian automobile industry was beginning to suffer. Sales of Japanese cars were high in Canada in spite of a tariff barrier and, from time to time, certain non-tariff barriers. In recent years Canada has negotiated a quota of automobile imports from Japan. In order to overcome Canada's import barriers, Japanese auto companies have built factories in Canada: Toyota at Cambridge, Honda at Alliston, and Suzuki with General Motors, at

Figure 11.8 *Members of the EEC*

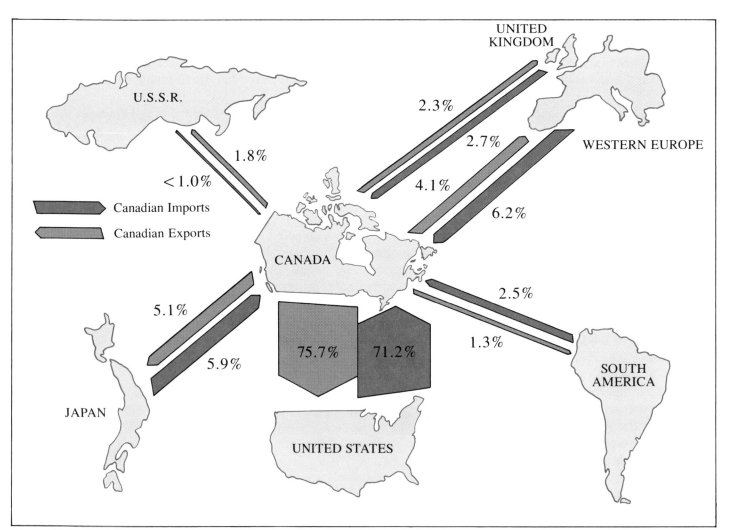

UNITED
KINGDOM

U.S.S.R.

2.3%

2.7%

WESTERN EUROPE

1.8%

4.1%

<1.0%

6.2%

■ Canadian Imports

■ Canadian Exports

CANADA

5.1%

2.5%

5.9%

1.3%

75.7%   71.2%

SOUTH
AMERICA

JAPAN

UNITED STATES

Figure 11.9 *Canadian Import and Export Trade with Leading Trade Partners*

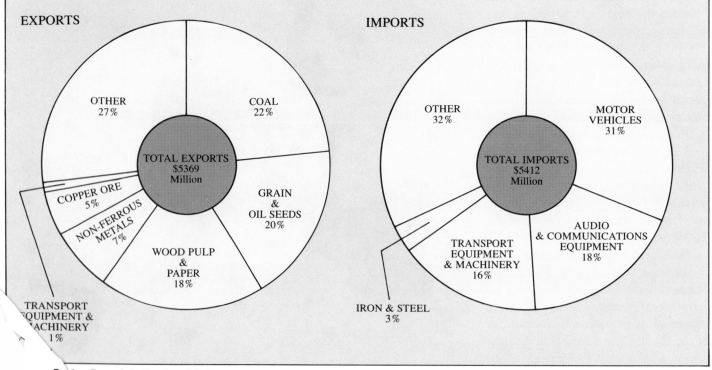

EXPORTS

OTHER
27%

COAL
22%

COPPER ORE
5%

TOTAL EXPORTS
$5369
Million

NON-FERROUS
METALS
7%

GRAIN
&
OIL SEEDS
20%

WOOD PULP
&
PAPER
18%

TRANSPORT
EQUIPMENT &
MACHINERY
1%

IMPORTS

OTHER
32%

MOTOR
VEHICLES
31%

TOTAL IMPORTS
$5412
Million

TRANSPORT
EQUIPMENT
& MACHINERY
16%

AUDIO
& COMMUNICATIONS
EQUIPMENT
18%

IRON & STEEL
3%

Ingersoll. All of these plants are in southern Ontario, where the largest part of the Canadian automotive industry is located. Even though most of the auto parts will come from Japan, these new plants will create employment in Canada.

Many Canadian industrialists and business people believe that Canada could benefit greatly by expanding its trade with Pacific Rim countries. Many of those countries have growing populations and growing economies that could provide a market for Canadian products. However, selling in Asian countries is difficult. The language, culture, and ways of doing business in Asian countries pose problems for Canadians.

Since 1984, Canada's trade across the Pacific has exceeded its trade across the Atlantic.

Considering the size of the U.S.S.R., and its closeness to Canada, there is less trade between these two countries than one would expect. In some years, Canada exports large amounts of wheat to the Soviet Union. Canada also exports some offshore drilling equipment to the U.S.S.R. for use in the Arctic. Canada is one of the few countries in the world with Arctic drilling experience, but the Soviet Union will not buy more from us until

---

F O C U S

You Can't Just Go with an Order Book

Mr. Sarsons first visited Japan in 1969, when he was director of the industrial division of the Saskatchewan Wheat Pool.

Since that first trip—to promote Canadian Canola and help the Japanese establish a crushing plant—he has been to the Far East more than 20 times. His several journeys a year to market Canola and its by-products have taken him beyond Japan to Korea, Taiwan, and China . . .

"You can't just go with an order book if you expect to do business in that part of the world," said Mr. Sarsons, a director of both the Asia-Pacific Foundation and the Canadian branch of the Pacific Basin Economic Council.

"You must also understand language and culture so that you can extend the proper courtesies and be sure that you are talking to the right people. Furthermore, when trade delegations from the Far East visit Canada, it is vital to provide them with the *amenities* that are important to them."

He said Japanese business people almost always have a Canadian flag on display when they greet business people from this country in Tokyo board rooms. But Japan's flag is never visible when Canadian executives are host to Japanese in this country.

"We should not be neglecting their flag. It is this kind of small but thoughtful gesture that makes people feel welcome." . . .

Mr. Sarsons believes Canada can substantially increase trade with emerging industrial countries such as Taiwan, South Korea, Singapore, Malaysia, Indonesia, China, and India. But he said there will be difficulties in penetrating those markets unless Canadians are taught more about Asian cultures at school and university.

"Traditionally, our young people have learned about the Atlantic countries, which are growing much more slowly than those in the Pacific. The challenge is to make them as comfortable with Tokyo, Seoul, and Hong Kong as they are with London, Paris, and Berlin. We must also aim for excellence in translation, and perhaps the solution is to harness better the talents of our ethnic minorities."

—Roger Newman,
Globe and Mail,
September 1987 (Adapted)

1. Name two difficulties that Canadians must overcome before Canada can "substantially increase trade with emerging industrial countries such as Taiwan, South Korea, Singapore, Malaysia, Indonesia, China, and India."

2. How many students do you know who are studying a language of some Asian country? Why might it be useful for a Canadian to learn an Asian language?

3. Why does China offer "enormous potential" for Canadian farm products? Why is it hard for Canadians to do business with China?

4. What did Mr. Sarsons mean by "You can't just go with an order book if you expect to do business in that part of the world"?

5. Working in small groups of "Canadian business people", plan to entertain for a day "business people" from one of the Far Eastern countries Mr. Sarsons mentioned. Prepare a schedule and list arrangements you will make to welcome these people and promote a business connection.

we buy more from them. Canada imports very little from the Soviet Union.

There are several reasons for the small amount of trade between these two countries. Language is a serious barrier. Canada's participation in Western European and American defence pacts has tended to alienate Canada from the Soviet Union. Until very recently, too, the Soviet Union has not been an ''open'' society, and it did not allow foreign business people to enter freely. In the past, the Soviet government closely supervised travel by foreigners in the U.S.S.R. But since the Soviet government has adopted the policies of *glasnost* and **perestroika**, a number of Canadians have opened business in the Soviet Union. In the future, trade may increase a great deal between Canada and the Soviet Union.

In 1985, the Hyundai motor company sold more automobiles to Canadians than did any other foreign company. Because South Korea was considered a developing country, no tariff was charged on imported Hyundai cars. This policy gave the company an advantage over other foreign auto makers. By 1987, Canada had placed a tariff on South Korean cars.

1. Approximately what percentage of Canada's total trade is represented by the countries (or areas) shown in Figure 11.9?
2. To which countries (or areas) does Canada export more than it imports? (Figure 11.9).

3. What percentage of Canada's exports to Japan come from mines, farms, and forests? (Figure 11.10).
4. Survey your class to discover the country of origin of most of the following products in your homes: radios, television sets, video cassette recorders, cameras, microwave ovens. Draw a general conclusion from the results of this survey.
5. There are many reasons for the large amount of trade between Canada and the United States. These reasons can be grouped under headings like those listed below. Working in small groups, write a short paragraph to explain each item on the list. Be prepared to read any of your paragraphs to the whole class. Discuss in class the reasons mentioned in the paragraphs read. Consider:
   - location
   - climate
   - natural resources
   - language
   - cultural heritage and customs
   - standard of living
   - transportation and communications
   - differences in degree of industrialization
   - patterns of recreational travel
   - U.S. branch plants in Canada
   - ease of border crossing
   - special trade agreements

Sergei Makarov of the Calgary Flames was one of the first Russian hockey players allowed to play for Canadian teams.

FREE TRADE WITH THE UNITED STATES

The large volume of trade between Canada and the United States has benefited the economy of both countries. The Canadian and U.S. governments believe that free trade (i.e., abolishing tariffs and non-tariff barriers) will make the two countries even more prosperous. In 1987, the two countries agreed on a ''Free Trade Accord''.

Two years later the Canadian Parliament and the United States Congress ratified the free trade agreement. Tariff reductions will be phased in over a 10-year period.

Not all Canadians (nor all Americans) are in favour of the Free Trade agreement. Some of the many arguments for and against free trade with the United States follow.

> Based on manufacturing value added per worker, Canada's productivity rating is 40 percent below that of the United States.

Arguments *for* Free Trade with the United States

1. Free trade opens a huge American market to Canadian products. The Canadian and American markets combined permit *economies of scale* not possible to suppliers of the small Canadian market alone.
2. Free trade allows Canada to specialize in products in which it has a comparative advantage (e.g., forest products, iron and steel) and to buy from the United States products which that country makes more efficiently (e.g., many manufactured goods).
3. Free trade reduces costs of production for Canadian *primary* and *secondary industries*, making them more competitive internationally.
4. Free trade reduces Canadian prices of *consumer goods*.
5. Free trade will allow the Canadian government to cancel many subsidies now paid to industry, thus reducing government spending and lowering taxes.
6. U.S. companies are allowed to invest more freely in Canada. Canada needs more foreign investment to develop its resources.
7. Before the Free Trade deal of 1989, there were few or no tariffs on primary products; there was free trade in farm machinery and defence supplies, and a special auto trade pact, as well. These arrangements benefited the economy of both countries.
8. Free trade eliminates tariff and non-tariff disputes between Canada and the United States.
9. Free trade may remove the irritation caused by limiting the amount of U.S. goods Canadian tourists can bring back free of *customs duties* from trips to the United States.
10. A free trade area that includes Canada and the United States combined will be better able to compete with other major world *trading blocs*, such as the European Economic Community.
11. Free trade offers highly skilled Canadian workers greater opportunities of finding suitable jobs at good pay in the United States.
12. If Canada were to revoke the free trade deal, the United States might freeze out many Canadian exports with tariff and non-tariff barriers. This could ruin Canada's economy.

F O C U S

Free Trade Is Not a New Idea

In the early days of the British Empire, there was free trade between Britain and its colonies. In 1846, Britain adopted a policy of free trade with the whole world, which ended the trade privileges her colonies had enjoyed with the mother country.

In 1854, a Reciprocity Treaty was negotiated between the British colonies in North America and the United States. This treaty resulted in free trade in natural resources and agricultural products. But free trade did not last long. Soon after Confederation, Canada adopted a high-tariff policy to protect its infant industries. Within this policy, a preference was arranged with Britain and members of the British Empire. This arrangement later became known as the Commonwealth Trade Preferences. These Commonwealth Preferences gradually decreased and disappeared when the United Kingdom joined the European Economic Community (EEC) in 1971.

The idea of Canada-U.S. free trade was raised again in the early part of the 20th century. An agreement was negotiated between the two countries, but Canadians voted to reject the free trade agreement in a federal election held in 1911.

In the 1930s, Canada and the United States signed ''most-favoured nation'' agreements. This meant that any trade concession made by Canada with any other country would be extended to the United States. The United States, of course, would do the same for Canada.

In 1987, the governments of Canada and the United States signed a ''Free Trade Accord''. This Accord is supposed to be fully implemented by 1999.

Arguments *against* Free Trade with the United States

1. Free trade opens up the Canadian market to U.S. firms. Smaller Canadian firms will not be able to compete and will be forced to close. Even some large companies will likely be forced out of business.

2. Many U.S. firms have surplus production capacity. This means that with little additional expense they can produce enough extra goods to supply the Canadian market. Thus they have a big advantage over Canadian firms, which must expand to compete.

3. Many U.S. companies have established branch plants in Canada in order to produce behind the Canadian tariff wall. Without tariffs, they need not keep their Canadian plants open.

4. Canadian manufacturing firms may decide to move their operations to the United States, where construction and heating costs are lower, and where they are closer to the largest markets. As a result, unemployment will increase in Canada.

5. Free trade requires the Canadian government to eliminate many subsidies to industries. Without subsidies, some industries will collapse, causing further unemployment.

6. The United States has complained that *regional economic development* grants to the poorer regions of Canada (e.g., a grant to encourage an industry to locate in the Atlantic Provinces) are subsidies that give Canadian industry an unfair advantage. Free trade requires that Canada's regional economic development program be cut.

7. Under free trade, Canada is under pressure to relax its pollution control and other environmental regulations because these add to the costs of Canadian industries, making them less competitive.

8. The Canadian government is under pressure to reduce subsidies to primary industries such as agriculture, forestry, fishing, and mining. This change will eliminate the price advantages these industries now enjoy over U.S. competitors.

9. The foregoing changes will result in massive unemployment in Canada. Hardest hit will be the unskilled workers in low-technology industries.

10. For free trade to work, there must be a "level playing field". This means that the costs of production in both countries must be about the same. Canadian citizens have much better medical insurance, unemployment insurance, and old age pensions than have American citizens. Free trade is applying pressure on Canada to weaken these programs.

11. Free trade is resulting in a Canadian loss of cultural identity. Canadian culture (literature, music, theatre, and general way of life) is being swallowed up by the much larger United States.

12. Free trade is a first step only. Because of the Free Trade deal, Canada will gradually lose control over its own economic policies. In time, Canada will form a political union with the United States, and our country will cease to exist as an independent nation.

---

1. a) Poll your class on the following question: "Do you think that Canada-U.S. free trade benefits Canada?" Record the vote.

   b) Have each class member do the following:

   For each argument *for* and each argument *against* free trade, assign a number to reflect your view of the importance of the argument. Use the following scale:

   > 0 – of no importance or not true
   > 1 – of little importance
   > 2 – important
   > 3 – very important

   c) Add up the *for* numbers and the *against* numbers that you have assigned. If the sums do not support the way you voted on the issue, consider why. Perhaps you will need to add some arguments, or you may change your mind after considering the arguments.

   d) When you have completed parts a) to c), take another vote on the question of free trade. In classroom discussion, explain any changes in the result of the second vote.

The percentage of industrial profit spent on research and development in Canada is lower than that spent in most other industrial nations.

Canada stands ninth in a list of 10 industrialized countries ranked according to the number of robots used in manufacturing for each 10 000 employees.

TRADE OUTLOOK

Where do we look for Canada's most favourable trade opportunities? Should we look to freer trade with our best trading partner, the United States? Across the Atlantic to the EEC and Africa? Toward the north to the Soviet Union? Or west to the Pacific Rim? Must Canada put "all its eggs in one basket": that is, depend almost wholly on trade with the United States?

Although governments work out formal trade relations, most trade is carried on by companies or individuals. In order to compete in world markets, Canadians must produce goods that are competitive in quality and

A Nation Of Techno-Peasants?

Galileo did his research by looking at the stars through a crude telescope. Sir Isaac Newton is said to have done some of his by watching an apple fall from a tree in his garden. Their research, though enormously important, cost little or nothing. But scientific research today is both complex and expensive, and the nations willing to support it are the industrial leaders of the world. Where does Canada stand among those nations?

In 1985, Canada's federal government made spending cuts to reduce the national deficit; science was one of the victims. The National Research Council (NRC) was forced to close research centres, cancel programs, and lay off employees. The cuts have continued. Provincial governments also began to reduce spending on research. Canada is now spending about 1.3 percent of its **gross national product** (GNP) on science. That percentage represents a

quarter of the percentage of its GNP that Japan spends, and half the percentage that the United States spends. In the middle level of industrial states, only Australia spends less than Canada as a proportion of GNP.

Private industry in Canada shows little interest in spending money on research. The reason is that many of our companies are branch plants with headquarters in the United States, and so the parent company does the research and the branch plants make use of the results . . .

Critics say that the lack of financial support will make Canada an also-ran in the race to compete in world markets. Without more money for research, they say, we are in danger of slipping back to just digging up rocks and chopping down trees to sell to more science-oriented countries. Canadians, says Leslie Millin, formerly secretary of the Science Council of Canada, could become a

nation of ''techno-peasants'', depending on the scientific know-how of more advanced societies.

—Charles White,
Canada and the World, December 1987
(Adapted)

1. What is meant by the statement: ''. . . we are in danger of slipping back to just digging up rocks and chopping down trees . . .''? How does this statement relate to ''Canadians are hewers of wood and drawers of water''? (See Chapter Three.)
2. What do you think ''techno-peasants'' means? What must Canada do to prevent Canadians from becoming techno-peasants?
3. Why is there little political incentive for a government to spend large amounts of money on scientific research?
4. Why is private industry in Canada not much interested in spending money on research?

---

price. To remain competitive or to increase our ability to compete, Canada must spend more on research and development than we now spend. We need research that will result in new and better products than those produced in other countries. We also need well-educated Canadians who know the ways and languages of foreign countries to sell those products.

Japan has a superb research force of 350 000 persons; Canada has 14 000 researchers.

CANADA AND THE CULTURAL WORLD

IMMIGRATION

Our nation of Canada owes its existence to immigration of peoples from around the world. In the 1700s, when the Native peoples had been living in North America for thousands of years, the British and French explored, settled, and fought over what is now Canada (Chapters Three and Four). In the 1800s and early 1900s, waves of immigrants came to Canada from the British Isles and continental Europe. Many Europeans migrated to the

United States first and then moved on to Canada. By 1950, Canada's heritage was still chiefly British and French, though a sizeable number of people had come to Canada from other European countries.

Until the 1960s, most immigrants to Canada were white. For many years, Canada had policies that discouraged the immigration of blacks and Asians. But some Chinese and Japanese settled in Victoria and Vancouver in the late 1800s. Between 1881 and 1885 more than 15 000 Chinese were admitted to Canada to provide the labour needed to build the CPR through the Western Cordillera. The white settlers of British Columbia did not welcome Chinese and Japanese immigrants, and in 1884, an ''entry'' tax of $100 per Asian immigrant was charged. In 1903, this tax was raised to $500, which in those days was a substantial sum. Even with the entry tax, there was more Asian immigration than the white population wanted. In 1923, federal legislation almost stopped Chinese immigration to Canada. At the same time, Canada asked Japan to set a quota of 400 Japanese per year who might emigrate to Canada.

The Chinese and Japanese who came to Canada faced racial discrimination. White Canadians who controlled Canada's government, business, industry, and professions treated the Asians shabbily. Chinese and Japanese were not permitted to enter professions such as medicine, law, and teaching. They were paid less than white Canadians for doing the same jobs and received less welfare assistance during the Great Depression of the 1930s. The number of fishing franchises given to Japanese Canadians was limited. Chinese Canadians were not allowed to vote in provincial and federal elections until 1947. Japanese Canadians were not granted the vote until 1949. This racial discrimination encouraged the Chinese and Japanese to settle in colonies or *ghettos* in Canadian cities.

The most serious Canadian act of discrimination against Asians was the removal of the people of Japanese descent from the coastal area of British Columbia in 1942. Canada was at war with Japan. The federal government believed that Japan might attack Canada's west coast. The Japanese Canadians living there were considered a threat to Canada's security, even though no Japanese Canadian was ever charged with disloyalty to Canada, and some fought with the Canadian forces overseas.

Over 20 000 Japanese Canadians were taken from their homes and relocated in camps in the interior of

Canada accepts refugees from many different countries.

British Columbia. The government then sold their homes, businesses, and possessions. When the Second World War ended, Japanese Canadians could choose between being deported to Japan or being moved east to other parts of Canada. Almost all of them stayed in Canada. It was not until 1988 that the Canadian government apologized to these Canadians of Japanese origin and made token payments to them for their property losses and the hardships they had endured.

In 1967, Canadian immigration laws were changed so that immigrants would no longer be refused because of their race or colour. Current regulations require that immigrants be admitted to Canada on the basis of their education, training, skills, and other special qualifications that would make them suitable citizens of Canada. But critics of Canada's immigration policies say that nothing much has changed. The skills in greatest demand in Canada are found in countries with a modern industrial society like our own, such as the United States and the countries of Western Europe. Therefore, say the critics, most Canadian immigrants will come from those areas. This criticism ignores the fact that a number of countries in southeast

Asia are now highly industrialized and have many highly skilled people.

Experience has not supported the critics. In 1986, out of a total of 98 000 immigrants to Canada, 41 000 came from Asian countries, and 9000 came from Caribbean countries. When immigrants from Africa are added, non-whites made up well over half of Canada's immigrants.

In addition to regular immigrants, Canada accepts *refugees* from other countries (Figure 11.11). Almost 100 000 refugees from Europe left homeless by the Second World War came to Canada after 1946. A special airlift brought 36 000 refugees from Hungary when the Soviet Union invaded that country in 1957. When the same thing happened to Czechoslovakia, in 1968, Canada opened the door to 10 000 refugees. In the 1970s and 1980s, Canada accepted refugees from Tibet, Uganda, Vietnam, Poland, and countries in Central and South America. In 1986, the United Nations High Commissioner for Refugees honoured the People of Canada by awarding them the Nansen medal for help given to refugees since the Second World War. It was the first time the award had been given to an entire nation.

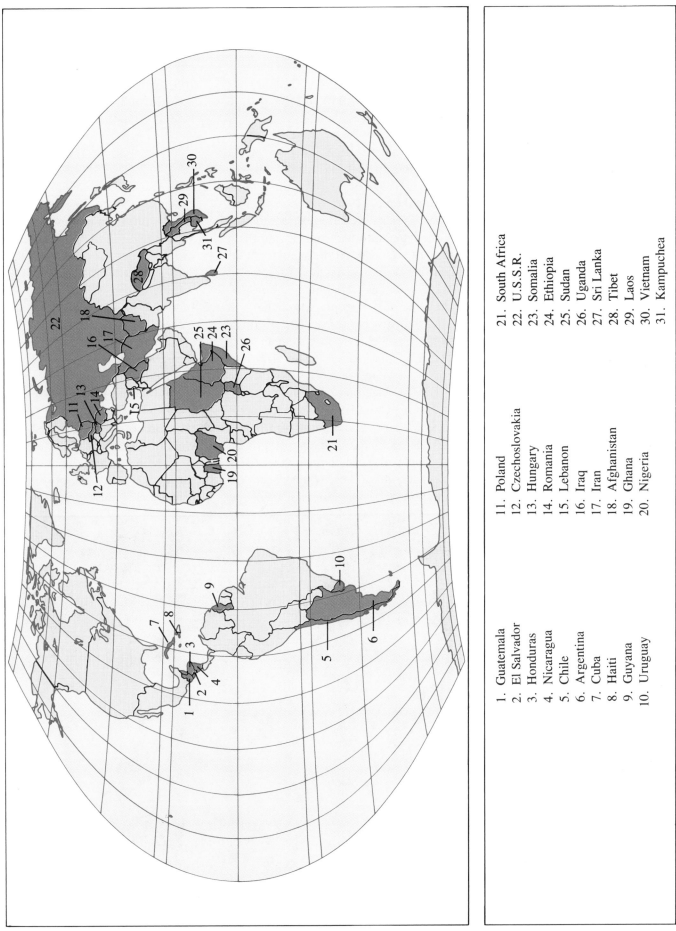

1. Guatemala
2. El Salvador
3. Honduras
4. Nicaragua
5. Chile
6. Argentina
7. Cuba
8. Haiti
9. Guyana
10. Uruguay

11. Poland
12. Czechoslovakia
13. Hungary
14. Romania
15. Lebanon
16. Iraq
17. Iran
18. Afghanistan
19. Ghana
20. Nigeria

21. South Africa
22. U.S.S.R.
23. Somalia
24. Ethiopia
25. Sudan
26. Uganda
27. Sri Lanka
28. Tibet
29. Laos
30. Vietnam
31. Kampuchea

Figure 11.11 *Refugees come to Canada from many parts of the world.*

In the 1980s, the numbers of **political refugees** who came to Canada seeking asylum became so great that immigration officers found it difficult to process them. A boat load of Tamils arrived from Sri Lanka. Thousands of Turks asked for admission. Refugees from Guatemala and El Salvador, who were refused a haven in the United States, came to Canada. The Canadian government was committed to accepting political refugees. Unfortunately, some of those who sought entry to Canada were not political refugees but claimed they were, to enter the country more promptly than they could have done through the regular immigration process.

Because the number of refugees awaiting processing in Canada became so large, the government introduced legislation that made it more difficult for refugees to enter the country. All refugees have to pass hearings of the Immigration and Refugee Board. Persons who are found not to have a legitimate claim to refugee status are refused permission to remain in Canada.

A MULTICULTURAL SOCIETY

As a result of more recent immigration trends, Canada is becoming a truly multicultural society, representing races from around the world. Multiculturalism is now the basis for Canada's national identity and nation building. Multiculturalism was enshrined in the *Canadian Charter of Rights and Freedoms*, in 1982. In 1988, the federal government passed a *Multicultural Act*. These Acts are meant to help preserve the cultural identity of immigrant groups and to discourage racial discrimination.

Multiculturalism is a valuable asset to a country. It provides a richness of culture and customs. Immigrants from other countries bring with them new ideas and skills, different viewpoints

and attitudes, and new human energy and **entrepreneurship**. By retaining their language and culture, new Canadians maintain contacts with various parts of the world. This is important now that the world has become a global village.

It is not easy for a country to follow a policy of multiculturalism. How does it preserve the culture of individual groups and at the same time retain national unity? A 1987 public opinion survey discovered that 61 percent of Canadians think that multiculturalism benefits Canada. At the same time, 75 percent do not want the character of Canadian society to change. But how do some of the people who believe in multiculturalism expect to attain it without any change in Canadian society? Canadian society, like all societies, has, in fact, *always* been gradually changing.

Some Canadians of European descent are concerned about the increasing visible minorities: groups of people who can be distinguished by racial features. These white Canadians fear that the visible minorities will one

day become a visible majority. Their fear shows racial prejudice. In 1986, the visible minorities made up about seven percent of the Canadian population. With current immigration trends, this will rise to about ten percent in the year 2000.

---

1. It has been said that all Canadians, except the Native peoples, are immigrants. What does this mean?
2. Why do you think the Canadians of European descent treated the early Chinese and Japanese settlers so badly?
3. In the Second World War, Canada was at war with both Germany and Japan. Why do you suppose the government expelled the Japanese Canadians from their homes but did not do the same to the Canadians of German descent?
4. "Canada is more interested in what immigrants can do for Canada than what Canada can do for immigrants." Support or refute this statement with facts.

Canada has become a multicultural country.

CANADA AND THE WORLD ENVIRONMENT

In a number of earlier chapters we discussed how people and their activities have affected Canada's natural environment. In recent years we have begun to see that human activities in one country can have serious effects on the global environment. Even drinking coffee or eating frogs' legs in Canada can affect the environment and living conditions of people in countries on the other side of the globe.

There is growing global concern about what humans are doing to world environment. The Worldwatch Institute has published a list of these environmental concerns. Any one of the changes listed by the Worldwatch Institute could be a catastrophe for humankind if we do not do something to reverse the present trends.

1. Working in small groups, prepare a report on one topic taken from the "State of the World 1988" chart. (Each group should report on a different topic.) Consult library sources, and old and current newspapers and news magazines. Present your report to the whole class. Your report might take the form of a poster.

2. a) Find a piece of popular music that has an environmental message, such as Bruce Cockburn's "Going to the Country". Bring an example of the music to the classroom on record, tape, or sheet music. Identify the issue highlighted in the music. In your opinion and that of your classmates, are people influenced by the work of popular artists? Discuss.
   b) Working as a class or in small groups, compose a poem or song about protecting the environment.

3. Over the last nine chapters you have been constructing a model of your community. Think of ways that you can make changes to your model in order to safeguard as much as possible existing vegetation, wildlife, and resources. What would you add to make your community a better place to live? How large do you think your community can grow before it significantly endangers the environment? Where can suburbs expand? Where should they not be allowed to expand? Make the changes to your model that will show how you would like your community to look 10 years from now.

State of the World, 1988

Environmental Indicator	Environmental Changes
Forest Cover	Tropical forests shrinking by 11 million hectares per year; 31 million hectares in industrial countries damaged, apparently by air pollution or acid rain
Topsoil on Cropland	An estimated 23.5 billion tonnes lost annually in excess of new soil formation
Desert Area	Some six million hectares of new desert formed annually by land mismanagement
Lakes	Thousands of lakes in the industrial north now biologically dead; thousands more dying
Fresh Water	Underground water tables falling in parts of Africa, China, India, and North America as demand for water rises above aquifer recharge rates
Species Diversity	Extinctions of plant and animal species together now estimated at several thousand per year; one-fifth of all species may disappear over next 20 years
Ground Water Quality	Some 50 pesticides contaminate ground water in 32 American states; some 2500 U.S. toxic waste sites need clean-up; extent of toxic contamination worldwide unknown
Climate	Mean temperature projected to rise between 1.5°C and 4.5°C between now and 2050
Sea Level	Projected to rise between 1.4 metres and 2.2 metres by 2100
Ozone Layer in Upper Atmosphere	Growing "hole" in the earth's ozone layer over Antarctica each spring suggests a gradual global depletion could be starting.

—Compiled by Worldwatch Institute from various sources

Recent clean air laws should help reduce scenes like this.

Frogs' Legs and Famine

Until about a year ago, most of the frogs' legs served in restaurants in Canada, the United States, Europe, and Japan came from India. Yet few connoisseurs of the delicacy knew this. Hardly anyone was aware of how the ecology of India was being destroyed and how the poor were being harmed.

Some 800 tonnes of frogs in India were slaughtered yearly to earn about $12 million. More than 100 000 men and women worked at catching the frogs. They received about $1 for a night's work, and they killed 100 million frogs a year.

Large hungry frogs are a farmer's best friend. The Indian bullfrog eats its own body mass in insect pests every day. Reducing the frog population increased the pest population, and so increased the threat of malaria and encephalitis, and caused damage to rice and fish stocks. And eliminating 100 million frogs created the need to import or manufacture thousands of tonnes of insecticides and pesticides.

In March 1987, after a long struggle by environmental groups, India banned the export of frogs. However, demand in the West remains, and now Bangladesh—the poorest of the poor countries—feeds the frog market.

In terms of Third World exports, frogs' legs are a fairly recent phenomenon and a small item in the scheme of things. But the exploitation of forests, lands, water, and natural resources in most parts of Africa, Asia, and Latin America, for the benefit and consumption of Europeans and North Americans, is part of colonial history.

Tea, coffee, sugar, cotton, peanut, and banana plantations all were set up by the imperial powers in their colonies. Colonial practices transformed nature and humankind's relationship with nature more drastically than thousands of years of nature use by the people who lived there.

Ironically, today, when hardly any colonies remain, several times more land is being used in the Third World to provide food for the West than was used in the 1940s. In the colonial period, cash crops were introduced under the threat of guns and whips, with the collaboration of the local ruling élite. Such changes sowed the seeds of starvation for the local populations for many decades to come.

In Gambia, before the Europeans arrived, rice farming was common. Then so much of the best land was taken over to grow peanuts for export that rice had to be imported. Northern Ghana, once famous for its yams and other foods, was forced to concentrate almost exclusively on cocoa. Food production in Dahomey and southeast Nigeria was all but abandoned in favor of palm oil. Tanzania had to focus on sisal, Uganda on cotton.

Some of these long-term changes in land use, reinforced by a new thrust for modernization, have come to threaten the people of many Third World countries . . .

In the past few years there has been much international concern about starvation in Ethiopia. Yet even as people there have been dying of hunger by the thousands and Westerners collect money to help feed the starving, Ethiopia has been exporting food. Only about six per cent of its agricultural industry can be described as modern—and almost all of it grows coffee for export rather than food for the people.

Indeed, coffee—the largest food item for export in the world—has become vitally important for 11 countries in the Third World. Colombia, Burundi, Rwanda, Ethiopia, and Uganda all earn more than half their foreign exchange from coffee, and little of this money is spent on ordinary people . . .

Another serious problem has resulted from exporting beef from countries in Central America. To make way for cattle ranching, more than one-quarter of all rainforest in Central America has been destroyed since 1960. Between 85 and 95 per cent of the beef produced has gone for cheap hamburgers, tinned meat, and pet food in North America. While their ecosystem has been destroyed, Central Americans' consumption of beef has fallen dramatically. Raising cattle is probably the worst use for the fragile soil on which the tropical rainforests grow; every five to seven years the productivity at the ranches slumps, and ranchers have to move on, destroying still more forests.

—Sehdev Kumar,
Globe and Mail, April 1988 (Adapted)

REDUCING TROPICAL RAIN FORESTS

There is not space in this book to discuss all of the Worldwatch Institute's list of environmental changes. Following are a few comments on the first change mentioned.

Tropical forests cover only seven percent of the earth's surface, but they are home to more than eighty percent of its plant and animal species (Figure 8.7). Because rain forests contain a great many species of plant and animal life, they are very stable ecosystems. (Review discussion of ecosystems in Chapter Two.) This means that rain forests can withstand the loss of one or more species without a catastrophic effect on the ecosystem. The food-chain links are many and complex.

Rain forests are stable when left in a natural state, but human actions can destroy them. Millions of people in tropical countries cut down about two million hectares of forest each year for firewood. Logging companies from industrialized countries cut large areas of forest each year for the valuable tropical hardwood. More than one-quarter of Central America's tropical forest has been cut to make way for grass to feed beef cattle. In recent years farmers have started clearing forests in the Amazon basin of Brazil. For cattle ranchers, burning the forest is the least expensive way of converting the forest to pasture. The fire destroys parasites and disease, and releases nutrients to the soil. But much of the land cleared for cattle raising is not very fertile. Once the trees are cleared, the soil is quickly eroded and leached. After about ten to fifteen years, the pasture is no longer very productive and more forest has to be burned to keep the cattle operation profitable.

As a result of human use, nearly half of the world's tropical rain forest has been destroyed in the last two centuries. As world population grows rapidly, the rate of destruction is increasing. Scientists estimate that most of the rest of the tropical rain forests could be destroyed within the next century.

Changes in the tropical rain forest can affect many other parts of the global environment. The destruction of much of the tropical rain forest affects world climate. Because the clearing of forests affects the water cycle, deforestation causes deserts to expand and water tables to drop. Destruction of the rain forest also destroys the habitat of many plant and animal species, and often leads to their extinction. The extinction of species can have an effect around the world. For example, more than one-quarter of modern prescription drugs are made from plants found only in the tropics. By destroying the tropical rain forest, we may be extinguishing some rare plant that could cure some current or future serious human disease.

When we think of the global problems that result from the destruction of forests, it is usually tropical forests that come to mind. But Canada is also losing forests at an alarming rate. Every four years we cut an area of Canada's forest equal to the size of Vancouver Island. Some of the clear-cut areas on steep mountain slopes in western Canada cannot be replanted and will not regrow in time to prevent most of the topsoil from being eroded away.

The Great Auk is one of the species that has become extinct as a result of human actions.

Since the turn of the century, the proportion of Ethiopia's land area in forest has been reduced from 40 percent to four percent.

The sea otter, too, has become an endangered species.

THE ULTIMATE GLOBAL POLLUTION

The danger of global nuclear contamination was not mentioned in "The State of the World, 1988". If you have seen pictures of what atomic bombs did to the city of Hiroshima and its people in 1945, you will appreciate the destructive power of nuclear bombs. Today's nuclear bombs are many times more powerful than were the bombs dropped in 1945, and they can be delivered to any place around the globe. There are now enough nuclear bombs to kill all the people in the world several times over.

There is also the possibility of serious radioactive pollution from accidents at nuclear power plants. In 1986, one nuclear accident at Chernobyl, in the Soviet Union, contaminated crops throughout Europe, and spread radioactive dust around the globe. Every country is trying to make its nuclear reactors as safe as possible. Many scientists fear, however, that human error could result in more disasters. Another concern is the wastes from nuclear reactors: we still have no safe way of disposing of them. Some people believe that the world would be better off in the long run if we phased out the use of nuclear power altogether.

Canada played a leading role at the Law of the Sea Conference in 1982. This conference led to an agreement by 60 countries that the resources of the seabed in international waters are part of the common heritage of all humankind.

A GLOBAL RESPONSE

In the 1960s and 1970s, many scientists began to express their alarm about what was happening to the global environment. News media began to make regular reports on major environmental catastrophes. Governments began to take notice. Environmental issues were debated in various United Nations agencies. The International Union for Conservation of Nature and Natural Resources (IUCN) was set up. It published an important document entitled "The 1980 World Conservation Strategy". The central idea of this strategy was labelled *sustainable development*. A plea was made to all nations to consider the effects on the ecology of all economic development. According to the strategy, all renewable resources should be developed in such a way that they could renew themselves and continue to be useful to future generations. A World Commission on Environment and Development was set up to educate the nations of the world about the long-run benefits of the principle of sustainable development.

Twenty-four nations signed a global agreement, in 1987, to control pollution that is destroying the earth's ozone layer.

Canada has been very active in these international conservation efforts. Canadian scientists helped to compile the 1980 World Conservation Strategy. Ottawa was the host city for the World Conservation Strategy Conference held in 1986. When, in 1987, the World Commission on Environment and Development published a report entitled *Our Common Future*, also known as "the Bruntland Report", Canada responded to the challenge.

"The world economy depends on the environment, and the environment is in bad shape."

—The Bruntland Report, 1987

The Bruntland Report called on the nations of the world to start solving environmental problems before it is too late. Canada's response was to establish the Task Force on Environment and Economy. In 1987, this Task Force published a report that urged "governments and business to co-operate in removing barriers to environmentally sound development". "All Canadians", the report said, "have a major role to play in making sustainable development a reality.

"Environment is where we all live; development is what we all do."

—Canadian Task Force on Environment and Economy, 1987

Let's treat Canada as though we plan to stay." The Task Force Report went on to ask every province and territory to have a conservation strategy in place by 1992. It recommended that a number of round-table conferences be held in each province and territory so that people from government, industry, business, and universities might discuss what should be included in these conservation strategy reports.

Following the task force's plan, a national conservation strategy will be prepared. This work will be submitted to a UN conference on the environment. Other nations will present their conservation strategies at the same time.

---

1. a) Discuss in class the slogan, "Think globally, act locally."
   b) Working in small groups, prepare a poster to illustrate some of the points made in your discussion.
2. a) Make a class collection of cartoons on global environmental problems.
   b) Create your own cartoon to make a point about some environmental problem in Canada that has a global impact.

WHAT LIES AHEAD?

Global environmental problems are immense. It is going to take much effort and a long time to change our ways and cease to ''foul our nest''. But it is heartening to see that international groups have recognized the problems and are starting to do something about them.

REVIEW QUESTIONS

1. In what ways have Canada's global location and the nature of its population increased the country's contacts with the rest of the world?

2. Why do you think Canada has played a leading role in international peace-keeping projects and in social and economic assistance programs for developing countries?

3. Explain why Canada's foreign-trade patterns have shifted a good deal in this century. What do you think the next major trade shift will be? Why?

4. Discuss: ''Multiculturalism in Canada can be considered a valuable resource.'' Do you agree or disagree? Explain the reasons for your answer.

5. Which of the environmental problems listed in ''State of the World, 1988'' do you think poses the greatest threat to humanity? Explain why.

6. At the Epcot Centre in Disney World in Florida, countries from around the world have built national showplaces. At these showplaces, each nation has tried to give visitors an experience similar to a visit to its country.

You and your classmates have been given the task of designing a Canadian showplace for the new Disney World near Paris, France. Your task is to present an image of Canada that would give millions of visitors a feeling that they have experienced a visit to our country. For each of the following categories, decide in detail what you would show, feed, or sell to the visitors. Make sure that your decisions reflect the nature of Canada's land, resources, industries, settlement, and people.
a) Building designs
b) Landscaping
c) Audio-visual displays
d) Restaurants
e) Gift shops

7. A friend from another country is coming to visit you. Your friend will be staying long enough to take a 10-day trip with you. You may start anywhere, and you needn't worry about how to get back.

Plan a trip along any 2000-km stretch of the Trans-Canada Highway that you could cover easily in 10 days. Try to pick a part of the highway that will show your friend some of the variety Canada offers. You might include visits to places important for forestry, mining, agriculture, fishing, scenic areas, and rural countryside, as well as cities. You should also include historic sites and tourist areas.
a) Plot your trip on a map of Canada.
b) For each of 10 days decide in detail the following:
i) Length of day trip
ii) Where to go
iii) What to see
iv) What to do
v) Where to eat
vi) Where to stay overnight

8. You have been asked to design a four-page brochure to advertise Canada in travel offices around the world.
a) Decide what kinds of information and photographs should be included in the brochure.
b) Prepare a mock-up of the brochure that contains the written text and sketches of the photographs you wish to use.

Suggested Readings

CHAPTER ONE

- *Book of the Road* (Montréal: Reader's Digest (Canada) Ltd., 1979).
- *Canada: A Portrait* (Ottawa: Statistics Canada, annual). Over 200 coloured photographs and much up-to-date information about Canada.
- Curtis, B. and J. Kraulis. *Canada From the Air* (Edmonton: Hurtig 1981). Excellent colour oblique aerial photographs with good geographic descriptions.
- Deutsch, G. and A. Swan. *Canada: A Symphony in Colour* (Guildford, Surrey England: Colour Library Books, 1986). Colour photographs of Canada with a good text on what to see and do.
- *Heritage of Canada* (Montréal: Reader's Digest (Canada) Ltd., 1978). Well illustrated background information about historic sites in Canada.
- Kraulis, J., ed. *Canada, A Landscape Portrait* (Edmonton: Hurtig, 1982). A portfolio by some of Canada's leading colour photographers.
- Lawrence, R.D. *Canada's National Parks* (Toronto: Collins, 1983). A picture of the environmental variety in parkland across Canada.
- Milne, B. *Trans-Canada Country* (Don Mills: Collins, 1986). A journey across Canada with colour photographs and descriptions.

CHAPTER TWO

- Andrews, W. and D. Moore. *Investigating Terrestrial Ecosystems* (Scarborough: Prentice-Hall, 1986). Chapters 8 to 13 provide information about the Biomes (ecosystems) of North America.
- *Canada Handbook* (Ottawa: Statistics Canada, 1986). See the environment section for a description and photos of land and climate.
- *Canada's Environment: An Overview* (Ottawa: Supply and Services Canada, 1986) Free colour booklet on ecosystem stresses.
- *Canadian Encyclopedia* (Edmonton: Hurtig 1985; 2nd ed. 1988). Geological Regions; Climate; Vegetation Regions; Soil Classification; Wildlife Conservation and Management; Climate Change; Parks, National.
- Fitzharris, T. and J. Livingston. *Canada, a Natural History* (Toronto: Royal Canadian Geographical Society and Penguin, 1988). An excellent picture ecology of Canada.
- *Human Activity and the Environment* (Ottawa: Supply and Services Canada, 1986). Environmental data organized on the basis of ecozones.

- Robinson, J. ''Sorting Out All the Mountains in B.C.'', in *Canadian Geographic* Vol. 107, No. 1, 1987.
- *State of the Environment Report for Canada* (Ottawa: Supply and Services Canada, 1986). An advanced look at stresses on the environment based on ecozones.

CHAPTER THREE

- Andrew, W., ed. *Canadians and Their Environment* (Toronto: McClelland and Stewart, 1974). Especially the section ''The North American Indian'', pp. 9–16, and Chapter 2, ''Early Canadian Attitudes''.
- *Canadian Encyclopedia* (Edmonton: Hurtig, 1985; 2nd ed. 1988). Agriculture history, Economic history, Fisheries history, Fur trade, Mining, Native people, Population, Timber trade history.
- Harris, R.C., ed. *A Historical Atlas of Canada* (Toronto: University of Toronto Press, 1987).
- Heidenreich, C.E. and A.J. Ray. *The Early Fur Trades* (Toronto: McClelland and Stewart, 1976).
- Kerr, D.G.G., ed. *A Historical Atlas of Canada* (Toronto: Nelson, 1961).
- Skeoch, A. and T. Smith. *Canadians and Their Society* (Toronto: McClelland and Stewart, 1973). Especially Part 3, ''Canadian Communities Past and Present''.
- *Thinking About Ontario: A Hosford Study Atlas* (Toronto and Edmonton: Hosford, 1981). ''Thinking about People'', pp. 821, ''Peoples of Ontario and Canada'', pp. 22–37.

CHAPTER FOUR

- *Canada and the World* (Toronto: MacLean Hunter) Vol. 52, No. 5, 1987. See special section on ''Native People''.
- *Canada Handbook* and *Canada Year Book* (Ottawa: Statistics Canada, various years). These source books contain a description of the operation and functions of the federal and provincial governments.
- *Canadian Encyclopedia*, (Edmonton: Hurtig, 1985; 2nd ed. 1988). Statistical, historical, and political data on each province and territory, Aboriginal Rights, Acadia, Confederation, *Constitution Act*, Indian, *Indian Act*, Indian Treaties, Inuit, Land Claims, Local Government, Lower Canada, Loyalist, Métis, Native people, Province of Canada, Province of Québec, Regionalism, regional disparities, regional economic policies, Separatism, Upper Canada.

CHAPTER FIVE

- Allaby, I. "GO Transit Moves a City", in *Canadian Geographic* Vol. 108, No. 6, 1989.
- Backhouse, F. "Le miracle de Sherbrooke, Québec", in *Canadian Geographic* Vol. 107, No. 4, 1987.
- Baine, R., and L. McMurray. *Toronto: An Urban Study* (Toronto: Irwin Publishing, 1984).
- Blair, C., and R. Simpson. *The Canadian Landscape* (Toronto: Copp Clark, 1978). A number of topographic maps and photographic studies of large and small Canadian urban centres.
- Bowden, F., and others. *Canadian Industrialization* (Toronto: McGraw-Hill Ryerson, 1983). An enquiry approach to industrial production, automobile manufacture, Anik communication satellites, and Kitimat, B.C., a planned resource town.
- Braund, B., and W. Blake. *Case Studies in Canadian Geography* (Toronto: McGraw-Hill Ryerson, 1982). Chapter 5, The Steel Industry; Chapter 6, The Automobile Industry; and Chapter 7, Place Ville Marie, Montréal (tertiary activity).
- Cameron, S. "Part of Halifax", in *Canadian Geographic* Vol. 108, No. 6, 1989.
- *Canadian Encyclopedia* (Edmonton: Hurtig, 1985; 2nd ed. 1988). Manufacturing, Transportation, Urban and Regional Planning, Urban Transportation, Urbanization. Also see a series of land-use maps and descriptions of metropolitan areas (and some smaller centres), their points of interest, and employment-by-industry graphs.
- Heine, W. "Canada from Space", (shows remote sensing of urban areas from satellites), in *Canadian Geographic* Vol. 106, No. 6, 1986.
- Leahy, G. "Quebec City", in *Canadian Geographic* Vol. 106, No. 6, 1986.
- Palmer-Benson, T. "Wind Breakers", (City Buildings), in *Canadian Geographic* Vol. 107, No. 1, 1987.
- Struzik, C. "Yellowknife and Whitehorse: Sister Cities North of Sixty", in *Canadian Geographic* Vol. 106, No. 3, 1986.
- Yeates, M. *Land in Canada's Urban Heartland* (Ottawa: Environment Canada, 1985).
- *Note:* A number of earlier issues of *Canadian Geographic* (1980s) contain interesting articles on the cities of Saint John, Ottawa-Hull, Toronto, Windsor, and Vancouver.

CHAPTER SIX

- *Acid Rain Story* (Ottawa: Environment Canada, 1984).
- *Current* Vol. 3, No. 1, 1982. A special issue on water including articles on pollution and Ontario's Conservation Authorities. (Available from Ontario Hydro.)
- Gorrie, P. "Taming the Great Lakes: Is It Really Necessary?" in *Canadian Geographic* Vol. 108, No. 5, 1988.
- _____ . "The James Bay Power Project" in *Canadian Geographic* Vol. 110, No. 1, 1990.
- *Great Lakes: An Environmental Atlas and Resource Book* (Ottawa: Environment Canada, 1987).
- "Great Lakes Toxic Hot Spots Poster Map" (Toronto: Pollution Probe Foundation).
- Keating, M. "Our Vanishing Wetlands", in *Canadian Geographic* Vol. 107, No. 4, 1987.
- Keating, M. *To the Last Drop* (Toronto: Macmillan, 1986).
- Kaye, M. "The Watershed Years", in *Landmarks* (Ontario's Natural Resources Magazine), Vol. 4, No. 3, 1986.
- Mandale, M. *Canada's Natural Resources and Their Use* (Halifax: Lighthouse Publications, 1982). Chapter 3, Water.
- Pearse, P. et al. *Currents of Change, Final Report* (Ottawa: Inquiry on Federal Water Policy, Supply and Services, 1985).
- *Primer on Water: Questions and Answers* (Ottawa: Environment Canada, 1990).
- Reid, R. "Saving the Great Lakes", in *Nature Canada* Vol. 18, No. 1, 1989.
- *Seasons* (Journal of the Federation of Ontario Naturalists). A special issue on the Great Lakes. Autumn, 1987.
- *Water Is a Mainstream Issue* (Ottawa: Inquiry on Federal Water Policy, Supply and Services, 1984).

CHAPTER SEVEN

- Bowden, F. and others. *Canadian Industrialization* (Toronto: McGraw-Hill Ryerson, 1983). Chapter 6, Grassy Narrows: A Study of Change and Conflict.
- Braund B., and W. Blake. *Case Studies in Canadian Geography* (Toronto: McGraw-Hill Ryerson, 1982). Chapter 4, Lunenburg: An Atlantic Fishing Port.
- Calhoun, S. "Acadia Snow Crabs", in *Canadian Geographic* Vol. 108, No. 6, 1988.
- Cameron, S. "Almighty Cod", in *Canadian Geographic* Vol. 108, No. 3, 1988.
- Cameron, S. D. "Net Losses—The Sorry State of Our Atlantic Fishery", in *Canadian Geographic* Vol. 110, No. 2, 1990.
- *Canadian Encyclopedia* (Edmonton: Hurtig, 1985; 2nd ed. 1988). Fisheries Resources, Fisheries History, and Fisheries Policy.
- Jackson, L. "Improving the Odds for Atlantic Salmon", in *Canadian Geographic* Vol. 106, No. 3, 1986.

- Koppel, T. "A Spectacular Year for Pacific Salmon", in *Canadian Geographic* Vol. 106, No. 3, 1986.
- Koppel, T. "Gooey-duck Galore", in *Canadian Geographic* Vol. 108, No. 5, 1988.
- McDaniel, N. "Life in the Fast Lane" (B.C. sea life), in *Equinox*, No. 41, 1988.
- Mowat, F. *Sea of Slaughter* (Toronto: McClelland and Stewart, 1984). A commentary on fish harvest problems.
- Surette, R. "Divvying Up The Fish: World Court Decision on Georges Bank", in *Canadian Geographic* Vol. 105, No. 3, 1985.
- *Underwater World* (Ottawa: Department of Fisheries and Oceans, 1980–90). A series of fact sheets on a variety of fish species.
- Wilcox, J. "Seafood's New Wave" (East Coast Shellfish Farms), in *Canadian Geographic* Vol. 105, No. 4, 1985.

CHAPTER EIGHT

- *Canadian Encyclopedia* (Edmonton: Hurtig, 1985; 2nd ed. 1988). Forests, Forest Economics, Forest Fires, Forest Harvesting, Forest Regions, Forestry, Pulp and Paper Industry.
- Donev, S. "Perpetual Paper" (new paper-making technology), in *Landmarks* Vol. 3, No. 3, 1985.
- Geddes, J. "The Battle for Carmanah" (B.C. forest conflicts), in *Financial Post* June 12, 1989.
- Gladstone, B. "Fuel for Thought" (firewood), in *Landmarks* Vol. 5, No. 1, 1987.
- Hoyt, E. "Paradise in Peril" (west coast forest resource issues), in *Equinox* No. 19, 1985.
- Kennedy, D. "B.C.'s Ancient Forests", in *Probe Post* Vol. 11, No. 3, 1988.
- Ladell, J. "Foresters Under Fire", in *Bridges* Vol. 3, No. 3-4, 1986.
- Lanken, D. "We're Killing Our Maples", in *Canadian Geographic* Vol. 107, No. 1, 1987.
- Mason, H. "The Maple Leaf Forever?" (acid rain damage), in *Landmarks* Vol. 4, No. 4, 1986.
- Mcgonigle, M. and T. Alden. "Wilderness Epitaph" (west coast forest resource issues), in *Equinox* No. 29, 1986.
- Moise, B. "Temagami Under Siege" (Northern Ontario forest conflicts), in *Canadian Geographic* Vol. 109, No. 1, 1989.
- Naczynski, J. "Life on the Fire Line", in *Landmarks* Vol. 5, No. 2, 1987.
- Rahtz, N. and S. Donev. "Operation Budworm", in *Landmarks* Vol. 4, No. 1, 1986.
- Schmidt, J. "Manitoba Burning", in *Equinox* No. 48, 1989.
- Wood, T. "The Art of Rebuilding Forests", in *Landmarks* Vol. 4, No. 3, 1986.
- Young, C. "Our Biggest and Oldest Trees", in *Canadian Geographic* Vol. 108, No. 3, 1988.
- Young, C. "The Last Stand", in *Canadian Geographic* Vol. 106, No. 1, 1986.

CHAPTER NINE

- Algie, J. "Plowman, Spare That Field", in *Canadian Geographic* Vol. 108, No. 5, 1988.
- Bowden, F., and others. *Canadian Industrialization* (Toronto: McGraw-Hill Ryerson, 1983). Chapter 4, The Food Industry of Canada.
- Cameron, S. "P.E.I.'s Mighty Spud . . .", in *Canadian Geographic* Vol. 104, No. 5, 1985.
- *Canadian Encyclopedia* (Edmonton: Hurtig, 1985; 2nd ed. 1988). Agricultural Economics, Agricultural Implements, Agricultural Research and Development, Agricultural Food Policy, Agriculture History.
- Cotte, D. and J. Dumanski. "The State of our Agricultural Soil Resource", in *Bridges* Vol. 2, No. 4, 1985.
- Keating, M. "Our Precious Fruitlands in Peril", in *Canadian Geographic* Vol. 106, No. 5, 1986.
- Manning, E. "Farmland: the Myth of Plenty", in *Bridges* Vol. 1, No. 3, 1984.
- Preservation of Agricultural Lands Society (pals) (P.O. Box 1090, St. Catharines, Ont., L2R 7A3). Write for up-to-date list of publications about urbanization of agricultural land. (PALS prefers only one request from each school.)
- Simpson-Lewis, W., and others. *Canada's Special Resource Lands* Map Folio. No. 4 (Ottawa: Lands Directorate, Environment Canada, 1982). First chapter on agriculture.
- *Southern Ontario Atlas of Agriculture* (Guelph: University of Guelph, Occasional Papers in Geography, No.7, 1985).
- Stark, M. "Soil Erosion Out of Control in Southern Alberta", in *Canadian Geographic* Vol. 107, No. 3, 1987.

CHAPTER TEN

- Bowden, F. and others. *Canadian Industrialization* (Toronto: McGraw-Hill Ryerson, 1983). Chapter 8, "The Alberta Oil Sands".
- Braund, W. and W. Blake. *Case Studies in Canadian Geography* (Toronto: McGraw-Hill Ryerson, 1982). Chapter 1, "The Petroleum and Natural Gas Industry" and Chapter 3, "A Mining Complex in the Canadian Shield".

- *Canadian Encyclopedia* (Edmonton: Hurtig, 1985; 2nd ed. 1988). Coal, Mineral Resources, Mining, Petroleum, Nuclear Energy.
- *Current* Vol. 2, No. 7, 1982. (Available from Ontario Hydro.) A special issue on mineral resources. Other special issues related to minerals are: Vol. 2, No. 1, 1981, on fossil fuels; Vol. 6, No. 1, 1985, on nuclear energy; Vol. 10, No. 1, 1990, on electric energy.
- Dwyer, R. and S. Penny. *Challenges in the Development of Resources* (Agincourt: Domini Press, 1984). Information and activities on Canadian mining.
- *Energy in Canada* (Ottawa: Energy, Mines and Resources Canada, 1987).
- Fisher, J. ''Heart of Gold'', in *Landmarks* Fall, 1984. Details on the Hemlo development.
- Little, B. ''The Next Oil Crunch'', in *Report on Business Magazine* May, 1987.
- *Mining in Canada: Facts and Figures* (available annually, free of charge from The Mining Association of Canada, 350 Sparks St., Suite 809, Ottawa, Ontario, K1R 7S8).
- *Mining: What it Means to Canada* (available annually, free of charge from The Mining Association of Canada, 350 Sparks St., Suite 809, Ottawa, Ontario, K1R 7S8).
- ''The Oslo Factor'' (Another oil-sands project) in *Review* (Imperial Oil) Summer, 1989.
- *Our Petroleum Challenge* (available free of charge from the Petroleum Resources Communication Foundation 2030, 801-6th Ave., S.W., Calgary, Alberta, T2P 3W2).
- *Principal Mineral Areas of Canada* (Ottawa: Energy Mines and Resources Canada, annual). An official map of all current mining operations and active oil and gas fields.

CHAPTER ELEVEN

- *Background Readings in Selected Global Issues* (Don Mills: Fitzhenry & Whiteside, 1980). A series of three reports on global disparities.
- Boyd, A. *An Atlas of World Affairs* (New York: Methuen, 1988).
- *Canada and the World* (Maclean-Hunter). A magazine that discusses Canada's role in controversial world issues.
- *Canada Handbook* (Ottawa: Statistics Canada, most recent year). See sections on foreign affairs, defence, and economic relations.
- *Canadian Encyclopedia* (Edmonton: Hurtig, 1985; 2nd ed. 1988). Commonwealth, Foreign Investment, Francophonie, United Nations, and other items.
- *Canadian Green Consumer Guide: How you can help* (Toronto: McClelland and Stewart, 1989). This book, produced by the Pollution Probe Foundation, recommends ''responsible shopping that won't cost the earth''.
- *Development* (Public Affairs Branch, CIDA, Hull, Québec). A journal that contains articles on Canada's assistance to developing countries . The same source has collections of newspaper clippings on foreign aid to developing countries.
- *Gaia: An Atlas of Planet Management* (Garden City, New York: Anchor Press, Doubleday and Co., 1984).
- Hunter, W.T. *Canada in the International Economy* (Toronto: The Canadian Studies Foundation, 1983).
- *Junior Encyclopedia of Canada* (Edmonton: Hurtig, 1990).
- Kidron, M. and R. Segal. *New State of the World Atlas* (London and Sydney: Pan Books, 1984). A set of 57 world maps shows how Canada compares to other countries in things such as military spending, export of grain, protection and extinction of species, use of nuclear power, and many more.
- Rabbior, C. *Export Canada: Opportunities and Challenges in the World Economy* (Toronto: Canadian Foundation for Economic Education, 1984).
- Stark, L. *Signs of Hope: Progress towards our Common Future* (Don Mills: Oxford University Press, 1990). This book documents progress in solving global environmental problems.
- *The World: Our Market* (Ottawa: External Affairs, 1987).

Glossary

A

aggregate: loose rock material, varying from fine sand to coarse gravel, used in construction

air mass: a large body of air consistent in moisture and temperature

alloy: a metal made by fusing two or more metals

ambassador: the official representative of one country to another

amenities: goods and facilities that make life easier and more pleasant

anadromous [fish]: that leave the sea and swim up rivers to spawn

anglophone: a person whose principal language is English

annual allowable cut (AAC): the volume of timber that government regulations allow a given logging company to harvest in a given year

apartheid: South Africa's policy of keeping different racial groups separated

aquatic environment: the habitat and all living things found in any body of water

aquifer: underground layers of sand or gravel or very porous rock in which water moves freely

asphalt: pavement made of a mixture of crushed rock and a crude oil product

assimilate: absorb; gradually make like others in customs and outlook

avalanche: a large mass of snow or of soil and rock sliding down a mountain

B

Bacillus thuringiensis (Bt): a biological insecticide that harms only the spruce budworm and no other living organism in the forest

bank: an elevated area on the bottom of an ocean, sea, or river, sometimes connected with the shore, but not high enough to interfere with shipping. Such areas provide ideal feeding and spawning grounds for many species of fish, including shellfish.

base metals: non-precious metals, such as lead, zinc, iron or tin

basin: a large, dish-shaped area; such an area on the ocean floor that traps the remains of tiny plant and animal organisms between layers of sedimentary rock (These organisms, under pressure over a long time, form crude oil and natural gas.)

benches: a series of terraces or levels cut into solid rock in an open-pit mine

beneficiation: a process of crushing and grinding both metallic and non-metallic minerals to separate the **tailings** (waste material) from the ore

biomass: organic matter that can be burned or chemically changed to produce energy

biotechnology: the application of biological knowledge to improve the productivity of plant and animal species

biotic composition: the variety of living organisms that inhabit any environment

bog: low-lying, poorly drained land in which there is a great deal of dead vegetative matter. After thousands of years, the vegetation turns into peat. In northern Canada, large areas of peat bog are called muskeg. *See* **marsh**, **swamp**, and **muskeg**.

booms: rafts of logs floated on water

boreal: of, or relating to, the north

C

CANDU: Canada Deuterium Uranium Reactor (a Canadian nuclear reactor using deuterium oxide or heavy water and uranium)

capillary action: the upward movement of ground water through dry soil

carnivore: a meat-eating creature

Census Metropolitan Area (CMA): an area containing a city of 100 000 or more people, plus the surrounding area within easy commuting distance for workers

census subdivisions: parts of larger census divisions (areas designated by government for the collection of data)

central business district (CBD): a concentration of service buildings, near the centre of an urban community

central place functions: services provided by urban centres for the people who live there and in the surrounding areas

clearcutting: logging all the trees in an area at the same time

coal: a fuel formed from peat and various sediments under great pressure

coalition: a union of groups that have agreed to work together in a common cause

coke: a fuel made from bituminous coal that is used for melting iron ore

commercial farming: farming that produces surplus products that can be sold

commercial fishing: catching marketable fish for profit

commercial forest: woodland area with trees that are large enough and accessible enough to make harvesting them a profitable operation

commercial land use: use of land to provide locations for stores and other service businesses

commercial strip: a series of shops and service buildings lining a street or road; **ribbon development; strip plaza**

common-property resource: a resource that belongs to everyone

compensation: a satisfactory return for a loss or injury

concentrates: ore or minerals from which rock, sand, or other impurities have been removed

concentrating plant: that part of a mine operation where rock, sand, and other non-metallic materials are removed from ore

confederacy: an alliance of several political groups

confederation: a union of political units in which there are two levels of government, federal and provincial/state

conifer: tree or shrub that bears its seeds in cones

coniferous: cone-bearing [tree]

conservation authorities: groups of people appointed by government to plan the wise use of resources in a given region (often a river basin)

conserver society: a society that favours using resources as efficiently as possible by practising conservation of energy and recycling

consumer goods: products that people use to satisfy their needs or wants

consumptive: relating to a process that consumes [a resource] in using [it] (e.g., using water for irrigating crops)

continental climate: climate typical of the interior of large land masses (i.e., hot in summer and cold in winter)

continental drift: the movement of continental plates

continental glacier: an ice mass that grew from separate ice centres to cover large areas of a continent

continental shelf: a gently sloping extension of a continent under the ocean to a depth of about 200 m. (The shallow water above a continental shelf usually supports plenty of fish.)

continuous cropping: cultivating fields every year, but rotating crops in order to control weeds and conserve soil

contour farming: plowing and planting crops so that the rows run across a slope instead of up and down the slope. In contour farming, the furrows form a series of small dams that tend to block the run-off, instead of a series of small channels that allow rainwater and meltwater to run off freely.

contour lines: lines drawn on maps by cartographers to join sites at the same height in relation to sea level

cosmopolitan: relating to a city in which dwellers have come from many parts of the world

the Crown: the authority and power of a king or queen or of the elected officials who exercise that authority

crown land: land belonging to the monarch or to the government that exercises the monarch's authority; government-owned or public land

crude oil: *See* **petroleum.**

crustaceans: shellfish found in lakes (e.g., crayfish) and in oceans (e.g., lobster and shrimp)

customs clearance procedures: compliance with government regulations for importing goods and materials

customs duties: taxes payable on imported goods

D

deciduous: broad-leaved [trees] that shed their leaves each year

defoliate: remove leaves from a plant

deforestation: clearing trees from an area (to gain timber, farmland, or building space)

delta: a roughly triangular deposit of earth and sand that may build up at the mouth of a river as sediment is carried downstream. Delta soils are usually very fertile.

de-oxygenated water: water from which a significant amount of oxygen has been removed

deposition: the depositing of particles moved by erosion

devalue currency: officially reduce the value of one's country's money in relation to foreign currencies (in order to gain some economic advantage)

developed country: a country with an industrialized economy and a healthy standard of living for its citizens

developing country: a country working to achieve an improved economy (through industrialization) and a healthy standard of living for its citizens

dieback: the effect of a disease of trees that causes the twigs and tips of branches to die first

diorama: a scene (to be viewed through a window-like opening) showing a painted background and a foreground occupied by three-dimensional figures (life-size or smaller) of people, animals, and appropriate accessory objects

disk-packer: a (farm) tilling implement that does not turn over the soil like a plough or cultivator, but leaves the soil packed down with some stubble trash on the surface

drainage basin: an area drained by a river and its tributaries

drumlin: an oval-shaped hill formed of materials deposited by moving ice

durum wheat: a kind of wheat used in making pasta products

E

earthquake: movement of the earth's surface resulting from movement of the earth's plates

ecology: the study that investigates how parts of an ecosystem relate to one another

economic sanctions: trade restrictions imposed by one or more nations against another in order to force it to change a policy

economic sectors: major divisions of a country's economy—the primary industrial sector (e.g., mining); the secondary industrial sector (e.g., manufacturing steel); and the tertiary economic sector (e.g., providing garage services for automobiles)

economy of scale: a lowering of the per unit cost of production in proportion to an increase in the overall output of an operation

ecosystem: a group of plants and animals in which all the living parts interact with one another and with their environment in a way that makes them close to self-sufficient

embargo: a government-imposed ban on the import of a certain product

embassy: an ambassador and supporting staff; the residence or office of an ambassador in a foreign country

entrepreneurship: organization and management of a business or industrial enterprise in the hope of making a profit but risking a loss

environment: all the surrounding conditions and systems that affect the development of a living thing

environmental impact assessment: expert investigation and conclusion concerning the likely effect on the environment of a project or event

erosion: the wearing down of the earth's surface

erratic blocks: *See* **erratics**.

erratics: large boulders, foreign to an area, deposited by moving ice

escarpment: a steep cliff formed by erosion (*See* **faulting**.)

esker: a steep-sided, winding ridge formed by sand or gravel deposited in meltwater streams flowing through tunnels within and below glacial ice

estuary: the broad mouth of a river flowing into the sea, at the point where the river current meets the tide and is influenced by it

European Economic Community (EEC): a group of European countries which have free trade among themselves and common customs duties on imported products

eutrophication: the process in which plant growth uses up oxygen from rivers and lakes

evaporate: the process by which water turns from liquid into vapour (invisible moisture in the air)

exotics: non-native species introduced into a new habitat either on purpose or by accident

extraction: removal of minerals from the earth by the process of mining

F

fabricate: make raw materials into finished products

fallow [land]: farmland cultivated but left unplanted for one or two years to store up scarce soil moisture for the next grain crop

faulting: the vertical movement of surface rock along a crack or fault in the earth's crust

finish [cattle]: feed grain to stock to fatten them for market

fish landing: volume of fish brought ashore from a fishing boat

flail: beat stalks of grain with jointed sticks to break the heads from the stalks; the jointed stick used for this purpose

flake: a wooden platform built for drying cod

flood plains: flat land on either side of river channels that is built up by periodic flooding

floor price: the lowest price for which a product can be sold at a profit

folding: the buckling of layers of sedimentary rock, under pressure, into ridges and valleys

food chain: a pattern of the transfer of food energy from plants through a series of animals

forester: a person who works in the forest; a person who is trained in the science of forestry

fossil fuels: *See* **hydrocarbons.**

francophone: a person whose principal language is French

front [relating to weather]: the line of contact where a warmer, lighter air mass meets a colder, heavier air mass

frost-free period: all the days between the last "killing frost" of spring and the first one of autumn

full-tree logging: the removal of the whole tree from the forest to a central location to be de-limbed and topped

G

galvanized: (metal) covered with a thin coating of zinc to prevent rust

gateway: geographic feature giving access to one or more regions

geologist: a person who is trained in the study of the rock that forms the earth's crust, and of its history

geology: the study of the rock that forms the earth's crust, and the history of that crust

geothermal: relating to or coming from the heat of the earth's interior (Some of this heat escapes to the earth's surface through steam vents.)

ghetto: a part of a city occupied by a minority group obliged to live there for economic, social, or political reasons (e.g., because of poverty, prejudice, or repression)

glacial meltwater: water produced by the melting of glaciers

glacier: "river" of ice formed from the compression of many layers of unmelted snow

glasnost: a Russian word meaning "openness"; the Soviet policy, begun under President Gorbachev, of "openness" with the Soviet people and the Western nations

Golden Horseshoe: the densely populated area of high industrial development around the western end of Lake Ontario

government procurement policies: government policies restricting their departments to buying from intra-national (not foreign) suppliers

great circle route: the shortest possible air route connecting any two points on the globe

grist mills: mills that grind grain into flour

gross national product (GNP): the total market value of a nation's goods and services

groundfish: fish that live and feed near the bottom of the ocean

ground water: water that soaks deep into the ground and accumulates in layers of sand and gravel or porous rock

ground water recharge: supply of ground water added periodically/seasonally as a result of heavy precipitation or run-off

growing degree day: a measurement of the potential for the daily growth of plants, calculated on a base of 5.6°C. Each degree Celsius above 5.6°C equals one growing degree day.

growing season: the days in any year with an average temperature of 5.6°C or higher

H

hardware [computer]: machines that process computer data

hard wheat: wheat with a hard kernel, used for making bread flour

hardwoods: wood produced from broad-leaved trees such as maple and oak

heartland: (a term often used in contrast to hinterland); a highly urbanized region containing cities with a large population, a great deal of economic activity, and many transportation services

herbicide: a chemical spray developed to kill weeds or other unwanted vegetation

herbivore: a plant-eating creature

hewed: cut or shaped with an axe (or adze or similar tool)

hinterland: (a term often used in contrast to heartland); regions beyond intensely developed urban areas but within their sphere of influence

humidex: a index of discomfort resulting from the combination of humidity and heat

humus: decomposing plant material that enriches the parent soil material

hybrid: the product of a cross of two varieties or species that differ in their genetic composition

hydraulic power: energy generated in a hydro-electric generating station that is operated by water pressure

hydrocarbons: fuels formed when fossilized plant and animal matter trapped in sedimentary rock layers was compressed. Chemical changes produced coal, crude oil (petroleum), or natural gas.

I

igneous rock: rock formed by the cooling and hardening of molten rock

industrial land use: use of land to provide locations for manufacturing plants, and for storage and distribution facilities

industrial park: landscaped and serviced areas of land set aside for one-storey industrial buildings

inshore fishery: ocean fishing close enough to the coast to allow small boats to leave port and return with their catch within a single day

institutional land use: use of land to provide locations for institutions (e.g., schools, colleges, hospitals, government offices)

Inuit: a Native people that inhabits the far North

Inuktitut: the language spoken by the Inuit who live in the Canadian Arctic

isotherm: a line drawn on a map to join all places with the same average temperature

J

jet stream: a narrow ''river'' of air moving from west to east in the upper atmosphere

K

kayak: traditional Inuit boat made by covering a light wooden frame with seal skins

L

labrusca: variety of grapes originating in North America (These grapes are very hardy and make good juice, but they do not produce high-quality wine.)

landfill sites: places set aside for the disposal of municipal and industrial garbage and other refuse. The refuse is dumped at these sites and then covered with earth.

landform region: *See* **physiographic region.**

landing: *See* **fish landing.**

landmark: a special feature that helps to identify an area

larva: the immature stage of some animals with very different appearance and way of life from the adults of the species

leaching: the process by which rain water dissolves some of the nutrients in topsoil and carries them to the lower depths of the parent material and into springs and streams

lichen: an extremely hardy plant formed from algae and fungus growing together in a permanent relationship

limestone: a sedimentary rock formed from the shell remains of sea animals and from lime left when the seas evaporated

liquified natural gas (LNG): natural gas reduced to liquid form for transport by ship

loam: topsoil composed of a mixture of sand, silt, and clay

longhouse: a communal dwelling built by the Natives of southern Ontario and some areas of the United States. Such a dwelling was constructed by covering a framework of wooden poles with bark.

longitudinal: relating to the distance east or west on the earth's surface as measured in degrees from the prime meridian

low pressure: low barometric pressure resulting from the meeting of a warm air mass with a cold air mass. As the warm air rises, the pressure on it drops; moisture, now too heavy for it to hold, falls as rain.

M

mammal: a creature that suckles its young

manufacture: develop raw or processed materials into semi-processed goods in mills or plants, or develop semi-processed goods into finished products in assembly plants

manufacturing industry: an industry that processes raw materials or partly processed goods into a refined or finished product

map projection: the way a sphere or globe is represented on a flat surface

market gardening: a type of intensive farming in which fruits and vegetables are grown to be sold as fresh produce in a nearby city

marketing boards: organizations formed to regulate the price of products by controlling the supply

marsh: very wet **swamp**

mass transit: a public transportation system organized and equipped to move large numbers of people

metallics: minerals found in some metamorphic, igneous rocks that can be processed into metals

metamorphic rock: igneous or sedimentary rock changed in composition, texture, or inner structure by pressure, heat, or other forces

Métis: people of mixed Native Indian-European descent

metropolis: a large urban centre with an active business district, high population density, extensive shopping facilities, and various industries, serving a wide tributary area

metropolitan city: a federation of several adjacent municipalities that together form a large urban area

micro-chip: silicone chip that stores information in a computer

mill [wheat]: grind wheat into flour

minerals: solid or liquid inorganic substances, like salt or petroleum, found in rock, soil, or sediment

mixed farming: farming that produces a variety of crops and livestock or their products

monopoly: exclusive control held by one company over the sale of a product or the provision of a service

moraine: a mass of mixed rock débris, ranging from boulders to clay, deposited by a glacier

muskeg: Algonquian term for wetlands such as marshes and bogs. Today the term usually refers to northern peat bogs. *See* **bog**, **swamp**, and **marsh**.

N

National Policy: the name given to the Canadian government's policy of high tariffs, introduced in 1878. These tariffs were imposed to protect the Canadian manufacturing industry from having to meet the keen competition of much cheaper imported goods.

natural resources: parts of the natural environment that people find useful, such as water, soil, plants, animals, and minerals

natural vegetation: the mixture of uncultivated plants that grows in any given region, undisturbed by people

nitrous oxides (NO_x): colourless gases formed when petroleum products are burned (Nitrous oxides mix with the moisture in the air to form nitrous acids.)

nomad: a person who follows a lifestyle of moving about constantly rather than living in a fixed place

nomadic: constantly moving about rather than living in a fixed place

non-consumptive: relating to a process that uses [a resource] without consuming it (e.g., generating electricity by means of water power)

non-metallics: minerals found in some metamorphic, sedimentary rocks that contain no fuel or metallic traits (e.g., asbestos or potash) (These minerals have special uses in construction.)

non-renewable [resources]: resources that cannot renew themselves

non-status Indians: Canadian Indians who have not been registered with Canada's federal government

no-till cropping: planting crops without tilling the soil ahead of time; **zero-till cropping**

nuclear reactor: a device used in a nuclear generating station to produce controlled nuclear energy instead of an explosion

nurseries: facilities where tree seedlings are grown

nutrients: mineral substances in soil and water that plants absorb through their roots and use for growth

O

offshore fishing: ocean fishing far enough from home ports to allow trawlers to spend several days at sea and catch a full load of fish

open-pit mining: a surface mining method used to extract irregularly shaped deposits of minerals lying close to the earth's surface

ore: rock or other geological material containing, in its raw (unprocessed) state, a mineral deposit valuable enough to be worth mining

outports: small fishing settlements on the Newfoundland coast

overburden: soil and rock above a mineral deposit which must be removed in order to begin mining

P

pack ice: sea ice that is not firmly attached to any shore

palisade: a defensive wall made of upright wooden poles often sharpened at the top

paradox: a statement that seems to say two contradictory things

parent material: ground up rock material on the earth's surface

parkland: areas of tall grasses and groves of aspen trees

patriate: to bring home (Canada's Constitution was patriated when the British government handed over responsibility for it to the Canadian government.)

peat: a substance (fuel) formed from the remains of ancient swamp vegetation

pelagic: [of fish] living in the ocean and feeding near its surface

perennial [plant]: plant that lives longer than two years

perestroika: a Russian word meaning "restructuring" (a term adopted by President Gorbachev to define political and economic changes begun in his régime)

permafrost: permanently frozen soil

petrochemical: the part of refined petroleum used to make certain substances including synthetic rubber, fibreglass, and styrofoam

petroleum: a liquid mineral developed from decaying plant and animal material, extracted from the ground and used for fuel; crude oil

photosynthesis: the process by which plants use sunlight to convert carbon dioxide, water, and minerals into organic substances (food)

physiographic region: a large area of the earth's surface that has similar landforms

phytoplankton: microscopic plant organisms that live in water

piling (pile): heavy beam driven upright into the earth, often under water, to support a bridge, wharf, or building

planing mill: a mill where logs or rough lumber is smoothed and shaped into many building materials

plankton: microscopic animal or plant life that lives in salt- or fresh water in great masses, providing food for fish and whales

planning boards: groups of citizens appointed by local governments to advise them on issues relating to land-use planning

plate: a section of the earth's crust

plateau: a high, fairly flat landform often cut by river valleys

plethora: excessive number; too much/many

plywood: board made of several thin layers of wood glued together

political refugee: a person who has fled her/his country for safety because of a fear of persecution *See* **refugee**.

polynya: a large area of open water, in arctic seas, surrounded by **pack ice**

prairie: a large area of flat or gently rolling plain covered with grass but few or no trees

precious metals: metals prized for their high value, especially gold, platinum, and silver

precipitation: moisture that falls to earth in the form of rain, snow, hail, or sleet

predator: a meat-eating creature that searches out its prey

primary industries: industries that process raw materials

primary resources: raw materials available for processing

primary sewage treatment: removal of solids only from sewage

process [verb]: by means of some special method, prepare natural resources/products for a particular use

projection: *See* **map projection**.

public transportation: transportation provided by mass transit vehicles

public utility commission: a group of people elected in a municipality to be responsible for the provision of such utilities as electricity and water

Q

quaking bog: a thick mass of floating vegetation in an oxygen-starved lake

quota: a limit on the quantity of a resource that may be harvested; a limit on the quantity of a product that may be imported

R

rain shadow: an area on the lee side of mountains that receives less precipitation than does the windward side

reactor: *See* **nuclear reactor**.

reclamation: redeveloping (land or other resources that have been damaged or depleted through use) for other uses

recreational land use: use of land to provide locations for various types of recreation services and facilities

reeve: the elected head of government of a village or township (The position is similar to that of a mayor of a town or city.)

referendum: a direct vote by citizens to accept or reject a specific proposal

refinery: a plant where minerals are purified or refined

reforestation: the replanting of trees in logged or burnt-over forest areas

refugee: a person who has fled his or her home to find refuge or safety. *See* **political refugee**.

regenerate: give new life to; grow again

regional economic development: economic expansion funded by federal government grants to poorer regions of the country

regional economic disparities: differences among regions in degree of economic welfare

regional shopping centre: large commercial plaza that draws shoppers from many kilometres around

regionalism: a distinct sense/policy of promoting regional identity

relief food: food supplied free of charge to persons at risk of starvation

remote sensing: relating to equipment that while orbiting in space receives radiation from the earth and converts that radiation into coloured images that represent different features on the ground

renewable resources: natural resources that replace themselves (e.g., water, forests, fish, and agricultural land). If managed properly, these resources can be used forever without running out or being destroyed.

reserves: small areas of land set aside for the use of bands of Native peoples only

residential land use: use of land to provide locations for various types of housing

resource development: human use of natural resources

ribbon development: growth of business and commercial enterprises along the main streets and highways leading into or out of an urban centre; **commercial strip**

river channels: depressions in river valleys in which rivers flow

rivershed: a high ridge of land that divides areas drained by different river systems; **watershed**

roundwood: timber (logs) before it is squared or cut into lumber

row crops: crops planted in widely spaced rows

run-off: rainwater or melted snow that runs off the land surface instead of soaking into the ground

rural: relating to the countryside

S

salinization: a build-up of salt in the soil

sandstone: a sedimentary rock formed of compressed sand

sapling: a young tree

school board: a group of citizens elected to be responsible for the school system in a municipality

secondary industries: industries that produce finished products from resources processed by **primary industries**

secondary sewage treatment: removal of both solids and nutrients from sewage

sections: areas of prairie farmland originally surveyed into sections of one square mile or 640 acres (The metric equivalents are 2.59 km² or 259 ha. Each section is bounded on all sides by a road or right-of-way for a road.)

sedimentary rock: rock formed of eroded rock particles compressed or cemented together

seedling: a young plant grown from a seed

seed potatoes: sprouted potatoes from which new crops of potatoes are grown

seigneurial system: a traditional way of distributing and occupying land in (France and) New France. The owner of the land was called the *seigneur*; he allocated parcels of land to tenants, called (*paysans* or) *habitants*, who had to pay him certain dues, rents, and taxes, sometimes in the form of services.

seismic: relating to shock waves or earth tremors caused by earthquakes or by explosions resulting from mining explorations

sensible temperature: the temperature that our bodies seem to feel

separatism: a political movement that would lead to an established political unit (e.g., a province) separating itself from a larger unit (e.g., Canada) and becoming politically independent

service industries: businesses that provide services rather than producing goods

settling ponds: ponds where mine **tailings** or waste materials are dumped. The ponds keep the tailings from seeping into lakes and rivers. As the liquid wastes evaporate, only solid waste remains.

shaft: the main vertical opening that gives access to an underground mine (The shaft is used for moving miners in and out, and for hauling ore to the surface.)

shale: a sedimentary rock formed of compressed clay

shopping plaza: a concentration of retail stores and services, with parking facilities, in an urban area

shore leads: ocean currents forming channels of open water that may be covered with thin winter ice. These channels parallel the shoreline.

sill: an underwater ridge deposited by a glacier that creates shallow depths at the entrance to inlets, fiords, and straits

silviculture: the management of forests

skidding: dragging harvested logs behind tractors out of the forest to the roadside

slag: waste rock left after metal is separated from ore by melting

slough: an inlet, backwater, or pond in a grassland region that often dries up by the end of the summer

smelt: melt ore and separate the metal it contains from the liquid waste rock, or **slag**

smelter: a furnace for melting ore and separating the metal it contains from the liquid waste rock, or **slag**

smokestack scrubbers: devices installed in smokestacks to remove the gases that, when combined with moisture, form acid rain

snowshed: a sturdy wooden structure built over railway tracks to protect the trains from avalanches

sod mat: an almost impenetrable layer formed by the intertwining root systems of many grass plants

software [computer]: computer programs

softwoods: wood produced from needle-leaved trees such as pine and spruce

solar power: energy generated directly or indirectly by sunlight (Swimming pools or water used to heat buildings may be warmed by solar power. Energy obtained by solar collectors and stored in photoelectric cells can be used to generate a small electric current.)

soup kitchen: a centre offering low-cost food, often soup, at no charge, to persons in extreme need

sovereignty association: political independence for Québec combined with economic association with the rest of Canada. The achievement of this combination was the primary aim of the Parti Québécois.

spawn: reproduce [of fish] by laying or fertilizing eggs

sphagnum moss: peat moss

spile: a short tube or spout for drawing off sap from sugar maple trees

sport fishing: catching fish for fun rather than for profit

spring wheat: wheat sown in the spring for fall harvest in the same year

squatter slums: poorly constructed, insanitary housing built wherever the occupants can find space and materials

status Indians: Canadian Indians registered with Canada's federal government

stope: a cell in an underground mine where a mineral is excavated; the opening at the end of a tunnel

striations: scratches on bedrock surfaces made by moving rock carried by the ice of glaciers

strip cropping: planting crops in strips across the path of prevailing winds in order to reduce soil erosion

strip mining: surface mining in which dragline cranes dig trenches to expose minerals lying in horizontal layers near the earth's surface

strip plaza: a concentration of shops and services, with parking facilities, lining a street or road in an urban centre; **commercial strip**

subsidy: payment made by government to industry, usually to help the industry meet the costs of production

subsoil: the layer of soil immediately below the top soil

suburb: a residential section just outside or very near a city or town

sulphur dioxide (SO₂): colourless gas formed when fossil fuels (which contain sulphur) are burned (Sulphur dioxide mixes with the moisture in the air to form sulphuric acid.)

summer-fallowing: the practice of harvesting a crop every other year and cultivating the land in the years when no crop is sown

sunrise industries: modernizing industries that are producing more efficiently goods in greater demand

sunset industries: less efficient industries that are being replaced by others using more advanced processes

supply management: using quotas to control the amount of a product that may be marketed

surplus: an amount that exceeds basic necessities

sustainable development: economic expansion through harvesting or using a renewable resource in such a way as to avoid depleting it significantly or destroying it

swamp: an area of poorly drained, wet land often supporting trees, shrubs, grasses, and sedges

T

tailings: pieces of crushed waste rock left over after the mining of ore

tariff: tax on goods being imported

tender fruit crops: fruit crops (such as peaches, apricots, and sweet cherries) that tend to be easily injured by low temperatures

tertiary sewage treatment: removal of all impurities from sewage

thermal electricity: electrical current generated when water is heated (by burning of coal, oil, or natural gas) to produce steam that turns turbines. These turbines spin the generators that produce the electricity.

tidal power: electricity generated by the energy of tidal flows at suitable seacoast locations

till plain: a flat landscape formed from glacial deposits, mostly of sand, silt, and clay

timber range: land covered with a mix of grass and trees in mountainous areas, where cattle are pastured in late summer

ton: an imperial unit for measuring weight (In Canadian measurement, a ton equals 2000 pounds, or the equivalent of a mass of about 907 kg.)

topsoil: upper part of the parent soil material that contains humus

total allowable catch (TAC): the quantity (per fishing boat) of a particular variety of fish that may be harvested annually (The TAC is based on an estimate of the numbers of fish that can be caught without significantly reducing the fish population.)

toxic chemicals: substances poisonous to all forms of life

trading bloc: a group of several countries formed to promote specific trade policies that benefit all the member countries

transformer station: an electrical installation that changes the voltage of electric current (The voltage is set higher for transmission and lower for consumer use.)

transition zones: areas where one region gradually blends into the next (These areas contain a mix of natural vegetation, soils, and wildlife found in neighbouring regions.)

transpiration: a process in plants that parallels breathing in animals (When plants transpire, they give off moisture.)

travois: a frame made of poles for hauling loads (A loaded travois could be dragged by a dog or a horse.)

trawler: a large, ocean-going, fishing boat capable of catching many tonnes of fish

tree line: a climate boundary beyond which trees will not grow

tributary areas: areas that "feed" primary products to urban centres

tundra: mixture of low shrubs, sparse grasses, mosses, and lichens that make up the vegetative groundcover in parts of the Arctic or high mountain regions

tunnel: a horizontal passage in an underground mine that leads from the **shaft** to the **stope**, where ore is extracted

turbine: a water- or steam-driven machine that causes an electrical generator to turn

U

urban: relating to cities or towns

urban system: network of urban areas that provide goods and services to a large region

urbanization: the process of change from rural to urban land use

utilities: necessities such as water, sewers, and electricity supplied to citizens by public bodies

V

value added: increase of value through a manufacturing process

veneer: a thin layer of fine wood used to cover a cheaper grade of wood

vertical integration: an arrangement by which one company becomes involved in the production, processing, and distribution of goods

vinifera: varieties of grapes, originating in Europe, that produce high-quality wines

voyageurs: men who travelled in the service of the French fur-trading companies

W

watershed (rivershed): a high ridge of land that divides areas drained by different river systems

water table: the top level of the water-saturated zone of the earth

weir: a fence of stakes or broken branches blocking (part of) a stream or channel, to catch fish

welfare: financial assistance provided by municipalities to local people in need

wetland: area of waterlogged land that is covered by shallow water; a **marsh**, **bog**, or **swamp**

windbreak: row of trees planted to provide protection from wind and wind erosion

wind chill: the chilling effect on the human body of strong winds combined with cool temperatures

winnow: separate kernels of grain from chaff by tossing the grain into the air or shaking it in a screened frame to let the wind blow the chaff away

winter wheat: a type of wheat that is sown and sprouts in the fall, winters over, regenerates in early spring from an established root system, and is harvested in early summer

Y

yarding: collecting harvested trees in one central location, by means of a spar pole, cables, and a winch

York boat: a heavy, flat-bottomed, wooden rowboat used by the Hudson's Bay Company in the fur trade

Z

zero-till cropping: *See* **no-till cropping**.

zooplankton: tiny animals that live in the sea and eat phytoplankton

Index

Acknowledgements

Care has been taken to trace the ownership of copyright material used in this text. The publishers will welcome any information enabling them to correct any reference or credit in subsequent printings. All photos not cited are courtesy of authors John Koegler and Ralph Krueger.

Abbreviations

DEMR/SM & RS—Department of Energy, Mines & Resources/Survey, Mapping & Remote Sensing Sector; OMAF—Ontario Ministry of Agriculture & Food; OMNR—Ontario Ministry of Natural Resources; PAC—Public Archives of Canada; PFRA—Prairie Farm Rehabilitation Administration

Photographs

Front and Back Cover: Bill Brooks/Masterfile; **Front Cover Inset:** J. A. Kraulis/Masterfile; **Back Cover Inset:** Sherman Hines/Masterfile.

Chapter One Photos: C-1 D.C. Productions/The Image Bank; 1.1 G. Elgin/Miller Comstock; 1.2 Gary Cralle/The Image Bank; 1.4 Her Majesty The Queen in Right of Canada, DEMR/SM & RS; 1.5 Focus Stock Photo; 1.6 CN Rail; 1.10 S. Satushek/The Image Bank; 1.11 Paul Coates/Canapress; 1.12 Canapress; 1.14 Westcoast Energy Inc./Lloyd Sutton; 1.19 National Air Photo Library/DEMR/SM & RS; 1.22 Provincial Archives of Manitoba (Reinfeld Archive Photo); 1.23 Peter Goerzen/Mennonite Village, Manitoba; 1.25 Courtesy The Issacs Gallery, Toronto; 1.26 CN Rail; 1.27 The Port of Thunder Bay; 1.29 The National Gallery of Canada, Ottawa; 1.32 Denison Mines Ltd.; 1.34 OMNR; 1.36 John Lewis Stage/The Image Bank; 1.37 DSS Photo Centre (76-2291K); 1.38 Metro Toronto Visitors Convention; 1.39 Ontario Place, Toronto, Ontario. 1.40 OMAF; 1.43 G.V. Faint/The Image Bank; 1.47 General Motors of Canada; 1.44 Deal Fisher Heli Photo/Courtesy U.S. Army Corps of Engineers; 1.49 Gary Cralle/The Image Bank; 1.50 Guido Alberto Rossi/The Image Bank; 1.51 Alain Choisnet/The Image Bank; 1.52 Port of Montréal; 1.54 Canadian Arctic Producers; 1.55 DEMR/SM & RS; 1.57 John Lewis Stage/The Image Bank; 1.58 Guido Alberto Rossi/The Image Bank; 1.59 Steve Dunwell/The Image Bank; 1.60 M. Romanelli/The Image Bank; 1.61 Alcan Aluminium Ltd.; 1.63 Gary Cralle/The Image Bank; 1.64 Jurgen Vogt/The Image Bank; 1.65 Jurgen Vogt/The Image Bank; 1.67 H. Wendler/The Image Bank; 1.68 Tom King/The Image Bank; 1.69 Yuri Dojc/The Image Bank; 1.70 Wayne Barrett/P.E.I. Tourism; 1.71 Eric Hayes/Miller Comstock; 1.72 G.V. Faint/The Image Bank; 1.73 Nova Scotia Tourism & Culture; 1.74 Nova Scotia Tourism & Culture; 1.76 Krueger Inc.; 1.79 G.V. Faint/The Image Bank. **Figures:** 1.3 Canada Centre for Remote Sensing, Energy, Mines & Resources Canada.

Chapter Two: pp. 36-7 Hans Wendler/The Image Bank; p. 43 Quebec Ministry of Tourism; p. 44 (B) Canada Post Corporation; p. 46 (T) DSS Photo Centre (77-134K); p. 65 G. & J Images/The Image Bank; p. 69 (TL) Tom Walker/Canapress; (BL) Marc Solomon/The Image Bank; p. 72 (T) Valan Photos, (B) James M. Richards; p. 74 Canapress; p. 75 James D. Markou/Miller Comstock; p. 76 Brett Froomer/The Image Bank; p. 80 Canada Centre for Remote Sensing, Energy, Mines & Resources Canada.

Chapter Three: pp. 84-5 The Confederation Life Gallery of Canadian History; p. 88 (T) Vancouver Art Gallery, (B) Public Archives of Canada (C403); p. 89 (TR) British Columbia Archives & Records Services (74524), (BL) PAC/Geological Survey of Canada (400-C-3), (BR) Mike Beedell/Miller Comstock; p. 90 (T) PAC (C1912), (BR) Royal Ontario Museum, Toronto; p. 92 W. Griebeling/Miller Comstock; p. 93 PAC (C-17338); p. 94 PAC (C1229); p. 96 (T) PAC (C13320), (B) Glenbow Museum; p. 99 Manitoba Museum of Man & Nature; p. 100 (BR) DC Productions/The Image Bank, (TR) OMNR; p. 102 Canapress; p. 103 B. C. Archives & Records Services (A-2070); p. 104 (T) Archives of Ontario (Acc 2380/S5422), (B) OMAF/Photo by R. R. Sallows; p. 106 (TL) PAC (11569), (C) PAC (C8891), (B) Provincial Archives of Manitoba; p. 109 M. Beedell/DSS Photo Centre (EXT-11452); p. 113 (TL) Devries Mikkelsen/DSS Photo Centre (801-998-007-003), (BR) Dawn Goss/First Light, (Others) National Air Photo Library/DEMR/SM & RS; p. 116 (BR & BL) National Air Photo Library/DEMR/SM & RS; p. 117 M. Romanelli/The Image Bank.

Chapter Four: pp. 120-1 Canapress; p. 122 G.A. Rossi/The Image Bank; p. 123 Jessie Parker/First Light; p. 125 PAC/Cartographic Archives (NMC 1908); p. 127 PAC (C73709); p. 130 (T) Harold Rosenberg, (B) Canapress; p. 134 Canapress; p. 136 PAC (C2366); p. 139 Canapress; p. 141 PAC; p. 144 Provincial Archives of Manitoba; p. 145 PAC (PA 168131); p. 146 (T) Canapress, (BL & BR) B.K. Deans/Canapress; p. 149 DSS Photo Centre (81-2256K).

Chapter Five: pp. 152-153 Janet Dwyer/First Light; p. 156 (B) Grant V. Faint/The Image Bank; p. 157 (T & B) Bill Woods; p. 158 (T & B) Canapress; p. 160 Canapress; p. 162 Thomas Kitchin/First Light; p. 164 Canadian Centre for Remote Sensing; p. 165 (T) Kay Chernush/The Image Bank, (B) John de Visser/DSS Photo Centre; p. 167 (T) H. Ekmekjian/DSS Photo Centre, (BL) Terry Waterfield/DSS Photo Centre, (BR) G. Hunter/DSS Photo Centre; p. 170 Via Rail; p. 172 (T) Courtesy Moss Foods Ltd. & Morris Rollie, Mayor of Mossbank, (B) Courtesy Morris Rollie, Mayor of Mossbank; p. 175 R. & M. Magruder/The Image Bank; p. 176 (BR) Brian Milne/First Light; p. 180 (BR) West Edmonton Mall; p. 179 (BR) Mel Digiacomo/The Image Bank, (BL) M. Beedell/DSS Photo Centre; p. 184 H. Kalen/DSS Photo Centre; p. 185 (TL & TR) Toronto Transit Commission, (BL) Timothy Hudson/GO Transit.

Chapter Six: pp. 188-9 Miller Comstock; p. 191 (B) J. Vogt/The Image Bank; p. 193 C. R. Potter/Miller Comstock; p. 194 Miller Comstock; p. 195 (T) Canapress, (B) Esther Schmidt/Valan Photos; p. 197 (T) Ontario Hydro, (BR) OMNR, (TL) Canapress, (TR) OMNR, (BL) G. Eligh/Miller Comstock; p. 200 Service de l'enviroment de la communaute urbain de Montréal; p. 201 (TL) Canapress, (TR) J.A. Wilkinson/Valan Photos, (B) Thomas Kitchin/Valan Photos; p. 203 (TR) J. Irwin/Miller Comstock, (BL) Val Wilkinson/Valan Photos; p. 207 Canapress; p. 210 Canapress; p. 212 Metropolitan Water Reclamation District of Greater Chicago; p. 213 B. C. Parks.

Chapter Seven: pp. 216-7 George Hunter/Miller Comstock; p. 218 (T) W. Griebling/Miller Comstock, (B) PAC/NMC (C-3686); p. 221 (T) J.A. Wilkinson/Valan Photos, (B) Harold V. Green/Valan Photos; p. 223 Patrick Morrow/First Light; p. 224 Fred Bruemmer; p. 226 Gordon Photographic/Miller Comstock; p. 227 Stephen Homer/First Light; p. 230 W.P. Wittman/Miller Comstock; p. 231 (T) Francis Lepine/Valan Photos, (B) J.R. Page/Valan Photos; p. 232 Frank W. Grant/Miller Comstock; p. 235 (T) The Image Bank.

Chapter Eight: pp. 240-1 Provincial Archives of B.C.; p. 244 Forestry Canada, Ontario; p. 246 Val Wilkinson/Valan Photos; p. 247 (T) Forestry Canada, Ontario, (inset) Abitibi Price Inc., (B) Forestry Canada, Ontario; p. 248 (TL) Abitibi Price Inc., (TR) Forestry Canada, Ontario, (B) Canada Centre for Remote Sensing, Energy, Mines & Resources Canada; p. 249 Forestry Canada, Quebec; p. 250 (TL) Irwin Barrett/Valan Photos, (BR) Y.R. Tymstra/Valan Photos; p. 252 (T) Forestry Canada, Quebec, (B) Canada Centre for Remote Sensing, Energy, Mines & Resources Canada; p. 253 (B) Canada Centre for Remote Sensing, Energy, Mines & Resources Canada; p. 254 Thomas Kitchin/Valan Photos; p. 255 (T) Kennon Cook/Canapress, (B) Canapress; p. 256 (BL) Y. R. Tymstra/Valan Photos, (TR) Kennon Cooke/ Valan Photos (BR) Forestry Canada, Quebec; p. 257 Tom W. Parkin/ Valan Photos; p. 258 Stone Consolidated Inc.; p. 259 (TL) Abitibi Price Inc., (BL) Thomas Kitchin/Valan Photos; p. 260 Forestry Canada, Ontario; p. 263 John Reeves/Canapress.

Chapter Nine: pp. 264-5 Canapress; p. 272 (C) Tom W. Parkin/ Valan Photos, (BL) G. Hunter/Miller Comstock, (BR) G. V. Faint/ The Image Bank; p. 273 (T) Canada Centre for Remote Sensing, Energy, Mines and Resources Canada, (CR) Canapress, (BL) D.W. Schmidt/Valan Photos, (BR) Gary Cralle/The Image Bank; p. 274 (C) John Fowler/Valan Photos, (B) J.K. Page/Valan Photos; p. 275 (T) Kennon Cooke/Valan Photos, (CR) OMAF, (BL) OMAF; p. 276 (TL) OMAF, (TR) OMAF, (BL) OMAF, (CR) V. Whelan/Valan Photos, (BR) V. Wilkinson/Valan Photos; p. 277 (T) Wouterloot Gregoire/ Valan Photos; p. 281 Karen D. Rooney/Valan Photos; p. 282 (B) University of Guelph/Department of Soil & Water Conservation; p. 283 (T) Alberta Archives, (B) OMAF; p. 284 (TL) Alberta Archives, (B) Alberta Archives, (TR) PFRA; p. 291 Kennon Cooke/ Valan Photos; p. 293 John Fowler/Valan Photos; p. 294 PAC (C34438).

Chapter Ten: pp. 296-7 Canapress; p. 299 Gary Cralle/The Image Bank; p. 300 (T) Geological Survey of Canada, (B) Gary Cralle/The Image Bank; p. 301 Geological Survey of Canada; p. 303 (T) Geological Survey of Canada; p. 304 The Coal Association of Canada; p. 305 D.S. Henderson/The Image Bank; p. 313 INCO Ltd; p. 314 (T) Tom Skudra/Canapress, (B) Barry Dursley/Canadian Petroleum Association/Esso Resources; p. 316 (B) Coal Association of Canada; p. 318 Canadian Petroleum Association; p. 320 Lloyd Sutton Photo/ Westcoast Energy Inc.; p. 321 Canadian Petroleum Association; p. 323 Ontario Hydro; p. 325 John Reeves/Canapress; p. 327 Dan Roitner/Canapress.

Chapter Eleven: pp. 328-9 Canapress; p. 331 (BL) Mahaux Photography/The Image Bank, (BR) Roger Lemoyne/CIDA; p. 332 David Barbour/CIDA; p. 334 Canapress; p. 337 David Jeffrey/The Image Bank; p. 338 Canapress; p. 339 (TR) World Vision, (TL) CARE Canada; p. 343 (TR) Bombardier Inc., (BL) Mary Lyons/The Image Bank; p. 344 Revenue Canada/Customs & Excise; p. 348 Canapress; p. 352 Fred Sharp/Sharp Images; p. 354 Fred Sharp/Sharp Images; p. 357 (T) Royal Ontario Museum (B) John Sabean.

Text

Chapter One Photos: "This Land is Your Land" words and music by Woody Guthrie. TRO — Copyright © 1956 (renewed) 1958 (renewed) and 1970 by Ludlow Music, Inc. New York, N.Y. Reprinted by permission.

Chapter Three: Instructions for track casting reprinted by permission of the Federation of Ontario Naturalists. "Within the Fantastic Frontiers: A Geographer's Thoughts on Canadian Unity" from an article by Cole Harris; *Canadian Geographer,* Vol. 23, No. 3, 1979. Reprinted by permission of Canadian Society of Geographers.

Chapter Four: "A Tale of Two Bands" by Mark Zuehlke. Reprinted by permission of *Canada and the World* magazine, Oakville, Ontario.

Chapter Five: "Montreal's Vietnamese" by Janice Hamilton. Appeared originally in *Canadian Geography.* Reprinted by permission of the author. "Hodgeville: A Dying Village" reprinted by permission of the *Globe and Mail.* "Housing: Search for a Roof" by Ken Mark. Reprinted by permission of *Canada and the World* magazine, Oakville, Ontario. "City Politics: Sewers Not Circuses" by Rupert J. Taylor. Reprinted by permission of *Canada and the World* magazine, Oakville, Ontario. "Skydome: A Family Affair" Reprinted by permission of the *Financial Times. The Myth of the North American City: From The Myth of the North American City Continentalism Challenged* by Michael A. Goldberg and John Mercer. Copyright © 1986 by the University of British Columbia Press. Reprinted by permission of the publisher.

Chapter Nine: Figure 9.2 is reproduced with the permission of the Ministry of Supply and Services Canada, 1990. "Down and Out on the Farm" by Mary Janigan. Reprinted by permission from *Maclean's,* May 14, 1987.

Chapter Ten: "Our Fossil Fuel Savings Account" from *Current,* Ontario Hydro's Energy Education magazine. Reprinted by permission.

Chapter Eleven: Map projections from *Third World Atlas* (Open University Press, 1983). Reprinted by permission of the publisher. Figure 11.5 from a map entitled "Armed Conflicts in the World 1989" by Project Ploughshares. Reproduced by permission of *Compass* and Project Ploughshares. "You Can't Just Go With An Order Book" from an article originally entitled "Better Appreciation of Asian Mores is Urged" by Roger Newman. From the *Globe and Mail,* September 18, 1987. Reprinted by permission. "A Nation of Techno-Peasants?" by Charles White. Reprinted by permission of *Canada and the World* magazine, Oakville, Ontario. "Frogs' Legs and Famine" from an article originally entitled "Third World Toils to Feed the West" by Sehdev Kumar, the *Globe and Mail,* April 15, 1988. Reprinted by permission of the author.